KT-428-015

COMMON MARKET LAW OF COMPETITION

FOURTH EDITION

FIRST SUPPLEMENT

General Editor: P. M. ROTH, Barrister

CONTRIBUTORS

RUPERT ANDERSON
Barrister

FRANCES BARR
Solicitor

JOHN BOYCE
Solicitor

LAURA CARSTENSEN
Solicitor

PHILIPPE CHAPPATTE
Solicitor

RAYMOND HILL
Barrister

PAUL McGEOWN
Solicitor

GEORGE PERETZ
Barrister

VIVIEN ROSE
Barrister

WILLIAM SIBREE
Solicitor

JENNIFER SKILBECK
Barrister

RHODRI THOMPSON
Barrister

JONATHAN TURNER
Barrister

CHRISTOPHER VAJDA
Barrister

CHARLES WILLIAMS
Barrister

Published in Great Britain by
Sweet & Maxwell Limited
100 Avenue Road,
London NW3 3PF
Computerset by
Mendip Communications Ltd, Frome, Somerset
Printed by Bath Press

MAIN WORK ISBN 0421 48930 8
SUPPLEMENT ISBN 0421 56510 1

PREFACE

This Supplement, covering under four years, is considerably larger than the first edition of *Bellamy & Child* that was published in 1973. This in itself is a striking indication of the expansion of Community competition law, both in the pace of its development and the quantity of decisions involved in its implementation.

Why, then, a Supplement and not a new edition? In part, there was a sense that it might be unreasonable to expect the users of *Bellamy & Child* to purchase a replacement volume so soon after they had acquired the 4th edition. Furthermore, it seems appropriate for a complete revision of the existing work to await the replacement, or at least modification, of the existing block exemptions for exclusive distribution agreements, exclusive purchasing agreements and franchising agreements that is likely to follow the Commission's Green Paper on vertical agreements, now expected in early 1997. There is also the possibility of major change in the treatment of joint ventures, as set out in the Commission's legislative proposal on amendment of the Merger Regulation presented in September 1996, following the earlier Green Paper on concentrations. These anticipated developments, affecting substantial areas with which *Bellamy & Child* is concerned, can be better described in a new edition without postponing a supplement to the existing text, which the extent of legislation and case-law since 1993 clearly merits.

As with the 4th edition, this volume is a collaborative work. The individual contributors each prepared separate chapters as follows: George Peretz (Article 85(3)); Rhodri Thompson (common horizontal agreements); Laura Carstensen (co-operative joint ventures); John Boyce (mergers and acquisitions); Raymond Hill and Jennifer Skilbeck (vertical agreements affecting distribution or supply); Paul McGeown (intellectual property rights); Rupert Anderson (Article 86); Jonathan Turner (enforcement of competition rules in the Member States); Charles Williams (notification and its effects); Vivien Rose (enforcement and procedure); William Sibree (regulated industries; agriculture; and coal and steel); Philippe Chappatte (transport); Frances Barr (energy); Christopher Vajda (State aids). As general editor, I was responsible for the Introduction and the general chapter on Article 85(1). As Frances Barr, George Peretz, Vivien Rose and Charles Williams at the time of writing were working, respectively, at the Department of Trade and

Industry, the Office of Fair Trading, the Treasury Solicitor's and at Directorate-General IV of the European Commission, it should be made clear that any views expressed in the chapters for which they are primarily responsible, as indeed in this volume as a whole, are purely personal and not to be attributed to any of those institutions.

We are grateful to Rebecca Haynes, barrister, for considerable work on State aids; and to Jessica Jones, barrister, for assistance regarding the new United Kingdom trademark legislation. My thanks go also to my predecessor as general editor, Vivien Rose, who in addition to producing her own chapter gave assistance far beyond the call of duty; to Ann-Kristin Hanssen, of the EFTA Surveillance Authority, who promptly responded to my many requests for information; and to Lambros Kilaniotis for general help in research. Yvonne Cocklin and Gina Finer were invaluable in their assistance with not only typing but also the amalgamation of drafts produced on different word-processing systems. Our editors at Sweet & Maxwell have been most conscientious in overseeing publication to a tight timetable.

We have attempted to take account of all developments up to 1 July 1996. However, it has proved possible to incorporate reference to some major subsequent developments, such as the decision of the Court of First Instance in *Métropole Télévision*, annulling the grant of exemption to the *EBU/Eurovision* agreements; the judgment of the Court of Justice in the French express post case on State aids; the Commission's decision in *ADALAT* (finally published on 8 August 1996), on the scope of an agreement for the purpose of Article 85(1); and the "Mitigation" Notice on the level of fines.

As the lamentable gap, that omitted judgments from late 1992–1993, in the English edition of the European Court Reports is at last being closed, reference is given to the ECRs for all decisions from that period, in the expectation that the English version should have been published by early 1997. The pagination is of course the same as in the original French edition of the *Recueil de la Jurisprudence.* Where reference is made to the *Report on the application of the competition rules in the European Union*, published for the first time by DG IV in 1995, that can be found appended to the Commission's XXVth Report on Competition Policy.

P.M. Roth
Monckton Chambers,
Gray's Inn

CONTENTS

	Page
Preface	v
Table of Cases	xii
A. Alphabetical List	xii
B. European Court of Justice	xxiv
C. European Court of First Instance	xxvii
D. Merger Decisions	xxx
E. National Cases	lxxviii
Table of Legislation	lxxx
F. European Community Treaties and Conventions	lxxx
G. Regulations	lxxxii
H. Directives	lxxxvi
I. Decisions	lxxxvi
J. Notices, Guidelines and Other Informal Texts	lxxxvii
K. Rules of Procedure	xc
L. National Legislation	xc
M. International Treaties and Conventions	xci

1. THE COMMUNITY CONTEXT
   1. Historical Background — 1
   2. The Institutional Structure of the European Community — 3
   3. The EC Treaty — 6
   4. Sources of EC Competition Law — 9
   5. The Aims of the Community Rules on Competition — 12

2. ARTICLE 85(1) — 13
   2. Undertakings — 13
   3. Agreements, Decisions and Concerted Practices — 14
   4. Agreements with Subsidiary Undertakings — 19
   5. Restriction of Competition — 20
   6. Effect on Trade between Member States — 25
   7. Appreciable Effect — 26
   8. The Territorial Ambit of Article 85(1) — 27

3. ARTICLE 85(3) — 31
   1. Introduction — 31
   2. Block Exemption — 32
   3. Individual Exemption — 35

4. ARTICLE 85: COMMON HORIZONTAL AGREEMENTS — 48
   1. Introduction — 48
   2. Agreements on Selling Prices and Conditions — 49

3. Information Agreements 53
4. Agreements to Limit Production 54
5. Agreements on Technical Standards 54
6. Agreements to Limit or Share Markets 55
7. Collective Exclusive Dealing 57
8. Joint Purchasing 58
9. Joint Selling 60

5. CO-OPERATIVE JOINT VENTURES (INCLUDING SPECIALISATION AGREEMENTS) 61
1. Introduction 61
2. Production Joint Ventures 63
3. R&D Joint Ventures 73
3A. Strategic Alliances 75
4. Specialisation Agreements 76

6. MERGERS AND ACQUISITIONS 77
1. Introduction 77
2. Concentrations 80
3. Joint Control, Concentrative and Co-operative Joint Ventures 85
4. Community Dimension 92
5. The Commission's Appraisal of Concentrations 95
7. Notification of Concentrations 98
8. Conduct of Formal Investigations 101
9. Principle of Exclusivity of Jurisdiction 106
10. Mergers and Acquisitions under Articles 85 and 86 111

7. VERTICAL AGREEMENTS AFFECTING DISTRIBUTION OR SUPPLY 113
1. Introduction 113
2. Agency 113
3. Distribution Agreements 114
4. Selective Distribution Systems 117
5. Exclusive Purchasing Agreements for Resale 127
6. Franchising 136
7. Other Purchase and Supply Agreements 137
8. Sub-contracting 137

8. INTELLECTUAL PROPERTY RIGHTS 138
1. Introduction 138
2. The Effect of the Rules on Free Movement on Infringement Actions 139
3. The Effect of Articles 85 and 86 on Infringement Actions 145
4. Patent Licences Under Article 85 146
5. Regulation 2349/84 148
6. Know-how Licence Agreements Under Article 85 149
6A. Regulation 240/96 149

	7. Other Licence Agreements Under Article 85	156
9. Article 86		160
	1. Introduction	160
	2. Dominant Position	161
	3. Abuse of Dominant Position	166
10. The Enforcement of the Competition Rules in the Member States		174
	2. Applications of Articles 85 and 86 in the Courts of the United Kingdom	174
	3. The Effect of Community Law on National Competition Law	183
	4. Application of Competition Law in the United Kingdom	184
11. Notification and Its Effects		187
	1. Notification and Application for Negative Clearance	187
	2. Notification of New Agreements not Falling Within Article 4(2) of Regulation 17	189
	3. New Agreements Within Article 4(2) of Regulation 17	190
	4. Transitional Rules	190
	5. Notification Procedure	192
	6. Post-Notification Procedure	196
12. Enforcement and Procedure		199
	1. The Commission's Powers of Investigation	199
	2. Complaints	202
	3. Commission's Formal Procedure Prior to an Adverse Decision	204
	4. Interim Measures of the Commission	210
	5. The Commission's Power to Terminate Infringements	210
	6. Fines for Substantive Infringements	211
	7. Control by the Court of First Instance	219
	8. Appeals to the Court of Justice	223
	9. The EFTA Court	223
13. The Role of the State in Regulated Industries		224
	1. Introduction	224
	2. State Monopolies of a Commercial Character	224
	3. Public Undertakings: Article 90	225
	4. Military Equipment	230
14. Agriculture		232
	1. Generally	232
	2. Regulation 26	232
	3. State Aids in Agriculture	234
15. Transport		235
	1. Introduction	235
	2. Rail, Road and Inland Waterway Transport	235

3. Sea Transport 238
4. Air Transport 241
16. ENERGY 247
1. Introduction 247
2. Electricity 249
3. Nuclear Energy 253
4. Gas 254
5. Oil 255
17. COAL AND STEEL 257
1. Production Quotas and Pricing 257
2. Restrictive Agreements 258
3. Concentrations 259
4. Abuse of Dominant Position under Article 66(7) 259
5. State Aids under the ECSC Treaty 260
18. STATE AIDS 261
1. Introduction 261
2. The Concept of an Aid 262
3. Aids that are Compatible with the Common Market 265
4. Aids that may be Compatible with the Common Market 265
5. Supervision under Article 93 269
6. Article 94 273
7. Judicial Remedies 274
8. The Relationship Between Articles 92 to 94 and Other Provisions of the EC Treaty 279

APPENDICES 281
THE EC TREATY PROVISIONS (AS AMENDED BY THE TEU)
1. General Principles: Articles 1–3; 3b–6; 7a–7c 281
THE BLOCK EXEMPTIONS
2. Commission Regulation 1475/95 (motor vehicle distribution and servicing agreements). 284
3. Commission Explanatory Brochure on Regulation 1475/95. 296
4. Commission Regulation 240/96 (technology transfer agreements) 323
PROCEDURAL MATTERS
5. Article 25 of Council Regulation 17, as amended 338
6. Commission Regulation 3385/94 (new Form A/B) 339
7. Commission Decision on Terms of Reference of Hearing Officers 374
8. Commission Notice on the non-imposition or reduction of fines in cartel cases 378

CONTROL OF CONCENTRATIONS
9. Commission Regulation 3384/94 (new Form CO) 381
10. Commission Notice on Concentrative and Co-operative Joint Ventures (the Interface Notice) 412
11. Commission Notice on the Notion of a Concentration 418
12. Commission Notice on the Notion of Undertakings Concerned 427
13. Commission Notice on Calculation of Turnover 438
TRANSPORT
14. Commission Regulation 870/95 (block exemption for consortia agreements) 452
STATE AIDS
15. Commission Directive 93/84 (amending Directive 80/723 on transparency of financial relations) 463
16. Commission's Notice on Co-operation Between National Courts and the Commission in the State Aid Field 467
INDEX 475

TABLE OF CASES

A. ALPHABETICAL LIST

AAC and Others v. Commission (T–442/93) [1995] II ECR 1329 .... 18–027, 18–050
ABB/Daimler Benz (M.580) Decn. of 18 October 1995 6–076
——/Renault Automation (M.409) Decn. of 9 March 1994 6–016
ACI OJ 1994 L224/28 .... 3–034, 3–052, 4–054, 4–096, 5–019, 5–042, 15–006, 15–008, 15–040A, 15–042
ADALAT, OJ 1996 L201/1 [1996] 5 CMLR 416 .... 2–017, 7–019, 12–092
AITEC and Others v. Commission (T–447/93 etc.) [1995] II ECR 1971 ... 18–014, 18–019, 18–027, 18–048, 18–052, 18–055
AKZO Chemicals Press Release IP (93) 893 of 19 October 1993 [1993] 5 CMLR 431 12–014
——/Nobel Industrier (M.390) Decn. of 10 January 1994 6–050
ASPEC and Others v. Commission (T–435/93) [1995] II ECR 1281 .... 18–027, 18–050, 18–055
ATR/BAe (M.551) Decn. of 27 July 1995 .... 3–045, 5–019
Press Release IP (95) 952 of 12 September 1995 [1995] 5 CMLR 377 6–033
AWS Benelux v. Commission (T–38/92) [1994] II ECR 211 [1995] 4 CMLR 43 .... 12–043, 12–092, 12–111
Accession to the European Convention for the Protection of Human Rights and Fundamental Freedoms (Op. 2194) [1966] I ECR 1759 [1996] 2 CMLR 265 ... 1–026, 1–050
Agreement on Finnish Forestry, Re, OJ 1994 C337/21 [1995] 4 CMLR 104 ....4–001A
Agreement regarding the ferry service between Dragør and Lumhamn OJ 1995 C350/16 15–017
Ahlström v. Commission (C–89/85 etc.) judgment of 31 March 1993 [1993] I ECR 1307 [1993] 4 CMLR 407 2–043
Ahmed Saeed (66/86) [1989] ECR 803 [1990] 4 CMLR 102 15–053
Aid for audio-visual productions, ESA Annual Report 1995, point 4.7.4.2 18–016
Aid for restructuring the Italian Steel industry XXIVth Report on Competition Policy (1994), Annex II.E, p. 503–4 17–020
Air France v Commission (T–2/93) [1994] II ECR 323 .... 6–009, 6–140, 12–104, 15–053, 15–058
—— v. —— (T–3/93) [1994] II ECR 121 .... 6–050, 6–140
——/Sabena (M.157) Decn. of 5 October 1992 15–057
Albacom (M.604) Decn. of 15 September 1995 .... 6–032A
Alcan/Inespal/Palco (M.322) Decn. of 14 April 1993 6–054
Alenia/Honeywell XXIIIrd Report on Competition Policy (1993), point 216 .... 2–116, 5–019, 5–051, 5–056
Allied Signal/Knorr-Bremse (M.337) Decn. of 14 September 1993 6–076
Almelo (C–393/92) [1994] I ECR 1477 ... 2–079, 2–134, 2–144, 7–111, 7–113, 9–002, 9–005, 9–029, 9–039, 9–057, 13–004, 13–023, 13–025, 13–027, 16–006, 16–009, 16–011, 16–012, 16–020
American Home Products/American Cyanamid (M.500) Decn. of 19 September 1994 6–064
Aristrain v. Commission (T–156/94R) [1994] II ECR 717 .... 4–014A
Asahi/St. Gobain OJ 1994 L354/87 .... 3–033, 3–045, 5–019, 5–053, 5–088, 5–106
Aspen (Elf Atochen/Union Carbide Corporation) Report on application of competition rules in the EU (1995) 5–019
Atlantic Containers Line and Others v. Commission (T–395/94); *See* [1995] II ECR 595 (partial suspension of Commission decision); *on appeal* Case C–149/95P (R) 4–003, 4–038, 11–017, 12–130, 15–004, 15–019, 15–024
Atlas OJ 1995 C337/2 [1996] 4 CMLR 265 .... 3–045, 5–040A, 5–131B
Atlas OJ 1996 L239/23 .... 3–045, 3–052, 5–019, 5–040A, 5–131B
Auditer OJ 1993 L306/50 [1995] 5 CMLR 719; *on appeal* Case T–66/94 .... 3–043, 4–075, 5–039
—— v. Commission (T–66/94) [1995] II ECR 239 .... 3–043, 4–075, 5–039, 12–046
Avesta II (M.452) Decn. of 9 June 1994 6–011

Avesta III (M.504) Decn. of 20 October 1994 6–011
BASF and Others v. Commission (T–80/89 etc.) [1995] II ECR 729 .... 4–011, 12–043
BASF Lacke & Farben/Accinauto OJ 1995 L272/16 [1996] 4 CMLR 811 ... 7–019, 12–072
BBC Enterprises OJ 1993 C105/6 [1993] 5 CMLR 300, XXIIIrd Report on Competition Policy (1993), p. 459 .... 8–060, 8–173A
BEMIM v. Commission (T–114/92) [1995] II ECR 147 [1996] 4 CMLR 305 .... 8–052, 12–022, 12–023, 12–026
BEUC and NCC v. Commission (T–37/92) [1994] II ECR 285 [1995] 4 CMLR 167 .... 12–021, 12–023, 12–024
BMSC/UPSA (M.464) Decn. of 6 September 1994 6–064
BMW v. ALD [1995] I ECR 3439 (C-70/93) [1996] 4 CMLR 478 ... 7–098, 7–100, 7–107A, 10–051, 10–060
BPB Industries and British Gypsum v. Commission (T–65/89) [1993] II ECR 389 [1993] 5 CMLR 32; *on appeal* Case C–310/93P 9–002, 9–045, 9–057, 12–036, 12–091
—— v. —— (C–310/93P) [1995] I ECR 865 ...... 2–091, 9–002, 9–006, 9–036, 9–045, 9–057, 9–077, 12–036
BSB/Football Association OJ 1993 C94/6, XXIIIrd Report on Competition Policy (1993), p. 459 .... 4–095, 8–060, 8–173
BT/MCI OJ 1994 L223/36 [1995] 5 CMLR 285 .... 3–031, 3–039, 3–045, 5–013, 5–019, 5–035, 5–040A, 5–056, 5–060, 5–062, 5–131B, 6–165
Banco Exterior de Espana (C–387/92) [1994] I ECR 877 [1994] 3 CMLR 473 ...... 13–021, 18–003, 18–009, 18–027, 18–062
Banks (C–128/92) [1994] I ECR 1209 [1994] 5 CMLR 30 .... 10–006, 10–022, 10–041, 10–047, 16–001, 17–005, 17–017
—— v. British Coal Corporation, judgment of 19 July 1994 (QBD) 10–006, 17–005, 17–017
Banque Nationale de Paris/Dresdner Bank, OJ 1996 L188/37 .... 3–037, 3–050, 5–131B
Baustahlgewebe v. Commission (T–145/89) [1995] II ECR 987 .... 12–080, 12–119
Bayer v. Commission (T–12/90) [1991] II ECR 219 [1993] 4 CMLR 30; *on appeal* Case C–195/91P 2–098, 2–121
—— v. —— (T–41/96R) [1996] 5 CMLR 290 .... 2–017, 7–019, 12–091
—— v. —— (C–195/91P) [1994] I ECR 5619 [1996] 4 CMLR 32 .... 2–098, 2–121, 7–020, 12–043, 12–117, 12–130
Bayer/BP Chemicals OJ 1988 L150/35 [1989] 4 CMLR 24 5–135
—— (No. 2) OJ 1994 L174/34 .... 3–052, 4–040, 5–019, 7–069
Bayer/Monsanto OJ 1995 C298/8 11–058
Bayerische Motorenwerke AG v. ALD Auto-Leasing *See* BMW v. ALD Auto-Leasing.
Bayo-n-OX OJ 1990 L21/71 [1990] 4 CMLR 930; *on appeal* Case T–12/90 .. 2–098, 2–121, 7–020, 7–021, 10–060
Becton Dickinson/Cyclopore, XXIIIrd Report on Competition Policy (1993), point 241 .... 8–114A
Beecham Group plc v. Europharm of Worthing Ltd (C–268/95), not yet decided 8–018
Behringwerke/Armour Pharmaceutical (M.495) Decn. of 3 April 1995 6–064
Belgium v. Commission (C–56/93) [1996] I ECR 1029 18–010
—— v. —— (C–291/95) 9–016A, 9–020; 9–041; 13–018
BEMIM v. Commission [1995] II ECR 147 [1996] 4 CMLR 305 10–023
Bodson v. Pompes funèbres (30/87) [1988] ECR 2479 [1989] 4 CMLR 984 3–039
Boël v. Commission (T–142/89) [1995] II ECR 867 12–099
Bosman. *See* Union Royale Belge des Sociétés de Football Association v. Bosman.
BP Bayer (L150/35) [1989] 4 CMLR 24 5–018
Bourgoin SA v. Ministry of Agriculture Fisheries and Food [1986] QB 716 10–038
Brasserie de Haecht v. Wilkin (No. 1) (23/67) [1967] ECR 407 [1968] CMLR 26 .. 16–020
Brasseriè du Pêcheur v. Germany (C–46/93) [1996] I ECR 1029 [1996] 1 CMLR 889 [1996] All ER (EC) 493 .... 10–039, 18–046A
Bristol-Myers Squibb and Others v. Paranova (C–472/93 etc), judgment of 11 July 1996 .... 8–010, 8–030, 8–035, 8–036
British Aerospace/VSEL (M.528) Decn. of 24 November 1994 13–035
British Airways/DanAir (M.278) Decn. of 30 October 1992; *on appeal* Case T–3/93 6–154
——/TAT (M.259) Decn. of 27 November 1992; *on appeal* Case T–2/93 6–009
British Cattle and Sheep Breeders' Associations, XXIInd Report on Competition Policy (1992), point 167 and Annex III, p. 416 14–005

British Iron and Steel Producers' Association v. Commission (T–150/95) XXIVth Report on Competition Policy (1994), Annex II. E, p. 504 17–020
British Steel v. Commission (T–243/94), not yet decided 17–020
British Sugar Plc v. Director General of Fair Trading, judgment of 9 August 1995 (Restr. Pr. Ct.) 10–059
British Telecom/Banco Santander (M.425) Decn. of 28 March 1994 .... 6–031, 6–032A
Brunner, 12 October 1993 [1994] 1 CMLR 57 (German Fed. Const. Ct.) 1–006
Brussels Airport OJ 1995 L216/8 [1996] 4 CMLR 232; *on appeal* Case C-291/95 .... 9–016A, 9–020, 9–041, 9–063A, 13–018, 15–053
Buchmann v. Commission (T–295/94) [1994] II ECR 1265 .... 2–034, 4–014B, 12–036, 12–077, 12–091, 12–092, 12–129
Building and Construction Industry in the Netherlands OJ 1992 L92/1; *on appeal* Case T–29/92 .... 2–132, 2–146, 3–024, 3–039, 3–043, 4–002, 4–021, 4–022, 4–036, 4–055, 4–070
Bundeskartellamt v. Volkswagen and VAG Leasing (C–266/93) [1995] I ECR 3439, 3477 [1996] 4 CMLR 478 .... 7–005, 7–098, 7–100, 10–051, 10–060
CB v. Commission (T–275/94) [1995] II ECR 2169 [1995] 5 CMLR 410 [1995] All ER (EC) 717 .... 4–017, 12–077, 12–097, 12–099, 12–103
CB and Europay v. Commission (T–39 & 40/92) [1994] II ECR 49 ... 2–033, 3–021, 3–037, 3–043, 4–017, 4–025, 12–083
CBA OJ 1995 C211/11 [1995] 5 CMLR 734 .... 8–078, 8–177
CCE de la Société Générale des Grandes Sources v. Commission (T–96/92R) [1992] II ECR 2579 (T–96/92) [1995] II ECR 1213 .... 6–122, 6–140A, 12–104
CCE de Vittel v. Commission (T–12/93) [1995] II ECR 1247 12–104
CCE Vitel and CE Pierval v. Commission (T–12/93R) [1993] II ECR 785 .... 6–122, 6–140A
CdF Chimie AZF v. Commission (C–169/84) [1990] IECR 3083 [1992] 1 CMLR 177 18–010
CHEETAH Trademark [1993] FSR 263 8–037
CIA OJ 1994 C130/3, XXIVth Report on Competition Policy (1994), point 191 ... 15–008, 15–011
CIRFS and Others v. Commission (C–313/90) [1993] I ECR 1125 .... 18–024, 18–052, 18–055
CNSD (T–513/93) not yet decided 2–021, 4–016
—— OJ 1993 L203/27 [1995] 5 CMLR 495; *on appeal* Case T–513/93 .... 2–008, 2–012, 2–021, 4–016, 4–020, 4–022
COAPI OJ 1995 L122/37 [1995] 5 CMLR 468 .. 2–008, 2–032, 2–128, 2–134, 3–024, 4–016, 4–020, 4–022
COFAZ v. Commission (169/84) [1986] ECR 391 [1986] 3 CMLR 385 18–055
Campina, XXIst Report on Competition Policy (1991), point 83 14–005
Carlsberg/Allied Lyons, XXIInd Report on Competition Policy (1992), points 131–137 7–135
——/Interbrew XXIVth Report on Competition Policy (1994), points 198 and 201 and Annex II, p. 351 .... 4–065, 7–144, 9–009, 9–040, 9–075
——Tetley OJ 1992 C97/21, XXIInd Report on Competition Policy (1992), point 116 11–058
Cartonboard OJ 1994 L243/1 [1994] 5 CMLR 547; *on appeal* Cases T–295/94 etc. 2–003, 2–033, 2–034, 4–005, 4–014B, 4–036, 4–038, 4–055, 12–036, 12–046, 12–077, 12–086, 12–091, 12–092
Cascades v. Commission (T–308/94R) [1995] II ECR 265 12–129
Casillo Grani v. Commission (T–443/93) [1995] II ECR 1375 18–055
Cement Cartel, OJ 1994 L343/1 [1995] 4 CMLR 327; *on appeal* Cases T–25/95 etc 2–033, 2–034, 2–151, 4–005, 4–014C, 4–036, 4–038, 4–055, 4–058, 12–092
Centre d'Insemination de la Crespelle v. Coopérative de la Mayenne (C–323/93) [1994] I ECR 5077 .... 9–002, 9–029, 13–016
Centro Servizi Spedi porto (C–96/94) [1995] I ECR 2883 [1996] 4 CMLR 613 2–021
Cewal, Cowac and Ukwal OJ 1993 L34/20; *on appeal* Cases T–24/93 etc. 15–018, 15–021, 15–024
Chanel OJ 1994 C334/11 [1995] 4 CMLR 108 7–084
Channel Five (M.673) Decn. of 22 December 1995 6–032
Charterhouse/Porterbrook (M.669) Decn. of 11 December 1995 6–024
Chemidus Wavin v. TERI [1978] 3 CMLR 514 (CA) 10–028
Chiron Corp. v. Murex Diagnostics Ltd (No. 2) [1994] FSR 187 [1994] 1 CMLR 410 (CA); [1993] FSR 324 [1992] 3 CMLR 813 (High Ct.)8–072, 10–033
Cicra/Fiat Auto Spa, XXIVth Report on Competition Policy (1994), Annex II, p. 361 .... 7–106, 7–108I

Coditer v. Cine Vog Films (No. 2) (262/81) [1982] ECR 3381 [1983] 1 CMLR 49 .. 8–173
Cold-rolled Stainless Steel Flat Products, OJ 1990 L220/28 17–008
Commission v. Atlantic Container Line & Others (C–149/95 P (R)) [1995] I ECR 2165 [1995] All ER (EC) 853 .... 4–003, 12–130, 15–004
—— v. BASF and Others Case (C–137/92 P) [1994] I ECR 2555 .... 4–011, 12–043, 18–027
—— v. Council (C–122/94) [1996] I ECR 881 18–026
—— v. France (C–159/94), not yet decided 16–038
—— v. Italy (C–348 and 350/93) [1995] I ECR 673 & 679 18–042
—— v. —— (C–349/93) [1995] I ECR 343 18–042
Compagnia di Navigazione Marittima v. Compagnie Maritime Belge (C–339/95), not yet decided 15–004, 15–023, 15–025
Compagnie Maritime Belge v. Commission (T–24/93 etc.) not yet decided 2–151, 12–084, 15–018
Cook v. Commission (C–198/91) [1993] I ECR 2487 [1993] 3 CMLR 206 .... 18–031, 18–050, 18–055
Cooperation agreements between Peugeot and Fiat involving the Sevel joint venture, XXIIIrd Report on Competition Policy (1993), point 227 *see also* PSA/Fiat (Sevel) agreement 5–122
Corbeau v. Belgian Post Office (C–320/91) [1993] I ECR 2533 [1995] 4 CMLR 621 ... 9–029, 13–016, 13–025, 13–027
Corsica Ferries (C–18/93) [1994] I ECR 1783 .... 9–002, 9–016A, 9–041, 9–055, 13–016, 13–018, 15–021
Crédit Lyonnais OJ 1995 L308/92, XXVth Report on Competition Policy (1995), point 197, *on appeal* Cases T–31 & 32/96 18–024
Crown Cork & Seal/Camaud-Metalbox (M.603) OJ 1996 L75/38 .... 6–124, 6–138
DIPA and Others (Cases C–140 & 142/94) [1995] I ECR 3257 [1996] 4 CMLR 157 ... 2–021, 9–039
DSB/SFL/SJ, XXIInd Report on Competition Policy (1992), Annex III, p. 418 15–017
DSM v. Commission (T–8/89 Rev) [1992] II ECR 2399; *on appeal* Case C–5/93P ... 2–044, 4–010
Danish Shipowner's v. CEWAL OJ 1993 L34/1 [1995] 5 CMLR 198, *on appeal* Cases T–24/93, etc 12–084, 12–082
Decoster (C–69/91) [1993] I ECR 5335 13–033
Delta Schiffarts-und Speditionsgesellschaft (C–153/93) [1994] I ECR 2517 [1996] 4 CMLR 21 .... 1–027, 2–021
Deutsche Bahn v. Commission (T–229/94) 4–075
Deutsche Renault (C–317/91) [1993] I Rec. 6227 [1995] 1 CMLR 461 .... 8–028, 8–030, 8–040
Diego Cali & Figli v. Servizi Ecologico Porto di Genova (C–343/95), not yet decided 9–016A
Dijkstra and Others (C–319/93 etc.) [1995] I ECR 4471 .. 10–016, 10–019, 10–023, 14–006, 14–007
Dillenhofer v. Germany (178/94), not yet decided 18–046A
Director General of Fair Trading v. Publishers' Association, judgment of 9 August 1995 (Restr. Pr. Ct.) 10–059
Disma, XXIIIrd Report on Competition Policy (1993) points 223–224 .... 5–019, 16–046
Distribution of railway tickets by travel agents OJ 1992 L366/47; *on appeal* Case T–14/93 .... 2–032, 4–003, 7–005, 12–109
Ducros/DHL OJ 1994 C165/10, XXIVth Report on Competition Policy (1994), point 192 and Annex II, pp. 3701–3771 .... 4–067, 15–011
Dunlop Slazenger v. Commission (T–43/92) [1994] II ECR 441 .... 2–017, 2–048, 7–013, 7–020, 7–021, 12–044, 12–088
Dutch gas tariffs XXIInd Report on Competition Policy (1993), points 388 & 533 18–004
EBU/Eurovision OJ 1993 L179/23 [1995] 4 CMLR 56; *on appeal* Cases T–528/93 etc 3–032, 3–039, 3–042, 3–052, 4–086, 4–095, 8–060, 8–173, 13–025
EFIM OJ 1993 C267/11 18–011
EISA v. Commission (T–239/94R) [1994] II ECR 703 17–020
ETSI interim IPR policy OJ 1995 C76/5 [1995] 5 CMLR 352 .... 8—179
East African Conference OJ 1994 L378/17, XXIIIrd Report on Competition Policy (1993), points 230–31 .... 4–086, 15–024
Eco System/Peugeot OJ 1992 L66/1; *on appeal* Case T–9/92 .... 7–098, 7–107, 7–107A
Elders/Grand Metropolitan, XXIst Report on Competition Policy (1991), point 86 7–135

Electricidade de Portugal/Pego Project, XXIIIrd Report on Competition Policy (1993), point 222 .... 5–019, 5–055, 16–009, 16–019A, 16–020
Electrolux/AEG OJ 1993 C269/4 .... 5–041, 5–135
Elf Atochem/Rütgers (M.442) Decn. of 29 July 1994 .... 6–032A, 6–103, 6–113
Elsinore, Port of; see Port of Elsinore
Empresa Nacional Siderurgica SA and the Aristrain Group OJ 1993 L48/54 17–006
Eudim OJ 1996 C111/8 [1996] 4 CMLR 871 .... 4–031, 4–067
Eurim-Pharm v. Beiersdorf (C–71/94), judgment of 11 July 1996 .... 8–010, 8–035, 8–036
Eurocheque: Helsinki Agreement OJ 1992 L95/50; *on appeal* Cases T–39 & 40/92 ... 3–037, 4–017, 4–025, 12–083
European Night Services OJ 1994 L259/20 [1995] 5 CMLR 76; *on appeal* Cases T–374/94 etc. 3–034, 3–052, 4–054, 4–096, 5–019, 5–040A, 5–042, 15–006, 15–008
European producers of beams OJ 1994 L116/1 [1994] 5 CMLR 353; *on appeal* Cases T–134/94 etc. 17–005, 17–008
Européenne Automobile v. Commission (T–9/96) not yet decided 7–107A
Eurotunnel III OJ 1994 L354/66 [1995] 4 CMLR 801; *on appeal* Cases T–79 & 80/95 ... 3–034, 3–043, 3–050, 3–052, 4–054, 4–102, 5–040A, 15–004, 15–005, 15–008, 15–011
Exxon/Shell OJ 1994 L144/20 ...... 3–024, 3–031, 3–033, 3–039, 3–043, 3–052, 4–040, 5–013, 5–019, 5–022, 5–038, 5–041, 5–045, 5–046, 5–053
Factortame III. *See* R. v. Secretary of State for Transport ex p. Factortame Ltd.
Far Eastern Freight Conference OJ 1994 L378/17 .. 3–024, 4–003, 12–084, 12–088, 15–004, 15–005, 15–013, 15–023
Fédération Francaise des Sociétés d'Assurance (C–244/94) [1995] I ECR 4013 2–004
Fenex, OJ 1996 L181/28 [1996] 5 CMLR 332 .... 4–004, 15–004
Fiatagri and New Holland Ford v. Commission (T–34/92) [1994] II ECR 905; *on appeal* Case C–7/95P 2–122, 4–029, 4–034, 12–043
Fletcher Challenge/Methanex (M.331) Decn. of 31 March 1993 6–032
Florimex v. Commission (C–70 & 71/92) 4–079
Ford/Hertz (M.397) Decn. of 7 March 1994 6–013
Ford New Holland Ltd OJ 1993 L20/1 [1995] 5 CMLR 89 12–084
Ford/Volkswagen OJ 1993 L20/14 [1993] 5 CMLR 617; *on appeal* Case T–17/93 .... 3–031, 3–039, 5–007, 5–018, 5–074
France v. Commission (C–325/91) [1993] I ECR 3283 .... 18–007, 18–008
—— v. —— (C–327/91) [1994] I ECR 364 [1994] 5 CMLR 517 ...... 1–070, 11–057, 12–046
—— v. —— (C–68/94), not yet decided 6–140
—— v. —— (C–174/94R) [1994] I ECR 5229 12–130
Francovich v. Italian Republic (C–6 & 9/90) [1991] I ECR 5337 [1993] 2 CMLR 66 [1995] ICR 722 .... 10–038, 10–041
French-West African Shipowners' Committees OJ 1992 L134/1; *on appeal* Cases T–24/93 etc. 2–151
Fresenius OJ 1994 C21/04 18–011
Fritz Egger Spanplatten industrie OJ 1994 C–369/6 18–011
Fujitsu/AMD Semiconductor OJ 1994 L341/66 .... 3–031, 5–019, 5–035, 5–056, 5–060
GE/Nuovo Pignore (M.440) Decn. of 6 May 1994 6–103
GEC/VSEL (M.529) Decn. of 24 November 1994 13–035
GKN Brambles/Leto Recycling (M.448) Decn. of 7 June 1994 6–011
GSM radiotelephony services in Italy OJ 1995 L280/49 [1996] 4 CMLR 700 .... 9–010, 13–017
Galileo and Covia CRSs OJ 1993 C107/4 [1993] 4 CMLR 638 15–043
Gehe/Lloyds (M.716) Decn. of 22 March 1996 6–146
Gencor/Lonrho (M.619) Decn. of 24 April 1996 6–066
General Electric Plastics/BASF, Report on application of competition rules in the EU (1995) 5–019
Generics BV v. Smith, Kline & French Laboratories (C–316/95), not yet decided 8–025
Germany v. Commission (C–400/92) [1994] I ECR 4701 [1995] 2 CMLR 461 18–025
Germany and Pleuger Worthington v. Commission (C–324 & 342/90) [1994] I ECR 1173 [1994] 3 CMLR 521 .... 18–039, 18–051
Gestevision Telecino v. Commission (T–543/93R) [1993] II ECR 1409 12–130
Glaxo/Wellcome (M.555) Decn. of 28 February 1995 .... 6–064, 6–113
Global Logistics System OJ 1993 C76/5 15–043
Goldstein v. General Medical Council [1994] 4 CMLR 492 12–048
Gøttrup-Klim v. Dansk Landbrugs Grovvareselskab AmbA (C–250/92) [1994] I ECR 5641 [1996] 4 CMLR 191 .... 2–063, 2–091, 4–090, 9–002, 14–003

Grand Garage Albigeois v. Garage Massol (C–226/94) [1996] I ECR 651 7–098
Greenpeace and Others v. Commission (T–585/93) [1995] II ECR 2205, *on appeal* Case C–321/95P 18–055
Grundig OJ 1985 L233/1 [1988] 4 CMLR 865 (proposal to renew exemption: OJ 1992 C181/3); (exemption renewal OJ 1994 L20/15 [1995] 4 CMLR 658) 7–086
—— (No. 2) OJ 1994 L20/15 [1995] 4 CMLR 658 .... 3–039, 3–042, 3–050, 3–052, 7–046, 7–075, 7–084, 7–086, 7–089, 7–093
Guérin automobiles v. Commission (T–186/94) [1995] II ECR 1753 [1996] 4 CMLR 685; *on appeal* Case C–282/95P 7–107A, 12–023, 12–024
HOV SVZ/MCN OJ 1994 L104/34; *on appeal* Case T–229/94 .... 4–075, 4–096, 9–008, 9–020, 12–084, 15–010
Hansa Ferry OJ 1996 C118/5 15–017
Herlitz v. Commission (T–66/92) [1994] II ECR 531 [1995] 5 CMLR 458 .... 2–098, 7–019, 12–068
Higgins v. Marchant & Eliot Underwriting Ltd, judgment of 21 December 1995 (CA) 2–137, 10–029
Hilti v. Commission (T–30/89) [1991] II ECR 1439 [1992] 4 CMLR 16; *on appeal* Case C–53/92P 9–002, 9–008, 9–062
—— v. —— (C–53/92P) [1994] I ECR 667 [1994] 4 CMLR 614 .... 9–002, 9–008, 9–014, 9–046, 9–057, 9–062, 9–071, 12–132
Hoechst/Marion Merrell Dow (M.587) Decn. of 22 June 1995 6–064
Holderim/Cedest (M.460) Decn. of 6 July 1994 .... 6–076, 6–116, 6–146, 6–148
Holmsund Golv OJ 1994 C398/8 [1995] 4 CMLR 673 .... 7–011, 7–027
Hoogovens/Klöckner (M.578) Decn. of 11 April 1995 .... 6–040, 6–042
Hopkins v. National Power (C-18/94) [1996] 4 CMLR 745 .... 16–001, 16–013, 17–004A
Hugin v. Commission (22/78) [1979] ECR 1869 [1979] 3 CMLR 345 9–014
IATA-Cargo Surcharge, XXIIIrd Report on Competition Policy (1993), point 238 4–003
IATA-Currency Rules, XXIIIrd Report on Competition Policy (1993), point 237 4–082
IBM v. Phoenix International [1994] RPC 251 (Ch D) 8–072
——/France/CGI (M.336) Decn. of 19 May 1993 6–150
ICI v. Commission (T–36/91) [1995] II ECR 1847 [1995] All ER (EC) 600: on appeal Case–286/95P 2–025, 2–037, 4–055, 4–064, 12–029 12–036, 12–046
—— v. —— (T–37/91) [1995] II ECR 1901; *on appeal* Case C–286/95P etc .. 4–064, 7–192, 9–057, 9–073, 12–035, 12–036, 12–043
——/Tioxide (M.023) Decn. of 28 November 1990 [1991] 4 CMLR 792 6–011
IHT Internationale Heitztechnik v. Ideal Standard (C–9/93) [1994] I ECR 2789 .... 8–005, 8–010, 8–021, 8–029, 8–034, 8–067, 8–165
IJsselcentrale OJ 1991 L28Ø32 [1992] 5 CMLR 154; *on appeal* Case T–16/91 .... 16–010, 16–011
ING/Barings (M.573) Decn. of 14 March 1995 6–023
——/—— (M.573) Decn. of 11 April 1995 6–110
ISAB Energy OJ 1996 C138/3 [1996] 4 CMLR 889 .... 16–019A
Iberian UK Ltd v. BPB Industries PLC [1996] 2 CMLR 601 (Ch D) 10–022, 10–047
Ingersoll-Rand/Clark Equipment (M.388) Decn. of 15 May 1995 6–049
——/MAN (M.479) Decn. of 28 July 1994 6–016
Inntrepreneur Estates v. Boyes [1993] 47 EG 140 [1994] 68 P&CR 77 (CA) 7–128, 10–028
—— v. Mason [1993] 2 CMLR 293 [1994] 68 P & CR 53 (QBD) 7–128, 11–022, 11–064
Inntrepreneur-GM-Courage OJ 1993 C206/2 [1993] 5 CMLR 517 ..... 7–126, 7–135, 7–162
Intergraph Corp. v. Solid Systems CAD Services Ltd, judgment of 7 December 1993 (Ch D) 10–043
International Energy Agency OJ 1994 L68/35 .... 3–024, 3–050, 4–059, 16–043
International Private Satellite Partners OJ 1994 L354/75 .... 5–019, 5–060, 5–062
Intrax, XXIIIrd Report on Competition Policy (1993), point 218 .... 5–019, 5–040A
Irish Club Rules OJ 1993 C263/6 XXIIIrd Report on Competition Policy (1993), point 233 .... 4–037, 15–019
Irish Continental Group v. CCI Morlaix [1995] 5 CMLR 177 .... 9–016A, 9–063A , 12–048
Italy v. Commission (C–364/90) [1993] I ECR 2097 18–051
—— v. —— (C–47/91) [1994] I ECR 4635 .... 18–027, 18–039, 18–053
Ivoclar (No. 2) OJ 1993 C251/3 [1994] 4 CMLR 578 ..... 7–027, 7–075, 7–090, 7–094, 7–095
Jefferson Smurfit/Munksjo (M.613) Decn. of 31 July 1995 6–013
Johnbeere v. Commission (T–35/92) [1994] II ECR 957; *on appeal* Case C–8/95P ... 2–122, 4–029, 4–034

KNP BT/Société Générale (M.640) Decn. of 3 October 1995 6–040
Kali & Salz/MdK/Treuhand (M.308) OJ 1994 L186/386–054, 6–074A, 6–076, 6–077, 6–140, 6–140A
Kall-Kwik Printing (UK) Ltd v. Rush [1996] FSR 114 (Ch D) 7–177
Keck and Mithouard (C–267 & 268/91) [1993] I ECR 6097 [1995] 1 CMLR 101 ... 1–036
Kenwood Electronics Deutschland OJ 1993 C67/9 [1993] 4 CMLR 389 7–084
Kimberley-Clark OJ 1995 C283/2 18–011
Kirklees MBC v. Wickes Building Supplies Ltd [1993] AC 227 (HL) 10–038
Koelman v. Commission [1996] 4 CMLR 636 .... 10–023, 12–023, 12–024, 12–026
Kruidvat v. Commission (T–87/92) not yet decided 2–019, 7–075, 7–085, 7–089, 9–015
Krupp/Thyssen/Riva/Falck/Tadfin/AST (M.484) OJ 1995 L251/18 6–103
LdPE OJ 1989 L74/21 [1990] 4 CMLR 382; *on appeal* Cases T–80/89, etc. .. 4–011, 12–043
LH/SAS OJ 1996 L54/28 [1996] 4 CMLR 845; *on appeal* Case T–37/96 .... 3–034, 3–045, 3–050, 3–052, 5–131B, 15–057
La Cinq v. Commission (T–44/90) [1992] II ECR 1 [1992] 4 CMLR 449 12–048
La Roche/Syntax (M.457) Decn. of 20 June 1994 6–064
Laakmann Karton v. Commission (T–301/94R) [1994å II ECR 1279 12–129
Ladbroke v. Commission (T–74/92) [1995] II ECR 115 .... 12–023, 12–024
Ladbroke Racing v. Commission (T–548/93) [1995] II ECR 2565 [1996] 4 CMLR 549; *on appeal* Cases C–359 & 379/95P 12–024
—— v. —— (C–359 & 379/95P) 12–024
Lagauche (C–46/90 and C–93/91) [1993] I ECR 5267 .... 13–004, 13–015, 13–033
Langnese-Iglo OJ 1993 L183/19 [1994] 4 CMLR 83 ..... 3–027, 3–039, 3–045, 7–109, 7–118, 7–123, 7–124, 7–127, 7–135, 12–054
—— v. Commission (T–24/92R) [1992] II ECR 1839 .... 7–111, 12–048
—— v. —— (T–7/93) [1995] II ECR 1533 [1995] 5 CMLR 602 [1995] All ER (EC) 902; *on appeal* Case C–279/95P ... 2–079, 2–104, 2–105, 2–106, 2–135, 2–144, 3–021, 3–032, 7–109, 7–111, 7–123, 7–127, 9–073, 11–066, 12–054
Langnese-Iglo and Schöller v. Commission (T–7 & T–9/93R) [1993] II ECR 131 .. 7–111
Le Nouveau Garage v. Commission (T–199/95) not yet decided 7–107A
Leclerc v. Commission (T–19/92) not yet decided 2–143, 2–145, 7–075, 7–085, 7–089, 9–015
Lener Ignace SA v. Beauvois [1994] 2 CMLR 419 (French Cour de Cass.) 18–037
Leyland DAF v. Automotive Products [1994] 1 BCLC 245 (CA) 9–059
Luftartsfunktionaererne v. Commission (T–37/96) [1996] 4 CMLR 845 (*on appeal*, T–37/96) 3–034, 3–050, 5–131B, 12–022, 15–057
Lyonnaise des Eaux/Northumbrian Water (M.567) Decn. of 21 December 1995 ... 6–153
MSG Media Services (M.469) OJ 1994 L364/1 6–146
MTV Europe v. BMG Records (UK) Ltd, judgment of 17 July 1995 (CA) [1995] 1 CMLR 437 (Ch D) 10–016, 10–022
McCormick/CPC/Rabobank/Ostmann (M.330) Decn. of 3 November 1993 .. 6–146, 6–147
McDermott/ETPM (M.648) Decn. of 27 November 1995 6–052
Mannesmann/Vallourec/Ilva (M.315) OJ 1994 L102/15 .... 6–065, 6–076
March & Elliot (Underwriting) Ltd v. Higgins [1996] 1 Lloyd's Rep. (QBD) on appeal: [1996] 2 Lloyd's Rep. 31 (CA) 2–063, 10–029
Marconi/Finmeccanica (M.496) Decn. of 5 September 1994 6–054
Masterfoods Ltd t/a Mars Ireland v. HB Ice Cream Ltd [1992] 3 CMLR 830 (Ir. High Ct) 7–111, 7–128, 10–047
Matra v. Commission (C–225/91) [1993] I ECR 3203 ...... 18–011, 18–013, 18–031, 18–050, 18–055, 18–061
Matra Hachette v. Commission (T–17/93) [1994] II ECR 595 .... 2–064, 3–003, 3–017, 3–021, 3–027, 3–028, 3–031, 3–033, 3–038, 3–039, 5–007, 5–019, 5–077, 12–036, 12–046, 18–061
Maxims v. Dye [1978] 2 All ER 55 [1977] 1 WLR 1155 (Ch.D) 8–045
Mediobanca/Generali (M.159) Decn. of 19 December 1991; *on appeal* Case T–83/92 6–140
Merci Convenzionali Porto di Genova (C–179/90) [1991] I ECR 5891 .... 9–016, 15–021
Merck & Co. Inc. v. Prime-crown Ltd (C–267/95), not yet decided 8–018
Metro SB-Grossmärkte v. Cartier (C–376/92) [1994] I ECR 15 [1994] 5 CMLR 331 7–075
Métropole Télévision and Others v. Commission (T–528/93 etc) [1996] SCMLR 386 (*on appeal*: Case C–320/96P) 3–021, 3–032, 3–042, 4–086, 4–095, 8–173, 13–025
Microsoft, XXIVth Report on Competition Policy (1994), p. 364 ...... 8–096, 8–109, 8–178, 9–043
Milk Marketing Board, XXIInd Report on Competition Policy (1992), points 161–167 14–005

Montedison/Groupe Vernes/SCI (M.630) Decn. of 8 December 1995 6–011
Motor Vehicle Grouping OJ 1994 C130/3, XXIVth Report on Competition Policy (1994), Annex II, p. 369 4–003
NALOO v. Commission. *See* National Association of Licensed Opencast Operators v. Commission.
NMH Stahlwerke GmbH and Others v. Commission (T–134/94), not yet decided 17–005
Namur-les Assurances du Crédit v. OND (C-44/93) [1994] I ECR 33829 18–027
National Association of Licensed Opencast Operators v. British Coal Corporation [1993] 4 CMLR 615; *on appeal* Case T–57/91 .... 16–013, 17–005, 17–017
—— v. Commission (T–57/91) [1993] 5 CMLR 124 .... 12–046, 16–013, 17–017
Neste/Statoil (M.361) Decn. of 17 February 1994 6–138
Nestlé/Pemer (M.190) OJ 1992 L356/1; *on appeal* Case T–12/93 .... 6–140A
Nestlé/Perrier (Case IV/M.190), OJ 1992 L356/1 6–122
Net Book Agreement (Ir. Comp. Authority Decn. of 10 June 1994) 7–036
Newitt/Dunlop Slazenger International OJ 1992 L131/32; *on appeal* Case T–43/92 ... 7–013, 7–020, 7–021
Newspaper Publishing (M.423) Decn. of 14 March 1994 6–151
Night Services. *See* European Night Services.
Nissan France v. Dupasquier (C–53/95) [1996] I ECR 677 7–098
Nokia/SP Tyres (M.548) Decn. of 14 March 1995 6–032
Nordic Capital/Transpool (M.625) Decn. of 23 August 1995 6–011
Nordick Satellite Distribution (M.490) Decn. of 19 July 1995 6–138
Novell/Microsoft, XXIVth Report on Competition Policy (1994), point 200 9–040
Nuclear Electric/British Nuclear Fuels OJ 1996 C89/4 [1996] 4 CMLR 716 16–032
Oliebranchens Fadlesrad, XXIVth Report on Competition Policy (1994), Annex II, A.2(j) 16–046
Olivetti/Digital OJ 1994 L309/24 .... 3–031, 3–033, 3–039, 5–131B, 7–112
Omnitel (M.538) Decn. of 24 February 1995 6–040
Organon, XXVth Report on Competition Policy (1995), points 37–38 7–020
Orkla/Volvo (M.582) OJ 1996 L66/17 .... 6–124, 6–138, 6–142
Ortscheit (C–320/93) [1994] I ECR 5243 8–025
Otto v. Postbank (C–60/92) [1993] I ECR 5683 12–016
Oude Luttikhuis v. Coberco Case C–399/93 [1995] I ECR 4515 [1996] 5 CMLR 178 14–006
P&I Clubs OJ 1995 C181/16 11–058
PMI-DSV OJ 1995 L221/34 .... 8–060, 8–175
PSA/Fiat (Sevel agreement, Report on application of competition rules in the EU (1995) 5–019, 5–074
PVC OJ 1989 L74/1 [1990] 4 CMLR 345; *on appeal* Cases T–79/89 etc 4–011, 12–043
PVC Cartel, Re, (T–79/89 etc) [1992] II ECR 315 [1992] 4 CMLR 357; *on appeal* Cases C–137/92P 12–043
PVC II OJ 1994 L239/14; *on appeal* Cases T–305/94 etc 4–011, 12–043
—— (T–305/94 etc) 4–011
Pack Service/4PEF, Tribunal de Defensa de la Competencia (Spain) XXIVth Report on Competition Policy (1994), point 90 .... 8–119, 12–046
Panayiotou v. Sony Music Entertainment Ltd [1994] EMLR 229 (Ch D) 10–047
Papeteries de Golbey, XXIIIrd Report on Competition Policy (1993), point 244 ... 5–019, 5–035, 5–051
Parfums Givenchy OJ 1992 L236/11; *on appeal* Case T–87/92 .... 2–019, 7–075, 7–085, 7–087, 9–015
Parker Pen v. Commission (T–77/92) [1994] II ECR 549 [1995] 5 CMLR 435 .... 2–098, 2–099, 7–019, 12–037, 12–068, 12–078, 12–090
Pasteur Mérieux/Merck OJ 1994 L309/1 .... 3–025, 3–033, 5–019, 5–045, 5–046, 5–049, 5–052, 5–056, 5–060, 5–088, 5–094
Pechiney World Trade/Minemet (M./473) Decn. of 20 July 1994 6–049
Pelikan/Kyocera, XXVth Report on Competition Policy (1995), points 86–7 9–014
Petrogal (C–39/92) [1993] I ECR 5659 .... 7–145, 7–155
Peugeot v. Commission (T–9/92) [1993] II ECR 493 [1995] 5 CMLR 696; *on appeal* Case C–322/93P 7–098, 7–100, 7–107
—— v. —— (C–322/93P) [1994] I ECR 2727 .... 7–098, 7–107
Pharma v. Rhône-Poulenc (C–232/94) judgment of 11 July 1996 .... 8–010, 8–035, 8–036
Phil Collins (C–92 & 326/92) [1993] I ECR 5145 [1993] 3 CMLR 773 8–002
Philips/Grundig (M.382) Decn. of 3 December 1993 6–032
——/Matsushita DCC OJ 1992 C333/8 [1995] 4 CMLR 286 .... 8–115, 8–116

Philips/Osram OJ 1994 L378/37 [1996] 4 CMLR 48 ..... 3–031, 3–033, 3–045, 5–019, 5–041, 5–045, 5–060
——/Thomson/SAGEM XXIIIrd Report on Competition Policy (1993), point 215 ... 3–025, 5–019, 5–046, 5–049, 5–051
Phoenix/GlobalOne, OJ 1996 L239/57 .... 3–045, 3–052, 5–018, 5–040A
Pilkington-Techint/SIV (M.358) OJ 1994 L158/24 6–076
Pitney Bowes v. Francotyp-Postalia [1990] 3 CMLR 466 (Ch D) 10–033
Port of Elsinore, Press Release IP (96) 205, 6 March 1996 [1996] 4 CMLR 728 ... 1–026A, 13–018, 15–021
Port of Rødby OJ 1994 L55/52 [1994] 5 CMLR 457 .... 9–016A, 9–039, 9–041, 9–063A, 13–018
Postbank v. Commission (T–353/94R) [1994] II ECR 1141 12–046
Premiair, Report on the application of the competition rules in the EU (1995) 5–019
Procordia/Erbamont (M.323) Decn. of 29 April 1993 6–064
Procter & Gamble/VP Schickedanz (M.430) Decn. of 21 June 1994 OJ 1994 L354/32 .... 6–064, 6–113A, 6–138
Profil ARBED; *on appeal* Case T–150/95 17–020
Publishers' Association v. Commission (T–66/89) [1992] 5 CMLR 120; *on appeal* Case C–360/92P 2–129
—— v. —— (C–360/92P) [1995] I ECR 23 [1995] 5 CMLR 33 [1996] ICR 121 .... 2–129, 3–021, 3–024, 3–027, 3–032, 3–043, 4–023, 7–036, 8–055, 12–132
—— – Net Book Agreement OJ 1989 L22/12; *on appeal* Case T–66/89 8–055
R v. HM Treasury, ex p British Telecommunications (C–392/93) [1996] I ECR 1631 [1996] All ER (EC) 411 .... 18–046A
—— v. Minister of Agriculture Fisheries and Food, ex p Hedley Lomas (Ireland) Ltd (C–5/94) [1996] All ER (EC) 493 .... 10–039, 10–041, 18–046A
—— v. Secretary of State for Foreign and Commonwealth Affairs, ex p Rees-Mogg [1994] QB 552 [1994] 1 All ER 457 [1993] 3 CMLR 101
—— v. Secretary of State for Trade and Industry, ex p Airlines of Britain [1993] BCC 89 6–161
R. v. Secretary of State for Transport ex p. Factortame (C–48/93) [1996] I ECR 1029 [1996] 1 CMLR 889 [1996] All ER (EC) 301 .... 10–039, 18–046A
—— v. Stock Exchange, ex p Else Ltd [1993] QB 534 (CA) 10–010
REN/Turbogás OJ 1996 C118/7 [1996] 4 CMLR 881 .... 16–019A
Rev Norsk Hydro v. Commission (T–106/89) [1994] II ECR 419 12–043
RTE and ITP v. Commission (C–241 & 242/91P) [1995] I ECR 743 [1995] 4 CMLR 718 [1995] All ER (EC) 416 .... 1–068, 8–064, 8–176, 9–002, 9–007, 9–014, 9–032, 9–065, 9–639, 10–033, 12–055
RTL/Veronica/Endemol (M.533) Decn. of 20 September 1995; *on appeal* Case T–221/95 6–154
RTZ/CRA (M.660) Decn. of 7 December 1995 6–007
Radio Telefis Eireann v. Commission (T–69/89) [1991] II ECR 485 [1991] 4 CMLR 586; *on appeal* Cases C–241 & 242/91P 1–068, 9–007, 9–014, 9–032, 9–041, 9–063A, 9–065
Ready Mixed Concrete Agreements, Re (1996) Tr LR 78 10–056
Reiff (C–185/91) [1993] I ECR 5801 [1995] 5 CMLR 145 ..... 1–027, 2–021, 10–064, 15–003
Rendo v. Commission (T–16/91) [1992] II ECR 2417; *on appeal* Case C–19/93P 2–021, 2–053, 4–027, 4–071
—— v. —— (C–19/93P) [1995] I ECR 3319 ...... 2–021, 2–053, 4–027, 4–071, 7–113, 7–118, 16–010
Rendo I (T–2/92) 4–071
Repola/Kymmene (M.646) Decn. of 30 October 1995 6–113
Revlon v. Cripps & Lee [1980] FSR 85 (CA) 8–027
Rhône-Poulenc/Cooper (M.426) Decn. of 18 April 1994 6–064
——/Fisons (M.632) Decn. of 21 September 1995 6–049
——-SNIA/Nordfaser (M.399) Decn. of 3 February 1994 6–076
——/SNIA II (M.355) Decn. of 8 September 1993 6–076
Richard Cound Ltd v. BMS (GB) Ltd, judgment of 10 May 1995 (CA) 2–022, 7–107A, 10–028
Rouffeteau and Badia (C–314/93) [1994] I ECR 3257 13–033
Rover Group, XXIIIrd Report on Competition Policy (1993), point 228 7–036
Royal Bank of Scotland/Bank of Ireland (M.681) Decn. of 5 February 1996 6–031
SAS/Icelandair OJ 1994 C201/9 [1994] 5 CMLR 480 15–058
SAT Fluggesellschaft v. Eurocontrol (C–364/92) [1994] I ECR 43 [1994] 5 CMLR 208 .... 2–004, 2–010, 2–012, 13–023

SCK and FNK OJ 1994 L117/30 and OJ 1995 L312/79 [1996] 4 CMLR 565; *on appeal* Case T–18/96, not yet decided 2–003, 2–134, 3–024, 3–027, 3–043, 4–004, 4–075, 11–017, 12–073, 12–088, 12–095
SEP v. Commission (C–36/92P) [1994] I ECR 1911 .... 11–047, 12–005, 12–008, 12–018, 12–046
SFEI and Others v. La Poste and Others (C–39/94) [1996] All ER(EC) 685 .... 18–003, 18–004, 18–046A
SFEI v. Commission (C–39/93P) [1994] I ECR 2681 .... 12–023, 12–024, 12–132
SGA v. Commission (T–189/95) not yet decided 7–107A
SGS/Thomson (M.216) Decn. of 22 February 1993 ....6–009A
SICASOV OJ 1995 C95/8 [1995] 5 CMLR 100 .... 8–089, 8–177
SIDE v. Commission (T–49/93) [1995] II ECR 2501 .... 18–016, 18–031, 18–039, 18–041, 18–050, 18–051, 18–061
SNCF and British Rail v. Commission (T–79 & 80/95R) [1995] II ECR 1433 [1996] 5 CMLR 26 .... 3–034, 3–050, 4–130, 12–130, 15–008
SPO v. Commission (C–137/95P) [1996] I ECR 1611 .... 1–026A, 2–132, 2–146, 3–021, 3–024, 3–028, 3–039, 3–043, 4–002, 4–021, 4–036, 4–055, 4–070, 11–025, 12–077
SPO and Others v. Commission (T–29/92) [1995] II ECR 289; *on appeal* Case C–137/95P 1–026A, 2–106, 2–132, 2–146, 3–021, 3–024, 3–028, 3–039, 3–048, 4–002, 4–021, 4–036, 4–055, 4–070, 11–025, 12–043
Sabre/Air France and Iberia XXIIIrd Report on Competition Policy (1993), point 239 .... 4–082, 15–047
Salt Union v. Commission Case T–330/94 [1995] II ECR 2881 18–055
Sammelrevers OJ 1996 C54/2, Reuters E.U. Briefing 8 August 1994 .... 3–024, 3–043, 4–023, 7–036
Sanofi/Kodak (M.480) Decn. of 12 August 1994 6–064
——/Sterling Drug (M.072) Decn. of 10 June 1991 6–064
Scheepvaart v. Commission Case T–398/94 judgment of 5 June 1996 18–055
Schöller v. Commission (T–28/92R) 7–111, 12–048
—— v. —— (T–9/93) [1995] II ECR 1611 [1995] 5 CMLR 659 .... 2–079, 2–104, 2–105, 2–106, 2–135, 2–144, 3–021, 3–032, 7–109, 7–111, 7–123, 7–127, 7–162, 11–066, 12–054
Schöller Lebensmittel OJ 1993 L183/1 [1994] 4 CMLR 51 ...... 3–039, 3–045, 7–109, 7–118, 7–123, 7–127, 7–135, 7–162, 12–054
Schott-Zweisel-Glaswerke OJ 1993 C111/4 [1993] 5 CMLR 85 7–084
Scottish Football Association v. Commission (T–46/92) [1994] II ECR 1039 .... 12–003, 12–005
Scottish Nuclear/British Nuclear Fuels OJ 1996 C89/6 [1996] 4 CMLR 718 16–032
Scottish Salmon Board OJ 1992 L246/37 [1993] 5 CMLR 602 .... 14–004, 14–005
Scottish Salmon Growers Association v. EFTA Surveillance Authority (E–2/94) [1994–5] Rep. EFTA Ct. 59 [1995] 1 CMLR 851 .... 12–111, 12–134B, 18–055
Sea Containers v. Stena Sealink OJ 1994 L15/8 [1995] 4 CMLR 84 .... 9–016A, 9–063A, 12–048
Service Station Agreements in Austria, ESA Annual Report 1994, point 4.9.2 .... 7–147, 7–153, 7–155, 7–162
Service Station Agreements in the Canary Islands XXIIIrd Report on Competition Policy (1993), point 226(a) 7–147, 7–155
Service Station Agreements in Spain XXIIIrd Report on Competition Policy (1993), point 226, XXIVth Report on Competition Policy (1994), Annex II p. 361 .... 7–147, 7–153, 7–155
Shell Unimie/Elf Atochem (M.474) Decn. of 22 December 1994 .... 6–034, 6–076
Shell/Montecatini (M.269) OJ 1994 L332/48 .... 6–064A, 6–140A
Siemens v. Commission (T–459/93) [1995] II ECR 1675 .... 18–022, 18–042, 18–042A, 18–043, 18–050
Sloman Neptune (C–72 & 73/91) [1993] I ECR 887 [1995] 2 CMLR 97 ..... 18–004, 18–009
Société Commerciale des Potasses et de L'Azote v. Commission (T–88/94R) [1994] II ECR 401 .... 6–140, 6–140A, 12–130
Société Générale v. Commission (T–34/93) [1995] II ECR 545 [1996] 4 CMLR 665 12–005
Société Generalé de Belgique/Générale de Banque (M.343) Decn. of 3 August 1993 6–013
Society of Lloyd's v. Clementson [1995] CLC 117 (CA), judgment of 7 May 1996 (QBD) 2–063, 2–128, 10–047
Soda-ash-ICI OJ 1991 L152/40 [1994] 4 CMLR 645; *on appeal* Case T–37/91 .... 7–192, 9–057, 9–072

Soda-ash-Solvay OJ 1991 L152/21 [1994] 4 CMLR 645; *on appeal* Case T-32/91 .... 2-131, 7-192, 9-057, 9-073
—— Solvay, CFK OJ 1991 L152/16; *on appeal by Solvay* Case T-31/91 2-016
—— Solvay, ICI OJ 1991 L152/1 [1994] 4 CMLR 454 *on appeal* Cases T-30/91, T-36/912-025, 2-037, 2-046, 4-055
Sogecable v. Commission (T-52/96), not yet decided 6-111, 6-140A
Solvay v. Commission (T-30/91) [1995] II ECR 1775 [1996] 5 CMLR 57 [1995] All ER (EC) 600 .... 2-025, 2-037, 4-055, 4-064, 12-029, 12-036, 12-046
—— v. —— (T—31/91) [1995] II ECR 1821; *on appeal* Case C-286/95P 2-016, 4-064, 12-043
—— v. —— (T—32/91) [1995] II ECR 1825 [1996] 5 CMLR 91; *on appeal* Case C287/95P 2-131, 4-064, 7-192, 9-057, 9-073
Solvay-Laporte/Interox (M.197) Decn. of 30 April 1992 6-016
Sony Espana OJ 1993 C275/3 [1994] 4 CMLR 581 .... 7-069, 7-075, 7-084, 7-087
Sony Pan-European Dealer Agreement OJ 1993 C321/11 [1994] 5 CMLR 101 (Notice), Press Release IP (95) 736, 12 July 1995 [1995] 5 CMLR 126 .... 7-084, 7-087
Sotralentz v. Commission (T-149/89) [1995] II ECR 1127 12-094
Spa Monopole/GDB XXIIIrd Report on Competition Policy (1993), point 240, [1994] 4 CMLR 20 4-084
Spain v. Commission (C-278/92 etc.) [1994] I ECR 4103 .... 18-004, 18-007, 18-014, 18-023, 18-030, 18-042, 18-052
—— v. —— (C-42/93) [1994] I ECR 4175 [1995] 2 CMLR 702 XXIVth Report on Competition Policy (1994), point 344, XXVth Report (1995), point 159 ..... 18-007, 18-012, 18-022, 18-023
—— v. —— (C-135/93) [1995] I ECR 1651 .... 18-024, 18-048
Spain and Portugal v. Commission (C-11 & 12/96), not yet decided 13-033
Standard Seed Production and Sales Agreement OJ 1990 C6/3 8-089
Steelbeams OJ 1994 416/1 [1994] 5 CMLR 353; *on appeal* Cases T-137/94 etc 2-034, 4-005, 4-014A, 4-027, 4-036, 4-038, 4-040, 4-055, 12-084, 12-088
Stena Tor Line OJ 1996 C-209/5 15-017
Stergios Delimitis v. Henninger Brau AG (C-234.89) [1991] I ECR 935 [1992] 5 CMLR 210 .... 7-111, 7-127, 7-128, 16-020
Stichting Baksteen OJ 1994 L131/15 [1995] 4 CMLR 646 .... 3-031, 3-034, 3-039, 3-045, 4-040
Stoke-on-Trent v. B&Q (C-169/91) [1992] I ECR 6635 [1993] 1 CMLR 426 1-036
Swissair/Sabena (M.616) Decn. of 20 July 1995 .... 6-113, 6-113A, 15-057
Synthomer/Yule Catto (M.376) Decn. of 22 October 1993 6-011
Sytraval and Brink's France v. Commission (T-95/94) [1995] II ECR 2651
—— v. —— (C-367/95P) 18-031, 18-051
TBT/BT/Tele Danmark/Telnor (M.570) Decn. of 24 April 1995 6-040
TWD Textilwerke Deggendorf (C-188/92) [1994] I ECR 833 [1995] 2 CMLR 145 .... 18-037, 18-047, 18-055
—— v. Commission (T-244 & 486/93) [1995] II ECR 2265 [1996] 1 CMLR 332; *on appeal* Case C-355/95P 18-036A, 18-043
—— (No. 1) OJ 1986 L300/34 .... 18-036A
—— (No. 2) OJ 1991 L215/16; *on appeal* Case T-244/93 .... 18-036A
—— (No. 3) OJ 1992 L183/36; *on appeal* Case T-486/93 .... 18-036A
Taillandier (C-92/91) [1993] I ECR 5383 13-033
Tax aid for investment (Basque country) OJ 1993 L134/25 .... 18-009, 18-010
Tetra Pak II OJ 1992 L72/1 [1992] 4 CMLR 551; *on appeal* Case T-83/91 ... 1-075, 2-121, 9-002, 9-010, 9-045, 9-046, 9-047, 9-055, 9-073, 9-075, 12-079
Tetra Pak v. Commission (T-83/91) [1994] II ECR 755; *on appeal* Case C-333/94P ... 1-075, 2-121, 9-002, 9-008, 9-010, 9-017, 9-040, 9-044, 9-045, 9-046, 9-047, 9-054, 9-055, 9-056, 9-059, 9-073, 9-074, 9-075, 12-037, 12-077, 12-082, 12-093
Tetra Pak Rausing v. Commission (T-51/89) [1990] II ECR 309 [1991] 4 CMLR 334 9-046
Texaco Ltd, XXIIIrd Report on Competition Policy (1993), point 225 .... 7-165, 7-177
Texaco/Norsk Hydro (M.511) Decn. of 9 January 1994 6-033
The State (Belgium) v. Tubemeuse [1994] 3 CMLR 93 (Belg. Cour de Cass.) 18-047
Tiercé Ladbroke v. Commission (T-471/93) [1995] II ECR 2537; *on appeal* Case C-353/95P 12-024, 18-004
Tractebel/Distrigaz II (M.493) Decn. of 1 September 1994 .... 6-009A
——/Synatom (M.466) Decn. of 30 June 1994 .... 6-009A

Trans-Atlantic Agreement OJ 1994 L376/1; *on appeal* Case T–395/94R 4–003, 4–038, 15–004, 15–019, 15–024
Tréfil Europe Sales v. Commission (T–141/89 etc.) [1995] II ECR 791 etc; *on appeal* Cases C–185 & 219/95P 2–016, 2–020, 2–033, 2–034, 2–099, 2–133, 2–151, 4–004
Tréfilunion v. Commission (T–148/89) [1995] II ECR 1063 12–035
Tremblay and Others v. Commission (T–5/93) [1995] II ECR 185 [1996] 4 CMLR 305 .... 8–052, 12–023
Tretorn and Others OJ 1994 L378/45; *on appeal* Case T–49/95 .... 7–019, 7–021
Tsimenta Chalkidos v. Commission Case T–104/95R [1995] II ECR 2235 12–129
UBC-Almirall, XXIVth Report on Competition Policy (1994), Annex II, p. 362 .... 7–116, 9–057, 9–073
Ukwal OJ 1992 L121/45 [1993] 5 CMLR 632 12–004
Unilever/Deversey (M.704) Decn. of 20 March 1996 6–076
Unilever France/Ortiz Miko (M.422) Decn. of 15 March 1994 .... 6–076, 6–113, 6–113A, 6–064
Union Carbide v. Commission (T–322/94R) [1994] II ECR 1159 .... 6–140A, 12–130
——/Enichem (M.550) Decn. of 13 March 1995 .... 6–064A
Union Internationale des Chemins de Fer v. Commission (T–14/93) [1995] II ECR 1503 [1906] 5 CMLR 40; *on appeal* Case C–264/95P .. 2–032, 4–003, 7–005, 12–109, 15–004, 15–011
Union Royale Belge des Sociétés de Football Association v. Bosman (C–415/93) [1995] I ECR 4921 [1996] 1 CMLR 645 .... 2–063, 2–128, 3–003
Unisource/Telefónica (M.544) Decn. of 6 November 1995 .... 6–031, 6–034, 6–042
United Kingdom Agricultural Tractor Exchange OJ 1992 L68/19; *on appeal* Cases T–34 & 35/92 .... 2–122, 4–029, 4–034
Upjohn/Pharmacia (M.631) Decn. of 28 September 1995 6–064
VGB v. Commission (T–77/94) not yet decided 4–079
Van Den Bergh Foods OJ 1995 C211/4 [1995] 5 CMLR 734 ... 7–111, 7–128, 9–055, 9–073
Van Megen Sports Group v. Commission (T–49/95), not yet decided 7–019, 7–021
Vereingegen Unwesen in Handel und Gewerbe Köln v. Mars (C–470/92) [1995] I ECR 1923 8–038
Vesunis/Wülfrath (M.472) Decn. of 5 September 1994 6–103
Vichy v. Commission (T–19/91) [1992] II ECR 415 11–017
Viho v. Commission (T–102/92) [1995] II ECR 17 [1995] ICR 1050 [1995] All ER (EC) 371; *on appeal* Case C–73/95P 2–005, 2–054
Viho/Parker Pen OJ 1992 L233/27; *on appeal* Cases T–6 and 77/92 .... 2–098, 7–019
Voith/Sulzer II (M.478) Decn. of 29 July 1994 6–040
Volvo v. Erik Veng (UK) Ltd (C–238/87) [1980] ECR 6211 [1989] 4 CMLR 122 ... 8–072, 8–073, 10–033
Welded Steel Mesh OJ 1989 L260/1 [1991] 4 CMLR 13; *on appeal* Cases T–141/89 etc 2–020, 2–033, 2–034, 2–099, 2–133, 4–004
Wellcome Foundation v. Discpharm Ltd [1993] FSR 433 (Patent Cty. Ct.) 8–018
Westdeutsche Landesbank v. Islington B.C. [1994] 1 WLR 938 (CA) 10–030
Winterthur/DBV (M.429) Decn. of 30 May 1994 6–016
Wirtschaftsvereinigung Stahl and Others v. Commission (T–244/94) 17–020
Wood Pulp II. *See* Ahlström v. Commission 2–043
Yves Saint Laurent Parfums OJ 1992 L12/24 [1993] 4 CMLR 120; *on appeal* Case T–19/92 .... 2–143, 2–145, 7–075, 7–085, 7–087, 9–015
Zerz/Montedison OJ 1993 L272/28 [1995] 5 CMLR 320 .... 7–013, 7–021
Zunis Holding and Others v. Commission (T–83/92) [1993] II ECR 1169 [1994] 5 CMLR 154; *on appeal* Case C–480/93P 6–013, 6–140, 12–104
—— v. —— (C–480/93P) [1996] I ECR 1, [1996] 5 CMLR 219 .... 6–013, 6–140, 12–104, 12–105

B. EUROPEAN COURT OF JUSTICE

23/67, Brasserie de Haecht v. Wilkin (No. 1) [1967] ECR 407 [1968] CMLR 26 16–020
22/78, Hugun v. Commission [1979] ECR 1869 [1979] 3 CMLR 345 9–014
262/81, Coditel v. Curie Vog Films (No. 2) [1982] ECR 3381 [1983] 1 CMLR 49 .. 8–173
C–169/84, CdF Chimie AZF v. Commission [1990] I ECR 3083 [1992] 1 CMLR 177 18–010
169/84, COFAZ v. Commission [1986] ECR 391 [1986] 3 CMLR 385 18–055
C–89/85, etc., Ahlström v. Commission [1993] I ECR 1307 [1993] 4 CMLR 407 2–043
66/86, Ahmed Saeed [1989] ECR 803 [1990] 4 CMLR 102 15–053
30/87, Bodson v. Pompes Funèbres [1988] ECR 2479 [1989] 4 CMLR 984 3–039
C–234/89, Stergios Delimitis v. Hanninger Brau AG [1991] I ECR 935 [1992] 5 CMLR 210 .... 7–111, 7–127, 7–128, 16–020
C–238/87, Volvo v. Erik Veng (UK) Ltd [1988] ECR 6211 [1989] 4 CMLR 122 ..... 8–072, 8–073, 10–033
C–6 & 9/90, Francovich v. Italian Republic [1991] I ECR 5337 [1993] 2 CMLR 66 .... 10–038, 10–041
C–179/90, Merci Convenzionali Porto di Genova [1991] I ECR 5891 .... 9–016, 15–021
C–313/90, CIRFS and Others v. Commission [1993] I ECR 1125 .. 18–024, 18–052, 18–055
C–324 & 342/90, Germany and Pleuger Worthington v. Commission [1994] I ECR 1173 [1994] 3 CMLR 521 .... 18–039, 18–051
C–364/90, Italy v. Commission [1993] I ECR 2097 18–051
C–46/90 & 93/91, Lagauche [1993] I ECR 5267 .... 13–004, 13–015, 13–033
C–47/91, Italy v. Commission [1994] I ECR 4635 .... 18–027, 18–039, 18–053
C–69/91, Decoster [1993] I ECR 5335 13–033
C–72 & 73/91, Sloman Neptune [1993] I ECR 887 [1995] 2 CMLR 97 .... 18–004, 18–009
C–92/91 Taillander [1993] I ECR 5383 13–033
C–169/91, Stoke-on-Trent v. B&Q [1993] 1 CMLR 426 1–036
C–185/91, Reiff [1993] I ECR 5801 [1995] 5 CMLR 145 .... 1–027, 2–021, 10–064, 15–003
C–195/91P, Bayer v. Commission [1994] I ECR 5619 [1996] 4 CMLR 32 ..... 2–098, 2–121, 7–020, 12–043, 12–117
C–198/91, Cook v. Commission [1993] I ECR 2487 [1993] 3 CMLR 206 ... 18–031, 18–050, 18–055
C–225/91 Matra v. Commission [1993] I ECR 3203 .... 18–011, 18–013, 18–031, 18–050, 18–055, 18–061
C–241 & 242/91P, RTE and ITP v. Commission [1995] I ECR 743 [1995] 4 CMLR 718 [1995] All ER (EC) 416 .... 1–068, 8–064, 8–176, 9–002, 9–007, 9–014, 9–032, 9–065, 9–639, 10–033, 12–055
C–267 & 268/91, Keck and Mithouard [1993] I ECR 6097 1–036
C–317/91, Deutsche Renault [1993] I ECR 6227 [1995] 1 CMLR 461 .... 8–028, 8–030, 8–040
C–320/91, Corbeau v. Belgian Post Office [1993] I ECR 2523 [1995] 4 CMLR 621 ... 9–029, 13–016, 13–025, 13–027
C–325/91, France v. Commission [1993] I ECR 3283 .... 18–007, 18–008
C–372/91, France v. Commission [1994] I ECR 364 [1994] 5 CMLR 517 .... 1–070, 11–057, 12–046
C–36/92P, SEP v. Commission [1994] I ECR 1911 .... 11–057, 12–005, 12–008, 12–018, 12–046
C–39/92, Petrogal [1993] I ECR 5659 .... 7–145, 7–155
C–53/92P, Milti v. Commission [1994] I ECR 667 [1994] 4 CMLR 614 .... 9–002, 9–008, 9–014, 9–046, 9–057, 9–062, 9–071, 12–132
C–60/92, Otto v. Postbank [1993] I ECR 5683 12–016
C–70 & 71/92, Florimex v. Commission 4–079
C–92 & 326–92, Phil Collins [1993] I ECR 5145 [1995] 3 CMLR 773 8–002
C–128/92, Banks [1994] I ECR 1209 [1994] 5 CMLR 30 .. 10–006, 10–022, 10–041, 10–047, 16–001, 17–005, 17–017
C–137/92P, Commission v. BASF and Others [1994] I ECR 2555 .... 4–011, 12–043, 18–027
C–188/92, TWD Textilwerke Deggendorf [1994] I ECR 833 [1995] 2 CMLR 145 .... 18–037, 18–047, 18–055
C–250/92, Gøttrup-Klim v. Dansk Landbrugs Grorrareselskab AmbA [1994] I ECR 5641 [1996] 4 CMLR 191 .... 2–063, 2–091, 4–090, 9–002, 14–003

C–278/92, etc., Spain v. Commission [1994] I ECR 410318–004, 18–007, 18–014, 18–023, 18–030, 18–042, 18–052
C–360/92P, Publishers' Association v. Commission [1995] I ECR 23 [1995] 5 CMLR 33 .... 2–129, 3–021, 3–024, 3–027, 3–032, 3–043, 4–023, 7–036, 8–055, 12–132
C–364/92, SAT Fluggesellschaft v. Eurocontrol [1994] I ECR 43 [1994] 5 CMLR 208 .... 2–004, 2–010, 2–012, 13–023
C–376/92, Metro SB Grossmärkte v. Cartier [1994] I ECR 15 [1994] 5 CMLR 331 7–075
C–387/92, Banco Exterior de Espana [1994] I CMLR 877 [1994] 3 CMLR 473 ..... 13–021, 18–003, 18–009, 18–027, 18–062
C–393/92, Almelo [1994] I ECR 1477 ..... 2–079, 3–134, 2–144, 7–111, 7–113, 9–002, 9–005, 9–029, 9–039, 9–057, 13–004, 13–023, 13–025, 13–027, 16–006, 16–009, 16–011, 16–012, 16–020
C–400/92, Germany v. Commission [1994] I ECR 4701 [1995] 2 CMLR 461 18–025
C–5/93P, DSM v. Commission, not yet decided 2–044, 4–010
C–9/93, IHT Internationale Heitztechnik v. Ideal Standard [1994] I ECR 2789 ...... 8–005, 8–010, 8–021, 8–029, 8–034, 8–067, 8–165
C–18/93, Corsica Ferries [1994] I ECR 1783 .... 9–003, 9–016A, 9–041, 9–055, 13–016, 13–018, 15–021
C–19/93P, Rendo v. Commission [1995] I ECR 3319 ... 2–021, 2–053, 4–027, 4–071, 7–113, 16–010
C–39/93P, SFEI v. Commission [1994] I ECR 2681 .... 12–023, 12–024, 12–132
C–42/93, Spain v. Commission [1994] I ECR 4175 [1995] 2 CMLR 702 XXIVth Report on Competition Policy (1994), point 344 and XXVth Report (1995), point 159 .... 18–007, 18–012, 18–022, 18–023
C–44/93, Namur-les Assurances du Crédit v. OND [1994] I ECR 3829 18–027
C–46 & 48/93, Brasserie du Pêcheur v. Germany and Factortame III [1996] I ECR 1029 [1996] 1 CMLR 889 [1996] All ER (EC) 493 .... 10–039, 18–046A
C–56/93, Belgium v. Commission [1996] I ECR 723 18–010
C–70/93, BMW v. ALD Auto-Leasing [1996] 4 CMLR 478 .... 7–098, 7–100, 7–107A, 10–051, 10–060
C–135/93, Spain v. Commission [1995] I ECR 1651 .... 18–024, 18–048
C–153/93, Delta Schiftartes-und Speditiongesellschaft [1994] I ECR 2517 [1996] 4 CMLR 21 .... 1–027, 2–021
C–266/93, Bundeskartellamt v. Volkswagen and VAG Leasing [1996] 4 CMLR 478 .... 7–005, 7–098, 7–100, 10–051, 10–060
C–310/93P, BPB Industries and British Gypsum v. Commission [1995] I ECR 865 .... 2–091, 9–002, 9–006, 9–045, 9–057, 9–077, 12–036
C–314/93, Roufteteau and Badia [1994] I ECR 3257 13–033
C–319/93, etc., Dijkstra and Others [1995] I ECR 4471 ... 10–016, 10–019, 10–023, 14–006, 14–007
C–320/93, Ortscheit [1994] I ECR 5243 8–025
C–322/93P, Peugeot v. Commission [1994] I ECR 2727 .... 7–098, 7–107
C–323/93, Centre d'Insemination de la Crespelle v. Coopérature de la Mayenne [1994] I ECR 5077 .... 9–002, 9–029, 13–016
C–348 & 350/93, Commission v. Italy [1995] I ECR 673 & 679 18–042
C–349/93, Commission v. Italy [1995] I ECR 343 18–042
C–392/93, R v. HM Treasury, ex p British Telecommunications [1996] All ER (EC) 411 .... 18–046A
C–399/93 Oude Luttikhuis v. Coberco [1995] I ECR 4515 [1996] 5 CMLR 178 14–006
C–415/93, Union Royale Belge des Sociétés de Football Association v. Bosman [1995] I ECR 4921 [1996] 1 CMLR 645 [1996] All ER (EC) 97 .... 2–063, 2–128, 3–003
C–470/93, Vereingegen Unwesen in Handel und Gewerbe Köln v. Mars [1995] I ECR 1923 8–038
C–472/93, etc., Bristol-Myers Squibb and Others v. Paranova 8–010, 8–030, 8–036
C–480/93P, Zunis Holding and Others v. Commission 6–013, 6–140, 12–104, 12–105
C–18/94, Hopkins v. National Power [1996] 4 CMLR 745 .... 16–001, 16–013, 17–004A
C–39/94, SFE1 and Others v. La Poste and Others [1996] All ER (EC) 685 .... 18–003, 18–004, 18–046A
C–68/94, France v. Commission, not yet decided 6–140
C–71/94, Eurim-Pharm v. Beiersdorf judgment of 11 July 1996 8–025
C–96/94, Centro Servizi Spediporto [1995] I ECR 2883 [1996] 4 CMLR 613 2–021
C–122/94 Commission v. Council [1996] I ECR 881 18–026

B. EUROPEAN COURT OF JUSTICE

C–140 & 142/94, DIP Spa v. Commune di Bassani del Grappa [1995] I ECR 3257 [1996] 4 CMLR 1572–021, 9–039
C–159/94, Commission v. France, not yet decided 16–038
C-174/94R, France v. Commission [1994] I ECR 5229 12–130
C–178/94, Dillenhofer v. Germany, not yet decided 18–046A
C–226, 94, Grand Garage Albigeois v. Garage Massol [1996] I ECR 651 7–098
C–244/94, Fédération Francaise des Sociétés d'Assurance [1995] I ECR 4013 2–004
C–333/94P, Tetra Pak v. Commission 1–075, 2–121, 9–045, 9–046, 9–047, 9–055, 9–073, 12–082
C–5/95, R v. Minister of Agriculture Fisheries and Food, ex p. Hedley Lomas (Ireland) Ltd [1996] All ER (EC) 493 .... 10–039, 10–041, 18–046A
C–7/95P, Fiatagn and New Holland Ford v. Commission, not yet decided ... 2–122, 4–029, 4–034
C–8/95P, John Deere v. Commission 2–122, 4–029, 4–034
C–53/95, Nissan France v. Dupasquier [1996] I ECR 677 7–098
C–73/95P, Viho v. Commission 2–054
C–137/95P, SPO v. Commission [1996] I ECR 1611 .. 1–026A, 2–132, 2–146, 3–021, 3–024, 3–028, 3–039, 3–043, 4–002, 4–021, 4–036, 4–055, 4–070, 11–025
C–149/95P(R), Commission v. Atlantic Container Line and Others [1995] I ECR 2165 [1995] All ER (EC) 853 .... 4–003, 4–038, 12–130, 15–004
C–185/95P & 219/95P, Tréfileurope Sales v. Commission, etc. 2–033, 2–099, 2–133, 4–004
C–232/94 Pharma v. Rhône-Poulenc 8–025
C–264/95P, Union Internationale des Chemins de Fer v. Commission 2–032, 4–003, 12–109, 15–004
C–267/95, Merck & Co. Inc. v. Primecrown Ltd, not yet decided 8–018
C–268/95, Beecham Group plc v. Europharm of Worthing Ltd, not yet decided ... 8–018
C–279/95P, Langnese-Iglo v. Commission 2–079, 2–135, 2–104, 2–105, 2–106, 2–144, 3–021, 3–032, 9–073
C–282/95P, Guérin Automobiles v. Commission 12–023, 12–024
C–286/95P, etc., Solvay v. Commission 2–016, 4–064, 7–192, 9–073
C–288/95P, ICI v. Commission 4–064, 7–192, 9–073
C–291/95, Belgium v. Commission 9–016A, 9–020, 9–041, 13–018
C–316/95, Generics BV v. Smith, Kline & French laboratories, not yet decided 8–025
C–321/95P, Greenpeace and Others v. Commission 18–055
C–339/95, Compagnia di Navigazione Maritime v. Compagnie Maritime Belge, not yet decided 15–004, 15–023, 15–025
C–343/95, Diego Cali & Figli v. Servizi Ecologico Porto di Genora, not yet decided 9–016A
C–353/95P, Tiercé Ladbroke v. Commission 12–024, 18–004
C–359 & 379/95P, Ladbroke Racing Ltd v. Commission 12–024
C–367/95P, Sytraval v. Commission 18–031, 18–051
C–11 & 12/96, Spain and Portugal v. Commission, not yet decided 13–033

C. EUROPEAN COURT OF FIRST INSTANCE

T–8/89, Rev., DSM v. Commission [1992] II ECR 2399; *on appeal* Case C–5/93P ... 2–044, 4–010
T–30/89, Hilti v. Commission [1991] II ECR 1439 [1992] 4 CMLR 16; *on appeal* Case C–53/92P ... 9–002, 9–008, 9–062
T–39 & 40/92, CB and Europay v. Commission [1994] II ECR 49 ..... 2–033, 3–021, 3–037, 3–043, 4–017, 4–025, 12–083
T–51/89, Tetra Pak Rausing v. Commission [1990] II ECR 309 [1991] 4 CMLR 334 9–046
T–65/89, BPB Industries and British Gypsum v. Commission [1993] II ECR 389 [1993] 5 CMLR 32; *on appeal* Case C–310/93P 9–002, 9–045, 9–057, 12–036, 12–091
T–145/89, Baustahlgewebe v. Commission [1995] II ECR 987 .... 12–080, 12–119
T–66/89, Publishers' Association v. Commission [1992] 5 CMLR 120; *on appeal* Case C–360/92P ... 2–129
T–69/89, Radio Telefis Eireann v. Commission [1991] II ECR 485 [1991] 4 CMLR 586; *on appeal* Cases C–241 & 242/91P 1–068, 9–007, 9–014, 9–032, 9–041, 9–063A, 9–065
T–79/89, etc., Re PVC Cartel [1992] II ECR 315 [1992] 4 CMLR 357; *on appeal* C–137/92P ... 12–043
T–80/89, etc., BASF and Others v. Commission [1995] II ECR 729 judgment of 6 April 1995 ... 4–011, 12–043
T–106/89, REV Novsk Hydro v Commission [1994] II ECR 419 ... 12–043
T–141/89, etc., Tréfileurope Sales v. Commission [1995] II ECR 791 etc; *on appeal* Cases C–185 & 219/95P 2–016, 2–020, 2–033, 2–034, 2–099, 2–133, 2–151, 4–004
T–142/89, Boël v. Commission [1995] II ECR 867 ... 12–099
T–145/89, Baustahlgewebe v. Commission [1995] II ECR 937 .... 12–080, 12–119
T–148/89, Tréfilunion v. Commission, judgment of 6 April 1995 ... 12–035
—— v. —— (T–148/89) [1995] II ECR 1063 ... 000
T–149/89, Sotralentz v. Commission [1995] II ECR 1127 ... 12–094
T–12/90, Bayer v. Commission [1991] II ECR 219 æ1993] 4 CMLR 30; *on appeal* Case C–195/91P ... 2–098, 2–121
T–44/90, La Cinq v. Commission [1992] II ECR 1 [1992] 4 CMLR 449 ... 12–048
T–16/91, Rendo v. Commission [1992] II ECR 2417; *on appeal* Case C–19/93P 2–021, 2–053, 4–027, 4–071
T–19/91, Vichy v. Commission [1992] II ECR 415 ... 11–017
T–30/91, Solvay v. Commission [1995] II ECR 1775 [1996] 5 CMLR 57 .... 2–025, 2–037, 4–055, 4–064, 12–029, 12–036, 12–046
T–30/91 etc., Solvay, ICI [1995] II ECR 1775, 1821, 1825, 1847, 1901 .... 2–131, 7–192, 9–057, 9–073
T–31/91, Solvay v. Commission [1995] II ECR 1821; *on appeal* Case C–286/95P 2–016, 4–054, 4–064, 12–043
T–32/91, Solvay v. Commission [1995] II ECR 1825 [1996] 5 CMLR 91; *on appeal* Case C–287/95P ... 2–131, 4–064, 7–192, 9–057, 9–073
T–36/91, ICI v. Commission [1995] II ECR 1847 [1995] All ER (EC) 600 .... 2–025, 2–037, 4–055, 4–064, 12–029, 12–036, 12–046
T–37/91, ICI v. Commission [1995] II ECR 1901; *on appeal* Cases C–286/95P etc. ... 4–064, 7–192, 9–057, 9–073, 12–035, 12–036
T–52/96 Sogecable v. Commission ... 6–111, 6–140A
T–57/91, National Association of Licensed Opencast Operators v. Commission [1993] 4 CMLR 124 ... 12–046, 16–013, 17–017
T–83/91, Tetra Pak v. Commission [1994] II ECR 755; *on appeal* Case C–333/94P ... 1–075, 2–121, 9–002, 9–008, 9–010, 9–017, 9–040, 9–044, 9–045, 9–046, 9–047, 9–054, 9–055, 9–056, 9–059, 9–073, 9–074, 9–075, 12–037, 12–077, 12–082, 12–093
T–2/92, Rendo I ... 4–071
T–9/92, Peugeot v. Commission [1993] II Rec. 493 [1995] 5 CMLR696; *on appeal* Case C–322/93P ... 7-098, 7–100, 7–107
T–19/92, Leclerc v. Commission, not yet decided 2–143, 2–145, 7–075, 7–085, 7–089, 9–015
T–24/92R, Langnese-Iglo v. Commission [1992] II Rec. 1839 ... 7–111, 12–048

T–28/92R, Schöller v. Commission7–111, 12–048
T–29/92, SPO and Others v. Commission [1995] II ECR 289; *on appeal* Case C–137/95P 1–026A, 2–106, 2–132, 2–146, 3–021, 3–024, 3–028, 3–039, 3–043, 4–002, 4–021, 4–036, 4–055, 4–070, 11–025, 12–043
T–34/92, Fiatagri and New Holland Ford v. Commission [1994] II ECR 905; *on appeal* Case C–7/95P 2–122, 4–029, 4–034, 12–043
T–35/92, John Deere v. Commission [1994] II ECR 957; *on appeal* Case-C–8/95P ... 2–122, 4–029, 4–034
T–37/92, BEUC and NCC v. Commission [1994] II ECR 285 [1995] 4 CMLR 167 .... 12–021, 12–023, 12–024
T–38/92, AWS Benelux v. Commission [1994] II ECR 211 [1995] 4 CMLR 43 ...... 12–043, 12–092, 12–111
T–39 & 40/92, CB and Europay v. Commission [1994] II ECR 49 ..... 2–033, 3–021, 3–037, 3–043, 4–017, 4–025, 12–083
T–43/92, Dunlop Slazenger v. Commission [1994] II ECR 441 .... 2–017, 2–048, 7–013, 7–020, 7–021, 12–044, 12–088
T–46/92, Scottish Football Association v. Commission [1994] II ECR 1039 .... 12–003, 12–005
T–66/92, Herlitz v. Commission [1994] II ECR 531 [1995] 5 CMLR 458 ...... 2–098, 7–019, 12–068
T–74/92, Ladbroke v Commission [1995] II ECR 115 .... 12–023, 12–024
T–77/92, Parker Pen v. Commission [1994] II ECR 549 [1995] 5 CMLR 435 .... 2–098, 2–099, 7–019, 12–037, 12–068, 12–078, 12–090
T–83/92, Zunis Holding and Others v. Commission [1993] II ECR 1169 [1994] 5 CMLR 154; *on appeal* Case C–480/93P 6–013, 6–140, 12–104, 12–105
T–87/92, Kruitvat v. Commission, not yet decided 2–019, 7–075, 7–085, 7–089, 9–015
T–96/92, CCE de la Société Générale des Grandes Sources v. Commission [1995] II ECR 1213 and T–96/92R, [1992] II ECR 2579 .... 6–140A, 12–104
T–102/92, Viho v. Commission [1995] II ECR 17 [1995] ICR 1050 [1995] All ER (EC) 371; *on appeal* Case C-73/95P 2–005, 2–054
T–114/92, BEMIM v. Commission [1995] II ECR 147 [1996] 4 CMLR 305 .... 8–052, 10–023, 12–022, 12–023, 12–026
T–2/93, Air France v. Commission [1994] II ECR 323 .... 6–009, 6–140, 12–104, 15–053, 15–058
T–3/93, Air France v. Commission [1994] II ECR 121 .... 6-050, 6–140
T–5/93, Tremblay and Others v. Commission [1995] II ECR 185 [1996] 4 CMLR 305 .... 8–052, 12–023
T–7/93, Langnese-Iglo v. Commission [1995] II ECR 1533 [1995] 5 CMLR 602 [1995] All ER (EC) 902; *on appeal* Case C–279/95P 2–079, 2–104, 2–105, 2–106, 2–135, 2–144, 3–021, 3–032, 7–109, 7–111, 7–123, 7–127, 9–073, 11–066, 12–054
T–7 & 9/93R, Langnese-Iglo and Schöller v. Commission [1993] II ECR 131 7–111
T–9/93, Schöller v. Commission [1995] II ECR 1611 [1995] 5 CMLR 659 .... 2–079, 2–104, 2–105, 2–106, 2–135, 3–021, 3–032, 7–109, 7–111, 7–123, 7–127, 7–162, 11–066, 12–054
T–12/93, CCE de Vittel v. Commission [1995] II ECR 1247 12–104
T–12/93R, CCE Vittel and CE Pierval v. Commission [1993] II ECR 785 .... 6–140A
T–14/93, Union Internationale des Chemins de Fer v. Commission [1995] II ECR 1503 [1996] 5 CMLR 40; *on appeal* Case C–64/95P 2–032, 4–003, 7–005, 12–109, 15–004, 15–011
T–17/93, Matra Hachette v. Commission [1994] II ECR 595 .. 2–064, 3–003, 3–017, 3–021, 3–027, 3–028, 3–031, 3–033, 3–038, 3–039, 5–007, 5–019, 5–077, 12–036, 12–046, 18–061
T–24/93, etc., Compagnie Maritime Belge v. Commission, not yet decided 2–151, 12–084, 15–018
T–32/93, Ladbroke v. Commission [1994] II ECR 1015 .... 13–024, 13–029
T–34/93, Société Générale v. Commission, judgment of 8 March 1995 12–005
T–49/93, SIDE v. Commission [1995] II ECR 2501 .... 18–016, 18–031, 18–039, 18–041, 18–050, 18–051, 18–061
T–244 & 486/93, TWD Textilwerke Deggendorf v. Commission; *on appeal* Case C–355/95P 18–036A, 18–043
T–435/93, ASPEC and Others v. Commission [1995] II ECR 1281 .... 18–027, 18–050, 18–055
T–442/93, AAC and Others v. Commission [1995] II ECR 1329 .... 18–027, 18–050
T–443/93, Casillo Grani v Commission [1995] II ECR 1375 18–055

T–447/93, etc., AITEC and others v. Commission [1995] II ECR 1971 judgment of 22 May 199618–014, 18–019, 18–027, 18–048, 18–052, 18–055
T–459/93, Slemeins v. Commission [1995] II ECR 1675 .... 18–022, 18–042, 18–042A, 18–043, 18–050
T–471/93, Tiercé Ladbroke v. Commission, judgment of 18 September 1995; *on appeal* Case C–353/95P 12–024, 18–004
T–513/93, CNSD, not yet decided 2–021, 4–016
T–528/93, etc., Metropole Télévision and Others v Commission, judgment of 11 July 1996 (*on appeal*: C–320/96P) 3–021, 3–032, 4–086, 4–095
T–543/93R, Gestevision Telecino v. Commission [1993] II ECR 1409 12–130
T–549/93, Ladbroke Racing Ltd v. Commission [1996] 4 CMLR 549; *on appeal* Cases C–359 & 379/95P 12–024
T–575/93 Koelman v. Commission [1996] 4 CMLR 636 10–023
T–585/93, Greenpeace and Others v. Commission [1995] II ECR 2205; *on appeal* Case C–321/95P 18–055
T–66/94, Auditer v. Commission [1995] II ECR 239 .... 3–043, 4–075, 5–039, 12–046
T–77/94, VGB v. Commission, not yet decided 4–079
T–88/94R, Société Commerciale des Potasses et de l'Azote v. Commission [1994] II ECR 401 .... 6–140, 6–140A, 12–130
T–95/94, Sytraval and Brink's France v. Commission [1995] II ECR 2651; *on appeal* Case C–367/95P 18–031, 18–051
T–134/94, NMH Stahlwerke GmbH and Others v. Commission 17–005
T–137/94, etc., Steelbeams 2–034, 4–014A, 4–027, 4–040
T–156/94R, Aristrain v. Commission [1994] II ECR 717 .... 4–014A
T–186/94, Guérin Automobiles v. Commission [1995] II ECR 1753 [1996] 4 CMLR 685; *on appeal* Case C–282/95P 7–107A, 12–023, 12–024
T–229/94, Deutsche Bahn v. Commission 4–075
T–239/94R, EISA v. Commission [1994] II ECR 703 17–020
T–243/94, British Steel v. Commission, not yet decided 17–020
T–244/94, Wirtschaftsvereingung Stahl and Others v. Commission 17–020
T–275/94, CB v. Commission [1995] II ECR 2169 [1995] 5 CMLR 410 [1995] All ER (EC) 717 .... 4–017, 12–097, 12–099, 12–103
T–295/94R, Buchmann v. Commission [1994] II ECR 1265 .... 2–034, 4–014B, 12–036, 12–077, 12–091, 12–092, 12–129
T–301/94R, Laakmann Karton v. Commission [1994] II ECR 1279 12–129
T–305/94, etc., PVC II 4–011
T–307/94, etc., Re PVC Cartel [1995] 4 CMLR 15 12–043
T–308/94R, Cascades v. Commission [1995] II ECR 265 12–129
T–330/94 Salt Union v. Commission [1995] II ECR 2881 18–055
T–332/94R, Union Carbide v. Commission [1994] II ECR 1159 .... 6–140A, 12–130
T–353/94R, Postbank v. Commission [1994] II ECR 1141 12–046
T–374/94, etc., European Night Services 3–034, 3–052, 4–054, 5–019, 15–006
T–395/94, Atlantic Containers Line and Others v. Commission; *See* [1995] II ECR 595 (partial suspension of Commission Decision); *on appeal* Case C–149/95P (R) 4–003, 4–038, 11–017, 12–130, 15–004, 15–019, 15–024
T–395/94, Atlantic Container Line and Others v. Commission, not yet decided 4–003, 4–038
T–395/94R, —— (partial suspension of Commission Decision) [1995] II ECR 595, *on appeal*, Case C–149/95 PCR) 4–003, 4–038, 12–130
T–395/94RII, —— (re: withdrawal of immunity from fines) [1995] II ECR 2893 ..... 4–003, 11–017
T–398/94 Scheepvaart v. Commission, judgment of 5 June 1996 18–055
T–25/95, etc., Cement 2–034, 2–151, 4–014C
T–49/95, Van Megen Sports Group v. Commission, not yet decided 7–019, 7–021
T–79 & 80/95R, SNCF and British Rail v. Commission [1995] II ECR 1433 .... 3–034, 3–050, 4–054, 12–130, 15–008
T–150/95, British Iron and Steel Producers' Association v. Commission, XXIVth Report on Competition Policy (1994), Annex II.E, p. 504 17–020
T–189/95, SGA v. Commission, not yet decided 7–107A
T–199/95, Le Nouveau Garage v. Commission, not yet decided 7–107A
T–9/96, Européenne Automobile v. Commission, not yet decided 7–107A
T–37/96, Luftfartesfunktionaererne v. Commission [1996] 4 CMLR 845 ...... 3–034, 3–050, 5–131B, 15–057
T–52/96, Sagecable v. Commission, not yet decided 6–111, 6–140A

D. EC MERGER REGULATION CASES

NB. The Commission's Annual Reports on Competition Policy contain additional information on procedural and substantive issues raised by cases viewed as significant by the Commission.

Recent cases marked below are those where the public decision is not yet on the file.*

1990 NOTIFICATIONS

	Parties (Case No.)	Notice of notification and Phase I decision	Decision (date) OJ and CMLR references	Business sector
1.	Renault/Volvo (IV/M.004)	OJ 1990 C254/3 OJ 1990 C281/2	1. Clearance 2. No jurisdiction (7 November 1990) [1991] 4 CMLR 297	Motor vehicles: 1. Trucks and buses 2. Cars
2.	AG/Amev (IV/M.018)	OJ 1990 C268/8 OJ 1990 C304/27	Clearance (21 November 1990) [1991] 4 CMLR 847	Insurance
3.	ICI/Tioxide (IV/M.023)	OJ 1990 C278/15 OJ 1990 C304/27	Clearance (28 November 1990) [1991] 4 CMLR 792	Chemical (titanium dioxide)
4.	Arjomari-Prioux/ Wiggins Teape Appleton (IV/M.025)	OJ 1990 C285/18 OJ 1990 C321/16	No jurisdiction (10 December 1990) [1991] 4 CMLR 854	Paper and pulp
5.	Promodes/Dirsa (IV/M.027)	OJ 1990 C290/16 OJ 1990 C321/16	Clearance (17 December 1990) [1992] 5 CMLR M25	Food retailing
6.	Cargill/Unilever (IV/M.026)	OJ 1990 C293/8 OJ 1990 C327/14	Clearance (20 December 1990) [1992] 4 CMLR M55	Agricultural merchanting
7.	Mitsubishi/UCAR (IV/M.024)	OJ 1990 C300/8 OJ 1991 C5/7	Clearance (4 January 1991) [1992] 4 CMLR M50	Carbon and graphite
8.	Matsushita/MCA (IV/M.037)	OJ 1990 C307/2 OJ 1991 C12/15	Clearance (10 January 1991) [1992] 4 CMLR M36	Consumer electronics and entertainment

	Parties (Case No.)	Notice of notification and Phase I decision	Decision (date) OJ and CMLR references	Business sector
9.	AT&T/NCR (IV/M.050)	OJ 1990 C310/23 OJ 1991 C16/20	Clearance (18 January 1991) [1992] 4 CMLR M41	Computers
10.	Alcatel/Telettra (IV/M.042)	OJ 1990 C315/13 IP/91/50	Phase II: Conditional clearance (12 April 1991) OJ 1991 L122/48 OJ 1991 C127/2 [1991] 4 CMLR 778 (Art. 9 request made)	Telecommunications equipment
11.	Magneti Marelli/CEAc (IV/M.043)	OJ 1990 C315/14 IP/91/51	Phase II: Conditional clearance (29 May 1991) OJ 1991 L222/38 OJ 1991 C209/11	Automotive parts (starter batteries)
12.	Dresdner Bank/Banque Nationale de Paris (IV/M.021)	OJ 1991 C5/7 OJ 1991 C34/20	Clearance (4 February 1991)	Banking (Hungary)

1991 NOTIFICATIONS

	Parties (Case No.)	Notice of notification and Phase I decision	Decision (date) OJ and CMLR references	Business sector
1.	Baxter/Nestlé/Salvia (IV/M.058)	OJ 1991 C7/3 OJ 1991 C37/11	No jurisdiction (6 February 1991) [1992] 5 CMLR M33	Clinical nutrition
2.	Fiat Geotech/ Ford New Holland (IV/M.009)	OJ 1991 C8/7 OJ 1991 C118/14	Clearance (8 February 1991)	Agricultural machinery
3.	ASKO/Omni (IV/M.065)	OJ 1991 C18/13 OJ 1991 C51/12	Clearance (21 February 1991) [1992] 5 CMLR M30	Office services
4.	Aérospatiale/MBB (IV/M.017)	OJ 1991 C18/14 OJ 1991 C59/13	Clearance (25 February 1991) [1992] 5 CMLR M70	Helicopters
5.	Digital/Kienzle (IV/M.057)	OJ 1991 C18/15 OJ 1991 C56/16	Clearance (22 February 1991) [1992] 4 CMLR M99	Computers
6.	Tetra Pak/Alfa-Laval (IV/M.068)	OJ 1991 C36/15 IP/91/235	Phase II: Clearance (19 July 1991) OJ 1991 L290/35 OJ 1991 C275/6 [1992] 4 CMLR M81	Food processing and packaging
7.	Kyowa/Saitama Banks (IV/M.069)	OJ 1991 C36/15 OJ 1991 C66/13	Clearance (7 March 1991) [1992] 4 CMLR M105	Banking
8.	Otto/Grattan (IV/M.070)	OJ 1991 C51/5 OJ 1991 C93/6	Clearance (21 March 1991) [1992] 5 CMLR M49	Mail order retailing
9.	Varta/Bosch (IV/M.012)	OJ 1991 C55/4 IP/91/304	Phase II: Conditional clearance (31 July 1991) OJ 1991 L320/26 OJ 1991 C302/6 [1992] 5 CMLR M1	Automotive parts (starter batteries)

	Parties (Case No.)	Notice of notification and Phase I decision	Decision (date) OJ and CMLR references	Business sector
10.	Usinor/ASD (IV/M.073)	OJ 1991 C84/7 OJ 1991 C193/34	Clearance (29 April 1991)	Steel stockholding
11.	Elf/Ertoil (IV/M.063)	OJ 1991 C84/8 OJ 1991 C124/13	Clearance (29 April 1991)	Oil refining and marketing
12.	La Redoute/Empire (IV/M.080)	OJ 1991 C87/10 OJ 1991 C156/10	Clearance (25 April 1991) [1992] 5 CMLR M39	Mail order retailing
13.	ASKO/Jacobs/ADIA (IV/M.082)	OJ 1991 C100/18 OJ 1991 C132/13	Clearance (16 May 1991) [1993] 4 CMLR M14	Office services
14.	Conagra/Idea (IV/M.010)	OJ 1991 C118/14 OJ 1991 C175/18	Clearance (30 May 1991) [1992] 5 CMLR M19	Meat products
15.	RVI/VBC/Heuliez (IV/M.092)	OJ 1991 C119/12 OJ 1991 C149/15	Clearance (3 June 1991) [1992] 5 CMLR M63	Trucks and buses
16.	VIAG/Continental Can (IV/M.081)	OJ 1991 C119/13 OJ 1991 C156/10	Clearance (6 June 1991)	Packaging
17.	Sanofi/Sterling Drug (IV/M.072)	OJ 1991 C123/28 OJ 1991 C156/10	Clearance (10 June 1991) [1993] 5 CMLR M1	Pharmaceuticals
18.	Elf/Occidental (IV/M.085)	OJ 1991 C126/7 OJ 1991 C160/20	Clearance (13 June 1991) [1993] 4 CMLR M9	Oil and gas exploration and production
19.	Aérospatiale-Alenia/de Havilland (IV/M.053)	OJ 1991 C128/13 IP/91/554	Phase II: Prohibition (2 October 1991) OJ 1991 L334/42 OJ 1991 C314/7 [1992] 4 CMLR M2	Turbo-prop aircraft

	Parties (Case No.)	Notice of notification and Phase I decision	Decision (date) OJ and CMLR references	Business sector
20.	Elf/BC/CEPSA (IV/M.098)	OJ 1991 C132/12 OJ 1991 C172/8	Clearance (18 June 1991)	Oil refining and marketing
21.	Péchiney/Usinor-Sacilor (IV/M.097)	OJ 1991 C135/15 OJ 1991 C175/18	Clearance (24 June 1991)	Metallurgy (sintered alloy parts)
22.	Apollinaris/Schweppes (IV/M.093)	OJ 1991 C137/18 OJ 1991 C203/14	No jurisdiction (24 June 1991) [1992] 4 CMLR M78	Non-alcoholic drinks
23.	Nissan/R. Nissan (IV/M.099)	OJ 1991 C142/10 OJ 1991 C181/21	Clearance (28 June 1991) [1992] 4 CMLR M46	Motor vehicle distribution
24.	Dräger/IBM/HMP (IV/M.101)	OJ 1991 C142/11 OJ 1991 C236/6	Clearance (28 June 1991) [1993] 4 CMLR M77	Hospital software
25.	Lyonnaise de Eaux Dumez/Brochier (IV/M.076)	OJ 1991 C156/9 OJ 1991 C188/20	Clearance (11 July 1991) [1992] 5 CMLR M66	Pipelines and water supply
26.	ICL/Nokia Data (IV/M.105)	OJ 1991 C162/10 OJ 1991 C236/6	Clearance (17 July 1991)	Computers
27.	EDS/SD-Scicon (IV/M.112)	OJ 1991 C162/11 OJ 1991 C237/44	Clearance (17 July 1991) [1993] 4 CMLR M77	Information technology services
28.	Elf/Enterprise (IV/M.088)	OJ 1991 C166/16 OJ 1991 C203/14	No jurisdiction (24 July 1991) [1992] 5 CMLR M66	Oil and gas exploration and production
29.	BP/Petromed (IV/M.111)	OJ 1991 C172/9 OJ 1991 C208/24	Clearance (29 July 1991) [1993] 4 CMLR M71	Oil refining and marketing
30.	Eridania/ISI (IV/M.062)	OJ 1991 C175/19 OJ 1991 C204/12	Clearance (30 July 1991)	Sugar

	Parties (Case No.)	Notice of notification and Phase I decision	Decision (date) OJ and CMLR references	Business sector
31.	Kelt/American Express (IV/M.116)	OJ 1991 C189/25 OJ 1991 C223/38	Clearance (20 August 1991) [1993] 5 CMLR M38	Oil and gas exploration and production
32.	BNP/Dresdner Bank (IV/M.124)	OJ 1991 C198/27 OJ 1991 C226/28	Clearance (26 August 1991)	Banking (Czechoslovakia)
33.	Digital/Philips (IV/M.129)	OJ 1991 C206/9 OJ 1991 C235/13	Clearance (2 September 1991) [1994] 4 CMLR M4	Computers
34.	ABC/Générale des Eaux/Canal+/ W H Smith TV (IV/M.110)	OJ 1991 C209/17 OJ 1991 C244/5	Clearance (10 September 1991) [1993] 4 CMLR M1	TV broadcasting (cable TV)
35.	Delta Air Lines/Pan Am (IV/M.130)	OJ 1991 C213/20 OJ 1991 C289/14	Clearance (13 September 1991) [1992] 5 CMLR M56	Air transport
36.	Mannesmann/Boge (IV/M.134)	OJ 1991 C223/39 OJ 1991 C265/8	Clearance (23 September 1991)	Automotive parts (shock absorbers)
37.	Metallgesellschaft/Feldmühle (IV/M.119)	OJ 1991 C242/7 OJ 1991 C276/4	Clearance (14 October 1991)	Various (explosives, heating and building technology, automotive parts, chemicals, metals)
38.	Paribas/MTH/MBH (IV/M.122)	OJ 1991 C245/16 OJ 1991 C277/18	Clearance (17 October 1991)	Electrical goods
39.	Thomson/Pilkington (IV/M.086)	OJ 1991 C250/31 OJ 1991 C279/19	Clearance (23 October 1991)	Optronic systems
40.	BankAmerica/Security Pacific (IV/M.137)	OJ 1991 C251/10 OJ 1991 C289/14	Clearance (22 October 1991)	Banking
41.	UAP/Transatlantic/Sun Life (IV/M.141)	OJ 1991 C264/12 OJ 1991 C296/12	Clearance (11 November 1991)	Insurance
42.	Metallgesellschaft/Safic Alcan (IV/M.146)	OJ 1991 C265/7 OJ 1991 C300/22	Clearance (8 November 1991)	Rubber

	Parties (Case No.)	Notice of notification and Phase I decision	Decision (date) OJ and CMLR references	Business sector
43.	TNT/Canada Post, DBP Postdienst, La Poste, PTT Post and Sweden Post (IV/M.102)	OJ 1991 C284/24 OJ 1991 C322/19	Clearance (2 December 1991)	Postal services
44.	Cereol/Continentale Italiana (IV/M.156)	OJ 1991 C288/13 OJ 1992 C7/7	No jurisdiction (27 November 1991)	Oil seed, vegetable oil and grain storage
45.	Alcatel/AEG Kabel (IV/M.165)	OJ 1991 C292/16 OJ 1992 C6/23	Clearance (18 December 1991) (Art. 9 request rejected)	Telecommunications and power cables
46.	Lucas/Eaton (IV/M.149)	OJ 1991 C293/11 OJ 1991 C328/15	Clearance (9 December 1991)	Automotive parts (heavy duty braking systems)
47.	Mannesmann/VDO (IV/M.164)	OJ 1991 C297/10 OJ 1991 C88/13	Clearance (13 December 1991)	Automotive parts (various)
48.	Accor/Wagons-Lits (IV/M.126)	OJ 1991 C298/23 IP/91/1169	Phase II: Conditional clearance (28 April 1992) OJ 1992 L204/1 OJ 1992 C184/2 [1993] 5 CMLR M13	Hotels and motorway restaurant services
49.	Eurocom/RSCG (IV/M.147)	OJ 1991 C300/21 OJ 1991 C332/16	Clearance (18 December 1991)	Advertising
50.	Campsa (IV/M.138)	OJ 1991 C302/19 OJ 1991 C334/23	Clearance (19 December 1991)	Oil retailing
51.	Courtaulds/SNIA (IV/M.113)	OJ 1991 C304/18 OJ 1991 C333/16	Clearance (19 December 1991)	Textile fibres (acetate filament yarns)
52.	Ingersoll-Rand/Dresser (IV/M.121)	OJ 1991 C304/19 OJ 1992 C86/15	Clearance (18 December 1991) [1993] 5 CMLR M67	Industrial pumps
53.	Gambogi/Cogei (IV/M.167)	OJ 1991 C304/20 OJ 1991 C334/23	Clearance (19 December 1991)	Construction

	Parties (Case No.)	Notice of notification and Phase I decision	Decision (date) OJ and CMLR references	Business sector
54.	VIAG/EB Brühl (IV/M.139)	OJ 1991 C306/17 OJ 1991 C333/16	Clearance (19 December 1991)	Automotive parts (engine blocks and cylinder heads)
55.	Mediobanca/Generali (IV/M.159)	OJ 1991 C310/35 OJ 1991 C334/23	No jurisdiction (19 December 1991) [1994] 4 CMLR M1	Insurance
56.	Sunrise (IV/M.176)	OJ 1991 C312/23 OJ 1992 C18/15	No jurisdiction (13 January 1992)	TV broadcasting and advertising
57.	Saab Ericsson Space (IV/M.178)	OJ 1991 C314/24 OJ 1992 C17/10	Clearance (13 January 1992)	Electronic equipment
58.	Volvo/Atlas (IV/M.152)	OJ 1991 C320/12 OJ 1992 C17/10	Clearance (14 January 1992)	Hydraulic components
59.	Inchape/IEP (IV/M.182)	OJ 1991 C325/26 OJ 1992 C21/27	Clearance (21 January 1992) [1994] 4 CMLR M11	Motor vehicle distribution, hire and leasing
60.	Ericsson/Kolbe (IV/M.133)	OJ 1991 C329/23 OJ 1992 C27/14	Clearance (22 January 1992)	Telecommunications (digital transmission equipment)
61.	Schweizer Rück/ELVIA (IV/M.183)	OJ 1991 C331/19 OJ 1992 C27/14	Clearance (14 January 1992)	Insurance
62.	Steetley/Tarmac (IV/M.180)	OJ 1992 C1/13 OJ 1992 C50/25	1. Art. 9 referral to UK 2. Clearance (12 February 1992)	Building materials: 1. bricks and clay tiles 2. concrete products
63.	SPAR/Dansk Supermarked (IV/M.179)	OJ 1992 C6/21 OJ 1992 C29/18	Clearance (3 February 1992)	Food retailing

1992 NOTIFICATIONS

	Parties (Case No.)	Notice of notification and Phase I decision	Decision (date) OJ and CMLR references	Business sector
1.	Grand Metropolitan/Cinzano (IV/M.184)	OJ 1992 C6/22 OJ 1992 C47/23	Clearance (7 February 1992)	Drinks
2.	James River/Rayne (IV/M.162)	OJ 1992 C11/10 OJ 1992 C43/19	Clearance (13 February 1992)	Tissue paper
3.	BSN-Nestlé/Cokoladovny (IV/M.090)	OJ 1992 C16/15 OJ 1992 C47/23	No jurisdiction (17 February 1992)	Food products
4.	Torras/Sarrio (IV/M.166)	OJ 1992 C21/26 OJ 1992 C58/20	Clearance (24 February 1992)	Paper and pulp
5.	Ifint/EXOR (IV/M.187)	OJ 1992 C27/15 OJ 1992 C88/13	Clearance (2 March 1992)	Bottled water
6.	Henkel/Nobel (IV/M.186)	OJ 1992 C52/16 OJ 1992 C96/23	Clearance (23 March 1992)	Cosmetics asnd toiletries
7.	Nestlé/Perrier (IV/M.190)	OJ 1992 C53/19 OJ 1992 C80/11	Phase II: Conditional clearance (22 July 1992) OJ 1992 L356/1 OJ 1992 C319/3 [1993] 4 CMLR M17	Bottled water
8.	Generali/BCHA (IV/M.189)	OJ 1992 C62/3 OJ 1992 C107/24	Clearance (6 April 1992)	Insurance
9.	Flachglas/VEGLA (IV/M.168)	OJ 1992 C68/21 OJ 1992 C120/30	No jurisdiction (13 April 1992)	Glass recycling
10.	BSN/EXOR (IV/M.211)	OJ 1992 C72/24 OJ 1992 C115/43	Withdrawn (1 April 1992)	Bottled water
11.	Banesto/Totta (IV/M.192)	OJ 1992 C73/18 OJ 1992 C107/24	Clearance (14 April 1992)	Banking
12.	Thorn EMI/Virgin Music (IV/M.202)	OJ 1992 C75/12 OJ 1992 C120/30	Clearance (27 April 1992)	Music publishing and recording

	Parties (Case No.)	Notice of notification and Phase I decision	Decision (date) OJ and CMLR references	Business sector
13.	Eureko (IV/M.207)	OJ 1992 C75/13 OJ 1992 C113/12	No jurisdiction (27 April 1992)	Insurance
14.	Herba/IRR (IV/M.188)	OJ 1992 C77/15 OJ 1992 C120/30	No jurisdiction (23 April 1992)	Rice
15.	Solvay-Laporte/Interox (IV/M.197)	OJ 1992 C82/11 OJ 1992 C165/26	1. Clearance 2. No jurisdiction (30 April 1992)	Peroxygen products
16.	Mondi/Frantschach (IV/M.210)	OJ 1992 C92/12 OJ 1992 C124/19	Clearance (12 May 1992)	Paper and pulp
17.	Eucom/Digital (IV/M.218)	OJ 1992 C103/22 OJ 1992 C140/20	Clearance (18 May 1992)	Telecommunications (value added network services)
18.	Scott/Mölnlycke (IV/M.208)	OJ 1992 C107/22 OJ 1992 C135/20	Withdrawn	Adult incontinence products
19.	Volvo/Lex (1) (IV/M.224)	OJ 1992 C107/23 OJ 1992 C142/18	Clearance (21 May 1992)	Vehicle distribution
20.	ABB/BREL (IV/M.221)	OJ 1992 C109/10 OJ 1992 C142/18	Clearance (26 May 1992)	Rail transport (rolling stock)
21.	Hong Kong & Shanghai Bank/ Midland (IV/M.213)	OJ 1992 C113/11 OJ 1992 C157/18	Clearance (21 May 1992)	Banking
22.	Du Pont/ICI (IV/M.214)	OJ 1992 C116/13 OJ 1992 C144/10	Phase II: Conditional clearance (30 September 1992) OJ 1993 L7/13 OJ 1993 C8/2 [1993] 5 CMLR M41	Textile fibres (nylon)
23.	Bibby/Finanzauto (IV/M.220)	OJ 1992 C139/17 OJ 1992 C275/8	Clearance (29 June 1992) [1993] 5 CMLR M11	Earth moving equipment

	Parties (Case No.)	Notice of notification and Phase I decision	Decision (date) OJ and CMLR references	Business sector
24.	Mannesmann/Hoesch (IV/M.222)	OJ 1992 C142/17 IP/92/575	Phase II: Clearance (12 November 1992) OJ 1993 L114/34 OJ 1993 C128/4 (Art. 9 request made)	Steel tubes (gas-line pipes)
25.	Ericsson/Ascom (IV/M.236)	OJ 1992 C151/14 OJ 1992 C201/26	Clearance (8 July 1992)	Telecommunications equipment
26.	Eurocard/Eurocheque-Europay (IV/M.241)	OJ 1992 C182/19 OJ 1992 C193/12	No jurisdiction (13 July 1992)	Financial services
27.	Promodes/BRMC (IV/M.242)	OJ 1992 C152/23 OJ 1992 C232/14	Clearance (13 July 1992)	Food and non-food retailing
28.	GECC/Avis Lease (IV/M.234)	OJ 1992 C153/18 OJ 1992 C201/26	Clearance (15 July 1992)	Motor vehicle leasing
29.	Thomas Cook/LTU/West LB (IV/M.229)	OJ 1992 C154/29 OJ 1992 C199/12	Clearance (14 July 1992)	Travel agencies
30.	Elf Atochem/Rohm & Haas (IV/M.160)	OJ 1992 C161/31 OJ 1992 C201/27	Clearance (28 July 1992)	Acrylic glass
31.	Rhône-Poulenc/SNIA (IV/M.206)	OJ 1992 C177/20 OJ 1992 C212/23	Clearance (10 August 1992)	Textile fibres (nylon filament yarn)
32.	Péchiney/VIAG (IV/M.198)	OJ 1992 C181/21 OJ 1992 C307/17	Clearance (10 August 1992)	Metallurgical products
33.	Northern Telecom/Matra Telecommunication (IV/M.249)	OJ 1992 C181/22 OJ 1992 C240/15	Clearance (10 August 1992)	Telecommunications equipment
34.	Koipe-Tabacalera/Elosua (IV/M.117)	OJ 1992 C185/17 OJ 1992 C227/10	No jurisdiction (28 July 1992)	Olive and sunflower oils

	Parties (Case No.)	Notice of notification and Phase I decision	Decision (date) OJ and CMLR references	Business sector
35.	BTR/Pirelli (IV/M.253)	OJ 1992 C186/31 OJ 1992 C265/5	Clearance (17 August 1992)	Automotive parts (weatherseals)
36.	Pepsico/General Mills (IV/M.232)	OJ 1992 C187/18 OJ 1992 C228/6	Clearance (5 August 1992)	Snack foods
37.	Elf Acquitaine-Thyssen/Minol (IV/M.235)	OJ 1992 C200/18 OJ 1992 C232/14	Clearance (4 September 1992)	Oil distribution
38.	Avesta/British Steel/NCC/AGA/ Axel Johnson (IV/M.239)	OJ 1992 C204/12 OJ 1992 C258/9	Clearance (4 September 1992)	Stainless steel
39.	Allianz/DKV (IV/M.251)	OJ 1992 C207/19 OJ 1992 C258/9	Clearance (10 September 1992)	Insurance
40.	Volvo/Lex(2) (IV/M.261)	OJ 1992 C208/15 OJ 1992 C239/11	Clearance (4 September 1992)	Motor vehicle distribution
41.	CCIE/GTE (IV/M.258)	OJ 1992 C225/14 OJ 1992 C258/10	Clearance (25 September 1992)	Lighting
42.	Ahold/Jerónimo Martins (IV/M.263)	OJ 1992 C226/8 OJ 1992 C261/10	Clearance (29 September 1992)	Food retailing
43.	Siemens/Philips Kabel (IV/M.238)	OJ 1992 C227/9 OJ 1992 C300/14	Withdrawn then re-notified (see no. 51 below)	Cables
44.	Linde/Fiat (IV/M.256)	OJ 1992 C227/10 OJ 1992 C258/10	Clearance (28 September 1992)	Fork lift trucks
45.	Air France/Sabena (IV/M.157)	OJ 1992 C232/15 OJ 1992 C272/5	Clearance (5 October 1992) [1994] 5 CMLR M1	Air transport
46.	VTG/BPTL (IV/M.265)	OJ 1992 C240/14 OJ 1992 C279/8	No jurisdiction (12 October 1992)	Oil distribution
47.	Fortis/La Caixa (IV/M.254)	OJ 1992 C261/9 OJ 1992 C297/4	Clearance (5 November 1992)	Insurance

	Parties (Case No.)	Notice of notification and Phase I decision	Decision (date) OJ and CMLR references	Business sector
48.	British Airways/TAT (IV/M.259)	OJ 1992 C283/10 OJ 1992 C326/16	Clearance (27 November 1992)	Air transport
49.	Rhône-Poulenc Chimie/SITA (IV/M.266)	OJ 1992 C288/6 OJ 1992 C319/6	Clearance (26 November 1992)	Waste management
50.	Del Monte/Royal Foods/Anglo American (IV/M.277)	OJ 1992 C298/10 OJ 1992 C331/13	Clearance (9 December 1992)	Food and drink
51.	Siemens/Philips Kabel (IV/M.238)	OJ 1992 C300/14 OJ 1993 C11/5	Phase II: Re-notification withdrawn (see no. 43 above) (Art. 9 request made)	Cables
52.	Waste Management International – SAE (IV/M.283)	OJ 1992 C307/7 OJ 1993 C10/5	Clearance (21 December 1992)	Waste management
53.	Sextant/BGT-VDO (IV/M.290)	OJ 1992 C312/8 OJ 1993 C9/3	Clearance (21 December 1992)	Aircraft instruments
54.	Pepsico/KAS (IV/M.289)	OJ 1992 C315/2 OJ 1993 C8/2	Clearance (21 December 1992)	Carbonated soft drinks
55.	Crédit Lyonnais/BFG Bank (IV/M.296)	OJ 1992 C322/16 OJ 1993 C45/18	Clearance (11 January 1993)	Banking
56.	British Airways/Dan Air (IV/M.278) (Art. 22 request)	OJ 1992 C328/4 OJ 1993 C68/5	Clearance (17 February 1993) [1993] 5 CMLR M61	Air transport
57.	KNP/Bührmann-Tetterode/VRG (IV/M.291)	OJ 1992 C329/2 IP/93/29	Phase II: Conditional clearance (4 May 1993) OJ 1993 L217/35 OJ 1993 C231/5	Printing presses, paper and board

	Parties (Case No.)	Notice of notification and Phase I decision	Decision (date) OJ and CMLR references	Business sector
58.	Philips/Thomson/SAGEM (IV/M.293)	OJ 1992 C331/14 OJ 1993 C22/2	No jurisdiction (18 January 1993)	Electronics
59.	Tesco/Catteau (IV/M.301)	OJ 1993 C4/2 OJ 1993 C45/18	Clearance (4 February 1993)	Food retailing
60.	Volkswagen/VAG(UK) (IV/M.304)	OJ 1993 C5/3 OJ 1993 C38/12	Clearance (4 February 1993)	Vehicle distribution

1993 NOTIFICATIONS

	Parties (Case No.)	Notice of notification and Phase I decision	Decision (date) OJ and CMLR references	Business sector
1.	Sara Lee/BP Food Division (IV/M.299)	OJ 1993 C9/3 OJ 1993 C39/12	Clearance (8 February 1993)	Meat products
2.	CEA Industrie/France Télécom/Finmeccanica/ SGS-Thomson (IV/M.216)	OJ 1993 C27/3 OJ 1993 C68/5	Clearance (22 February 1993)	Electronics (semi-conductors)
3.	Sanofi/Yves Saint Laurent (IV/M.312)	OJ 1993 C46/10 OJ 1993 C89/3	Clearance (15 March 1993)	Cosmetics and fragrances
4.	Ericsson/Hewlett-Packard (IV/M.292)	OJ 1993 C48/9 OJ 1993 C83/5	Clearance (12 March 1993)	Telecommunications
5.	Matra/Cap Gemini Sogeti (IV/M.272)	OJ 1993 C52/5 OJ 1993 C88/8	Clearance (17 March 1993)	Defence information technology
6.	SITA-RPC/Scori (IV/M.295)	OJ 1993 C53/10 OJ 1993 C88/9	Clearance (19 March 1993)	Waste management
7.	Kingfisher/Darty (IV/M.300)	OJ 1993 C55/11 OJ 1993 C87/8	Clearance (22 March 1993)	Retailing of electrical goods
8.	Zürich/MMI (IV/M.286)	OJ 1993 C64/3 OJ 1993 C112/4	Clearance (2 April 1993)	Insurance
9.	Fletcher Challenge/Methanex (IV/M.331)	OJ 1993 C64/3 OJ 1993 C98/12	Clearance (31 March 1993)	Methanol
10.	Degussa/Ciba-Geigy (IV/M.317)	OJ 1993 C66/14 OJ 1993 C104/10	Clearance (5 April 1993)	Colours for ceramics and glass
11.	GEHE/OCP (IV/M.328)	OJ 1993 C67/12 OJ 1993 C114/5	Clearance (5 April 1993)	Pharmaceutical wholesaling
12.	Thomson/Shorts (IV/M.318)	OJ 1993 C71/7 OJ 1993 C136/4	Clearance (14 April 1993)	Missiles

	Parties (Case No.)	Notice of notification and Phase I decision	Decision (date) OJ and CMLR references	Business sector
13.	Alcan/Inespal/Palco (IV/M.322)	OJ 1993 C75/11 OJ 1993 C114/5	Clearance (14 April 1994)	Packaging (aluminium foil containers)
14.	Ahold/Jerónimo Martin/Inovaçao (IV/M.320)	OJ 1993 C79/5 OJ 1993 C117/2	Clearance (19 April 1993)	Food retailing
15.	Procordia/Erbamont (IV/M.323)	OJ 1993 C88/9 OJ 1993 C128/5	Clearance (29 April 1993)	Pharmaceuticals
16.	Schweizerische Kreditanstalt/Schweizerische Volksbank (IV/M.335)	OJ 1993 C91/5 OJ 1993 C147/6	Clearance (29 April 1993)	Banking
17.	Harrisons & Crosfield/AKZO (IV/M.310)	OJ 1993 C91/6 OJ 1993 C128/5	Clearance (29 April 1993)	Chemicals (including PVC processing additives)
18.	DASA/Fokker (IV/M.237)	OJ 1993 C104/10 OJ 1993 C136/4	Clearance (10 May 1993)	Regional aircraft
19.	Hoechst/Wacker (IV/M.284)	OJ 1993 C105/4 OJ 1993 C171/4	Clearance (10 May 1993)	PVC
20.	IBM France/CGI (IV/M.336)	OJ 1993 C113/2 OJ 1993 C151/5	Clearance (19 May 1993)	IT services and software
21.	Codan/Hafnia (IV/M.344)	OJ 1993 C120/2 OJ 1993 C171/4	Clearance (28 May 1993)	Insurance
22.	Deutsche Bank/Banco de Madrid (IV/M.341)	OJ 1993 C121/5 OJ 1993 C175/11	Clearance (28 May 1993)	Banking
23.	Aegon/Scottish Equitable (IV/M.349)	OJ 1993 C147/7 OJ 1993 C181/4	Clearance (25 June 1993)	Insurance
24.	Toyota Motor Corp/ Walter Frey/Toyota France (IV/M.326)	OJ 1993 C154/8 OJ 1993 C187/4	Clearance (1 July 1993)	Vehicle distribution

	Parties (Case No.)	Notice of notification and Phase I decision	Decision (date) OJ and CMLR references	Business sector
25.	West LB/Thomas Cook (IV/M.350)	OJ 1993 C157/4 OJ 1993 C216/4	Clearance (30 June 1993)	Travel agencies
26.	JCSAT/Sajac (IV/M.346)	OJ 1993 C158/4 OJ 1993 C219/14	Clearance (30 June 1993)	Satellite communications
27.	Pasteur-Mérieux/Merck (IV/M.285)	OJ 1993 C159/2 OJ 1993 C188/10	No jurisdiction (5 July 1993)	Human vaccines
28.	Costa Crociere/ Chargeurs/Accor (IV/M.334)	OJ 1993 C173/15 OJ 1993 C204/5	Clearance (19 July 1993)	Tourism (cruises)
29.	Société Générale de Belgique/Générale de Banque (IV/M.343)	OJ 1993 C188/9 OJ 1993 C225/2	Clearance (3 August 1993)	Banking
30.	Commerzbank/CCR (IV/M.357)	OJ 1993 C191/6 OJ 1993 C221/4	Clearance (9 August 1993)	Banking
31.	Kali und Salz/MdK/Treuhand (IV/M.308)	OJ 1993 C196/9 IP/93/707	Phase II: Conditional clearance (14 December 1993) OJ 1994 L186/38 OJ 1994 C199/5	Potash and salts
32.	Rhône-Poulenc/SNIA(II) (IV/M.355)	OJ 1993 C205/4 OJ 1993 C272/6	Clearance (8 September 1993)	Textile fibres (nylon filament yarn)
33.	BHF/CCF/Charterhouse (IV/M.319)	OJ 1993 C209/6 OJ 1993 C247/4	Clearance (30 August 1993)	Banking
34.	Alcatel/STC (IV/M.366)	OJ 1993 C209/17 OJ 1993 C225/2 OJ 1993 C259/3	No jurisdiction (13 September 1993)	Submarine cables

	Parties (Case No.)	Notice of notification and Phase I decision	Decision (date) OJ and CMLR references	Business sector
35.	Pilkington-Techint/SIV (IV/M.358)	OJ 1993 C213/13 IP/93/724	Phase II: Clearance (21 December 1993) OJ 1994 L158/24 OJ 1994 C173/4	Flat glass
36.	British Telecom/MCI (IV/M.353)	OJ 1993 C226/3 OJ 1993 C259/3	No jurisdiction (13 September 1993)	Telecommunications
37.	Nestlé/Italgel (IV/M.362)	OJ 1993 C226/4 OJ 1993 C270/5	Clearance (15 September 1993)	Ice cream and food products
38.	Mannesmann/Valourec/Ilva (IV/M.315)	OJ 1993 C228/17 OJ 1993 C265/5	Phase II: Clearance (17 December 1993) OJ 1994 L102/15 OJ 1994 C111/6	Stainless steel tubes
39.	Arvin/Sogefi (IV/M.360)	OJ 1993 C235/10 OJ 1993 C305/11	Clearance (23 September 1993)	Automotive parts (exhaust systems)
40.	American Cyanamid/Shell (IV/M.354)	OJ 1993 C243/2 OJ 1993 C273/6	Clearance (1 October 1993)	Agrochemicals
41.	Thyssen/Balzer (IV/M.365)	OJ 1993 C244/5 OJ 1993 C276/18	Clearance (30 September 1993)	Steel tempering and coating
42.	Volvo/Procordia (IV/M.196)	OJ 1993 C252/3 OJ 1993 C281/5	Clearance (11 October 1993)	Food, drink, matches
43.	McCormick/CPC/Rabobank/ Ostmann (IV/M.330)	OJ 1993 C256/3	Art. 9 referral to Germany	Herbs and spices
44.	Allied Signal/ Knorr-Bremse (IV/M.337)	OJ 1993 C257/2 OJ 1993 C298/6	Clearance (15 October 1993)	Automotive parts (air brake systems)

	Parties (Case No.)	Notice of notification and Phase I decision	Decision (date) OJ and CMLR references	Business sector
45.	Synthomer/Yule Catto (IV/M.376)	OJ 1993 C262/3 OJ 1993 C303/5	Clearance (22 October 1993)	Synthetic rubber
46.	Fortis/CGER (IV/M.342)	OJ 1993 C278/3 OJ 1993 C23/13	Clearance (15 November 1993)	Banking/insurance
47.	Continental/Kaliko/ DG Bank/Benecke (IV/M.363)	OJ 1993 C298/6 OJ 1993 C336/11	Clearance (29 November 1993)	Automotive parts (plastic and foam panelling)
48.	UAP/VINCI (IV/M.384)	OJ 1993 C300/11 OJ 1993 C3/5	Clearance (1 December 1993)	Insurance
49.	Philips/Grundig (IV/M.382)	OJ 1993 C302/3 OJ 1993 C336/11	Clearance (3 December 1993)	Electronic equipment
50.	Hoechst/Schering (IV/M.392)	OJ 1993 C321/12 OJ 1993 C9/3	Clearance (6 January 1994)	Agrochemicals
51.	Mannesmann/RWE/Deutsche Bank (IV/M.394)	OJ 1993 C321/13 OJ 1994 C9/3	Clearance (22 December 1993)	Telecomunications
52.	BAI/Banca Popolare di Lecco (IV/M.391)	OJ 1993 C324/2 OJ 1994 C4/3	Clearance (20 December 1993)	Banking
53.	Akzo/Nobel Industrier (IV/M.390)	OJ 1993 C332/6 OJ 1994 C19/13	Clearance (10 January 1994)	Chemicals and paints (decorative, automotive and industrial coatings)
54.	SNECMA/TI (IV/M.368)	OJ 1993 C339/13 OJ 1994 C42/12	Clearance (17 January 1994)	Aircraft equipment (landing gear)
55.	Procter & Gambler/VP Schickendanz I (IV/M.398)	OJ 1993 C341/13 OJ 1994 C19/15	Withdrawn then renotified (see 1994 no. 3 below)	Sanitary protection products

	Parties (Case No.)	Notice of notification and Phase I decision	Decision (date) OJ and CMLR references	Business sector
56.	Unilever France/ Ortiz Miko (I) (IV/M.388)	OJ 1994 C5/3 OJ 1994 C39/5	Withdrawn then renotified (see 1994 no. 12 below)	Ice cream
57.	Rhône-Poulenc-SNIA/ Nordfaser (IV/M.399)	OJ 1994 C6/3 OJ 1994 C42/13	Clearance (3 February 1994)	Textile fibres (nylon filament yarn)

1994 NOTIFICATIONS

	Parties (Case No.)	Notice of notification and Phase I decision	Decision (date) OJ and CMLR references	Business sector
1.	Shell/Montecatini (IV/M.269)	OJ 1994 C8/4 IP/94/87	Phase II: Conditional clearance (8 June 1994) OJ 1994 L332/48	Polypropylene
2.	Generali/Central Hispano-Generali (IV/M.404)	OJ 1994 C11/3 OJ 1994 C57/3	Clearance (9 February 1994) (see 1992, no. 8 above)	Insurance
3.	Procter & Gamble/VP Schickendanz (II) (IV/M.430)	OJ 1994 C19/15 IP/94/143	Phase II: Conditional clearance (21 June 1994) OJ 1994 L354/32 OJ 1994 C379/12	Sanitary protection products
4.	Neste/Statoil (IV/M.361)	OJ 1994 C22/6 OJ 1994 C99/13	Clearance (17 February 1994)	Petrochemicals
5.	CWB/Goldman Sachs/Tarkett (IV/M.395)	OJ 1994 C26/4 OJ 1994 C67/11	Clearance (21 February 1994)	Floor coverings
6.	RWE/Mannesmann (IV/M.408)	OJ 1994 C30/11 OJ 1994 C68/5	Clearance (28 February 1994)	Telecommunications (Mobile data transmission)
7.	Rütgerswerke/Hüls Troisdorf (IV/M.401)	OJ 1994 C40/5 OJ 1994 C95/6	Clearance (2 March 1994)	Copper-clad laminates
8.	Ford/Hertz (IV/M.397)	OJ 1994 C42/13 OJ 1994 C121/4	No jurisdiction (7 March 1994)	Vehicle leasing
9.	ABB/Renault Automation (IV/M.409)	OJ 1994 C49/10 OJ 1994 C80/11	Clearance (9 March 1994)	Automation systems (motor vehicle production)
10.	BMW/Rover (IV/M.416)	OJ 1994 C49/11 OJ 1994 C93/23	Clearance (14 March 1994)	Motor vehicles
11.	Newspaper Publishing (IV/M.423)	OJ 1994 C54/12 OJ 1994 C85/6	Clearance (14 March 1994)	Newspapers

	Parties (Case No.)	Notice of notification and Phase I decision	Decision (date) OJ and CMLR references	Business sector
12.	Unilever France/Ortiz Miko (II) (IV/M.422)	OJ 1994 C55/5 OJ 1994 C109/3	Clearance (15 March 1994)	Frozen food and ice cream
13.	Philips/Hoechst (IV/M.406)	OJ 1994 C55/6 OJ 1994 C81/3	Clearance (11 March 1994)	Optical storage media
14.	GE/Nuovo Pignone (IV/M.405)	OJ 1994 C67/11 OJ 1994 C105/7	Withdrawn then renotified (see no. 21 below)	Gas turbines
15.	BS/BT (IV/M.425)	OJ 1994 C68/4 OJ 1994 C134/4	No jurisdiction (28 March 1994)	Telecommunication (managed data network services)
16.	Rhône-Poulenc/Cooper (IV/M.426)	OJ 1994 C80/3 OJ 1994 C113/2	Clearance (18 April 1994)	Agrochemical pharmaceuticals, medical implements
17.	CGP/GEC Alsthom/KPR/Kone (IV/M.420)	OJ 1994 C85/7 OJ 1994 C110/4	Clearance (14 April 1994)	Cranes
18.	AGF/La Unión y El Félix (IV/M.403)	OJ 1994 C92/11 OJ 1994 C155/7	Clearance (25 April 1994)	Insurance
19.	Allied Lyons/HWE-Pedro Domecq (IV/M.400)	OJ 1994 C93/25 OJ 1994 C126/10	Clearance (28 April 1994)	Wine and spirits
20.	Hüls/Phenolchemie (IV/M.439)	OJ 1994 C105/6 OJ 1994 C142/4	Clearance (6 May 1994)	Chemicals
21.	GE/ENI/Nuovo Pignone (II) (IV/M.440)	OJ 1994 C105/7 OJ 1994 C162/7	Clearance (6 May 1994) (see no. 14 above)	Gas turbines
22.	VIAG/Bayernwerk (IV/M.417)	OJ 1994 C106/3 OJ 1994 C168/11	Clearance (5 May 1994)	Electricity and gas supply
23.	ERC/NRG Victory (IV/M.433)	OJ 1994 C119/6 OJ 1994 C165/8	Clearance (27 May 1994)	Reinsurance

	Parties (Case No.)	Notice of notification and Phase I decision	Decision (date) OJ and CMLR references	Business sector
24.	Winterthur/DBV (IV/M.429)	OJ 1994 C121/6 OJ 1994 C168/11	Clearance (30 May 1994)	Insurance
25.	Sidmar/Klöckner Stahl (IV/M.444)	OJ 1994 C121/7 OJ 1994 C165/9	Clearance (30 May 1994) (see no. 92 below)	Steel products (tubes, pipes)
26.	Medeol/Elosua (IV/M.431)	OJ 1994 C124/4 OJ 1994 C169/10	Clearance (6 June 1994)	Edible oils
27.	BSN/Euralim (IV/M.445)	OJ 1994 C126/9 OJ 1994 C269/6	Clearance (7 June 1994)	Food (ready-prepared meals)
28.	GKN/Brambles/Leto Recycling (IV/M.448)	OJ 1994 C126/9 OJ 1994 C165/9	Clearance (7 June 1994)	Hazardous waste management
29.	Avesta II (IV/M.452)	OJ 1994 C135/6 OJ 1994 C179/7	Clearance (9 June 1994)	Stainless steel
30.	Banco de Santander/Banesto (IV/M.455)	OJ 1994 C138/3 OJ 1994 C178/16	Clearance (13 June 1994)	Banking
31.	Rhône-Poulenc/Caffaro (IV/M.427)	OJ 1994 C139/9 OJ 1994 C259/2	Clearance (17 June 1994)	Technical plastics (nylon)
32.	Daimler Benz/RWE (IV/M.441)	OJ 1994 C139/10 OJ 1994 C178/15	Clearance (20 June 1994)	Solar energy
33.	La Roche/Syntex (IV/M.457)	OJ 1994 C143/4 OJ 1994 C178/15	Clearance (20 June 1994)	Pharmaceuticals, diagnotic systems
34.	Electrolux/AEG (IV/M.458)	OJ 1994 C143/5 OJ 1994 C187/14	Clearance (21 June 1994)	Domestic electrical applicances (white goods)
35.	AGF/Assubel (IV/M.450)	OJ 1994 C150/8 OJ 1994 C215/13	Clearance (27 June 1994)	Insurance
36.	PowerGen/NRG Energy/Morrison Knudsen/Mibrag (IV/M.402)	OJ 1994 C150/9 OJ 1994 C189/5	Clearance (27 June 1994)	Brown coal

	Parties (Case No.)	Notice of notification and Phase I decision	Decision (date) OJ and CMLR references	Business sector
37.	Holdercim/Cedest (IV/M.460)	OJ 1994 C151/11 OJ 1994 C211/5	1. Art 9 referral to France 2. Clearance (6 July 1994)	Building materials: 1. ready mixed concrete 2. cement
38.	Voith/Sulzer (IV/M.443)	OJ 1994 C151/12 OJ 1994 C183/9	Withdrawn then renotified (see no. 44 below)	Paper machinery
39.	Elf Atochem/Rütgers (IV/M.442)	OJ 1994 C153/21 OJ 1994 C235/5	Clearance (29 July 1994)	Tar products
40.	Tractebel/Distrigaz (IV/M.418)	OJ 1994 C157/3 OJ 1994 C185/3	Withdrawn then renotified (see no. 57 below)	Energy
41.	Tractebel/Synatom (IV/M.466)	OJ 1994 C157/4 OJ 1994 C185/3	Clearance (30 June 1994)	Nuclear fuel handling
42.	MSG Media Service (IV/M.469)	OJ 1994 C160/4 IP/94/675 19 July 1994	Phase II: Prohobition (9 November 1994) OJ 1994 L364/1 OJ 1994 C379/35 (Art. 9 request made)	TV broadcasting (pay TV and cable)
43.	Pechiney World Trade/Minemet (IV/M.473)	OJ 1994 C178/14 OJ 1994 C212/3	Clearance (20 July 1994)	Metals trading
44.	Voith/Sulzer (II) (IV/M.478)	OJ 1994 C183/9 OJ 1994 C225/3	Clearance (29 July 1994) (see no. 38 above)	Paper-making machinery
45.	Ingersoll-Rand/MAN (IV/M.479)	OJ 1994 C183/10 OJ 1994 C231/6	Clearance (28 July 1994)	Air compressors
46.	Schneider/AEG (IV/M.447)	OJ 1994 C189/6 OJ 1994 C270/3	Clearance (1 August 1994)	Electronic components

	Parties (Case No.)	Notice of notification and Phase I decision	Decision (date) OJ and CMLR references	Business sector
47.	Kirch/Richemont/Telepiù (IV/M.410)	OJ 1994 C189/6 OJ 1994 C225/3	Clearance (2 August 1994)	TV broadcasting (pay TV)
48.	Vesuvius/Wülfrath (IV/M.472)	OJ 1994 C189/7 OJ 1994 C259/2	Clearance (5 September 1994)	Refractory products
49.	Holdercim/Origny-Desvroise (IV/M.486)	OJ 1994 C193/3 OJ 1994 C238/3	Clearance (5 August 1994)	Building materials
50.	Sanofi/Kodak (IV/M.480)	OJ 1994 C200/3 OJ 1994 C252/3	Clearance (12 August 1994 (see 1991, no. 17)	Pharmaceuticals
51.	Delhaize/PG (IV/M.471)	OJ 1994 C201/11 OJ 1994 C239/13	Clearance (22 August 1994)	Food retailing
52.	GE/CIGI (IV/M.465)	OJ 1994 C209/3 OJ 1994 C271/3	Clearance (29 August 1994)	Insurance
53.	Gencor/Shell (IV/M.470)	OJ 1994 C211/6 OJ 1994 C271/3	Clearance (29 August 1994)	Metals and minerals
54.	Krupp/Thysen/Riva/ Falck/Tadfin/AST (IV/M.484)	OJ 1994 C214/3 OJ 1994 C311/4	Phase II: Clearance (21 December 1994) OJ 1995 L251/18 OJ 1995 C274/3	Stainless steel
55.	Klöckner/Computer 2000 (IV/M.492)	OJ 1994 C221/11 OJ 1994 C303/5	Clearance (5 September 1994)	Computers
56.	Matra Marconi Space/British Aerospace Space Systems (IV/M.437)	OJ 1994 C221/12 OJ 1994 C245/9	Clearance (23 August 1994)	Space systems (satellites)
57.	Tractebel/Distrigaz (II) (IV/M.493)	OJ 1994 C222/4 OJ 1994 C249/3	Clearance (1 September 1994) (see no. 40 above)	Energy, cable TV, water supply, real estate
58.	Marconi/Finmeccanica (IV/M.496)	OJ 1994 C223/7 OJ 1994 C253/10	Clearance (5 September 1994)	Radio-communications (military and civil)

	Parties (Case No.)	Notice of notification and Phase I decision	Decision (date) OJ and CMLR references	Business sector
59.	BMSC/UPSA (IV/M.464)	OJ 1994 C227/6 OJ 1994 C284/3	Clearance (6 September 1994)	Pharmaceuticals
60.	Bertelsmann/News International/Vox (IV/M.489)	OJ 1994 C227/7 OJ 1994 C274/9	Clearance (6 September 1994) (see also no. 87 below)	TV broadcasting, publishing
61.	Commercial Union/ Groupe Victoire (IV/M.498)	OJ 1994 C229/6 OJ 1994 C299/5	Clearance (12 September 1994)	Insurance
62.	American Home Products/ American Cyanamid (IV/M.500)	OJ 1994 C236/6 OJ 1994 C278/3	Clearance (19 September 1994)	Pharmaceuticals
63.	Colonia/Lefac/Breuer/ KMK-CCI (IV/M.494)	OJ 1994 C238/2 OJ 1994 C274/9	Withdrawn (16 September 1994)	Mobile cranes
64.	Jefferson Smurfit/ St Gobain (IV/M.499)	OJ 1994 C243/3 OJ 1994 C284/3	Clearance (19 September 1994)	Paper and packaging
65.	VAG/SAB (IV/M.502)	OJ 1994 C246/3 OJ 1994 C280/3	Clearance (19 September 1994)	Motor vehicle assembly
66.	Rheinelektra/Cofira/ DEKRA (IV/M.485)	OJ 1994 C247/3 OJ 1994 C284/4	No jurisidiction (26 September 1994)	Telecommunications (mobile phones)
67.	CINVen/CIE Management II/ BP Nutrition (IV/M.459)	OJ 1994 C248/3 OJ 1994 C299/5	Clearance (29 September 1994)	Animal foodstuffs
68.	Siemens/Italtel (IV/M.468)	OJ 1994 C264/4 OJ 1994 C292/13	Phase II: Clearance (17 February 1995) OJ 1995 L161/27 OJ 1995 C176/3	Telecommunications equipment

	Parties (Case No.)	Notice of notification and Phase I decision	Decision (date) OJ and CMLR references	Business sector
69.	Mercedes-Benz/ Kässbohrer (IV/M.477)	OJ 1994 C264/5 IP/94/952	Phase II: Clearance (14 February 1995) OJ 1995 L211/1 OJ 1995 C232/2	Buses
70.	Matra Marconi Space/Satcomms (IV/M.497)	OJ 1994 C296/5 OJ 1994 C307/3	Clearance (14 October 1994)	Space systems (satellites)
71.	Avesta (III) (IV/M.504)	OJ 1994 C271/4 OJ 1994 C326/4	Clearance (20 October 1994)	Stainless steel
72.	General Re/Kölnische Rück (IV/M.491)	OJ 1994 C274/8 OJ 1994 C312/5	Clearance (24 October 1994)	Reinsurance
73.	BHF/CCF (II) (IV/M.508)	OJ 1994 C281/6 OJ 1994 C318/7	Clearance (28 October 1994)	Banking
74.	UAP/Provincial (IV/M.512)	OJ 1994 C281/7 OJ 1994 C322/7	Clearance (7 November 1994)	Insurance
75.	British Steel/Svensk Stål/NSD (IV/M.503)	OJ 1994 C283/4 OJ 1994 C350/3	Clearance (7 November 1994)	Steel stockholding
76.	Rhône-Poulenc Italia/Ambiente (IV/M.513)	OJ 1994 C283/5 OJ 1994 C322/5	Clearance (7 November 1994)	Sulphuric acid recycling
77.	Ericsson/Raychem (IV/M.519)	OJ 1994 C297/5 OJ 1994 C350/3	Clearance (21 November 1994)	Telecommunications (fibre optic transmission systems)
78.	KKR/Borden (IV/M.517)	OJ 1994 C303/6 OJ 1994 C364/6	Clearance (24 November 1994)	Food and non-food products

	Parties (Case No.)	Notice of notification and Phase I decision	Decision (date) OJ and CMLR references	Business sector
79.	Sappi/DLJMB/UBS/ Warren (IV/M.526)	OJ 1994 C307/4 OJ 1995 C57/5	Clearance (14 December 1994)	Paper and financial services
80.	Scandinavian Project (IV/M.522)	OJ 1994 C308/9 OJ 1994 C343/13	Clearance (28 November 1994)	Vegetable oils, fork lift trucks, automotive parts
81.	Thomson CSF/ Deutsche Aerospace (IV/M.527)	OJ 1994 C312/6 OJ 1995 C65/4	Clearance (2 December 1994)	Armaments, missiles
82.	British Aerospace/VSEL (IV/M.528)	OJ 1994 C312/7 OJ 1994 C348/6	Clearance (24 November 1994)	Aeronautical and oil/gas engineering
83.	GEC/VSEL (IV/M.529)	OJ 1994 C320/6 OJ 1994 C368/20	Clearance (7 December 1994)	Aeronautical and oil/gas engineering
84.	Shell/Monteshell (IV/M.505)	OJ 1994 C325/6 OJ 1994 C107/2	Clearance (16 December 1994)	Lubricants, liquified petroleum gas
85.	Shell Chimie/Elf Atochem (IV/M.475)	OJ 1994 C328/2 OJ 1995 C35/4	Clearance (22 December 1994)	Flexible PVC (for packaging)
86.	Mannesmann Demag/ Delaval Stork (IV/M.535)	OJ 1994 C333/4 OJ 1995 C23/4	Clearance (21 December 1994)	Gas compressors, steam turbines and feed water pumps
87.	Vox II (IV/M.525)	OJ 1994 C333/5 OJ 1995 C57/5	Clearance (18 January 1994) (see also no. 60 above)	TV broadcasting, publishing
88.	Viag/Sanofi (IV/M.521)	OJ 1994 C334/8 OJ 1995 C57/6	Clearance (21 December 1994)	Food additives, animal waste
89.	Bayer/Hoechst (IV/M.534)	OJ 1994 C334/9 OJ 1994 C379/34	Clearance (21 December 1994)	Dyestuffs (for textiles)
90.	Cable & Wireless/ Schlumberger (IV/M.532)	OJ 1994 C334/10 OJ 1995 C34/2	Clearance (22 December 1994)	Telecommunications services

	Parties (Case No.)	Notice of notification and Phase I decision	Decision (date) OJ and CMLR references	Business sector
91.	Texaco/Norsk Hydro (IV/M.511)	OJ 1994 C347/3 OJ 1995 C23/3	Clearance (9 January 1995)	Gasoline and oil wholesaling and retailing
92.	Sidmar/Klöckner (II) (IV/M.537)	OJ 1994 C347/4 OJ 1995 C37/3	Clearance (9 January 1995) (see also no. 25 above)	Steel products (tubes, pipes)
93.	Direct Line/Bankinter (IV/M.520)	OJ 1994 C350/4 OJ 1994 C1345/5	Clearance (12 January 1995)	Non-life insurance
94.	Akzo Nobel/Monsanto (IV/M.523)	OJ 1994 C359/6 OJ 1995 C37/3	Clearance (19 January 1995)	Chemicals (for industrial rubber)

1995 NOTIFICATIONS

	Parties (Case No.)	Notice of notification and Phase I decision	Decision (date) OJ and CMLR references	Business sector
1.	Recticel/CWW-Gerko Akustik (IV/M.531)	OJ 1995 C7/3 OJ 1995 C187/10	Clearance (3 February 1995)	Sound absorption materials
2.	TWD/Akzo Nobel-Kuagtextil (IV/M.533)	OJ 1995 C14/3 OJ 1995 C46/5	Clearance (10 February 1995)	Textile fibres (polyester filament yarns)
3.	Cegelec/AEG (IV/M.540)	OJ 1995 C20/6 OJ 1995 C71/7	Clearance (20 February 1995)	Industrial control systems (drives and projects)
4.	Svenska Cellulosa/PWA (IV/M.549)	OJ 1995 C20/7 OJ 1995 C57/6	Clearance (20 February 1995)	Paper and packaging products
5.	Glaxo/Wellcome (IV/M.555)	OJ 1995 C31/3 OJ 1995 C65/3	Clearance (28 February 1995)	Pharmaceuticals
6.	Zurigo/Banco di Napoli (IV/M.543)	OJ 1995 C31/4 OJ 1995 C58/4	Clearance (22 February 1995)	Life insurance
7.	Union Carbide/Enichem (IV/M.550)	OJ 1995 C40/3 OJ 1995 C123/3	Clearance (13 March 1995)	Polyethylene resins
8.	Dalgety/Quaker Oats (IV/M.554)	OJ 1995 C40/4 OJ 1995 C82/4	Clearance (13 March 1995)	Pet food
9.	Winterthur/Schweizer Rück (IV/M.518)	OJ 1995 C44/3 OJ 1995 C73/18	Clearance (14 March 1995)	Insurance
10.	La Rinascente/ Cedis Migliarini (IV/M.558)	OJ 1995 C46/3 OJ 1995 C71/7	Clearance (15 March 1995)	Food/non-food retailing
11.	Nokia/SP Tyres UK (IV/M.548)	OJ 1995 C46/4 OJ 1995 C163/9	No jurisdiction (14 March 1995)	Tyres
12.	British Steel/UES (IV/M.563)	OJ 1995 C48/4 OJ 1995 C105/7	Clearance (17 March 1995)	Steel products (forgings, blight bar, cylinders)

	Parties (Case No.)	Notice of notification and Phase I decision	Decision (date) OJ and CMLR references	Business sector
13.	Securicor Datatrak (IV/M.561)	OJ 1995 C48/5 OJ 1995 C82/4	Clearance (20 March 1995)	Vehicle tracking services
14.	CGI/Dassault (IV/M.571)	OJ 1995 C51/3 OJ 1995 C100/3	Clearance (24 March 1995)	Computer defence electronic
15.	Nordic Satellite* Distribution (IV/M.490)	OJ 1995 C53/6 OJ 1995 C104/6	Phase II: Prohibition (19 July 1995) IP/95/801	TV broadcasting (satellite and cable TV)
16.	Torrington/NSK (IV/M.536)	OJ 1995 C53/7 OJ 1995 C104/7	Clearance (28 March 1995)	Automotive parts (steering column systems)
17.	Omnitel (IV/M.538)	OJ 1995 C53/8 OJ 1995 C96/3	No jurisdiction (27 March 1995)	Telecommunications (mobile phones)
18.	GEHE/AAH (IV/M.572)	OJ 1995 C58/5 OJ 1995 C117/8	Clearance (3 April 1995)	Pharmaceutical wholesaling
19.	Allianz/Elvia/ Lloyd Adriatico (IV/M.539)	OJ 1995 C61/2 OJ 1995 C180/4	Clearance (3 April 1995)	Insurance
20.	Behringwerke/Armour Pharmaceutical (IV/M.495)	OJ 1995 C61/3 OJ 1995 C134/4	Clearance (3 April 1995)	Pharmaceuticals (plasma derivatives)
21.	Alfred C. Toepfer/ Champagne Céréales (IV/M.577)	OJ 1995 C63/8 OJ 1995 C104/7	Clearance (6 April 1995)	Malting barley
22.	Havas Voyage/ American Express (IV/M.564)	OJ 1995 C69/3 OJ 1995 C117/8	Clearance (6 April 1995)	Travel services
23.	ING/Barings (IV/M.573)	OJ 1995 C70/4 OJ 1995 C114/6	Clearance (11 April 1995)	Banking
24.	Hoogovens/Klöckner (IV/M.578)	OJ 1995 C71/6 OJ 1995 C243/5	No jurisdiction (11 April 1995)	Steel and non-ferrous metal stockholding

	Parties (Case No.)	Notice of notification and Phase I decision	Decision (date) OJ and CMLR references	Business sector
25.	Solvay/Wienerberger (IV/M.565)	OJ 1995 C73/19 OJ 1995 C170/6	Clearance (12 April 1995)	Plastic pipes and fittings
26.	TBT/BT/Tele Danmark/Telenor (IV/M.570)	OJ 1995 C76/3 OJ 1995 C154/4	Clearance (24 April 1995)	Telecommunications
27.	Volvo/VME (IV/M.575)	OJ 1995 C76/4 OJ 1995 C104/7	Clearance (11 April 1995)	Earth moving and construction equipment
28.	Burda/Blockbuster (IV/M.579)	OJ 1995 C78/15 OJ 1995 C129/5	Clearance (27 April 1995)	Rental and sale of video film and games
29.	Kirch/Richemont/ Multichoice/Telepiù (IV/M.584)	OJ 1995 C82/5 OJ 1995 C129/6	Clearance (5 May 1995)	TV broadcasting (pay TV)
30.	GE/Power Controls (IV/M.577)	OJ 1995 C86/5 OJ 1995 C163/8	Clearance (28 April 1995)	Electrical equipment
31.	EDS/Lufthansa (IV/M.560)	OJ 1995 C91/4 OJ 1995 C163/8	Clearance (11 May 1995)	Information technology services (for airline and other travel industries)
32.	Ingersoll-Rand/Clark Equipment (IV/M.588)	OJ 1995 C94/2 OJ 1995 C154/4	No jurisdiction (15 May 1995)	Loaders and construction equipment, paving machines
33.	CLT/Disney/Super RTL (IV/M.566)	OJ 1995 C96/3 OJ 1995 C144/23	Clearance (17 May 1995) IP/95/535	TV broadcasting and productions
34.	Orkla/Volvo (IV/M.582)	OJ 1995 C100/3 IP/95/534	Phase II: Conditional Clearance (20 September 1995) IP/95/1021	Beer
35.	Saudi Aramco/MOH (IV/M.574)	OJ 1995 C106/4 OJ 1995 C158/4	Clearance (23 May 1995)	Oil refining and trading
36.	Inchcape/Gestetner (IV/M.583)	OJ 1995 C108/3 OJ 1995 C201/3	Clearance (1 June 1995)	Office automation products

	Parties (Case No.)	Notice of notification and Phase I decision	Decision (date) OJ and CMLR references	Business sector
37.	Seagram/MCA (IV/M.589)	OJ 1995 C111/5 OJ 1995 C149/11	Clearance (29 May 1995)	Entertainment, film production and distribution
38.	RTL/Veronica/ Endemol (IV/M.553) (Art. 22 request)	OJ 1995 C112/4 IP/95/526	Phase II; Prohibition (20 September 1995) IP/95/995 IP/96/653	TV and radio production and broadcasting
39.	EDF/Edison-ISE (IV/M.568)	OJ 1995 C115/4 OJ 1995 C241/4	Clearance (8 June 1995)	Electricity
40.	Ferruzzi Finanziaria/ Fondiaria (IV/M.576)	OJ 1995 C118/6 OJ 1995 C158/4	Clearance (9 June 1995)	Insurance and financial services
41.	Generali/COMIT/ Robert Flemings (IV/M.586)	OJ 1995 C121/3 OJ 1995 C263/3	Clearance (15 June 1995) (see also no. 59 below)	Financial services
42.	ABB/Daimler-Benz* (IV/M.580)	OJ 1995 C122/3 IP/95/668	Phase II: Conditional clearance (18 October 1995) IP/95/1126	Rail transport (locomotives train sets, metros, trams)
43.	Hoechst/Marion Merrell Dow (IV/M.587)	OJ 1995 C129/3 OJ 1995 C193/5	Clearance (22 June 1995)	Pharmaceuticals
44.	Swissair/Sabena (IV/M.562)	OJ 1995 C129/4 OJ 1995 C162/5	Withdrawn then renotified (see no. 56 below)	Air transport
45.	Swiss Bank Corporation/ S.G. Warburg (IV/M.597)	OJ 1995 C129/5 OJ 1995 C180/4	Clearance (28 June 1995)	Banking and financial services
46.	Volvo/Henlys (IV/M.593)	OJ 1995 C132/2 OJ 1995 C177/7	Clearance (27 June 1995)	Coaches and bus shells
47.	Daimler-Benz/Carl Zeiss (IV/M.598)	OJ 1995 C134/4 OJ 1995 C276/10	Clearance (27 June 1995)	Military technical optronics

	Parties (Case No.)	Notice of notification and Phase I decision	Decision (date) OJ and CMLR references	Business sector
48.	RWE-DEA/Enichem Augusta (IV/M.592)	OJ 1995 C134/5 OJ 1995 C162/5	Withdrawn then renotified (see no. 58 below)	Surfactants and other raw materials for detergents
49.	Employers Reinsurance/ Franktona Rück (IV/M.600)	OJ 1995 C141/7 OJ 1995 C272/5	Clearance (30 June 1995)	Reinsurance
50.	Employers Reinsurance/ Aachener Rück (IV/M.601)	OJ 1995 C141/8 OJ 1995 C272/5	Clearance (30 June 1995)	Reinsurance
51.	Babcock/Siemens/BS Railcare (IV/M.542)	OJ 1995 C146/4 OJ 1995 C186/8	Clearance (30 June 1995)	Rail transportation (vehicle maintenance and refurbishment)
52.	Voest Alpine/Davy International (IV/M.585)	OJ 1995 C146/5 OJ 1995 C246/2	Clearance (7 July 1995)	Hot connect systems for steam production plants
53.	Dow/Buna (IV/M.591)	OJ 1995 C148/4 OJ 1995 C181/17	Clearance (4 July 1995)	Petrochemicals and electrochemicals
54.	Mitsubishi Bank/Bank of Tokyo (IV/M.596)	OJ 1995 C156/3 OJ 1995 C198/5	Clearance (17 July 1995)	Banking and financial services
55.	ATR/BAe (IV/M.551)	OJ 1995 C162/6 OJ 1995 C264/8	No jurisdiction (25 July 1995)	Military and commercial aerospace industries
56.	Swissair/Sabena (IV/M.616)	OJ 1995 C165/4 OJ 1995 C200/10	Clearance (20 July 1995) (see no. 44 above)	Air transport
57.	Crown Cork & Seal/ Carnaud Metal Box (IV/M.603)	OJ 1995 C165/5 IP/95/856	Phase II: Conditional Clearance (14 November 1995)	Packaging (tinplate aerosol cans, food cans)
58.	RWE-DEA/Enichem Augusta (IV/M.612)	OJ 1995 C168/10 OJ 1995 C207/11	Clearance (27 July 1995) IP/95/831 (see no. 48 above)	Surfactants and other raw materials for detergents

	Parties (Case No.)	Notice of notification and Phase I decision	Decision (date) OJ and CMLR references	Business sector
59.	Generali/COMIT (Previnet) (IV/M.606)	OJ 1995 C169/10 OJ 1995 C263/4	Clearance (26 July 1995) (see also no. 41 above)	Financial services (pension funds)
60.	Jefferson Smurfit Group/Munksjo (IV/M.613)	OJ 1995 C169/11 OJ 1995 C252/3	Clearance (31 July 1995)	Paper
61.	Dresdner Bank/ Kleinwort Benson (IV/M.611)	OJ 1995 C170/5 OJ 1995 C207/11	Clearance (28 July 1995)	Banking and financial services
62.	Cable & Wireless/VEBA (IV/M.618)	OJ 1995 C185/3 OJ 1995 C231/3	Clearance (16 August 1995)	Telecommunications
63.	Crédit Local de France/ Hypothekenbank in Berlin (IV/M.617)	OJ 1995 C188/6 OJ 1995 C241/4	Clearance (10 August 1995)	Banking (loans to local authorities)
64.	Generali/France Vie – france Iard (IV/M.614)	OJ 1995 C193/5 OJ 1995 C244/9	Clearance (21 August 1995)	Insurance
65.	Thomson-CSF/ Teneo/Indra (IV/M.620)	OJ 1995 C194/15 OJ 1995 C264/9	Clearance (22 August 1995)	Computer and IT services, space and air traffic systems, defence systems including military simulators
66.	UAP/Sun Life (IV/M.627)	OJ 1995 C195/3 OJ 1995 C292/8	Clearance (21 August 1995)	Insurance
67.	Frantschach/Bischof & Klein (IV/M.581)	OJ 1995 C197/4 OJ 1995 C238/3	Clearance (5 September 1995)	Flexible packaging products

	Parties (Case No.)	Notice of notification and Phase I decision	Decision (date) OJ and CMLR references	Business sector
68.	Nordic Capital/ Transpool (IV/M.625)	OJ 1995 C199/14 OJ 1995 C243/5	Clearance (23 August 1995)	Air transport and travel agency
69.	Noranda Forest/Glunz (IV/M.599)	OJ 1995 C207/10 OJ 1995 C298/6	Clearance (8 September 1995)	Wood-based panel board products
70.	Kimberly-Clark/Scott (IV/M.623)*	OJ 1995 C212/5 IP/95/968	Phase II: Conditional clearance (16 January 1996) IP/96/48	Tissues, personal care and cleaning products
71.	Ricoh/Gestetner (IV/M.622)	OJ 1995 C215/5 OJ 1995 C264/9	Clearance (12 September 1995)	Photocopiers, fax machines and cameras
72.	Albacom (IV/M.604)	OJ 1995 C219/3 OJ 1995 C278/8	No jurisdiction (15 September 1995)	Telecommunications
73.	Rhône-Poulenc Rorer/ Fisons (IV/M.632)	OJ 1995 C221/11 OJ 1995 C263/4	Clearance (21 September 1995)	Pharmaceutical and horticultural products
74.	Generale Bank/Crédit Lyonnais Nederland (IV/M.628)	OJ 1995 C226/8 OJ 1995 C289/10	Clearance (25 September 1995)	Banking
75.	Upjohn/Pharmacia (IV/M.631)	OJ 1995 C232/3 OJ 1995 C294/9	Clearance (28 September 1995)	Pharmaceuticals
76.	KNP BT/Société Générale (IV/M.640)	OJ 1995 C239/4 OJ 1995 C274/3	Clearance (3 October 1995)	Computer distribution and maintenance services
77.	Ericcson/Ascom (IV/M.608)	OJ 1995 C241/7 OJ 1995 C292/8	Withdrawn then renotified (see no. 109 below)	Telecommunications
78.	Henkel/Schwarzkopf (IV/M.630)	OJ 1995 C247/5 OJ 1995 C298/7	Clearance (31 October 1995)	Haircare products
79.	Rhône-Poulenc/ Engelhard (IV/M.615)	OJ 1995 C255/6 OJ 1995 C293/7	Clearance (23 October 1995)	Catalytic converter recycling

	Parties (Case No.)	Notice of notification and Phase I decision	Decision (date) OJ and CMLR references	Business sector
80.	CGER-Banque/SNCI (IV/M.643)	OJ 1995 C255/7 OJ 1995 C293/8	Clearance (23 October 1995)	Banking and financial services
81.	Swiss Life/INCA (IV/M.644)	OJ 1995 C258/8 OJ 1995 C307/17	Clearance (25 October 1995)	Life insurance and financial services
82.	Repola/Kymmene (IV/M.646)	OJ 1995 C260/3 OJ 1995 C318/3	Clearance (30 October 1995)	Forestry products, including newsprint, pulp and paper sacks
83.	Chase Manhattan/ Chemical Bank (IV/M.642)	OJ 1995 C260/4 OJ 1996 C33/7	Clearance (26 October 1995)	Financial services (investment and commercial banking)
84.	Unisource/Telefónica (IV/M.544)	OJ 1995 C263/5 OJ 1996 C13/3	No jurisdiction (6 November 1995)	Telecommunications
85.	GE Capital/Sovac (IV/M.659)	OJ 1995 C276/10 OJ 1995 C322/21	Clearance (17 November 1995)	Financial services (automobile and equipment financing)
86.	Seagate/Conner (IV/M.656)	OJ 1995 C278/8 OJ 1995 C334/3	Clearance (17 November 1995)	Computers (hard disk drives)
87.	McDermott/ETPM (IV/M.648)	OJ 1995 C289/9 OJ 1995 C330/9	Clearance (27 November 1995)	Marine construction services (for offshore oil and gas industry)
88.	Canal+/UFA/MDO (IV/M.655)	OJ 1995 C290/4 OJ 1996 C15/4	Clearance (13 November 1995)	TV broadcasting (cable)
89.	CEP/Groupe de la Cité (IV/M.665)	OJ 1995 C292/9 OJ 1995 C338/3	Clearance (29 November 1995)	Publishing and newspapers
90.	RTZ/CRA (IV/M.660)	OJ 1995 C298/6 OJ 1996 C22/10	Clearance (7 December 1995)	Mining, metals and minerals

	Parties (Case No.)	Notice of notification and Phase I decision	Decision (date) OJ and CMLR references	Business sector
91.	Johnson Controls/Roth Frères (IV/M.666)	OJ 1995 C298/7 OJ 1996 C3/17	Clearance (5 December 1995)	Automotive parts (seats)
92.	Montedison/Group Vernes/SCI (IV/M.639)	OJ 1995 C302/4 OJ 1995 C347/17	Clearance (8 December 1995)	Agro-food products (including sugar)
93.	Charterhouse/Porterbrook (IV/M.669)	OJ 1995 C309/7 OJ 1995 C350/18	Clearance (11 December 1995)	Rail transportation (rolling stock)
94.	GRS Holding (IV/M.664)	OJ 1995 C309/8 OJ 1996 C8/4	Clearance (11 December 1995)	Rail transportation (passenger rolling stock)
95.	SBG/Rentenanstalt (IV/M.650)	OJ 1995 C314/12 OJ 1996 C23/5	No jurisdiction (20 December 1995)	Banking and insurance
96.	Gencor/Lonrho* (IV/M.619)	OJ 1995 C314/14 OJ 1995 C347/18	Phase II: Prohibition (24 April 1996) IP/96/346	Mining, metals and minerals
97.	Elsag Bailey/Hartmann & Braun (IV/M.670)	OJ 1995 C314/15 OJ 1995 C24/7	Clearance (20 December 1995)	Industrial process control equipment and nuclear radiation measurement equipment
98.	Channel Five (IV/M.673)	OJ 1995 C317/6 OJ 1996 C57/3	No jurisdiction (22 December 1995)	TV broadcasting
99.	Demag/Komatsu (IV/M.674)	OJ 1995 C318/4 OJ 1996 C38/17	Clearance (21 December 1995)	Mining, digging and excavating machinery
100.	Alumix/Alcoa* (IV/M.675)	OJ 1995 C318/5 IP/95/1471	Clearance (21 December 1995)	Bauxite mining and aluminium
101.	BLG/BAWAG (IV/M.621)	OJ 1995 C319/3 OJ 1996 C23/5	Clearance (21 December 1995)	Banking
102.	Strabag/Bank Austria/Stuag (IV/M.661)	OJ 1995 C321/2 OJ 1996 C38/17	No jurisdiction (15 January 1996) (Art. 9 request made)	Construction of buildings and roads

	Parties (Case No.)	Notice of notification and Phase I decision	Decision (date) OJ and CMLR references	Business sector
103.	Leisureplan* (IV/M.662)	OJ 1995 C321/3	Clearance (10 January 1996)	Travel services, media and publishing software
104.	Minorco/Tilcon (IV/M.678)	OJ 1995 C322/20 OJ 1996 C24/7	Clearance (22 December 1995)	Quickline, aggregates and coated stone
105.	Philips/Origin (IV/M.668)	OJ 1995 C322/18 OJ 1996 C58/3	Clearance (22 December 1995)	Information technology services and software
106.	Lyonnaise des Eaux/ Northumbrian Water (IV/M.567)	OJ 1995 C322/19 OJ 1996 C11/3	Clearance (22 December 1995)	Water supply and waste management
107.	Röhm/Ciba-Geigy-TFL* (IV/M.657)	OJ 1995 C324/17 OJ 1996 C60/9	Clearance (22 December 1995)	Chemical products
108.	BT/VIAG (IV/M.595)	OJ 1995 C324/18 OJ 1996 C15/4	Clearance (22 December 1995)	Telecommunications
109.	Ericsson/Ascom II (IV/M.676)	OJ 1995 C324/19 OJ 1996 C19/10	Clearance (22 December 1995) (see also no. 77 above)	Telecommunications (on-site paging systems)
110.	Skanska/Securum* (IV/M.677	OJ 1995 C325/9 OJ 1996 C54/3	Clearance (8 January 1996)	Hotels
111.	Kvaerner/Amec* (IV/M.680)	OJ 1995 C325/10 OJ 1996 C8/4	Withdrawn (22 December 1995)	Engineering and construction

1996 NOTIFICATIONS

	Parties (Case No.)	Notice of notification and Phase I decision	Decision (date) OJ and CMLR references	Business sector
1.	Nokia/Autoliv* (IV/M.686)	OJ 1996 C7/8 IP/96/110	Clearance (5 February 1996)	Electronics and automotive safety devices
2.	RB of Scotland/Bank of Ireland (IV/M.681)	OJ 1996 C7/9 OJ 1996 C57/3	No jurisdiction (5 February 1996)	Banking and financial services
3.	AT&T Philips Electronics NV* (IV/M.651)	OJ 1996 C7/10	Clearance (5 February 1996)	Telecommunications
4.	Siemens/Lagardère* (IV/M.685)	OJ 1996 C8/3 IP/96/133	Clearance (8 February 1996)	Transport and technology
5.	BP/Sonatrach* (IV/M.672)	OJ 1996 C13/3 IP/96/139	Clearance (12 February 1996)	Oil and gas
6.	Elektrowatt/Landis & Gyr* (IV/M.692)	OJ 1996 C13/5 IP/96/138	Clearance (12 February 1996)	Energy, commercial and residential building control, security
7.	SFK/INA/WPB* (IV/M.694)	OJ 1996 C23/4 IP/96/152	Clearance (19 February 1996)	Automotive parts (water pumps)
8.	Dow/Du Pont* (IV/M.663)	OJ 1996 C24/6 IP/96/163	Clearance (21 February 1996)	Textile fibres (synthetic elastomers)
9.	Lockheed Martin/Loral* (IV/M.697)	OJ 1996 C33/10 IP/96/277	Clearance (28 March 1996)	Defence systems
10.	ADSB/Belgacom* (IV/M.689)	OJ 1996 C33/11 IP/96/192	Clearance (29 February 1996)	Telecommunications
11.	Starck/Wienerberger* (IV/M.702)	OJ 1996 C35/3 IP/96/199	Clearance (1 March 1996)	Hard metals, abrasives and fireproof materials
12.	Toro Assicurazioni/ Banca di Roma* (IV/M.707)	OJ 1996 C36/2 OJ 1996 C76/16	Clearance (5 March 1996)	Banking, insurance

	Parties (Case No.)	Notice of notification and Phase I decision	Decision (date) OJ and CMLR references	Business sector
13.	Tomkins/Gates* (IV/M.699)	OJ 1996 C38/18	Clearance (4 March 1996)	Automotive and industrial rubber products
14.	GTS-Hermes Inc./ Hit Rail BV* (IV/M.683)	OJ 1996 C41/6 IP/96/211	Clearance (8 March 1996)	Telecommunications
15.	GEHE/Lloyds Chemists* (IV/M.716)	OJ 1996 C43/8 IP/96/254	Art. 9 referral to UK (22 March 1996)	Pharmaceutical production, wholesaling and retailing
16.	Generali/Unicredito* (IV/M.711)	OJ 1996 C44/5	No jurisdiction (25 March 1996)	Banking and insurance
17.	NAW/Saltano/Contrac* (IV/M.698)	OJ 1996 C49/8	Clearance (26 February 1996)	Airport ground handling equipment
18.	Preussag/ELCO Looser* (IV/M.714)	OJ 1996 C53/3 IP/96/236	Clearance (14 March 1996)	Various (steel production, energy and raw materials, heating systems, paints and varnishes)
19.	Unilever/Diversey (IV/M.704)	OJ 1996 C55/4 IP/96/253	Clearance (20 March 1996)	Industrial cleaning product
20.	Textron/Valois* (IV/M.721)	OJ 1996 C58/3 IP/96/252	Clearance (22 March 1996)	Automotive parts and aerospace and defence components
21.	Viacom/Bear Stearns* (IV/M.717)	OJ 1996 C60/8 IP/96/276	Clearance (28 March 1996)	TV broadcasting
22.	Phoenix/Comifar* (IV/M.718)	OJ 1996 C62/2 IP/96/251	Clearance (20 March 1996)	Pharmaceutical wholesaling
23.	Zeneca/Vanderhave* (IV/M.556)	OJ 1996 C70/8 IP/96/303	Clearance (10 April 1996)	Agrochemicals (seeds)
24.	Deutsche Telekom/ SAP-S* (IV/M.705)	OJ 1996 C70/9 IP/96/283	Clearance (29 March 1996)	Telecommunications services and software

	Parties (Case No.)	Notice of notification and Phase I decision	Decision (date) OJ and CMLR references	Business sector
25.	Bosch/Allied Signals* (IV/M.726)	OJ 1996 C71/3 IP/96/304	Clearance (10 April 1996)	Automotive parts (air brakes and hydraulic brakes)
26.	Téneo/Merill Lynch/ Bankers Trust* (IV/M.722)	OJ 1996 C81/13	No Jurisdiction (18 April 1996)	Air transport, banking and financial services
27.	Kvaerner/Trafalgar* (IV/M.731)	OJ 1996 C83/9 IP/96/320	Clearance (17 April 1996)	Shipping, oil and gas and engineering
28.	Nordic Capital/Euroc* (IV/M.732)	OJ 1996 C85/18 IP/96/323	Clearance (19 April 1996)	Building materials and hardware products
29.	GEC/Alsthom/Tarmac/ Central IMU* (IV/M.729)	OJ 1996 C86/7 IP/96/335	Clearance (18 April 1996)	Engineering and railway infrastructure services
30.	Natwest/Schroder/ Sheffield* (IV/M.738)	OJ 1996 C89/4 IP/96/334	Clearance (24 April 1996)	Steel
31.	Sandoz/Ciba-Geigy* (IV/M.737)	OJ 1996 C102/18 IP/96/652	Phase II: Clearance (17 July 1996)	Pharmaceuticals and agrochemicals
32.	Krupp II* (IV/M.740)	OJ 1996 C104/4 IP/96/385	Clearance (3 May 1996)	Steel
33.	BHF-Bank/Crédit Commercial de France* (IV/M.710)	OJ 1996 C105/4 IP/96/386	Clearance (3 May 1996)	Banking (vehicle and other leasing)
34.	Frantschach/B+K/ Volfin* (IV/M.733)	OJ 1996 C106/3 IP/96/427	Clearance (20 May 1996)	Industrial sacks and packaging (paper, paper board and flexible packaging)
35.	GEC/Thomson-CSF (II)* (IV/M.724)	OJ 1996 C114/7 IP/96/426	Clearance (20 May 1996)	Sonar equipment (non-military activities)

	Parties (Case No.)	Notice of notification and Phase I decision	Decision (date) OJ and CMLR references	Business sector
36.	Thomson/Daimler-Benz* (IV/M.744)	OJ 1996 C114/8 IP/96/434	Clearance (21 May 1996)	Gallium arsenide based components
37.	CGEA/NSC* (IV/M.748)	OJ 1996 C116/9 IP/96/435	Clearance (22 May 1996)	Road and rail transport services
38.	Hoechst Klöckner-werke/Hartfolien* (IV/M.605)	OJ 1996 C118/9 IP/96/438	Clearance (23 May 1996)	Chemical and pharmaceutical products, plastics and films
39.	Ford/Mazda* (IV/M.741)	OJ 1996 C121/12 IP/96/439	Clearance (24 May 1996)	Motor vehicles
40.	Toro Assicurazioni/ Nuova Tirrena* (IV/M.742)	OJ 1996 C121/13 IP/96/437	Clearance (23 May 1996)	Insurance
41.	Emerson/Caterpillar* (IV/M.700)	OJ 1996 C130/2	Clearance (31 May 1996)	Diesel generator sets
42.	Cereol/Aceprosa* (IV/M.720)	OJ 1996 C140/3 IP/96/483	Clearance (7 June 1996)	Oil seeds
43.	Creditanstalt/Koramic* (IV/M.755)	OJ 1996 C146/5	Clearance (18 June 1996)	Building materials (bricks)
44.	Exxon/DSM* (IV/M.708)	OJ 1996 C148/18 IP/96/516	Clearance (14 June 1996)	High-grade polymers (polyethylene and plastomers)
45.	Sun Alliance/Royal Insurance* (IV/M.759)	OJ 1996 C148/19 IP/96/531	Clearance (18 June 1996)	Insurance
46.	Sara Lee/Aoste Holding SA* (IV/M.758)	OJ 1996 C154/26 IP/96/565	Clearance (25 June 1996)	Processed meat products
47.	ADIA/ECCO* (IV/M.765)	OJ 1996 C155/12 IP/96/542	Clearance (24 June 1996)	Temporary personnel services
48.	Credit Agricol/Banque Indosuez*	OJ 1996 C157/10 IP/96/573	Clearance (1 July 1996)	Banking and financial services

	Parties (Case No.)	Notice of notification and Phase I decision	Decision (date) OJ and CMLR references	Business sector
49.	Hong Kong Aero Engine Services — "HAESEL"* (IV/M.775)	OJ 1996 C162/04 OJ 1996 C226/05	Clearance (1 July 1996)	Mechanical engineering and aero-engines
50.	Röhm/Rohm and Haas* (IV/M.719)	OJ 1996 C162/03 IP/96/574	Clearance (28 June 1996)	Chemicals and petrochemicals
51.	Bayernwerk/Gaz de France* (IV/M.745)	OJ 1996 C165/04 IP/96/572	Clearance (2 July 1996)	Oil and gas exploration and production
52.	BPB/Isover* (IV/M.735)	OJ 1996 C165/03	No jurisdiction (3 July 1996)	Building materials
53.	Telefónica/Sogecable/ Cablevisión* (IV/M.709)	OJ 1996 C167/05	Phase II: Pending	TV broadcasting (cable and satellite) and telephone and data transmission
54.	St. Gobain/Poliet* (IV/M.764)	OJ 1996 C168/12 IP/96/601	Clearance (4 July 1996)	Building materials
55.	Bayer/Hüls-Newco* (IV/M.751	OJ 1996 C168/13 IP/96/602	Clearance (3 July 1996)	Latex
56.	IP/Reuters* (IV/M.730)	OJ 1996 C168/14 IP/96/613	Clearance (9 July 1996)	Information services
57.	Lucas/Varity* (IV/M.768)	OJ 1996 C177/03 IP/96/643	Clearance (11 July 1996)	Automotive and aerospace equipment
58.	Swissair/Allders International* (IV/M.782)	OJ 1996 C184/11 IP/96/679	Clearance (17 July 1996)	Duty-free retailing
59.	3M/Hoechst* (IV/M.757)	OJ 1996 C187/05 IP/96/680	Clearance (18 July 1996)	Chemicals and films
60.	PTT Post/TNT-GD NET* (IV/M.787)	OJ 1996 C187/07 IP/96/699	Clearance (24 July 1996) (see 1991 no. 43)	Postal services

	Parties (Case No.)	Notice of notification and Phase I decision	Decision (date) OJ and CMLR references	Business sector
61.	Enderly/SBE* (IV/M.789)	OJ 1996 C187/06 IP/96/678	Clearance (15 July 1996)	Electronics
62.	AMB/Rodutch Holdings* (IV/M.771)	OJ 1996 C189/07 IP/96/640	Clearance (11 July 1996)	Insurance
63.	Chevron/British Gas/ NOVA/NGC* (IV/M.747)	OJ 1996 C191/05 IP/96/725	Clearance (30 July 1996)	Gas
64.	Melitta/Dow* (IV/M.734)	OJ 1996 C193/03	Clearance (25 July 1996)	Household packaging
65.	Kesko/Tuko* (Art. 22 request) (IV/M.784)	OJ 1996 C193/04 IP/96/717	Phase II: Pending	Food retailing
66.	Norsk Hydro/Arnyca (Enichem Agricoltura)* (IV/M.769)	OJ 1996 C194/05	Clearance (29 July 1996)	Agrochemicals
67.	IFIL/Worms/Saint Louis* (IV/M.750)	OJ 1996 C194/03 IP/96/705	Clearance (25 July 1996)	Sugar, paper
68.	Saint-Gobain/Wacker-Chemie/NOM* (IV/M.774)	OJ 1996 C200/03	Phase II: Pending	Silicon carbide
69.	Thomson-CSF/Finmeccanica/ Elettronica* (IV/M.767)	OJ 1996 C201/03 IP/96/775	Clearance (5 August 1996)	Electronic warfare systems
70.	BP/Mobil* (IV/M.727)	OJ 1996 C202/06 IP/96/790	Clearance (8 August 1996)	Oil and gas
71.	Thomas Cook/Sunworld* (IV/M.785)	OJ 1996 C203/09 IP/96/792	Clearance (9 August 1996)	Travel agency services

	Parties (Case No.)	Notice of notification and Phase I decision	Decision (date) OJ and CMLR references	Business sector
72.	CCB/CLF* (IV/M.736)	OJ 1996 C208/06	Clearance (12 August 1996)	Banking
73.	General Electric/CompuNet* (IV/M.798)	OJ 1996 C208/07 IP/96/798	Clearance (20 August 1996)	Information networks and services
74.	Siemens/Sommer Allibert Industrie* (IV/M.800)	OJ 1996 C213/03 IP/96/797	Clearance (20 August 1996)	Car parts
75.	Klöckner/ARUS* (IV/M.760)	OJ 1996 C216/05 IP/96/799	Clearance (20 August 1996)	Steel, building supplies
76.	Blokker/Toys R Us* (IV/M.801) (Article 22 request)	OJ 1996 C216/06	No jurisdiction (22 August 1996)	Retailing (toys)
77.	British Airways/TAT* (IV/M.806)	OJ 1996 C218/03 IP/96/803	Clearance (27 August 1996)	Air transport
78.	Grant Rail Limited* (IV/M.797)	OJ 1996 C221/06	Clearance (23 August 1996)	Railways
79.	Rewe/Billa* (IV/M.803)	OJ 1996 C221/07	Clearance (28 August 1996)	Food retailing
80.	AGF/Camat* (IV/M.777)	OJ 1996 C224/12	No jurisdiction (28 August 1996)	Insurance
81.	Infra Leuna* (IV/M.796)	OJ 1996 C224/13	Clearance (23 August 1996)	Infrastructure services
82.	Auchan/Pâo de Açúcar* (IV/M.804)	OJ 1996 C226/02	Clearance (28 August 1996)	Food retailing

	Parties (Case No.)	Notice of notification and Phase I decision	Decision (date) OJ and CMLR references	Business sector
83.	Creditanstalt-Bankverein/ Treibacher* (IV/M.811)	OJ 1996 C226/03	Clearance (6 September 1996)	Corundum
84.	Cegelec/AEG II* (IV/M.762)	OJ 1996 C228/03	Clearance (13 September 1996)	Engineering
85.	GEC Alsthom/AEG* (IV/M.706)	OJ 1996 C229/8	Clearance (13 September 1996)	Power transmission and distribution equipment
86.	AgrEvo/Maruberi* (IV/M.788)	OJ 1996 C229/9	Clearance (13 September 1996)	Crop protection and environmental health
87.	Coca-Cola Enterprises/ Amalgamated Beverages GB* (IV/M.794)	OJ 1996 C241/4	Phase II: Pending	Soft drinks bottling
88.	n-tv* (IV/M.810)	OJ 1996 C241/6	[Pending]	TV broadcasting
89.	Schering/Gehe-Jenapharm* (IV/M.781)	OJ 1996 C241/3	Clearance (17 September 1996)	Pharmaceuticals
90.	British Aerospace/Lagardère SCA* (IV/M.820)	OJ 1996 C250/4	[Pending]	Guided missiles
91.	Allianz Aktiengesellschaft Holding/Hermes Kredit Versicherungs-AG* (IV/M.813)	OJ 1996 C258/3	[Pending]	Insurance
92.	Temic/Leica AG/ADC (IV/M.792)	OJ 1996 C258/4	[Pending]	Automotive parts (Electronics)
93.	CGEA/SET (IV/M.816)	OJ 1996 C262/4	[Pending]	Rail transport services

	Parties (Case No.)	Notice of notification and Phase I decision	Decision (date) OJ and CMLR references	Business sector
94.	Bertelsmann/CTL	OJ 1996 C265/3	[Pending]	TV broadcasting
95.	British gas/Group 4 Securitas	OJ C268/5	[Pending]	Gas
96.	John Deere Capital Corp/ Lombard North Central	OJ C271/17	[Pending]	Banking (agricultural equipment leasing)

E. NATIONAL CASES

Belgium

The State (Belgium) v. Tubemeuse [1994] 3 CMLR 93 (Belg. Court de Cass.) 18–047

France

Lener Ignace S.A. v. Beauvois [1994] 2 CMLR 419 (French Court. de Cass.) 18–037

Germany

Brunner, 12 October 1993 [1994] 1 CMLR 57 (Fed. Const. Ct.) 1–006

Ireland

Irish Competition Authority Decision No. 336 of 10 June 1994 7–036
Masterfoods Ltd t/a Mars Ireland v. HB Ice Cream Ltd [1992] 3 CMLR 830 (Ir. High Ct.) 7–111, 7–128, 10–047

Spain

Case 1236/1992 [1994] 3 CMLR 101 (Const. Ct.) 1–006
Pack Service/4PEF, Tribunal de Defensa de la Competencia, XXIVth Report on Competition Policy (1994), point 90 .... 8–119, 12–046

United Kingdom

Banks v. British Coal Corporation judgment of 19 July 1994 (QBD) 10–006, 17–005, 17–017
Bourgoin SA v. Ministry of Agriculture Fisheries and Food [1985] 3 WLR 1027 (CA) 10–038
British Sugar Plc v. Director General of Fair Trading, judgment of 9 August 1995, (Restr. Pr. Ct.) 10–059
CHEETAH Trademark [1993] FSR 263 8–037
Chemidus Wavin v. TERI [1978] 3 CMLR 514 (CA) 10–028
Chiron Corp. v. Murex Diagnostics Ltd. (No. 2) [1994] FSR 187 [1994] 1 CMLR 410 (CA) [1993] FSR 324 [1992] 3 CMLR 813 (High Ct.) 8–072, 10–033
Director General of Fair Trading v. Publishers Association, judgment of 9 August 1995 (Restr. Pr. Ct.) 10–059
Higgins v. Marchant & Eliot Underwriting Ltd, judgment of 21 December 1995 (CA) 2–137, 10–029
IBM v. Phoenix International [1994] RPC 251 (Ch D) 8–072
Iberian UK Ltd v. BPB Industries PLC, judgment of 18 April 1995 (Ch D) 10–022, 10–047
Inntrepreneur Estates v. Boyes [1993] 47 EG 140 [1993] 68 P&CR 77 (CA) [1994] 68 P&CR 53 (QBD) 7–128, 10–028
—— v. Mason [1993] 2 CMLR 293 [1994] 68 P&CR 53 (QBD) 7–128, 11–022, 11–064
Intergraph Corp. v. Solid Systems CAD Services Ltd, judgment of 7 December 1993 (Ch D) 10–043
Kall-Kwik Printing (UK) Ltd v. Rush [1996] FSR 114 (Ch D) 7–177
Kirklees MBC v. Wickes Building Supplies Ltd [1993] AC 227 (HL) 10–038
Leyland DAF v. Automotive Products [1994] 1 BCLC 245 (CA) 9–059
MTV Europe v. BMG Records (UK) judgment of 17 July 1995 (CA) Ltd [1995] 1 CMLR 437 (Ch D) 10–016, 10–022
Maxims v. Dye [1978] 2 All ER 55 8–045
Panayiotou v. Sony Music Entertainment Ltd, judgment of 23 June 1994 (Ch D) 10–047
Putney Bowes v. Francotyp-Postalia [1990] 3 CMLR 466 (Ch D) 10–033
R v. Secretary of State for Foreign and Commonwealth Affairs, ex p Rees-Mogg [1994] QB 552 [1994] 1 All ER 457 [1993] 3 CMLR 101

E. NATIONAL CASES

R. v. Secretary of State for Trade and Industry, ex p Airlines of Britain [1993] BCC 89 6–161
—— v. Stock Exchange ex p Else Ltd [1993] QB 534 (CA) 10–010
Ready Mixed Concrete Agreements, Re (1996) Tr LR 78 10–056
Revlon v. Cripp's & Lee [1980] FSR 85 (CA) 8–027
Richard Cound Ltd v. BMW (GB) Ltd, judgment of 10 May 1995 (CA) .. 2–022, 7–107A, 10–028
Society of Lloyd's v. Clementson, [1995] CLC 117 (CA), judgment of 7 May 1996, QBD 2–063, 2–128, 10–047
Wellcome Foundation v. Discpharm Ltd [1993] FSR 433 (Patent Cty. Ct.) 8–018
Westdeutsche Landesbank v. Islington BC [1994] 1 WLR 938 (CA) 10–030

TABLE OF LEGISLATION

F. EUROPEAN COMMUNITY TREATIES AND CONVENTIONS

1951 Paris. Treaty establishing the European Coal and Steel Community (ECSC Treaty) (18 April) .. 1–006, 10–006, 10–022, 10–041, 16–001, 17–001
Art. 2 17–019
Arts. 3–7 17–019
Art. 3 17–020
Art. 4 .... 16–013, 17–020
Art. 41 17–005
Art. 58 .... 4–014A, 4–040
Art. 63 .... 17–004A
(1) 16–013, 17–004A
Art. 65 .... 4–014A, 12–084, 17–004A, 17–005
(1) 2–034
(2) 17–006
Art. 66 .... 17–004A
(7) 16–013, 17–017, 17–004A, 17–005
Art. 80 17–005
Art. 95 17–020

1957 Rome. Treaty establishing the European Atomic Energy Community (Euratom) (25 March) ... 1–006, 16–001, 16–021
Rome. Treaty establishing the European Economic Community (EEC Treaty) (25 March) 16–001
Pt. II 1–029
Art. 3(d) 14–001
(e) 15–002
(f) 1–026, 1–039, 2–108, 9–002
Art. 7 .... 1–023, 1–028
Art. 8(9) 1–024, 16–002
Arts. 67–73 1–029
Art. 92(3)(d) 18–016
Art. 114 1–038

1992 Maastricht. Treaty on European Union (TEU) (7 February) OJ 1992 C191/1 [1992] 1 CMLR 719 .... 1–001, 1–002, 1–003, 1–006, 1–008, 1–009, 1–022, 2–108, 10–003, 14–001, 15–002, 16–001, 16–021, 18–001, 18–016, 18–044
Art. D 1–010
Art. F 1–050
2 1–050

1992 Maastrict. Treaty on European Union (TEU) (7 February) OJ 1992 C191/1 [1992] 1 CMLR 719—*cont.*
Art. G 1–002
Art. L 1–050
European Community Treaty (EC Treaty) (Incorporating amendments introduced by TEU) ... 1–022, 10–041, 10–047, **App. 1**
Pt. I 1–022, 1–023
Pt. II 1–022, 1–029
Pt. III 1–022, 1–029
Art. 1 .... **App. 1**
Art. 2 .... 1–023, 1–024, **App. 1**
Art. 3 .... 1–023, 16–001, **App. 1**
(b) .... 1–026A, **App. 1**
(e) 14–001
(f) 14–001, 15–002
(g) 1–026, 1–039, 2–108, 9–002, 14–001
(l) 4–016
Art. 4 .... 1–023, **App. 1**
(a) .... **App. 1**
(b) .... **App. 1**
Art. 5 .... 4–016, **App. 1**
Art. 6 .... 1–023, 1–028, 8–002, 12–023, **App. 1**
Art. 7(a) ... 1–024, 1–029, 16–002, **App. 1**
(b) .... **App. 1**
(c) .... **App. 1**
Art. 8 .... 1–011, 1–029
Art. 19(3) 4–031, 15–043
Arts. 30–36 1–036
Art. 30 .... 1–036, 8–025, 18–046A
Art. 36 8–025
Art. 37 .... 13–004, 16–011, 16–038
(1) 13–005
(5) 13–008
Art. 39 .... 14–001, 14–005, 14–007
Art. 42 14–003
Art. 48 3–003
Art. 52 .... 18–010, 18–046A
Art. 65 10–006
Art. 66 10–006
Art. 73(b) 1–029
(g) 1–029
Art. 84(1) 15–002
(2) 15–002

1992 European Community Treaty (EC Treaty) (Incorporating amendments introduced by TEU)—*cont.*
Arts. 85–86 .. *Reference should be made to the index under the appropriate subject heading*
Art. 88 1–045
Art. 89 .... 1–046, 15–057
Art. 90 .... 2–004, 12–024, 13–017, 13–023, 18–062
(2) 7–113, 13–016, 13–021, 13–025, 13–027, 16–012, 18–062
(3) .. 12–024, 13–017, 13–028, 13–029, 13–031, 13–033
Art. 92 ... 12–024, 13–021, 18–001, 18–009, 18–037, 18–044, 18–050, 18–051, 18–061, 18–062
(1) 18–024, 18–044A
(2) 18–015
(a) 18–015
(3) 18–016
(b) 18–019
(c) 18–016, 18–022
(e) 18–016
Art. 93 ... 21–024, 13–021, 18–044, 18–061, 18–062
(1) 18–024
(2) .. 18–001, 18–026, 18–031, 18–037, 18–042A, 18–048, 18–050, 18–052, 18–055
(3) .. 18–031, 18–041, 18–044, 18–044A, 18–053, 18–062
Art. 94 18–044
Arts. 109(j)–109(l) 1–024
Art. 113 18–014
(4) 1–038
Arts. 117–125 1–038
Art. 128 1–038
Art. 129 1–038
(a) 1–038

1992 European Community Treaty (EC Treaty) (Incorporating amendments introduced by TEU)—*cont.*
Art. 129(b)(d) 1–038, 16–001, 16–006
Art. 138(e) 1–009
Art. 158(2) 1–009
Art. 168(a) 12–101
Art. 169 13–009
Art. 172 12–103
Art. 173 .... 7–107A, 10–022, 12–024, 12–105, 12–130, 18–037, 18–048, 18–055
Art. 175 .... 7–107A, 12–023, 12–024, 12–122, 12–125, 18–048
Art. 177 .... 9–039, 10–010, 15–004, 15–025, 16–011, 16–013
Arts. 188(a)–(c) 1–008
(b) 1–009, 16–006, 16–045
(c) 1–009
Art. 223 13–035
(1)(b) 13–035
Art. 338 1–070

1994 Treaty of Accession to the European Communities (Austria, Finland, Sweden) (24 June) 1–004, 2–029
Act annexed to the Treaty of Accession
Arts. 138–141 14–008
Art. 142 14–008
Art. 172 3–057
Protocol 3 1–005

1995 Association Agreement between Community and Israel (November) OJ 2–167

G. REGULATIONS

Reg. 1/58, JO 1958 1-7, 385; OJ 1973 L2/1 11–048
Art. 3 12–035
Reg. 26 JO 1962 993, OJ 1959–1962 *Spec. Ed.* 129 .... 14–003, 14–005
Art. 2 14–006
(1) 14–004, 14–005, 14–007
(2) 14–007
Reg. 17 OJ 1959–1962 *Spec. Ed.* 87 ... 6–165, 7–108G, 11–001A, 11–005, 11–008, 12–002, 12–046, 12–109, 15–004
Art. 3 10–033
Art. 4(2) 3–056, 11–018, 11–024, 11–044, 12–073
Art. 6 11–003
(1) 11–018, 11–038
(2) 11–036, 11–038, 11–044
Art. 7(1) 11–036, 11–039, 11–044
Art. 10 12–046
(1) 11–057
Art. 15(6) 11–017
Art. 19(3) 3–019, 11–058, 18–061
Art. 20 .... 11–057, 12–046
Art. 25 .. 1–052, 11–033, 11–035, 11–044, **App. 5**
(2) 11–044
(3) 11–036, 11–038
(6) 11–008, 11–034
Reg. 27, OJ 1959–1962, *Sped. Ed.* 132 .... 1–053, 11–046
Reg. 141, JO 1962, 2751 15–004
Reg. 99/63, JO 1963, 2268 12–030
Reg. 19/65, OJ 1965–66, *Sped. Ed.* 35
Art. 20 12–046
Reg. 1017/68, OJ 1968 175/1 .... 3–005, 3–034, 3–050, 4–003, 4–067, 7–005, 12–084, 12–109, 15–002, 15–004, 15–011
Art. 1 15–004
Art. 3 15–006
Reg. 2988/74, OJ 1974 L319/1 .... 12–088, 12–096
Reg. 1360/78, OJ 1978 L166/1
Art. 17 14–007
Reg. 3796/81 14–005
Reg. 1983/83, OJ 1983 L173/1 .... 3–016A, 7–011
Reg. 1984/83, OJ 1983 L173/5 .... 3–016A, 7–011, 7–111, 7–117, 7–117A, 7–124, 7–153, 7–154, 12–054, 16–044
Art. 14 .... 7–067, 7–124
(a) 7–124
(b) 7–124
Reg. 2349/84, OJ 1984 L219/15 [1993] 4 CMLR 177 .... 1–022, 1–071, 2–113, 3–008, 3–016A, 3–024, 3–031, 8–007, 8–090, 8–093, 8–118, 8–119, 8–125, 8–150, 8–164A, 8–164C, 8–164E, 8–164L–M, 8–174U–W
Art. 9(2) 8–164F
Reg. 123/85, OJ 1985 L15/16 .... 1–071, 2–022, 3–016A, 7–100, 7–107A, 7–108A, 7–108G, 7–108H, 10–028
Art. 1 .... 3–009, 7–108C
Art. 2 .... 7–108C
Art. 3(11) 7–100
Reg. 417/85, OJ 1985 L53/1 [1993] 4 CMLR 155 .... 3–016A
Reg. 418/85, OJ 1985 L53/5 [1993] 4 CMLR 164 .... 3–016A, 5–018, 5–088, 5–121, 5–122
Art. 3(1) 5–053
(2) 5–053
Reg. 4056/86, OJ 1986 L378/4 .... 15–002, 15–013
Art. 3 .... 15–019, 15–024
Art. 12 15–017
Art. 18 12–004
Reg. 3975/87, OJ 1987 L374/1 .... 1–046, 15–002, 15–011, 15–031
Art. 6(1) 3–050
Reg. 3976/87, OJ 1987 L374/9 15–045
Reg. 4078/88, OJ 1988 L359/46 .... 3–016A, 7–172, 7–177
Reg. 4261/88, OJ 1988 L376/10 .... 15–033, 15–034
Reg. 556/89, OJ 1989 L61/1 [1993] 4 CMLR 195 .... 3–016A, 3–024, 3–031, 8–007, 8–118, 8–151, 8–164A–C, 8–164F, 8–174L–M, 8–164U–V
Reg. 4064/89 (Merger Regulation) OJ 1989 L395/1 and OJ 1990 L257/14 ... 2–095, 3–018, 4–001, 5–009, 5–009A, 5–013, 5–023, 5–025, 5–035, 5–046, 6–003, 6–004, 6–004A, 6–005A, 6–009A, 6–016, 6–032A, 6–034, 6–036, 6–044, 6–064, 11–014, 12–130, 13–035, 15–053, 15–057
Recital (13) 6–077
Art. 1 6–003
Art. 3 6–003
(1)(a) 6–007
(5) 6–021
(c) 6–024, 6–027
Art. 4 6–147
(3) 11–058
Art. 5 6–003
(2) 6–050
(4)(b) 6–051, 6–055
Art. 6(1)(b) 6–116

Reg. 4064/89 (Merger Regulation) OJ 1989 L395/1 and OJ 1990 L257/14—*cont.*
Art. 7(2) 6–108
Art. 8(2) 6–123A
Art. 9 .... 6–005A, 6–116, 6–146, 6–148
Art. 10(1) 6–147
(6) 6–147
Art. 13(2) 6–120
Art. 20 6–120
Art. 21(3) 6–150
Art. 22 ....6–005A
Reg. 2367/90 (Implementing Reg. 4064/89) OJ 1990 L219/5 .... 1–056, 6–003, 6–004A
Reg. 83/91, OJ 1991 L10/9 3–012
Reg. 84/91, OJ 1991 L10/14 .... 3–012, 15–048
Reg. 479/92, OJ 1992 L55/3 .. 3–004, 3–016, 15–027
Reg. 2408/92, OJ 1992 L240/8 15–029
Reg. 3932/92, OJ 1992 L398/7 ...... 3–016A, 4–081
Reg. 151/93, OJ 1993 L21/8 [1993] 4 CMLR 151 ....3–016A
Reg. 1617/93, OJ 1993 L155/18 .... 3–012, 3–016A, 15–029, 15–048
Art. 1 15–048
Art. 3 15–048
Art. 6 15–048
Art. 7 15–048
Reg. 3089/93, OJ 1993 L278/1 and OJ 1995 L17/18 15–043
Reg. 3652/93, OJ 1993 L333/37 .... 3–012, 3–016A 15–029, 15–046
Art. 1 15–047
Art. 3 15–047
Art. 4 15–047
Art. 6 15–047
Art. 7 15–047
Art. 9 15–047
Art. 10 15–047
Art. 11 15–047
Art. 12 15–047
Art. 13 15–047
Art. 14 15–047
Art. 15 15–047
Reg. 3666/93, OJ 1993 L336/1 .... 11–046, 15–034
Art. 4 15–033
Reg. 40/94, OJ 1994 L11/1 .... 8–002, 8–027
Reg. 2100/94, OJ 1994 L227/1 .... 8–002, 8–177
Reg. 2349/94 .... 3–008A, 8–007
Reg. 3288/94, OJ 1994 L394/83 .... 8–002, 8–027
Reg. 3384/94 (revised reg. implementing reg. 4064/89) ...... 1–056, 6–003, 6–004A, 6–096, 6–097, **App. 6**
Preambles .... **App. 6**
Recital (8) 11–047
Art. 1 .... **App. 6**
Art. 2 .... **App. 6**
Reg. 3384/94 (revised reg. implementing reg. 4064/89—*cont.*
Art. 2(2) 6–096, 6–097
(3) 11–048
Art. 3 .... **App. 6**
(1) 6–099
(2) 6–102
Art. 4 .... **App. 6**
(3) 6–099
Art. 5 .... **App. 6**
Art. 6 .... **App. 6**
(1) 6–112
(2) 6–119
Art. 7 .... **App. 6**
(4) 6–119
Art. 8 .... 6–119, **App. 6**
Art. 9 .... **App. 6**
Art. 10 .... 6–118, **App. 6**
Art. 11 .... 6–121, **App. 6**
Art. 12 .... 6–108, 6–110, **App. 6**
Art. 13 .... **App. 6**
(2) 6–121
(3) 6–121
(4) 6–122
Art. 14 .... 6–123, **App. 6**
Art. 15 .... 6–123, **App. 6**
Art. 16 .... **App. 6**
(1) 6–123
(2) 6–123
(3) 6–123
Art. 17 .... **App. 6**
Art. 18 .... 6–123A, **App. 6**
Art. 19 .... 6–118, **App. 6**
Art. 20 .... 6–108, 6–110, **App. 6**
Art. 21 .... **App. 6**
(3) 6–103
Art. 22 .... 6–112, 6–119, **App. 6**
Art. 23 .... **App. 6**
Art. 24 .... **App. 6**
Annex (Form CO) .... **App. 6**
Reg. 3385/94 .... 1–053, 6–049, 8–164V, 11–046, 11–051
Recital (4) 11–050
Recital (6) 11–047
Art. 1(1) 11–048
(2) 11–046
(3) 11–048
(4) 11–048
Art. 2(1) 11–046
(2) 11–048
(3) 11–048
(4) 11–048
(5) 11–048
Art. 3(1) 11–050
(2) 11–005, 11–046
(3) 5–009, 11–050
Art. 4(1) 11–054
(2) 11–049, 11–054
(3) 11–050, 11–055
(5) 11–049, 11–054
Annex Introduction, Point 1 5–012
Reg. 70/95, OJ 1995 L12/13 .... 3–008, 3–016A, 8–125

Reg. 870/95 .... 3–015A, 3–016, 3–016A, 15–015, 15–028A, 15–028B, **App. 13**
Preambles .... **App. 13**
Art. 1 .... 15–028A, **App. 13**
Art. 2 .... 15–028A, **App. 13**
Art. 3 .... 15–028A, **App. 13**
(2) 3–015A
Art. 4 .... 15–028A, **App. 13**
Art. 5 .... 15–028A, **App. 13**
Art. 6 .... 15–028B, **App. 13**
Art. 7 .... 15–028B, **App. 13**
Art. 8 .... **App. 13**
Art. 9 .... 15–028B, **App. 13**
Art. 10 .... **App. 13**
Art. 11 .... **App. 13**
Art. 12 .... **App. 13**
Art. 13 .... **App. 13**
Reg. 1475/95 .... 1–071, 3–009, 7–096, 7–107A, 7–108A–J, 11–006, **App. 2**, **App. 3**
Preambles .... **App. 2**
Recital (9) 7–108D
Recitals (20)–(28) 7–108H
Recital (26) 7–108E
Art. 1 .... 3–009, 7–108C, **App. 2**
Art. 2 .... 7–108C, **App. 2**
Art. 3 .... **App. 2**
(3) 7–108D
(4) 7–108D
(8) 7–108D
(10) 7–108D
(11) 7–108D
Art. 4 .... **App. 2**
(1)(3)–(5) 7–108J
(3) 7–108E
(4) 7–108E
(5) 7–108E
Art. 5 .... **App. 2**
(2)(2) 7–108F
(3) 7–108F, 7–108J
Art. 6 .... 3–024, 7–108I, **App. 2**
(1) 7–108H
(2) 7–108H
(3) 7–108H
(4) 7–108H
(5) 7–108H
(6)–(12) 7–108I
(6) 7–108I
(7) 7–108D–E, 7–108I
(8) 7–108I
(9) 7–108I
(10) 7–108I
(11) 7–108I
(12) 7–108I
(2) 7–108H–I
(3) 7–108I
Art. 7 .... 7–108A, **App. 2**
Art. 8 .... 7–108G, **App. 2**
Art. 9 .... **App. 2**
Art. 10 .... **App. 2**
(12) 7–108D
(13) 7–108D
Art. 11 .... **App. 2**
Art. 12 .... **App. 2**
Reg. 1475/95—*cont.*
Art. 13 .... 7–108, 7–108A, **App. 2**
Reg. 2131/95, OJ 1995 L214/6 .... 3–008, 3–016A, 8–125
Reg. 3094/95 18–025
Reg. 240/96 .... 1–033, 1–071, 2–024, 2–113, 3–008, 3–008A, 8–007, 8–090, 8–093, 8–116, 8–125, 8–150, 8–151, 8–164A–W, 11–006, **App. 4**
Preambles .... **App. 4**
Recital (3) 8–164A
Recital (10) 3–031
Recital (25) 8–164V
Art. 1 .... 3–008A, 8–164C, 8–164G, 8–164U, **App. 4**
(1) 8–164B, 8–164G
(1) 8–164H
(2) 8–164H
(3) 8–164I
(4) 8–164I
(7) 8–164K
(8) 8–164K
(2) 8–164H, 8–164J, 8–164T
(3) 8–164H, 8–164T
(4) 8–164H
(5) 8–164G
Art. 2 ... 8–093, 8–164C, 8–164U, **App. 4**
(1) 8–164L
(4) 8–164L
(7) 8–164L
(13) 8–164L, 8–164Q
(17) 8–164L
(18) 8–164L, 8–164O
Art. 3 .... 3–008A, 3–024, 8–093, 8–164C, 8–164M, 8–164U, **App. 4**
(1) 8–164N
(2) 8–164L, 8–164O
(3) 8–164P
(4) 8–164Q
(5) 8–164R
(6) 8–164L, 8–164S
(7) 8–164T
Art. 4 3–008A, 3–020, 8–164C, 8–164W, **App. 4**
(1) 8–164U
(2) 8–164U
(5) 8–164U
Art. 5 .... 8–164C, 8–164D, **App. 4**
(1)(1) 8–164D
(2) 8–164E
(3) 8–164D
(2)(1) 8–164E
(2) 8–164D
(3) 8–164E
Art. 6 .... **App. 4**
(1) 8–164B
(2) 8–164B
(3) 8–164B
Art. 7 .... 3–008A, 8–164C, 8–164F, **App. 4**
(1) 8–164F
(2) 8–164F
(3) 8–164F
Art. 7 .... **App. 4**

Reg. 240/96—*cont.*
Art. 7(1) 8–164B
Art. 9 .... **App. 4**
Art. 10 .... **App. 4**
(1) 8–164B
(15) 8–164B
Art. 11 .... 8–164A, **App. 4**

Reg. 240/96—*cont.*
Art. 11(1) 3–014
(2) 3–008A
(3) 8–164A
Art. 12 .... **App. 4**
Art. 13 .... 8–164A, **App. 4**

H. DIRECTIVES

Dir. 80/723, OJ 1980 L195/35, OJ 1985 L229/20 .... 13–032, 18–008
Art. 5 18–007
(a) 18–029
Dir. 88/301, OJ 1977 L131/73 13–033
Art. 3 13–033
Art. 6 13–033
Dir. 89/104, OJ 1989 L40/1 8–027
Dir. 90/388, OJ 1990 L192/10 13–033
Dir. 90/684, OJ 1990 L380/27 18–025
Dir. 91/250, OJ 1991 L122/42, OJ 1993 L11/20 8–063
Dir. 92/100, OJ 1992 L346/61 8–047
Dir. 93/38, 1993 OJ L199/84 16–006
Dir. 93/83, OJ 1993 L248/15 .. 8–002, 8–047
Dir. 93/84 .... 13–032, 18–008, 18–029, **App. 14**
Preambles .... **App. 14**
Art. 1 .... **App. 14**
Art. 2 .... **App. 14**
Art. 3 .... **App. 14**
Art. 5a(3) 13–032
Dir. 93/98, OJ 1993 L290/9 .... 8–002, 8–063
Art. 1(1) 8–063
Dir. 94/46, OJ 1994 L268/15 [1996] 4 CMLR 87 .... 13–014, 13–033
Dir. 95/46, OJ 1995 L281/31 8–002
Dir. 95/51, OJ 1995 L256/49 13–033
Dir. 96/2, OJ 1996 L20/59 13–033
Dir. 96/19, OJ 1996 L74/13 13–033

I. DECISIONS

Decn. 2064/86, OJ 1986 L177/1 17–019
Decn. 3855/91, OJ 1991 L362/57 and OJ 1994 L112/45 17–020
Art. 6(4) 18–001
Decn. 93/350, OJ 1993 L144/21 18–048
Decn. 3632/93, OJ 1993 L329/12 17–019
Decn. 94/149, OJ 1994 L66/29 12–101
Decn. 94/810 .... **App. 7**
Art. 1 .... **App. 7**
Art. 2 .... **App. 7**
Art. 3 .... **App. 7**
Art. 4 .... **App. 7**
Art. 5 .... **App. 7**
Art. 6 .... **App. 7**
Decn. 94/810—*cont.*
Art. 7 .... **App. 7**
Art. 8 .... **App. 7**
Art. 9 .... **App. 7**
Art. 10 .... **App. 7**
Art. 11 .... **App. 7**
Art. 12 .... **App. 7**
Decn. 94/824, OJ 1994 L349/201 8–047
Decn. 95/1, OJ 1995 L1/1 .... 11–033, 11–048, 15–029, 15–033
Decn. 95/145, OJ 1995 L95/45 [1995] 4 CMLR 707 11–057
Decn. 95/208, OJ 1995 L131/33 12–132

J. NOTICES, GUIDELINES AND OTHER INFORMAL TEXTS

Notice on Cooperation Agreements, OJ 1968 C75/3 and C93/14 11–064
Notice on Subcontracting Agreements, OJ 1979 C1/2 11–064
Notice on Agreements of Minor Importance, OJ 1986 C231/2 .. 11–064
Commission Notice on Ancillary Restrictions, OJ 1990 C203/5 6–003
Commission Notice on concentrature and co-operative operations, OJ 1990 C203/10 1–056
Commission's Report on the implementation of the Merger Regulation, 28 July 1993, (COM (93) 385 final) 6–004
Community guidelines on State aid for environmental protection, OJ 1994 C72/3 18–024
EFTA Surveillance Authority Notice regarding exclusive distribution and exclusive purchasing agreements, OJ 1994 L153/1 [1994] 4 CMLR 317, as amended by OJ 1994 L186/57 ... 2–079, 7–050
EFTA Surveillance Authority Notice regarding block exemption, OJ 1994 L153/1 [1994] 4 CMLR 332 7–096
EFTA Surveillance Authority Notice on application of Art. 53(1) of EEA Agreement, OJ 1994 L153/1 [1994] 4 CMLR 339 .... 2–115, 7–004
EFTA Surveillance Authority Notice on sub-contracting agreements, OJ 1994 L153/1 [1994] 4 CMLR 353 .... 2–115, 7–198
EFTA Surveillance Authority Notice on assessment of co-operative joint ventures under Article 53 of EEA Agreement, OJ 1994 L186/57 .... 2–059, 2–093, 2–114, 5–009
EFTA Surveillance Authority Notice on exclusive distribution and exclusive purchasing agreements (as modified), OJ 1994 L186/57 7–129
EFTA Surveillance Authority Notice regarding motor vehicle intermediaries, OJ 1994 L186/57 7–097
EFTA Surveillance Notice on scope of activities of intermediaries within Reg. 123/85, Art. 3(11), OJ 1994 L186/57 7–100
EFTA Surveillance Authority Guidelines on application and interpretation of the State aid provisions of the EEA Agreement, OJ 1994 L231/1 18–017
Commission guidelines for the examination of State aids in the fisheries and aquaculture sector, OJ 1994 C260/3 14–008
Community guidelines on State aid for rescuing and restructuring firms in difficulty OJ 1994 C368/12 18–024
EFTA Surveillance Authority State Aid Guidelines, OJ 1994 L383/1
Commission's Notice on the distinction between concentrative and cooperative joint venture undertaking's (the reused Interface Notice), OJ 1994 C385/1 ..... 5–009, 5–012, 5–019, 6–003, 6–0235, 6–027, 6–028, 6–034, 6–035, 6–036, 6–041, 6–164
  points 12–16 6–033
  point 13 .... 5–020, 6–025, 6–033
  point 16 6–033
  point 17 *et seq* 6–040
  point 18 .... 6–037, 6–038, 6–040
  point 20 6–042
  point 33 6–039
  point 47 6–019
Commission Green Paper For a European Union Energy Policy (23 February) (COM (94) 659) 16–003, 16–004, 16–005, 16–036, 16–041
Commission Notice 94/C 385/01 ..... **App. 9**
  Pt. I .... **App. 9**
  Pt. II .... **App. 9**
  Pt. III .... **App. 9**
Commission Notice 94/C 385/02 ... **App. 10**
  Pt. I .... **App. 10**
  Pt. II .... **App. 10**
  Pt. III .... **App. 10**
  Pt. IV .... **App. 10**
  Pt. V .... **App. 10**
Commission Notice 94/C 385/03 ... **App. 11**
  Pt. I .... **App. 11**
  Pt. II .... **App. 11**
  Pt. III .... **App. 11**
Commission Notice 94/C 385/04 ... **App. 12**
  Pt. I .... **App. 12**
  Pt. II .... **App. 12**
  Pt. III .... **App. 12**
Letter from Commission to Member States, s 9(94)D/2484 22 February 1994 18–028

ECJ Opinion 2/94 Accession to the European Convention for the Protection of Human Rights and Fundamental Freedoms [1996] 2 CMLR 265 .... 1–026A, 1–050
OECD Report Competition Policy and Vertical Restraints: Franchising Agreements (1994) 7–003, 7–163, 7–185
Council approval for co-operation Agreement within United States, OJ 1995 L95/45, OJ 1995 L131/38 [1995] 4 CMLR 707 1–070
EFTA Surveillance Notice on cooperation between national courts and ESA in applying Articles 53 & 54 of EEA Agreement, OJ 1995 C112/7 [1995] 5 CMLR 358 ... 10–015, 10–017, 10–023
Council's Agreement to adopt the Commission's proposal for a Directive on access to the ground handling markets at community airports, OJ 1995 C142/7 15–030
Commission Communication to member states on repayment of illegally granted aid, OJ 1995 C–156/5 18–041
Council Adoption of Common Position (EC) No. 12/95 on Guidelines for trans-European gas and electricity networks, OJ 1995 C216/31 16–006
Commission's Notice on the application of the EC Competition rules to cross-border credit transfers, OJ 1995 C251/3 [1995] 5 CMLR 551 ...... 4–016, 4–025, 4–047, 4–086
Commission Proposal to modify Reg. 1617/93, OJ 1995 C322/15, XXVth Report on Competition Policy [1995], points 74–75 3–012
Commission's employment aid guidelines, OJ 1995 C–334/4 18–024
Commission's draft guidelines on possible exemption from fine, OJ 1995 C341/8 [1996] 4 CMLR 593 12–086
Commission Green Paper on Utility models (COM (95) 370) 8–002
Commission Green Paper on Copyright and Related Rights in the Information Society, (COM (95) 382) 8–002
Commission Notice on Co-operation between National Courts and the Commission in the State Aid, Field C(95) 2436 final .... 18–044A, 18–046, **App. 15**
Pt. I .... **App. 15**
Commission Notice on Co-operation between National Courts and the Commission in the State Aid, Field C(95) 2436 final—*cont.*
Pt. II .... **App. 15**
Pt. III .... **App. 15**
Pt. IV .... **App. 15**
Pt. V .... **App. 15**
Pt. VI .... **App. 15**
Pt. VII .... **App. 15**
Commission Communication on interest rates to apply when recovering illegal aid, Press Release IP (95) 87 of 1 February 1995 .... 18–042A
US Department of Justice and Federal Trade Commission Antitrust Guidelines for the Licensing of Intellectual Property, [1995] 7 EIPR supplement 8–080
Explanatory Brochure on Reg. 1475/95 .... **App. 3**
Pt. I.1 .... **App. 3**
Pt. I.2 .... **App. 3**
Pt. I.3 .... **App. 3**
Pt. I.4 .... **App. 3**
Pt. II.1 .... **App. 3**
Pt. II.2 .... **App. 3**
Pt. II.3 .... **App. 3**
Pt. II.4 .... **App. 3**
Pt. II.5 .... **App. 3**
Pt. III.1 .... **App. 3**
Pt. III.2 .... **App. 3**
Pt. IV.1 .... **App. 3**
Pt. IV.2 .... **App. 3**
Pt. IV.3 .... **App. 3**
Pt. V .... **App. 3**
Annex .... **App. 3**
Commission's proposed Directive to introduce rational planning techniques in electricity and gas distribution sectors and to reduce CO2 emissions, OJ 1996 C1/6 10–006
Commission Notice Setting out a de minimis rule on State Aid, OJ 1996 C68/9 18–013
Commission revised guidelines on State Aid for small and medium-sized enterprises, OJ 1966 18–013
Commission Green Paper on the review of the Merger Regulation (31 January) (COM (96) final) .. 2–095, 5–009A, 6–005A, 6–144
Pt. IV 5–009A
Proposed Commission Green Paper on vertical restraints on Trade, XXVth Report on Competition Policy (1995) point 44; Parliamentary answer of September 11, 1995 [1996] 4 CMLR 20 .... 3–016, 7–048, 7–117, 7–172

Commission Notice (96/C 207/04) .. **App. 8**
Pt. A(1) .... **App. 8**
(2) .... **App. 8**
(3) .... **App. 8**
(4) .... **App. 8**
(5) .... **App. 8**
Pt. B(a) .... **App. 8**
(b) .... **App. 8**
(c) .... **App. 8**
(d) .... **App. 8**
(e) .... **App. 8**
Pt. C .... **App. 8**
Pt. D(1) .... **App. 8**
(2) .... **App. 8**
Pt. E(1) .... **App. 8**
(2) .... **App. 8**
(3) .... **App. 8**
(4) .... **App. 8**
Commission Notice expanding on the text of Articles 1 and 5 of the Merger Regulation (The Turnover Notice) 6–003, 6–049
Pt. I 6–049
Pt. II 6–049
Pt. III 6–049
point 27 6–050
points 30–31 6–050
points 32–35 6–050
points 36–42 6–051
point 38(3) 6–050, 6–055
point 40 6–051
point 42 6–053
points 43–44 6–054
point 51 6–056
point 52 6–056
points 54–58 6–056
points 59–61 6–057
points 62–64 6–058
points 65–68 6–056
Commission Notice interpreting the notion of a concentration under Article 3 of the Merger Regulation (The Concentration Notice) ... 6–003, 6–006, 6–007, 6–008, 6–009, 6–009A, 6–027, 6–028, 6–164
points 6–7 6–164
points 12 *et seq* 6–010
points 13–14 6–164
point 15 6–164
point 16 6–016
points 18 *et seq* 5–013, 6–164
Commission Notice interpreting the notion of a concentration under Article 3 of the Merger Regulation (The Concentration Notice)—*cont.*
point 19 6–030
point 20 6–032
point 21 6–031
point 22 6–030
point 23 6–030
point 24 6–030
point 25 6–030
point 26 6–030
point 27 6–030
point 29 6–030
points 30–35 6–032
point 37 6–031
point 38 .... 6–032A
points 41–45 6–021
Commission Notice on Cooperation between National Courts and the Commission in applying Articles 85 and 86 of the EC Treaty 18–044A
Commission Notice on interpretation of the notion of undertakings concerned under Articles 1 and 5 of the Merger Regulation (The Undertakings Concerned Notice) ... 6–003, 6–006, 6–016, 6–019, 6–044, 6–048
points 24–25 6–017
points 26–29 6–055
points 30–32 6–011
points 33–45 6–011
points 55–56 .... 6–009A
Commission Notice on the notion of a concentration 5–019
EFTA Surveillance Authority Notice on Ancillary Restrictions 6–004A
EFTA Surveillance Authority Notice on Concentrative and Cooperative Operations 6–004A
EFTA Surveillance Authority Notice interpreting Reg. 1984/83 .... 7–117A
Guidance Note I to the revised Form Co 6–056
Guidance Note II to the revised Form Co 6–056

K. RULES OF PROCEDURE

Rules of Procedure (ECJ) OJ 1991 L176/7, as corrected at OJ 1992 L383/117 and as amended at OJ 1995 L44/61 1–017
Rules of Procedure (CFI) – amendment re intellectual property matters, OJ 1994 L249/17, OJ 1995 L44/64, OJ 1995 172/3 12–116
Statute of the Court of Justice Protocol – as amended re intellectual property matters Protocol, OJ 1995 L131/33 12–116
Statute of the Court of Justice of the European Communities Protocol
Art. 46 12–132
Statute of the CFI
Art. 47 6–140
Statute of the EFTA Court Protocol 5 .... 12–134A

L. NATIONAL LEGISLATION

United Kingdom

Statutes

1938 Trade Marks Act (c.22) 8–027
1972 European Communities Act (c.68)
s.1(1) 10–003
(2) 10–003
(k) 1–050
1973 Fair Trading Act (c.41)
Pt. V 6–151
1976 Restrictive Trade Practices Act (c.34) 10–059, 10–060, 11–053
1993 European Communities (Amendment) Act (c.32) 1–002, 10–003
European Economic Area Act (c.51) 10–003
1994 Trade Marks Act (c.26) 8–027
s.9 8–027
s.10 8–027
(6) 8–027
s.11(2) 8–027
1994 Trade Marks Act—*cont.*
s.12 8–027
(2) 8–027

Statutory Instruments

1989 Supply of Beer (Loan, Licensed Premises and Wholesale Prices) Order (SI 1989 No 2258) 7–131
1994 Registration of Restrictive Trading Agreements (EEC Documents) (Revocation) Regulations (SI 1994 No 1095) 11–053
1996 Restrictive Trade Practices (Non-notifiable Agreements) (EC Block Exemptions) Order (SI 1996 No 349) ... 10–057, 10–060

Netherlands

1989 Dutch Electricity Law 16–010

M. INTERNATIONAL TREATIES AND CONVENTIONS

1950 European Convention for the Protection of Human Rights and Fundamental Freedoms (November 4) 213 U.N.T.S 221, U.K.T.S 71 (1953) 1–026A, 1–050

1991 EEC–USA Competition Laws Cooperation Agreement (September 23) [1991] 4 CMLR 823 ..... 2–156, 12–008B, 12–017
Art. III 12–046
(3) 12–008B
Art. VIII 12–046
EEC/Hungary Agreement (16 December) 2–168
EEC/Poland Agreement (16 December) OJ 1991 L111/11 2–168

1992 Treaty on a European Economic Area (the EEA Agreement) (May 2) CM 2073, [1992] 1 CMLR 921, [1992] 1 CLE 277 .. 1–007, 2–158, 2–165, 3–053, 3–055, 3–056, 4–001A, 6–004A, 10–003, 11–001A, 11–046, 12–134B, 15–029, 15–033, 15–047, 18–016
Art. 4(2) 11–018
Art. 6 11–018
Art. 8 6–142
(3) 11–008
Art. 53 .... 2–059, 2–093, 2–114, 5–009, 7–011, 7–048, 7–096, 7–108A, 7–117A, 7–172, 11–001A, 11–008, 11–033, 11–034, 11–034A, 11–035, 11–038
(1) 2–029, 2–115, 3–003A, 3–055, 5–121, 7–004, 11–006, 11–010, 11–034, 11–035
(3) . 3–003A, 3–016A, 3–047, 3–053, 3–055, 11–018
Art. 54 .... 11–001A
Art. 56 .... 3–003A, 11–001A
Art. 58 .... 12–008A
Art. 60 ... 3–003A, 6–004A, 7–011
Art. 61 18–001
(1) 18–001
Art. 98 .... 3–016A
Art. 102 .... 3–016A
Art. 108 .... 1–007, 2–160
(2) 12–134A
Art. 109 .... 12–008A, 18–001
Annex XIII
point 7 15–002

1992 Treaty on a European Economic Area (the EEA Agreement) (May 2) CM 2073, [1992] 1 CMLR 921, [1992] 1 CLE 277—*cont.*
point 50 .... 15–002, 15–013
Annex XIV 3–003A, 3–016A, 6–004A, 11–006
points 2–3 7–011
point 2 .... 3–016A, 7–048
point 3 .... 3–016A, 7–117A
point 4 .... 3–016A, 7–096
point 5 .... 3–016A
point 6 .... 3–016A
point 7 .... 3–016A
point 8 .... 3–016A, 7–172
point 9 .... 3–016A
point 11a 3–016A
point 11b 3–016A
point 11c 3–016A
point 15a 3–016A, 4–081
Protocol 1 11–006
Protocol 3 6–142
Protocol 21 ...... 11–001A, 11–018
Art. 1 .... 11–001A
Art. 4(2) 3–056, 11–006, 11–024, 11–044
Arts. 5–7 .... 11–034A
Art. 5(1) 3–055, 11–044
Art. 6 .... 3–055, 3–056, 11–056, 11–038, 11–044
Art. 7(1) . 11–036, 11–039, 11–044
Art. 8 3–054
Art. 9 11–036
Arts. 11–12 .... 11–034A
Art. 11 3–055
Art. 12 3–055
Art. 13 3–053
Protocol 23 .... 12–008A
Art. 12 11–048
Protocol 24 .... 12–008A
Protocol 27 18–001
Swiss Protocol 2–158
Protocol of 1993 10–003

1993 EEC/Romania Agreement (1 February) 2–168
EEC/Bulgaria Agreement (8 March) 2–168
EEC/Czech Republic Agreement (4 October) 2–168
EEC/Slovakia Agreement (4 October) 2–168

1994 Agreement on Trade-Related Aspects of Intellectual Property Rights 15 April 1994, U.K.T.S. No. 10 (1996) Cm. 3046 .... 8–007A
Pt. II 8–007A

1994 Agreement on Trade-Related Aspects of Intellectual Property Rights 15 April 1994, U.K.T.S. No. 10 (1996) Cm. 3046—*cont.*
Art. 3 .... 8–007A
Art. 4 .... 8–007A
Art. 6 .... 8–007A
Art. 40(1) 8–007A
(2) 8–007A
(3) 8–007A
Agreement between EFTA States on the establishment of a Surveillance Authority and a Court of Justice (The EFTA Surveillance Agreement) OJ 1994 L344/1 [1994] 4 CMLR 180 ...... 1–007, 2–160, 11–001A, 12–002, 12–134B
Art. 16 12–111
Arts. 27–41 .... 12–134A
Protocol 4 .... 11–001A
Chap. II 11–001A, 12–002
Art. 6 11–003
Art. 19(3) 3–019
Chap. IV 12–030
1994 Agreement between EFTA States on the establishment of a Surveillance Authority and a Court of Justice (The EFTA Surveillance Agreement) OJ 1994 L344/1 [1994] 4 CMLR 180—*cont.*
Chap. V 12–096
Chap. XI 15–002
Chap. XIV 6–004A
Chap. XVI
Art. 2 11–003
1995 Interpretative letter re EEC–USA Competition Laws Cooperation Agreement 1995 OJ L95/45 1995 OJ L131/38 [1995] 4 CMLR 707 12–046
EFTA Adjustment Agreement 12–134A
EFTA Transitional Arrangements Agreement 12–134A
Energy Charter Treaty 16–002
OECD Agreement 18–025

CHAPTER 1

THE COMMUNITY CONTEXT

1. HISTORICAL BACKGROUND

The ECSC Treaty **1–001**

n. 2. For the text of the Treaty as further amended by the TEU, see *Encyclopedia of European Union Law (Constitutional Texts)* (Sweet & Maxwell, 1996), Vol. 1, §§ 10.0010 *et seq.*; Rudden and Wyatt (eds.), *Basic Community Laws* (6th ed., Clarendon Press, 1996).

The EEC Treaty. Further substantial amendments were made to the Treaty of Rome by the Treaty on European Union ("TEU") which entered into force on 1 November 1993. The amendments include the replacement of the term "European Economic Community" by "European Community": TEU, Article G (A). Accordingly, the current term "EC Treaty" is used throughout this Supplement. Other amendments made by the TEU are considered in more detail at para. 1–006, *infra*. **1–002**

n. 3. The TEU amendments take effect in the UK under the European Communities (Amendment) Act 1993. The amended EC Treaty is appended to the fully annotated text of the UK statute in *Current Law Statutes Annotated*: *1993* (Sweet & Maxwell), Vol. 2, c. 32; see also *Encyclopedia of European Union Law (Constitutional Texts)*, Vol. 1, §§ 12.0034 *et seq.*; Rudden and Wyatt, *op. cit.* For general works, see now Hartley, *op. cit.* (3rd ed., 1994); Craig and de Burca, *EC Law: Text, Cases, and Materials* (Clarendon Press, 1995); Weatherill & Beaumont, *EC Law* (2nd ed., Penguin, 1995).

The Euratom Treaty **1–003**

n. 7. For an annotated text of the Treaty incorporating the amendments made by the TEU see *Encyclopedia of European Union Law (Constitutional Texts)*, Vol. 1, §§ 1.0001 *et seq.*

1–004 **The Accession Treaties.** Austria, Finland and Sweden acceded to the European Community with effect from 1 January 1995. The Treaty of Accession signed at Corfu on 24 June 1994 was signed also by Norway but the subsequent Norwegian referendum voted against accession. The Treaty provided that the annexed Act of Accession could be amended in such circumstances by unanimous decision of the Council of the European Union, which duly took place so as to remove those aspects relating to Norway. For the text of the Treaty and Act of Accession, see *Encyclopedia of European Union Law (Constitutional Texts)*, Vol. 2, paras. 23.0034 *et seq*.

1–005 **The Member States.** Following the accession of Austria, Finland and Sweden, the EC Treaty now extends to 15 Member States. As regards Finland, the Treaty does not apply to the Åland Islands (but provision was made for its extension to those Islands subject to derogations). Protocol 3 to the Act of Accession of Austria, Finland and Sweden makes special provision for protection of the traditional way of life of the Sami people in accordance with commitments undertaken by Finland and Sweden.

1–006 **The Treaty on European Union.** The Treaty came into force on 1 November 1993, when ratifications by the then 12 Member States of the Community took effect. This followed constitutional challenges under national law before the courts in England: *R. v. Secretary of State for Foreign and Commonwealth Affairs, ex p. Rees-Mogg* [1994] QB 552 [1994] 1 All ER 457, [1993] 3 CMLR 101 (D.C.); France: Case 92–308 of 9 April 1992 [1993] 3 CMLR 345 and, following a constitutional amendment, Case 92–312 of 2 September 1992 (1992) JORF 12095 (Conseil Constitutionnel); Germany: *Brunner*, 12 October 1993 [1994] 1 CMLR 57 (Fed. Const. Ct.); and Spain: Case 1236/1992 [1994] 3 CMLR 101 (Const. Ct.).

The political pressures and compromises reached at Maastricht resulted in a Treaty with an unsatisfactory and inelegant structure. The basic provisions are lettered, not numbered, and those substantive provisions of the Treaty are followed by 11 Protocols and 32 Declarations, some of them of considerable significance. For the text of the TEU, see *Encyclopedia of European Union Law (Constitutional Texts)*, Vol. 1, paras. 13.0001 *et seq*. and Vol. 6, paras. 97.001 *et seq*.

The most striking change introduced by the TEU was the establishment of the European Union which, despite popular misconceptions, has not replaced the European Community. The Community, along with the Coal and Steel Community and the European Atomic Energy Community, continues in its pre-Maastricht structure although the EC Treaty, along with the ECSC and Euratom Treaties, is subject to numerous detailed amendments made by the TEU. The European Union is a broader, albeit loose, entity that embraces the European Community as the first of its "Three Pillars". The Second Pillar is the Common Foreign and Security Policy: Article J; and the Third Pillar comprises Co-operation in the Fields of Justice and Home Affairs: Article K. The latter two pillars are not part of the *Community* legal order, which is kept clearly distinct, and the jurisdiction of the European Court of Justice does not apply to them: Article L. However, in political and administrative respects, a single set of institutions applies to all aspects of the European Union: the European Parliament, the Council of Ministers and the European Commission: Article C. See paras. 1–008 *et seq.* of the main work.

The role of the Parliament has been increased as a result of the amendments made to the decision-making process under the EC Treaty. The TEU also gives further recognition to the role of the European Council (not to be confused with the Council of Ministers), a summit of the Heads of Government of the Member States (accompanied by their Foreign Ministers) and the President of the Commission: Article D.

1–007 **Treaty on a European Economic Area.** The EEA Treaty is here referred to by its more usual term, the EEA Agreement. It came into force on 1 January 1994. The accession of Austria, Finland and Sweden to the European Community on 1 January 1995 reduced the number of non-EC signatory States to two: Iceland and Norway. Liechtenstein, which had withdrawn from the EEA along with Switzerland, joined the EEA after the Agreement had been suitably amended, on 1 May 1995. Accordingly, the non-EC signatory states are now Iceland, Liechtenstein and Norway. For the text of the EEA Agreement as amended by the "Swiss Protocol" (to take account of the absence of Switzerland), see *Encyclopedia of European Union Law (Constitutional Texts)*, Vol. 2, paras. 30.0042 *et seq.* Article 108 of the EEA Agreement was implemented by the Agreement between the EFTA States on the establishment of a Surveillance Authority and a Court of Justice. For the text as amended (to take account of the withdrawal of Switzerland and then Austria, Finland and Sweden), see *ibid.*, Vol. 5, paras. 82.0277 *et seq.* For general commentary, see Norberg *et al., EEA Law: A Commentary on the EEA Agreement* (Fritzes, 1993).

2. THE INSTITUTIONAL STRUCTURE OF THE EUROPEAN COMMUNITY

1–008 **The institutions of the EC** Following the Maastricht amendment made by the TEU, the Court of Auditors was established as a Community institution. Its powers are set out in Articles 188a–188c of the EC Treaty. It has no impact on competition law and its activities are therefore not discussed here.

n. 26. See now *Vacher's European Companion* (quarterly). For the European Council, see § 1–006, *supra*.

1–009 **The European Parliament.** The importance of the European Parliament was considerably enhanced by the amendments to the EC Treaty made by the TEU. In particular, through the so-called "co-decision" procedure, the Parliament now has a substantive role alongside the Council of Ministers in adoption of legislation in certain areas. The relevant provisions of the EC Treaty are complex and beyond the scope of this work, but the areas of co-decision include the internal market and consumer affairs. See Articles 189b and 189c and Hartley, *op. cit.*, pages 38–48. The European Parliament is also empowered to appoint an Ombudsman: Article 138e; and nominations for appointment of Commissioners and the President of the Commission must be approved by vote of the Parliament: Article 158(2). The European Parliament now has 626 members who sit in party political groups and not as national delegations.

1–010 **The Council**

n. 31. For the European Council, now constituted under Article D of the TEU, see § 1–006, *supra*.

1–011 **Functions of the Council.** For the requirement of co-decision making in certain areas of legislation introduced by the Maastricht amendments, see para. 1–009, *supra*. The position under Article 8 regarding competition matters is unchanged.

1–012 **The Commission.** Following the accession of Austria, Finland and Sweden, the Commission now comprises 20 members: Article 157(1).

1–014 **The services of the Commission.** The Secretariat-General and the Legal Service form part of the Commission and are both responsible directly to the President of the Commission.

There are now 24 Directorates-General and changes have been made to their areas of responsibility, as follows:

DG III	Industrial Affairs
DG V	Employment, Industrial Relations and Social Affairs
DG XV	Internal Market and Financial Services
DG XXII	Education, Training and Youth
DG XXIV	Consumer Policy

1–015 **The Directorate-General for Competition.** DG IV now comprises seven Directorates:

A General competition policy and co-ordination
B Merger Task Force

C Information, communication and multimedia:
- (1) Post and telecommunications and information society co-ordination
- (2) Media and music publishing
- (3) Information industries and consumer electronics

D Services:
- (1) Financial services (banking, insurance)
- (2) Transport
- (3) Distributive trades (including mass marketing), tourism and other services.

E Basic industries:
- (1) Steel, non-ferrous metals, non-metallic mineral products, construction, timber, paper and glass industries
- (2) Basic and processed chemical products and rubber industries
- (3) Energy (coal, oil and gas, electricity)
- (4) Cartels and inspection

F Capital and consumer goods industries:
- (1) Mechanical and electrical engineering and other manufacturing industries
- (2) Motor vehicles and other means of transport, and associated mechanical manufactured products
- (3) Agricultural, food and pharmaceutical products, textiles and other consumer goods industries

G State aids

The Merger Task Force. The Merger Task Force is now a separate Directorate within DG IV: para. 1–015, *supra*. **1–016**

The European Courts **1–017**

n. 46. The Rules of Procedure of the ECJ set out at OJ 1991 L176/7 were corrected at OJ 1992 L383/117 and amended by OJ 1995 L44/61. See the legislative consolidation in *Encyclopedia of European Union Law (Constitutional Texts)*, Vol. 4, §§ 60.0580 *et seq.* The Rules of Procedure of the CFI have been successively amended: OJ 1994 L249/17; OJ 1995 L44/64 and OJ 1995 L172/3.

The Court of First Instance. Following the accession of Austria, Finland and Sweden, the Court now has 15 judges, one from each Member State. **1–018**

The Court of Justice. Following the accession of Austria, Finland and Sweden, the Court of Justice also has 15 judges, one from each Member State, and the number of Advocates General has been increased to nine. **1–019**

3. THE EC TREATY

1–022 **The provisions of the EC Treaty.** Following the Maastricht amendments made by the TEU, the structure of the EC Treaty has been altered. The first three Parts of the Treaty are now: Part One "Principles" (Articles 1 to 7c); Part Two "Citizenship of the Union" (Articles 8 to 8e); Part Three "Community policies" (Articles 9 to 130y).

n. 55. Reg. 2349/84 has been replaced by the technology transfer block exemption, Reg. 240/96: §§ 8–164A *et seq. infra.*

1–023 **Part One of the EC Treaty.** As stated above, this now comprises Articles 1 to 7c: see Appendix 1, *post.* The statement of the tasks of the Community set out in Article 2 has been amended, notably by introducing as one of the tasks, the establishment of "an economic and monetary union" as opposed to merely a "closer relationship" between the Member States: *cf.* the previous text in Appendix 2 to the main work. The list of activities set out in Article 3 has been considerably expanded. The Court of Auditors has been established as a fifth Community institution under Article 4. The prohibition of discrimination on the grounds of nationality, previously Article 7, is now Article 6.

1–024 **The aims of the EC Treaty.** For the amended text of Article 2, see Appendix 1, *post.* Although this remains controversial in the United Kingdom, one aim of the Community as set out in the amended Treaty is an economic and monetary union, including a single currency: see Articles 109j to 109l. The former Article 8a is now Article 7a.

1–026 **Article 3(f).** Article 3(f) has become Article 3(*g*).

1–026A **Article 3b: Subsidiarity.** The Maastricht amendments enshrined in the Treaty the principle of subsidiarity, expressed as follows in the new Article 3b (second paragraph):

> "In areas which do not fall within its exclusive competence, the Community shall take action, in accordance with the principle of subsidiarity, only if and in so far as the objectives of the proposed action cannot be sufficiently achieved by the Member States and can, therefore, by reason of the scale or effects of the proposed action, be better achieved by the Community."

The principle expressed in this paragraph does not itself limit the scope of Community law. *Cp.* the first paragraph of Article 3b *infra.* Subsidiarity is, rather a principle of allocation of jurisdiction to apply the Community objectives set out in the Treaty. See generally, O'Keefe and Twomey (eds.), *Legal Issues of the Maastricht Treaty* (Wiley Chancery, 1994). Although it is arguable that subsidiarity has no application to the Community competition rules, because they concern a matter within the Community's exclusive competence, the better view is that subsidiarity should apply to the enforcement of EC competition law. It is only reasonable that the principle of subsidiarity should apply to the Community's enforcement jurisdiction as well as to its legislative jurisdiction.

The Commission has accepted that subsidiarity applies in the field of competition law. It has pointed out that the principle of subsidiarity "does not mean that everything should be handled by the authorities in the Member States, but rather that the most appropriate authority should take action". The Commission draws a distinction, in the context of the competition rules, between the rules applicable to Member States and those applicable to enterprises. As regards the rules applicable to the Member States, the Commission considers that "subsidiarity is not feasible, since it is not possible for the Member States to be required to monitor themselves or each other". In the case of enterprises, a more flexible approach can be adopted. XXIVth Report on Competition Policy (1994), point 23. See also XXVth Report (1995), points 90–92.

Indeed, the Commission already applied a principle of subsidiarity in certain respects prior to the entry into force of Article 3b. See, *e.g. Port of Elsinore*, Press Release IP (96) 205 of 6 March 1996 [1996] 4 CMLR 728. After receiving a complaint regarding restriction of access to facilities for a ferry service from the port, the Commission first considered that the matter might be more effectively solved by the Danish government and therefore took no action; although the Danish Competition Council then made an appropriate recommendation, the Commission found that this was not enforceable and accordingly it then intervened. However, it is only since Article 3b entered into force that subsidiarity became a principle of Community law that can be relied upon in seeking to challenge a Commission decision. See Case T–29/92 *SPO v. Commission* [1995] II ECR 291, appeal dismissed Case C–137/95P [1996] I ECR 1611 where the Court of First Instance rejected the contention that the Commission violated the principle of subsidiarity in not leaving it to the Dutch competition authorities to investigate a building industry cartel in the Netherlands, on the grounds that Article 3b had not yet entered into force when the Commission took its decision and is not to be given retroactive effect (paras. 330–32).

In practice, it seems unlikely that a Commission decision establishing a violation of Community law would be quashed on the grounds that investigation should have been left to the national authorities on the basis of subsidiarity. See generally, Harrison, "Subsidiarity in Article 3b of the EC Treaty—Gobbledegook or Justiciable Principle?" (1996) 45 ICLQ 431.

Article 3b also provides, in the first paragraph, that:

"The Community shall act within the limits of the powers conferred upon it by this Treaty and of the objectives assigned to it therein."

This provision was relied on by the Court of Justice in Opinion 2/94 *Accession to the European Convention for the Protection of Human Rights and Fundamental Freedoms* [1996] I ECR 1759 [1996] 2 CMLR 265, holding that the Community did not have competence to accede to the Convention. The principles enshrined in the Convention have already been accepted as general principles of Community law. For the Community to go further and enter the distinct institutional system provided for by the Convention would require an amendment to the EC Treaty.

1–027 **Article 5: duties of Member States**

n. 67. See also Case C–185/91 Reiff [1993] I ECR 5801 [1995] 5 CMLR 145; Case C–153/93 *Delta Schiffarts- und Speditionsgesellschaft* [1994] I ECR 2517 [1996] 4 CMLR 21.

1–028 **Article 7: non-discrimination.** Article 7 has been re-numbered Article 6, following the amendments made by the TEU.

1–029 **Part Two of the EC Treaty.** The new Part Two, "Citizenship of the Union", comprises Articles 8 to 8e and concerns the rights that result from citizenship of the European Union that is bestowed on the citizens of each Member State: *e.g.* the right to vote and stand as a candidate in municipal (but not national) elections. The former Part Two discussed in para. 1–029 of the main work is accordingly now Part Three.

The provisions on free movement of capital are now set out in Articles 73b to 73g, which superseded Articles 67 to 73 with effect from 1 January 1994: Article 7a.

1–030 **Free movement of goods**

n. 74. See now Oliver, *Free Movement of Goods in the European Community* (Sweet & Maxwell, 3rd ed. 1996).

n. 77. See now Hartley, *op. cit.* (Clarendon Press, 3rd ed. 1994), pp. 195–233.

1–032 **Measures within Article 30**

n. 87. See now Oliver, *op. cit.*, Annex II.

1–034 **The *Cassis de Dijon* principle**

n. 8. See now Oliver, *op. cit.*, Annex II.

Article 36 **1–036**

n. 16. The *Stoke-on-Trent* decision is reported at [1992] I ECR 6635 [1993] 1 CMLR 426. The Sunday trading legislation and other national measures relating to matters extrinsic to the goods themselves gave rise to a number of cases in which the traditional analysis under Articles 30 to 36 was strained. In Cases C–267 & 268/91 *Keck and Mithouard* [1993] I ECR 6097 [1995] 1 CMLR 101, the Court of Justice clarified the position by modifying the approach to be adopted. The issue there was whether French legislation that prohibited traders from selling goods at a loss infringed Article 30 of the Treaty. The Court distinguished between "rules that lay down requirements to be met by goods" and "selling arrangements". The former are to be dealt with on the basis of the previous case law whereas rules under the latter are subject to different principles. The Court held that rules in the second category, like the legislation in *Keck* itself, fall outside the scope of Article 30 altogether provided that they "apply to all affected traders operating within the national territory and provided that they affect in the same manner, in law and in fact, the marketing of domestic products and of those from other Member States". For analysis of the judgment and its relevance in the area of free movement of goods in general, see Oliver, *op. cit.*, pp. 100–110.

1–038 **Other relevant Treaty provisions.** Article 114 has been repealed and its relevant provisions are now found at Article 113(4).

The social policy provisions are now at Articles 117 to 125. The new Treaty provisions on culture (Article 128); public health (Article 129) and consumer protection (Article 129a) are to be noted.

Of particular significance to competition policy are the new Articles 129b to 129d on the promotion of trans-European networks in the field of transport, telecommunications and energy infrastructures: see para. 16–006, *infra*.

4. SOURCES OF EC COMPETITION LAW

(a) *The provisions of the Treaty*

1–039 **Generally.** Article 3(*f*) is now Article 3(*g*). Articles 85 and 86 became directly effective in Austria, Finland and Sweden on 1 January 1995.

1–045 **Article 88.** Article 88 continues to have application in the fields of air transport between Community and third country airports and international maritime tramp vessel services, in respect of which no implementing regulations have been made under Article 87. In August

1996, the UK government rushed through secondary legislation enabling the UK competition authorities, pursuant to Article 88, to exercise jurisdiction under Articles 85 and 86 in those areas: EC Competition Law (Articles 88 and 89) Enforcement Regulations 1996 (SI 1996 No. 2199). This was prompted by the Commission's announcement of an investigation under Article 89 into the alliance between British Airways and American Airlines.

1–046 **Article 89.** The Commission's initiation in July 1996 of investigations into six trans-Atlantic alliances between airlines has awoken interest in Article 89. As Regulation 3975/87, which provides for enforcement of the competition rules in the air transport sector, applies only to transport between Community airports, the Commission has sought to take this action under its residual powers found in Article 89. See para. 15–057, *infra*.

1–050 **The interpretation of the Treaty.** The principles of the European Convention for the Protection of Human Rights and Fundamental Freedoms have been formally stated to be general principles of Community law by Article F.2 of the TEU. (They are also specifically referred to under the Second and Third Pillars.) Paradoxically, Article F is in a part of the TEU that is expressly excluded from consideration by the Court of Justice: Article L. Nonetheless, there is nothing to preclude consideration of Article F by national courts of the Member States, and it has probably been enacted into law in the United Kingdom by the amended section 1(2)(k) of the European Communities Act 1972.

See also Court of Justice's Opinion 2/94 *Accession to the European Convention for the Protection of Human Rights and Fundamental Freedoms* [1996] I ECR 1759 [1996] 2 CMLR 265.

n. 42. For the principle of proportionality see now Art. 3b (3rd para.) of the EC Treaty, inserted by the TEU: App. 1, *post*.

(b) *Regulations and Directives*

1–052 **Regulation 17**

n. 50. For the amended Art. 25 of Reg. 17 (concerning transitional arrangements), see Appendix 5, *post*.

1–053 **Other procedural regulations.** Regulation 27 was replaced by Regulation 3385/94: Appendix 6, *post*.

1–056 **Mergers and concentrations.** Regulation 2367/90 has been replaced by Regulation 3384/94: Appendix 9, *post*.

n. 59. The Notice on concentrative and co-operative operations has been replaced by the Notice on the distinction between concentrative and co-operative joint ventures: Appendix 10, *post*. Three further Notices have been issued: see § 6–003, *infra*.

(c) *Decisions and pronouncements of The Commission*

The Commission's decisions. There should be added to the list: (v) decisions granting or refusing authorization to State aids: see Chapter 18 of the main work and *infra*. **1–058**

Other pronouncements by the Commission. Since 1994, the Commission has also published an *EC Competition Policy Newsletter* three times a year. **1–061**

n. 72. The Commission emphasised the importance that it attaches to achieving greater transparency in its XXIVth Report on Competition Policy (1994), points 30–33.

(e) *Other sources*

Treaties with third countries. For agreements with Central and East European countries, see para. 2–168, *infra*. **1–067**

International conventions and codes of practice **1–068**

n. 85. The decision of the CFI in Case T–69/89 was upheld in Cases C–241 & 242/91P *RTE and ITP v. Commission* [1995] I ECR 743, [1995] 4 CMLR 718, [1995] All ER (EC) 416.

Competition laws of the Member States. An increasing number of Member States have adopted, or are in the process of adopting, competition legislation modelled on the provisions of the EC Treaty: *e.g.*, Belgium, Ireland, Italy and Spain. In August 1996, the UK Department of Trade and Industry published legislative proposals, expressly based on Article 85, to prohibit anti-competitive agreements: *Tackling Cartels and the Abuse of Market Power: A draft Bill.* **1–069**

United States antitrust law. In Case C–327/91 *France v. Commission* [1994] I ECR 3641 [1994] 5 CMLR 517, the Court of Justice held that the conclusion of the Co-operation Agreement with the United States, as an **1–070**

international agreement, was *ultra vires* the Commission's powers under Article 228 of the Treaty, whereby such an agreement must be concluded by the Council of Ministers. The Council thereupon gave the necessary approval so as to conclude the Agreement with minor amendments appended to the text and an exchange of interpretative letters to deal with the problem of protection of confidentiality. See OJ 1995 L95/45, OJ 1995 L131/38, [1995] 4 CMLR 707.

5. THE AIMS OF THE COMMUNITY RULES ON COMPETITION

1–071 **Purpose of the rules on competition.** The liberalisation of previously monopolised or regulated markets, such as utilities and telecommunications, has increasingly attracted the attention of the Commission which seeks to ensure that effective competition at Community level is introduced and that the new arrangements which replace former state monopolies do not in themselves stifle competitive development: see XXVth Report on Competition Policy (1995), points 5 to 11. The approach to joint ventures and the Treaty provisions on State aids assume particular significance in that regard: see Chapters 5 and 18 of the main work and *infra*. Tariff reforms introduced by the monopoly operator in anticipation of new competitors entering the market will also attract scrutiny under Article 86: see Press Release IP (96) 543 of 26 June 1996 [1996] 5 CMLR 121.

n. 92. See now Whish, *op. cit.* (3rd ed., 1993).

n. 93. The promotion of "fair dealing" is still more evident in the new block exemption for motor vehicle distribution agreements, Reg. 1475/95, that has replaced Reg. 123/85. Reg. 2349/84 has been replaced by the technology transfer block exemption, Reg. 240/96.

1–075 **Importance of trading by intermediaries**

n. 98. The Commission's decision in *Tetra Pak II* was upheld by the CFI: Case T–83/91 *Tetra Pak v. Commission* [1994] II ECR 755, on further appeal Case C–333/94P.

CHAPTER 2

ARTICLE 85(1)

2. UNDERTAKINGS

Undertakings. The Commission has expressed the view that an undertaking for the purpose of the Treaty's competition rules need not possess separate legal personality but may refer to any entity engaged in economic activity, *e.g.*, a division comprising several companies in a corporate group could in certain circumstances constitute an undertaking: *Cartonboard*, OJ 1994 L234/1 [1994] 5 CMLR 547, para. 140 (on appeal Cases T–295/94, etc.). However, in practice the Commission will address any decision to a body that has legal personality so as to avoid potential problems of enforcement. **2–003**

n. 9. See also *SCK and FNK*, OJ 1995 L312/79 [1996] 4 CMLR 565 (private law certification organisation).

Economic or commercial activity. The question whether an international organisation is an undertaking for the purpose of the competition rules of the Treaty is to be answered by consideration of the nature and aim of its activities and the rules to which they are subject. In Case C–364/92 *SAT Fluggesellschaft v. Eurocontrol* [1994] I ECR 43 [1994] 5 CMLR 208, the Court of Justice held that Eurocontrol, whose activities concerned co-operation between contracting states in the field of air navigation, but included the provision of traffic control services and the collection of route charges, was not an undertaking for the purpose of Articles 86 and 90. Its activities taken as a whole were not of an economic nature but were derived from the power of the contracting states to supervise and control air space, were financed by contributions from those states, and were carried out in the public interest of furthering air navigation safety. The collection of route charges could not be separated from Eurocontrol's other activities and make it an undertaking. **2–004**

n. 11. But *cf.* Case C–244/94 *Fédération Française des Sociétés d'Assu-*

rance [1995] 1 ECR 4013: a non-profit making organisation managing an optional supplementary old-age insurance scheme under rules laid down by public authorities was an undertaking within Art. 85 as it carries on an economic activity financed out of contributions and in competition with life assurance companies.

2–005 **Subsidiary companies.** See the Commission's discussion of the situation of a corporate group of companies in *Cartonboard, supra.* The Commission there suggests that the economic unit is itself to be treated as an "undertaking".

n. 12. See also Case T–102/92 *Viho v. Commission*: § 2–054, *infra.*

2–008 **Individuals as undertakings.** In *CNSD*, OJ 1993 L203/27 [1995] 5 CMLR 495, on appeal Case T–513/93, the Commission held that customs agents in Italy, classified under Italian law as a liberal profession, were nonetheless undertakings for the purpose of Article 85(1). Similarly, the Commission concluded that industrial property agents in Spain, who practised their profession as self-employed persons, constituted undertakings: *COAPI*, OJ 1995 L122/37 [1995] 5 CMLR 468. The Commission has stated that "one can expect a growing number of cases" regarding the application of the competition rules to the practices of the liberal professions: XXVth Report on Competition Policy (1995), point 88.

2–010 **Member States**

n. 27. See now the ECJ's decision in *SAT Fluggesellschaft v. Eurocontrol*, § 2–004, *supra.*

2–012 **Other statutory bodies**

n. 31. See also *CNSD, supra.*

3. AGREEMENTS, DECISIONS AND CONCERTED PRACTICES

(a) *Agreements*

2–016 **Agreements may be informal.** A "gentlemen's agreement" is an agreement for the purpose of Article 85(1): Case T–141/89 *Tréfileurope Sales v. Commission* [1995] II ECR 791.

n. 37. The decision in *Soda-ash—Solvay, CFK* was annulled as regards

Solvay for procedural irregularity: Case T–31/91 *Solvay v. Commission* [1995] II ECR 1821, on appeal by the Commission Case C–286/95P.

Incorporation of terms in an agreement. The question of when the refusal to supply products with the intention of preventing parallel trade constitutes a term of an agreement is likely to receive full consideration in the pending appeal against the Commission's decision in *ADALAT*, OJ 1996 L201/1 [1996] 5 CMLR 416. The Commission relied on the *Sandoz* case in finding that reductions in the volume of supplies by Bayer of this major coronary medicinal product to its leading wholesalers in France and Spain, in an effort to prevent parallel exports by those wholesalers to the United Kingdom, amounted to the incorporation of an export ban as "an integral element in the continuous commercial relations between the parties" (para. 186). Although no export restriction was imposed, the wholesalers were made aware of the reason why supplies to them were curtailed and responded by seeking to demonstrate that their level of orders related to their domestic markets. The Commission held that this was sufficient to bring the circumstances within Article 85(1) and imposed a substantial fine. Bayer appealed and the President of the Court of First Instance granted an interim suspension of the Commission's decision, noting that the appeal disclosed a *prima facie* case: Case T–41/96R *Bayer v. Commission* [1996] 5 CMLR 290. **2–017**

n. 44. See also Case T–43/92 *Dunlop Slazenger v. Commission* [1994] II ECR 441.

Standard conditions of sale **2–019**

n. 48. The Commission's decision in *Parfums Givenchy* granting exemption was challenged in Case T–87/92 *Kruidvat v. Commission*, not yet decided.

Agreements under duress. The argument raised on appeal by one of the participants in the *Welded Steel Mesh* cartel, that it took part in discussions against its will under pressure from other producers, was robustly dismissed by the Court of First Instance. The company should have complained to the competent national authorities or the Commission instead of taking part. *Tréfileurope Sales v. Commission, supra*, para. 58. **2–020**

Government measures. There is a distinction between national legislation which in itself restricts competition (which will not give rise to a violation of Articles 85 or 86) and legislation that facilitates or seeks to legitimise anti-competitive conduct by enterprises (which conduct may contravene Articles 85 or 86 notwithstanding the legislation). Where under a national **2–021**

measure rates are fixed by a commission that includes members appointed by enterprises or trade associations, the decisions of the commission will not give rise to an agreement between undertakings if the members act in their personal capacity in the public interest; but the position will be otherwise if they act as representatives of the associations or enterprises that appointed them. See Case C–185/91 *Reiff* [1993] I ECR 5801 [1995] 5 CMLR 145 (fixing of road haulage tariffs in Germany); Case C–153/93 *Delta Schiffarts- und Speditionsgesellschaft* [1994] I ECR 2517 [1996] 4 CMLR 21 (commission fixing inland waterways tariffs in Germany). In that regard it is relevant if the industry-appointed members of the commission are in a minority: Case C–96/94 *Centro Servizi Spediporto* [1995] I ECR 2883 [1996] 4 CMLR 613 (road haulage tariffs in Italy); Cases C–140/94, etc. *DIP and Others* [1995] I ECR 3257 [1996] 4 CMLR 157 (committees advising local authorities on trading licences).

n. 52. The judgment in Case T–16/91 *Rendo v. Commission* [1992] II ECR 2417 was partially set aside by the ECJ, who referred the matter back to the CFI: Case C–19/93P [1995] I ECR 3319.

n. 57. See also *CNSD*, OJ 1993 L203/27 [1995] 5 CMLR 495, on appeal Case T–513/93 (tariff decisions of association of customs agents ratified by Ministerial decree).

2–022 **Unilateral action.** The last two sentences of this paragraph were cited with approval by the English Court of Appeal in *Richard Cound Ltd v. BMW (G.B.) Ltd*, judgment of 10 May 1995. The court held that the giving of notice of termination by the importer to a dealer, under a motor vehicle distribution agreement, was unilateral conduct outside the ambit of Article 85(1). The provision of an agreement governing the conditions for termination could fall within Article 85(1); but in *Cound* the notice provision satisfied the conditions of the motor vehicle block exemption (Regulation 123/85) and the prescribed 12 months notice was given. However, where an agreement is terminated pursuant to a policy to restrict distribution to a limited number of dealers, this may in certain circumstances constitute a concerted practice: see para. 2–049 of the main work.

2–024 **Assignments and exclusive licences**

n. 70. See now Reg. 240/96: §§ 8–164A *et seq.*, *infra*.

2–025 **Terminated or "spent" agreements**

n. 72. The decision in *Soda-ash—Solvay, ICI*, has been annulled on procedural grounds: Case T–30/91 *Solvay v. Commission* [1995] II ECR 1775 [1996] 5 CMLR 57; Case T–36/91 *ICI v. Commission* [1995] II ECR 1847; [1995] All ER (EC) 600 (both): see § 12–036, *infra*.

Judicial settlements. For the third sentence of this paragraph in the main work, substitute the following: **2–026**

> The Court rejected the argument, advanced by the Commission, that such a clause should be regarded as compatible with Article 85(1) when it is included in an agreement to settle pending court proceedings provided that the existence of the industrial property right in question was genuinely in doubt. There the clause was part of an out-of-court settlement and the Court of Justice pointed out that "Article 85(1) makes no distinction between agreements whose purpose is to put an end to litigation and those concluded with other aims in mind" (para. 15). See also the Opinion of Advocate General Darmon at para. 11.

Accession Agreements. Austria, Finland and Sweden acceded to the community on 1 January 1995. However, the position is complicated because of those States' prior membership of the EEA. For Accession Arguments as regards the accession of Austria, Finland and Sweden, see para. 11–034, *infra*. **2–029**

(b) *Decisions by associations of undertakings*

Associations of undertakings **2–031**

n. 90. See also the cases cited at § 2–021, *supra*.

Decisions **2–032**

n. 92. See also *COAPI*, OJ 1995 L122/37 [1995] 5 CMLR 468 (internal regulations of professional association of agents of industrial property).

n. 95. The decision in *Distribution of railway tickets by travel agents* was annulled on procedural grounds: Case T–14/93 *Union Internationale des Chemins de Fer v. Commission* [1995] II ECR 1503 [1996] 5 CMLR 40, on appeal Case C–264/95P.

Association as party to agreement. In its major decision in *Cement*, OJ 1994 L343/1 [1995] 4 CMLR 327, the Commission discussed, at para. 44, the application of Article 85(1) to associations and to associations of associations. Along with producers of cement, a number of national cement associations and the European Cement Association, Cembureau, were fined for their involvement in market-sharing arrangements. The decision is on appeal, Cases T–25/95, etc. See also Cases T–39 & 40/92 *CB and Europay v. Commission* [1994] II ECR 49, where the Court of First Instance upheld the determination by the Commission that the Groupement des Cartes Bancaires 'CB', an economic grouping of French banks, **2–033**

had infringed Article 85(1) by reason of its agreement with Eurocheque International concerning the basis of acceptance of Eurocheques in France.

In *Cartonboard*, OJ 1994 L243/1 [1994] 5 CMLR 547, on appeal Cases T–295/94, etc., the Finnish board mills association, Finnboard, was found to have been directly involved in the producers' cartel, along with its members, through its role as a joint sales agency and was fined 20 million ECU. The members were held to be jointly and severally liable with the Finnboard for that part of the fine that corresponded to their proportionate share of Finnboard's sales.

n. 98. The appeals by some of the individual companies against the Commission decision in *Welded Steel Mesh* were unsuccessful save for reduction of some of the fines: Cases T–141/89, etc. *Tréfileurope Sales v. Commission*, etc., [1995] II ECR 791, etc.; on further appeal in Cases C–185/95P and 219/95P.

(c) *Concerted practices*

2–034 In general

n. 6. See also the Commission's decisions in *Steel beams*, OJ 1994 L116/1 [1994] 5 CMLR 353, on appeal Cases T–137/94, etc., (under the equivalent Art. 65(1) of the ECSC Treaty); *Cartonboard*, OJ 1994 L243/1 [1994] 5 CMLR 547, on appeal Cases T–295/94, etc.; *Cement, supra*. The appeals in *Welded Steel Mesh* were largely unsuccessful: *supra*.

2–037 Sugar

n. 16. The Commission's decision in *Soda-ash—Solvay, ICI* was annulled for breaches of the rights of defence: Case T–30/91 *Solvay v. Commission* [1995] II ECR 1775 [1996] 5 CMLR 57; Case T–36/91 *ICI v. Commission* [1995] II ECR 1847 [1995] All ER (EC) 600 (both): see 12–036, *infra*.

2–043 Proof of concerted practice

n. 35. *Wood Pulp II* is reported in [1993] I ECR 1307 [1993] 4 CMLR 407.

2–044 Burden of proof

n. 38. The CFI dismissed an application by DSM NV for revision of the judgment: Case T–8/89 Rev. *DSM v. Commission* [1992] II ECR 2399, which decision is on appeal in Case C–5/93P.

Relevance of parallel behaviour **2–046**

n. 50. The Commission's decision in *Soda-ash—Solvay, ICI* was annulled for breaches of the rights of defence: *supra.*

n. 51. See also *Cement*, OJ 1994 L343/1 [1995] 4 CMLR 327 (§ 45(8)), on appeal Cases T–25/95, etc.

Acting on complaints **2–047**

n. 55. The Commission's decision in *Newitt/Dunlop Slazenger* was substantially upheld by the CFI: Case T–43/92 *Dunlop Slazenger v. Commission* [1994] II ECR 441. However, the Court held that the duration of the infringement was shorter than that found by the Commission and the fine was therefore reduced from 5 million to 3 million ECU.

Duration of concerted practice **2–048**

n. 57. See also *Dunlop Slazenger v. Commission*, *supra.*

4. AGREEMENTS WITH SUBSIDIARY UNDERTAKINGS

Undertaking comprises whole "economic unit" **2–053**

n. 66. The judgment in Case T–16/91 *Rendo I* was partially set aside by the ECJ which referred the matter back to the CFI: Case C–19/93P *Rendo and Others v. Commission* [1995] I ECR 3336.

Application of the rule. Instructions given by the parent company of a group to its subsidiaries not to supply third parties accordingly do not come within the scope of Article 85(1). The Court of First Instance upheld the dismissal by the Commission of a complaint against Parker Pen Ltd for prohibiting its subsidiaries in different Member States from distributing products to customers outside their allocated territory. The Court noted that such conduct may contribute towards partitioning the market but concluded (at para. 54): **2–054**

> "It is not for the Court, on the pretext that certain conduct . . . may fall outside the competition rules, to apply Article 85 to circumstances for which it is not intended in order to fill a gap which may exist in the system of regulation laid down by the Treaty."

Case T–102/92 *Viho v. Commission* [1995] II ECR 17 [1995] ICR 1050

[1995] All ER (EC) 371, on appeal Case C–73/95P; *cf.* the position as regards the export ban in Parker Pen's agreement with its independent distributor in Germany: para. 7–019, *infra.*

5. RESTRICTION OF COMPETITION

(a) *Some conceptual issues*

2–057 **Some conceptual issues**

n. 74. See now *Chitty on Contracts* (27th ed., 1994) Vol. I § 16–067 and Vol. II §§ 40–052 to 40–062.

2–059 **Horizontal restrictions**

n. 79. The EFTA Surveillance Authority has issued a Notice on the assessment of co-operative joint ventures under Article 53 of the EEA Agreement equivalent to the Commission's Notice: OJ 1994 L186/57.

2–063 **Rule of reason: market analysis and "essential" restrictions.** In Case C–250/92 *Gøttrup-Klim v. Dansk Landbrugs Grovvareselskab AmbA* [1994] I ECR 5641 [1996] 4 CMLR 191, the Court of Justice held that the rules of a Danish agricultural co-operative purchasing organisation that prohibited members from joining competing co-operatives, and so obtaining supplies elsewhere, may have an adverse effect on competition; but that this will not constitute a violation of Article 85(1) if the prohibition goes no further than is necessary to ensure that the co-operative functions properly and maintains its purchasing power in relation to producers. In his Opinion in that case, Advocate General Tesauro considered how, in the light of the Court's jurisprudence, the criteria of anti-competitive object or effect are to be applied to an agreement: see at paras. 14–16. He emphasised that the concept of an anti-competitive object is not to be applied to a contractual provision in the abstract but by analysis of the function of the provision in its specific context of the legal relationship between the parties. See also the discussion of the concept of a "rule of reason" by Advocate General Lenz in Case C–415/93 *Bosman* [1995] I ECR 4921, [1996] 1 CMLR 645, Opinion at paras. 266–69 (citing this passage of the main work).

In *Society of Lloyd's v. Clementson* (QBD), judgment of 7 May 1996, Cresswell J. held, citing this passage from the main work, that the rule of reason applied to the Central Fund arrangements of Lloyd's. In *Marchant & Eliot (Underwriting) Ltd. v. Higgins* [1996] 1 Lloyd's Rep. (QBD), Rix J. followed the above analysis of Advocate General Tesauro, holding that it was not arguable that the "pay first, sue later" provisions of a Lloyd's agency agreement had an anti-competitive object or effect within Article 85(1). The decision was upheld on appeal: [1996] 2 Lloyd's Rep. 31 (CA).

(b) *The main decisions*

Generally **2–064**

n. 87. See Case T–17/93 *Matra Hachette v. Commission* [1994] II ECR 595 § 85, where the CFI stated that in principle the Commission had power to exempt any anti-competitive practice if the conditions of Art. 85(3) were fulfilled.

***Delimitis*: comment.** It is now established that the approach set out in *Delimitis* is relevant to all sectors: Case C–393/92 *Almelo* [1994] I ECR 1477. The Court of First Instance applied such a detailed analysis of the cumulative effect of a network of exclusive purchasing agreements for impulse ice-cream in Germany, instead of the simpler approach that had been adopted by the Commission, in Case T–7/93 *Langnese-Iglo v. Commission* [1995] II ECR 1533 [1995] 5 CMLR 602 [1995] All ER (EC) 902, on appeal Case C–279/95P; Case T–9/93 *Schöller v. Commission* [1995] II ECR 1611 [1995] 5 CMLR 659. See para. 7–111, *infra*. **2–079**

n. 28. The EFTA Surveillance Authority has issued an equivalent Notice modifying its previous Notice on exclusive distribution and exclusive purchasing agreements: OJ 1994 L168/57, 69.

The Court's decision in *Metro (No. 1)*: "workable competition" **2–082**

n. 34. See now Whish, *Competition Law* (3rd ed., 1993) pp. 10–11.

Comment on *Pronuptia* **2–091**

n. 65. See also Case C–250/92 *Gøttrup-Klim v. Dansk Landburgs Grovvaresalskab AmbA*: § 2–063, *supra*.

Elopak/Metal Box-Odin **2–093**

n. 67. The EFTA Surveillance Authority has issued a Notice on the assessment of co-operative joint ventures under Article 53 of the EEA Agreement equivalent to the Commission's Notice: OJ 1994 L186/57.

Comment on *Elopak/Metal Box-Odin*. The Commission has noted the increasing number of co-operative arrangements entered into between **2–095**

major enterprises, often now described by the parties not as a joint venture but a "strategic alliance". These are a particular feature of newly liberalised and international markets, such as telecommunications. Such arrangements often involve a number of different agreements, and may include intellectual property licences, arrangements for joint research, development and marketing, and provision for equity participation. The Commission has stated that it intends "to maintain a favourable approach" to forms of co-operation that strengthen the efficiency and thus the competitiveness of the parties. It will not adopt an unduly analytical approach to the component elements of such arrangements but will consider the operation as a whole and assess each aspect in conjunction with the others. The Commission will in particular consider whether the agreements include anti-competitive aspects that go beyond what is necessary to achieve the objective sought. XXIVth Report on Competition Policy (1994), point 17. However, in this context, the concept of ancillary restrictions has more often been applied in practice in the context of a decision to grant exemption under Article 85(3) to the alliance or joint venture than to negative clearance under Article 85(1). See further paras. 5–054 *et seq. infra.*

The Commission's legislative proposals for amendment of the Merger Regulation, presented in September 1996, would largely remove the distinction in treatment as between concentrative and co-operative joint ventures may be simplified: para. 5–009A, *infra.*

(c) *The present law*

2–098 Objects restrictive *per se*

n. 82. The Commission's decision in *Viho/Parker Pen* was upheld by the CFI, save that the fine on Parker Pen was reduced: Case T–66/92 *Herlitz v. Commission* [1994] II ECR 531 [1995] 5 CMLR 458 and Case T–77/92 *Parker Pen v. Commission* [1994] II ECR 549 [1995] 5 CMLR 435.

n. 83. Bayer's appeal to the CFI against the Commission's decision in *Bayo-n-ox* was ruled inadmissible: Case T–12/90 *Bayer v. Commission* [1991] II ECR 219, [1993] 4 CMLR 30; a further appeal to the ECJ was dismissed: Case C–195/91P *Bayer v. Commission* [1994] I ECR 5619 [1996] 4 CMLR 32.

2–099 How far object alone sufficient

n. 87. See also the CFI decisions dismissing the appeals as to liability from the Commission's decision on the *Welded Steel Mesh* cartel: Cases T–141/89, etc., *Tréfileurope Sales v. Commission*, etc., [1995] II ECR 791, etc., on further appeal in Cases 185/95P and 219/95P.

n. 92. Accordingly, although an agreement that prohibits exports, by its very nature, constitutes a restriction of competition, an analysis of the parties' position on the market was necessary to determine whether this restriction could cause an appreciable effect on trade between Member States so as to constitute a violation of Art. 85(1): Case T–77/92 *Parker Pen v. Commission* [1994] II ECR 549 [1995] 5 CMLR 435.

Whole economic context **2–104**

n. 23. See also *Langnese-Iglo v. Commission* [1995] II ECR 1533 [1995] 5 CMLR 602 [1995] All ER (EC) 902, on appeal Case C–279/95P and Case T–9/93 *Schöller v. Commission* [1995] II ECR 1611 [1995] 5 CMLR 659 (effect of the network of agreements with retailers of the two leading suppliers of ice-cream on the German market); for further analysis see § 7–111, *infra*.

Appreciable effect. The ceiling under the Commission's *de minimis* notice has been raised to 300 million ECU: OJ 1994 C368/20. **2–105**

n. 31. The CFI held that it could not be assumed that an agreement has an appreciable effect merely because the Commission's five per cent ceiling was exceeded: *Langnese-Iglo* (§ 98) and *Schöller* (§ 75), *supra* and § 7–111, *infra*.

Relevant product market. For products that have only a very limited storage life, the place of consumption may be relevant to determination of the relevant product market. In the German ice-cream cases, *Langnese-Iglo* and *Schöller*, *supra*, the applicants challenged as too narrow the Commission's determination of the market as impulse ice-cream sold through all distribution channels except for doorstep delivery services. The Court of First Instance upheld the Commission's determination that industrial ice-cream for supply at catering establishments and "take-home" ice-cream to be stored in consumers' homes should be excluded. But the Court considered that "scooping" ice-cream, *i.e.* ice-cream for bulk-buying customers intended for sale in individual portions in the street, formed part of the same product market as impulse ice-cream as they are largely interchangeable from the consumer's point of view in making purchase decisions. The fact that the products may differ in their production technology was not sufficient to delineate two separate markets where consumers do not take that difference into account. However, it was not necessary to annul the decision on this ground as exclusion of such ice-cream did not substantially affect the assessment of the agreements at issue. **2–106**

n. 38. In Case T–29/92 *SPO and Others v. Commission* [1995] II ECR 295, the CFI stated (at § 74) that the approach to defining the relevant market differs according to whether Art. 85 or Art. 86 is to be applied. *Sed* *quaere*: although the purpose of market definition is different as between the two provisions, it is not clear how it is suggested that the definition itself should be different.

2–108 **Distortion of competition.** Under the Maastricht amendments made by the TEU, Article 3(*f*) is now 3(*g*).

2–113 **Restrictions in licences of intellectual property rights**

n. 52. Reg. 2349/84 has been replaced by Reg. 240/96: Appendix 4, *post*.

2–114 **Restrictions not within Article 85(1)**

n. 63. The EFTA Surveillance Authority has issued an equivalent Notice on the assessment of co-operative joint ventures under Article 53 of the EEA Agreement: OJ 1994 L186/57.

2–115 **Other restrictions outside Article 85(1)**

n. 65. The EFTA Surveillance Authority has issued an equivalent notice as regards the application of Article 53(1) of the EEA Agreement: OJ 1994 L153/1 [1994] 4 CMLR 339.

n. 66. The EFTA Surveillance Authority has issued an equivalent Notice on sub-contracting agreements: OJ 1994 L153/1, 30 [1994] 4 CMLR 353.

2–116 **Permitted co-operation**

n. 72. See also *Alenia/Honeywell*, XXIIIrd Report on Competition Policy (1993), point 216 (comfort letter sent in respect of JV for production and sale of space control products: the parent companies were not actual or potential competitors in the satellite field; however the Commission indicated clearance only after the agreements had been amended to remove stringent post-termination non-compete obligations that were not considered to be ancillary).

2–121 **"Unfair" competition not deserving protection**

n. 91. The appeal against the Commission's decision in *Tetra Pak II* was dismissed by the CFI in Case T–83/91 *Tetra Pak International v. Commission* [1994] II ECR 755, on appeal Case C–33/94P.

n. 98. For the appeals against the Commission's decision in *Bayo-n-ox*, see § 2–098, n. 83, *supra*.

National laws distorting competition **2–122**

n. 99. The CFI dismissed the appeals against the Commission's decision in *UK Agricultural tractor registration Exchange*: Case T–34/92 *Fiattagari and New Holland Ford v. Commission* [1994] II ECR 905 and Case T–35/92 *John Deere v. Commission* [1994] II ECR 957; on appeal in Cases C–7 & 8/95P.

6. EFFECT ON TRADE BETWEEN MEMBER STATES

Member States. With effect from 1 January 1995, Austria, Finland and Sweden joined the Community, bringing the total number of Member States to fifteen. **2–127**

Trade. In *COAPI*, OJ 1995 L122/37; [1995] 5 CMLR 468, Article 85 was applied to the services of self-employed industrial property agents in Spain and there was no dispute that such services constituted "trade". The Commission has stated that "one can expect a growing number of cases" regarding the application of the competition rules to the practices of the liberal professions: XXVth Report on Competition Policy (1995), point 88. **2–128**

n. 22. See also *Society of Lloyd's v. Clementson* [1995] C.L.C. 117, 125 (C.A.).

n. 32. In Case C–415/93 *Union Royale Belge des Sociétés de Football Association v. Bosman* [1995] I ECR 4921 [1996] 1 CMLR 645, concerning footballers' contracts and transfer system, Advocate General Lenz summarily rejected the submission that such arrangements did not constitute "trade", stating that this expression in Arts. 85 and 86 "covers all economic relations between the Member States" (Opinion at § 261). The ECJ did not address this issue.

The basic test: alteration of trade flows **2–129**

n. 36. The decision of the CFI in *Publishers' Association v. Commission* was annulled by the ECJ on other grounds (refusal of exemption under Art. 85(3)): Case C–360/92P [1995] I ECR 23 [1995] 5 CMLR 33.

Altering the structure of competition **2–131**

n. 63. The Commission's decision in *Soda-ash—Solvay* was annulled on procedural grounds: Case T–32/91 *Solvay v. Commission* [1995] II ECR 1825 [1996] 5 CMLR 91.

2–132 **Degree of effect required**

n. 76. The successive appeals against the Commission's decision in *Building and construction industry in the Netherlands* were dismissed: Case T–29/92 *SPO and others v. Commission* [1995] II ECR 289 (CFI), Case C–137/95P [1996] I ECR 1611 (ECJ).

2–133 **Effect of agreement as a whole**

n. 79. The appeals against the Commission decision in *Welded Steel Mesh* were unsuccessful save for reduction of the fines: Cases T–141/89, etc., *Tréfileurope Sales v. Commission,* etc. [1995] II ECR 791, etc.; on further appeal in Cases C–185/98P and C–219/95P.

2–134 **Agreements covering one Member State**

n. 83. See also Case C–393/92 *Almelo* [1994] I ECR 1477 (national electricity distribution system); *SCK and FNK*, OJ 1995 L312/79 [1996] 4 CMLR 565 (§ 31), on appeal Case T–18/96 (Dutch crane-hire association); *COAPI*, OJ 1995 L122/37 [1995] 5 CMLR 468 (§ 40) (regulations of national association of industrial property agents).

2–135 **Barriers to entry**

n. 89. See also the CFI's decisions in Case T–7/93 *Langnese-Iglo v. Commission* [1995] II ECR 1533 [1995] 5 CMLR 602, on appeal Case C–279/95P and Case T–9/93 *Schöller v. Commission* [1995] II ECR 1611, [1995] 5 CMLR 659: § 7–111, *infra.*

2–137 **Effects confined to one Member State: *Hugin***

n. 99. See also *Higgins v. Marchant & Eliot Underwriting Ltd* (C.A.), [1996] 2 Lloyd's Rep. 31: funding arrangements between Name at Lloyd's and the managing agents of the syndicate of which he is a member.

7. APPRECIABLE EFFECT

2–139 **In general**

n. 4. See § 2–142, *infra*, for the amendment to the Notice.

2–142 **The Commission's Notice.** In December 1994, the Commission amended the Notice by raising the turnover ceiling from 200 million to 300 million ECU: OJ 1994 C368/20.

Relevance of parallel networks of agreements: *Delimitis*

n. 27. The Commission's decision in *Yves Saint Laurent Parfums* was challenged by retailers that were not admitted to the network: Case T–19/92 *Leclerc v. Commission*, not yet decided. **2–143**

Application of *Delimitis* and the Commission's Notice. It is now established that the *Delimitis* decision extends to all exclusive purchasing agreements: see, *e.g.* Case C–393/92 *Almelo* [1994] I ECR 1477. **2–144**

In Case T–7/93 *Langnese-Iglo v. Commission* [1995] II ECR 1533, [1995] 5 CMLR 602, on appeal Case C–279/95P, and Case T–9/93 *Schöller v. Commission* [1995] II ECR 1611, [1995] 5 CMLR 659, the Court of First Instance held that the Commission's Notice was not conclusive as regards the effect of a network of agreements where the five per cent ceiling is exceeded. It is necessary to examine the cumulative effect of the agreements and other similar agreements in their economic and legal context, according to the principles set out in *Delimitis*, in order to determine whether or not trade between Member States is affected to more than an insignificant extent. Having conducted such an analysis, the Court found that the network of agreements in each case had an appreciable effect on competition and consequently all the agreements in the network were caught by Article 85(1), even if some of them, on their own, might not have an appreciable anti-competitive effect.

Commission decisions on market weakness **2–145**

n. 36. For the appeal against *Yves Saint Laurent Parfums*, see n. 27, *supra*.

Other reason for lack of appreciable effect **2–146**

n. 44. The successive appeals against the Commission's decision in *Building and construction industry in the Netherlands* were dismissed: Case T–29/92 *SPO and others v. Commission* [1995] II ECR 289 (CFI); Case C–137/95P [1996] I ECR 1611 (ECJ).

8. THE TERRITORIAL AMBIT OF ARTICLE 85(1)

(b) *Trade from the Community to third countries*

Examination of individual circumstances required **2–151**

n. 65. See also *Cement*, OJ 1994 L343/1 [1995] 4 CMLR 327 (§§ 5862), on appeal Cases T–25/95, etc.

n. 67. The decision in *French-West African shipowners' committees* is on appeal, Cases T–24/93, etc., not yet decided.

n. 68. See also Case T–141/89 *Tréfileurope Sales v. Commission* [1995] II ECR 791 (§§ 140–44).

(c) *Jurisdiction over undertakings outside the Community*

2–154 **"Effects doctrine" versus "territoriality principle"**

n. 74. See also the article by Roth cited at § 2–147, n. 47, of the main work.

2–156 **International comity.** See the US-EC Competition Laws Enforcement Agreement, that is designed in part to avoid conflicts of jurisdiction, at least so far as concerns public enforcement of Community or United States competition or antitrust law: para. 1–170 of the main work and *supra.*

(d) *Treaties with third countries*

2–158 **The Agreement on the European Economic Area**

n. 79. The EEA Agreement came into force on 1 January 1994. However, Austria, Finland and Sweden subsequently acceded to the European Community on 1 January 1995 which reduced the number of non-EC signatory States to two: Iceland and Norway. Liechtenstein, which had withdrawn from the EEA along with Switzerland, joined the EEA after the Agreement had been suitably amended, on 1 May 1995. Accordingly, the non-EC signatory states are now Iceland, Liechtenstein and Norway. For the text of the EEA Agreement as amended by the "Swiss Protocol" (to take account of the absence of Switzerland), see *Encyclopedia of European Union Law (Constitutional Texts)*, Vol. 2, §§ 30.0042 *et seq.* For general commentary, see Norberg *et al., EEA Law: A Commentary on the EEA Agreement* (Fritzes, 1993).

2–160 **Institutions of the EEA.** Article 108 of the EEA Agreement was implemented by the Agreement between the EFTA States on the establishment of a Surveillance Authority and a Court of Justice ("the EFTA Surveillance Agreement"). For the text as amended (to take account of the withdrawal of Switzerland and then Austria, Finland and Sweden), see *Encyclopedia of European Union Law (Constitutional Texts)*, Vol. 5, paras. 82.0277 *et seq.* The EFTA Court originally sat in Geneva but has now moved to Luxembourg.

The competition provisions of the EEA. It is to be noted, however, that by Article 8(3) EEA, various products are outside the scope of the EEA Agreement. The competition provisions therefore do not apply, in particular, to basic agricultural products or to some processed products. **2–161**

The issue of Notices by the EFTA Surveillance Authority corresponding to those of the EC Commission is noted at the relevant subject entry in this Supplement. For the adoption by the EEA of EC block exemption regulations, see para. 3–016A, *infra*. See generally Blanchet, Piipponen and Westman-Clément, *The Agreement on the European Economic Area (EEA): A Guide to the Free Movement of Goods and Competition Rules* (Clarendon Press, 1994); Stragier "The Competition Rules of the EEA Agreement and their Implementation" (1993) 1 E.C.L.R. 30.

Procedure under the EEA **2–163**

n. 88. See § 11–001A, *infra*.

The EFTA Treaties **2–165**

n. 90. For the texts of the treaties with Switzerland, Iceland and Norway, see *Encyclopedia of European Union Law (Constitutional Texts)* Vol. 3, §§ 41.0006 *et seq.* However, the treaties with Iceland and Norway have effectively been superseded by the EEA Agreement.

The Treaty with Israel. An Association Agreement was signed on 20 November 1995 between the European Communities, their Member States and Israel which replaces the Treaty of 1975 and which contains prohibitions on anti-competitive practices and State aids analogous to those in Articles 85, 86 and 92. Those provisions are to be implemented by rules to be adopted within three years by an Association Council established by the Agreement. The Agreement requires ratification by each Member State. To provide for the period until that process is completed, the Community concluded an Interim Agreement with Israel on 18 December 1995 that entered into force on 1 January 1996: OJ 1996 L71/1. **2–167**

Other treaties with third countries. The Community has concluded so-called Europe Agreements with the countries of Central and Eastern Europe that contain substantive competition provisions similar to those of the EC Treaty and which provide for implementation of the rules on State aids and the rules on undertakings. See the treaties with Poland, 16 December 1991; Hungary, 16 December 1991; Czech Republic, 4 October 1993; Slovakia, 4 October 1993; Bulgaria, 8 March 1993; and Romania, 1 February 1993: *Encyclopedia of European Union Law (Constitutional* **2–168**

Texts), Vol. 3, paras. 43.0006 *et seq.* Free Trading Agreements were concluded on 18 July 1994 with the three Baltic states, Latvia, Lithuania and Estonia, that contain competition provisions: see *ibid.* paras. 42.1672, *et seq.* Those came into force on 1 January 1995 but will be replaced by Europe Agreements signed in June 1995. See XXVth Report on Competition Policy (1995), points 221–22.

n. 5. For the text of the Lomé IV Convention, see *Encyclopedia of European Union Law (Constitutional Texts)*, Vol. 3, §§ 41.0024 *et seq.*

CHAPTER 3

ARTICLE 85(3)

1. INTRODUCTION

Relationship between Article 85(3) and Article 86. The Court of First Instance has expressly reserved its opinion as to whether the Commission should reject a request for an individual exemption where there is a substantiated infringement of Article 86. See Case T–17/93 *Matra Hachette v. Commission* [1994] II ECR 595, paras. 124 and 153–54, where the Court held that a risk that the parties to an agreement might thereby achieve a collective dominant position could not in itself justify refusal of exemption. **3–003**

The relationship between Article 85(3) and Article 48 (free movement of workers) was briefly discussed by Advocate General Lenz in Case C–415/93 *Union Royale Belge des Sociétés de Football Association v. Bosman* [1995] I ECR 4921 [1996] 1 CMLR 645, Opinion at para. 278. Although it was "theoretically conceivable" for the Commission to grant an exemption under Article 85(3) to an agreement which was in breach of Article 48, it should take into account the breach of Article 48 and "a uniform result should be aimed at in any case [which] would mean that an exemption under Article 85(3) would also have to be ruled out". The Court of Justice did not address this point.

The EEA Agreement: Article 53(3). Article 53(3) of the EEA Agreement provides for the exemption of certain agreements or categories of agreements from the prohibition in Article 53(1) of the EEA Agreement: see para. 2–161 of the main work, *supra*. Article 53(3) mirrors Article 85(3) of the E.C. Treaty. Individual exemption under Article 53(3) may be granted either by the Commission or by the EFTA Surveillance Authority and Article 56 of the EEA Agreement sets out the basis upon which jurisdiction to do so is divided between them: see para. 2–162 of the main work. Pursuant to Article 60, block exemptions under **3–003A**

Article 53(3) are listed in Annex XIV to the EEA Agreement as amended from time to time: see para. 3–016A, *infra*.

2. BLOCK EXEMPTION

3–004 **Council Regulations.** Council Regulation 479/92, OJ 1992 L55/3, empowers the Commission to grant block exemption to agreements that have the object of promoting or establishing co-operation in the joint operation of maritime transport services between liner shipping companies.

3–005 **Commission Regulations**

n. 14. The Commission took five decisions granting or renewing exemption under Article 85(3) in 1992, two in 1993, 11 in 1994 (the last figure does not include three further exemptions relating to rail services granted in 1994 under Reg. 1017/68), and three in 1995.

3–006 **Bilateral exclusive distribution agreements: Regulation 1983/83.** The extension of Regulation 1983/83 by a further two years to 31 December 1999 is now expected but, at the time of writing, has not yet been announced.

3–007 **Bilateral exclusive purchasing agreements: Regulation 1984/83.** The extension of Regulation 1984/83 by a further two years to 31 December 1999 is now expected but, at the time of writing, has not yet been announced.

3–008 **Patent licences: Regulation 2349/84.** The life of this Regulation was extended retroactively by Regulation 70/95 (OJ 1995 L12/13) to 30 June 1995 and then extended again to 31 December 1995 by Regulation 2131/95 (OJ 1995 L214/6). It was further extended to 31 March 1996 by Regulation 240/96 which then replaced it. See para. 3–008A, *infra*.

3–008A **Technology transfer agreements: Regulation 240/96.** Made on 31 January 1996 Regulation 240/96 (Appendix 4, *post*) took effect on 1 April 1996 (save for Article 11(2) that took effect retroactively 1 January 1996 and extended the validity of Regulation 2349/94). The Regulation replaces both the patent licence block exemption and the know-how licence block exemption with a single block exemption, thereby avoiding some of the previous difficulties of determining which of the two block exemptions was applicable to an agreement. The Regulation applies to certain patent licensing, know-how licensing and mixed patent and know-how licensing agreements to which only two undertakings are party. It includes agreements which contain "ancillary provisions" relating to intellectual property rights other than patents. The exemption covers agreements containing provisions which, essentially, restrain the licensee for a time from actively promoting or selling the licensed product outside his territory, or restrain the licensor from exploiting the licensed product, or licensing others to do so, in the territory (see Article 1). Article 3 lists provisions which, if included, will take the agreement outside the exemption (such as price or quantity restrictions or provisions designed to prevent parallel imports). Article 4 sets out an opposition procedure which will apply if certain restrictions are included. Article 7 allows the Commission to withdraw the benefit of the exemption where the effect of the agreement is to prevent competition to the licensed products in the territory—which may in particular occur where the licensee's market share exceeds 40 per cent. See further paras. 8–164A *et seq., infra.*

3–009 **Selective distribution for motor vehicles: Regulation 123/85.** Regulation 1475/95 (Appendix 2, *post*) extended the life of Regulation 123/85 to 30 September 1995, and applies in its place as from 1 October 1995. The passage quoted from Article 1 of Regulation 123/85 in para. 3–009 of the main work (describing the class of agreements that potentially benefit from the block exemption) is repeated in Article 1 of Regulation 1475/95 save for the addition of the word "new" in front of "motor vehicles". For discussion, see paras. 7–108A *et seq., infra.* Regulation 1475/95 expires on 30 September 2002.

3–012 **Certain agreements regarding air transport.** Regulations 83/91 and 84/91 have now been replaced by Regulations 1617/93 and 3652/93. Regulation 1617/93, OJ 1993 L155/18, entered into force on 1 July 1993 but was amended by Regulation 1523/96, OJ 1996 L190/11, to exclude freight tariffs. It now applies to certain agreements which have as their purpose:

(a) the joint planning and co-ordination of the schedule of an air service between Community airports;
(b) the joint operation of a scheduled air service on a new or low-density route between Community airports;
(c) the holding of consultations on tariffs for the carriage of passengers, with their baggage, on scheduled air services between Community airports; or
(d) slot-allocation and airport scheduling so far as they concern air services between airports in the Community.

Regulation 3652/93, OJ 1993 L333/37, applies from 1 January 1994 to agreements for the joint purchasing or development of computerised reservation systems, or for the creation of a "system vendor" to operate or market such a system, or for the regulation of the provision by the system vendor or distributors of facilities such as information, making reservations and issuing tickets. See para. 15–047, *infra.*

Both Regulations expire on 30 June 1998.

3–014 **Know-how licences: Regulation 556/89.** This Regulation was repealed with effect from 1 April 1996 by Article 11(1) of Regulation 240/96, the technology transfer block exemption: see para. 3–008A, *supra*.

3–015A **Liner consortia: Regulation 870/95.** Regulation 870/95 (Appendix 14, *post*) came into force on 22 April 1995 and exempts certain activities (listed in Article 3(2)) of liner consortia, *i.e.* agreements between carriers of international cargo freight for the joint operation of a maritime transport service. It applies only to consortia which provide international liner transport services from or to one or more Community ports. See paras. 15–028A–B, *infra*.

3–016 **Proposed block exemptions.** For the block exemption in the field of consortium agreements in sea transport, see Council Regulation 479/92, para. 3–004, *supra*, which enabled the introduction of Regulation 870/95, para. 3–015A, *supra*.

As set out in the main work, the two main block exemptions concerning "vertical" agreements are due to expire on 31 December 1997. However, a two years extension of Regulations 1983/83 and 1984/83 is now likely. This follows delay in publication of the Commission's Green Paper on vertical restraints on trade, covering the operation of the block exemptions on exclusive distribution, exclusive purchasing and franchising agreements, which the Commission had intended to publish in 1996: XXVth Report on Competition Policy (1995), point 44; see also the Parliamentary answer of 11 September 1995 [1996] 4 CMLR 20.

3–016A **The EEA Agreement: block exemptions.** The EEA Agreement, Annex XIV, adopts (with necessary amendments) various of the block exemptions that apply under Article 85(3) of the EC Treaty as similar exemptions under Article 53(3) of the EEA Agreement. Under Article 98 of the EEA Agreement, the EEA Joint Committee may by decision amend Annex XIV. Under Article 102, *ibid.* the EEA Joint Committee is required to take such a decision as closely as possible to the adoption of new EC legislation. As of 1 September 1996, Annex XIV as amended adopts the following EC block exemption Regulations as block exemptions under the EEA Agreement (the relevant point of Annex XIV is given in each case):

Regulation 1983/83	point 2
Regulation 1984/83	point 3
Regulation 2349/84	point 5
Regulation 123/85	point 4
Regulation 417/85	point 6
Regulation 418/85	point 7

Regulation 4087/88	point 8
Regulation 556/89	point 9
Regulation 3932/92	point 15a
Regulation 1617/93	point 11b
Regulation 3652/93	point 11a
Regulation 870/95	point 11c
Regulation 1475/95	point 4a

Points 11a, 11b and 15a were added to Annex XIV by EEA Joint Committee Decision 7/94 (OJ 1994 L160/1: see Annex 12 at 129), and these additions came into force on 1 July 1994 (see OJ 1994 C208/7). Decision 7/94 also amended points 5, 6, 7 and 9 to reflect the changes to the relevant Regulations made by Regulation 151/93. EEA Joint Committee Decisions 23/95 (OJ 1995, L139/14) and 65/95 (OJ 1996 L8/36) amended point 5 of Annex XIV to reflect the extensions to the validity of Regulation 2349/84 created by Regulations 70/95 and 2131/95 respectively. Point 11c was added by EEA Joint Committee Decision 12/96 (OJ 1996 L124/13). Point 4a was added by EEA Joint Committee Decision 46/96.

3. INDIVIDUAL EXEMPTION

(a) *Powers of the Commission*

3–017 **Powers of the Commission.** In Case T–17/93 *Matra Hachette v. Commission* [1994] II ECR 595, the Court of First Instance said that in principle the Commission had power to exempt any anti-competitive practice, whatever the extent of its effects on a given market, provided that the conditions set out in Article 85(3) were fulfilled and that the practice had been properly notified to the Commission (para. 85).

3–018 **The problem of delay.** In January 1993, the Commission introduced an expedited procedure for structural co-operative joint ventures: see para. 5–009, *infra*. This procedure is clearly inspired by the procedure and time-limits set out in Regulation 4064/89 (the merger regulation), and aims to reduce the disparity between the relatively rapid treatment of concentrative joint ventures falling under that Regulation and the treatment of co-operative joint ventures falling to be examined under Article 85(3). The procedure incorporates a two months deadline within which the Commission aims to inform the parties whether it has "serious doubts" that the notified joint venture is compatible with the competition rules. However, the Commission's success in implementing this expedited procedure has been mixed. In 1994, the Commission failed to meet the two months deadline in six out of 18 cases that qualified for expedition: see the XXIVth Report on Competition Policy (1994), Annex III, where it was said that new internal procedures were being introduced to improve this performance. Of the remaining 12 cases, ten cases were dealt with by comfort letter, and two by warning letters. The position appears to have improved in 1995: Report on the application of the competition rules in the EU, page 307.

3–019 **Comfort letters.** The EFTA Surveillance Authority similarly issues "comfort letters" and there is an equivalent provision to Article 19(3) of Regulation 17 at Article 19(3) of Chapter II of Protocol 4 to the EFTA Surveillance Agreement: see para. 11–001A, *infra.*

n. 78. In 1995, the Commission issued 197 comfort letters: Report on the application of the competition rules in the EU (1995), p. 305. For the ESA see § 3–057, *infra.*

3–020 **Opposition procedures**

n. 80. See also Reg. 240/96 (technology transfer agreements) Art. 4, §§ 8–164U *infra.*

n. 81. According to the XXIIIrd Report on Competition Policy (1993), in 1993 the opposition procedure was invoked once in relation to specialisation agreements, once in relation to know-how licensing agreements, three times in relation to franchising agreements, and not at all in relation to patent licensing agreements or research and development agreements. In the case of one of the notifications, the agreement was found not to fall under Art. 85(1); the remainder were still under examination at the end of the year.

3–021 **The Commission's margin of appreciation**

n. 82. For other cases where the grant of an exemption was challenged, see Case T–17/93 *Matra Hachette v. Commission* [1994] II ECR 595; Cases T–528/93, etc., *Métropole Télévision and Others v. Commission*, [1996] 5 CMLR 386 (on appeal, Case C–320/96P).

n. 83. See also Cases T–39 & 40/92 *CB and Europay v. Commission* [1994] II ECR 49 §§ 109–10; *Matra Hachette, supra*, § 104: Case T–29/92 *SPO and others v. Commission* [1995] II ECR 289 § 288 (further appeal dismissed, Case C–137/95P, [1996] I ECR 1611); Case T–7/93 *Langnese-Iglo v. Commission* [1995] II ECR 1533 [1995] 5 CMLR 602 [1995] All ER (EC) 902 § 178 (on appeal Case C–279/95P) and Case T–9/93 *Schöller v. Commission* [1995] II ECR 1611 [1995] 5 CMLR 659 § 140. In *Métropole Télévision, supra*, § 93, the CFI stated that the Commission's power of appraisal made it even more important for the Commission to examine all the relevant aspects of the case carefully and impartially.

n. 85. Further examples where the Commission's decision to refuse an exemption was upheld by the CFI include *CB and Europay, SPO*, and *Langnese-Iglo, supra*. But *cf.* Case C–360/92P *Publishers' Association v. Commission* [1995] I ECR 23 [1995] 5 CMLR 33 [1996] ICR 121, where the ECJ set aside the judgment of the CFI and also annulled the decision of the Commission in so far as it refused exemption under Art. 85(3). See also *Métropole Télévision, supra*, where the grant of an exemption was annulled by the CFI on the application of third parties; the Commission has appealed against the decision.

(b) *The Commission's policy*

Agreements unlikely to gain exemption. See now Article 3 of Regulation 240/96 relating to technology transfer agreements (and replacing Regulations 2349/84 and 556/89), and Article 6 of Regulation 1475/95 granting block exemption to certain categories of motor vehicle distribution and servicing agreements. **3–024**

n. 98. See also *Far Eastern Freight Conference*, OJ 1994 L378/17 (fixed or minimum prices for freight carriage) and *COAPI*, OJ 1994 L122/37 [1995] 4 CMLR 468 (collective fixing of minimum prices by industrial property agents). The decision in *Building and Construction Industry in the Netherlands* was upheld by the CFI and ECJ in *SPO, supra*.

n. 99. The Commission objected to the original form of the notified joint venture in *Exxon/Shell*, OJ 1994 L144/20, on the ground that it could have encouraged the exchange of market information between the participants; the agreement was varied so as to meet this objection. But *cf.* para. 4–031, *infra*.

n. 2. The exemption granted in *International Energy Agency* has been renewed: OJ 1994 L38/35.

n. 5. See also *SCK and FNK*, OJ 1995 L312/79 [1996] 4 CMLR 565 (on appeal, Case T–18/96): Dutch crane hire association's ban on hiring extra cranes from non-members.

n. 10. However, in Case C–360/92P *Publishers Association v. Commission* [1995] I ECR 23 [1995] 5 CMLR 33 [1996] ICR 121, the ECJ set aside the judgment of the CFI and annulled the decision of the Commission in so far as the decision refused exemption under Art. 85(3). *Cf. Sammelrevers* (Reuters EU Briefing, 8 August 1994), where the Commission surprisingly issued a "provisional" comfort letter in respect of the rpm agreements between German and Austrian publishers and

German and Austrian booksellers. The comfort letter was limited to 30 June 1996 but indicated that there were sufficient grounds for exemption; however, the Commission has more recently stated that this does not represent its definitive position and that it will take a formal decision on whether or not the conditions of Art. 85(3) are satisfied: OJ 1996 C54/2.

3–025 **Large undertakings**

n. 17. See also *Philips-Thomson-Sagem*, XXIIIrd Report on Competition Policy (1993), point 215 (JV closed by comfort letter under expedited procedure).

n. 18. See also *Pasteur-Mérieux/Merck*, OJ 1994 L309/1.

(c) *The criteria for exemption*

(i) *The benefits of the agreement*

3–027 **Objective benefits must outweigh reduction in competition.** See the discussion of the way in which the Commission views agreements with environmental objectives in the XXVth Report on Competition Policy (1995), points 84–85.

n. 20. In *Publishers Association*, *supra*, § 29, the ECJ stated that nothing in Art. 85(3) suggested that it was a condition of exemption that the benefits occur only on the territory of the Member States in which the parties to the agreement are established.

n. 21. See also *Matra Hachette*, *supra*, § 135; *Langnese-Iglo*, *supra*, § 180.

n. 23. In *SCK and FNK*, *supra*, the Commission pointed out that the rules for which benefits were claimed added nothing to the requirements of Dutch law, compliance with which was monitored by the public authorities, and therefore constituted an insufficient improvement to justify exemption.

3–028 **The burden of proof.** When the Commission rejects an application for exemption, it is required only to mention the matters of fact and law and the considerations which prompted it to take that decision. The Commission cannot be criticised for failing to put forward alternative solutions which might gain the agreement an exemption. Case T–29/92 *SPO and others v. Commission* (para. 262); appeal dismissed, Case C–137/95P [1996] I ECR 1611.

n. 27. See also *Matra Hachette, supra*, § 104.

Improvements in production. In *Matra Hachette, supra*, at para. 109, the Court of First Instance stated that the bringing to the EC of an enhanced manufacturing process, recommended by experts in the field, clearly fell within the benefits contemplated in this limb of Article 85(3). **3–031**

For the reference to Regulations 2349/84 and 556/89, substitute Regulation 240/96, Recital (10).

n. 41. See also *Fujitsu/AMD Superconductor*, OJ 1994 L341/66.

n. 42. See also BT/MCI, OJ 1994 L223/36 [1995] 5 CMLR 283.

n. 45. See also *Olivetti/Digital*, OJ 1994 L309/24; *Exxon/Shell, supra*; *Philips/Osram* OJ 1994 L378/37 [1996] 4 CMLR 48.

n. 50. See also *Stichting Baksteen*, OJ 1994 L131/15 [1995] 4 CMLR 646.

n. 58. The application to annul the Commission's grant of exemption in *Ford/Volkswagen* was dismissed: *Matra Hachette, supra.*

Improvements in distribution. In the parallel Cases T–7/93 *Langnese-Iglo v. Commission* [1995] II ECR 1533 [1995] 5 CMLR 602 [1995] All ER (EC) 902 and T–9/93 *Schöller v. Commission* [1995] II ECR 1611 [1995] 5 CMLR 659, the Court of First Instance upheld the finding of the Commission that the exclusive purchasing agreements at issue (between leading ice-cream manufacturers and retail outlets) would not improve distribution; they would not lead to the intensification of competition but rather had the effect of foreclosing the market. The Court noted that similar agreements had not been found necessary in certain other Member States. (The judgment in Langnese-Iglo is on appeal, Case C-279/95P.) In *EBU/Eurovision*, OJ 1993 L179/23 [1995] 4 CMLR 56, the Commission found that an agreement for the joint negotiation by public service broadcasters of rights to televise sporting events, and for the sharing of such rights, led to an improvement in distribution because it: (i) assisted broadcasters in smaller Member States to obtain access to the televising of sporting events; (ii) made it much easier for broadcasters established in one Member State to broadcast sporting events into other Member States; and (iii) allowed quasi-permanent coverage to be given to major sporting events, by making it easier for different broadcasters in one Member State to alternate coverage of sporting events. The Commission's decision has now been annulled on other grounds by the Court of First Instance: Cases T–528/93, etc., *Métropole Télévision and Others v. Commission* [1996] 5 CMLR 386; see para. 4–095, *infra*. **3–032**

n. 72. See now Case C–360/92P *Publishers Association v. Commission* [1995] I ECR 23 [1995] 5 CMLR 33 [1996] ICR 121.

3–033 **Technical progress.** Other cases where the Commission has found that an agreement contributes to promoting technical progress include: *Pasteur-Mérieux/Merck* OJ 1994 L309/1 (development of better and higher-performing multivalent vaccines); *Exxon/Shell, supra* (reduction in pollution, use of raw materials and output of waste products); *Asahi/St Gobain*, OJ 1994 L354/87 (safer glass for motor cars); and *Philips/Osram, supra* (reduction in requirements for lead glass and consequent reduction in pollution and energy use). The Commission has stated that "improving the environment is regarded as a factor which contributes to improving production or distribution or to promoting economic or technical progress": XXVth Report on Competition Policy (1995), point 85. In *Olivetti/Digital, supra*, the Commission held that the rapid dissemination of the computer hardware technology that was the subject of the agreement would encourage the development of appropriate software and therefore promote technical progress. The Court of First Instance in Case T–17/93 *Matra Hachette v. Commission* [1994] II ECR 595, para. 110, upheld the Commission's view that technical progress would be promoted by bringing together in one model of car technical improvements found in isolation in other models.

3–034 **Economic progress.** The Commission found that the agreements under consideration contributed to promoting economic progress in a number of decisions granting individual exemption, subject to conditions, related to the Channel Tunnel project. See *Eurotunnel III*, OJ 1994 L354/66 [1995] 4 CMLR 801, on appeal Cases T–79 & 80/95 *SNCF and British Railways v. Commission:* the agreements contributed to the project's financial stability by helping to protect the very large investment by the rail companies in specialised equipment for services through the Channel Tunnel and also provided a guaranteed revenue stream to the Channel Tunnel concessionaires; *Night Services* OJ 1994 L259/20 [1995] 5 CMLR 76, on appeal Cases T–374/94, etc., where the Commission found that the provision of greater competition with airlines constituted economic progress; *ACI*, OJ 1994 L224/28 (joint marketing of combined road and rail transport through the Channel Tunnel; exemption granted under Regulation 1017/68). In *Stichting Baksteen, supra*, the Commission considered that the agreement contributed to promoting economic progress by permitting the necessary restructuring of the Dutch brick industry to be carried out under acceptable social conditions. In *LH/SAS*, OJ 1996 L54/28, on appeal Case T–37/96 *Lufartsfunktionaererne v. Commission*, the Commission held that a co-operation agreement between Lufthansa and SAS contributed to economic progress because the pooling of the two airlines' complimentary networks, and associated rationalisation, should improve the services offered to consumers and achieve substantial cost savings.

3–037 **Exemptions in the banking sector.** In *Banque Nationale de Paris/Dresdner Bank*, OJ 1996 188/37, the Commission found that the co-operation agreement between these two banks would lead to an improvement in cross-border payment systems, a general policy objective of the Commission.

n. 97. On appeal, the Commission's decision in *Eurocheque: Helsinki Agreement* was varied by the CFI as regards the Groupement des Cartes Bancaires and annulled on procedural grounds as regards Eurocheque International: Cases T–39 & 40/92 *CB* and *Europay v. Commission* [1994] II ECR 49.

(ii) *The benefits for consumers*

In general. Under this head of Article 85(3), the Commission must decide objectively whether or not the agreement allows consumers a fair share of the resulting benefit. At this stage in the analysis, it is not appropriate to compare the benefits to consumers which arise as a result of the agreement with the benefits which consumers could have received had the parties chosen economically viable or technically possible alternatives: those are matters which go to the separate question of whether the restrictions are indispensable: *Matra Hachette, supra*, para. 122. **3–038**

A fair share. In *EBU/Eurovision, supra*, the Commission regarded the fact that the parties were public service broadcasters who were largely non-profit-making as an indication that the benefits of the agreement to the parties would be passed on to the viewing public; the parties would spend the resulting cost-savings on the acquisition of more or better programmes. However the Court of First Instance has now annulled the Commission's decision: see para. 4–095, *infra.* **3–039**

n. 2. *Ford/Volkswagen* was upheld by the CFI in *Matra Hachette, supra.* See also *Exxon/Shell*, OJ 1994 L144/20 and *Olivetti/Digital, supra.* In Case T–29/92 *SPO and others v. Commission* [1995] II ECR 289 (upheld on appeal Case C–137/95P [1996] I ECR 1611) at 384–85 the CFI upheld the Commission's finding in *Building and Construction Industry in the Netherlands* that a fair share of the benefits would not be passed on to consumers because the agreement was designed to eliminate competition in the industry.

n. 6. See also *BT/MCI, supra* (the strategic nature of the services to be provided to multi-national companies meant that stability of supply was particularly important).

n. 10. In *Grundig (No. 2)*, OJ 1994 L20/15 [1995] 4 CMLR 658, the Commission found that it was still a benefit for consumers to have the choice of going to a specialist electrical retailer who could provide personal contact and advice, despite the widespread availability of written sources of advice and the fact that consumers were now better informed about electrical goods. *Cf. Langnese-Iglo*, OJ 1993 L183/19 and *Schöller Lebensmittel*, OJ 1993 L183/1 [1994] 4 CMLR 51 (upheld on appeal: see para. 3–032, *supra*), where the Commission regarded the limitation of choice at each outlet caused by the series of exclusive purchase agreements as detracting from any benefit; in the impulse ice-cream market, consumers were unlikely to shop around and it was important for them to have a choice in each outlet.

n. 11. See also *Stichting Baksteen, supra.*

n. 13. See also *SPO, supra:* the CFI upheld the Commission's finding that the alleged benefit of a reduction in tender costs would, for certain customers, be outweighed by the other costs arising as a result of the agreement.

3–040 **Resulting benefit.** See the cases mentioned in paras. 3–031 to 3–033, *supra.*

(iii) *Restrictions indispensable*

3–042 **Indispensable restrictions.** A requirement not to negotiate separately was held by the Commission to be indispensable to a joint negotiating arrangement, provided that parties are free to do so once joint negotiations have failed: *EBU/Eurovision*, OJ 1993 L179/23 [1995] 4 CMLR 56. In that arrangement, participation was restricted to public-service broadcasters; this was considered by the Commission to be indispensable because wide national coverage in each Member State was an important selling point to event organisers, and because the arrangement relied on participants being prepared to provide coverage of events occurring in their State to other parties even if they saw no profit in that coverage for themselves. However, the decision has now been annulled: Cases T–528/93, etc., *Métropole Télévision and Others v. Commission* [1996] 5 CMLR 386 (on appeal Case C–320/96P). The Court of First Instance stated that the Commission had not adequately examined whether public service broadcasters necessarily provided wider national coverage than commercial broadcasters.

n. 24. The exemption granted to Grundig has been renewed: *Grundig (No. 2), supra.*

3–043 **Some unnecessary restrictions.** Further examples of cases where certain restrictions were not indispensable are: *Exxon/Shell, supra* (provision requiring other party to consent before a party could invest in the joint venture or take over the other party's unused production rights); *Auditel*, OJ 1993 L306/50 [1995] 5 CMLR 719, on appeal case T–66/94 (provision requiring parties to use only Auditel's market research data even for purely internal purposes); *Eurotunnel III, supra* (provision reserving all train paths available for international train services through the Channel tunnel for BR or SNCF); *SCK and FNK*, OJ 1995 L312/79 [1996] 4 CMLR 565 (restriction did no more than duplicate a requirement of Dutch law enforced by the public authorities); *SPO, supra* (unnecessary for the parties to have a closed procedure to designate a contractor from among themselves, as the customer was well placed to decide for itself what the lowest tender was); and *CB and Europay, supra* (provision requiring banks to charge a commission to traders on collection of foreign Eurocheques). In *BNP/Dresdner Bank, supra*, the Commission stated that it did not regard the right to veto the other's participation in a co-operation agreement with a competitor as indispensable; exemption was granted after the veto right was limited to the sharing of know-how, which the Commission accepted was an indispensable restriction in the context of the exchange of information and linking of computer systems that was at the core of this agreement.

n. 33. In Case C–360/92P *Publishers Association v. Commission* [1995] I ECR 23 [1995] 5 CMLR 33 [1996] ICR 121, the ECJ set aside the judgment of the CFI. It also annulled the decision of the Commission insofar as the decision refused exemption under Art. 85(3). *Cf. Sammelrevers* (Reuters E.U. Briefing, 8 August 1994), where the Commission surprisingly issued a "provisional" comfort letter in respect of the rpm agreements between German and Austrian publishers and German and, Austrian booksellers, stating that there were sufficient grounds for exemption; this was limited to 30 June 1996 and the Commission has stated that a formal decision under Art. 85(3) will be taken: OJ 1996 C54/2. The appeals against the decision in *Building and Construction Industry in the Netherlands* were dismissed: Case T–29/92 *SPO and others v. Commission* [1995] II ECR 289; Case C–137/95P [1996] I ECR 1611.

(iv) *No substantial elimination of competition*

3–045 **Conditions to be satisfied.** In *BT/MCI*, OJ 1994 L223/36 [1995] 5 CMLR 283, the Commission took account of the fact that BT was extensively regulated under United Kingdom law and MCI under US law. Those national regulatory constraints made it less likely that the parties could eliminate competition by, *e.g.* cross-subsidisation or discriminating in the terms upon which they provided access to their networks to potential competitors of the joint venture; *cf.* the discussion of *Atlas/Phoenix* in the XXVth Report on Competition Policy (1995) point 57, and the grant of exemption in those cases: *Atlas*, OJ 1996 L239/23; *Phoenix/GlobalOne*, OJ 1996 L239/57. In *Stichting Baksteen*, OJ 1994 L131/15 [1995] 4 CMLR 646, the Commission accepted that a co-ordinated reduction in capacity would not eliminate competition, since (i) the parties would otherwise remain free to compete, *e.g.* on price, and (ii) the parties would bear in mind in their dealings with customers the prospect of the restoration of full competition at the expiry of the five year period of the exemption. In the parallel cases of *Langnese-Iglo*, OJ 1993 L183/19 and *Schöller Lebensmittel*, OJ 1993 L183/1 [1994] 4 CMLR 51, exemption was refused where the Commission found that competition between ice-cream manufacturers who supplied the German market was effectively duopolistic; the exclusive purchase agreements at issue created barriers to any entrant who wished to compete with the duopoly. (This point was not considered by the Court of First Instance on appeal.) In *LH/SAS*, OJ 1996 L54/28 [1996] 4 CMLR 845, on appeal Case T–37/96 *Luftfartsfunktionaererne v. Commission*, the Commission imposed conditions to ensure the contestability of routes that would now be operated only by the two parties to the agreement.

n. 38. See also *BT/MCI, supra; Philips/Osram* OJ 1994 L378/37 [1996] 4 CMLR 48; *ATR/BAe* [1995] 5 CMLR 377 (comfort letter).

n. 40. In both *Philips/Osram, supra*, and *Asahi/St Gobain*, OJ 1994 L354/87, the parties to the joint ventures held over 50 per cent of the European market.

(d) *Duration and conditions of exemption*

3–047 **Retroactive effect.** For the powers of the Commission and of the EFTA Surveillance Authority to declare that exemptions under Article 53(3) of the EEA Agreement shall have effect retroactively, see paras. 3–055 *et seq., infra.*

3–050 **Likely duration of exemption.** Article 6(1) of Regulation 3975/87 concerning air transport (App. 46 to the main work) states that normally an exemption shall be for not less than six years. In both *LH/SAS, supra*, and *BNP/Dresdner Bank, supra*, an exemption of 10 years was granted. In the former case, the Commission noted that the benefit of the restructuring involved would be achieved only in the long term; in the later, the Commission noted that implementation of the complex agreement would take several years.

n. 54. Of the 16 decisions granting or renewing exemption in 1993 and 1994 (including those granted under Reg. 1017/68), two were for three years, five were for five years (in one case this period would begin to run only when the joint venture began production in the EC, but would end at the latest 13 years from notification), one for eight years, six for 10 years, one for 13 years and one for 30 years (with some of the provisions to be reviewed after 12 years).

n. 55. In *Eurotunnel III*, OJ 1994 L354/66 [1995] 4 CMLR 801, on appeal Cases T–79 & 80/95 *SNCF and British Railways v. Commission*, exemption was granted for 30 years to reflect the need for stability over the long financing period for the project.

n. 59. See also *International Energy Agency* OJ 1994 L68/35 and *Grundig (No. 2)*, OJ 1994 L20/15 [1995] 4 CMLR 658.

3–052 **Conditions and obligations.** In *Eurotunnel III, supra*, the Commission imposed a condition on BR and SNCF requiring them to surrender to third parties at least 25 per cent (or more if they did not use it) of rail paths in the Channel Tunnel available for international railway services. In *European Night Services*, OJ 1994 L259/20 [1995] 5 CMLR 76, on appeal Cases T–374/94, etc., it was a condition of exemption that the parties supply locomotives, crew and train paths to a new entrant on the same terms as they did to the joint venture. Non-discrimination conditions were also imposed in *ACI*, OJ 1994 L224/28. In *EBU/Eurovision*, OJ 1993 L179/23 [1995] 4 CMLR 56, an obligation was imposed that non-parties be allowed access to broadcast sports events under the parties' access scheme (the decision has now been annulled by the Court of First Instance: see para. 4–095, *infra*.) In *Exxon/Shell*, OJ 1994 L144/20, an obligation was imposed requiring the parties to notify the Commission of any stoppages in production and of the reasons for them. In *LH/SAS, supra*, the Commission imposed, as conditions of the exemption, detailed requirements for the making available of slots and a limitation of the parties' frequencies on routes between Germany and Scandinavia so as to assist entry onto those routes by other airlines. Detailed requirements were also imposed as conditions for the exemptions granted in *Atlas*, OJ 1996 L239/23 and *Phoenix/GlobalOne*, OJ 1996 L239/57: the parties were required to establish access to their public networks on a non-discriminatory basis and specific conditions were included to ensure that the parents and the joint ventures dealt at arms' length and without cross-subsidisation or bundling of the parents' and the JVs' products.

n. 60. The conditions in *Bayer/BP Chemicals* were amended in *Bayer/BP Chemicals (No. 2)*, OJ 1994 L174/34: changes in product range meant that closure of a particular plant could be postponed until after the date set out in the original exemption.

n. 62. See also *Eurotunnel III* and *Exxon/Shell, supra*.

n. 63. See also *EBU/Eurovision* and *Exxon/Shell, supra*.

n. 65. The requirement on Grundig was imposed again on renewal of the exemption: *Grundig (No. 2), supra*.

n. 69. See also *EBU/Eurovision, supra*.

(e) *Individual exemptions under Article 53(3) of the EEA Agreement*

3–053 **Agreements exempted under Article 85(3) of the EC Treaty before the coming into force of the EEA Agreement.** Article 13 of Protocol 21 to the EEA Agreement provides that agreements previously exempted under Article 85(3) of the EC Treaty are exempted under Article 53(3) of the EEA Agreement until the exemption under Article 85(3) expires or is withdrawn.

3–054 **Agreements notified to the Commission before the coming into force of the EEA Agreement.** Agreements notified to the Commission before the coming into force of the EEA Agreement are deemed to have been properly notified under the EEA Agreement: Article 8 of Protocol 21 to the EEA Agreement.

3–055 **Other agreements falling under Article 53(1) of the EEA Agreement and in force before the coming into force of the EEA Agreement.** A period of six months (*i.e.* to 30 June 1994) was allowed for parties either to notify such an agreement to the EFTA Surveillance Authority, in which case the agreement could be exempted retrospectively to the entry into force of the EEA Agreement: Articles 5(1) and 6 of Protocol 21 to the EEA Agreement; or to modify the agreement so that it would fall outside Article 53(1) or within a block exemption granted under Article 53(3), in which case Article 53(1) would not apply to the agreement: Articles 11 and 12 of Protocol 21 to the EEA Agreement.

3–056 **Agreements coming into force after the coming into force of the EEA Agreement.** In these cases, the EFTA Surveillance Authority generally has no power to grant an exemption backdated to earlier than the date of notification: Article 6 of Protocol 21 to the EEA Agreement. However, it may grant an exemption backdated to a date before notification where the agreement falls within Article 4(2) of Protocol 21 to the EEA Agreement, which is equivalent to Article 4(2) of Regulation 17: see paras. 11–042 *et seq.* of the main work.

3–057 **Practice of the EFTA Surveillance Authority.** The EFTA Surveillance Authority has not so far granted any individual exemptions. In 1994 it issued Notices under Article 19(3) in three cases and issued three comfort letters: ESA Annual Report '94, point 4.9.2. Under Article 172 of the Treaty of Accession of Austria, Finland and Sweden to the European Union, the EFTA Surveillance Authority transmitted to the Commission those cases before it which it had not finalised by 1 January 1995 and which, as a result of the accession of these States to the Community, fell under the jurisdiction of the Commission. In consequence, 71 of the 109 cases pending before the EFTA Surveillance Authority were transferred to the Commission. The Authority was left with 35 pending notifications requesting negative clearance or exemption and received five further notifications in 1995: ESA Annual Report '95, point 3.4.

CHAPTER 4

ARTICLE 85: COMMON HORIZONTAL AGREEMENTS

1. INTRODUCTION

4–001 **Scope of this chapter.** There has been an increasingly marked tendency by the Commission to adopt a two-tier approach to horizontal agreements; XXIIIrd Report on Competition Policy (1993), points 209–10. In relation to cartels, particularly those involving "hard core" infringements such as price-fixing or market sharing, the Commission adopted several major decisions imposing unprecedentedly high fines: XXIVth Report on Competition Policy (1994), points 132 to 143, and see paras. 4–014A–14C, *infra*. At the same time, the Commission has taken steps to simplify and accelerate its procedures for other types of arrangement, in particular those involving co-operative joint ventures falling outside the scope of the Merger Regulation: see para. 5–009, *infra*.

4–001A **Application of the EEA Agreement.** The competition rules in the EEA Agreement entered into force on 1 January 1994. The EFTA Surveillance Authority has acted in a number of cases to bring cartel arrangements to an end, in particular in Austria, where the national competition rules are relatively lenient, and in Scandinavia, where price cartels were prevalent in the forestry sector: ESA Annual Report '94, point 4.9.2; see also *Re the Agreement on Finnish Forestry*, OJ 1994 C337/21 [1995] 4 CMLR 104 (Article 19(3) Notice in respect of a Finnish price agreement that had been amended to comply with the Authority's requirements).

2. AGREEMENTS ON SELLING PRICES AND CONDITIONS

Price-fixing prohibited **4–002**

n. 4. The appeal to the CFI against the Commission's decision in *Building and construction industry in the Netherlands* was dismissed: Case T–29/92 *SPO and others v. Commission* [1995] II ECR 289, and the ECJ dismissed a further appeal: Case C–137/95P, [1996] I ECR 1611.

What constitutes price-fixing **4–003**

n. 5. Express restrictions on price relating to "multimodal" transport entered into in the context of liner conferences were condemned in *Trans-Atlantic Agreement*, OJ 1994 L376/1, and *Far Eastern Freight Conference*, OJ 1994 L378/17. The decision in *Trans-Atlantic Agreement* is on appeal and in Case T–395/94R *Atlantic Container Line and others v. Commission* [1995] II ECR 595 the President of the CFI granted interim measures suspending the operation of the Commission's decision in so far as it related to inland-price-fixing (affirmed on appeal by the President of the ECJ, Case C–149/95 P(R) *Commission v. Atlantic Container Line and Others* [1995] I ECR 2165 [1995] All ER (EC) 853). A further application to the CFI seeking interim measures in relation to the Commission's intention to withdraw immunity from fines in respect of an amended version of the agreement was rejected by the President: Case T–395/94RII [1995] II ECR 2893.

n. 9. The decision in *Distribution of railway tickets by travel agents* was annulled by the CFI on the basis that the case did not fall within the scope of Art. 85 but rather within Reg. 1017/68: Case T–14/93 *Union Internationale des Chemins de Fer v. Commission* [1995] II ECR 1503 [1996] 5 CMLR 40, on appeal Case C–264/95P: see § 15–004, *infra*.

n. 22. See also *IATA-Cargo Surcharge*, XXIIIrd Report on Competition Policy (1993), point 238; *Motor vehicle grouping*, XXIVth Report on Competition Policy (1994), Annex II, p. 369, 1994 OJ C130/3.

Price recommendations. See also *SCK and FNK*, OJ 1995 L312/79 [1996] 4 CMLR 565: publication by the Dutch crane hire association of cost calculations and recommended rates based upon them, together with an obligation on the members to charge "reasonable rates" (fine of 11.5 million ECU imposed); on appeal Case T–18/96, not yet decided (application for interim measures refused: Case T–18/96R [1996] 5 CMLR 307). In *Fenex*, OJ 1996 L181/28 [1996] 5 CMLR 332, the practice of a Dutch association of freight forwarders in circulating recommended tariff increases to its members was similarly held to violate Article 85(1). **4–004**

n. 23. The appeals against the Commission decision in *Welded Steel Mesh* were unsuccessful save for reduction in some of the fines: Cases T–141/89, etc., *Tréfileurope Sales v. Commission*, etc., [1995] II ECR 791, etc., on further appeal, Cases C–185/95P and C–219/95P.

4–005 **Inter-State price cartels.** The Commission adopted three major decisions in 1994, *Steel beams, Cartonboard* and *Cement*: see paras. 4–014A to 14–014C, *infra*.

4–010 **Polypropylene: the appeals**

n. 31. The CFI dismissed an application by DSM NV to revise its judgment, Case T–8/89 Rev. *DSM v. Commission* [1992] II ECR 2399, which decision is under appeal to the ECJ: Case C–5/93P.

4–011 **The *PVC* and *LdPE* decisions.** The Court of Justice annulled the Court of First Instance's holding that the Commission's decision was "non-existent" but also annulled the *PVC* decision for serious procedural irregularity: Case C–137/92P *Commission v. BASF and others* [1994] I ECR 2555. The Commission then adopted a further decision in identical terms: *PVC II*, OJ 1994 L239/14, which is now also on appeal in Cases T–305/94, etc.

The *LdPE* decision has been annulled by the Court of First Instance, following the approach of the Court of Justice to the *PVC* decision: Cases T–80/89, etc., *BASF and others v. Commission* [1995] II ECR 729.

4–014A **Steel beams.** This decision under Article 65 of the ECSC Treaty related to a joint attempt to align prices in the different Member States in order to preserve existing market shares. The arrangements involved producers of approximately two-thirds of deliveries in the Community and were entered into between 1984 and 1991. Fines totalling 104,364,350 ECU were imposed on 14 different companies for infringements after 30 June 1988, the date of termination of crisis measures adopted pursuant to Article 58 of the ECSC Treaty: OJ 1994 L116/1 [1994] 5 CMLR 353, on appeal Cases T–137/94, etc. See also Case T–156/94R *Aristrain v. Commission* [1994] II ECR 717 (partial suspension of the fine).

4–014B **Cartonboard.** The *Cartonboard* decision related to a systematic attempt to fix prices and control production between 1986 and 1991, resulting in six-monthly co-ordinated price increases throughout the industry. Fines totalling 132 million ECU were imposed on 22 producers of cartonboard: OJ 1994 L243/1 [1994] 5 CMLR 547, on appeal Cases T–295/94, etc.

4–014C **Cement.** A large number of major producers of cement, national cement associations and the European Cement Association, Cembureau, were found to be involved in general market-sharing arrangements. The arrangements were entered into in the context of Cembureau meetings and concerned the maintenance of a "home market rule" and exchange of price information with a view to aligning prices so as to maintain market shares. These general arrangements were combined with bilateral arrangements between national producers to counter specific difficulties, in particular exports from Greek producers into other Community markets. Fines totalling 248 million ECU were imposed on Cembureau, eight national associations and 33 cement producers. OJ 1994 L343/1 [1995] 4 CMLR 327, on appeal Cases T–25/95, etc.

Price agreements in service industries. In *CNSD*, OJ 1993 L203/27 [1995] 5 CMLR 495, on appeal Case T–513/93, the Commission condemned a compulsory tariff established by a trade association representing customs agents in Italy. In *COAPI*, OJ 1995 L122/37 [1995] 5 CMLR 468, the target of the decision was minimum rates for services established by the Spanish professional association of agents of industrial property. Both cases are significant in that the services in question were classified as "professions" under national law and the price-fixing arrangements were expressly provided for (although not specifically required) by national legislation governing those services. Furthermore, the Commission proceeded to examine the compatibility of the Italian legislation at issue in *CNSD* with Articles 3(*f*) and 5, read in conjunction with Article 85, of the EC Treaty: XXIIIrd Report on Competition Policy (1993), point 219. **4–016**

See also the Commission's *Notice on the application of the EC competition rules to cross-border credit transfers*, OJ 1995 C251/3 [1995] 5 CMLR 551, in which the Commission indicates that multinational pricing agreements between banks who participate in such transfers may fall within Article 85(1). In order to obtain Article 85(3) exemption, such arrangements must not only be necessary to achieve some identifiable benefit, for example to avoid double charging, but must also (i) relate to average additional costs and (ii) be subject to alternative bilateral arrangements between participants.

Eurocheque: Helsinki Agreement. On appeal, the Court of First Instance upheld the Commission's conclusion that the Helsinki Agreement required the French participating banks to charge a commission in respect of Eurocheques additional to that provided for under the package deal Agreement, but found that the *amount* of such commission was not fixed by the Helsinki Agreement; the fines imposed on the banks were therefore reduced to two million ECU; the decision in respect of Eurocheque was annulled on procedural grounds: Cases T–39 & 40/92 *CB and Europay v. Commission* [1994] II ECR 49. See also as regards default interest on the fines Case T–275/94 *CB v. Commission* [1995] II ECR 2169 [1995] 5 CMLR 410. **4–017**

Domestic price agreements extending to imports or exports. For two national price-fixing regimes for services, see *CNSD*, para. 4–016, *supra* **4–020**

(scheme relating to goods imported into or exported from Italy); and *COAPI, ibid.* (minimum scale of charges affected non-Spanish residents seeking to register intellectual property rights in Spain and Spanish residents seeking to register such rights abroad).

4–021 **Domestic price agreements not extending to imports or exports**

n. 60. The CFI and the ECJ dismissed successive appeals against the Commission's decision in *Building and construction industry in the Netherlands*: Case T–29/92 *SPO and others v. Commission* [1995] II ECR 289; Case C–137/95P [1996] I ECR 1611.

4–022 **Domestic price agreements covering a whole Member State**

n. 64. See also *CNSD* and *COAPI*, 4–016, *supra*. The appeal against the Commission's decision in *Building and construction industry in the Netherlands* was dismissed: n. 60, *supra*.

4–023 **Collective resale price maintenance**

n. 66. The ECJ allowed the appeal in Case C–360/92P *Publishers Association v. Commission* [1995] I ECR 23 [1995] 5 CMLR 33 [1996] ICR 121, finding that the Commission had incorrectly evaluated the conditions for exemption under Art. 85(3): see § 3–021, *supra*. However, the Net Book Agreement was subject to scrutiny by the national competition authorities in both Ireland and the United Kingdom in 1994 and has now been abandoned by United Kingdom publishers. *Cf. Sammelrevers* (1994), the somewhat surprising issue of a "provisional" comfort letter in respect of the rpm agreements between German/Austrian publishers and German/Austrian booksellers, in which the Commission stated that there were sufficient grounds for exemption under Art. 85(3) until 30 June 1996: Reuters EU Briefing, 8 August 1994. The Commission is now to take a formal decision on the arrangement: OJ 1996 C54/2.

4–025 **Collective fixing of trading conditions**

n. 69. For the appeals in *Eurocheque: Helsinki Agreement*, see § 4–017, *supra*. See also the Commission's *Notice on the application of the EC competition rules to cross-border credit transfers*, OJ 1995 C251/3 [1995] 5 CMLR 551.

4–027 **Price agreements under Article 85(3).** In *Steel Beams*, OJ 1994 L116/1 [1994] 5 CMLR 353, on appeal Cases T–137/94, etc., the fact that there had been delivery and production quotas and minimum prices imposed by the Commission between October 1980 and June 1988 was not accepted as any justification for the price-fixing and production limitations agreed by the producers themselves (although no fine was imposed in relation to that period).

n. 76. The judgment in Case T–16/91 *Rendo v. Commission* [1992] II ECR 2417 was partially set aside by the ECJ, who referred the matter back to the CFI: Case C–19/93P [1995] I ECR 3319.

3. INFORMATION AGREEMENTS

Information agreements. The Court of First Instance considered the operation of such agreements in detail in determining the appeals against the Commission's decision in *United Kingdom Agricultural Tractor Registration Exchange*, OJ 1992 L68/19. Although the exchange of information between the main suppliers did not directly concern prices or "underpin any other anti competitive arrangement", the Court accepted the Commission's argument that the regular and frequent sharing of information regarding registered vehicles and their place of registration served to reduce uncertainty and impair competition on such a highly concentrated oligopolistic market. An important further objection to the arrangement was that participation in the exchange of information was in practice limited to the major suppliers. Case T–34/92 *Fiatagri and New Holland Ford v. Commission* [1994] II ECR 905, para. 91, and Case T–35/92 *John Deere v. Commission* [1994] II ECR 957, para. 51; on appeal Cases C–7 & 8/95P. **4–029**

Exchange of information between distributors. Where a market is *not* oligopolistic, the Commission is prepared to accept even the exchange of individual and confidential information concerning sales volumes and market shares: *Eudim* OJ 1996 C111/8 [1996] 4 CMLR 871 (Article 19(3) Notice). **4–031**

Information on output and sales. See also *Fiatagri* and *John Deere*, para. 4–029, *supra*. **4–034**

Other exchanges of information **4–036**

n. 97. See *Steel Beams, Cartonboard*, and *Cement*, §§ 4–014A to 14–014C, *supra*, for examples of a very widespread sharing of information to enable price-fixing, market sharing and production limitation arrangements to operate successfully.

The CFI and ECJ dismissed the appeals against the Commission's decision in *Building and construction industry in the Netherlands*: Case T–29/92 *SPO and others v. Commission* [1995] II ECR 289, and Case C–137/95P [1996] I ECR 1611.

4–037 **Information agreements under Article 85(3)**

n. 99. The Commission closed its file and sent a comfort letter to the parties with respect to the amended *Irish Club Rules*, OJ 1993 C263/6, XXIIIrd Report on Competition Policy (1993), point 233.

4. AGREEMENTS TO LIMIT PRODUCTION

4–038 **Limitation of production.** The three major cartels in *Steel beams, Cartonboard* and *Cement, supra*, are classic examples of production limitations combined with wider cartel agreements to fix prices or share markets. See also *Trans-Atlantic Agreement*, OJ 1994 L376/1 (agreement limiting capacity on container shipments between northern Europe and the USA), on appeal Case T–395/94 *Atlantic Containers Line and others v. Commission* and see at [1995] II ECR 595 (interim measures suspending in part the operation of the Commission's decision), upheld on appeal, Case C–149/95 P(R) [1995] I ECR 2165 [1995] All ER(EC) 853.

4–040 **Restructuring agreements.** *Stichting Baksteen*, OJ 1994 L131/15 [1995] 4 CMLR 646, illustrates the Commission's approach to such an agreement. In order to resolve the crisis of overcapacity in the Dutch brick industry, the major producers concluded an agreement providing for a collective reduction in production, with co-ordination and compensation for the cost of closures placed in the hands of a foundation financed by the 16 participating manufacturers. The Commission found that the agreement fell within Article 85(1) but after the agreement was amended to remove the provision for production quotas the Commission granted an exemption for five years on condition that the parties to the agreement did not divulge to one another any data in respect of individual outputs and deliveries.

Even where a restructuring agreement is in operation, the competition rules remain in force: *Steel Beams*, OJ 1994 L116/1 [1994] 5 CMLR 353, on appeal Cases T–137/94, etc. (where crisis measures were adopted pursuant to Article 58 ECSC).

n. 9. See the further decision in *Bayer/BP Chemicals*, OJ 1994 L174/34; and *cf. Exxon/Shell*, OJ 1994 L144/20 (production joint venture for linear polyethylene).

5. AGREEMENTS ON TECHNICAL STANDARDS

4–047 **Agreements on technical standards.** See the Commission's *Notice on the application of the EC competition rules to cross-border credit transfers*, OJ

1995 C251/3 [1995] 5 CMLR 551, paras. 30 to 34, for the Commission's views on the applicability of Article 85(1) and Article 85(3) to agreements between participants in cross-border credit transfer systems on common operational standards. See also XXVth Report on Competition Policy (1995) points 47–48.

6. AGREEMENTS TO LIMIT OR SHARE MARKETS

Limitation of markets. The opening of the Channel Tunnel has provided the occasion for a series of decisions relating to agreements to share access to an "essential facility": **4–054**

(a) In *ACI*, OJ 1994 L224/28, British Railways ("BR"), SNCF and Intercontainer (a combined transport operator owned by 24 railway undertakings) agreed to the joint marketing of combined road and rail services between the United Kingdom and continental Europe via the Channel Tunnel. The Commission considered that the three parent companies were potential competitors on the relevant market and that there was a risk that access to BR and SNCF networks and services would be limited. However, a five year exemption was granted subject to conditions, the most significant being an obligation on BR and SNCF to supply services to competitors of ACI on a non-discriminatory basis.

(b) In *Night Services*, OJ 1994 L259/20 [1995] 5 CMLR 76, on appeal Cases T–374/94, etc., BR, SNCF and the Dutch and German public railway undertakings set up a joint venture to operate night passenger services between the United Kingdom and continental Europe on four specific routes. The Commission granted an eight-year exemption on similar conditions to those imposed in *ACI*.

(c) *Eurotunnel III*, OJ 1994 L354/66 [1995] 4 CMLR 801, concerned the agreement by Eurotunnel, the company responsible for the Channel Tunnel, to grant BR and SNCF exclusive rights to 50 per cent of the capacity of the Channel Tunnel (the remainder being reserved to Eurotunnel itself). This severe restriction on access to the Tunnel was considered unacceptable by the Commission but a 30-year exemption was eventually granted to an agreement whereby at least 25 per cent of the capacity not reserved to Eurotunnel remained available to other undertakings. The decision is on appeal and an application for interim measures was refused: Cases T–79 & 80/95R *SNCF and British Railways v. Commission* [1995] II ECR 1433 [1996] 5 CMLR 26.

n. 31. The decision in *Soda-ash—Solvay, CFK* was annulled as regards Solvay for procedural irregularity: Case T–31/91 [1995] II ECR 1821: see § 12–043, *infra*. CFK did not appeal and the reference to Case T–32/91 should be deleted.

4–055 **Market sharing between producers.** See also *Steel beams, Cartonboard* and *Cement*, paras. 4–014A–14C, *supra*.

n. 33. The Commission's decision in *Soda-ash—Solvay, ICI* was annulled for breaches of the rights of defence: Case T–30/91 *Solvay v. Commission* [1995] II ECR 1775, Case T–36/91 *ICI v. Commission* [1995] II ECR 1847; [1995] All ER (EC) 600: see § 12–036, *infra*. The appeals against the Commission's decision in *Building and construction industry in the Netherlands* were dismissed: Case T–29/92 SPO *and others v. Commission* [1995] II ECR 289; Case C–137/95P [1996] I ECR 1611.

4–057 **Collective exclusive dealing between manufacturers**

n. 37. See n. 33, *supra*.

4–058 **Eastern Aluminium.** See also the attempts to prevent cheap imports from Greek suppliers in *Cement*, para. 4–014C, *supra*.

4–059 **Emergency allocation of supplies.** See now *International Energy Agency*, OJ 1994 L68/35 (exemption renewed for a further period of 10 years).

4–064 **Bilateral market sharing: *Soda Ash*.** All the decisions have been annulled as regards Solvay and ICI by the Court of First Instance on procedural grounds: Cases T–30, 31 & 32/91 *Solvay v. Commission* [1995] II ECR 1775, 1821, 1825 [1996] 5 CMLR 57, 91; Cases T–36 & 37/91 *ICI v. Commission* [1995] II ECR 1847, 1901. See paras. 12–036 and 12–043, *infra*. The Commission has appealed against the judgments in Cases T–31, 32 and 37/91: Cases 286/95P, etc.

4–065 **Exclusive selling rights to competitor.** See also *Carlsberg/Interbrew*, where the Commission required significant amendments to an agreement between the leading suppliers of beer in Denmark and Belgium/ Luxembourg giving exclusive rights for the Belgium/Luxembourg market. XXIVth Report on Competition Policy (1994), Annex II, p. 351, and see para. 7–144, *infra*.

4–067 **Market division between distributors.** See *Ducros/DHL*, for a co-operation agreement between express delivery services whereby a French company, Ducros, pooled its services in France with services provided by DHL and its German subsidiary, Elan, in other Member States. The parties agreed to operate under a common name and to grant each other reciprocal exclusive rights with regard to services in their respective territories. The Commission treated the agreement as a transport agreement and a three-year exemption was authorised under the opposition procedure pursuant to Regulation 1017/68. XXIVth Report on Competition Policy (1994), Point 192 and Annex II, pp. 370–71, OJ 1994 C165/10.

In *Eudim*, OJ 1996 C111/8 [1996] 4 CMLR 871, the Commission adopted a favourable position towards the agreements constituting an association of national distributors of plumbing, heating and sanitary products which limited membership to one per country and provided for extensive exchange of information, after the parties to those agreements adopted a formal declaration that they were "free to sell their products and to establish their businesses wherever they feel is appropriate".

Domestic market sharing agreements — 4–070

n. 64. The appeal to the CFI against the Commission's decision in *Building and construction industry in the Netherlands* was dismissed: Case T–29/92 *SPO and others v. Commission* [1995] II ECR 289; and the ECJ dismissed a further appeal Case: C–137/95P [1996] I ECR 1611.

Control over imports and exports — 4–071

n. 66. The judgment in Case T–16/91 *Rendo I* was partially set aside by decision of the ECJ which referred the matter back to the CFI: Case C–19/93P [1995] I ECR 3319. The application in Case T–2/92 was rejected as inadmissible by unpublished Order of the CFI dated 29 March 1993.

7. COLLECTIVE EXCLUSIVE DEALING

Collective exclusive dealing agreements under Article 85(1) — 4–075

n. 71. See also *Auditel*, OJ 1993 L306/50 [1995] 5 CMLR 719, on appeal Case T–66/94 *Auditel v. Commission* (agreement by Auditel shareholders, comprising in practice television broadcasters and advertising associations, to use exclusively the Italian audience ratings provided by Auditel); *HOV–SVZ/HCN*, OJ 1994 L104/34, on appeal Case T–229/94 *Deutsche Bahn v. Commission* (a case primarily under Art. 86 but also involving a joint marketing agreement between five rail and transport companies on the basis of a joint tariff grid); *SCK and FNK*, OJ 1995 L317/79 [1996] 4 CMLR 565, on appeal Case T–18/96 (Dutch crane-hirers affiliated to the domestic certification institution prevented from engaging non-affiliated crane hirers as sub-contractors).

Auctions — 4–079

n. 79. The appeal in *Florimex v. Commission* was struck out. See Case T–77/94 *VGB v. Commission*, not yet decided, for a subsequent demand for further action by the Commission against the VBA.

4–081 **Collective exclusive dealing in financial services**

n. 82. Reg. 3932/92 applies, subject to necessary amendments, with regard to the EEA competition rules: EEA Agreement, Annex XIV, point 15a.

4–082 **Collective exclusive dealing in the airline industry.** In *IATA-Currency Rules*, rules that prevented purchases by consumers from outside the country of travel origin were modified after intervention by the Commission so as not to apply to travel within the EC and Norway: XXIIIrd Report on Competition Policy (1993), point 237. See also *Sabre/Air France and Iberia* (refusal by Air France and Iberia to participate in a competing computerised reservation system): XXIIIrd Report on Competition Policy (1993), point 239; and see at para. 15–043, *infra*.

4–084 **Unreasonable refusal of membership.** See also *Spa Monopole/GDB*: rules of the German association of mineral waters were changed to allow non-German suppliers of mineral water access to the German pool of refillable glass bottles, after the Commission had commenced proceedings (under Articles 85 and 86) following changes to German national legislation requiring the use of such containers. XXIIIrd Report on Competition Policy (1993), point 240 [1994] 4 CMLR 20.

4–086 **The Commission's attitude to membership rules.** See also *East African Conference*, OJ 1994 L378/17, where the Commission was concerned at the effects of a requirement of six months' notice to *leave* a liner conference: XXIIIrd Report on Competition Policy (1993), points 230–31. The Commission's *Notice on the application of the EC competition rules to cross-border credit transfers*, OJ 1995 C251/3, [1995] 5 CMLR 551, requires cross-border credit transfer systems to be open to further members and to have objectively justified membership rules where they represent an "essential facility" for a bank to compete on the relevant market. The Court of First Instance has now made clear that in order for the Commission to be able to assess whether membership rules were indispensible within the meaning of Article 85(3), it is necessary for the rules to be objective and sufficiently determinate, and capable of non-discriminatory application: Cases T–528/93, etc., *Métropole Télévision and others v. Commission* [1996] 5 CMLR 386, at para. 102, annulling the Commission's decision in *EBU/Eurovision System*; see further para. 4–095, *infra*.

8. JOINT PURCHASING

4–090 **Collective purchasing of raw materials.** See now Case C–250/92 *Gøttrup-Klim v. Dansk Landbrugs Grovvareselskab AmhA* [1994] I ECR

5641 [1996] 4 CMLR 191, where the European Court of Justice ruled that a provision in the rules of a co-operative purchasing organisation forbidding its members to participate in other forms of organised co-operation which are in direct competition with it, is not caught by Article 85(1), so long as the abovementioned rule is restricted to what is necessary to ensure that the cooperative functions properly and maintains its contractual power in relation to producers. The Court considered that the rules in question were necessary in that case to enable individual farmers to combine their limited individual purchasing power in the face of very powerful world suppliers of fertilisers "joint control" and plant protection products.

Joint purchasing in the audiovisual media. In *EBU/Eurovision System*, OJ 1993 L179/23 [1995] 4 CMLR 56, the Commission finally issued a decision in its long-running proceedings against the European Broadcasting Union, an association of national public interest broadcasters in relation to a scheme for the joint acquisition of rights to televise international sports events together with a scheme ("the Eurovision System") for the exchange of programmes between members of the EBU. The case raised far-reaching questions concerning the future of television in the context of the rapidly developing market for commercial television making use of satellite and cable transmission. The combined purchasing power of the national broadcasters was considered by the Commission to restrict competition (i) between EBU members in so far as they transmitted to the same national audiences (as is the case in Belgium, France, Denmark, Germany and the UK) and (ii) in relation to non-EBU members. However, the Commission recognised considerable public interest benefits in the Eurovision System that provided free exchange and access (and particularly benefited the smaller public service broadcasters). The Commission therefore decided to grant a five year exemption subject to a detailed access scheme whereby individual EBU members are required to give third parties access to the acquired rights under specified minimum conditions (*e.g.* relating to live access, specified periods of delay and news access). The Commission also noted developments in the co-operation between *commercial* broadcasters but indicated that it was not yet able to evaluate how those would be assessed under the competition rules. However the *EBU/Eurovision System* decision has been annulled by the Court of First Instance on two fundamental grounds: Cases T–528/93, etc. *Métropole Télévision and others v. Commission* [1996] 5 CMLR 386. The Court held that the criteria for membership of the EBU were too vague and imprecise to enable the Commission to assess whether those criteria were indispensable within the meaning of Article 85(3) and, secondly, that it was a misinterpretation of Article 85(3) to treat fulfilment of a particular public mission as a criterion for granting exemption: see paras. 102 and 123 of the judgment. The Commission has appealed against this decision to the Court of Justice: Case C–320/96P, not yet decided. **4–095**

See also *BSB/Football Association*: joint acquisition of exclusive rights to English Football Association matches for four years by BSkyB (formerly BSB) and the BBC; after the removal of a similar exclusivity for foreign football matches, the Commission stated that exemption was justified to facilitate BSkyB's entry into the market. XXIIIrd Report on Competition Policy (1993), Annex III page 459.

9. JOINT SELLING

4–096 **Joint selling.** Both *ACI* and *Night Services*, para. 4–054, *supra*, contained aspects of joint selling. See also the arrangement between transport operators in HOV–SVZ/MCN, para. 4–074, *supra*.

4–102 **Working partnerships on specific orders**

n. 13. In *Eurotunnel III*, the exemption was renewed for 30 years, on stipulated conditions, in view of the exceptional nature of the tunnel and the need to create a successful environment for its successful use: see § 4–054, *supra*.

CHAPTER 5

CO-OPERATIVE JOINT VENTURES (INCLUDING SPECIALISATION AGREEMENTS)

1. INTRODUCTION

The application of a "rule of reason" to co-operative joint ventures. The Court of First Instance has considered a production joint venture in Case T–17/93 *Matra Hachette v. Commission* [1994] I ECR 595, a challenge by Matra of the exemption given to the *Ford/Volkswagen* JV: see para. 5–077 *infra*. However, there was no discussion of the "rule of reason" as it was common ground that the agreement fell within Article 85(1). **5–007**

Evolving treatment of JVs: impact of the Merger Regulation. The shift in the Commission's treatment of structural co-operative joint ventures so as to approximate to the type of market-based analysis adopted in relation to concentrations falling under the Merger Regulation has continued. See further at para. 5–025, *infra*. **5–008**

The Commission's initiatives on co-operative JVs. The procedure for "fast track" treatment introduced in January 1993 (see n. 15 of the main work) is now well established, both for structural co-operative JVs notified under Article 85(1) and for those originally notified under the Merger Regulation but found not to be concentrative and "converted" to an Article 85 notification. The usual practice in such cases is for a brief preliminary notice inviting third party comments to be published in the *Official Journal* (in the same form as the equivalent notices published under the Merger Regulation). Such a notice, which is not required under the legislation, is sometimes referred to as a *Carlsberg* notice: see para. 11–058 *infra*. Within two months of the completed notification, the Commission endeavours to inform the parties of the results of its initial analysis and whether it has "serious doubts" that the JV is compatible with the competition rules. It may state that it intends to proceed to a formal decision in the case or alternatively issue a comfort letter: see para. **5–009**

11–059 *et seq* of the main work. Where a formal decision is envisaged, the Commission will give the parties a timetable. The issuance of a comfort letter may be accompanied by a Commission press notice or noted in the next annual Report on Competition Policy but in some cases no publicity attends a comfort letter. In 1993 the Commission handled 25 cases under this accelerated procedure (XXIIIrd Report on Competition Policy (1993) point 208); in 1994 there were 18 such cases, of which 12 were dealt with within the two months period (XXIVth Report on Competition Policy (1994) Annex III, point 4.2); and in 1995 there were 15 such cases, of which seven were dealt within two months (Report on the application of the competition rules in the EU (1995), p. 307).

The new Form A/B introduced as from 1 March 1995 (paras. 11–046 *et seq., infra* and Appendix 6, *post*) has institutionalised this approach. Where the parties seek accelerated consideration of a structural JV they are required to provide more detailed market information as specified in Chapter III of the Form A/B (which is modelled on the Form CO for notifying concentrations under the Merger Regulation): see Point D of the Introduction to the Form A/B. The Commission may dispense with the requirement to furnish all the information requested: Regulation 3385/94, Article 3(3) and see also XXIVth Report on Competition Policy (1994), point 114.

The EFTA Surveillance Authority has issued a Notice on the assessment of co-operative joint ventures under Article 53 of the EEA Agreement equivalent to the Commission's Notice: OJ 1994 L186/57.

n. 18. A new Notice on concentrative and cooperative joint ventures (the Interface Notice) was introduced in 1994: App. 10, *post.*

5–009A **Commission review of the Merger Regulation.** The distinction between concentrative and co-operative joint ventures has been one of the most difficult aspects of the EC merger control regime, reflecting the different implementing regulations applicable to concentrative and co-operative joint ventures. Following consultation on its Green Paper on review of the Merger Regulation published at the beginning of 1996, the Commission presented in September 1996 legislative proposals for amending the Merger Regulation (COM (96) 313 Final). Although in part concerned with the treatment of concentrations (see para. 6–005A, *infra*), the Commission also proposes that all full-function joint ventures should be brought under the regime of the Merger Regulation. It is further proposed that insofar as a joint venture leads to co-ordination of competitive behaviour of companies that remain independent, (*e.g.* of the JV parents in the same or related markets), the Commission should be able to apply the criteria of Articles 85(1) and (3) within the procedure of the Merger Regulation. Adoption of this proposal would fundamentally change the way in which full-function joint ventures are assessed. Such joint ventures falling above the thresholds of the Merger Regulation would be subject to a single decision following the procedure, and tight timetable, of that Regulation. As regards joint ventures falling below the thresholds, the concentrative aspects would fall within the exclusive jurisdiction of the Member States whereas the co-ordination aspects would continue to be considered by the Commission as at present.

"Joint ventures". See now the definition of structural co-operative JVs, in the new Form A/B: a JV that "involves an important change in the structure and organisation of the business assets of the parties to the agreement. This may occur because the JV takes over or extends existing activities of the parent companies or because it undertakes new activities on their behalf. Such operations are characterised by the commitment of significant financial, material and/or other non-tangible assets such as intellectual property rights and know how". Annex to Regulation 3385/94, Introduction, Point D: Appendix 6, *post*. **5–012**

n. 20. The Notice in Appendix 30 to the main work has been replaced: see now the Notice on the distinction between concentrative and co-operative joint ventures (the Interface Notice), Appendix 10, *post*. That in turn refers (at § 11) to the extensive definition of "joint control" in the new Notice on the notion of a concentration, Appendix 11, *post*: see at §§ 18–38.

Functional diversity of joint ventures. See at para. 5–012, *supra*. As stated in n. 23, analysis of joint control in Article 85(1) JV cases has traditionally been absent or limited since, for Article 85(1) to apply, only an agreement between undertakings is necessary (*cf.* the Merger Regulation and the definition of joint control in the Concentration Notice, paras. 18–38, Appendix 11, *post*). However, in developing its approach to co-operative JVs, the Commission has recognised that joint control over an identified undertaking is an essential characteristic of a JV as compared to a looser co-operation: "... joint control [is] the pre-requisite of every JV", JV Notice, para. 9. Explicit joint control over an identified undertaking is a more comfortable concept for the Commission than a less defined and focused collaboration between still independent undertakings that could otherwise be expected to compete with one another. Accordingly, decisions on JVs under Article 85 now commonly contain a section establishing the presence of joint control, based on Merger Regulation precepts: *cf.* paras. 6–028 to 6–032, *infra* and see, *e.g.* *Exxon/Shell*, OJ 1994 L144/20, paras. 44–49; *BT/MCI*, OJ 1994 L223/36; [1995] 5 CMLR 285, para. 22 (a 75 per cent/25 per cent JV). **5–013**

2. PRODUCTION JOINT VENTURES

(a) *Generally*

Commission's policy and approach to production JVs **5–019**

n. 32. There should be added to the list the following. **Cases:** *Exxon/Shell*, OJ 1994 L144/20 (production-only JV akin to capacity-sharing for low density and linear, low density polyethylene, exempted for 10 years following modifications); *Night Services*, OJ 1994 L259/20; [1995] 5 CMLR 76, on appeal Cases T–374/94, etc. (JV between the national railways of the UK, France, Belgium, the Netherlands and Germany for passenger rail services via the Channel Tunnel exempted for eight years subject to conditions concerning non-discriminatory supply by parents of necessary facilities to emergent competitors); *Asahi/St. Gobain*, OJ 1994 L354/87 (JV for R&D, production and technology licensing in the new field of bi-layer safety glass products exempted by analogy with Reg. 418/85 after the duration was reduced from 30 years to five years following first commercial production); *Philips/Osram,* OJ 1994 L378/37 [1996] 4 CMLR 48 (input JV for production and supply mainly to parents of lead glass for incandescent and fluorescent lamps which would be sold by parents separately, exempted for 10 years); *BT/MCI*, OJ 1994 L223/36 [1995] 5 CMLR 285 (JV to provide value-added global telecommunications services to business users exempted for seven years; provisions discouraging competition between the parents' basic public telephony in their "home" geographic markets seen as non-ancillary but exempted for five years); *ACI*, OJ 1994 L224/28 (JV limited to joint marketing of international combined rail transport services via the Channel Tunnel exempted for five years with conditions concerning non-discriminatory supply to competitors of rail services/wagons); *Pasteur Mérieux/Merck*, OJ 1994 L309/1 (JV in human vaccines encompassing joint R&D and sale, with certain exclusive distribution agreements for France and Germany between JV and third parties, exempted for 12 years after modifications); *Fujitsu/AMD Semiconductor*, OJ 1994 L341/66 (input JV to design, build and operate a plant in Japan to produce new generation semiconductor wafers for supply mainly to JV parents partly negatively cleared and partly exempted for 20 years); *International Private Satellite Partners*, OJ 1994 L354/75 (JV to provide international business telecommunications services using JV's own satellites negatively cleared); *Bayer/BP Chemicals*, OJ 1994 L174/34 (variation of conditions attached to original exemption of production JV so as to permit deferral of plant closure in light of changed market conditions: *cf.* OJ 1988 L150/35 [1989] 4 CMLR 24). *Premiair*, Report on the application of the competition rules in the EU (1995), page 134 (JV to establish airline to supply flights for tour operators belonging to the JV parent groupings exempted for six years); *Atlas*, OJ 1996 L239/23, and *Phoenix/GlobalOne*, OJ 1996 L239/57 (linked JVs between (a) the French and German public telecommunications operators and (b) that JV and the United States Sprint Corporation, for the purpose of supplying various forms of corporate and global traveller telecommunications services: exemptions granted, subject to conditions, for, respectively, five and seven years from the date when two or more licences for alternative infrastructure come into force in Germany and France). See also Case T–17/93 *Matra Hachette v. Commission*, § 5–077, *infra*, in which the CFI upheld the decision in *Ford/Volkswagen*.

Cases concluded by comfort letter included: *Intrax*, XXIIIrd Report on Competition Policy (1993), point 218 (satellite news-gathering); *Papete-*

ries de Golbey, *ibid.*, point 244 (production only JV for newsprint; originally extended to selling but Commission required JV to be limited to production in light of parties' market positions); *Disma, ibid.*, points 223–224 (JV between airport manager and oil companies to install and operate jet fuel store and transfer system at airport merited exemption); *Electricidade de Portugal/Pego project, ibid.*, point 222 (JV to build, own and operate power station with associated long-term output supply contract merited exemption after modification in exclusivity restrictions in supply contract); *Alenia/Honeywell, ibid.*, point 216 (JV to design, develop, produce and sell space control products for satellites merited negative clearance after deletion of stringent post-termination non-compete obligations); *Philips/Thomson/Sagem, ibid.*, point 215 (JV to design produce and sell active matrix liquid crystal displays merited exemption); and *ATR/BAe*, Report on the application of competition rules in the EU (1995) (JV to pool marketing and sales in regional aircraft; sector and to conduct R&D and feasibility studies into new aircraft). *Aspen (Elf Atochem/Union Carbide Corporation), ibid.*, at p. 123 (JV to produce specialty polyethylene resins and compounds, to be marketed by JV parents as agents, merited exemption); *General Electric Plastics/ BASF, ibid.*, at p. 124 (JV to produce polybutylene terephthalate merited exemption as enabling the parents to invest in increased capacity that would not be warranted by each acting alone); and *PSA/Fiat (Sevel) agreement, ibid.*, at p. 127 (JV to produce a medium-sized commercial vehicle). Further cases are described in the XXIIIrd Report on Competition Policy (1993), Annex III(A); XXIVth Report (1994), Annex II(A) and in the Report on the application of the competition rules in the EU (1995), section 1(A, 2.1).

Materials: Commission Notice on the Distinction between concentrative and co-operative undertakings (the new Interface Notice), Appendix 10, *post*; Commission Notice on the notion of a concentration, Appendix 11, *post*, particularly on identifying joint control: para. 5–012 n. 20, *supra*.

Analytical approach to different types of JV. The new Form A/B includes the following definition of a "structural" co-operative JV, at point D: **5–020**

> "one that involves an important change in the structure and organisation of the business assets of the parties to the agreement. This may occur because the joint venture takes over or extends existing activities of the parent companies or because it undertakes new activities on their behalf. Such operations are characterised by the commitment of significant financial, material and/or non-tangible assets such as intellectual property rights and know-how. Structural joint ventures are therefore normally intended to operate on a medium or long-term basis.
>
> This concept includes certain 'partial function' joint ventures which take over one or several specific functions within the parents' business activity without access to the market, in particular research and development and/or production. It also covers those 'full function' joint ventures which give rise to coordination of the competitive behaviour

of independent undertakings, in particular between the parties to the joint venture or between them and the joint venture".

Therefore a "limited function" JV as well as a "full function" JV may be classified as "structural". See also the new Interface Notice, Appendix 10, *post*, para. 13, for a definition of "full function". For the development of the Commission's analytical approach to structural JVs, see para. 5–025, *infra*.

5–021 **Function of JV.** The Commission has categorised production JVs as "input-product JVs", where the JV supplies its product to the parents for incorporation into a fixed product that they will produce and sell separately; and "final product JVs" where the product manufactured by the JV is ready for distribution to customers: XXIVth Report on Competition Policy (1994), point 164. The distinction may be significant when analysing spill-over effects: para. 5–041, *infra*.

5–022 **Character of JV.** *Exxon/Shell*, OJ 1994 L144/20, concerned a production-only JV which was more akin to capacity-sharing between two competing producers than to a production JV, (*i.e.* it was a final product JV with separate distribution where both parents would have been capable of setting up production facilities independently). The approach of the Commission was accordingly more "hostile" to the arrangements both insofar as the case commenced with the issue of a Statement of Objections (following which the arrangements were notified) and in that it proceeded on the basis of an analytical approach unlike that typically adopted in relation to a structural JV, *e.g.* the parents' loss of decisional autonomy was identified as a relevant consideration in assessing the JV under Article 85(1) and modifications to the arrangements had to be made in order to minimise that effect so far as possible (paras. 39 and 54 of the Decision).

5–023 **Determining Compatibility**

n. 39. For statistics showing the increase in JVs by sectors, see the XXIIIrd Report on Competition Policy (1993), Annex IV, Table 1. Numerically, JV cases have declined since the entry into force of the Merger Regulation which has removed JVs susceptible of being classified as concentrative (and whether or not possessing a "Community dimension") from the ambit of Art. 85.

(b) *Application of Article 85(1) to the agreement to form the JV itself*

5–025 **Generally.** The analysis cautiously identified at paras. 5–026 to 5–029 of the main work is now reasonably consistently adhered to and the doctrine of ancillary restrictions is established (in practice, on the basis of shared jurisprudence with the Merger Regulation). A more economically realistic approach to the concepts of potential competition, foreclosure effect and "appreciable effect" continues in evidence. Equally, there continues to be an equation in such cases of the Article 85(3) prohibition test (that no substantial elimination of competition be involved) with the corresponding Merger Regulation test (that no creation or strengthening of a dominant position likely significantly to impede effective competition be involved). This has enabled the Commission to take exemption decisions or give Article 85(3) comfort letters in JV cases involving high individual market shares and oligopolistic market structures: see XXIVth Report on Competition Policy (1994), points 163–177.

Restriction of competition (as between the parents and as between any parent and the JV). The Commission has accordingly required the parties to change the scope of a production JV so as to exclude distribution from its activities where that carried a risk of co-ordination of competitive behaviour and market sharing between the parties: *Papeteries de Golbey*, XXIIIrd Report on Competition Policy (1993), point 244 (comfort letter issued in respect of amended JV). See also "Spillover", para. 5–041, *infra*. It is now settled law in relation to concentrative JVs under the Merger Regulation that provided no more than one of the JV parents remains in actual or potential competition with the JV then (a) that does not operate to render the JV co-operative rather than concentrative (contrary to early case law under the Merger Regulation); and (b) it will be expected that co-ordination will or may occur between that parent and the JV and any agreement to that effect will in principle be regarded as an ancillary restriction. It would seem rational that this principle should also apply to assessment of structural JVs under Article 85; however, it is not consistently so applied by the Commission, *e.g. Fujitsu/AMD Semiconductor*, OJ 1994 L341/66 at para. 30. **5–035**

n. 60. See also *BT/MCI*, OJ 1994 L223/36 [1995] 5 CMLR 285, where the Commission held that the agreement whereby BT acquired a 20 per cent shareholding was drafted in such a way as to prevent the possibility of its exercising influence or control.

Loss of parents' decisional autonomy in JV field **5–038**

n. 64. But note *Exxon/Shell*, OJ 1994 L144/20, where the limited function of the JV led the Commission to regard this issue as relevant:

> "Although the Court of Justice has not yet taken a specific position on joint ventures, the Commission has to bear in mind the central rôle of the independence of business operators with respect to their business decisions which must not be subject to reciprocal influence" (§ 54).

5–039 **Foreclosure effects on third parties as a result of the JV**

n. 69. See also *Auditel*, 1993 OJ L306/50 [1995] 5 CMLR 719 (on appeal Case T–66/94), where exemption was refused to an agreement between Italian public and private TV channels to take audience measurement figures exclusively from the JV that they owned: this restriction placed the JV in a *de facto* monopoly position. (See also *Auditel v. Commission*; [1995] II ECR 239: order permitting complainant to intervene in support of the Commission.)

5–040A **Parent in a special or dominant position.** The process of liberalisation of the various telecommunications markets in the E.U. has involved the Commission in reviewing several JVs that involve the incumbent monopolist telecommunications operator (TO) linking up with a partner in order to tackle particular sub-markets or adjacent markets. In such cases, "... on top of the traditional analysis of co-operative joint ventures under the competition rules, the Commission must examine whether the still existing special and/or exclusive rights of the TO in question cause its participation in the joint venture company to place the latter in an unjustifiably favourable position *vis-à-vis* competitors": XXIIIrd Report on Competition Policy (1993), point 218. Key concerns in such cases are the scope for cross-subsidy and the potential for withholding access to essential network facilities by third parties wishing to compete. See *Intrax*, XXIIIrd Report, point 218 (Netherlands-based satellite news-gathering service: comfort letter giving negative clearance); *BT/MCI*, OJ 1994 L223/36 [1995] 5 CMLR 285 (JV to market new, global value-added telecommunications services, exempted for seven years) where assurances were given as to non-discriminatory access by third parties; *Atlas*, OJ 1996 239/23 (JV in global telecommunications services for business between France Télécom and Deutsche Telekom) and *Phoenix/Global-One*, OJ 1996 L239/57 (a limited JV between Atlas and the US telecommunications company, Sprint). This response by the Commission followed changes made to the agreements and assurances given by the French and German governments regarding the liberalisation of infrastructure to enable the provision of competing services. See also the cases concerning the Channel Tunnel: para. 5–042, *infra*

5–041 **"Spillover" effect.** The Commission has set out a more analytical approach to spillover effect in its XXIVth Report on Competition Policy (1994) at point 165:

> "In the cases involving input joint ventures decided by the Commission, the spill-over effects on the final product market depended principally on two factors: the importance of the jointly produced input in the cost of the final product (ratio common cost/total final cost) and the market position of the parents. The higher the common cost and the combined market share of the parents in the final product market, the greater the risk of spill-over effects is likely to be. In the case of final product joint

ventures, the commonality of costs and proximity of the parents' co-operation to the final product market are such that appreciable spill-over effects are very likely to occur (for instance by alignment of sales prices), in particular where the parties have important market shares or operate in an oligopolistic market."

For application of this approach see, *e.g. Exxon/Shell, supra* (a final product JV) at para. 63; *cf. Philips/Osram,* OJ 1994 L378/37 [1996] 4 CMLR 48 (input product JV), at para. 18. For the special spillover concerns posed by strategic alliances, see para. 5–131B, *infra.*

n. 74. In *Electrolux/AEG*, OJ 1993 C269/4 [1994] 4 CMLR 112, specialisation agreements between major manufacturers of domestic appliances originally contained provisions for reciprocal board representation. The Commission noted that this could have given each party strategic information and the potential to influence the other's entire competitive behaviour. After those provisions were deleted in the course of the proceedings the Commission published an Art. 19(3) notice indicating its intention to take a favourable view of the agreements.

5–042 **Parallel interlocking JVs (network effect).** See *Night Services*, OJ 1994 L259/20 [1995] 5 CMLR 76: five public railway undertakings agreed to participate, in varying degrees, in JVs for the operation of goods and passenger transport services, to market night passenger trains on four routes between the United Kingdom and continental Europe. The Commission granted a conditional exemption for a transitional period of eight years to the agreements. Similar issues were raised in *ACI*, OJ 1994 L224/28, in which the JV was granted conditional exemption for five years. Both cases involved the creation of a network of JVs for transport services via the Channel Tunnel. The Commission remarked in its XXIVth Report on Competition Policy (1994), point 187, that such networks of JVs can have a restrictive effect on competition by intensifying "the effects of individual JVs on the policy of the parent undertakings on the market position of third parties". According to the Commission, competition between the parent undertakings is reduced as a result of closer ties between them formed by each new JV. However, regard was had by the Commission in granting exemption in these cases to the introduction of new, high quality rail services through the Channel Tunnel as a competitive alternative to the existing cross-Channel sea and air services.

(c) *Exemption of JVs under Article 85(3)*

5–045 **Individual exemption for production JVs.** In its XXIVth Report on Competition Policy (1994), point 155, the Commission set out its general attitude to co-operative JVs:

"In line with the general principles set out in its notice concerning the assessment of co-operative joint ventures pursuant to Article 85, the Commission is generally favourable to R&D and production joint ventures which promote the development and production of *new* products or services which did not exist before or which improve the quality of existing products and thus increase the output on the market and the choices available to consumers. Such joint ventures create new competition which normally outweighs possible disadvantages for competition overall, provided there remains effective competition from other competitors on the market, even if the market is characterised by an oligopolistic structure."

Significantly, in 1994 the Commission by formal decisions gave individual exemption to a number of JVs between important competitors in oligopolistic markets, *e.g. Philips/Osram, supra* (parents had 66 per cent market share); see also *Exxon/Shell, supra*; *Pasteur Mérieux/Merck*, OJ 1994 L309/1.

5–046 **Substantial elimination of competition.** *Exxon/Shell, supra*, concerned an oligopolistic market (the thermoplastics LdPE and LLdPE) in which the parties had a combined market share of 22 per cent. Nonetheless, the Commission concluded that the size of the remaining competitors "guarantees that workable competition is not eliminated" and, referring to the JV Notice and the fact that the 20 per cent threshold was only marginally exceeded, concluded that an exemption was possible (para. 81).

n. 91. Further examples of the Art. 85(3) prohibition test (whether the agreement in question may lead to a substantial elimination of competition) being taken to equate to the Merger Regulation test (whether a dominant position likely to significantly impede effective competition will be created or strengthened) are: *Philips/Thomson/Sagem*, XXIIIrd Report on Competition Policy (1993), point 215; *Pasteur-Mérieux/Merck, supra* (a fast-track case converted to Art. 85 from the Merger Regulation where Merger Regulation terminology is plainly used as well as a robust, merger-type analysis: see §§ 95–101).

5–048 **Improvements in competitive structure.** The Commission has now stated that it is "generally favourable" to JVs that relate to the development and production of entirely new products "because they create new competition and additional output on the market": XXIVth Report on Competition Policy (1994), point 177.

5–049 **Advanced technology products.** In *Pasteur-Mérieux/Merck, supra*, the Commission in exempting took account of the fact that the JV would be the first entity with access to the full range of antigens necessary to develop new generation multivalent vaccines so accelerating the availability of such vaccines in Europe: XXIVth Report on Competition Policy (1994), point 174.

n. 3. See also *Philips/Thomson/Sagem*, XXIIIrd Report on Competition Policy (1993), point 215: the market was worldwide with strong competition from Japanese producers. The Commission also relied on the sophisticated nature of the purchasers as a relevant consideration that justified exemption.

Joint distribution and sale. Although it is no longer hostile to the notion of a JV that extends to distribution and sale, when the Commission indicates that such a "full function" JV gives rise to "serious doubts" then removal of the distribution and sales elements, thereby converting the JV to a "limited function", may enable exemption to be granted under Article 85(3): see *Papeteries de Golbey*, XXIIIrd Report on Competition Policy (1993), point 244. **5–051**

n. 9. See also *Philips/Thomson/Sagem*, *supra* (comfort letter indicating exemption); *Alenia/Honeywell*, XXIIIrd Report on Competition Policy (1993), point 216 (comfort letter indicating negative clearance).

Indispensability. See the lengthy discussion in *Pasteur-Mérieux/Merck*, OJ 1994 L309/1, at paras. 91–94, in particular as regards distribution by the JV of the product of its R&D where Merck did not have its own Europe-wide distribution network and joint distribution was held to facilitate co-operation on R&D. **5–052**

Duration and conditions. In *Asahi/St. Gobain*, OJ 1994 L354/87 (an R&D plus production and licensing JV) in the light of the parties' combined position holding (over 30 per cent of the world market for vehicle safety glass), the Commission limited exemption to a period expiring five years after the earlier of 2005 or first commercial production (by analogy with Articles 3(1) and (2) of Regulation 418/85 which could not apply due to the market share thresholds being exceeded). Note also the reporting obligations imposed as a condition of exemption in *Exxon/Shell*, OJ 1994 L144/20. **5–053**

(d) *Application of Articles 85(1) and 85(3) to specific restrictions*

Specific restrictions (including ancillary restrictions). The Commission has clarified its approach in its XXIVth Report on Competition Policy (1994) at point 166: **5–054**

> "Ancillary restrictions are restrictions only imposed on the parties or the joint venture (not on third parties) which are objectively necessary for the successful functioning of the joint venture and thus by their very nature inherent in the operation concerned (*e.g.* non-compete obligation of the parents towards their joint venture). Such ancillary

restrictions are not assessed separately under Article 85(1) of the Treaty if the joint venture itself does not infringe Article 85(1) or is exempted under Article 85(3). While ancillary restrictions are normally only accepted for a limited period of time, in the context of joint ventures they are usually allowed for the whole duration of the joint venture."

5–055 **Restrictions falling within Article 85(1).** On non-compete restrictions, see at para. 5–054, *supra*.

n. 16. See also *Electricidade de Portugal/Pego project*, XXIIIrd Report on Competition Policy (1993), point 222, where the Commission required substantial amendment of the proposed 28 year exclusive supply obligation in favour of one of the parents of a JV to purchase and operate a power station, before issuing a comfort letter indicating exemption under Art. 85(3).

5–056 **Application of Article 85(3).** A non-compete restriction in respect of the JV field of activity accepted by the parents for the life of the JV will be regarded as ancillary and so share the fate of the JV itself. In *BT/MCI*, OJ 1994 L223/36 [1995] 5 CMLR 285, the arrangements included financial disincentives to either parent competing in basic public telephony in the other parent's "home" market (*i.e.* for MCI the Americas and for BT the rest of the world). However, that was not a JV activity and the provision therefore could not be regarded as an ancillary restriction but was granted individual exemption for five years.

n. 19 and **n. 23.** In *Fujitsu/AMD Semiconductor*, OJ 1994 L341/66, a two year post-termination, non-compete covenant that applied if either party sold its interest in the first 10 years of the JV was regarded as ancillary. *Cf. Alenia/Honeywell,* XXIIIrd Report on Competition Policy (1993), point 216, where certain "very stringent" post-termination non-compete obligations which were not regarded as ancillary to the JV (itself considered suitable for negative clearance) had to be modified or deleted. In *Pasteur-Mérieux/Merck*, OJ 1994 L309/1, Merck accepted a post-termination restriction on supplying or licensing to a third party a JV product or a competing product for five years (para. 41). This restriction was not dealt with in the legal analysis or operative parts of the Decision.

5–060 **Further ancillary restrictions.** Other examples of restrictions accepted as ancillary are: obligation on the parents to source all or most of their requirements from the JV (*BT/MCI*, *supra*; *Philips/Osram*, OJ 1994 L378/37 [1996] 4 CMLR 48); requirement on production JV to treat parents preferentially in case of capacity shortage (*Philips/Osram*); post JV restriction on assigning jointly-developed intellectual property rights without the other party's consent (*Fujitsu/AMD Semiconductor, supra*);

"most favoured nation" obligation imposed on JV for parents' benefit (*International Private Satellite Partners*, OJ 1994 L354/75); preference to be given by JV to parents as suppliers in relation to certain invitations to tender to the JV (*International Private Satellite Partners*). In *Pasteur-Mérieux/Merck*, each parent accepted a restriction on soliciting JV employees for three years after disposal of its JV interest or termination of the JV but the Decision does not clarify the status of such a restriction. See also *Fujitsu/AMD Semiconductor* (two year non-solicitation covenant). In principle, a non-solicitation restriction should not fall within Article 85(1) unless the circumstances are such that it is tantamount to a form of non-compete covenant.

As regards a territorial restriction on active sales, see *Fujitsu/AMD Semiconductor*: five year restriction granted exemption along with the JV agreement.

Appreciable effect. See also *International Private Satellite Partners, supra*, para. 60 (exclusivity rights for Austria and Italy granted to one of the partners held to be non-appreciable). In *BT/MCI, supra*, the Commission concluded that, given the current state of development of the overall market for telecommunications, restrictions affecting "the Americas" would produce no appreciable effect in the EEA. **5–062**

(e) *Some leading JV cases*

Exemption of JV for development and production (but not marketing) between major competitors: *Ford/Volkswagen* **5–074**

Ford/Volkswagen is reported at OJ 1993 L20/14 [1993] 5 CMLR 617. See also *PSA/Fiat (Sevel) agreement*, Report on the application of competition rules in the EU (1995), at p. 127.

***Ford/Volkswagen:* conditions for exemption**. The challenge by Matra to the Commission decision was rejected by the Court of First Instance, which held that the Commission's reasoning as regards the grant of exemption was not vitiated by error: Case T–17/93 *Matra Hachette v. Commission* [1994] II ECR 595. **5–077**

3. R&D JOINT VENTURES

(a) *Generally*

Introduction. Relatively few "pure R&D" joint ventures are established compared to the number of fuller function JVs (R&D plus production or **5–087**

R&D and production through to sales). The analysis in Part Two of this Chapter, as up-dated above, should therefore be consulted.

5–088 **R&D agreements**

n. 59. There have been no Decisions on pure R&D joint ventures since January 1993. However, some JVs notified to the Commission were exempted only after they had been amended to reduce the significance of the non-R&D elements. See *Asahi/St. Gobain*, OJ 1994 L354/87 (JV for bi-layer automotive safety glass that covered both R&D and a period for joint exploitation of the results: agreement amended to expire five years after commercial production commenced, and then granted exemption by analogy with Reg. 418/85); *Pasteur-Mérieux/Merck*, OJ 1994 L309/1 (JV that covered R&D and distribution of human vaccines, but not production which was to be undertaken by the parents who were to supply the product at cost to the JV for onward sale: exemption for 12 years after the parties agreed to grant distribution and manufacturing rights to third parties for Germany and France).

(b) *Application of Article 85(1)*

5–094 **Co-operation extending downstream of R&D.** In *Pasteur-Mérieux/Merck, supra*, a JV for human vaccines that encompassed joint distribution of products manufactured by the parents on the basis of R&D by the JV was granted exemption although the parents had very high market shares in a number of relevant product markets. The Commission found that distribution was closely linked to development, for example as regards pharmacovigilance (the need to observe unexpected effects of vaccination so that any adverse health risks can be avoided). However, in this case it was also relevant that Merck did not already have a developed distribution network in Europe outside Germany.

(c) *Individual Exemption under Article 85(3)*

5–106 **Generally**

n. 9. See also *Asahi/St. Gobain*, OJ 1994 L354/87: 30 year agreement amended to expire in effect five years after commercial production commenced, in order to gain exemption.

(e) *Regulation 418/85*

5–121 **In general.** Regulation 418/85 applies, with necessary modifications, to agreements falling within Article 53(1) of the EEA Agreement: Annex XIV, point 7, to the EEA Agreement.

The agreements covered **5–122**

n. 28. See *Co-operation agreements between Peugeot and Fiat involving the Sevel joint venture*, XXIIIrd Report on Competition Policy (1993), point 227: the agreement for joint production of multi-purpose vehicles and light commercial vehicles was notified for individual exemption but found by the Commission to come within Reg. 418/85.

3A. STRATEGIC ALLIANCES

5–131A **Strategic alliances.** The term "strategic alliances" is often used by the parties themselves to cover transactions ranging from partial concentrations or focused joint ventures to wider-ranging alliances. The Commission recognises that "strategic alliances can be co-operative arrangements of varying scope involving the creation of several contractual and structural links, such as the creation of a joint venture specialisation in certain markets, joint R&D, technology transfer, cross supply agreements, commitments to co-operate in other fields in the future and the acquisition of cross-shareholdings": XXIVth Report on Competition Policy (1994), point 156. Such arrangements are a particular feature of the telecommunications sector, prompted by the liberalisation of national regimes, the international potential and the convergence or complementarity of information technologies, media and telecommunications. The Commission has described the treatment of these alliances as "one of the major challenges for EU competition policy in recent years": XXVth Report on Competition Policy (1995), point 55.

5–131B **The Commission's approach.** Strategic alliances between actual or potential competitors give rise to particular spillover concerns because they may create a tendency for the parties to seek to co-operate rather than to compete in general. However, alliances can lead to the creation of new services, reductions in costs, and establishment of trans-European networks; and they may be essential to enable the participants to remain competitive in a dynamic, global market. The Commission attempts to assess those aspects and has shown particular concern that the creation of an alliance does not unduly strengthen the position of participant telecommunications operators against competitors in their domestic market. See *BT/MCI* OJ 1994 L223/36 [1995] 5 CMLR 285 (strategic alliance involving creation of a JV to develop and market international value-added telecommunications services for large multinational companies and a reciprocal territorial non-compete clause; exemption granted for seven years in respect of the JV itself and five years in respect of the territorial non-compete clause); and *Atlas*, OJ 1996 L239/23 and *Phoenix/GlobalOne*, OJ 1996 L239/57 (linked JVs and related distribution and agency arrangements involving France Télécom, Deutsche Telekom and Sprint Corporation; after the agreements were modified exemptions were granted for, respectively, five and seven years subject to a series of conditions, including non-discriminatory access, restrictions on cross-subsidies and the divestiture by France Télécom of its corporate service provider in Germany; moreover, the commencement of the period of exemption was contingent upon the further liberalisation of the telecommunications markets which the French and German governments had undertaken to carry out). For the arrangements agreed between airlines as part of the restructuring of European air transport, see XXVth Report on Competition Policy (1995), point 76 and *LH/SAS*, OJ 1996 L54/28; [1996] 4 CMLR 845 (exemption granted for the establishment of an integrated air transport system on routes between Scandinavia and Germany, subject to conditions to ease market entry for competitors), on appeal Case T–37/96 *Luftfartsfunktionaererne v. Commission*. For decisions on strategic alliances in other fields, see *Banque Nationale de Paris/Dresdner Bank*, OJ 1996 L188/37 (exemption for 10 years to co-operation agreement between fourth largest French bank and second largest German bank, that includes exchange of information and joint EDP developments on their home markets and joint activity in third country markets) and *Olivetti/Digital*, OJ 1994 L309/24 (strategic alliance involving co-operation to develop and promote operating systems and software given negative clearance; linked requirements purchasing contract exempted for four years; minority stake held by Digital in Olivetti negatively cleared). See paras. 6–164 *et seq*. of the main work for the relevant principles under Article 85 on minority stakes.

4. SPECIALISATION AGREEMENTS

(b) *Application of Article 85(1)*

5–135 **Generally**

n. 76. See also *Electrolux/AEG*, OJ 1993 C269/4 [1994] 4 CMLR 112 (Art. 19(3) Notice concerning agreements for specialisation of production and reciprocal supply of washing machines and dishwashers by major manufacturers; the agreements were amended in the course of the proceedings to delete provisions for reciprocal board representation).

The conditions for exemption in *Bayer/BP Chemicals*, OJ 1988 L150/35; [1989] 4 CMLR 24, were modified in the light of change in demand trends for polyethylene: OJ 1994 L174/34.

(e) *Regulation 417/85*

5–155 **In general.** Regulation 417/85 applies, with necessary modifications, to agreements falling within Article 53(1) of the EEA Agreement: Annex XIV, point 6, to the EEA Agreement.

CHAPTER 6

MERGERS AND ACQUISITIONS

1. INTRODUCTION

The EC and ECSC Treaties. At the end of 1994 the responsibilities of the Merger Task Force (see para. 6–100 of the main work) were extended with the addition of mergers falling within the scope of the ECSC Treaty. As a result the administration of mergers falling under both EC and ECSC jurisdictions has been simplified. **6–001**

Commission Implementing Regulation and guidelines. At the end of 1994, the Commission adopted various new measures. The Commission measures related to the Merger Regulation are now as follows: **6–003**

(i) *The revised Implementing Regulation.* The Commission has adopted a revised Implementing Regulation, Regulation 3384/94: see Appendix 9, *post.* The new Regulation, which entered into force on 1 March 1995, replaces Regulation 2367/90. It clarifies certain ambiguities in the old text and has introduced procedural changes regarding the calculation of deadlines, material changes in facts relating to notifications, and the rights of parties to be heard in the course of proceedings. It has also introduced a time limit for the submission of undertakings by parties to resolve competition problems identified by the Commission. The new Regulation includes a revised version of the questionnaire form—Form CO—which must be answered by parties notifying a concentration with a Community dimension to the Commission.

(ii) *The revised Interface Notice.* The Commission has adopted a revised Notice on the distinction between concentrative and co-operative joint venture undertakings: see Appendix 10, *post.* The Notice provides guidance as to how the Commission applies the Merger Regulation to joint ventures.

(iii) *The Concentration Notice.* The purpose of this new Notice is to provide guidance as to how the Commission interprets the notion of a concentration under Article 3 of the Regulation: see Appendix 11, *post*.

(iv) *The Undertakings Concerned Notice*. The purpose of this new Notice is to clarify the Commission's interpretation of the notion of undertakings concerned under Articles 1 and 5 of the Merger Regulation: see Appendix 12, *post*.

(v) *The Turnover Notice*. The purpose of this new Notice is to expand upon the text of Articles 1 and 5 of the Merger Regulation and in so doing elucidate certain procedural and practical questions which have caused doubt or difficulty: see Appendix 13, *post*.

(vi) *The Ancillary Restrictions Notice*. The Commission's 1990 Notice, providing guidelines on restrictions which are considered to be ancillary to concentrations, has not been revised: see Appendix 29 to the main work.

6–004 **Interpretative notes and decided cases.** The new and revised Notices are based on the experience gained by the Commission in applying the Merger Regulation since it came into force on 21 September 1990. They follow a report on the implementation of the Merger Regulation, sent to the Council on 28 July 1993 (COM (93) 385 final), in which the Commission undertook to make changes to its own procedures to improve efficiency, clarity and legal certainty, pending the formal review (see para. 6–005A, *infra*) in 1996. The changes were adopted by the Commission on 21 December 1994 and entered into force on 1 March 1995. Further guidance on the interpretation of the Merger Regulation can be obtained from the Commission's decisions in the considerable number of cases notified under the Merger Regulation. An updated list of cases notified under the Merger Regulation is provided in Table [D] of the Table of Cases.

n. 10. These interpretative statements are also reproduced in a booklet, *Merger control law in the European Union*, published by the Commission in 1995, which contains the text of the Merger Regulation, the revised Implementing Regulation and all the Notices.

n. 11. In May 1996 the Commission changed its practice for the dissemination of merger decisions. Non-confidential versions of merger decisions are now available from the Office for Official Publications of the European Communities (and in the United Kingdom from HMSO), and in electronic form through the Community's CELEX database. They are also collected in *EEC Merger Control Reporter* (Kluwer, 1991 and supp.). Summaries of the principal cases are included in the Commission's annual Reports on Competition Policy: see XXIInd Report (1992), points 7 to 15 and 221 to 264; XXIIIrd Report (1993), points 245 to 326 and 356a to 356b; XXIVth Report (1994), points 261 to 336, 484 to 489 and Annex II.D(2). The revised format of the XXVth Report (1995) gives a more selective summary at points 131–44, but see the appended Report on the application of the competition rules in the EU, section III.A. For textbooks, see now Cook and Kerse, *EC Merger Control* (Sweet & Maxwell, 2nd ed. 1996).

6–004A **The EEA regime.** For the allocation of jurisdiction over mergers under the EEA Agreement, see para. 6–142 of the main work. The Merger Regulation, with necessary adaptations, has effect within the EEA, pursuant to Article 60 and Annex XIV to the EEA Agreement. Chapter XIV of Protocol 4 to the EFTA Surveillance Agreement contains provisions equivalent to the original Implementing Regulation 2367/90: OJ 1994 L344/12 [1994] 4 CMLR 180, *Encyclopaedia of European Union Law (Constitutional Texts)*, Vol. 5, paras. 82.1651 *et seq.* Although Chapter XIV has not been amended to reflect Regulation 3384/94, the revised Form CO may be used: see Articles 2(1), 3(1). The EFTA Surveillance Authority issued Notices on Ancillary Restrictions and on Concentrative and Co-operative Operations corresponding to those of the Commission but those Notices have not been revised: [1994] 4 CMLR 295, 304. However, as of 1 September 1996, the EFTA Surveillance Authority had not had any merger cases.

6–005A **Commission review of the Merger Regulation.** Following consultation on its Green Paper on the review of the Merger Regulation (COM (96) 19 final), the Commission adopted in September 1996 a legislative proposal which was presented to the Council (COM(96) 313 final). The Commission's proposal may be summarised as follows:

(i) *Community dimension thresholds.* The Commission suggests a dual approach. The present worldwide threshold of 5,000 million ECU and Community-wide threshold of 250 million ECU should be reduced, respectively, to 3,000 million ECU and 150 million ECU. Those thresholds, however, would be "intermediate" levels. Below those levels but above thresholds of 2,000 million ECU and 100 million ECU, the Commission would have exclusive jurisdiction if the concentration would otherwise be subject to notification to three or more national competition authorities. This would go some way to meet the difficulty faced by parties that presently have to notify several Member State authorities under national merger control rules (see para. 6–141 of the main work).

(ii) *Joint Ventures.* The distinction between concentrative and co-operative joint ventures has been one of the more difficult aspects of the EC merger control regime (see para. 6–025 of the main work). These difficulties reflect the different implementing regulations applicable to concentrative and co-operative joint ventures. The Commission therefore proposes that all full-function joint ventures (whether concentrative or co-operative) should be subject to the Merger Regulation. Full-function joint ventures above the Regulation's thresholds would fall within the exclusive jurisdiction of the Commission. Below those thresholds, the concentrative aspects of full-function joint ventures would fall within the jurisdiction of the Member States but the treatment of the co-operative aspects would be unchanged.

(iii) *Procedural improvements.* A number of other procedural changes are proposed. These include:

- Clarification and improvements to the procedures for referring jurisdiction to and from Member States under Articles 9 and 22;
- Clarification of the Regulation to reflect the Commission's practice of accepting commitments from notifying parties during the initial investigation period (see para. 6–113 of the main work), so avoiding the cost and delay of a "serious doubts" investigation;
- Simplification of the method of calculating turnover for banks and other financial institutions and the geographic allocation of this turnover: *cf.* para. 6–056 of the main work.

2. CONCENTRATIONS

(a) *Mergers and acquisitions of control*

6–006 **In general.** The notion of a "concentration" is considered in some detail in the new Concentration Notice. The notion of an "undertaking" is discussed in the new Undertakings Concerned Notice. The concept of acquiring "parts" of an undertaking can extend to merely acquiring specific assets which in themselves could constitute a business, *e.g.* in certain cases brands or licences to which a market turnover can clearly be attributed (Undertakings Concerned Notice, point 14 and footnote 15).

6–007 **Mergers.** The concept of a "merger" within the meaning of Article 3(1)(a) is discussed at point 7 of the Concentration Notice. In *RTZ/CRA* (Case IV/M.660, Decision of 7 December 1995) the parties established a dual listed company structure, involving special shares and cross-guarantees; the Commission concluded that the proposed structure of ownership and control constituted a merger according to Article 3(1)(a).

6–008 **Acquisitions of control: "decisive influence".** The concept of control is discussed further at points 8 *et seq.* of the Concentration Notice.

6–009 **Rights not conferring decisive influence: options, loans**

n. 17. In *British Airways/TAT*, the Commission held that when deciding whether there was a situation of joint or sole control it should not take account of a 49.9 per cent shareholder's option to purchase the outstanding shares, nor of a put option exercisable by the other shareholder some 4½ years later, since it was not certain whether these options would be exercised. This was upheld by the CFI in Case T–2/93 *Air France v. Commission* [1994] II ECR 323 §§ 70–72. For further observations on options to purchase or convert shares, see point 15 of the new Concentration Notice. See also § 6–032A, *infra*, regarding joint venture structures involving put and call options indicating joint control for a limited period only.

Control and role of the State. The prerogatives exercised by a State (including regional or local authorities and other emanations of the State) acting as a public authority rather than as a shareholder, in so far as they are limited to the protection of the public interest, do not constitute control within the Merger Regulation. This is on the basis that such prerogatives have neither the aim nor the effect of enabling the State to exercise decisive influence over the activity of the undertaking. This was considered by the Commission in *Tractebel/Synatom* (Case IV/M.466, Decision of 30 June 1994) and *Tractebel/Distrigaz* II (Case IV/M.493, Decision of 1 September 1994); see also Concentration Notice, point 17. A State or State-controlled undertaking may, however, acquire decisive influence over the activity of another undertaking through the acquisition of voting rights, contractual rights or other means. In this regard State-owned undertakings are treated in exactly the same way as privately-owned undertakings. In situations where a State-owned company merges with or acquires control of another company controlled by the same State, the issue arises whether these should be treated as concentrations or merely public sector group reorganisations. The Commission's practice in this regard is to look not at ultimate legal ownership (the State) but rather at whether the companies are part of the same industrial holding (economic group or undertaking); see *SGS/Thomson* (Case IV/M.216, Decision of 22 February 1993) and points 55 to 56 of the Undertakings Concerned Notice. **6–009A**

(b) *Nature of control*

Sole control and joint control. The concepts of sole control and joint control are discussed further at points 12 *et seq.* of the Concentration Notice. **6–010**

Changes in the nature of control. Commission practice has continued to confirm that any durable structural change in the quality of control of an undertaking will give rise to a concentration. The Undertakings Concerned Notice (at points 30 to 32) refers to *ICI/Tioxide* as an example of a change in the nature of control from joint control to sole control. The Notice also refers (at points 33 to 45) to changes in shareholdings in cases **6–011**

of joint control of an existing joint venture undertaking. The Notice emphasises that each case must be examined on its facts with a view to determining whether the operation leads to a change in the quality of control. The Notice distinguishes between three circumstances:

(i) *Reduction in the number of shareholders leading to passage from joint to sole control.* Where the number of shareholders is reduced, there may be passage from joint control to sole control.

(ii) *Reduction in the number of shareholders not leading to passage from joint to sole control.* If an operation involves a reduction in the number of shareholders having joint control, without leading to a passage from joint control to sole control, the Commission will normally presume there not to be a change in the quality of control. However, if there is a significant change in the rights enjoyed by the shareholders, this may represent a change in the quality of control. In *Avesta II* (Case IV/M.452, Decision of 9 June 1994) the number of joint controlling shareholders decreased from four to three, leading to one of these shareholders, British Steel, acquiring negative veto rights (which it had not previously enjoyed). This acquisition of full veto rights, although falling short of *de facto* sole control, was considered by the Commission to represent a change in the quality of control. Subsequently, in *Avesta III* (Case IV/M.504, Decision of 20 October 1994) the Commission cleared an increase in British Steel's shareholding in circumstances which gave it sole control.

(iii) *Any other changes in the composition of the shareholding.* The Commission presumes that an operation will lead to a change in the quality of control if—irrespective of whether the number of shareholders decreases, increases or remains the same—it results in one or more shareholders acquiring control. This may arise if a new shareholder acquires a controlling interest, a non-controlling shareholder acquires a controlling interest, or a shareholder transfers its controlling interest to a third party. The Commission takes the view that any such operation leads to a change in the nature of control of the whole joint venture, and therefore a concentration, rather than being comparable to the simple acquisition of part of a business. The undertakings concerned in such cases are the controlling shareholders (both existing and new) and the joint venture undertaking itself. An example of such a case is *Synthomer/Yule Catto* (Case IV/M.376, Decision of 22 October 1993) in which one of the two shareholders sold its shareholding in the joint venture company to a third party. See also *GKN/Brambles/Leto Recycling* (Case IV/M.448, Decision of 7 June 1994) and *Montedison/Groupe Vernes/SCI* (Case IV/M.630, Decision of 8 December 1995). *Nordic Capital/Transpool* (Case IV/M.625, Decision of 23 August 1995) is an example of a change from joint control by two parties to joint control by three parties. Transpool had previously been jointly controlled by two shareholders, KF and Fortos. Under the operation, Nordic Capital (and Electra) injected new capital into Transpool in the form of subordinated loan stock convertible into a 50 per cent shareholding within a year, an option which these new investors intended to exercise. The new investors also had board representation from the outset and all indications were that they would take a long term interest in Transpool. The Commission therefore considered that a new control structure had been established on a lasting basis such that the resulting JV had a concentrative character.

(c) *Minority shareholdings*

Minority shareholdings **6–012**

n. 23. See now the Concentration Notice, point 14.

Sole control through minority shareholding. In *Société Générale de Belgique/Générale de Banque* (Case IV/M.343, Decision of 3 August 1993) the Commission considered an increase in SGB's shareholding from 20.94 per cent to 25.96 per cent where over half the shares in Générale de Banque were held by small investors. At the previous three annual general meetings SGB's stake of 20.94 per cent had represented between 43 and 47 per cent of the votes present or represented. On this basis the Commission concluded that a holding of 25.96 per cent would give SGB more than half the votes present or represented at future general meetings, so concluding that the increase in shareholding conferred sole control. In *Jefferson Smurfit/Munksjo* (Case IV/M.613, Decision of 31 July 1995) the Commission concluded that a 29 per cent shareholding conferred sole control of the particular publicly listed company, taking account of shareholder attendances at previous annual general meetings. In *Ford/Hertz* (Case IV/M.397, Decision of 7 March 1994) the Commission considered that Ford's 49 per cent stake in Hertz, when combined with the fact that Ford had the unconditional right to obtain a majority on the board of Hertz, conferred *de facto* sole control (notwithstanding that in practice Ford had only appointed four of the nine directors on the board). Accordingly, an increase in Ford's shareholding to 54 per cent did not bring about a change in control. **6–013**

n. 27. In Case T–83/92 *Zunis Holding and Others v. Commission* [1993] II ECR 1169 [1994] 5 CMLR 154, the CFI held that the application was inadmissible. The decision was upheld by the ECJ in Case C–480/93P [1996] I ECR 1 [1996] 5 CMLR 219.

(d) *Operations involving two or more concentrations*

In general. Operations involving two or more concentrations are considered in the Undertakings Concerned Notice. This considers joint **6–016**

acquisitions with a view to demerger as well as asset swaps and joint venture break-ups (referring to the *Solvay-Laporte/Interox* decision, *cf.* para. 6–020 of the main work). The Concentration Notice (at point 16) also refers to operations involving the acquisition of joint control of one part of an undertaking and sole control of another part, confirming that in principal these should be regarded as two separate concentrations for the purposes of the Merger Regulation. This was the approach adopted in *ABB/Renault Automation* (Case IV/M.409, Decision of 9 March 1994) and *Ingersoll-Rand/MAN* (Case IV/M.479 Decision of 28 July 1994).

n. 37. See also *Winterthur/DBV* (Case IV/M.429, Decision of 30 May 1994) where the Commission examined a concentration consisting of a series of transactions to be carried out over a period of months. The Commission concluded that the various arrangements were part of one binding agreement and so treated it as one single operation for Merger Regulation purposes.

6–017 **Joint acquisitions with a view to break-up**

n. 39. See now the Undertakings Concerned Notice, points 24–25.

6–019 **Asset swaps and rationalisation agreements**

n. 42. In practice the Commission has tended to treat asset swaps as giving rise to two (or more) independent concentrations, rather than seeking to apply Art. 85 to the overall swap arrangements. This is recognised at point 49 of the Undertakings Concerned Notice. Indeed point 47 of the old Interface Notice has not been reproduced in the new Notices.

(e) *Deemed absence of concentration*

6–021 **In general.** The three exceptional situations set out at Article 3(5) of the Merger Regulation, where the acquisition of a controlling interest is deemed not to constitute a concentration under the Merger Regulation, are considered at points 41 to 45 of the Concentration Notice.

6–023 **Liquidations.** An example of an acquisition of control by a liquidator not giving rise to a concentration is referred to in *ING/Barings* (Case IV/M.573, Decision of 14 March 1995 at point 8).

6–024 **Acquisitions by financial holding companies.** The concept of "financial holding companies" within the meaning of Article 3(5)(c) of the Merger

Regulation was considered by the Commission in *Charterhouse/ Porterbrook* (Case IV/M.669, Decision of 11 December 1995) at points 6 to 13).

3. JOINT CONTROL, CONCENTRATIVE AND CO-OPERATIVE JOINT VENTURES

(a) *Generally*

The basic distinction **6–025**

n. 52. The new Interface Notice does not set out a specific definition of "undertaking"; but see point 13 which addresses the issue of autonomy (discussed at § 6–033 *infra*).

n. 53. For further explanation of the basic distinction between concentrative and co-operative joint ventures, see the new Interface Notice, especially at points 5 to 8, and XXIVth Report on Competition Policy (1994), point 278.

The Interface Notice. The Commission's Notice on the distinction between concentrative and co-operative operations was revised and reissued in December 1994: Appendix 10, *post*. This new Interface Notice reflects and takes account of the Commission's practice in individual cases examined under the Merger Regulation. The principles for determining joint control are now set out in a separate notice, the Concentration Notice: Appendix 11, *post*. **6–027**

(b) *Joint control*

Joint control **6–028**

n. 61. The concepts of sole and joint control are now considered in the Concentration Notice (and not the Interface Notice): see §§ 6–008 *et seq. supra*.

Factors indicative of joint control. The Concentration Notice, at point 19, provides that joint control exists "where two or more undertakings or persons have the possibility to exercise decisive influence over another undertaking. Decisive influence in this sense normally means the power to block actions which determine the strategic commercial behaviour of an undertaking". These veto rights must go beyond the veto rights **6–030**

normally accorded to minority shareholders, relating to matters such as "changes in the statute, increase or decrease of the capital or liquidation" (Concentration Notice, point 22). Veto rights which confer joint control "typically include decisions on issues such as the budget, the business plan, major investments or the appointment of senior management" (*ibid.*, point 23). The crucial element is not the day-to-day running of the undertaking but whether the veto rights are sufficient to enable the shareholders to influence the undertaking's strategic business behaviour. The Concentration Notice first considers (at point 25) the significance of veto rights over the appointment of management and the determination of the budget, described as "normally the most important veto rights", a view subsequently reaffirmed by the Commission in *Albacom* (Case IV/M.604, Decision of 15 September 1995). The Notice proceeds to consider veto rights over the business plan (point 26) and investments (point 27). It also clarifies that it is not necessary to have all the veto rights mentioned. Depending on the facts, it may be sufficient if only some or even only one of these rights exists (points 24 and 29).

6–031 **Control based on agreement.** The Concentration Notice refers, at point 21, to the possibility of veto rights being set out in the statute of the undertaking or being conferred by agreement between its parent companies. It provides that joint control exists "where minority shareholders have additional rights which allow them to veto decisions which are essential for the strategic commercial behaviour of the joint venture". See *RB of Scotland/Bank of Ireland* (Case IV/M.681, Decision of 5 February 1996) where the minority shareholder had agreed the company's initial strategic business plan and would have a right to be consulted and comment on subsequent more detailed annual budgets and business plans; these rights were not sufficient on the facts to confer joint control. For joint control to exist there should not be a casting vote for one parent company only; however, *de facto* joint control may exist if the casting vote can only be exercised after a process of arbitration and attempts at reconciliation: Concentration Notice, point 37, and *British Telecom/Banco Santander* (Case IV/M.425, Decision of 28 March 1994). In *Unisource/Telefónica* (Case IV/M.544, Decision of 6 November 1995 the parties established a JV for various telecommunications activities including value added telecom services. Unanimity was required at the supervisory board level for the JV's activities except those relating to data communications (where two individual shareholders would decide separately on two distinct budgets and business plans for the business in question). The Commission therefore held that joint control existed only for the remaining activities covered by the operation.

6–032 **Control in absence of agreement**

n. 66. See now Concentration Notice, point 20.

n. 67. *Ibid.* points 30 to 35. This emphasises that, leaving aside deadlock joint ventures between two undertakings, joint control in the absence of an agreement is exceptional. See, *e.g. Nokia/SP Tyres* (Case IV/M.548, Decision of 14 March 1995) where the Commission concluded that Nokia and SP Tyres did not have sufficiently common interests to imply joint control. *Cf. Fletcher Challenge/Methanex* (Case IV/M.331, Decision of 31 March 1993) and *Philip/Grundig* (Case IV/M.382, Decision of 3 December 1993) where the facts were sufficient to imply joint control. The greater the number of shareholders involved, the less likely that there is a situation of *de facto* joint control. Thus in *Channel Five* (Case IV/M.673, Decision of 22 December 1995) the Commission, having examined the surrounding facts, concluded that the four shareholders (whose individual holdings ranged from 20 per cent to 32 per cent) did not have a strong common interest which would create a situation of *de facto* joint control amongst all four of them.

6–032A **Joint control for a limited period.** Some joint venture structures may provide that the undertaking will be subject to joint control for an initial starting-up period. However, if legally-binding agreements provide that this temporary joint control structure will then convert to sole control by one of the shareholders, then the whole operation will normally be treated as an acquisition of sole control (Concentration Notice, point 38). In *British Telecom/Banco Santander*, *supra*, the Commission considered a JV structure involving a put option and reduced veto rights for one parent after three years. On the facts the Commission found that joint control would exist for only three years and concluded that this was not sufficiently permanent for a situation of joint control. The Commission therefore treated the JV operation as an acquisition of sole control giving rise to a concentration without a Community dimension. Likewise, in *Albacom*, *supra*, the Commission considered a JV structure where the minority shareholder had permanent veto rights over various aspects of the JV's business but where its veto rights over the appointment of management and the determination of the budget would be limited to only the first three years. The Commission considered that this period was insufficient to bring about a lasting change with regard to the participation of the minority shareholder and therefore concluded that the majority shareholder (British Telecom) had acquired sole control for the purposes of the Merger Regulation. In *Elf Atochem/Rütgers* (Case IV/M.442, Decision of 29 July 1994) the Commission considered a JV structure involving a put option exercisable between two-and-a-half and four-and-a-half years after formation of the joint venture. On the facts, however, implementation of the option was only possible after five years and this was held to be sufficiently permanent for the company to be deemed to be jointly controlled.

(c) *Autonomy*

6–033 **Autonomous full-function entity.** Although the term "autonomy" might suggest independence of a jointly controlled undertaking *vis-à-vis* its parents, it is now clearly established that the concept merely requires that there should be an undertaking "performing the functions normally carried out by other undertakings operating on the same market": new Interface Notice, point 13. JV undertakings which satisfy this criterion are commonly described as "full-function" undertakings. For example, in *Texaco/Norsk Hydro* (Case IV/M.511, Decision of 9 January 1994) the Commission considered a JV operating on distribution markets which were viewed as separate from upstream trading markets. In *ATR/BAe* (Case IV/M.551, Decision of 27 July 1995) the Commission concluded that the JV would not be a full-function undertaking in the first stage of its existence. This was because there was uncertainty over the outcome of the feasibility studies and the combining of the parties' existing aircraft activities did not, at least initially, amount to more than a joint sales agency.

n. 70. See now the new Interface Notice at points 12 to 16.

n. 71. See also the new Interface Notice, point 16: a JV established in order to construct a specific project such as a power plant, but without involvement in the operation of the plant once constructed, will not be considered to operate on a lasting basis.

6–034 **Functional independence.** The new Interface Notice confirms that joint ventures which merely take over one specific function within their parent companies' business activities (*e.g.* R&D or production), without access to the market, will be considered auxiliary and not full-function.

n. 74. The revised Interface Notice considers the issue of autonomy or "structural changes of the undertakings" at points 12 to 16.

n. 75. See also *Shell Chimie/Elf Atochem* (Case IV/M.475, Decision of 22 December 1994).

n. 77. In *Unisource/Telefónica* (Case IV/M.544, Decision of 6 November 1995: see § 6–031, *supra*) the Commission concluded that some of the activities which would be jointly controlled would in fact involve the JV company either performing only the role of a management company for its parents or only providing services to its parents. These operations therefore fell outside the scope of the Merger Regulation.

6–035 **Legal dependence.** The revised Interface Notice no longer implies that the joint venture undertaking need be in a position to plan, decide and act independently of its parents. By making it clear that "autonomy" merely requires there to be a full-time undertaking (see para. 6–033 *supra*), albeit subject to the "control" of its parents, the Commission has removed the tension which had previously existed.

(d) *Concentrative and co-operative joint ventures*

Complete and partial mergers. The concepts of complete and partial mergers, which pre-date the Merger Regulation but remained in the old Interface Notice, are not referred to in the revised Interface Notice. These concepts are effectively redundant. It is now clearly established that commercial agreements between undertakings fall into two broad categories for Community competition law purposes: **6–036**

(i) *Operations involving jointly-controlled full-function undertakings.* The French and German language terms "entreprise commune" and "Gemeinschaftsunternehmen" are perhaps more precise than the English term "joint venture" in encapsulating the requirements of the first two criteria considered at sub-Sections (b) and (c) above. In short, there must be an identifiable undertaking which is both "jointly controlled" and "full-function". The Merger Regulation regime provides for differing jurisdictional analysis depending on whether such a joint venture undertaking is:
    (a) "concentrative", in which case Article 85(1) is not applicable. The Merger Regulation will only apply to such a concentrative operation if it has a "Community dimension"; or
    (b) "co-operative", in which case Article 85(1) is applicable (unless there is no appreciable effect on trade between Member States). The Merger Regulation will not apply to such an operation.

    The criteria applied in establishing whether or not such an undertaking is "concentrative" or "co-operative" are considered at paras. 6–037 *et seq.*, *infra*. Co-operative joint venture undertakings are discussed further in Chapter 5.
(ii) *Other operations.* Where an operation fails to satisfy one (or both) of the criteria considered at sub-sections (b) and (c) above, the transaction will not be analysed as a "concentrative" or "co-operative" joint venture undertaking. Rather, it may be analysed as:
    (a) a concentration involving an acquisition of "sole control", *i.e.* falling short of "joint control". The Merger Regulation will only apply if the operation has a "Community dimension"; or
    (b) a "co-operation" involving two or more undertakings, *i.e.* falling short of establishing a "full-function undertaking". Article 85(1) may be applicable to such an operation; or
    (c) a combination of both (a) and (b).

Absence of co-ordination on the market **6–037**

n. 82. Revised Interface Notice, point 18, first indent.

n. 83. Revised Interface Notice, point 18, second indent.

n. 86. Revised Interface Notice, point 18, third indent. See also § 6–039, *infra.*

6–038 **Related markets**

n. 88. Revised Interface Notice, point 18, fourth to seventh indents. See also § 6–039, *infra.*

6–039 **One parent active in related market.** The presumption at point 33 of the old Interface Notice, which was not followed by the Commission in practice, has been removed from the revised Interface Notice: see para. 6–040, *infra.*

6–040 **Focus on risk of co-ordination between parents.** The revised Interface Notice (at point 17 and subsequently) focuses on the need to determine whether there is "co-ordination between the parent companies in relation to prices, markets, output or innovation". It recognises that co-ordination between the parent companies and the JV is relevant "only in so far as it is an instrument for producing or reinforcing the co-ordination between the parent companies". This involves an assessment of whether the parents are in fact actual or realistic potential competitors of one another in the product and geographic markets affected by the joint venture. The Notice states (at point 18) that "there is normally a high probability of co-ordination where two or more parent companies retain to a significant extent activities in the same product market as the joint venture itself insofar as those activities are in the same geographic market". Thus in *Hoogovens/Klöckner* (Case IV/M.578, Decision of 11 April 1995) both parent companies were active in the same product and geographic market as the JV itself (steel stockholding in an area encompassing the Netherlands, Belgium and north-west Germany) which gave rise to "a high probability of co-ordination of competitive behaviour". Similarly, in *Omnitel* (Case IV/M.538, Decision of 24 February 1995), the Commission found that a JV offering GSM mobile phone services in Italy was "likely to create or reinforce a co-operation amongst those of its parents that are already active (as well as those which are likely to be active in the near future) in the GSM service provision". *Cf. Voith/Sulzer II* (Case IV/M.478, Decision of 29 July 1994), which concerned a worldwide paper machinery JV where both parents retained certain paper machinery businesses outside the joint venture. On the facts of that case the Commission concluded that there was no scope for co-ordination between these retained businesses, so the operation was assessed as a concentration. See also *KNP BT/Société Générale* (Case IV/M.640, Decision of 3 October 1995) where both parents kept their Belgian computer activities outside the JV. However, those activities were marginal both in actual terms and in relative terms (and had been kept outside the JV for purely practical reasons): the Commission concluded that no co-ordination of competitive behaviour was likely. Similarly, in *TBT/BT/Tele Danmark/Telenor* (Case IV/M.570, Decision of 24 April 1995), the Commission found that a telecommunications JV in Sweden between the principal providers of telephone services in the UK, Denmark and Norway, would not involve any appreciable likelihood of co-ordination between the parents' activities outside the JV.

Significance of market definition **6–041**

n. 98. Observations on the risks of co-ordination where the parent companies and the joint venture are active in the same product market but in different geographic markets are contained at point 19 of the revised Interface Notice.

***De minimis* considerations.** Conversely, a high accumulation of minor elements of co-ordination may lead to a situation where the operation as a whole has to be considered as co-operative. This is recognised at point 20 of the revised Interface Notice. Thus in *Unisource/Telefónica* (Case IV/M.544, Decision of 6 November 1995: see paras. 6–031 and 6–034 *supra*) the Commission considered the JV's activities which were jointly controlled and full-function. The Commission concluded that there was a likelihood of co-ordination of competitive behaviour between the parents in the fields of mobile telephony, card services and voice telephony but not in the area of satellite services. In the circumstances, the notified operation could not be regarded as concentrative. **6–042**

n. 1. See also point 20 of the revised Interface Notice. In *Hoogovens/Klöckner*, *supra*, the Commission considered whether the co-operative elements were of minor economic importance in relation to the operation as a whole. As the parent companies had an appreciable market share outside the JV, the Commission concluded that the co-operative elements were not *de minimis*.

(e) *Interests in pre-existing joint ventures*

Separate investigations. The new Undertakings Concerned Notice records the Commission's view that the Merger Regulation gives it jurisdiction over changes in the composition of shareholdings in pre-existing concentrative joint venture undertakings, if a new shareholder acquires a controlling interest, a non-controlling shareholder acquires a controlling interest or a shareholder transfers its controlling interest to a third party: see para. 6–011, sub-paragraph (iii), *supra*. This jurisdictional issue remains to be clarified by the Court. There may be circumstances in which the new controlling shareholder has activities outside the JV which may result in a "concentrative" JV becoming "co-operative". Likewise, **6–044**

depending on the turnovers of the undertakings concerned the operation, if concentrative, may not have a "Community dimension".

4. COMMUNITY DIMENSION

(a) *In general*

6–045 **Community dimension**

n. 5. 5,000 million ECU is approximately £4,100 million or U.S.$6,500 million (at September 1996 exchange rates).

n. 6. 250 million ECU is approximately £205 million or U.S.$325 million (at September 1996 exchange rates).

6–046 **Jurisdictional criteria.** The review of the turnover thresholds by the Council has been deferred until the end of 1996. See para. 6–005A, *supra*.

6–048 **Aggregation of turnover: the undertakings concerned.** The notion of "undertakings concerned" is considered at some length in the Commission's new Undertakings Concerned Notice, Appendix 12, *post*.

6–049 **Relevant turnover.** The Commission has issued a new Turnover Notice, Appendix 13, *post*. Part I of the Notice (points 9 to 44) considers the "accounting" calculation of turnover. It explains the concept of turnover as applied to goods and services and how the calculation must correspond to "ordinary activities" of the undertakings concerned. Thus in *Pechiney World Trade/Minemet* (Case IV/M.473, Decision of 20 July 1994) the Commission concluded that the activity of commercial representation by means of an agency constituted the provision of services corresponding to an ordinary activity of the undertakings concerned. Part I of the Notice also explains how the calculation of relevant turnover involves the deduction of rebates and taxes and of "internal" turnover, as well as explaining other adjustments which are relevant for different types of operations. Difficulties can arise in cases where part of the target business is disposed of before the acquisition is completed: see *Ingersoll-Rand/ Clark Equipment* (Case IV/M.388, Decision of 15 May 1995) and *Rhône Poulenc/Fisons* (Case IV/M.632, Decision of 21 September 1995). Part II of the Notice (points 45 to 50) considers the geographic allocation of turnover and the method of converting turnover into ECU. Part III considers the special rules applying to credit and other financial institutions and to insurance undertakings, as considered further at paras. 6–056 *et seq., infra*.

n. 13. The revised Form CO, annexed to the revised Implementing Reg. 3385/94 (Appendix 9, *post*), includes four guidance notes on the calculation of turnover.

Sale of part **6–050**

n. 17. See also the Turnover Notice, points 30 to 31, regarding acquisitions of parts of companies. In considering a case where a part of the operations of the undertaking to be acquired was discontinued as a condition of the merger, the CFI held that the purpose of Art. 5(2) is "to determine the real dimension of the concentration" so that "only the turnover in respect of activities effectively forming the subject-matter of the transaction" are taken into account: Case T–3/93 *Air France v. Commission* [1994] II ECR 121, 170–71. The CFI accordingly upheld the Commission's determination that the acquisition by British Airways of Dan Air did not have a Community dimension by reason of the exclusion of Dan Air's charter operations, the discontinuance of which had to be completed as a pre-condition under the merger agreement. See now the Turnover Notice, point 27.

n. 19. See also *Akzo/Nobel Industrier* (Case IV/M.390, Decision of January 10, 1994), where the parties had already agreed an assets swap prior to the public bid; and the Turnover Notice, points 32 to 35 ("staggered operations").

Aggregate turnover. Guidance is now set out in the Commission's Turnover Notice at points 36 to 42. Where two (or more) companies jointly have in the undertaking concerned the rights or powers listed at Article 5(4)(b) the Commission's practice has been to include the turnovers of both (or all) those companies in calculating relevant aggregate turnover: see point 38(3) of the Turnover Notice. **6–051**

Jointly controlled undertakings **6–052**

n. 23. See also the Turnover Notice, point 40, which confirms that the Commission's practice "so far" has been to apply equivalent criteria when calculating the aggregate turnover of undertakings controlled jointly with third parties; and *McDermott/ETPM* (Case IV/M.648, Decision of November 27, 1995) at point 18.

The power to appoint more than half the board **6–053**

n. 24. See also Turnover Notice, point 42.

State-controlled undertakings **6–054**

n. 28. See also *Kali+Salz/MdK/Treuhand* (Case IV/M.308, OJ 1994 L186/38) at point 9; *Alcan/Inespal/Palco* (Case IV/M.322, Decision of 14

April 1993); *Marconi/Finmeccanica* (Case IV/M.496, Decision of 5 September 1994) at point 5; and the Turnover Notice, points 43 to 44.

6–055 **Acquisitions by jointly controlled undertakings.** The Commission has further clarified the manner in which it applies the turnover rules to acquisitions by jointly controlled undertakings:

(i) *The undertakings concerned.* The Commission's new Notice on Undertakings Concerned, at points 26 to 29, confirms that "the Commission will look at the economic reality of the operation" in determining whether or not to "lift the corporate veil".

(ii) *Aggregation of turnover.* In circumstances where no individual parent holds in the jointly controlled undertaking any of the rights or powers listed at Article 5(4)(b), the Commission's practice has nevertheless been to aggregate the turnovers of the parents which enjoy those rights or powers jointly: see para. 6–051 *supra* and point 38(3) of the Turnover Notice.

(b) *Special rules for calculating turnover*

6–056 **Credit institutions and other financial institutions**

n. 33. See also Turnover Notice, point 51.

n. 34. See also Turnover Notice, points 51 to 52.

n. 35. See now Guidance Note I to the revised Form CO and points 54 to 58 of the Turnover Notice (which includes observations on the calculation of the turnover of leasing companies and fund management companies). For observations on the geographic allocation of turnover of banking undertakings and on the method of converting to ECU, see the Turnover Notice, points 65 to 68.

6–057 **Insurance companies**

n. 37. See now Guidance Note II to the revised Form CO and points 59 to 61 of the Turnover Notice (which includes observations on the concept of gross premiums written and the treatment of investments). For observations on the geographic allocation of turnover of insurance companies and the method of converting to ECU, see the Turnover Notice, points 65 to 68.

6–058 **Groups with mixed activities**

n. 38. See also Turnover Notice, points 62 to 64, regarding financial holding companies.

5. THE COMMISSION'S APPRAISAL OF CONCENTRATIONS

(b) *Relevant market*

Relevant product market. The Commission has continued to lay emphasis on "demand side" substitutability, making use of qualitative methods (*e.g.* looking at products' characteristics and intended use) and of quantitative techniques (*e.g.* examining price trends and cross price elasticities and other econometric tests). For example, in *Unilever France/Ortiz-Miko* (Case IV/M.422, Decision of 15 March 1994) the Commission relied essentially on qualitative methods in identifying three distinct markets for ice-cream in France: the take-home, restaurant and impulse ice-cream markets. In *Procter & Gamble/VP Schickedanz* (Case IV/M.430, Decision of 21 June 1994) the Commission had to examine various quantitative data submitted by Procter & Gamble and interested third parties, including supermarket scanner data of cross-price elasticities and cross-promotional elasticities in the German market for feminine sanitary protection products. The Commission eventually concluded that this quantitative evidence supported qualitative evidence that the German market for sanitary towels constituted a separate product market, distinct from the markets for tampons and pantyliners. **6–064**

In some market sectors, particularly those where there have been a number of mergers notified under the Merger Regulation, the Commission's methodology for defining the relevant product market is well established. For example, in the pharmaceuticals sector there have now been several cases where the Commission has adopted the same approach of analysing the parties' portfolios of drugs by therapeutic class using the third level of the Anatomical Therapeutic Classification (ATC) recognised and used by the World Health Organisation: see *Sanofi/Sterling Drug* (Case IV/M.072, Decision of 10 June 1991); *Procordia/Erbamont* (Case IV/M.323, Decision of 29 April 1993); *Rhône-Poulenc/Cooper* (Case IV/M.426, Decision of 18 April 1994); *La Roche/Syntax* (Case IV/M.457, Decision of 20 June 1994); *Sanofi/Kodak* (Case IV/M.480, Decision of 12 August 1994); *BMSC/UPSA* (Case IV/M.464, Decision of 6 September 1994); *American Home Products/American Cyanamid* (Case IV/M.500, Decision of 19 September 1994); *Glaxo/Wellcome* (Case IV/M.555, Decision of 28 February 1995); *Behringwerke/Armour Pharmaceutical* (Case IV/M.495, Decision of 3 April 1995); *Hoechst/Marion Merrell Dow* (Case IV/M.587, Decision of 22 June 1995); *Upjohn/Pharmacia* (Case IV/M.631, Decision of 28 September 1995). The pharmaceutical sector is one in which research and development is particularly important, so the Commission will also take account of the parties' R&D activities with a view to identifying possible competitive overlap in pipeline products: see *Glaxo/Wellcome*, *supra* and *Upjohn/Pharmacia*, *supra*.

Other industries for which there is a body of Merger Regulation case-law illustrating the Commission's methodology for defining the relevant market include the banking and insurance sectors, air transport, TV broadcasting (including satellite and cable TV), telecommunications, automotive parts, textile fibres, paper and packaging: see business sector descriptions in the list of cases at Table [D]. See also the XXIVth Report on Competition Policy (1994), points 280 to 283, for further observations on defining the relevant product market.

6–064A **Markets for technology licensing.** In *Shell/Montecatini* (Case IV/M.269, OJ 1994 L332/48), the Commission concluded that there was a market for the licensing of polypropylene technology, involving the licensing and use of catalysts and technological processes, distinct from the market for the production and sale of polypropylene (para. 44). In *Union Carbide/Enichem* (Case IV/M.550, Decision of 13 March 1995), the Commission similarly concluded that there was a market for the licensing of polyethylene technology distinct from the market for the production and sale of polyethylene. This approach to market definition may have similar applications in other technology-driven industries, particularly where licensing is an accepted form of exploiting technology.

n. 46. This definition of the relevant product market is now reproduced at Section 6 of the revised Form CO.

6–065 **Relevant geographic market.** As well as having regard to general qualitative indicators (such as trade flows and market share variations between Member States) and specific demand-side and supply-side factors, the Commission has occasionally considered the merits of various quantitative econometric techniques developed with a view to delineating the market. Price correlations, for example, can measure the extent to which price movements in one geographical area correspond to those in another area. The Commission has stated that a weak price correlation tends to indicate separate geographical markets as it shows that suppliers are able to discriminate in their prices for the same products. However, the Commission considers that the converse is not necessarily the case (*e.g.* in the absence of similar structures of supply and demand, different regions may well not constitute a homogenous market), and has also stressed the importance of selection of reliable and representative data to found such analysis. See XXIVth Report on Competition Policy (1994), point 291. In *Mannesmann/Vallourec/Ilva* (Case IV/M315, OJ 1994 L102/15) the Commission rejected an argument that western Europe and the United States should, on the basis of econometric price correlation data, be considered a single geographic market. In that case the Commission also considered shipment data on trade flows between western Europe and the United States. In rejecting econometric arguments based on the so-called Elzinga-Hogarty test (which assumes that a given area belongs to a wider geographic market if either 10 per cent of production is exported or 10 per cent of consumption is imported), the Commission observed that this risked defining markets widely even if interpenetration was not mutual (para. 33).

n. 51. This definition of the relevant geographic market is now reproduced at Section 6 of the revised Form CO, subject to the clarificatory substitution of "neighbouring geographic areas" instead of "neighbouring areas".

The dynamic approach to geographic markets **6–066**

n. 54 See also *Gencor/Lonrho* (Case IV M.619, Decision of 24 April 1996).

(c) *Factors taken into account in assessing compatibility*

Failing firm defence. There may be circumstances in which a merger between two undertakings is seen as the only sensible option because one of the parties is a failing firm and would otherwise go out of business. If the other party is already the dominant undertaking in the market, then the Commission will inevitably be concerned at the prospect of the failing firm's share going to the dominant firm. In *Kali+Salz/MdK/Treuhand* (Case IV/M.308, OJ 1994 L186/38) the Commission accepted that in exceptional circumstances the "failing firm defence" may justify such a concentration "if, even in the event of the merger's being prohibited, the acquirer would inevitably achieve or reinforce a dominant position" (para. 71). On that basis, there is "a lack of causality" between the concentration and the creation or strengthening of the dominant position. The Commission takes the line that, given the exceptional nature of the failing firm defence, the burden of proof for demonstrating a lack of causality lies with the notifying parties (*ibid.*, para. 72). This involves demonstrating three elements: that "the acquired undertaking would in the near future be forced out of the market if not taken over by another undertaking"; that "the acquiring undertaking would take over the market share of the acquired undertaking if the latter were forced out of the market; and that "there is no less anti-competitive alternative purchase". After a detailed investigation, the Commission concluded in *Kali+Salz/MdK/Treuhand* that these three elements were demonstrated as regards the German market for agricultural potash. **6–074A**

(d) *Oligopoly issues*

Oligopoly control under the Merger Regulation. Generally the increase in concentration levels arising from the notified operation itself will need to be significant before the Commission will analyse oligopolistic dominance. In *Mannesmann/Vallourec/Ilva* (Case IV/M.315, OJ 1994 L102/15) the Commission was concerned by the duopoly position which would arise following the merger, with DMV and Sandvik together **6–076**

having 70 per cent of the Western European market and no other existing competitor holding more than 13 per cent. Nevertheless the Commission took account of the potential for increased competition from Japan and Eastern Europe, concluding that this ongoing threat undermined the creation and stability of any possible anti-competitive parallel behaviour. Concerns that a concentration may lead to a situation of oligopolistic dominance may be prompted by the existence of close links between the principal competitors; thus in *Kali+Salz/MdK/Treuhand*, *supra*, the Commission referred to JV and supply links between Kali+Salz and the SCPA group. In *Pilkington-Techint/SIV* (Case IV/M.358, OJ 1994 L158/24) the Commission took account of demand side purchasing power and excess capacity in the sector in finding that there was insufficient evidence to conclude that the market structure created by the concentration would facilitate anti-competitive parallel behaviour. Likewise, in *ABB/Daimler Benz* (Case IV/M.580, Decision of 18 October 1995) the Commission concluded that factors such as buyer power and the structure of competition from third parties other than Siemens meant that the concentration would not give rise to the creation or strengthening of a dominant duopoly.

n. 74. See also *Rhône-Poulenc/SNIA II* (Case IV/M.355, Decision of 8 September 1993); *Allied Signal/Knorr-Bremse* (Case IV/M.337, Decision of 14 September 1993), para. 45; *Rhône-Poulenc-SNIA/Nordfaser* (Case IV/M.399, Decision of 3 February 1994); *Unilever/Ortiz-Miko* (Case IV/M.422, Decision of 15 March 1994); *Holdercim/Cedest* (Case IV/M.460, Decision of 6 July 1994); *Shell Chimie/Elf Atochem* (Case IV/M.474, Decision of 22 December 1994); *Unilever/Diversey* (Case IV/M.704, Decision of 20 March 1996).

(e) *Industrial policy issues*

6–077 **Non-competition issues.** In justifying the final decision to approve the concentration in *Kali+Salz/MdK/Treuhand*, *supra*, the Commission made reference to the objectives referred to in recital 13 to the Merger Regulation. It referred specifically to "the severe structural weakness of the regions in East Germany which are affected by the proposed concentration, and the likelihood of serious consequences for them of the closure of MdK" (para. 95). The Commission was satisfied that the closure of MdK was inevitable "in the foreseeable future if it was not acquired by another undertaking".

7. NOTIFICATION OF CONCENTRATIONS

(a) *Form CO*

6–096 **Form CO.** The revised Form CO is annexed to the revised Implementing Regulation (Regulation 3384/94, Appendix 9, *post*). It has introduced the option of a short-form notification in the case of concentrative joint venture undertakings with turnover and assets of less than ECU 100 million in the EEA. Twenty-four copies of each notification must be supplied to the Commission (Article 2(2)).

Supporting documentation. The revised Implementing Regulation requires 19 copies of all the supporting documents to be supplied to the Commission (Article 2(2)). These documents (as listed at Section 5 of Form CO) comprise: **6–097**

(a) copies of the final (or most recent) versions of all documents bringing about the concentration;
(b) in a public bid, a copy of the offer document (which, if unavailable on notification, should be submitted as soon as possible and not later than when posted to shareholders);
(c) copies of the parties' most recent annual reports and accounts;
(d) where at least one "affected market" is identified, copies of analyses, reports, studies and surveys submitted to or prepared for any member(s) of the board of directors, the supervisory board, or the shareholders meeting, for the purpose of assessing or analysing the concentration with respect to competition conditions, competitors (actual or potential) and market conditions.

Language **6–098**

n. 17. Swedish and Finnish are now also official languages of the Community.

Need for full and accurate disclosure **6–099**

n. 18. See now the revised Implementing Reg., Art. 3(1).

n. 21. *Ibid.*, Art. 4(3). Where material changes could have a significant effect on the appraisal of the concentration, the notification may be considered by the Commission as becoming effective on the date on which the information on the material changes is received by the Commission.

(b) *Role of the Merger Task Force*

The Merger Task Force. The Merger Task Force now has the status of a Directorate (Directorate B) within DGIV. **6–100**

6–102 **Waivers regarding provision of information**

n. 25. See now revised Implementing Reg., Art. 3(2).

(c) *Obligation to notify*

6–103 **One week to notify**

n. 28. See now revised Implementing Reg., Art. 21(3).

n. 31. See also *GE/Nuovo Pignone* (Case IV/M.440, Decision of 6 May 1994) which had initially been notified as a sole control case); *Elf Atochem/Rütgers* (Case IV/M.442, Decision of 29 July 1994); *Vesuvius/Wülfrath* (Case IV/M.472, Decision of 5 September 1994); and *Krupp/Thyssen/Riva/Falck/Tadfin/AST* (Case IV/M.484, OJ 1995 L251/18).

(d) *Suspension period*

6–108 **The suspension period**

n. 37. The Commission used its Art. 7(2) powers on 12 occasions in 1994: XXIVth Report on Competition Policy (1994), point 330.

n. 38. See now revised Implementing Reg., Arts. 12 and 20.

6–110 **Derogation**

n. 40. A derogation was granted in *ING/Barings* (Case IV/M.573, Decision of 11 April 1995) where the Barings holding company was in administration and it was necessary for the acquisition to be rapidly completed to prevent substantial damage to Barings and third parties.

n. 41. See now revised Implementing Reg., Arts. 12 and 20.

6–111 **Completion in breach**

n. 43. See also Case T–52/96 *Sogecable v. Commission*, not yet decided; interim measures refused by order of 12 July 1996.

8. CONDUCT OF FORMAL INVESTIGATIONS

(a) *Initial investigation*

Initial investigation period **6–112**

n. 46. See now revised Implementing Reg., Arts. 6(1) and 22.

Scope for amendment of the transaction. Other examples of cases where changes were made to the initial transaction, allowing the Commission to take the view that serious doubts initially raised had been removed, include *Unilever France/Ortiz Miko* (Case IV/M.422, Decision of 15 March 1994, see also XXIVth Report on Competition Policy (1994) at point 319); *Elf Atochem/Rütgers* (Case IV/M.442, Decision of 29 July 1994, see also XXIVth Report on Competition Policy (1994) at point 323); *Glaxo/Wellcome* (Case IV/M.555, Decision of 28 February 1995); *Swissair/Sabena* (Case IV/M.616, Decision of 20 July 1995, see also XXVth Report on Competitive Policy (1995), point 143); *Repola/Kymmene* (Case IV/M.646, Decision of 30 October 1995). The Commission is prepared to accept commitments to modify the original concentration plan if these provide a clear definitive solution to the potential competition problem giving rise to the serious doubts. In such cases, however, the Commission tends to require the modifications to be transparent, so as to safeguard the rights of third parties and Member States. Accordingly, the Commission will generally inform interested third parties and Member States of any modifications made or commitments proposed, inviting their comments. **6–113**

Scope for withdrawal of notification. If the Commission is satisfied that the initially proposed transaction has been abandoned, the parties may withdraw a notification and then make a new notification of an amended transaction. This enables the Commission to commence a new initial investigation, including the publication of a new *Official Journal* notice specifying the main changes and inviting third party comments. Cases which have been the subject of such a second notification include *Unilever France/Ortiz Miko, supra*; *Procter & Gamble/VP Schickedanz* (Case IV/M.430, Decision of 21 June 1994) where a Stage II inquiry was launched in respect of the renotified transaction; and *Swissair/Sabena, supra*. **6–113A**

Mixed decisions. See also the *Holdercim/Cedest* merger (Case IV/M.460, Decision of 6 July 1994) which involved an Article 6(1)(b) decision in respect of cement and an Article 9 reference in respect of ready mixed concrete. **6–116**

6–118 **Communications of decisions**

n. 63. See now revised Implementing Reg., Art. 10.

n. 64. Documents (other than the initial notification) may also be transmitted by electronic mail: revised Implementing Reg., Art. 19.

n. 65. For publication of decisions, see § 6–004, n. 11, *supra*.

(b) *"Serious doubts" investigations*

6–119 **Duration of "serious doubts" investigation**

n. 67. See now Implementing Reg., Arts. 6(2) and 22.

n. 68. For holidays, see now Implementing Reg., Arts. 8, 7(4) and 22.

6–120 **Statement of objections**

n. 70. *Ibid.*, Art. 13(2).

n. 71. *Ibid.*, Art. 20.

6–121 **Rights of defence and access to file.** Article 11 of the revised Implementing Regulation distinguishes between four categories of parties for the purposes of the rights of defence: the "notifying parties", *i.e.* the persons or undertakings submitting the notification; "other involved parties", *i.e.* other parties to the concentration plan such as the vendor or the target; "third parties", *i.e.* natural or legal persons showing a sufficient interest such as customers, suppliers, competitors, the management of the undertakings concerned and recognised workers' representatives; and fourthly, any parties who may be subject to a fine or penalty for committing procedural or substantive infringements.

n. 74. See now Implementing Reg., Art. 13(2) and (3). The right of access to the file has been extended "in so far as may be necessary for the purposes of preparing their observations" to the other involved parties who must also be informed in writing of the Commission's objections.

6–122 **Reply**

n. 76. *Ibid.*, Art. 13(4).

6–123 **Oral hearing**

In Cases T–96/92 *CCE de la Société Générale des Grandes Sources and Others v. Commission* [1995] II ECR 1213 and T–12/93 *CCE de Vittel and*

Others v. Commission [1995] II ECR 1247, employees' representatives applied to the Court of First Instance for annulment of the Commission's conditional clearance of the concentration in *Nestlé/Perrier* (Case IV/M.190, OJ 1992 L356/1). The Court held that in the administrative procedure third parties do not have the right to be treated by the Commission in the same way as the parties to the concentration. Where an organisation representing employees of one of the parties had made a mere request for information rather than an application to be heard, the Commission was not obliged to inform it in writing of the nature and subject matter of the procedure before giving it an opportunity to make known its views; nor was the Commission obliged to give it access to the file.

n. 77. See now Implementing Reg., Arts. 14 and 15 which also refer to the rights of other involved parties.

n. 78. *Ibid.*, Art. 16(1) requires third parties to apply in writing to be heard without any requirement that they demonstrate a sufficient interest. Any such third party will be provided with a written explanation of the case (effectively a non-confidential version of the statement of objections) and given a time limit within which to comment. Art. 16(2) provides that the Commission may give these third parties an oral hearing.

n. 79. *Ibid.*, Art. 16(3).

Modifications to the concentration plan. Article 18 of the revised Implementing Regulation has introduced a new time limit for parties to put forward modifications to the concentration plan as a means of addressing the serious doubts raised by the Commission. Modifications which are intended by the parties to form the basis for a decision pursuant to Article 8(2) of the Merger Regulation must be submitted to the Commission within three months of the date on which proceedings were initiated. The Commission may extend this period in exceptional circumstances. **6–123A**

Decisions following "serious doubts" investigation **6–124**

n. 80. Of the 398 investigations commenced in the period to the end of 1995, the Commission opened Phase II proceedings in just 28 cases. Of those, seven resulted in unconditional clearances and 14 in conditional clearances. When a concentration is cleared subject to divestment or other conditions, the Commission has tended to publish the text of the parties' undertakings (or at least their salient facts) in its decision, *e.g.* the "hold separate" and divestment undertakings in *Orkla/Volvo* (Case IV/M.582, OJ 1996 L66/17) § 123 and *Crown Cork & Seal/Carnaud-Metalbox* (Case IV/M.603, OJ 1996 L75/38) § 115. See also XXIVth

Report on Competition Policy (1994), points 317–24, for the Commission's monitoring of commitments given in a number of cases.

n. 81. Other prohibition cases are identified in the list of cases in Table [D]. In the period to the end of 1995, four cases resulted in prohibition decisions.

(f) *Role of the EFTA Surveillance Authority and the EFTA States*

6–138 **Concentrations subject to co-operation.** The co-operation procedure was implemented for the first time in *Neste/Statoil* (Case IV/M.361, Decision of 17 February 1994). In *P&G/VP-Schickedanz* (Case IV/M.430, OJ 1994 L354/32) the co-operation procedure focused on the Austrian market for feminine hygiene products. In 1994 the Commission initiated the co-operation procedure with the EFTA Surveillance Authority on 21 occasions: XXIVth Report on Competition Policy (1994), point 265. This was before the accession of Austria, Finland and Sweden to the Community. The co-operation procedure continues to operate with regard to Norway, Iceland and Liechtenstein. In *Orkla/Volvo* (Case IV/M.582, OJ 1996 L66/17), where the parties each had turnover exceeding ECU 250 million in the territory of the signatory EFTA states, the Commission focused on the Norwegian beer market. Likewise in *Nordic Satellite Distribution* (Case IV/M.490, Decision of 19 July 1995) those EFTA turnover tests were met in a case where the Commission considered pay-TV markets in the Nordic countries. The Commission also used the co-operation procedure in *Crown Cork & Seal/Carnaud-Metalbox* (Case IV/M.603, OJ 1996 L75/38) although the various packaging markets affected by that merger in Europe were mainly outside the signatory EFTA states.

n. 12. See now *Encyclopaedia of European Union Law (Constitutional Texts)*, Vol. 1, §§ 30.1860 *et seq.* [1994] 5 CMLR 155.

(g) *Role of the Court*

6–140 **Appeals.** In Case T–83/92 *Zunis Holding v. Commission* [1993] II ECR 1169 [1994] 5 CMLR 154, the Court of First Instance rejected an appeal against the Commission's decision in *Mediobanca/Generali* (Case IV/M.159, Decision of 19 December 1991) brought by a group of minority investors in Generali. The Court held that the appeal was inadmissible since the investors were not directly and individually concerned by the Commission's decision. The decision was upheld by the Court of Justice on other grounds, but see the Opinion of Advocate General Lenz: Case C–480/93 [1996] I ECR 1 [1996] 5 CMLR 219. Conversely, in Case T–2/93 *Air France v. Commission* [1994] II ECR 323 and Case T–3/93 *Air France* *v. Commission* [1994] II ECR 121, the Court of First Instance accepted the admissibility of actions brought by Air France in respect of British Airways' acquisitions of TAT and Dan Air. This was essentially on the basis that Air France was a competitor of British Airways and had played a role in the administrative proceedings. In both cases, however, the Court rejected Air France's substantive arguments and upheld the Commission's decisions. In Cases T–96/92 *CCE de la Société Générale des Grandes Sources and others v. Commission* [1995] II ECR 1213 and T–12/93 *CCE de Vittel and others v. Commission* [1995] II ECR 1247, the fact that a third party had not directly intervened in the course of the administrative procedure was held not to preclude that third party from challenging the decision. However, the Court of First Instance held that as employees' representatives are not *directly* concerned by a decision authorising a concentration, they are not entitled to challenge the decision for breach of the substantive rules of the Merger Regulation. But they may challenge a decision on the ground that their rights to participate in the administrative procedure have not been respected.

In *Kali+Salz/MdK/Treuhand* (Case IV/M.308 OJ 1994 L186/38) the Commission declared the concentration compatible with the common market subject to compliance with certain conditions and obligations. One condition was that Kali+Salz and the joint venture must withdraw from Kali-Export, a joint venture with a third party SCPA for the export of potash outside the Community. The French government brought an action before the Court of Justice (as a Member State is entitled to do as of right) for partial annulment of this decision: Case C–68/94 *France v. Commission*, not yet decided. At the same time, SCPA (and its parent EMC) brought a similar action before the Court of First Instance. In these circumstances, the Court of First Instance renounced its jurisdiction under Article 47 of the Statute of the Court in favour of the Court of Justice to which it referred the case so that both actions could be heard together: Case T–88/94R *Société Commerciale des Potasses et de l'Azote and Entreprise Minière et Chimique v. Commission* [1995] II ECR 221.

6–140A

Interim measures. In the action for partial annulment of the Commission decision in *Kali+Salz/MdK/Treuhand*, *supra*, SCPA and EMC sought interim measures suspending operation of the decision. The President of the Court of First Instance ordered the suspension of the condition imposed by the Commission, pending the outcome of the main action: Case T–88/94R *Société Commerciale des Potasses et de l'Azote and Entreprise Minière et Chimique v. Commission* [1994] II ECR 401. This was on the basis that the withdrawal of Kali+Salz and the joint venture from Kali-Export would have effectively entailed its dissolution and that this was not necessary or appropriate to maintain effective competition within the Community.

In 1996 the Commission commenced infringement proceedings for failure to notify a concentration formed in Spain to provide multimedia services to local cable operators. The parties contended that the concentration did not have a Community dimension and had notified it to the Spanish authorities, who had given it clearance. In Case T–52/96 *Sogecable v. Commission*, not yet decided, one of the parties applied for annulment of the Commission's preparatory assessment, which had been communicated to the parties by letter, that the concentration appeared to have a Community dimension. Sogecable then applied for interim measures suspending the Commission's infringement proceedings. The President of the Court of First Instance dismissed the application without ruling on whether the letter at issue produced legal effects making it susceptible to review (see para. 12–107 of the main work). The Court would not normally intervene to prevent the Commission from exercising its powers of investigation and sanction set out in the Merger Regulation before the Commission had adopted any decision; and the applicant had not demonstrated the existence of exceptional circumstances that could justify such interference in the administrative procedure: Case T–52/96R, order of 12 July 1996. In the meantime the parties had formally notified the concentration under the Merger Regulation and the Commission formally opened Phase II proceedings (Case IV/M.709, *Telefónica/Sogecable/Cablevisión*).

Merger Regulation cases in which third parties have unsuccessfully sought interim measures from the Court of First Instance are Case T–96/92R *CCE de la Société Générale des Grandes Sources v. Commission* [1992] II ECR 2579 and Case T–12/93R *CCE Vittel and CE Pierval v. Commission* [1993] II ECR 785, both arising out of the Commission's decision in *Nestlé/Perrier* (Case IV/M.190, OJ 1992 L356/1); and Case T–322/94R *Union Carbide Corporation v. Commission* [1994] II ECR 1159, rejecting an application by a competitor for an interim order that the notifying parties refrain from carrying out the concentrative JV that had been declared by the Commission to be compatible with the common market, subject to compliance with certain conditions and obligations, in *Shell/Montecatini* (Case IV/M.269, OJ 1994 L332/48). For further discussion of interim relief from the Court, see paras. 12–127 *et seq.* of the main work.

9. PRINCIPLE OF EXCLUSIVITY OF JURISDICTION

(a) *Principle of exclusivity*

6–142 **European Economic Area.** In *Orkla/Volvo* (Case IV/M.582, OJ 1996 L66/17) the Commission had exclusive jurisdiction to assess a merger affecting the market for beer in Norway. In accordance with Article 8 of and Protocol 3 to the EEA Agreement, certain beers brewed from substances other than malt are not covered by the Agreement such that the Commission's decision did not relate to the Norwegian market for those products (*ibid.*, point 9).

6–143 **National rules.** A number of countries within the EEA have introduced or amended their merger control rules in recent years. An updated summary of the basic jurisdictional tests and notification requirements of the national merger control regimes is given in the following table.

MERGER CONTROL REGIMES IN EEA STATES

(position as at September 1996)

Country	Jurisdictional criteria	Notification requirements
Austria	Combined worldwide turnover of Sch. 150 million (c. 11m ECU)	Mandatory prior notification if: (a) combined worldwide turnover of Sch. 3,500m (c. 250m ECU); and (b) at least two parties each have worldwide turnover of Sch. 5m (c. 0.4m ECU). Otherwise mandatory post notification
Belgium	(a) Combined worldwide turnover of BF 3,000m (c. 70m ECU); and (b) Combined market share in Belgium of 25 per cent	Mandatory prior notification
Denmark	No specific merger control regime	
Finland	No specific merger control regime	
France	(a) Combined turnover in France of FF 7,000m (c. 1,000m ECU), provided at least two parties each have turnover in France of FF 2,000m (c. 300m ECU); or (b) Combined market share in France of 25 per cent	Voluntary notification
Germany	Combined worldwide turnover of DM 500m (c. 250m ECU)	Mandatory prior notification if: (a) at least one party has worldwide turnover of DM 2,000m (c. 1,000m ECU); or (b) at least two parties each have worldwide turnover of DM 1,000m (c. 500m ECU). Otherwise mandatory post notification.

Country	Jurisdictional criteria	Notification requirements
Greece	(a) combined turnover of 50m ECU and at least two parties have turnover in Greece of 5m ECU; or (b) combined market share in Greece of 25 per cent	Mandatory prior notifiction
Iceland	No specific merger control regime	
Ireland	(a) At least two parties each have gross assets of IR £10m (c. 12m ECU); or (b) At least two parties each have turnover of IR £20m (c. 25m ECU) .	Mandatory prior notification
Italy	(a) Combined turnover in Italy of Lire 636,000m (c. 300m ECU); or (b) Undertaking to be acquired has turnover in Italy of Lire 63,600m (c. 30m ECU)	Mandatory prior notification
Lichtenstein	No specific merger control regime	
Luxembourg	No specific merger control regime	
Netherlands (draft legislation)	Combined worldwide turnover of DFl 250m (c. 120m ECU), provided at least two parties have turnover in the Netherlands of DFl 30m (c. 14m ECU)	Mandatory prior notification
Norway	No specific merger control regime	
Portugal	(a) Combined turnover in Portugal of Esc. 30,000m (c. 180m ECU); or (b) Combined market share in Portugal of 30 per cent	Mandatory prior notification
Spain	(a) Combined turnover in Spain of Ptas 20,000m (c. 125m ECU); or (b) Combined market share in Spain of 25 per cent	Voluntary notification
Sweden	Combined worldwide turnover of SKr 4,000m (c. 430m ECU)	Mandatory prior notification

Country	Jurisdictional criteria	Notification requirements
United Kingdom	(a) Undertaking to be acquired has worldwide gross assets of £70m (c. 90m ECU); or (b) Results in or increases market share in UK (or substantial part) of 25 per cent or more	Voluntary notification

(b) *Referral to the national competition authorities*

Article 9. In December 1993 the Council agreed to the Commission's proposal to postpone the review of the Article 9 procedures to the end of 1996. The Commission has proposed a number of changes in its 1996 review of the Merger Regulation: see para. 6–005A *supra*. **6–144**

Decision **6–146**

n. 33. See also *MSG Media Services* (Case IV/M.469, OJ 1994 L364/1) where the Commission held that the proposed establishment of a concentrative JV in Germany in the provision of pay-TV services was incompatible with the common market.

n. 34. See also *McCormick/CPC/Rabobank/Ostmann* (Case IV/M.330, Decision of 3 November 1993) considered at n. 39 *infra*; *Holdercim/Cedest* (Case IV/M.460, Decision of 6 July 1994) considered at § 6–148, *infra*; and *Gehe/Lloyds* (Case IV/M.716, Decision of 22 March 1996) where the Commission agreed to an Art. 9 reference to the United Kingdom authorities because of concerns about the proposed merger's impact on competition in the wholesale and retail pharmaceutical markets in the United Kingdom; the United Kingdom Secretary of State subsequently referred the case to the Monopolies and Mergers Commission.

Timing **6–147**

n. 39. See *McCormick/CPC/Rabobank/Ostmann*, *supra*, where the Commission agreed to a request for referral from the German authorities. The Commission had intended to deal with the case itself by opening a Phase II inquiry. However, as a result of an error in the calculation of the Art. 10(1) deadline this option was foreclosed. Nevertheless, the possibility of an Art. 9 referral remained open pursuant to Art. 10(6) read in conjunction with Art. (4)(a).

Concept of distinct market. In *Holdercim/Cedest* (Case IV/M.460, Decision of 6 July 1994), the French authorities invoked the Article 9 procedure because of concerns about the impact of the concentration on **6–148**

the supply of ready-mixed concrete. The Commission agreed to the request, given that the geographic reference markets were separate markets within France and did not constitute a substantial part of the Community.

(c) *National investigations on grounds other than competition*

6–150 **Public security.** Article 21(3) was invoked for the first time in *IBM France/CGI* (Case IV/M.336, Decision of 19 May 1993) where the French authorities informed the Commission that they were taking measures to protect French legitimate interests linked to public security: XXIIIrd Report on Competition Policy (1993), point 321.

6–151 **Plurality of the media**

n. 50. See, *e.g.*, *Newspaper Publishing* (Case IV/M.423, Decision of 14 March 1994) where the jurisdiction of the United Kingdom authorities (under Part V of the Fair Trading Act 1973) related to issues such as the accurate presentation of news and the free expression of opinion.

6–153 **Other grounds**

n. 51. In *Lyonnaise des Eaux/Northumbrian Water*, the proposed bid was referred to the United Kingdom Monopolies and Mergers Commission in March 1995 for investigation under the Water Industry Act 1991. This United Kingdom legislative framework provides that there should be a sufficient number of independent water enterprises to allow the Director General of Water Services to make comparisons of efficiencies. In a decision of 29 March 1995 addressed to the United Kingdom government, the Commission accepted this as a legitimate interest, but specified that the Monopolies and Mergers Commission should concern itself solely with the issues set out in that Act: see MMC Report, Cm, 2936 (July 1995), App. 1.2. The MMC accordingly considered that in evaluating the proposed merger it could not take account of the potential implications of the merger for competition, employment or regional policy: *ibid.* para. 1.9. (Nonetheless, the MMC concluded that the merger would be expected to operate against the public interest.) The merger was subsequently approved by the Commission under the Merger Regulation (Case IV/M.567, Decision of 21 December 1995.

(d) *Article 22(3) requests from Member States*

6–154 **Investigation requested by Member State**

n. 52. See also *RTL/Veronica/Endemol* (Case IV/M.553, Decision of 20 September 1995), a case which affected the Dutch TV production and advertising markets and was referred to the Commission under Art. 22 by the Dutch authorities. The Commission prohibited the concentration, which had already been completed, but after Endemol then withdrew its participation the Commission subsequently cleared the joint venture in its modified form: IP (96) 653 of 17 July 1996 [1996] 5 CMLR 256. However, a challenge to the original decision before the CFI is being pursued: Case T–221/95 *Endemol Entertainment Holding v. Commission*, not yet decided. In *Kesko/Tuko* (Case IV/M.784), the Finnish authorities made a request under Article 22 in respect of a merge between two Finnish supermarket chains; the Commission opened Phase II proceedings in respect of that case. In *Blokker/Toys 'R' Us* (Case IV/M.801, Decision of 22 August 1996), the Dutch authorities again made a request under Art. 22. However, in that case the Commission declined jurisdiction on the basis that the proposed merger had yet to be the subject of a binding agreement. In *British Airways/DanAir*, the Commission found that the concentration did not create or strengthen a dominant position on the Brussels/London route, which was the only aspect that potentially affected competition in Belgium. That decision was not the subject of appeal; for Case T–3/93, see para. 6–050, n. 17, *supra*.

(e) *Mergers in the defence sector*

Member State involvement. In 1993 the French authorities relied on Article 223(1)(b) when they informed the Commission that they had requested the parties to a concentration with a Community dimension not to notify it to the Commission: see XXIIIrd Report on Competition Policy (1993), points 324 to 326. That merger concerned the manufacture of engines for missiles. After an informal inquiry the Commission was satisfied that the concentration would have no spillover effects on non-military products. Likewise, in 1994 the Commission accepted that the United Kingdom authorities could invoke Article 223(1)(b) in respect of the competing bids by GEC and British Aerospace for VSEL: see XXIVth Report on Competition Policy (1994), point 336. However, the Commission requested that the two bids should be notified in respect of VSEL's non-military activities although those activities represented only an extremely limited part of the operation: *British Aerospace/VSEL* (Case IV/M.528, Decision of 24 November 1994), *GEC/VSEL* (Case IV/M.529, Decision of 7 December 1994); see further para. 13–035, *infra*. **6–157**

10. MERGERS AND ACQUISITIONS UNDER ARTICLES 85 AND 86

(b) *The current position on concentrations*

Scope of implementing regulations **6–161**

n. 68. *R. v. Secretary of State for Trade and Industry, ex p. Airlines of Britain* is reported at [1993] BCC 89.

(c) *The current position on non-concentrative transactions*

6–164 **Minority shareholdings and other links not conferring control**

n. 76. The revised Interface Notice deals only with operations involving joint control. The new Concentration Notice refers to management links and cross-shareholdings (points 6 to 7), minority shareholdings (points 13 to 14) and options (point 15), considering circumstances where these may give rise to sole control or (in combination with factors considered at points 18 *et seq.*) joint control.

6–165 **Article 85.** In *BT/MCI*, OJ 1994 L223/36 [1995] 5 CMLR 285, a complex alliance proposed between two leading United Kingdom and US telecommunications operators was originally notified as a concentration under the Merger Regulation but the Commission found that it did not constitute a concentration and therefore converted the notification to an application for negative clearance or exemption under Regulation 17. One aspect of the arrangement was the acquisition by British Telecom of a 20 per cent shareholding in MCI, with corresponding board representation. This agreement included a 'standstill' provision whereby BT undertook for 10 years not to acquire any further ownership interest or to seek to control or influence MCI. Having regard to that prohibition, and also to the provisions of U.S. anti-trust law that prevented misuse by BT of MCI's confidential information, the Commission concluded that the investment did not come within the scope of Article 85.

CHAPTER 7

VERTICAL AGREEMENTS AFFECTING DISTRIBUTION OR SUPPLY

1. INTRODUCTION

The distribution sector under Article 85. For an overview of the pro- and anti-competitive effects of different restrictions commonly found in vertical agreements, see the OECD report, *Competition Policy and Vertical Restraints: Franchising Agreements* (1994). The report concludes that all types of vertical restraints may either increase or decrease economic efficiency, depending crucially on market structure and the extent of inter-brand competition from other brands and retailers. **7–003**

2. AGENCY

True agency agreements fall outside Article 85(1). The EFTA Surveillance Authority has issued an equivalent notice as regards the application of Article 53(1) of the EEA Agreement: OJ 1994 L153/1 [1994] 4 CMLR 339. **7–004**

n. 5. For the reference to App. 16 in the main work, substitute App. 21.

Where an agent is an independent trader **7–005**

n. 11. See also Case C–266/93 *Bundeskartellamt v. Volkswagen and VAG Leasing* [1996] 4 CMLR 478 § 19.

n. 13. The Commission's decision in *Distribution of railway tickets by travel agents* was annulled by the CFI on the grounds that the activities concerned "operations of providers of services ancillary to transport" within the scope of Regulation 1017/68: Case T–14/93 *Union Inter-*

nationale des Chemins de Fer v. Commission [1995] II ECR 1503 [1996] 5 CMLR 40, on appeal by the Commission Case C–264/95P: see § 15–004, *infra*.

3. DISTRIBUTION AGREEMENTS

(a) *Generally*

7–011 **Exclusive distribution.** The block exemptions, Regulations 1983/83 and 1984/83, apply also with regard to Article 53 of the EEA Agreement subject to necessary modifications: Article 60 and Annex XIV, points 2–3, of the EEA Agreement. And see, *e.g. Holmsund Golv*, OJ 1994 C398/8 [1995] 4 CMLR 673, for an Article 19(3) Notice indicating the EFTA Surveillance Authority's intention to take a favourable view of an exclusive distribution agreement.

7–013 **Territorial protection of the distributor.** For the use of product differentiation as a means of preventing parallel imports, where the formulation of a product requires approval under national law, see *Zera/Montedison*, para. 7–021, *infra*.

n. 31. The Commission's decision in *Newitt/Dunlop Slazenger International* was substantially upheld by the CFI, Case T–43/92 *Dunlop Slazenger v. Commission* [1994] II ECR 441.

7–014 **The Community approach**

n. 38. See also XXIIIrd Report on Competition Policy (1993), points 211–12.

(b) *Measures obstructing parallel imports*

7–019 **Export bans prohibited**

n. 53. The appeals against the Commission's decision in *Viho/Parker Pen* were dismissed by the CFI, save that the fine on Parker Pen was reduced: Case T–66/92 *Herlitz v. Commission* [1994] ECR II 531 [1995] 5 CMLR 458 and Case T–77/92 *Parker Pen v. Commission* [1994] II ECR 549 [1995] 5 CMLR 435.

n. 54. See also: *BASF Lacke+Farben/Accinauto*, OJ 1995 L272/16, in which a fine of 2.7m ECU was imposed on BASF for prohibiting its exclusive dealer in Belgium from exporting to lower priced markets, in particular the United Kingdom; *ADALAT*, OJ 1996 L201/1 [1996] 5 CMLR 416, on appeal Case T–41/96 *Bayer v. Commission*, in which a fine of three million ECU was imposed on Bayer for refusing to supply wholesalers engaged in parallel trade; and *Tretorn and others*, OJ 1994 L378/45, on appeal by one defendant, Case T–49/95 *Van Megen Sports Group v. Commission.*

Pricing to restrict exports. The Commission's decision in *Newitt/Dunlop Slazenger International* was substantially upheld by the Court of First Instance, Case T–43/92 *Dunlop Slazenger v. Commission* [1994] II ECR 441. However, the Court held that the duration of the infringement was shorter than that found by the Commission and the fine was therefore reduced from five million to three million ECU. **7–020**

n. 60. The appeal against the decision in *Bayo-n-ox* was dismissed for being out of time: Case C–195/91P *Bayer v. Commission* [1994] I ECR 5619 [1996] 4 CMLR 32. See also *Organon*, XXVth Report on Competition Policy (1995), points 37–38 (only contraceptive pills to be sold in the United Kingdom, not those intended for export, qualified for discount).

Other measures impeding parallel imports. Product differentiation can be used to give absolute territorial protection contrary to Article 85(1). The Commission held that where the formulation of a herbicide requires approval under the law of one Member State in order to be sold, offering slightly different formulations in other Member States has the effect of a ban on parallel imports: *Zera/Montedison* OJ 1993 L272/28 [1995] 5 CMLR 320 and see XXIIIrd Report on Competition Policy (1993), point 212. **7–021**

n. 62. *Newitt/Dunlop Slazenger International* was substantially upheld by the CFI: Case T–43/92 *Dunlop Slazenger v. Commission*, *supra*. See also *Tretorn and others* OJ 1994 L378/45 (marking of products to identify origin of parallel imports and refusal of supplies), on appeal by one defendant, Case T–49/95 *Van Megen Sports Group v. Commission.*

n. 67. The appeal against the decision in *Bayo-n-ox* was dismissed: n. 60, *supra*.

n. 71. For *Newitt/Dunlop Slazenger International*, see § 7–020, *supra*.

(c) *Individual agreements under Article 85(1)*

Exclusive supply to distributor. See also *Holmsund Golv*, OJ 1994 398/8 [1995] 4 CMLR 673: Article 19(3) Notice by the EFTA Surveillance **7–027**

Authority indicating its intention to take a favourable view of a mixed exclusive and non-exclusive distribution system.

n. 85. See now *Ivoclar (No. 2)*, OJ 1993 C251/3 [1994] 4 CMLR 578: Art. 19(3) Notice stating intention to extend the exemption.

7–036 **Resale Price Maintenance.** On further appeal, the Court of Justice held that both the Commission and the Court of First Instance had erred in not taking account of the evidence relating to the effects on competition of the net book agreement in the United Kingdom and, in particular, the findings of the English Restrictive Practices Court in 1962, and remitted the case back to the Commission: Case C–360/92P, *Publishers Association v. Commission* [1995] I ECR 23 [1995] 5 CMLR 33 [1996] ICR 121. However, the net book agreement was referred by the United Kingdom authorities back to the Restrictive Practices Court and was held by the Irish Competition Authority to be contrary to Irish competition law (Decision No. 336 of 10 June 1994). The agreement has now been abandoned.

Cf. Sammelrevers (1994), in which the Commission issued what appears to have been a "provisional" comfort letter in respect of the resale price maintenance agreements between German and Austrian publishers and German and Austrian booksellers. The Commission stated that the agreements came within Article 85(1) but, somewhat surprisingly, found that there were grounds for exemption under Article 85(3): the arrangement contributed to an improvement in the distribution of goods and to the promotion of books as cultural items. However, the closure of the file was limited to 30 June 1996 and the Commission has more recently stated that this was not its definitive position but that it intends to take a formal decision on whether or not the conditions for exemption under Article 85(3) were in fact fulfilled: OJ 1996 C54/2.

See also *Rover Group*, XXIIIrd Report on Competition Policy (1993), point 228: maximum levels of discount.

7–046 **Customer and guarantee service.** In its decision renewing individual exemption for Grundig's selective distribution network, the Commission records that, pending the introduction of a Europe-wide contractual warranty, the company had undertaken that its distributors would allow consumers to claim in their country of residence the benefit of statutory warranty rights under the law of the country of purchase: *Grundig (No. 2)*, OJ 1994 L20/15 [1995] 4 CMLR 658, para. 19.

(d) *Regulation 1983/83*

7–048 **In general.** Regulation 1983/83 applies to Article 53 of the EEA Agreement, subject to necessary amendments: EEA Agreement, Annex XIV, point 2.

Regulation 1983/83 would expire on 31 December 1997, but at the time of writing, it is expected to be extended by a further two years. The Commission was due to publish in 1996 a Green Paper on vertical restraints on trade, to cover the operation of the block exemptions on exclusive distribution, exclusive purchasing and franchising agreements: XXVth Report on Competition Policy (1995), point 44; however, that is now expected in 1997.

The Commission's Notice. The EFTA Surveillance Authority has issued an equivalent Notice as regards exclusive distribution and exclusive purchasing agreements: OJ 1994 L153/1 [1994] 4 CMLR 317, as amended (in respect of beer tie agreements) by OJ 1994 L186/57. **7–050**

Revocation. See the observations by the Court of First Instance as regards Article 14 of Regulation 1984/83, which gives the Commission equivalent power to withdraw the benefit of the block exemption for exclusive purchasing agreements: para. 7–124, *infra*. **7–067**

(e) *Individual exemption under Article 85(3)*

Individual exemptions under Article 85(3) **7–069**

n. 21. See also *Sony Espana*, OJ 1993 C275/3 [1994] 4 CMLR 581, where the Commission issued an Art. 19(3) Notice expressing the intention to grant exemption to the closed distribution network being established by Sony's Spanish subsidiary for professional electronic equipment that combined exclusive distribution of some products and selective distribution of other products. Note *Bayer/BP Chemicals (No. 2)*, OJ 1994 L174/34, amending the conditions for plant closure included in the previous decision.

4. SELECTIVE DISTRIBUTION SYSTEMS

(b) *Some leading cases*

Basic principles. In Case C–376/92 *Metro SB-Grossmärkte v. Cartier* [1994] I ECR 15 [1994] 5 CMLR 331, the Court of Justice held that where a selective distribution system satisfies the conditions for validity under Article 85(1), the manufacturer's restriction of his guarantee to products purchased from authorised dealers is also valid as it imposes no greater a restriction on competition than the restriction on sales. The Court also held that a selective distribution system is not incompatible with Article **7–075**

85 only because the products may be imported into the Community after being obtained from a supplier outside in a country where no selective distribution system exists.

n. 33. There should be added to the list of Commission decisions: *Sony Espana*, OJ 1993 C275/3 [1994] 4 CMLR 581 (proposed exemption); *Grundig (No. 2)*, OJ 1994 L20/15 [1995] 4 CMLR 658 (renewal of exemption for a further 10 years); *Ivoclar (No. 2)*, OJ 1993 C251/3 [1994] 4 CMLR 578 (proposal to extend the exemption). Judgments are pending in appeals against the Commissioner's grant of exemption in *Yves St Laurent*, Case T–19/92 *Lelerc v. Commission*; and *Parfums Givenchy*, Case T–87/92 *Kruidvat v. Commission.*

(b) *Article 85(1)*

7–084 **Objective technical requirements: suitable products**

n. 75. See now *Grundig (No. 2)*, OJ 1994 L20/15 [1995] 4 CMLR 658 (renewal of exemption) and also *Sony Pan-European Dealer Agreement*, OJ 1993 C321/11; [1994] 5 CMLR 101 (Notice), Press Release IP (95) 736, July 12, 1995 [1995] 5 CMLR 126; *Sony Espana*, OJ 1993 C275/3 [1994] 4 CMLR 581 (professional electronic equipment); *Kenwood Electronics Deutschland*, OJ 1993 C67/9 [1993] 4 CMLR 389 (car audio equipment).

n. 76. See also *Chanel*, OJ 1994 C334/11, [1995] 4 CMLR 108.

n. 78. See also *Schott-Zwiesel-Glaswerke*, OJ 1993 C111/4, [1993] 5 CMLR 85.

7–085 **Luxury and prestige products.** The Commission's decisions in *Yves St Laurent Parfums* and *Parfums Givenchy* were challenged by retailers that were not admitted to the networks: see Case T–19/92 *Leclerc v. Commission* and Case T–87/92 *Kruidvat v. Commission*, not yet decided.

n. 87. The United Kingdom Monopolies and Mergers Commission followed the principles of *Yves Saint Laurent Parfums* in its report on *Fine Fragrances* (Cm. 2380, November 1993). See also, as regards a possible arbitration procedure, the written answer in the European Parliament, 14 September 1994 [1994] 5 CMLR 512.

7–086 **Qualitative criteria outside Article 85(1)**

n. 89. Grundig's exemption has been renewed in similar terms for a further 10 years, OJ 1994 L20/15 [1995] 4 CMLR 658.

Procedure for admission to the network. See also the Commission's approach to the notifications by Sony of selective distribution networks for electronic equipment. In *Sony Espana*, OJ 1993 C275/3, [1994] 4 CMLR 581, the Commission obtained Sony's agreement that a distributor would automatically be admitted to the network in Spain if their application had not been rejected, with written reasons, six months after application. In *Sony Pan-European Dealer Agreement*, OJ 1993 C321/11, [1994] 5 CMLR 101 (Notice), Press Release IP (95) 736, 12 July 1995 [1995] 5 CMLR 126, the Commission approved Sony's pan-European dealer agreement after it was changed to provide that Sony may not refuse to supply a product to an authorised distributor without written justification, and for an independent arbitration procedure to which a dealer refused authorisation may appeal. **7–087**

n. 96. The decisions in both *Yves St Laurent Parfums* and *Parfums Givenchy* are on appeal: see § 7–085, *supra*.

Additional obligations or restrictions within Article 85(1). In *Grundig (No. 2)*, OJ 1994 L20/15 [1995] 4 CMLR 658, the Commission held that requirements on dealers as to the range of products carried and levels of stock went beyond what was necessary for an "appropriate" distribution of the products and meant that dealers "must take sales promoting measures that restrict their commercial independence" (para. 35). These obligations therefore came within Article 85(1) but the exemption previously granted to the network agreement was renewed for 10 years. **7–089**

n. 4 and n. 10. For the appeal against the Commission's decision, see § 7–085, *supra*.

Territorial and other restrictions on resale **7–090**

n. 8. See also *Ivoclar (No. 2)*, OJ 1993 C251/3 [1994] 4 CMLR 578: Art. 19(3) Notice stating intention to extend the exemption.

(d) *Application of Article 85(3)*

Sales promotion obligations **7–093**

n. 17. See also *Grundig (No. 2)*, § 7–089, *supra*.

Territorial limitation of outlets **7–094**

n. 25. The Commission expressed its intention of granting *Ivoclar* continued exemption: OJ 1993 C251/3 [1994] 4 CMLR 578.

7–095 **Customer restrictions**

n. 28. See also *Ivoclar (No. 2)*, n. 25, *supra.*

(e) *Regulation 123/85*

7–096 **General.** Regulation 123/85 expired on 30 June 1995 but it continued to apply until 30 September 1995 under the terms of Regulation 1475/95 which replaces it: see Appendix 2, *post.* Commentary on Regulation 1475/95, insofar as it differs significantly from Regulation 123/85, follows in the next section (paras. 7–108A *et seq.*, *infra*), repeating the headings used in this section insofar as practicable. However, many of the provisions are in identical or similar form in both block exemptions and much of the commentary and case law relating to Regulation 123/85 therefore remains relevant to Regulation 1475/95. The authorities, all of which relate to agreements falling under Regulation 123/85, are referred to in respect of that Regulation and are not repeated in the commentary on Regulation 1475/95. Readers concerned with the operation of agreements under Regulation 1475/95 should therefore consult the commentary on both Regulations.

Regulation 123/85 applies with necessary modifications under Article 53 of the EEA Agreement: Annex XIV, point 4; and Regulation 1475/95 now similarly applies: Annex XIV, point 4a. The EFTA Surveillance Authority issued a notice with regard to the earlier block exemption equivalent to the Commission's Notice: OJ 1994 L153/1 [1994] 4 CMLR 332.

7–097 **Aims of Regulation 123/85**

n. 37. The ESA has issued an equivalent Notice regarding motor vehicle intermediaries: OJ 1994 L186/57.

7–098 **Agreements within Regulation 123/85.** Regulation 123/85 does not lay down mandatory provisions but prescribes conditions under which agreements between suppliers and approved distributors are removed from the prohibition in Article 85(1). Therefore, although the Regulation states what the supplier and dealer may or may not do in their relations with third parties, it does not regulate the activities of third parties themselves, who may operate outside the framework of Regulation 123/85. See Cases C–226/94 *Grand Garage Albigeois v. Garage Massol* [1996] I ECR 651 and C–53/95 *Nissan France v. Dupasquier* [1996] I ECR 677.

n. 35. Peugeot's appeals to the CFI and ECJ against the decision in *Eco System/Peugeot* were dismissed: Case T–9/92 *Peugeot v. Commission*

[1993] II ECR 493 [1995] 5 CMLR 696 and Case C–322/93P [1994] I ECR 2727.

n. 45. Leasing companies which do not offer an option to purchase are not resellers of motor vehicles within Reg. 123/45: Cases C–70/93 *BMW v. ALD* and C–266/93 *Bundeskartellamt v. Volkswagen* and *VAG Leasing* [1995] I ECR 3439, 3477 [1996] 4 CMLR 478.

Permitted restrictions on the authorised dealers. In Cases C–70/93 *BMW v. ALD Auto-Leasing* and C–266/93 *Bundeskartellamt v. Volkswagen and VAG Leasing* [1995] I ECR 3439, 3477, [1996] 4 CMLR 478, the Court of Justice held that a motor vehicle manufacturer was not permitted to restrict the dealers in its network as regards the supplies of vehicles to independent leasing companies. The requirement imposed by BMW on its dealers that vehicles would be supplied only if the lessee to whom they would be made available had its seat in the territory of the dealer in question was held to be contrary to Article 85(1) and outside any permitted exemption in Regulation 123/85. The requirement imposed by Volkswagen that its dealers should act as exclusive agents for its subsidiary leasing company was also contrary to Article 85(1). **7–100**

n. 51. See now Case T–9/92 *Peugeot v. Commission* [1993] II ECR 493 [1995] 5 CMLR 696, on appeal Case C–322/93P [1994] I ECR 2727. Dismissing Peugeot's appeal from the decision in *Eco System/Peugeot*, the CFI held that an undertaking which bears no legal and financial risk with regard to the motor vehicles purchased on behalf of customers is an intermediary for the purpose of Art. 3(11) although it carries on its activity as a business, promoting its services to the public and granting its customers credit by obtaining reimbursement of the purchase price only after paying the supplier.

n. 52. The ESA has issued an equivalent Notice: OJ 1994 L186/57.

Conditions to be satisfied by the authorised dealers. Provided that a motor vehicle is first supplied by an authorised dealer, it is not permissible to refuse guarantee services to a consumer who purchased the vehicle from a dealer outside the manufacturer's distribution network, (*e.g.* on a later sale). Because of the number of complaints received in this regard from parallel traders, the Commission sent warning letters to a number of manufacturers on this point: XXIVth Report on Competition Policy (1994), Annex II, p. 363. See also Press Release IP (94) 488 of 7 June 1994. **7–102**

Non-applicability of Regulation 123/85. For a parallel distribution network for spare parts that took a motor vehicle distribution network outside Regulation 123/85, see *Cicra/Fiat Auto SpA*, XXIVth Report on Competition Policy (1994), Annex II, p. 361. **7–106**

7–107 **Revocation of the block exemption**

n. 78. Peugeot's appeals to the CFI and ECJ against the decision in *Eco System/Peugeot* were dismissed: Case T–9/92 *Peugeot v. Commission* [1993] II ECR 493 [1995] 5 CMLR 696 and Case C–322/93P [1994] I ECR 2727.

7–107A **Enforcement and severance.** Once an agreement falls outside the terms of Regulation 123/85, all the provisions of the agreement restrictive of competition are void under Article 85(1) (subject only to the possibility of applying for individual exemption which in those circumstances is most unlikely to be granted). The result may be to deprive the dealer of many of the commercial safeguards in the agreement, *i.e.* the restrictive provisions designed for his benefit, or, where severance is impossible, to leave the dealer with no agreement at all. This has caused particular difficulty for dealers in those cases where the anti-competitive behaviour has been imposed by the supplier. Although unilateral action is not of itself within the scope of Article 85, ostensibly unilateral action has in certain circumstances been construed as part of a tacit agreement: see further paras. 7–066 and 7–083 of the main work; the Commission's decision in *Eco System/Peugeot, supra*, and Case C–70/93 *BMW v. ALD* [1995] I ECR 3439 [1996] 4 CMLR 478 paras. 15–18. A dealer may therefore be able to complain that apparently unilateral behaviour by the supplier takes the agreement outside the protection of the block exemption and is contrary to Article 85(1), but in so doing the dealer risks the entire agreement being held void.

In an English case, *Richard Cound Ltd v. BMW (GB) Ltd*, (C.A.) 10 May 1995, in which notice of termination had been given by BMW to the plaintiff dealer under an agreement benefiting from Regulation 123/85, the Court of Appeal held, first, that if the agreement fell within the block exemption the supplier could terminate the agreement on 12 months notice without applying objective qualitative criteria; secondly, that if the agreement were taken outside the block exemption on account of the anti-competitive practices alleged by the dealer, so many of the terms would be void as to render the remaining agreement of such a different character as to make it incapable of severance, and therefore void in its entirety, with the result that there would be no agreement left in respect of which the plaintiff could seek relief; and thirdly, that giving notice of termination was a unilateral act and therefore not one to which the provisions of Article 85 applied. *Cf.* para. 7–108I, *infra*, regarding the introduction of some limited protection for the dealer in this regard in Regulation 1475/95. For severance generally, see paras. 10–026 to 10–029 of the main work and *infra*.

A dealer may complain to the Commission and request it to take action in respect of infringements of Article 85(1) that fall outside the block exemption. The Commission is not necessarily obliged to investigate complaints but once it takes a decision, that is subject to challenge under Article 173 and in certain circumstances a complainant can apply to the

Court for a declaration under Article 175 that the Commission has failed to act: see Chapter 12 of the main work. The Commission's refusal to use its powers, or its slow response, upon complaints by motor vehicle distributors is the subject of a number of applications to the Court of First Instance. The Commission has declined to pursue such complaints on the grounds that the issue is the subject of an investigation in another complaint, (*e.g.* Case T–186/94, *Guérin Automobiles v. Commission* [1995] II ECR 1753 [1996] 4 CMLR 685 (action dismissed)), on appeal Case C–282/9SP; or has simply delayed (Case T–189/95 *SGA v. Commission* and Case T–199/95 *Le Nouveau Garage v. Commission*, not yet decided). See also Case T–9/96 *Européenne Automobile v. Commission*, not yet decided (damages claim against the Commission for failure to act).

7–108 **Transitional provisions.** Regulation 123/85 continued to apply until 30 September 1995: Regulation 1475/95, Article 13. See further para. 7–108A, *infra.*

(f) *Regulation 1475/95*

7–108A **Regulation 1475/95: transitional arrangements.** The first motor vehicle block exemption, Regulation 123/85, expired on 30 June 1995, and was replaced by Regulation 1475/95: Appendix 2, *post.* This entered into force on 1 July 1995 but applies from 1 October 1995 until 30 September 2002: Article 13. Transitional arrangements provide that agreements already in force on 1 October 1995 and which satisfy the requirements for exemption under Regulation 123/85 remain exempt until 1 October 1996: Article 7.

On 19 July 1996 Regulation 1475/95 was adopted by the EFTA States in the EEA so as to apply under Article 53 of the EEA Agreement: EEA Joint Committee Decision 46/96.

7–108B **Aims of Regulation 1475/95.** The underlying rationale of the block exemption remains as set out in paragraphs 7–096 to 7–097 of the main work. However, a number of significant changes were introduced in Regulation 1475/95 which reflect the substance of a large number of complaints to the Commission and extensive consultations with interested parties. Those complaints apparently mainly concerned constraints on inter-state trade, and unattainable sales targets: XXIVth Report on Competition Policy (1994), point 116. The Commission has issued an Explanatory Brochure (Appendix 3, *post*) which summarises the change of emphasis in the new block exemption as designed to:

(1) give dealers, the great majority of whom are small or medium sized enterprises, greater commercial independence *vis-à-vis* manufacturers;

(2) give independent spare-part manufacturers and distributors easier access to the various markets, notably the outlets provided by the car manufacturers' networks;
(3) improve the position of consumers in accordance with the principles underlying the internal market;
(4) make the dividing line between acceptable and unacceptable agreements and behaviour clearer.

See also the written answer by the Competition Commissioner in the European Parliament to a question concerning the difficulty experienced by German buyers in acquiring cars from dealers in Denmark at the lower Danish prices:

> "If the revised regulation were to bring about more flexible relationships between manufacturers and dealers, this would lead to the emergence of dealers who would be better able to resist the pressure by manufacturers and thus be more willing to supply new vehicles to customers from other Member States." 31 October 1994 [1994] 5 CMLR 514.

For commentary, see Van Overbeek, "Regulation 1475/95 relating to the Exclusive Selective Distribution of Motor Vehicles" (1996) ICCLR 185.

7–108C **Permitted restrictions on the supplier.** Articles 1 and 2 of Regulation 1475/95 reproduce Articles 1 and 2 of Regulation 123/85: see para. 7–099 of the main work.

7–108D **Permitted restrictions on the authorised dealers.** Regulation 1475/95 introduced some important changes to the restrictions which may be imposed on the dealers. *First*, there is a limitation on the supplier's right to require the dealer not to sell other marks. The dealer must now be able to sell competing makes of motor vehicle, although the supplier may require that they are sold on separate premises, under separate management, in the form of a distinct legal entity, and in a manner which avoids confusion between makes: Article 3(3). This provision must be read with Article 3(4) whereby the supplier may require the dealer not to permit a third party to benefit unduly from the use of a common workshop. *Secondly*, and providing scope for increased price competition between dealers, in place of the broad prohibition on dealers seeking customers for contract goods outside the territory there is permitted only a more limited restriction on "personalised advertising", *i.e.* direct canvassing by telephone or letter: Article 3(8) and Recital (9). *Thirdly*, Article 3(10) repeats the permitted restriction on supplying motor vehicles for resale only to other dealers in the network, but Regulation 1475/95 clarifies the meaning of resale in Article 6(1)(7) and in the definitions, Article 10(12) and (13): motor vehicles must be in a new condition, and "resale" includes any car offered by a lessor which includes purchase or an option to purchase (see further, para. 7–100, *supra*). The permitted restriction on sales to consumers purchasing through intermediaries remains unchanged

(Article 3(11)) and the Commission's Notice on that topic (App. 15 to the main work) continues to apply: Explanatory Brochure, page 26.

Other permitted provisions. Article 4(1)(3), (4) and (5) provides for a third party expert to adjudicate in case of disagreement between the parties over sales targets, levels of stocks to be maintained by the dealer or the range and number of demonstration vehicles to be kept by the dealer. This new provision is designed to ease the difficulty caused by suppliers setting unrealistic sales targets, but it refers to sales targets in the "territory" and thereby impliedly maintains the dealer's first responsibility to promote sales in his designated area rather than to engage in parallel trade. It seems that the refusal by a supplier to provide a dealer with motor vehicles in excess of his sales target, so as to restrict the dealer's deals outside his territory, would be covered by Article 6(1)(7) and constitute prohibited conduct; see also Recital (26). **7–108E**

Duration and termination. Where the agreement imposes minimum standards for the dealer as regards staff and facilities, as is customary, protection for the dealer's investment is given by the requirements of Regulation 1475/95 regarding duration and termination. Such an agreement must be either indefinite or for a period of at least five years: Article 5(2)(2); *cf.* the minimum period of four years in Regulation 123/85. If the parties conclude the agreement for an indefinite period, they must provide for at least a two year period of notice for termination: Article 5(2)(2); *cf.* the one year notice period in Regulation 123/85. Other provisions for termination remain unchanged, *e.g.* termination for cause (although reference is introduced to a party's failure to perform one of its "basic obligations"): Article 5(3). See further para. 7–1081, *infra*. **7–108F**

Revocation of the block exemption. Article 8 of Regulation 1475/95 allows the Commission to withdraw the benefit of the block exemption in certain circumstances, broadly similar to those in Regulation 123/85, where competition is ineffective, even if the agreement otherwise complies with its provisions. See paras. 7–104 and 7–107 of the main work. The Commission may also investigate complaints pursuant to the powers conferred by Regulation 17: see para. 7–107A, *supra*, and Chapter 12 of the main work. **7–108G**

Non-applicability of Regulation 1475/95. In addition to providing (as in Regulation 123/85) that the block exemption shall not apply if both parties, or their connected undertakings, are motor vehicle manufacturers, Article 6(1) sets out an extended list of prohibited clauses and practices (which the Commission persists in calling "black" practices and "black" clauses). The Commission's view of the purpose of these practices and clauses and their legal effect is set out in the Explanatory **7–108H**

Brochure (Appendix 3 *post*, pp. 5–8.) and in Recitals 20–28. The prohibited clauses are of broad scope and include any restrictions of competition agreed between the parties which are not expressly permitted by the Regulation (Article 6(1)(3)); or any restrictions or concerted practices which go beyond the scope of the block exemption, but which would otherwise be permitted by the Exclusive Purchasing or Exclusive Distribution block exemptions (Article 6(1)(4)). Other more specific prohibitions cover linking an otherwise exempt dealership agreement with provisions about products or services not referred to in Regulation 1475/95 (Article 6(1)(2)); and a reservation by the supplier of the right to add new dealerships to the contract territory or alter the contract territory (Article 6(1)(5)). Inclusion of any such prohibited clause renders the block exemption inapplicable to all the restrictions of competition in the agreement: Article 6(2).

7–108I **Prohibited practices and limited inapplicability.** The specified prohibited practices are, in relation to sales, those which directly or indirectly restrict the dealer's freedom to determine prices and discounts (Article 6(1)(6)) or measures designed to impede parallel trade (Article 6(1)(7) and 6(1)(8)); and, in relation to repairs and spare parts, practices limiting the availability of competing spare parts (Article 6(1)(9), 6(1)(10) and 6(1)(11)). (*Cf. Cicra/Fiat Auto Spa*, para. 7–106, *supra*.) Finally, manufacturers are prohibited from refusing (subject to appropriate payment and protection of intellectual property and know-how) repairers outside the network access to technical information required for repair or maintenance of the motor vehicles covered by the agreement and for the implementation of environmental protection measures (Article 6(1)(12)). These measures are designed to increase consumers' choice in accordance with the principles of the single market, an objective which requires, in the view of the Commission:

> "that consumers are able to buy a car and to have it maintained or repaired wherever in the European Union prices or terms are most favourable".

See XXVth Report on Competition Policy (1995), point 33.

In an important change, Regulation 1475/95 provides that a prohibited practice, if pursued by the manufacturer or supplier or another dealer in the network, has the effect of depriving only *that party* of the benefit of any clauses in the agreement restrictive of competition in that territory, and only for so long as the practice continues: Article 6(2) and (3).

This provision appears to be designed to assist the dealer in the event of specified breaches by the supplier by preserving the benefits of the block exemption for parts of the agreement. Not only can the dealer, to the extent permitted by Article 6(3), ignore the restrictions accepted in favour of the supplier and exploit any resulting commercial opportunities, but he can also take action for the supplier's breach of Article 85 in circumstances where, in the absence of Article 6(2) and (3), such action would merely have shown the agreement to be void.

Whilst Article 6 sets out the possible consequences of one party engaging in specified anti-competitive practices, it is not clear to what extent it can assist a dealer who is given notice of termination (without cause). If such termination results from the dealer's failure to comply with an anti-competitive practice urged upon it by the supplier and specifically proscribed by Article 6(1)(6) to (12) then Article 85 may provide a remedy; but if termination is not so based, Article 6 does not effect the supplier's right either to choose dealers or to remove dealers from the network (with notice) on any other basis. An earlier draft of Regulation 1475/95 provided that the agreement could be terminated only on objectively justifiable grounds but that general provision was not retained in the final version. See generally, Wijckmans and Vanderelst, "The EC Commission's Draft Regulation on Motor Vehicle Distribution: Alea Iacta Est?" (1995) 4 ECLR 225.

Arbitration. An important innovation in Regulation 1475/95 is the introduction of a reference to a third party expert in respect of disagreements over sales targets, stocks and demonstration vehicles (Article 4(1)(3)–(5)). The block exemption also provides that in the event of termination for cause, or on account of reorganisation of the dealership: **7–108J**

> "In each case the parties must, in the event of disagreement, accept a system for the quick resolution of the dispute, such as recourse to an expert third party or an arbitrator, without prejudice to the parties' right to apply to a competent court in conformity with the provisions of national law" (Article 5(3)).

It is not clear how these provisions will work in practice, but they appear designed to achieve alternative dispute resolution and potentially provide a solution to some of the practical difficulties faced by dealers over enforcement: para. 7–107A, *supra*.

5. EXCLUSIVE PURCHASING AGREEMENTS FOR RESALE

(a) *Generally*

In general. Exclusive purchasing agreements can indirectly restrict inter-brand competition by making it difficult or impossible to set up independent distribution structures that enable new entrants to gain access to the market: see the Commission's decisions in *Schöller Lebensmittel*, OJ 1993 L183/1 [1994] 4 CMLR 51, para. 69 and *Langnese-Iglo*, OJ 1993 Ll83/19 [1994] 4 CMLR 83, para. 72. The appeals against these decisions were largely dismissed: see para. 7–111, *infra*. See also Veltrop, "Tying and Exclusive Purchasing" (1994) C.M.L.Rev. 549 (who **7–109**

points out that control of exclusive purchasing agreements may also advance important non-competition EC policy goals).

7–111 **Anti-competitive effect.** It is now established that the *Delimitis* judgment is of general application. See, *e.g.*, Case C–393/92 *Almelo* [1994] I ECR 1477, which related to exclusive purchasing agreements in the Dutch electricity market.

The application of *Delimitis* has been clarified by the important judgments of the Court of First Instance on the appeals from the Commission's final decisions in *Schöller Lebensmittel* and *Langnese-Iglo*, *supra*. The cases concerned the network of agreements with retailers of the two leading suppliers of ice-cream on the German market, against whom a complaint had been brought by Mars. The Commission decided that the relevant agreements automatically had an appreciable effect on competition since the parties' market shares exceeded the five per cent limit set out in the Notice on Agreements of Minor Importance (Appendix 24 to the main work). It was not necessary to examine the cumulative effect of parallel networks of agreements of other ice-cream manufacturers on the German market. The Commission distinguished *Delimitis* as applying only where an undertaking's network of agreements did not have an appreciable effect on competition without taking into account the parallel networks of other undertakings. The Commission also held that all of the agreements were caught by Article 85(1): it could not be the case that part of a network of agreements did not have an appreciable effect on competition and thus fell outside Article 85(1). The Commission imposed a prohibition on the parties concluding further agreements of the same kind for five years.

On appeal, the Court of First Instance held that the Commission's Notice was not conclusive as regards the effect of a network of agreements where the five per cent ceiling is exceeded. The Court applied *Delimitis* and carried out an elaborate market analysis, which had regard not only to the parties' market shares but also to the cumulative effect of parallel networks of agreements on the market and considered the various barriers to entry for new competitors. The Court found that the network of agreements in each case had an appreciable effect on competition and consequently all the agreements in the network were caught by Article 85(1), even if some of them, on their own, might not have an appreciable anti-competitive effect. However, the Court held that the Commission had no legal power to prohibit undertakings from concluding agreements for the future. Moreover, such a prohibition would distort competition as competitors of the undertakings would remain free to conclude equivalent agreements. The decisions were annulled only to that extent. Case T–7/93 *Langnese-Iglo v. Commission* [1995] II ECR 1533 [1995] 5 CMLR 602 [1995] All ER (EC) 902, on appeal Case C–279/95P; Case T–9/93 *Schöller v. Commission* [1995] II ECR 1611 [1995] 5 CMLR 659.

For the further aspects of the judgments concerning Regulation

1984/83, see paras. 7–123 and 7–124, *infra*. See also the previous order in Cases T–7 & T–9/93R, *Langnese-Iglo and Schöller v. Commission* [1993] II ECR 131 (dismissal in large part of the applications to suspend enforcement of the Commission's decisions pending appeal); and Korah, "Exclusive Purchasing Obligations: Mars v. Langnese and Schöller" (1994) 3 ECLR 171.

Langnese-Iglo is the German ice cream subsidiary of Unilever. The Commission also commenced proceedings against Unilever's Irish-ice-cream subsidiary, which did not tie retail outlets but instead provided freezer cabinets to retailers without extra charge subject to a tying clause on the use of those cabinets. The Commission provisionally concluded that these practices infringed both Article 85 and Article 86 and Unilever then undertook to introduce a non-discriminatory differential pricing scheme in all Member States; to introduce a freezer hire-purchase scheme to enable retailers to buy their own freezer cabinets; and to sell off 20 per cent of the tied cabinets. On notification of its modified freezer exclusivity agreements, the Commission indicated that it intended to grant individual exemption. *Van Den Bergh Foods*, OJ 1995 C211/4 [1995] 5 CMLR 734 and see the Report on the application of the competition rules in the EU (1995), at p. 137. *Cf.* the approach to freezer exclusivity in *Masterfoods Ltd t/a Mars Ireland v. H B Ice Cream Ltd* [1992] 3 CMLR 830 (Ir. High Ct.); and the report of the United Kingdom Monopolies and Mergers Commission, *Ice Cream*, Cmnd. 2524 (1994).

n. 8. The interim measures decision was subsequently suspended by order of the President of the CFI, except insofar as it applied to retail outlets in petrol stations: Cases T–24 & T–28/92R *Langnese-Iglo and Schöller v. Commission* [1992] II ECR 1839.

Minimum quantities **7–112**

n. 9. See also *Olivetti/Digital*, OJ 1994 L309/24, where a four year commitment by Olivetti to purchase at least half its requirements of the relevant products was held to come within Art. 85(1) but was exempted as forming part of a strategic alliance which overall had a positive impact on the developing market for RISC computers.

Hindrance of imports **7–113**

n. 11. In Case C–19/93P *Rendo and Others v. Commission* [1995] I ECR 3319, the ECJ set aside the judgment of the CFI in so far as it had held that the Commission decision had had no legal effect in respect of the application of Art. 85 to the import restrictions applicable in the period before the 1989 Dutch Electricity Law came into effect, dismissed the remainder of the appeal and referred the case back to the CFI. See also the reference to the ECJ from parallel proceedings in the Dutch courts,

Case C–393/92 *Almelo* [1994] I ECR 1477, where the ECJ held that Art. 85(1) prevented a regional electricity distributor from using an exclusive purchasing clause so as to prohibit a local distributor from importing electricity for public supply, but that those restrictions might be justifiable under Art. 90(2): see §§ 16–011 and 16–012, *infra*.

7–116 **Article 86**

n. 15. See *UBC-Almirall*, XXIVth Report on Competition Policy (1994), Ann. II, p.362, where the Commission issued a comfort letter indicating individual exemption for a supply agreement between the dominant manufacturer of an active pharmaceutical ingredient (Piracetam) and the most important European purchaser of Piracetam, after the agreement had been amended to remove provisions which the Commission considered constituted an abuse of the manufacturer's dominant position.

7–117 **Agreements within Regulation 1984/83.** Regulation 1984/83 would expire on 31 December 1997, but a two year extension of the Regulation is to be proposed. For the Green Paper on vertical restraints on trade, see para. 7–048, *supra*.

n. 18. See § 7–111, *supra*.

7–117A **Application of Regulation 1984/83 in the EEA.** Regulation 1984/83 now also applies to Article 53 of the EEA Agreement, subject to necessary amendments: Annex XIV, point 3, to the EEA Agreement. An interpretative notice has been issued by the EFTA Surveillance Authority equivalent to the Commission's Notice: OJ 1994 L153/1 [1994] 4 CMLR 317, as amended (with respect to beer tie agreements) by OJ 1994 L186/57.

In 1994, the EFTA Surveillance Authority decided that the exclusive purchase agreements of various Austrian subsidiaries of oil companies with regard to their chains of service stations did not satisfy the requirements of the block exemption or meet the conditions for individual exemption (ESA Annual Report '94, para. 4.9.2.).

(b) *Title I agreements under Regulation 1984/83*

7–118 **The exclusive purchase obligation**

n. 20. In its decisions in *Schöller Lebensmittel* and *Langnese-Iglo*, *supra*, the Commission held that the goods covered by the agreement could be "specified" in an annual price list which could be unilaterally changed by the supplier (§§ 110–11 in both decisions). There were only a few annual changes to the list, so the range of goods covered by the exclusive purchase obligation continued to be clear-cut. This point was not considered by the CFI on appeal. *Cf.* Korah, *supra*, for criticism of the Commission's approach. See also § 7–135, *infra*.

Permitted duration **7–123**

n. 31. In the *Langnese-Iglo* and *Schöller* cases, *supra*, the CFI upheld the Commission's finding that agreements for a set duration of not more than two years, to be renewed automatically thereafter, were concluded for an indefinite duration and thus did not benefit from the block exemption. The fact that the agreements would probably not be renewed beyond the two year period, since retailers tended to terminate their exclusive purchase agreements as early as possible in order to obtain improved contractual conditions, did not affect this conclusion (*Langnese-Iglo* at §§ 137–38; *Schöller* at §§ 122–24).

Revocation by Commission. The Court of First Instance has pointed out **7–124** that withdrawal of the benefit of the block exemption under Article 14 of the Regulation is not equivalent to revocation of a decision granting individual exemption. Therefore the Commission is not required to consider whether there has been a change of circumstances. *Langnese-Iglo*, *supra*, at paras. 173–75.

In its decision in that case, the Commission withdrew the benefit of Regulation 1984/83 from Langnese-Iglo's agreements which were within its scope, on the grounds that those agreements made access to the retail level of the German ice-cream market very difficult. On appeal, Langnese-Iglo further argued:

(a) that the power of revocation in Article 14(a) and (b) of the Regulation was *ultra vires* as going beyond the conditions for exemption in Article 85(3);
(b) that the Commission was not entitled to withdraw the benefit of the block exemption from all the supply agreements since some of those agreements would qualify for individual exemption.

Both these arguments were rejected. As to the second argument, the Court of First Instance held that it was for Langnese-Iglo to produce evidence and prove that specific agreements satisfied the conditions in Article 85(3): *Langnese-Iglo* at para. 193.

(c) *Beer Supply agreements*

Brewery ties under Article 85(1) **7–126**

n. 33. In an oral reply in the European Parliament on 11 March 1992, the Commission stated that the United Kingdom Supply of Beer Orders were discussed between the United Kingdom authorities and the Commission before they were enacted: [1993] 4 CMLR 26. For further evidence of the close co-operation between the United Kingdom and EC competition authorities in the beer sector see the Commission's decision to suspend its investigation in *Inntrepreneur-GM-Courage* while the Office of Fair Trading carried out an enquiry into differential pricing by the major United Kingdom brewers: Press Release IP (95) 104, 8 February 1995, [1995] 4 CMLR 310.

n. 35. See now *Chitty on Contracts* (27th ed., 1994) Vol. I §§ 16–101 and 16–102.

7–127 **The *Delimitis* Case.** In its decisions in *Schöller Lebensmittel* and *Langnese-Iglo*, para. 7–109, *supra*, at paras. 77–94 and 80–93 respectively, the Commission held that the relevant product market included, in principle, all goods which were perceived by the consumer, on the grounds of their characteristics, price or intended purpose, as being similar. The Commission distinguished between ice cream stored at home and ice cream bought from retailers for immediate consumption: although the products in question were identical, they could still belong to different product markets if they satisfied a distinct consumer demand. The Commission also defined the market by reference to the different competitive conditions at different stages of distribution and in different distribution channels. The Commission excluded "scooping" ice-cream supplied in bulk for sale in individual portions, since grocery outlets were not generally geared to selling it and the product technology was different. On appeal, the Commission's analysis was upheld except as regards "scooping" ice cream, since a difference in production technology was not sufficient where there was no evidence of a difference in the pattern of demand from the consumer's point of view: *Langnese-Iglo v. Commission* and *Schöller v. Commission*, para. 7–111, *supra*, at paras. 60–72 and paras. 39–51, respectively.

7–128 **Effect of *Delimitis***

n. 41. Although they may be unable to take a final decision on the compatibility of the tying clauses of a beer supply agreement with Art. 85(1), this will not prevent the English courts from upholding the rent clause in the lease of the outlet in question: *Inntrepreneur Estates v. Mason* [1993] 2 CMLR 293 [1994] 68 P & CR 53 (QBD); *Inntrepreneur Estates v. Boyes* [1994] 68 P & CR 77 (CA). See MacCulloch, "Inntrepreneur Estates: Co-operative Application of the EC Competition Rules in the United Kingdom?" (1995) 6 ECLR 380.

n. 42. See also the decision of the Irish High Court in *Masterfoods Ltd v. H.B. Ice Cream Ltd* [1992] 3 CMLR 830, regarding freezer exclusivity agreements; *cf.* the Commission's subsequent provisional decision in *Van*

Den Bergh Foods, OJ 1995 C211/4 [1995] 4 CMLR 595 regarding the same agreements.

Commission's Notice on minor brewery networks. The EFTA Surveillance Authority has issued an equivalent Notice modifying its previous Notice on exclusive distribution and exclusive purchasing agreements: OJ 1994 L186/57, 69. **7–129**

Basic requirements for a permitted tie **7–131**

n. 45. In the United Kingdom, brewers with over 2,000 licensed premises have been prohibited since 1 May 1990 from tying beer over 1.2 per cent alcohol or any non-beer drink: The Supply of Beer (Tied Estate) Order 1989 (S.I. 1989 No. 2390).

Specified drinks **7–135**

n. 52. See also *Schöller Lebensmittel* and *Langnese-Iglo*, § 7–118 n. 20, *supra*; *Inntrepreneur-GM-Courage*, OJ 1993 C206/2 [1993] 5 CMLR 517: Art. 19(3) Notice indicating the Commission's intention to grant individual exemption for a tying agreement in which the tied beers were specified by description rather than by brand name. The actual brands supplied were specified in the brewery's price list, which could be unilaterally altered by the brewery. Despite adverse observations from third parties, the Commission subsequently announced that it had suspended investigations pending the enquiry by the United Kingdom Office of Fair Trading into differential pricing by the major United Kingdom brewers: Press Release IP (95) 104, 8 February 1995 [1995] 4 CMLR 310. (The OFT later announced that it intended to take no further action on the Inntrepreneur tenancy agreements: OFT Press Release, 16 May 1995 (1995) 5 ECLR 135.)

Exclusive purchase agreements between competing brewers. In *Carlsberg International and Interbrew*, XXIVth Report on Competition Policy (1994), Annex II, page 351, the Commission issued a statement of objections against both parties to an exclusive distribution agreement whereby the largest Belgian brewery enjoyed the exclusive right to distribute Carlsberg and Tuborg beers on the Belgian market. The Commission stated that the benefits of exclusive distribution agreements were outweighed by the disadvantages where an exclusive distribution right was granted to a brewery with a dominant position on its own market. The proceedings were terminated after the parties agreed to set up a second distribution channel by establishing a joint venture between Carlsberg and another Belgian company. See also *Elders/Grand Metropolitan*, XXIst Report on Competition Policy (1991), point 86; *Carlsberg/* **7–144**

Allied Lyons, XXIInd Report on Competition Policy (1992), points 131–137 (comfort letters issued after length of the ties were reduced).

7–145 **Transitional provisions.** For the application of Regulation 1984/83 to a Portuguese service station agreement entered into prior to Portuguese accession, see Case C–39/92 *Petrogal* [1993] I ECR 5659.

7–146 **Revocation.** See also para. 7–124, *supra*.

(d) *Service station agreements*

7–147 **Service station agreements under Article 85(1).** There have now been several cases concerning "solus" agreements for petrol stations. See *Service station agreements in Spain*, XXIIIrd Report on Competition Policy (1993), point 226, XXIVth Report on Competition Policy (1994), Annex II, page 361; *Service station agreements in the Canary Islands*, XXIIIrd Report on Competition Policy (1993), point 226(a); and the investigation by the EFTA Surveillance Authority, *Service station agreements in Austria*, ESA Annual Report '94, para. 4.9.2. See also *Petrogal*, para. 7–155, *infra*.

n. 71. See now *Chitty on Contracts* (27th ed., 1994) vol. I, §§ 16–098 to 16–100. For the undertakings given to the United Kingdom government by the oil companies regarding United Kingdom petrol retailers, see §§ 7–150, 7–155, 7–157 and 7–158, *infra*.

7–150 **Motor-vehicle and other fuels**

n. 74. In the United Kingdom, the oil companies have undertaken not to include kerosene for heating or lighting within the tie: Undertakings 6 and 23(ix) set out in the MMC Report, *The Supply of Petrol*, Cmnd. 972 (1990), App. 2.2.

7–153 **Lubricants.** In its investigations into *Service station agreements in Spain*, *supra*, the Commission found that service station agreements tying the sale of lubricants were incompatible with Regulation 1984/83. The Spanish oil companies agreed to amend their agreements. In *Service station agreements in Austria*, *supra*, the EFTA Surveillance Authority provisionally decided that the service station agreements of Austrian oil companies were incompatible with Regulation 1984/83 insofar as they involved the tying and price-fixing of lubricants and that the conditions for individual exemption appeared not to be met.

7–154 **Other goods must not be tied.** For the undertakings given by the oil companies in the United Kingdom (which go further than Regulation 1984/83), see the MMC Report, *The Supply of Petrol*, Cmnd. 972 (1990), Appendix 2.2.

Duration of the tie. In *Service station agreements in Spain*, *supra*, the Commission found that service station agreements lasting 10 years from the abolition of the national oil monopoly in December 1992, but which were mostly signed between 1986 and 1988, were incompatible with Regulation 1984/83 as being *de facto* concluded for a period longer than 10 years. See also *Service station agreements in the Canary Islands*, *supra*. In *Service station agreements in Austria*, *supra*, the EFTA Surveillance Authority provisionally found that agreements of over 10 years duration did not satisfy the conditions for individual exemption. *Cf.* Case C–39/92 *Petrogal* [1993] I ECR 5659, where the Court of Justice held that agreements relating to Spanish and Portuguese petrol stations entered into before the accession of those States to the EC in June 1985 could benefit from Regulation 1984/83 until 31 December 1997 even if they were of indeterminate length. (In the United Kingdom oil companies have given undertakings not to tie petrol stations (other than motorway service areas or as part of a tenancy) for a fixed term of more than five years: see the MMC Report, para. 7–154, *supra*.) **7–155**

Advertising. For the undertakings given by the oil companies in the United Kingdom as regards advertising restrictions, see the MMC Report, para. 7–154, *supra*. **7–157**

Minimum quantities. For the undertakings given by the oil companies in the United Kingdom in this regard, see the MMC Report, para. 7–154, *supra*. **7–158**

Transitional provisions. For the position as regards the Spanish and Portuguese accessions, see para. 7–155, *supra*. **7–160**

(e) *Individual exemption under Article 85(3)*

Individual exemptions under Article 85(3). In *Schöller Lebensmittel*, OJ 1993 L183/1 [1994] 4 CMLR 51, the Commission refused an individual exemption to Schöller's network of exclusive purchase agreements with ice cream retailers because the network constituted a major barrier to entry on the German market. This decision was upheld on appeal: Case T–9/93 *Schöller v. Commission* [1995] II ECR 1611 [1995] 5 CMLR 602. In *Service station agreements in Austria*, *supra*, the EFTA Surveillance Authority provisionally decided that a network of agreements entered **7–162**

into by Austrian oil companies with petrol retailers did not appear to satisfy the conditions for individual exemption, since the agreements contributed significantly to foreclosure of the market. See also *Inntrepreneur-GM-Courage* (20 year tie but no final decision on exemption taken): para. 7–135, *supra*.

6. FRANCHISING

(a) *Generally*

7–163 **Franchising.** See the OECD report, *Competition Policy and Vertical Restraints: Franchising Agreements* (1994). The report suggests that three different levels of competition law enforcement should be applied to franchising agreements, depending on the market share of the franchisor and the state of competition in the franchiser's market.

(b) *Franchising under Article 85*

7–165 **The Court of Justice's attitude to franchise agreements**

n. 86. See also *Texaco Ltd*, XXIIIrd Report on Competition Policy (1993), point 225 (franchised shops at petrol stations).

(c) *Regulation 4087/88*

7–172 **Application of the block exemption.** Regulation 4087/88 applies, subject to necessary amendments, to Article 53 of the EEA Agreement: Annex XIV, point 8, to the EEA Agreement.

For the Commission's Green Paper on vertical restraints on trade, covering the operation of Regulation 4087/88, as well as the block exemptions for exclusive purchasing and distribution agreements, see para. 7–048, *supra*.

7–177 **Sources of supply and competing goods.** In *Texaco Ltd*, *supra*, the Commission held that the following requirements in franchise agreements for the operation of service stations and integrated on-site shops were compatible with Regulation 4087/88:

(a) that only Texaco fuel be sold at the service stations;
(b) that the shops always stock certain brand products specified by Texaco, provided that the franchisee remained free to sell competing products that complied with minimum quality criteria;
(c) that part of the shop's shelf space be reserved for display of the branded products.

The Commission also held that an *optional* centralised purchasing system for the specified products complied with Regulation 4087/88. If a franchisee joined this system, he was required to purchase all of his requirements of the specified products from Texaco's designated suppliers.

Non-competition **7–179**

n. 29. See also *Kall-Kwik Printing (UK) Ltd v. Rush* [1996] FSR 114 (ChD).

Prices. The OECD report, *Competition Policy and Vertical Restraints: Franchising Agreements* (1994), states that the contrast in legal treatment of price and non-price restrictions on competition is not paralleled by a clear contrast in their likely effect on economic efficiency and that, depending on market circumstances, restrictions on price competition may increase economic efficiency by reducing free riding. The report suggests that franchisors with small market shares in unconcentrated markets be given permission to include either non-price or price restrictions in franchise agreements. See at pages 13 and 15. **7–185**

7. OTHER PURCHASE AND SUPPLY AGREEMENTS

Exclusive purchasing obligation. Note that an exclusive purchasing obligation on the parties to a co-operative joint venture in favour of the JV company may be an ancillary restriction and therefore outside Article 85(1) or may be exempted as "indispensible" under Article 85(3): see paras. 5–054 to 5–056 of the main work and para. 5–060, *supra*. **7–192**

n. 66. Solvay and ICI continued to enter into long-term arrangements with customers for the whole or substantially the whole of their requirements of soda ash. The Commission took proceedings against both companies for abuse of a dominant position, and imposed substantial fines for this and other infringements of Article 86: *Soda-ash—Solvay* and *Soda-ash—ICI*, OJ 1991 L152/21, 40 [1994] 4 CMLR 645, 681. The decisions were annulled by the CFI on procedural grounds and are on appeal to the ECJ: Case T–32/91 *Solvay v. Commission* [1995] II ECR 1825 on appeal Case C–287/95P; Case T–37/91 *ICI v. Commission* [1995] II ECR 1901 on appeal Case C–288/95P: see § 12–043, *infra*.

8. SUB-CONTRACTING

The Commission's view on sub-contracting. The EFTA Surveillance Authority has issued an equivalent Notice on sub-contracting agreements: OJ 1994 L153/1, 30 [1994] 4 CMLR 353. **7–198**

CHAPTER 8

INTELLECTUAL PROPERTY RIGHTS

1. INTRODUCTION

8–001 **In general**

n. 2. See now Cornish, *op. cit.* (3rd ed., 1996) and Tritton, *Intellectual Property in Europe* (Sweet & Maxwell, 1996).

8–002 **Free movement of goods.** Note that domestic intellectual property legislation may also fall foul of Article 6 of the Treaty (principle of non-discrimination): Cases C–92 & 326/92 *Phil Collins* [1993] I ECR 5145 [1993] 3 CMLR 773 in which the Court of Justice struck down provisions of German copyright legislation which accorded more favourable rights to German nationals.

n. 4. The Community Trade Mark Regulation was adopted on 20 December 1993 (Reg. 40/94, OJ 1994 L11/1) and has since been amended (Reg. 3288/94, OJ 1994 L349/83). It creates a single EC-wide right (CTM) alongside national marks. Application for a CTM, which will give its owner exclusive rights throughout the community can be filed with the Office for Harmonisation of the Internal Market in Alicante. (Further amendments to Reg. 40/94 have been proposed: COM(96)372.) In the field of copyright, Dir. 93/98 (OJ 1993 L290/9) seeks to harmonise the length of copyright protection in the Member States: the rights of the author of a literary or artistic work will last for 70 years after his or her death. A directive governing copyright and neighbouring rights relating to satellite broadcasting and cable transmission was adopted in September 1993 (Dir. 93/83, OJ 1993 L248/15); and in July 1995 the Commission issued a Green Paper on Copyright and Related Rights in the Information Society (COM(95)382). In October 1995, the Parliament and Council adopted a directive on the protection of individuals with regard to the processing of personal data (Dir. 95/46, OJ 1995 L281/31). A Green Paper on utility models has also been published (COM(95)370). Community plant variety rights are governed by Council Reg. 2100/94 (OJ 1994 L227/1).

The Community distinction between existence and exercise **8–003**

n. 3. See now Oliver, *op. cit.* (3rd ed., 1996).

Exhaustion of rights **8–005**

n. 11. See also Case C–9/93 *IHT Internationale Heitztechnik v. Ideal Standard* [1994] I ECR 2789: § 8–029, *infra.*

Licensing of intellectual property rights. With effect from 1 April 1996, the two block exemptions, Regulations 2349/84 and Regulation 556/89, were replaced by the new block exemption for technology transfer agreements, Regulation 240/96 made on 31 January 1996: Appendix 4, *post.* This is discussed in paras. 8–164A *et seq., infra.* **8–007**

n. 16. Reg. 2349/94 lapsed on 31 December 1994 and thereafter received several extensions. It expired on 31 March 1996 when Reg. 240/96 came into force. See para. 8–125, *infra.*

Trade-Related Aspects of Intellectual Property Rights. The Uruguay Round of the General Agreement on Tariffs and Trade was concluded on 15 December 1993. One of the trade agreements signed as part of the Uruguay Round was an Agreement on Trade-Related Aspects of Intellectual Property Rights (TRIPs), 15 April 1994, UKTS No. 10 (1996) Cm. 3046. The TRIPs Agreement came into force on 1 January 1995. Article 6 of TRIPs states that for the purposes of dispute settlement (but subject to Articles 3 and 4) nothing in the Agreement shall be used to address the issue of exhaustion of intellectual property rights (IPRs). Part II of TRIPs (Articles 9–40) addresses standards concerning the availability, scope and use of IPRs. In Article 40(1), Members acknowledge that some licensing practices which restrain competition may have an adverse effect upon trade. While Members remain free to take appropriate national measures to prevent or control anti-competitive licensing practices (Article 40(2)), provision is also made for consultation between governments where there is reason to believe that licensing practices are being abused by the owner of an IPR (Article 40(3)). **8–007A**

2. THE EFFECT OF THE RULES ON FREE MOVEMENT ON INFRINGEMENT ACTIONS

A chronological checklist. There should be added to the list: Case C–9/93 *IHT Internationale Heitztechnik v. Ideal Standard* [1994] I ECR 2789: the **8–010**

owner of a trademark in one Member State may prevent the import of products bearing the same trademark from another Member State where the manufacturer in the exporting state is the assignee of the local trademark and the owner of the mark in the importing state does not have the ability to control the quality of the goods to which the mark is applied in the exporting state. Cases C–427/93, etc., *Bristol-Myers Squibb and Others v. Paranova*, Cases C–71/94, etc., *Eurim-Pharm v. Beiersdorf* and Case C–232/94 *Pharma v. Rhône-Poulenc*, judgments of 11 July 1996: Article 7(2) of Directive 89/104 permits a trademark owner to oppose further marketing of a pharmaceutical product by an importer who has repackaged the product and reaffixed the owner's trademark, unless certain specified conditions are satisfied: see further para. 8–036, *infra*.

(a) *Patents*

8–018 **Exhaustion of rights where product not patentable in State of origin**

n. 61. See also Cases C–267 & 268/95 *Merck & Co. Inc. v. Primecrown Ltd* and *Beecham Group plc v. Europharm of Worthing Ltd*, not yet decided, on the rights of a patent holder to prevent, after the expiry of the Accession transitional period, imports of pharmaceutical products marketed by it in Spain and Portugal where patent protection was not available for those products. For an English case applying the transitional provisions see *Wellcome Foundation v. Discpharm Ltd* [1993] FSR 433 (Patent Cty. Ct.).

8–021 **What constitutes consent**

n. 73. But see Case C–9/93 *Ideal Standard*, discussed at § 8–029, *infra* in the context of the assignment of trademarks.

8–025 **Unjustified, discriminatory or disguised restrictions.** In Case C–320/93 *Ortscheit* [1994] I ECR 5243, the Court of Justice held that a German law prohibiting the advertising of pharmaceutical products which were not authorised by the German medical authority, but were lawfully imported into Germany, fell within Article 30 but was justified on grounds of public health under Article 36. See also Case C–316/95 *Generics BV v. Smith, Kline & French Laboratories*, not yet decided, concerning the compatibility of aspects of Dutch patent protection with Article 30.

(b) *Trademarks*

8–027 **Importation of trademarked goods under United Kingdom law.** The Trade Marks Act 1938 has been repealed by the Trade Marks Act 1994 which implements Council Directive 89/104 on the harmonisation of national trademark laws and contains provisions relating to the Community Trade Mark Regulation (Reg. 40/94, OJ 1994 L11/1 as amended by Reg. 3288/94, OJ 1994 L394/83). By sections 9 and 10 of the new Act, a United Kingdom registered trademark is infringed by any person who, without the consent of the registered proprietor, uses an identical sign in relation to identical goods or services or, where there exists a likelihood of confusion (including a likelihood of association), uses *either* an identical or similar sign in relation to similar goods or services *or* a similar sign in relation to identical goods or services. Section 10 also defines other infringing acts and gives examples of what may constitute "use" of a sign, such as importing or exporting goods under the sign.

Section 10(6) provides an exception to infringement for the use of a sign in order to identify goods or services as those of the proprietor provided that such use is in accordance with honest commercial practices. Section 12 sets out a much more limited exemption, giving specific effect to the principle of exhaustion of rights. It provides that, save in exceptional circumstances outlined in sub-section 12(2), there is no infringement if the sign is used in relation to goods which were originally marketed in another EEA country under the sign with the proprietor's consent. Section 12 is also restricted to goods. See generally Morcom, *A Guide to the Trade Marks Act 1994* (Butterworths, 1994); Kitchin and Mellor, *The Trade Marks Act 1994—Text and commentary* (Sweet & Maxwell, 1995).

n. 96. The position is unclear under the Trade Marks Act 1994 as regards goods originally marketed by a related company or licensee of the proprietor outside the EEA and imported into the United Kingdom. It has been suggested that ss.10(6) and 11(2) extend a similar protection to that provided for parallel imports from within the EEA by s.12 to parallel imports from outside the EEA in line with the decision in *Revlon v. Cripps & Lee* [1980] FSR 85 (CA). See Morcom, *op. cit.* § 7.7.

n. 97. The issue of consent, although important, is only one factor taken into consideration in deciding whether the goods can legitimately be identified as those of the proprietor; *e.g.* another factor is whether the character or quality of the goods differ from that which the United Kingdom consumer would usually associate with goods of the proprietor.

Summary of the rules on free movement affecting trademarks **8–028**

n. 2. See also Case C–317/91 *Deutsche Renault* [1993] I ECR 6227; [1995] 1 CMLR 461 where the ECJ held that the German trademarks law which allowed AUDI to register the word "Quattro", (*i.e.* the Italian for "four") as a trademark and to oppose use in Germany by Renault of the designation "Quadra" was compatible with Art. 30.

8–029 **Exhaustion of rights: trademarks.** The Court of Justice has drawn a distinction between the assignment and the licensing of trademarks in the context of exhaustion of rights. Case C–9/93 *IHT Internationale Heitztechnik v. Ideal Standard* [1994] I ECR 2789 concerned the trademark "Ideal Standard" as applied to heating equipment. The mark was originally held in Germany and France by the respective subsidiaries of the American Standard group. In 1984 the French subsidiary sold its heating equipment business together with the trademark for that sector to an unrelated company which later assigned it to the parent of IHT. When IHT started marketing in Germany heating equipment bearing the mark, the German subsidiary which still held the mark and applied it to sanitary equipment in Germany sued IHT for infringement of the German mark. The Court of Justice distinguished between the case where the imported goods were produced by an *assignee* which has no economic link with the owner of the mark in the importing State and the case where the goods were marketed by a *licensee or affiliate of the owner*. A contract of assignment by itself, in the absence of any economic link, does not give the assignor any means of controlling the quality of the products marketed by the assignee. The consent inherent in the assignment is not the consent required for the application of the doctrine of exhaustion of rights. For the latter, the owner of the right in the importing State must, directly or indirectly, be able to determine the products to which the trademark is affixed in the exporting State and to control their quality.

8–030 **Specific subject matter of the trademark**

n. 6. See also *Deutsche Renault, supra* at § 30, and Cases C–472/93, etc., *Bristol-Myers Squibb and Others v. Paranova*, judgment of 11 July 1996, at para. 44.

8–034 **The reasoning of the Court in *Hag II***

n. 22. See also *Ideal Standard, supra.*

8–035 **The problem of repackaging.** See now the three parallel judgments of the Court of Justice delivered on 11 July 1996: para. 8–036, *infra*.

8–036 **Repackaging: different packs or wrapping.** See now Cases C–472/93, etc., *Bristol-Myers Squibb and Others v. Paranova*, Cases C–71/94, etc., *Eurim-Pharm v. Beiersdorf* and Case C–232/94 *Pharma v. Rhône-Poulenc*, judgments of 11 July 1996, where the Court of Justice clarified the conditions set out in *Hoffman-La Roche.* Applying Article 7(2) of Directive 89/104 to parallel importation of pharmaceutical products, the Court stressed that any new packaging should identify the manufacturer and the repackager in print "such that a person with normal eyesight exercising a normal degree of attentiveness would be in a position to understand"; and that the presentation of the repackaged product must not be "defective, of poor quality or untidy", so as not to damage the reputation of the trademark.

Repackaging: different trademarks. In *CHEETAH Trademark* [1993] FSR 263, in the English High Court, Hoechst was the registered proprietor of the herbicide marks CHEETAH (in the United Kingdom) and PUMA (in France and Germany). Chemiculture imported PUMA from Belgium for resale in the United Kingdom, using the CHEETAH mark on product delivery notes and invoices. The court accepted that Hoechst's rights in PUMA were exhausted by its sale in Belgium and that Chemiculture was entitled to sell the herbicide under the PUMA mark in the United Kingdom. The court held, however, that the right to the CHEETAH mark had not been exhausted by Hoechst so that it was entitled to prevent Chemiculture from selling the PUMA product under the CHEETAH mark in the United Kingdom. **8–037**

Packaging: national law restrictions **8–038**

n. 35. For a recent labelling and packaging case see Case C–470/93 *Verein gegen Unwesen in Handel und Gewerbe Köln v. Mars* [1995] I ECR 1923.

The enforcement of national trademark rights where there is no exhaustion **8–040**

n. 41. See also Case C–317/91 *Deutsche Renault* [1993] I ECR 6227 [1995] 1 CMLR 461 (ECJ held it is for national law to set the criteria for assessing whether two marks are confusingly similar).

(c) *Passing off*

Passing off and unfair competition **8–042**

n. 44. See now Drysdale and Silverleaf, *op. cit.* (2nd ed., 1995); Wadlow, *The Law of Passing-Off* (Sweet & Maxwell, 2nd ed., 1995).

Reputation gained in other Member States. A foreign business may have a reputation in England that will found an action for passing off irrespective of Community law, and *Maxims v. Dye* was not decided on the basis of the restaurant's reputation outside England. **8–045**

n. 51. See now Drysdale and Silverleaf, *op. cit.* §§ 3.11 *et seq.*, § 10.18; Wadlow, *op. cit.* §§ 2.30–32, 7.24.

(d) *Copyright and similar rights*

8–047 **The Community's approach to copyright**

n. 57. See also Dir. 92/100 on rental and lending rights and certain rights related to copyright (OJ 1992 L346/61) and Dir. 93/83 on copyright and neighbouring rights relating to satellite broadcasting and cable retransmission (OJ 1993 L248/15). In the context of the Uruguay Round of GATT, further decisions on the protection of topographies of semiconductors have been adopted by the Council, in particular Dec. 94/824 (OJ 1994 L349/201).

(i) *Sound recordings*

8–052 **Subsequent judgments: performing rights**

n. 69. In Case T–114/92 *BEMIM v. Commission* [1995] II ECR 147 and Case T–5/93 *Tremblay and others v. Commission* [1995] II ECR 185; [1996] 4 CMLR 305 (both), the CFI found that the Commission had erred in failing to investigate allegations that an agreement between SACEM and copyright management societies in the other Member States could partition the market.

(ii) *Literary, dramatic, musical and artistic works*

8–055 **Literary works**

n. 75. In Case C–360/92P *Publishers Association v. Commission* [1995] I ECR 23 [1995] 5 CMLR 33, [1966] ICR 121, the ECJ set aside the CFI's judgment and annulled Arts. 2 to 4 of the Commission's decision in *Publishers Association—Net Book Agreements*, OJ 1989 L22/12; see further § 4–023 *supra*.

(iv) *Television*

8–060 **Television broadcasts.** There have been a number of investigations by the Commission under Article 85 concerning the licensing of rights to transmit television programmes: see *BBC Enterprises*, XXIIIrd Report on Competition Policy (1993), page 459 (licence to re-transmit UK programmes on cable in Ireland: comfort letter issued after the agreement was modified); *BSB/Football Association, ibid.* (5 year exclusive rights to cover national and international matches: considered to be appropriate for exemption under Article 85(3) in circumstances where the agreement facilitated entry into a new and developing market and the Commission closed the file without a formal decision); *PMI-DSV*, OJ 1995 L221/34, discussed at paras. 8–173 to 8–175, *infra*; and *KNVB/Sport 7*, OJ 1996 C228/4.

n. 85. The Commission granted exemption for a five year period to the EBU's rules governing the joint acquisition and sharing of television rights to certain sports events, OJ 1993 L179/23 [1995] 4 CMLR 56; but this decision was annulled by the CFI: Cases T–528/93, etc., *Métropole Télévision and Others v. Commission* [1996] 5 CMLR 386 on appeal Case C–320/96P, not yet decided.

(vi) *Computer programs*

Harmonisation Directive **8–063**

n. 96 and n. 97. Dir. 91/250 was amended by Dir. 93/98 (OJ 1993 L290/9). As a literary work, a computer program will be protected for 70 years from its author's death: Art. 1(1) of Dir. 93/98.

3. THE EFFECT OF ARTICLES 85 AND 86 ON INFRINGEMENT ACTIONS

Generally **8–064**

n. 99. See now Cases C–241 & 242/91P *RTE and ITP v. Commission:* § 8–071 *infra*. The ECJ did not find it necessary to examine the reasoning of the CFI as regards Art. 36.

Trademark infringement actions to divide markets **8–067**

n. 12. See also Case C–9/93 *IHT Internationale Heitztechnik v. Ideal Standard* [1994] I ECR 2789: Art. 85 may apply to a trademark assignment following a market-sharing agreement, but only after an analysis of the context, the commitments underlying the assignment, the intention of the parties and the consideration for the assignment (§ 59).

8–071 **Article 86: the *TV Guide* cases.** In April 1995 the Court of Justice dismissed the appeals of RTE and ITP against the decisions of the Court of First Instance: Cases C–241 & 242/91P *RTE and ITP v. Commission* [1995] I ECR 743 [1995] 4 CMLR 718 [1995] All ER (EC) 416. The Court repeated that mere ownership of an intellectual property right cannot confer a dominant position, but confirmed the Court of First Instance's finding of fact that RTE, ITP (and the BBC) enjoyed a *de facto* monopoly over the information used to compile listings (at §§ 46–47).

The Court ruled that the exercise of an exclusive right may, in exceptional circumstances, involve abusive conduct (at para. 50) and concluded that the refusal of RTE and ITP to provide basic information as to the channel, day, time and title of programmes in reliance upon national copyright law constituted an abuse under heading (b) of Article 86. See also at para. 9–065, *infra*. The Court also endorsed the Court of First Instance's finding that there was no justification for such refusal and concluded that the appellants had reserved to themselves the secondary market of weekly TV guides by excluding all competition on that market since they denied access to the basic information which is the raw material indispensable for the compilation of such a guide (para. 56). See Thompson (1995) 4 Ent. LR 143.

8–072 **Volvo v. Veng**

n. 25. *Chiron v. Murex Diagnostics Ltd* is reported at [1993] FSR 324 [1992] 3 CMLR 813 and the judgment of Aldous J. was upheld by the CA: [1994] FSR 187 [1994] 1 CMLR 410. See also *IBM v. Phoenix International* [1994] RPC 251 (ChD) (Art. 86 defence struck out because no nexus between alleged abuse and infringement).

8–073 ***Volvo v. Veng* distinguished**

n. 26. The CFI's analysis was endorsed by the ECJ (at §§ 48 *et seq.*) in dismissing the appeal: para. 8–071, *supra*.

4. PATENT LICENCES UNDER ARTICLE 85

(a) *Introduction*

8–078 **Limited licences: "Opening the door"**

n. 41. The "opening the door" theory has not been entirely discarded by the Commission; see *CBA*, OJ 1995 C211/11 [1995] 5 CMLR 734 (Art. 19(3) notice in the context of plant variety rights).

8–080 **Balancing the conflicts**

n. 43. See also the new *Antitrust Guidelines for the Licensing of Intellectual Property* issued on 6 April 1995 by the US Department of Justice and the Federal Trade Commission [1995] 7 EIPR Supplement.

(b) *Exclusive and territorial provisions in patent licences*

Export restrictions on licensees **8–089**

n. 82. In *SICASOV*, OJ 1995 C95/8, [1995] 5 CMLR 100 the Commission considered the successor arrangements to *Standard Seed Production and Sales Agreement* and indicated (in an Art. 19(3) notice) that it proposed to adopt a favourable decision in circumstances where exports of basic and certified seeds were severely restricted.

Sales by licensee in territory of licensor. Regulation 2349/84 has been replaced by Regulation 240/96. See paras. 8–164A *et seq. infra.* **8–090**

(c) *Other provisions in patent licences*

Generally. Regulation 2349/84 has been replaced with effect from 1 April 1996 by Regulation 240/96. The new block exemption has a similar structure to Regulation 2349/84, although it also covers know-how licensing agreements. For discussion of the permitted and precluded provisions under Articles 2 and 3 of Regulation 240/96, reference should be made to section 6A, *infra.* **8–093**

Minimum royalties **8–096**

n. 2. But *cf. Microsoft*, XXIVth Report on Competition Policy (1994), page 364, where the Commission suggested that a requirement that a licensee of software pay a minimum royalty regardless of actual use could contribute to the foreclosure of competitor licensors from the market.

Royalties on products not using the patent **8–109**

n. 37. *In Microsoft, supra*, the Commission expressed concern about the likely foreclosure effect of "per processor" and "per system" provisions in software licensing agreements which required payment of a royalty on every computer produced by a PC manufacturer regardless of whether a particular computer was shipped with pre-installed Microsoft-licensed software.

(d) *Other agreements involving patents*

Exploitation of patented technology. In *Becton Dickinson/Cyclopore*, XXIIIrd Report on Competition Policy (1993), point 241, Cyclopore (an **8–114A**

independent Belgian firm producing membranes based on a patent licence granted by the Université Catholique de Louvain) granted a US medical supply company the exclusive world-wide right to manufacture and sell Cyclopore membranes for use in tissue culture products. The licensee undertook to purchase all of its requirements of certain microporous membranes for use in tissue culture from Cyclopore and to make a minimum quantity of purchases. Cyclopore accepted an exclusive supply obligation in favour of the licensee which, following Commission intervention, was limited to five years. An Article 85(3) comfort letter was issued.

8–115 **Jointly held patents**

n. 54. See also *Philips/Matsushita DCC*, OJ 1992 C333/8, [1995] 4 CMLR 286, XXIIIrd Report, page 460 (Art. 85(3) comfort letter).

8–116 **Cross licences**

n. 61. Cross licensing of patents may, despite infringing Art. 85(1), benefit from an Art. 85(3) exemption: see Art. 19(3) notice in *Philips/Matsushita DCC, supra* (where the Commission was evidently influenced by the fact that the arrangements appeared "to contribute substantially to technical progress").

5. REGULATION 2349/84

(a) *Introduction*

8–118 **Regulation 2349/84.** Regulation 2349/84 lapsed on 31 December 1994. It was thereafter retroactively extended three times, until 31 March 1996: see para. 8–125, *infra*. With effect from 1 April 1996, both Regulation 2349/84 and Regulation 556/89 were replaced by a new block exemption for technology transfer agreements, Regulation 240/96: see Appendix 4, *post* and paras. 8–164A *et seq., infra*.

8–119 **Scope of Regulation 2349/84**

n. 70. The Spanish *Tribunal de Defensa de la Competencia* is reported as deciding that patent licensing agreements which also covered technical information, know-how and trademarks met the conditions required by Reg. 2349/84: *Pack Service/4PEF*, XXIVth Report on Competition Policy (1994), point 90.

8–125 **Duration of Regulation 2349/84.** Regulation 70/95 (OJ 1995 L12/13), adopted on 17 January 1995, extended the life of the block exemption from 1 January to 30 June 1995. Regulation 2131/95 (OJ 1995 L 214/6), adopted on 7 September 1995, extended the term from 1 July to 31 December 1995. Regulation 240/96, adopted on 31 January 1996, extended the term from 1 January to 31 March 1996: Appendix 4, *post*.

6. KNOW-HOW LICENCE AGREEMENTS UNDER ARTICLE 85

(a) *Introduction*

8–150 **Know-how licences generally.** Regulation 2349/84 was replaced with effect from 1 April 1996 by the technology transfer block exemption, Regulation 240/96 which also covers know-how licensing agreements. The new block exemption is discussed in paras. 8–164A *et seq., infra.*

8–151 **Protection of know-how.** Regulation 556/89 has been repealed and replaced with effect from 1 April 1996 by Regulation 240/96. See paras. 8–164A *et seq., infra.*

6A. REGULATION 240/96

(a) *Introduction*

8–164A **General.** Regulation 240/96 on the application of Article 85(3) to certain categories of technology transfer agreements was adopted on 31 January 1996: see App. 4, *post*. The new block exemption came into force on 1 April 1996 and supercedes both Regulation 2349/84 on patent licensing agreements (which expired on 31 March 1996) and Regulation 556/89 on know-how licensing agreements (which it repeals by Article 11). The new block exemption is intended both to simplify and harmonise the content of those two previous block exemptions and to combine them in a single block exemption: Recital (3). It also provides for new, permitted clauses: see para. 8–164L, *infra*. Pursuant to Article 11(3) of Regulation 240/96, agreements in force on 31 March 1996 which fulfil the requirements of either Regulation 2349/84 or Regulation 556/89 continue to benefit from the exemption. Regulation 240/96 expires on 31 March 2006 (Article 13). As of 1 September 1996, Regulation 240/96 had not been adopted under the EEA Agreement.

8–164B **Scope of Regulation 240/96.** Regulation 240/96 applies to pure patent licensing agreements, to know-how licensing agreements and to mixed patent and know-how licensing agreements (Article 1(1)). The Regulation also applies if the licensor is not the patentee or the holder of the know-how but himself a licensee with authority to grant a licence (Article 6(1)); if a technology transfer agreement is structured as an assignment but the risks associated with exploitation remain with the assignor (Article 6(2)); and if obligations are assumed by undertakings connected with the licensor or licensee (Article 6(3)). The fact that an agreement contains ancillary provisions relating to intellectual property rights other than patents (Article 1(1)) does not prevent Regulation 240/96 from applying. To be characterised as "ancillary", the relevant provisions must contain no obligations restrictive of competition other than those also attached to the licensed know-how or patents (Article 10(15)).

"Patents" are defined so as to include patent applications, utility models, applications for registration of utility models, French law *certificats d'utilité, certificats d'addition* and applications for such *certificats*, all of which were covered by Regulation 2349/84. However, Article 8(1) of Regulation 240/96 extends the scope of the previous definition to embrace topographies of semi-conductor products, supplementary protection certificates for medicinal products and plant breeder's certificates. "Know-how" is given the same definition as in Regulation 556/89: "a body of technical information that is secret, substantial and identified in any appropriate form" (Article 10(1)). See para. 8–156 of the main work.

8–164C **Structure of the block exemption.** Regulation 240/96 follows the broad structure of Regulations 2349/84 and 556/89. Article 1 sets out a list of restrictive contractual provisions which will automatically qualify for exemption, provided that the other conditions of the block exemption are satisfied. Article 2 lists a number of provisions which are not generally restrictive of competition and exempts them in case they should, because of particular circumstances, fall within the scope of Article 85(1). Article 3 describes a number of provisions the inclusion of which in any agreement takes that agreement outside the block exemption. Such provisions may only be exempted by an individual decision of the Commission. Article 4 of Regulation 240/96 provides for an accelerated "opposition procedure", to enable parties to obtain an individual exemption for agreements which fall outside the four corners of the block exemption but which do not contain any provisions listed in Article 3. Article 5 describes types of agreement which fall outside the scope of the block exemption. Article 7 empowers the Commission to withdraw the benefit of the block exemption in certain circumstances.

8–164D **Agreements not covered.** Regulation 240/96 will not ordinarily apply to agreements between members of a patent pool or know-how pool relating to pooled technology or to reciprocal cross-licensing agreements between parties who are competitors in relation to the products covered by the agreements (Articles 5(1)(1) and 5(1)(3), subject only to Article

5(2)(2)). Similarly, the Regulation does not apply to licensing agreements containing provisions relating to intellectual property rights other than patents which are not ancillary, nor to agreements entered into solely for the purpose of sale (Article 5).

Application to joint ventures. Article 5(1)(2) provides that where licensing agreements are concluded by competing manufacturers with interests in a joint venture (or by one parent and the joint venture) and those agreements relate to the activities of the joint venture, Regulation 240/96 will not apply unless certain conditions are satisfied. Those conditions, set out in Article 5(2)(1), are that the aggregate market share of the parents and their joint venture in the market for the licensed products does not exceed either 20 per cent of the relevant market (if the licence is limited to production) or 10 per cent of the relevant market (in the case of a licence covering production and distribution). As with Regulation 2349/84, the benefit of the block exemption will not be lost if, for two consecutive financial years, the relevant market share is exceeded by no more than one-tenth. Where the one-tenth threshold is exceeded, the block exemption lapses after six months from the end of the year in which it was exceeded (Article 5(3)). **8–164E**

Withdrawal of benefit of block exemption. As with other block exemptions, the Commission may withdraw the benefit of Regulation 240/96 in any particular case where it finds that an agreement that is otherwise exempted has effects which are incompatible with the common market. Article 7 sets out a number of circumstances in which the Commission may be minded to withdraw the benefit of the Regulation. These include cases where the parties obstruct parallel imports (Article 7(2) and (3)) and cases where "the effect of the agreement is to prevent the licensed products from being exposed to effective competition in the licensed territory" (Article 7(1)). Similar language can be found in Regulation 2349/84 (Article 9(2)) and in Regulation 556/89 (Article 7(2)). See para. 8–126 of the main work. Article 7(1) of Regulation 240/96 may assume greater practical importance, however, as it goes on to state that it may be appropriate for the Commission to withdraw the benefit of the block exemption in cases where the licensee's market share exceeds 40 per cent. (*Cf.* the much-criticised draft of the block exemption published at OJ 1994 C178/3, which would have circumscribed the availability of the block exemption by reference to market shares.) See also XXVth Report on Competition Policy (1995), point 65. **8–164F**

(b) *Permitted obligations*

Article 1 restrictions. Article 1 of Regulation 240/96 exempts a number of obligations relating to exclusivity and territorial protection. An **8–164G**

agreement which contains restrictions of the type referred to in Article 1(1) but of more limited scope also benefits from the block exemption (Article 1(5)).

8–164H **Restrictions on the licensor: exclusivity.** Obligations accepted by the licensor not to license other undertakings to exploit the licensed technology in the territory of the licensee, and not to do so itself, are exempted by Article 1(1)(1) and Article 1(1)(2). The territorial protection afforded to the licensee may last, in the case of a pure patent licensing agreement, for as long as the licensed product is protected by a patent in the territory of the licensee: Article 1(2). In the case of a pure know-how licensing agreement, the relevant period is no more than 10 years from the date when the licensed product is first put on the market within the common market by a licensee: Article 1(3). In the case of a mixed licensing agreement, the exemption applies in Member States in which the technology is protected by necessary patents for as long as the licensed product is protected in those Member States by patents if that period is longer than ten years: Article 1(4). In these cases, the exemption is available only for so long as the patents remain in force or to the extent that know-how remains secret and substantial, whichever is the longer.

8–164I **Restrictions on the licensee: exploitation of the licensed technology.** Obligations accepted by a licensee not to exploit the licensed technology in territories reserved to the licensor or not to manufacture or use the licensed product or process in territories within the common market licensed to other licensees are exempted by Article 1(1)(3) and (4). Again, the duration of the protection afforded to the licensor or other licensees depends upon the nature of the licensing agreement: for as long as there are parallel patents in force in the case of pure patent licensing agreements; for 10 years from the date of first marketing within the common market by a licensee in the case of pure know-how licensing agreements; and for the longer of those periods in the case of mixed agreements.

8–164J **Restrictions on the licensee: sales in the territory of other licensees.** Regulation 240/96, like its predecessors, distinguishes between active and passive sales. An obligation accepted by a licensee not to pursue an active policy of putting the licensed product on the market in the territory of another licensee within the common market is exempted for so long as there is a parallel patent in the other licensee's territory in the case of pure patent licensing agreements; for up to 10 years from the date of first marketing of the licensed product within the common market by a licensee in the case of pure know-how licensing agreements; or for the longer period in the case of a mixed agreement. For the block exemption to be available, any prohibition on passive sales (where the licensee merely responds to orders it receives) must last for no longer than five years from the date the licensed product is first put on the market in the common market by a licensee. The period will be shorter if parallel patent protection lapses before the expiry of that five year period: Article 1(2), final sentence.

Other permitted restrictions on the licensee. Provided that the licensee is not prohibited from identifying himself as manufacturer of the licensed products, that licensee may be required during the term of the agreement only to use the licensor's trademark or get up to distinguish the licensed product (for so long as the product is protected by a patent in the licensee's territory or for so long as the know-how remains secret and substantial): Article 1(1)(7). An obligation on a licensee to limit production of the licensed product to the quantities that he requires in manufacturing his own products likewise benefits from the block exemption, provided that the licensee is free to quantify its own requirements: Article 1(1)(8). **8–164K**

Provisions not generally restrictive of competition. Article 2(1) lists a number of obligations which do not generally restrict competition, but which are exempted should they fall, on the facts of a particular case, within the scope of Article 85(1). This list is longer in Regulation 240/96 than in Regulation 2349/84 and Regulation 556/89. Significantly, the list includes an obligation on the licensee to license the licensee's improvements to or new applications of the licensed technology provided that (i) the licensor undertakes to license his own improvements to the licensee and (ii) in the case of severable improvements, the licence-back to the licensor is non-exclusive: Article 2(1)(4). By contrast, an obligation on the licensee to assign rights to improvements to or new applications of the licensed technology to the licensor takes an agreement outside the block exemption by virtue of Article 3(6). **8–164L**

Article 2(1)(7) provides that an obligation on the licensee to continue paying royalties over a period going beyond the duration of the licensed patents does not ordinarily infringe Article 85(1) if the obligation is accepted in order to facilitate payment. In a further innovation, Article 2(1)(13) covers an obligation on a licensee to supply only a limited quantity of the licensed product to a specified customer, where the licence was granted to provide that customer with a second source of supply.

An obligation on a licensee to use its best endeavours to manufacture and market the licensed product (formerly a proviso to a prohibited provision) is now expressly permitted: Article 2(1)(17); so too is the reservation by the licensor of the right to terminate the licensee's exclusivity and to stop licensing improvements to him if the licensee competes with the licensor or with licensor group companies in respect of R&D, production, use or distribution of competing products: Article 2(1)(18); but *cf.* Article 3(2).

(c) *Prohibited restrictions*

8–164M **Prohibited restrictions.** For Regulation 240/96 to apply, it is essential that the technology transfer licensing agreement should not contain any of the provisions described in Article 3. The new "prohibited list" is considerably shorter than the corresponding provisions in Regulations 2349/84 and 556/89. Although not exempted, no-challenge clauses and tying provisions may now be notified to the Commission under the opposition procedure: para. 8–164U, *infra*.

8–164N **Price restrictions.** As was the case under the two earlier regulations, Regulation 240/96 does not apply where either party is restricted in the determination of prices, the components of prices or discounts for licensed products: Article 3(1).

8–164O **Non-compete obligations.** Where either party is restricted by contract from competing with the other within the common market in respect of R&D, production, use or distribution of competing products, the block exemption is not available: Article 3(2). However, a licensor may reserve the right to terminate the licensee's exclusivity and to stop licensing improvements to the licensee in these circumstances without the benefit of Regulation 240/96 being lost: Article 2(1)(18).

8–164P **Territorial restrictions: parallel imports.** Where one or both of the parties is required not to meet orders from users or resellers who would market products in other territories in the common market, or where the parties make it difficult for users or resellers to obtain products from other resellers (in either case without any objectively justified reason), the block exemption is not available: Article 3(3).

8–164Q **Customer allocation.** Where the parties were competing manufacturers, and one of them at the time the licence was granted is restricted as to the customers it may serve (*e.g.* not to supply certain classes of user or not to use certain distribution channels), then Regulation 240/96 may not apply: Article 3(4). However, this is subject to the permitted limitation on quantities to be supplied to a particular customer as a second source, as set out in Article 2(1)(13): see para. 8–146L, *supra*.

8–164R **Maximum quantities.** Subject to the obligation only to manufacture in quantities sufficient to meet own-demand or to provide a customer within a second source of supply, it is not permissible to include a contractual prohibition on the quantity of licensed products which a licensee may manufacture or sell: Article 3(5).

Assignments of improvements. Whereas it is permissible for a licensor to require its licensee to grant to the licensor a licence of the licensee's own improvements to the licensed technology (in certain circumstances), should the licensee be required to assign (either in whole or in part) its right to improvements to or new applications of the licensed technology to the licensor then Regulation 240/96 does not apply: Article 3(6). **8–164S**

Prolongation of restrictions. Under Article 3(7), the benefit of the block exemption is also lost if the licensor is prohibited, for a period exceeding that referred to in Article 1(2) (pure patent licensing agreements) and Article 1(3) (pure know-how licensing agreements), from licensing other undertakings to exploit the technology in a licensed territory or if either party is prohibited from exploiting the licensed technology in the territory of the other party or of other licensees. This provision refers to the possibility of such extension to the period of territorial restriction being achieved by a separate agreement or through automatic prolongation of the agreement by the inclusion of new improvements. **8–164T**

(d) *Opposition procedure*

Opposition procedure. The opposition procedure, common to both Regulation 2349/84 and Regulation 556/89 but rarely used, has been retained in Regulation 240/96. Where an agreement contains a restriction on competition not provided for in Articles 1 and 2 (and not proscribed by Article 3), that agreement will automatically benefit from the protection of the block exemption if it is notified to the Commission with an application for individual exemption and the Commission does not oppose such exemption within a period of four months from the date on which the notification takes effect: Article 4(1) (*cf.* the period of six months in Regulation 2349/84 and Regulation 556/89). The Commission has an obligation to oppose exemption when it receives a request to do so from a Member State, justified on the basis of the competition rules of the Treaty: Article 4(5). By way of illustration, Article 4(2) gives two examples of circumstances in which it may be appropriate to invoke the opposition procedure: (i) where the procurement of goods or services or the acceptance of licences not necessary for a technically satisfactory exploitation of the licensed technology is imposed upon a licensee; and (ii) where a licensee is prohibited from contesting the secrecy or substantiality of a licensor's know-how or from challenging the validity of a licensed patent. **8–164U**

Form of notification. The notification must be in accordance with Regulation 3385/94: see paras. 11–048 *et seq.*, *infra*. However, Recital (25) to Regulation 240/96 notes that the Commission may waive the obligation to supply specific information required in Form A/B but not necessary for **8–164V**

the Commission's examination of the case. It suggests that the Commission may be able to conduct its examination on the basis of the text of the agreement and an estimate (based on directly available data) of the market structure and of the licensee's market share. Unlike the position under Regulation 2349/84 or Regulation 556/89, it is no longer necessary expressly to refer to the opposition procedure when notifying in order for it to apply.

8–164W **Other provisions.** Article 4 contains further provisions concerning the opposition procedure that follow those in Regulation 2349/84. See paras. 8–147 to 8–149 of the main work.

7. OTHER LICENCE AGREEMENTS UNDER ARTICLE 85

(a) *Trademark licences*

8–165 **Trademark licences generally**

n. 18. See also Case C–9/93 *IHT Internationale Heitztechnik v. Ideal Standard* [1994] I ECR 2789, § 8–029, *supra*.

(b) *Copyright licences*

8–173 **Application of *Coditel (No.2)*.** The Commission has now had occasion to examine the acquisition of rights to certain international sporting events. In *EBU/Eurovision System*, OJ 1993 L179/23, the Commission found that the rules of the European Broadcasting Union governing the joint negotiation, acquisition and sharing of television rights to sporting events by a number of public-service broadcasters restricted or eliminated competition between EBU members and operated to the disadvantage of independent competitors. To alleviate these concerns, certain modifications were made to the access scheme operated for the benefit of third-party broadcasters. The Commission required that all rights acquisition agreements should make provision for the rights' owners, or the EBU or its members, to grant access to third parties in accordance with an approved scheme which allowed them access in return for a negotiated fee either to live transmissions (if the event is not broadcast live by the EBU member in the relevant country) or to deferred transmissions (should the local EBU member carry the broadcast live). The Commission exempted the amended rules for a five year period but that decision was annulled by the Court of First Instance: Cases T–528/93, etc., *Métropole Télévision and Others v. Commission* [1995] 5 CMLR 386. The

Court held that the Commission had failed to examine properly the membership rules of the EBU and to determine whether those rules were discriminatory (in particular because some members were not State-controlled channels). The Commission has appealed: Case C–320/96P, not yet decided.

In *BSB/Football Association*, OJ 1993 C94/6, XXIIIrd Report on Competition Policy (1993), page 459, the Commission indicated that, in order to allow all TV channels a fair chance to obtain access to major football matches, the duration of contracts between rights owners and broadcasters should as a general rule be limited to one football season. The notified agreements had granted BBC and BSB the exclusive television rights to all national and international matches of which the Football Association was the rights owner for a five-year term beginning with the 1988–89 season. The Commission concluded, however, that an exemption was justified since BSB (now BSkyB), which only became operational in April 1990, needed a longer-term contract in order to facilitate its entry into the new, developing market for direct-to-home satellite broadcasting. The Commission insisted that an additional provision granting the BBC and BSkyB exclusive permission to broadcast all foreign matches under the auspices of UEFA and FIFA be removed from the agreement as contrary to Articles 85 and 86. Following this amendment, the Commission closed the file. See also *KNVB/Sport 7*, OJ 1996 C228/4.

8–173A **Collective copyright licensing.** In *BBC Enterprises*, OJ 1993 C105/6, [1993] 5 CMLR 300 (Article 19(3) notice), the Commission examined a standard copyright licensing agreement designed to facilitate the retransmission of United Kingdom television programmes to subscribers in Ireland of cable TV and local distribution system networks. The licensors under the agreements were the United Kingdom terrestrial broadcasters and organisations representing the owners of copyright and related rights in TV programme services broadcast in the United Kingdom. The Commission required the parties to modify their agreements to ensure adequate access by broadcasters not originally party to the arrangements. However, the Commission accepted that collective licensing was the most effective means by which a cable TV operator (or other local service provider) could be sure of not infringing the intellectual property rights held in the programmes retransmitted to its subscribers. An Article 85(3) comfort letter was issued: XXIIIrd Report on Competition Policy (1993), page 459.

8–175 **Other restrictions.** The Commission has stated that a clause preventing the licensee from broadcasting the licensed material outside his contract area does not fall within Article 85(1) as it is an inherent part of the copyright. *PMI-DSV*, OJ 1995 L221/34, concerned the licence agreement between PMI, an association holding a licence from French racing organisations to exploit the rights to film and commentary of French horse races, and DSV, a German sports publisher. The original agreement, (that covered the former Federal Republic of Germany (FDR) and Austria), provided that pictures and news of French races would be relayed live to turf accountants appointed by DSV. The Commission objected to two clauses in this agreement which prevented DSV from sub-licensing the use of sound and pictures to corporate turf accountants or to betting shops which were not in existence at the time the agreement was concluded. The parties then notified a replacement agreement under which PMI granted DSV the exclusive operating licence in the former FDR and Austria for the pictures and commentary and DSV agreed to sub-contract the rights to turf accountants in the territory. The new agreement provided for a standard form of sub-licence to be used by DSV that contained a number of provisions which the Commission considered were contrary to Article 85(1):

(a) a requirement of honesty on the part of the subcontractor. The Commission thought this was too vague and the parties replaced it with a prohibition on the appointment of subcontractors found guilty of infringements of the law in the territories covered;
(b) a no-challenge clause requiring the subcontractors to recognise in all countries the ownership rights of the racing associations. This clause was deleted by the parties; and
(c) a requirement of disclosure of information imposed only on corporate sub-contractors. The Commission found this included highly confidential information and amounted to serious discrimination. The requirement was then limited to published documents.

Although various third parties objected to the prohibition on DSV relaying the sound and pictures it received to agencies outside the licensed territory, the Commission held that this did not fall within Article 85(1). A licensor must remain free to choose his licensee and the size of the licensed territory granted to him. If such a clause was not included, the licence would become a Europe-wide licence and the licensor would be unable to co-ordinate the management of all the relays of sound and pictures to the other Member States. The modified agreement was granted negative clearance.

8–176 **Copyright licences and Article 86.** The decision of the Court of First Instance was upheld by the Court of Justice: Cases C–241 & 242/91P *RTE and ITP v. Commission* [1995] I ECR 743 [1995] 4 CMLR 718 [1995] All ER (EC) 416. See para. 8–071, *supra*.

(c) *Licences of plant breeders' rights*

8–177 **Licences of plant breeders' rights**

n. 48. This approach would appear to be confirmed by the Art. 19(3) notices published in *SICASOV*, OJ 1995 C95/8 [1995] 5 CMLR 100 and

CBA, OJ 1995 C211/11 [1995] 5 CMLR 734. Plant variety rights may now be granted throughout the Community: Reg. 2100/94, OJ 1994 L227/1.

(d) *IPR licensing policies*

Software licensing policy. In *Microsoft*, XXIVth Report on Competition Policy (1994), page 364, the Commission expressed concern about: **8–178**

(a) the use by Microsoft of "per processor" or "per system" licences, *i.e.* clauses in software licences to PC manufacturers requiring payment of a royalty, regardless of whether any particular computer was shipped with pre-installed Microsoft software;
(b) provisions requiring licensees to pay a minimum royalty to Microsoft regardless of actual use of Microsoft products; and
(c) the duration of Microsoft licence agreements.

Microsoft gave an undertaking, for a period of six-and-a-half years, to modify its licensing practices. It would cease to include "per processor" clauses in its licences, abandon minimum commitment clauses, and not enter into licence contracts with a duration of more than one year. "Per system" licences will be granted only if licensees are given flexibility to purchase non-Microsoft products and to avoid the payment of royalties in such cases. (For the full text of the undertaking, see EU Bulletin 7/8–1994 at page 130).

European standards and IPR licensing policies. Under its original interim IPR policy, the European Telecommunications Standards Institute, whose task is to establish common European standard in the telecommunications sector, obliged its members to agree in advance to license any of their IPRs deemed "essential" to the development of an ETSI standard unless the IPR holder identified intellectual property which it wished to withhold for six months. Members were also required to grant licences for monetary consideration and to notify ETSI of the maximum royalty rate which they would apply. These provisions were the subject of a complaint as amounting to a compulsory licensing system and, following the Commission's intervention, were revised. ETSI adopted an amended interim policy providing that IPR holders should be adequately and fairly rewarded for the use of their IPRs, without requiring licensers to accept royalties from licensees. Where ETSI becomes aware of an essential IPR, it shall request from the IPR holder an undertaking that it is prepared to grant irrevocable licences on fair, reasonable and non-discriminatory terms; should the IPR holder refuse and should no viable alternative technology exist, ETSI shall cease work on that standard. Accordingly, there are no provisions for automatic licensing or specific licensing terms. The Commission issued a comfort letter indicating negative clearance. *ETSI Interim IPR Policy*, Report on the application of competition rules in the EU (1995), page 131. **8–179**

CHAPTER 9

ARTICLE 86

1. INTRODUCTION

(a) *General*

9–002 **Article 86 generally.** As a result of the amendments made by the TEU, the former Article 3(f) of the Treaty is now Article 3(g) and the wording has been revised to substitute "the internal market" for "the common market": see Appendix 1, *post.*

n. 1. There should be added to the list the following principal decisions by the ECJ and CFI:

Case C–53/92P *Hilti v. Commission* [1994] I ECR 667 [1994] 4 CMLR 614, (dismissing the appeal from Case T–30/89 [1991] II ECR 1439 [1992] 4 CMLR 16);
Case C–393/92 *Almelo* [1994] I ECR 1477;
Case C–18/93 *Corsica Ferries* [1994] I ECR 1783;
Case C–323/93 *Centre d'Insémination de la Crespelle v. Coopérative de la Mayenne* [1994] I ECR 5077;
Case T–83/91 *Tetra Pak v. Commission* [1994] II ECR 755, (upholding the Commission's decision in *Tetra Pak II*, OJ 1992 L72/1, [1992] 4 CMLR 551), on further appeal Case C–333/94P;
Case C–250/92 *Gøttrup-Klim v. Dansk Landbrugs Grovvareselskab AmbA* [1994] I ECR 5641 [1996] 4 CMLR 191;
Cases C–241 & 242/91P *RTE and ITP v. Commission* [1995] I ECR 743 [1995] 4 CMLR 718 [1995] All ER (EC) 416 (upholding Case T–69/89 [1991] II ECR 485 [1991] 4 CMLR 586 and Case T–76/89 [1991] II ECR 575 [1991] 4 CMLR 745);
Case C–310/93P *BPB Industries and British Gypsum v. Commission* [1995] I ECR 865 (dismissing the appeal from Case T–65/89 [1993] II ECR 389, [1993] 5 CMLR 32).

For published works, see now Whish, *op. cit.* (3rd ed., 1993); Van Bael and

Bellis *Competition Law of the European Community* (3rd ed., CCH 1994).

n. 5. See also *Gøttrup-Klim v. Dansk Landbrugs Grovvareselskab AmbA*, *supra*, § 49: "neither the creation nor the strengthening of a dominant position is in itself contrary to Art. 86 of the Treaty".

(b) *Relationship between Article 85 and Article 86*

Requirement of an additional element. It seems clear that use of a contractual term that has an anti-competitive effect by an undertaking in a dominant position may both constitute an abuse within Article 86 and bring the contracts incorporating that term within Article 85. In Case C–393/92 *Almelo* [1994] I ECR 1477, it was held that an exclusive purchasing obligation imposed by regional electricity distributors on local distributors and end users came within Article 85 and could also constitute an abuse if the regional distributors occupied a collective dominant position. **9–005**

Article 86 and exemptions under Article 85(3) **9–006**

n. 14. See also Case C–310/93P *BPB Industries and British Gypsum v. Commission* [1995] I ECR 865, *per* Advocate General Léger at §§ 63–69. His conclusions at those paragraphs were adopted by the ECJ.

2. DOMINANT POSITION

Definition and elements of dominance **9–007**

n. 19. The CFI's analysis in Case T–69/89 was upheld on appeal in Cases C–241 & 242/91P *RTE and ITP v. Commission* [1995] I ECR 743 [1995] 4 CMLR 718 [1995] All ER (EC) 416.

(a) *The relevant product market*

The relevant product market. *HOV-SVZ/MCN*, OJ 1994 L104/34, concerned the inland carriage of containers between Germany and the main ports in north-west Europe. Such containers could physically be carried by rail, road or inland waterway and when they are carried by rail, the bulk of traffic is organised by combined transport operators. These operators have invested considerable sums in dedicated wagons and handling equipment which can be used only for rail transport of **9–008**

containers, making it economically impossible for them to change their activity to provide road or inland waterway transport. The Commission held that the relevant market is therefore the supply of rail services (traction and access to rail network) in Germany (for which Deutsche Bundesbahn held a statutory monopoly).

n. 21. See now the CFI's decision in *Tetra Pak v. Commission*, § 9–010 *infra.*

n. 22. Case T–30/89 *Hilti v. Commission* was upheld on appeal in Case C–53/92P [1994] I ECR 667 [1994] 4 CMLR 614.

9–009 **The test of demand substitutability.** In *Carlsberg/Interbrew*, XXIVth Report on Competition Policy (1994), point 198, the beer market was regarded as separate from the market for other alcoholic and non-alcoholic beverages. The Commission did not need to take a view on whether high and low fermented beers, or luxury and standard beers, or beer consumed outside the home and that consumed at home, formed separate markets.

9–010 **Interchangeability must be more than "limited".** The Commission's decision in *Tetra Pak II* was upheld by the Court of First Instance: Case T–83/91 *Tetra Pak v. Commission* [1994] II ECR 755. The Court noted that each of the packaging products other than cartons was introduced in only one country, that it accounted for only a marginal share of the UHT-milk packaging market and that that share had not changed between 1987 and 1991. As regards non-aseptic packaging, the Court noted that since the cost of the package was only a very small proportion of the total price of the final carton of milk, containers of all kinds would be interchangeable only if there were an "an almost perfect substitution of final consumer demand" (para. 72). The interchangeability should be assessed on the basis of present demand and not on developments in demand that may take place at some unspecified time in the future: *GSM radiotelephony services in Italy*, OJ 1995 L280/49; [1996] 4 CMLR 700 (mobile radiotelephony a distinct market from traditional telephony).

9–014 **A narrow market may be justified.** In Case C–53/92P *Hilti* [1994] I ECR 667 [1994] 4 CMLR 614, the Court of Justice emphasized that *Hugin* did not intend to lay down criteria for determining whether a market for consumables is distinct from the market for the equipment for which they are intended: in that case, the purchasers of the relevant spare parts were independent repairers and therefore different from the purchasers of the cash registers themselves, so that the market for spare parts constituted a specific market "governed by its own rules of supply and demand" (§ 15). See also *per* Advocate General Jacobs at §§ 15–18.

The Commission has also indicated that "in-depth fact-finding exercise and analysis on a case-by-case basis" are required to determine whether a manufacturer is dominant in the supply of spare parts and consumables. It will take into account factors such as the price and life time of the primary product, transparency of prices of secondary products, prices of secondary products as a proportion of the value of the primary product and information costs: see comments on the rejection of the complaint in *Pelikan/Kyocera*, XXVth Report on Competition Policy (1995), points 86 and 87.

n. 34. Case T–69/89 *Radio Telefis Eireann v. Commission* was upheld on appeal in Cases C–241 & 242/91P *RTE and ITP v. Commission* [1995] I ECR 743 [1995] 4 CMLR 718 [1995] All ER (EC) 416.

Narrow market in "luxury" goods. The Commission's decisions in *Yves St Laurent Parfums* and *Parfums Givenchy* were challenged by retailers that were not admitted to the networks: see Case T–19/92 *Leclerc v. Commission* and Case T–87/92 *Kruidvat v. Commission*, not yet decided. **9–015**

Ports and airports. The Court of Justice has held that the organisation of port facilities for third parties at a single port may constitute a relevant market (see Case C–179/90 *Merci Convenzionali Porto di Genova* [1991] I ECR 5891) and that compulsory piloting services at that port may also constitute a relevant market: Case C–18/93 *Corsica Ferries* [1994] I ECR 1783. The Commission has held in a number of cases that services in a single port or airport constitutes a relevant market: *Sea Containers v. Stena Sealink*, OJ 1994 L15/8 [1995] 4 CMLR 84, (market for provision of port facilities over central corridor route between Ireland and Great Britain, *i.e.* between Holyhead and Dublin/Dun Laoghaire); *Port of Rødby*, OJ 1994 L55/52 [1994] 5 CMLR 457, (market for the organisation of port services in Denmark for ferry services operating on the Rødby–Puttgarden route); *Brussels Airport*, OJ 1995 L216/8 [1996] 4 CMLR 232, on appeal Case C–291/95 *Belgium v. Commission*, (market for services linked to access to airport infrastructure for which a fee is payable at Zaventem airport); *Irish Continental Group v. CCI Morlaix* [1995] 5 CMLR 177 (supply of port facilities in Brittany for operators of ferry services between Brittany and Ireland, where only the Port of Roscoff in France had the necessary facilities). See also Case C–343/95 *Diego Cali & Figli v. Servizi Ecologico Porto di Genova*, not yet decided. **9–016A**

Need to take account of competitive conditions **9–017**

n. 39. See also Case T–83/91 *Tetra Pak v. Commission* [1994] II ECR 755, where the CFI rejected the contention that machines for packaging liquid foods and cartons should be regarded as a single market (integrated packaging systems).

(b) *The relevant degree of economic power: dominance*

9–020 **Definition of dominance**

n. 47. See also *HOV SVZ/MCN*, OJ 1994 L104/34; *Brussels Airport*, OJ 1995 L216/8 [1996] 4 CMLR 232 (on appeal Case C–291/95 *Belgium v. Commission*).

9–029 **Private and public undertakings**

n. 73. See also the decisions cited at § 9–016A, *supra*.

n. 74. In Case C–323/93 *Centre d'Insémination de la Crespelle v. Co-opérative de la Mayenne* [1994] I ECR 5077, the ECJ held that by making the operation of insemination centres subject to authorisation and providing that each centre should have the exclusive right to serve a defined area, the national legislation created a dominant position in favour of the authorised undertakings, since the effect was to establish a contiguous series of monopolies territorially limited but together covering the whole of France. *Cf.* Case C–393/92 *Almelo* [1994] I ECR 1477 where the concessions granted by the state to the regional electricity distributors were nonexclusive so that it could not be assumed without further analysis that each such distributor held a dominant position.

n. 76. See also Case C–320/91 *Corbeau* [1993] I ECR 2533 [1994] 4 CMLR 621.

9–032 **Intellectual property rights.** The issue was considered further by the Court of Justice on the appeal against the decision in *Radio Telefis Eireann*. The Court reiterated that mere ownership of an intellectual property right cannot confer a dominant position. In that case the television stations, as programme broadcasters, were the only source of the basic information necessary for a third party to publish a weekly television listings magazine. Thus the television stations enjoyed a *de facto* monopoly over the information used to compile listings for television programmes and were in a position to prevent effective competition on the market in weekly television magazines. The Court of Justice accordingly upheld the judgment of the Court of First Instance: Cases C–241 & 242/91P *RTE and ITP v. Commission* [1995] I ECR 743 [1995] 4 CMLR 718 [1995] All ER (EC) 416.

(c) *One or more undertakings*

9–036 **Parent company liability**

n. 94. The appeal against this finding was dismissed by the ECJ: findings of fact made by the CFI could not be challenged on appeal: see Case

C–310/93P *BPB Industries and British Gypsum v. Commission* [1995] I ECR 865.

Subsequent decisions on collective dominance. In Case C–393/92 *Almelo* [1994] I ECR 1477, the Court of Justice on a preliminary ruling stated, relying on its earlier decision in Case 30/87 *Bodson* [1988] ECR 2479, that for a collective dominant position to exist, the undertakings in the group must be linked in such a way as to adopt the same conduct on the market. The Court held that a contractual exclusive purchasing obligation that amounted to a breach of Article 85 would also violate Article 86 if the suppliers were found together to hold a dominant position. *RTE and ITP v. Commission, supra*, appears to involve a hybrid between individual and joint dominance, in that it was not clear that any of the three broadcasting companies (BBC, ITV and RTE) held an individual dominant position in Ireland, nor was there any evidence of collusion between them. The Court of Justice upheld the finding of the Court of First Instance that the companies held a dominant position that was based on the proposition that each one had the negative power to block publication of a listings magazine by refusing to supply information on its programmes. **9–039**

n. 5. See also *Port of Rødby*, OJ 1994 L55/52 [1994] 5 CMLR 457, where the Commission held that the two ferry companies who operated services on Rødby–Puttgarden route were jointly dominant because they fixed common rates, co-ordinated their timetables and undertook joint marketing for the service. *Cf.* Cases C–140 & 142/94 *DIP and others* [1995] I ECR 3257 [1996] 4 CMLR 157, where the ECJ held on an Art. 177 reference that national rules limiting the number of shops in an area do not place all the permitted traders in a collective dominant position because they continue to compete against each other.

(d) *The relevant geographic market*

Relevant geographic market. In Case T–83/91 *Tetra Pak v. Commission* [1994] II ECR 755, the Court of First Instance upheld the Commission's definition of the relevant geographic market as comprising the whole Community for three main reasons. First, demand was stable and not insignificant for all the relevant products throughout the territory of the Community. Secondly, customers could obtain supplies of the machinery and cartons in other Member States. Thirdly, the low cost of transport for cartons and machines meant that they could be easily and rapidly traded between States. The local differences between individual Member States or regions in patterns of consumption or prices were not considered evidence of objective conditions of competition of a non-homogeneous nature, but rather were evidence of an artificial partitioning of the market by Tetra Pak. The Commission has stated that although most technical and fiscal barriers have disappeared or are in the process of being **9–040**

eliminated inside the Community, careful analysis is still needed in each case to determine whether producers in one Member State or in the Community are subject to effective competition from producers outside, *i.e.* whether consumers have a real economic choice: XXIVth Report on Competition Policy (1994), point 200.

n. 8. See also *Novell/Microsoft*, XXIVth Report on Competition Policy (1994), point 200: world market for computer software due to lack of import restrictions, low transport costs and the absence of technical barriers (the case was dealt with by undertakings without a formal decision). *Cf. Carlsberg/Interbrew*, *ibid.* point 201: Belgium was the relevant geographic market for beer as Belgian brewers are able to determine their competitive behaviour without sufficient competitive constraints from outside Belgium. Relevant factors included the existence of strong local brands, the variety of local beers available, the high costs of transportation, the barriers to entry created by exclusive beer agreements which count for a large proportion of sales and the high degree of concentration on general national markets.

9–041 **A substantial part of the common market**

n. 12. This finding in *Radio Telefis Eireann* was not challenged on the appeal to the ECJ.

n. 13. See also *Port of Rødby*, OJ 1994 L55/52 [1994] 5 CMLR 457 (Danish Government enjoyed a dominant position in relation to Danish port of Rødby); *Brussels Airport*, OJ 1995 L216/8 [1996] 4 CMLR 232 (the eleventh busiest airport in the Community constitutes a substantial part of the common market) (on appeal Case C–291/95 *Belgium v. Commission*); Case C–18/93 *Corsica Ferries* [1994] I ECR 1783 (piloting services in the port of Genoa was the relevant market, having regard to the volume of traffic in that port and its importance in relation to maritime import and export operations as a whole in Italy).

3. ABUSE OF DOMINANT POSITION

9–042 **General Considerations.** The responsibility of a dominant firm towards actual and potential competitors has been further developed in relation to access to 'essential facilities': see para. 9–063A, *infra* and the comments of the Commission in the XXIIIrd Report on Competition Policy (1993), point 213.

9–043 **Governing principles.** In the XXIVth Report on Competition Policy (1994), point 207, the Commission summarised its approach to the concept of abuse:

> "The existence of a dominant position is not itself against the rules of competition. Consumers can suffer from a dominant company exploiting this position, the most likely way being through prices higher than would be found if the market were subject to effective competition. However, the Commission in its decision-making practice does not normally control or condemn the high level of prices as such. Rather it examines the behaviour of the dominant company designed to preserve its dominance, usually directly against competitors or new entrants who would normally bring about effective competition and the price level associated with it. A dominant company therefore has a special obligation not to do anything that would cause further deterioration to the already fragile structure of competition or to unfairly prevent the emergence and growth of new or existing competitors who might challenge this dominance and bring about the establishment of effective competition."

The Commission cited the *Microsoft* case as an illustration of the above approach whereby it had sought to address the structure of the market rather than attack Microsoft's prices as such.

Abuse as an objective concept. In *Tetra Pak, infra*, the Court of First Instance reiterated the objective nature of the assessment of abuse under Article 86 and stated that the actual scope of the special responsibility imposed on an undertaking in a dominant position must be considered in the light of the specific circumstances of each case. **9–044**

Link between dominant position and abuse. The Commission's decision in *Tetra Pak II* was upheld by the Court of First Instance: Case T–83/91 *Tetra Pak v. Commission* [1994] II ECR 755, now on further appeal Case C–333/94P. **9–045**

n. 22. Case T–65/89 *BPB Industries v. Commission* was upheld on appeal in Case C–310/93P [1995] I ECR 865.

Exclusionary and exploitative abuse. If the conduct of a dominant undertaking does not constitute an abuse, the question of objective justification does not arise. Where that conduct does not fall within one of the established heads of abuse, determination of the ambit of the "special responsibility" placed on the dominant undertaking can be of some difficulty. But see the observations of Advocate General Kirschner in Case T–51/89 *Tetra Pak Rausing v. Commission* [1990] II ECR 309 at 331 to 338 [1991] 4 CMLR 334 at 358 to 365. **9–046**

n. 24. Hilti's appeal against the decision of the CFI was dismissed in Case C–53/92P *Hilti v. Commission* [1994] I ECR 667 [1994] 4 CMLR 614; the Commission's decision in *Tetra Pak II* was upheld in Case T–83/91 *Tetra Pak v. Commission* [1994] II ECR 755, on further appeal Case C–333/94P.

9–047 **Kinds of abuse.** *Tetra Pak*, *supra*, considers a number of the specific kinds of abuse discussed in the remaining paragraphs of this chapter, including exclusivity and other abusive clauses in contracts with customers, predatory pricing, and the application of discriminatory prices.

(ii) *Predatory pricing*

9–054 **Predatory pricing: subsequent decisions.** The decision of the Commission was upheld by the Court of First Instance in Case T–83/91 *Tetra Pak v. Commission* [1994] II ECR 755. The Court recognised that it may be acceptable for an undertaking in a dominant position to sell at a loss in certain circumstances, but not where such selling was predatory. The sale of Tetra Rex cartons in Italy for a period of seven years constantly below not only their total cost but also their variable direct cost was sufficient evidence that Tetra Pak pursued a policy of eviction.

(iii) *Price discrimination*

9–055 **Price discrimination generally.** In *Tetra Pak*, *supra*, the company contended that the differences in prices between Member States were not discriminatory on the grounds, *inter alia*, that the prices of cartons and machines could not be viewed separately and that the equilibrium between machine and carton prices varied from one Member State to another. That contention was rejected by the Court of First Instance because the differences were too great to be justified by local market conditions. See also Case C–18/93 *Corsica Ferries* [1994] I ECR 1783, where a tariff of charges for piloting services which in effect set different rates depending on the nationality of the vessel was condemned under Article 86. In *Van den Bergh Foods*, OJ 1995 C211/4 [1995] 5 CMLR 734, the Commission stated that the system of "inclusive pricing" operated by Unilever (whereby a freezer cabinet was supplied "free of charge" but the cost was included in the price of the ice cream, and that price was charged irrespective of whether the retailer actually took a freezer cabinet from Unilever) would be contrary to Article 86.

9–056 **Price discrimination in United Brands**

n. 51. See now Case T–83/91 *Tetra Pak v. Commission* [1994] II ECR 755.

(iv) *Fidelity rebates and similar practices*

9–057 **Fidelity rebates and similar practices.** In Case C–393/92 *Almelo* [1994] I ECR 1477, the Court of Justice reiterated that it is an abuse for a dominant undertaking to include a loyalty obligation in its contracts, even at the buyers' request. In its two decisions finding infringements of Article 86 in *Soda Ash, Solvay*, OJ 1991 L152/21, and *ICI*, OJ 1991 L152/40; [1994] 4 CMLR 645 (both), the Commission distinguished fidelity rebates from simple quantity discounts: the former "involves offering customers financial advantages in order to prevent them from obtaining their supplies from competing producers". The decisions were quashed by the Court of First Instance on procedural grounds but those judgments are on appeal by the Commission to the Court of Justice: Case T–32/91 *Solvay v. Commission* [1995] II ECR 1825 [1996] 5 CMLR 91, Case T–37/91 *ICI v. Commission* [1995] II ECR 1901, on appeal Cases C–286/95P, etc. See also *UCB/Almirall*, XXIVth Report on Competition Policy (1994), page 362: free samples as a fidelity discount.

n. 56. The appeal against the CFI judgment was dismissed in Case C–53/92P *Hilti v. Commission* [1994] I ECR 667 [1994] 4 CMLR 614.

n. 58. See now Case C–310/93P *BPB Industries and British Gypsum v. Commission* [1995] I ECR 865 (dismissing the appeal from Case T–65/89 [1993] II ECR 389 [1993] 5 CMLR 32).

(v) *Refusal to supply*

9–059 **In general.** On the question of how far Article 86 applies where the dominant firm has never previously supplied the customer in question, see the development of the concept of access to "essential facilities": para. 9–063A, *infra*. The refusal by a dominant undertaking to supply further goods to a customer when payment is overdue for supplies previously made does not constitute an abuse: *Leyland DAF v. Automotive Products* [1994] 1 BCLC 245 (C.A.).

n. 64. See now Case T–83/91 *Tetra Pak v. Commission* [1994] II ECR 755 in which the CFI upheld the Commission's decision.

9–062 **Refusal to supply in narrow markets: *Hugin***

n. 72. The appeal against Case T–30/89 *Hilti* was dismissed in Case C–53/92P *Hilti v. Commission* [1994] I ECR 667 [1994] 4 CMLR 614. See the Commission's comments on the analysis of abuse in secondary markets: XXVth Report on Competition Policy (1995), point 86.

9–063A **Refusal of access to "essential facilities".** The cases discussed in the preceding paragraphs concern actions where the dominant undertaking has refused to supply an existing customer. More recently, the Commission has developed a line of cases in which it has held that where a dominant undertaking owns or controls access to facilities which a competitor must use in order to provide a competing service, the dominant undertaking cannot refuse to make those facilities available to the new market entrant, unless it has an objective justification for that refusal. Thus in *Port of Rødby*, OJ 1994 L55/52 [1994] 5 CMLR 457, Stena ferry operators wished to start operating a service between Rødby in Denmark and Puttgarden in Germany. The service would compete with that offered by the Danish public undertaking, DSB, which also operated the port facilities at Rødby. Having analysed alternative routes, the Commission concluded that the relevant market was for the organisation of port services in Denmark for ferry services operating on the Rødby/Puttgarden route. It held, purporting to follow *Télémarketing*, that

> "an undertaking that owns or manages and uses itself an essential facility, *i.e.* a facility or infrastructure without which its competitors are unable to offer their service to customers, and refuses to grant them access to such facility is abusing its dominant position. Consequently, an undertaking that owns or manages an essential port facility from which it provides a maritime transport services may not, without objective justification, refuse to grant a shipowner wishing to operate on the same maritime route access to that facility without infringing Article 86" (para. 12).

The Commission arrived at a similar conclusion in *Sea Containers/Stena Sealink*, OJ 1994 L15/8, in the context of an application for interim measures, holding that Stena could not refuse access to the port facilities at Holyhead to Sea Containers, nor could it grant access only on terms less favourable than those which it gave its own services. This applied even where the competitor was a new entrant to the relevant market. The Commission has applied the same reasoning to access to airport facilities at Zaventem airport: *Brussels Airport*, OJ 1995 L216/8.

It is not clear from the current state of the law whether the obligation to make the facilities available arises only where the dominant undertaking itself operates a service with which the new entrant will be competing. This was included as an element in the formulation of the principle in the *Port of Rødby* and *Stena Sealink/Sea Containers* cases. However, in *Irish Continental Group v. CCI Morlaix* [1995] 5 CMLR 177, the Commission held that the relevant product market was the supply of port facilities in Brittany for operators of ferry services between Brittany and Ireland and found that Roscoff was the only port in Brittany which had suitable facilities for ICG to use. The port was managed by CCI Morlaix under a state concession and that company held a five per cent shareholding in Brittany Ferries, the principal user of the port. The Commission held, in an application for interim measures, that the refusal to grant access was an abuse even leaving aside any economic interest held by CCI Morlaix in Brittany Ferries. For a discussion of these cases, see Glasl "Essential Facilities doctrine in EC Anti-trust law" (1994) 6 ECLR 306.

(vi) *Abuse of intellectual property rights*

Refusal of licences: *Radio Telefis Eireann.* The appeals by RTE and ITP against the decisions of the Court of First Instance were dismissed. The Court of Justice affirmed that the exercise of an exclusive right by the proprietor may, in exceptional circumstances, involve abusive conduct. The conduct objected to was the television stations' reliance on copyright to prevent others from publishing on a weekly basis information (channel, day, time and title of programmes) together with commentaries and pictures obtained independently of the television stations. That refusal to provide basic information prevented the appearance of a new product, a comprehensive weekly guide to television programmes, which the television companies did not offer and for which there was a potential consumer demand. Such refusal constituted an abuse. Further, there was no justification for such refusal either in the activity of television broadcasting or in that of publishing television magazines. Finally, the television stations had reserved to themselves the secondary market of weekly television guides by excluding all competition on that market since they denied access to the basic information which was the raw material indispensable for the compilation of such a guide. Cases C–241 & 242/91P *RTE and ITP v. Commission* [1995] I ECR 743 [1995] 4 CMLR 718 [1995] All ER (EC) 416. **9–065**

Remedies ordered. The Court of Justice held that the Court of First Instance was right to find that a requirement to provide the information, with the possibility of making authorisation of publication dependent on certain conditions, including payment of royalties, was the only way of bringing the infringement to an end. **9–066**

(vii) *Tying clauses*

Tying clauses: *Hilti.* The Court of Justice dismissed Hilti's appeal, which was confined to challenging the Court of First Instance's appraisal of the relevant market and not the conduct objected to as being abusive: Case C–53/92P [1994] I ECR 667. **9–071**

Tying clauses: *Tetra Pak II.* The Commission's decision was upheld by the Court of First Instance in Case T–83/91 *Tetra Pak v. Commission* [1994] II ECR 755, on further appeal Case C–333/94P. **9–073**

n. 94. The distinction between ties and exclusive purchasing obligations is also illustrated by the cases concerning distribution of impulse ice cream. In the German market where ice cream suppliers entered into exclusive purchasing obligations with retail outlets, the Commission considered the matter under Art. 85: see, *e.g.* Case T–7/93 *Langnese-Iglo v. Commission* [1995] II ECR 1533 [1995] 5 CMLR 602 [1995] All ER (EC) 902, on appeal Case C–79/95P. In the Irish market, Unilever's practice was to supply a freezer cabinet "free of charge" to the retail outlet under an agreement which provided that only Unilever's ice cream products were to be stocked in the freezer. The Commission indicated that this was contrary to both Arts. 85 and 86: *Van den Bergh Foods*, OJ 1995 C211/4 [1995] 5 CMLR 734. See also the *Soda Ash* decisions: *Solvay*, OJ 1991 L152/21, and *ICI*, OJ 1991 L152/40 [1994] 4 CMLR 645 (both): it is an abuse for a dominant company to tie customers by an arrangement to supply all or substantially all of their requirements; even if the customer is free to purchase elsewhere, so that there is no legal "tie", such an agreement may constitute an abuse if it is of long duration. The decisions were quashed on procedural grounds: Case T–32/91 *Solvay v. Commission* [1995] II ECR 1825 [1996] 5 CMLR 91; Case T–37/91 *ICI v. Commission* [1995] II ECR 1901, on appeal Cases C–286/95P, etc. See also *UCB/Almirall*, XXIVth Report on Competition Policy (1994), at 362.

9–074 **Tying of ancillary services.** The Court of First Instance in *Tetra Pak*, *infra*, further accepted that the combined effect of the other contractual provisions which restricted the commercial freedom of users was an overall strategy aimed to make the customer totally dependent on Tetra Pak for the entire life of the machine, thereby excluding any possibility of competition at the level both of cartons and machines. Those clauses were considered to be abusive in themselves since their object was to make the sale of machines subject to the acceptance of additional services of a different type, such as maintenance and repair and the provision of spare parts.

(viii) *Other contractual conditions*

9–075 **Other anti-competitive conditions.** The Commission's decision in *Tetra Pak II* in relation to the additional clauses was upheld in Case T–83/91 *Tetra Pak v. Commission* [1994] II ECR 755 (see further para. 9–074, *supra*). See also *Carlsberg/Interbrew*, XXIVth Report on Competition Policy (1994), point 198, where the abuse consisted of an exclusive licence by Carlsberg to Interbrew to produce or distribute certain internationally known luxury beers. The Commission acknowledged that in other beer markets where there was effective competition, such exclusive licences between producers can be a highly effective way for producers in one Member State to penetrate markets in other Member States. In this case, however, the exclusivity extended the range of beers which Interbrew could offer to include a market segment which it had not penetrated with much success previously. The extension of Interbrew's range further increased barriers to entry for existing firms and potential new entrants since they would also need to offer a full range to compete effectively with

Interbrew. The exclusivity was all the more detrimental to competition because Carlsberg's (the licensor) beers represented around 76 per cent of the luxury pils segment.

(x) *Discrimination*

Different aspects of discrimination **9–077**

n. 12. The appeal to the ECJ was dismissed: Case C–310/93P *BPB Industries and British Gypsum v. Commission* [1995] I ECR 865.

CHAPTER 10

THE ENFORCEMENT OF THE COMPETITION RULES IN THE MEMBER STATES

2. APPLICATION OF ARTICLES 85 AND 86 IN THE COURTS OF THE UNITED KINGDOM

(a) *Generally*

10–002 **Direct effect and the supremacy of Community law**

n. 1. See now Hartley, *The Foundations of European Community Law* (Clarendon Press, 3rd ed., 1995). See also Brealey and Hoskins, *Remedies in EC Law* (Longman, 1994); Lewis, *Remedies and the Enforcement of European Community Law* (Sweet & Maxwell, 1996).

10–003 **The European Communities Act**

n. 4. For s.1(1) in the main work, substitute s.1(2). "The Treaties" as defined in that sub-section now includes also: the EEA Agreement of 1992 (together with the adjustment Protocol of 1993); and Titles II, III and IV of the Treaty of European Union of 1992 (together with the other provisions of the TEU so far as they relate to those titles) and the Protocols adopted at Maastricht annexed to the EC Treaty with the exception of the Protocol on Social Policy: see the European Economic Area Act 1993 and the European Communities (Amendment) Act 1993.

(b) *Matters affecting jurisdiction*

10–006 **Jurisdiction of national courts.** The position is different under the competition provisions of the ECSC Treaty. A decision by the

Commission finding an infringement of Articles 65 or 66 is a prerequisite to an action before a national court: see Case C–128/92 *Banks* [1994] 1 ECR 1209 [1994] 5 CMLR 30. Accordingly, in the related English proceedings, *Banks v. British Coal Corporation* (judgment of 19 July 1994), Mance J. struck out a claim for damages brought before such a determination by the Commission.

Article 177 references. In *R. v. Stock Exchange, ex p. Else Ltd* [1993] QB 534, 545 (C.A.), Sir Thomas Bingham MR set out as follows his understanding of the correct approach in principle of a national court (other than a final court of appeal) in deciding whether to make an Article 177 reference: **10–010**

> "... if the facts have been found and the Community law issue is critical to the court's final decision, the appropriate course is ordinarily to refer the issue to the Court of Justice unless the national court can with complete confidence resolve the issue itself. In considering whether it can with complete confidence resolve the issue itself the national court must be fully mindful of the differences between national and Community legislation, of the pitfalls which face a national court venturing into what may be an unfamiliar field, of the need for uniform interpretation throughout the Community and of the great advantages enjoyed by the Court of Justice in construing Community instruments. If the national court has any real doubt, it should ordinarily refer".

n. 23. See now Hartley, *The Foundations of European Community Law* (Clarendon Press, 3rd ed., 1995). See also Brealey and Hoskins, *Remedies in EC Law* (Longman, 1994), Ch. 10; Lewis, *Remedies and the Enforcement of European Community Law* (Sweet & Maxwell, 1996), Ch. 11; Anderson, *References to the European Court* (Sweet & Maxwell, 1995).

Where contract subject to law of non-Member State **10–011**

n. 27. See now Dicey and Morris, *The Conflict of Laws* (12th ed., 1993), Rule 177, esp. p. 1241.

(c) *Consistency and the duty of "sincere co-operation"*

Generally. The EFTA Surveillance Authority has issued a similar co-operation Notice as regards the application of Articles 53 and 54 of the EEA Agreement: see para. 10–017, *infra*. **10–015**

Avoidance of inconsistent decisions. In *MTV Europe v. BMG Records (U.K.) Ltd* [1995] 1 CMLR 437 (Ch.D.), the defendants applied for a stay of national court proceedings for damages for breach of Article 85, **10–016**

pending a decision by the Commission and any appeal from that decision to the Court of First Instance or onward appeal to the Court of Justice. The question of whether or not the Commission would grant an exemption under Article 85(3) was immaterial, since an exemption could at most relate back to the date of notification of the arrangements to the Commission, and notification had taken place some time after the matters alleged to give rise to a cause of action in the national proceedings.

Evans-Lombe J. held that he could not rule out the possibility that the Commission would grant negative clearance of the arrangements on the basis that there had been no infringement of Article 85, despite the expression by the Commission of a prima facie view that there had been infringement. However, the chances of the Commission granting negative clearance were not sufficient to justify refusing the plaintiff the right to press on with the preparation of its case in accordance with the rules. The judge nevertheless allowed an initial stay of proceedings until after the expected conclusion of the formal procedure before the Commission, to avoid the hardship of the defendants having to contest the same issue in two fora simultaneously. Thereafter, the national proceedings would be allowed to progress until the setting down stage. If at that point the Commission had still not reported, the national proceedings would be stayed until one month after publication of the Commission's decision.

On appeal, the Court of Appeal rejected the contention that unless a national court is able to find that a complaint of infringement of Articles 85 or 86 is clearcut, its only option is to stay all further national proceedings from that point forward until the Commission has made its decision (judgment of 17 July 1995, unreported). The Court held that the only concern of Community law was to avoid inconsistent decisions, and that there was no ground for seeking to prohibit the preparation of an action for trial so long as it did not lead to a decision in advance of a decision by the Commission.

n. 36. In Cases C–319/93, etc., *Dijkstra and Others* [1995] I ECR 4471 [1996] 5 CMLR 178, the ECJ stated that the practice of the Commission is to be discerned not only from its decisions but also from its annual Reports on Competition Policy and its communications (§ 32).

10–017 **The Commission's Notice: Articles 85(1) and 86.** The EFTA Surveillance Authority has issued an analogous Notice on co-operation between national courts and the EFTA Surveillance Authority in applying Articles 53 and 54 of the EEA Agreement: OJ 1995 C112/7 [1995] 5 CMLR 358.

10–019 **Assistance from the Commission.** See also Cases C–319/93, etc., *Dijkstra, supra*, para. 34. In its XXIVth Report on Competition Policy (1994), point 50, the Commission noted that a Queen's Bench Master had made a request for information to the Directorate-General for Competition. The information requested included (a) references to the relevant case law of the Court of Justice and the Court of First Instance, (b) decisions previously taken by the Commission in similar cases, (c) information on the state of proceedings in the handling by the Commission of a complaint relating to the matters before the Master, (d) information on the Commission's established practise regarding the relevant Community law, and (e) information on factual data: statistics, market studies and economic analyses. With the exception of questions relating to the interpretation of Community law, an answer to the request was provided by letter within six months.

Effect of earlier decision by Commissions. The question of the effect in national proceedings based on an alleged infringement of the EC rules on competition of an earlier decision by the Commission was addressed in *Iberian U.K. Ltd v. BPB Industries PLC* (ChD, [1996] 2 CMLR 601. Iberian sought damages against BPB in respect of an alleged abuse of BPB's dominant position on the United Kingdom market for plasterboard and claimed to be entitled to rely in the national proceedings on an earlier Commission decision, which had found abuse by BPB and had imposed substantial fines. (BPB's appeals against that decision had been unsuccessful). Laddie J. held that the earlier Commission decision must at least be *admissible* in the English proceedings, since otherwise the principle that a national court ought to stay its proceedings to await the outcome of parallel Commission proceedings (save in clearcut cases) would be pointless. He held further that, for the purpose of the national proceedings for damages, the decision of the Commission and the judgments of the European courts upholding it on appeal were *conclusive* so far as concerned (i) the findings of fact set out in them, and (ii) any issues relating to the interpretation and/or applicability of Article 86 in the case. He stated in particular: **10–022**

> "... where, as here, the parties have disputed the same issues before the Commission, and have had real and reasonable opportunities to appeal from an adverse decision, there is no injustice in obliging them to accept the result obtained in Europe ... Therefore, whether expressed in terms of res judicata or abuse of process, it would be contrary to public policy to allow persons who have been involved in competition proceedings in Europe to deny here the correctness of the conclusions reached there".

The Judge endorsed the views expressed by Advocate General Van Gerven on this question in Case C–128/92 *Banks* [1994] I ECR 1209 [1994] 5 CMLR 30 (a case concerning the ECSC Treaty where the Court of Justice did not itself rule on the question). The Advocate General considered that the addressee of a Commission decision, and persons to whom it was of direct and individual concern were bound to accept the findings of fact and law made in it: the only course of action open to them if they wished to challenge the decision would be to bring an action for annulment under Article 173. In other cases, the Advocate General considered that if a national court comes to the conclusion that the issues of fact and/or of law decided by the Commission are incorrect or insufficient, or at any rate if it has serious doubts in that regard, then it must take the following course of action: in the case of findings which carried no weight in the final decision and do not therefore underlie the reasoning of the Commission, the national court is at liberty to adopt a different interpretation (since in those circumstances the risk of conflicting decisions and the resulting impairment of the principle of legal certainty is extremely small). On the other hand, in the case of findings which had an influence on the final decision arrived at by the Commission, the national court should, in accordance with the provisions of its national procedural law, suspend the proceedings and seek the necessary information from the Commission or make a direct reference to the Court of Justice for a preliminary ruling concerning the validity of the decision in question or the interpretation of the relevant Community competition rules.

In *MTV Europe v. BMG Records (U.K.) Ltd* [1995] 1 CMLR 437 (Ch.D.), it was argued that a decision of the Commission granting negative clearance in respect of an agreement, as opposed to an exemption, is merely an indication that the Commission does not intend to take enforcement action on the basis of the information before them, so that a judgment of a national court concluding that there had been a breach of Article 85 would not be in conflict with the Commission's decision. The court held, however, that much will depend upon the terms and reasoning of the Commission's decision.

10–023 **Status of the Commission's informal view.** In Case T–114/92 *BEMIM v. Commission* [1995] II ECR 147 [1996] 4 CMLR 305, the Court of First Instance held that the provisional assessment by the Commission in an Article 6 letter rejecting a complaint could not affect the position of individuals in proceedings before national courts (para. 65). In Case T–575/93 *Koelman v. Commission* [1996] 4 CMLR 636, the Court of First Instance held that a decision by the Commission to reject a complaint has the same legal status as a "comfort letter". It followed that the assessments made by the Commission in a decision rejecting a complaint did not prevent a national court, which had to rule on the compatibility with Article 85(1) of the agreements or practices complained of, from declaring those agreements or practices to be automatically void under Article 85(2) having regard to the evidence before it. The fact that, unlike in the case of comfort letters, the Commission's assessment was contained in a challengeable measure did not affect that conclusion, since such an assessment entailed no definitive decision on the issue of whether Article 85(1) had been infringed or whether an exemption was to be granted under Article 85(3). See also the observations of the Court of Justice in Cases C–319/93, etc., *Dijkstra and Others* [1995] I ECR 4471: para. 10–016, n. 36, *supra*.

n. 55. For § 20 substitute § 14. There is no analogous provision in the EFTA Surveillance Authority's Co-operation Notice.

(d) *Voidness of contractual provisions*

Chemidus Wavin v. TERI. See now also *Richard Cound Ltd v. BMW (G.B.) Ltd* (C.A., judgment of 10 May 1995), where the plaintiff motor dealer contended that BMW's standard distribution agreement infringed Article 85(1) and was not covered by the motor vehicle block exemption, Regulation 123/85. Balcombe L.J. found that the effect of excising all the restrictive provisions of the distribution agreement would be that: **10–028**

> "Instead of being a dealership agreement under which [BMW G.B.] supplied BMW cars and BMW spare parts to [Cound], and [Cound] undertook to resell those cars and those spare parts to the public within a public area and to provide servicing facilities for BMW cars for anyone owning such a car, whether or not bought from [Cound], the agreement would become an agreement, the essence of which would be that [BMW G.B.] would be obliged to sell BMW cars and parts to [Cound] and [Cound] would be obliged to pay for them.... That is an agreement so different that, in my judgment, it is apt to regard the effect of severance as 'altering entirely the scope and intention of the agreement' or as removing the heart and soul of the agreement ..."

Cound's argument that the remainder of the agreement should survive the excision of its restrictive provisions because of an express "severance" clause in the contract was rejected: the severance clause was not apt to permit the excision of void terms in circumstances where the result would be entirely to alter the scope and intention of the agreement.

n. 75. See also *Inntrepreneur Estates v. Boyes* (1993) 47 EG 140 (1993) 68 P & CR 77 (C.A.).

Severance: a summary **10–029**

n. 79. In *Marchant & Eliot Underwriting Ltd v. Higgins* (CA) [1996] 2 Lloyd's Rep. 31, the Court of Appeal applied the English principles of severance in considering the enforceability of the payment obligations of a Lloyd's "Name" in the light of allegations that the Lloyd's Central Fund arrangement might contravene Art. 85.

Consequences of nullity as between the parties **10–030**

n. 83. See now Goff & Jones (4th ed., 1993) and *Westdeutsche Landesbank v. Islington B.C.* [1994] 1 WLR 938 [1994] 4 All ER 890 [1994] 4 All ER 890 (C.A.).

Existence of nexus: *Volvo v. Veng.* The Court of Appeal in *Chiron Corp. v. Murex Diagnostics Ltd (No. 2)* [1994] FSR 187 [1994] 1 CMLR 410, has **10–033**

cast doubt on the correctness of the wide view expressed by Hoffman J. in *Pitney Bowes* of the circumstances in which the court will find a sufficient nexus between the relief claimed by a plaintiff and the alleged breach by him of Article 85 or Article 86.

In *Chiron*, the holder of a patent relating to testing kits for Hepatitis C antibodies sued a number of defendants for infringement. The judge refused to strike out that part of one of the defences which alleged that the patentee was abusing its dominant position contrary to Article 86, in particular by charging excessive prices for licences and for its kits. The decision was upheld on the narrow procedural basis that the Court of Appeal would not interfere with the judge's decision unless it was satisfied that he was "plainly wrong" in his conclusion that there was a nexus sufficient to allow the pleading in the action to stand.

However, Staughton L.J. went further and chose to "grasp the nettle" of the nexus point himself. He held that in general the remedy for abuses such as were alleged in the instant case was not to refuse relief to the holder of the patent against an infringer, because that could be altogether lacking in proportionality. He added that it might give rise to a fluctuating situation whereby a patent was sometimes enforceable and sometimes not, depending on whether the patentee was charging a fair price or a price that was unfairly high. In the event, Staughton L.J. impliedly declined to follow the view of Hoffman J. in *Pitney Bowes* that the remedy for abuses of a dominant position in cases where the abuser's ability to act unlawfully is buttressed by an intellectual property right is that "the plaintiff may have to be deprived of the means of maintaining his dominant position". Instead, Staughton L.J. stated that there were other remedies available to the victim of an abuse of the kind alleged, such as the making of a complaint to the Commission under Article 3 of Regulation 17. He left open the possibility that there may be "extraordinary cases" where the Court should refuse relief to the patent-holder on the ground that he was in breach of Article 86, but there was nothing to indicate that the case before him fell into that class.

It is submitted that the "extraordinary cases" to which Staughton L.J. referred would properly include all cases where the abuse alleged was a consequence of the relief claimed in the particular action. Such an interpretation would accord with the judgments of the Court of Justice in *Volvo v. Veng*, and in Cases C–241 & 242/91P *RTE and ITP v. Commission* [1995] I ECR 743 [1995] 4 CMLR 718 [1995] All ER (EC) 416, that the exercise of an exclusive right by its proprietor may, in exceptional circumstances, itself involve abusive conduct. See para. 8–071, *supra.*

10–035 **Generally**

n. 6. See now Kerse, *EC Antitrust Procedure* (Sweet & Maxwell, 3rd ed., 1994).

10–038 **Bourgoin.** In *Kirklees MBC v. Wickes Building Supplies Ltd* [1993] A.C. 227, at 281–82, the House of Lords, *obiter*, doubted whether *Bourgoin* was correctly decided in the light of the Court of Justice's judgment in *Francovich*: see para. 10–040 of the main work.

Recent case law of the Court of Justice. In Cases C–46 & 48/93 *Brasserie du Pêcheur v. Germany* and *Factortame* III [1996] I ECR 1029 [1996] 1 CMLR 889 [1996] 1 All ER (EC) 301, the Court of Justice considered the nature and extent of State liability to make reparation to individuals for breaches of Community law. Although the cases therefore did not directly concern the liability of *individuals* for breaches of Community law (*e.g.* for breaches of Articles 85 or 86), the judgment was expressed in general terms which are apt to cover such a situation. **10–039**

The Court enunciated in particular the following principles to govern actions for damages for breaches of Community law:

(a) reparation for loss or damage caused to individuals as a result of breaches of Community law must be commensurate with the loss or damage sustained so as to ensure the effective protection for their rights (para. 82);
(b) the national court may inquire whether the injured person showed reasonable diligence in order to avoid the loss or damage or limit its extent and whether he availed himself in time of all the legal remedies available to him (para. 84);
(c) in the case of economic or commercial litigation, claims for loss of profit cannot be totally excluded (para. 87);
(d) a national court may award exemplary damages pursuant to a claim or an action founded on Community law if such damages could be awarded pursuant to a similar claim or action founded on domestic law (para. 89).

See also Case C–5/94 *R. v. Minister of Agriculture Fisheries and Food, ex p. Hedley Lomas (Ireland) Ltd* [1996] 2 CMLR 391 [1996] All ER (EC) 493, deciding that Member States have an obligation to compensate individuals for damages caused by the breach of a directly effective Treaty article, where the breach is sufficiently serious and there is a direct causal link between the breach and the damage sustained by the individuals. The Court of Justice held that Member States are obliged in those circumstances to make good the consequences of the loss or damage in accordance with their domestic law on liability. However, the conditions laid down by the applicable domestic laws must not be less favourable than those relating to similar domestic claims or framed in such a way as in practice to make it impossible or excessively difficult to obtain reparation.

Implications of *Francovich*. In Case C–128/92 *Banks* [1994] I ECR 1209 [1994] 5 CMLR 30, Advocate General Van Gerven directly addressed the question whether an individual suffering loss as the result of an infringement of his Community rights by another is entitled, *as a matter of* **10–041**

Community law, to compensation for that loss. Whilst that case concerned the ECSC Treaty, the Advocate General stated that his analysis might well also apply to the EC Treaty. This issue was not addressed in the judgment of the Court of Justice. According to the Advocate General, as a result of their obligation to ensure that Community law is fully effective and to protect the rights thereby conferred on individuals, national courts are under an obligation to award damages for loss sustained by an undertaking as a result of the breach by another undertaking of a directly effective provision of Community competition law. In the field of competition law, the only effective method whereby the national court can fully safeguard the directly effective provisions of Community law is by restoring the rights of an injured party by the award of damages. Moreover, such a rule on reparation helps to make the Community competition rules more *operational*, particularly since the Commission is dependent upon the co-operation of the national courts in enforcing those rules.

See also the Opinion of Advocate General Léger in Case C–5/94 *R. v. Minister of Agriculture Fisheries and Food, ex p. Hedley Lomas (Ireland) Ltd, supra*, at para. 87, strongly supporting a right to damages against an individual for breach of a directly effective provision of Community law and Van Gerven, "Bridging the Unbridgeable: Community and National Tort Laws after *Francovich* and *Brasserie*" (1996) 45 ICLQ 507.

(e) *Practice and procedure*

10–043 **Pleading.** In *Intergraph Corp. v. Solid Systems CAD Services Ltd* (Ch.D., judgment of 7 December 1993), Intergraph contended that Solid Systems should provide particulars of all facts and matters relied upon to justify the definition of the market that it had selected for the purposes of Article 85. Ferris J. held that the request was impermissible as constituting in reality a request for evidence. Moreover, as regards the allegation that the agreement at issue prevents, restricts or distorts competition within Article 85, the judge held that:

> "while any agreement can only be appraised by reference to its terms, I do not think that it is a requirement of pleading that every allegation as to the object or effect of an agreement must in every case attribute each object or effect to a particular identified clause of the agreement ... What is required, in my judgment, is that the factual allegations regarding effect on competition should be pleaded in such terms that it can be seen how the effect complained of flows from the agreement or concerted practice ..."

10–047 **Burden of proof and evidence.** As regards the standard of proof, other judges have applied the normal civil standard, (*i.e.* balance of probabilities) although without deciding the point as they held that the claims based on EC law failed in any event: *Panayiotou v. Sony Music*

Entertainment Ltd (Ch.D., [1994] EMLR 229 *Society of Lloyd's v. Clementson* (QBD., judgment of 7 May 1996). See also *Masterfoods Ltd v. H.B. Ice Cream Ltd* [1992] 3 CMLR 830 (Ir. High Ct.).

As regards evidence, in *Panayiotou, supra*, the successful pop recording artist George Michael claimed that exclusive recording agreements that he had entered into with Sony Music in 1988 were contrary to Article 85(1), and automatically void pursuant to Article 85(2). Jonathan Parker J. dismissed the claim, in a judgment which, although controversial in its statement of the substantive law, serves at least as a reminder of the need to take care to adduce cogent evidence underpinning a claim based on the competition rules of the EC Treaty. The judge emphasised that the plaintiff could succeed only if the parties conducted a detailed investigation of the surrounding circumstances of the recording agreements, including the nature and operation of the relevant economic market or markets.

In *Iberian U.K. Ltd v. BPB Industries PLC* (Ch.D., judgment of 18 April 1995), Laddie J. held that the findings of fact by the Commission, in proceedings in which the parties have participated, were not only admissible but conclusive evidence in subsequent proceedings before the English court: see para. 10–022, *supra.* Laddie J. relied in part on the observations of Advocate General Van Gerven in Case C–128/92 *Banks*, para. 10–041, *supra*, that national rules of evidence may not make it excessively difficult to obtain redress in an action for breach of Community law rights, particularly by means of presumptions or rules of evidence which place an unreasonably heavy onus of proof on the individual in question, or by means of special limitations concerning the form of the evidence to be adduced.

3. THE EFFECT OF COMMUNITY LAW ON NATIONAL COMPETITION LAW

In general **10–050**

n. 57. See also XXIIIrd Report on Competition Policy (1993), Annex V; XXIVth Report on Competition Policy (1994), points 53 to 104; Report on the application of the competition rules in the EU (1995), Part VI.

Difference of approach. The question whether national law may strike down an agreement which is exempted under Article 85(3) has now received an indicative answer in two Opinions of Advocate General Tesauro in Case C–70/93 *BMW v. ALD* [1995] I ECR 3439 and Case C–266/93 *Bundeskartellamt v. Volkswagen* and *VAG Leasing* [1995] I ECR 3477 [1996] 4 CMLR 478 (both). However, as the Court of Justice did not itself rule on the issue in either case, the matter must still be regarded as unsettled. **10–051**

Advocate General Tesauro considered that, as a consequence of the primacy of Community law, an agreement exempted under Article 85(3) may not be prohibited by national authorities on the basis of more restrictive national provisions, save possibly in exceptional circumstances where no conflict with Community law arises. He reasoned that since exempted agreements

> "are liable to affect trade between Member States and therefore fall in principle within the prohibition set out in Article 85(1), the exemption granted to them cannot but prevent the national authorities from ignoring the positive assessment put on them by the Community authorities. Otherwise, not only would a given agreement be treated differently depending on the law of each Member State, thus detracting from the uniform application of Community law, but the full effectiveness of a Community measure—which an exemption under Article 85(3) undoubtedly is—would also be disregarded"; (*BMW* case at para. 39).

He considered that the position was no different in respect of agreements protected under block exemptions.

4. APPLICATION OF COMPETITION LAW IN THE UNITED KINGDOM

10–055 **United Kingdom competition law.** The EC Competition Law (Articles 88 and 89) Enforcement Regulations 1996 (SI 1996 No. 2199) came into force on 28 August 1996. Those Regulations make provision for the investigation of, and the making and enforcement of decisions in respect of, agreements or practices on which it appears to the Secretary of State that the United Kingdom has a duty to rule under Article 88 of the EC Treaty. Article 88 applies to cases where the Council of Ministers has not made regulations under Article 87 giving effect to Articles 85 and 86. No implementing regulations have been made under article 87 in respect of air transport services between Member States and third countries, or in respect of international maritime tramp vessel services. The new Regulations also enable the Secretary of State to make orders where the Commission authorises the United Kingdom to take measures under Article 89 of the Treaty.

n. 78. See now *Chitty on Contracts* (27th ed., 1994) Vol. II, Chap. 40; Whish, *Competition Law* (3rd ed. 1993).

10–056 **Restrictive Trade Practices Act**

n. 90. See also *Re Ready Mixed Concrete Agreements* (1996) Tr.L.R. 78.

Statutory provisions relation to Community law. As a result of the operation of the Restrictive Trade Practices (Non-notifiable Agreements) (EC Block Exemptions) Order 1996 (S.I. 1996 No. 349), individuals are now relieved in certain circumstances from their duty to furnish to the Director particulars of restrictive agreements which benefit from the application of an EC block exemption, or which would so benefit if they fell within Article 85(1): see further para. 10–060, *infra.* **10–057**

Community principles in the application of United Kingdom competition law. The Restrictive Practices Court has refused applications for a stay of proceedings brought by the Director under the Restrictive Trade Practices Act 1976, pending the outcome of Commission proceedings under Article 85. **10–059**

In *Director General of Fair Trading v. Publishers Association* (judgment of 9 August 1995), the Publishers Association sought to stay the Director's application to the Restrictive Practices Court, in which he was seeking leave to apply for a variation of existing Court orders upholding the Net Book Agreement and resale price maintenance for books in general, on the grounds that an application by the Publishers Association for an exemption of the Net Book Agreement from the prohibition in Article 85(1) was pending before the Commission. The Court rejected the Publishers Association's submission that the fate of the Net Book Agreement would necessarily be determined in Brussels, holding (a) that the question of Community law as to how far national authorities may strike down an agreement exempted by the Commission was still unsettled (see para. 10–051, *supra*); and (b) that in any event the extent and terms of any exemption which might ultimately be granted by the Commission in respect of the Net Book Agreement were uncertain.

In *British Sugar Plc v. Director General of Fair Trading* (judgment of 9 August 1995), British Sugar sought a stay of proceedings before the Restrictive Practices Court pending the outcome of a Commission investigation into the commercial activities of itself and other suppliers of sugar. The Commission had served a Statement of Objections on British Sugar which covered ground considerably wider than that with which the Restrictive Practices Court was concerned. In refusing the application for a stay, the Court found that the nature of the tasks facing the Commission and the Court was very different.

In both cases, the Court was also influenced by the uncertainty as to the time which would elapse before the Commission gave its decision, and emphasised that a stay would hold up the progress of proceedings relating to the ascertainment of the public interest in accordance with the national law.

Agreements exempted under Article 85(3). For the question as to how far national authorities are free to strike down under national law agreements which benefit from individual or block exemption under Article 85(3), see now the Opinions of Advocate General Tesauro in Case C–70/93 *BMW v. ALD Auto-Leasing* and Case C–266/93 *Bundeskartellamt v. Volkswagen and VAG Leasing*: para. 10–051, *supra.* **10–060**

As a result of certain changes made to the United Kingdom Restrictive Trade Practices Act 1976 ("the Act of 1976") by the Deregulation and Contracting Out Act 1994 and the operation of the Restrictive Trade Practices (Non-notifiable Agreements) (EC Block Exemptions) Order 1996 (S.I. 1996 No. 349), which came into force on 19 March 1996, individuals are now relieved from their duty to furnish particulars of registrable agreements under the Act of 1976 (unless the Director requires them by serving a notice on the parties) in the case of:

(a) agreements which are exempt from Article 85(1) by virtue of the application of a block exemption; and
(b) agreements which do not fall within the prohibition in Article 85(1) but which, if they did so fall, would be exempt from that provision by virtue of the application of a block exemption.

10–064 **Application of the INNO principle.** See generally the Opinion of Advocate General Darmon in Case C–185/91 *Reiff* [1993] I ECR 5801 [1995] 5 CMLR 145, and the cases cited at para. 2–021, *supra*.

CHAPTER 11

NOTIFICATION AND ITS EFFECTS

1. NOTIFICATION AND APPLICATION FOR NEGATIVE CLEARANCE

Notification under the EEA Agreement. The Commission and the EFTA Surveillance Authority (ESA) have shared competence for applying the EEA competition rules: see para. 2–162 of the main work. Under the "one-stop shop" principle, notifications and applications are allocated to the Commission or to the ESA according to the provisions of Article 56 of the EEA Agreement. Point B of the new Form A/B (see para. 11–051, *infra*) gives guidance as to the authority to which a notification or application should be made. The procedural rules for applying Articles 53 and 54 EEA reflect those applicable to Articles 85 and 86 EC. Where the Commission is responsible for handling a notification or application in respect of an agreement falling within the EEA competition rules, the procedure is that set out in Regulation 17, subject to provisions in the EEA Agreement in particular Protocol 21. Where the ESA is responsible for handling an application or notification, it applies equivalent procedures (as required by Article 1 of Protocol 21). Except as specifically noted below, provisions equivalent to Regulation 17 as regards the EEA regime are set out in Chapter II of Protocol 4 to the Agreement between the EFTA States on the Establishment of a Surveillance Authority and a Court of Justice ("the EFTA Surveillance Agreement"), OJ 1994 L344/1, [1994] 4 CMLR 180, *Encyclopedia of European Union Law (Constitutional Texts)*, Vol. 5, paras. 82.0619 *et seq.* (It is to be noted that the constituent articles are not numbered consecutively throughout Protocol 4 but only within each chapter.) **11–001A**

Notification to obtain exemption **11–002**

n. 10. As at 31 December 1994, 604 applications or notifications were pending before the Commission. During 1994 the Commission received

236 notifications/applications and took 19 decisions of negative clearance or exemption: XXIVth Report on Competition Policy (1994), Annex III, section A. The ESA reported that in 1994, its first year of operation, it received 103 notifications/applications, the bulk of which (due to the transition period) were received in June and July. About two-thirds of the cases were transferred to the Commission at the beginning of 1995 as a result of the accession of Austria, Finland and Sweden: ESA Annual Report '94, point 4.9.2. Partly in consequence, the number of notifications registered by the Commission in 1995 increased to 368: XXVth Report on Competition Policy (1995), point 96. The ESA, with its reduced jurisdiction, received only five new notifications during 1995: ESA Annual Report '95, point 4.9.2.

11–003 **Other consequences of notification**

n. 14. Art. 6 of Chap. II and also Art. 2 of Chap. XVI of Protocol 4 to the EFTA Surveillance Agreement contain equivalent provisions to Art. 6 of Reg. 17.

11–004 **Comfort letters**

n. 16. In 1994, 197 cases were closed by comfort letter: XXIVth Report on Competition Policy (1994), Annex III, section A. In 1995, the number was 171: Report on the Application of the Competition rules in the EU (1995), p. 305. The ESA closed three cases by comfort letter: ESA Annual Report '94, point 4.9.2.

11–005 **Application for negative clearance**

n. 20. See now Art. 3(2) of Reg. 3385/94 which has replaced Reg. 17: Appendix 6, *post*.

11–006 **Agreements not required to be notified.** Article 4(2) of Protocol 21 to the EEA Agreement contains equivalent provisions to Article 4(2) of Regulation 17.

n. 23. There is now a new block exemption for the distribution of motor vehicles (Reg. 1475/95), see § 7–108A *et seq.*, *infra*; and the patent licensing and know-how licensing block exemptions have been replaced with a single block exemption for technology transfer agreements (Reg. 240/96), see § 8–164A *et seq.*, *infra*. Most of the EC block exemptions, with the adaptations contained in Protocol 1 and Annex XIV to the EEA Agreement, apply also to agreements falling within Art. 53(1) EEA: see § 3–016A, *supra*.

11–008 **Transitional rules for Accession agreements.** Austria, Finland and Sweden acceded on 1 January 1995. The new Article 25(6) of Regulation

17 excludes the application of the transitional rules to agreements which at that date already fell under Article 53 EEA: App. 5, *post*. The practical effect would seem to be that the Regulation 17 transitional rules apply only to restrictive agreements relating to products that are excluded from the scope of the EEA Agreement by virtue of its Article 8(3). Agreements which already fell under Article 53 benefited from transitional rules under the EEA Agreement: see para. 11–034A, *infra*.

2. NOTIFICATION OF NEW AGREEMENTS NOT FALLING WITHIN ARTICLE 4(2) OF REGULATION 17

(a) *Generally*

11–010 **New agreements.** As regards the accession of Austria, Finland and Sweden, "new agreements" will include those agreements entered into after 1 January 1994 and falling within Article 53(1) EEA, as well as those entered into after 1 January 1995 and falling within Article 85(1) EC.

11–014 **Likely time-scale.** The stark contrast with the short deadlines under the Merger Regulation led the Commission to introduce an optional accelerated procedure for handling notifications of co-operative joint ventures of a structural nature. Under this procedure the Commission aims within two months of receipt of the notification to inform the parties of the results of an initial assessment of the case: see para. 11–059A, *infra*. Changes to the notification procedure and a new Form A/B have also been introduced with a view to speeding up proceedings: see para. 11–046, *infra*.

(b) *Effect of notification of new agreement*

11–017 **Article 15(6) decisions.** Such a decision can be taken only in the case of a manifestly serious infringement of Article 85(1): Case T–19/91 *Vichy v. Commission* [1992] II ECR 415. An Article 15(6) decision removes protection from fines only in respect of the period following its notification to the parties concerned: Case T–395/94 R(II) *Atlantic Container Line and others v. Commission* [1995] II ECR 2893 order of the President of the CFI 1995, para. 53.

n. 50. See also the Art. 15(6) decision in *SCK and FNK*, OJ 1994 L117/30, which was followed by a decision imposing fines, *SCK and FNK*, OJ 1995 L312/79 [1996] 4 CMLR 565.

n. 52. See also Case T–19/91 *Vichy v. Commission* [1992] II ECR 415 (but § 3 of the headnote is misleading).

11–018 **Retroactive exemption.** Articles 4(2) and 6 of Protocol 21 EEA apply to exemptions under Article 53(3) EEA equivalent provisions to Articles 4(2) and 6(1) of Regulation 17.

11–022 **Civil validity if the Commission has issued a comfort letter**

n. 66. For the reference to App. 36 substitute App. 26. *Inntrepreneur Estates Ltd v. Mason* is reported at (1994) 68 P & CR 53 [1993] 2 CMLR 293.

(c) *Merits and demerits of notification*

11–023 **Merits and demerits of notification.** For a consideration of the commercial reasons for and against notification, see Brown, "Notification of Agreements to the EC Commission: Whether to Submit to a Flawed System" (1992) E.L. Rev. 323.

3. NEW AGREEMENTS WITHIN ARTICLE 4(2) OF REGULATION 17

11–024 **Function of Article 4(2).** Article 4(2) of Protocol 21 EEA contains equivalent provisions to Article 4(2) of Regulation 17.

11–025 **Intervention by the Commission against Article 4(2) agreements**

n. 80. See also Case T–29/92 *SPO and others v. Commission* [1995] II ECR 295, appeal dismissed Case C–137/95P [1996] I ECR 1611.

4. TRANSITIONAL RULES

(b) *Accession agreements falling outside Article 4(2)*

11–033 **Article 25 of Regulation 17.** As regards the accession of Austria, Finland and Sweden, the transitional provisions of Regulation 17 do not apply to agreements which at the date of accession already fell under Article 53 EEA: see paras. 11–034 and 11–034A, *infra*.

n. 13. Art. 25 of Reg. 17 was further amended by the Annex to Council Decision 95/1/EC, Euratom, ECSC, adjusting the instruments concerning the accession of new Member States to the European Union, OJ 1995 Ll/l: App. 5, *post*.

Accession agreements. Austria, Finland and Sweden acceded on 1 January 1995. Article 25(6) of Regulation 17 excludes the application of the transitional rules to agreements which at the date of accession already fell under Article 53 EEA. Agreements which already fell under Article 53 EEA benefited from transitional rules under the EEA Agreement: see para. 11–034A, *infra*. As regards the accession of Austria, Finland and Sweden, Accession agreements would therefore appear to comprise: **11–034**

(a) the narrow category of agreements in existence on 1 January 1995 which fell outside the scope of Article 53(1) EEA and which would have fallen outside the scope of Article 85(1) but for the accession. These are agreements relating to products to which the EEA Agreement does not apply by reason of Article 8(3) EEA (in practice all basic agricultural products and some processed products);
(b) agreements in existence on 1 January 1994 which fell under the scope of Article 53(1) EEA and benefited from transitional rules under the EEA Agreement: see para. 11–034A, *infra*.

EEA agreements. The EEA Agreement entered into force on 1 January 1994. In respect of agreements falling under Article 53 and already in existence on 1 January 1994, the EEA Agreement contains transitional rules similar to those in Regulation 17: Articles 5–7 of Protocol 21. In addition, Articles 11 and 12 of Protocol 21 gave parties six months until 30 June 1994 to modify existing agreements so as to bring them either within a block exemption or outside the scope of Article 53 EEA. **11–034A**

Date for notification under Article 25. As regards the accession of Austria, Finland and Sweden, the requirement of notification "within six months of accession", *i.e.* by 30 June 1995, applied to agreements in existence on 1 January 1995 which fell outside the scope of Article 53(1) EEA and which would have fallen outside the scope of Article 85(1) but for the accession. Agreements which fell within the scope of Article 53 EEA were required to be notified or modified within six months of the entry into force of the EEA Agreement: para. 11–034A, *supra*. **11–035**

Effect of timely notification **11–036**

n. 18. Art. 9 of Protocol 21 EEA contains equivalent provisions to Art. 25(3) of Reg. 17.

n. 19. Art. 6 of Protocol 21 EEA contains equivalent provisions to Arts. 25(1) and 6(2) of Reg. 17.

n. 20. Art. 7(1) of Protocol 21 EEA contains equivalent provisions to Art. 7(1) of Reg. 17.

11–038 **Retroactive exemptions.** Add: 1 January 1994 and 1 January 1995, as regards, respectively, agreements which fell within and outside the scope of Article 53 EEA.

n. 23. Art. 6 of Protocol 21 EEA contains equivalent provisions to Arts. 6(1), 6(2) and 25 of Reg. 17.

11–039 **Article 7(1).** Article 7(1) of Protocol 21 to the EEA Agreement contains equivalent provisions to Article 7(1) of Regulation 17.

11–041 **The *Perfumes* cases: loss of provisional validity on closure of file**

n. 31. See now Kerse, *EC Antitrust Procedure* (Sweet & Maxwell, 3rd ed., 1994) §§ 10.08 *et seq*.

(c) *Accession agreements within Article 4(2)*

11–044 **Accession agreements within Article 4(2).** Articles 4(2) and 7(1) of Protocol 21 EEA contain equivalent provisions to Articles 4(2) and 7(1) of Regulation 17.

n. 36. Art. 6 of Protocol 21 EEA contains equivalent provisions to Arts. 6(2) and 25 of Reg. 17.

n. 37. Art. 5(1) of Protocol 21 EEA contains equivalent provisions to Art. 25(2) of Reg. 17.

5. NOTIFICATION PROCEDURE

11–046 **Procedure generally.** Regulation 3385/94 has, with effect from 1 March 1995, replaced Regulation 27 and introduced a new Form A/B: see Appendix 6, *post*. The new Regulation and the new Form A/B have introduced changes modelled on the provisions for notifying mergers, with the aim in particular of speeding up proceedings before the Commission: XXIVth Report on Competition Policy (1994), point 114.

n. 41. Before its replacement by Reg. 3385/94, Reg. 27 had previously been further amended by Regulation 3666/93 (OJ 1993 L336/1) to take account of the EEA Agreement: see Kerse, *op. cit.* n. 31 *supra*, §§ 2.21 *et seq*.

n. 42. For negative clearance applications under Art. 86 see now Arts. 1(2), 2(1) and 3(2) of Reg. 3385/94.

n. 43. See also para. 11–057 *infra*.

Informal approaches. The Sixth Recital to Regulation 3385/94 specifically refers to the possibility of pre-notification discussions. This is modelled on Recital (8) to the merger Implementing Regulation: see para. 6–101 of the main work. **11–047**

Formal procedure. One original and 16 copies of the notification, including the last versions of all agreements which are the subject matter of the notification, are now required: Art. 2(2) of Reg. 3385/94 and Section 18 of the Form A/B. As regards copies of supporting documents, notifying parties are now required to confirm that the copies are true copies of the originals and complete: Art. 2(3) of Reg. 3385/94, which is modelled on Art. 2(3) of the merger Implementing Regulation. Another provision adopted from the merger procedure is that the language of the notification now becomes the language of the proceeding for the notifying party: Art. 2(4) of Reg. 3385/94. Supporting documents must be submitted in their original language, and, where that language is not an official language, be accompanied by a translation into the language of the proceeding: Art. 2(4) of Reg. 3385/94. For the new Form A/B: see para. 11–051, *infra*. **11–048**

n. 45. Now Art. 1(1) of Reg. 3385/94.

n 46. *Ibid.* Art. 1(4). See also Point G of the Form A/B.

n. 47. *Ibid.* Art. 1(3).

n. 48. See now Art. 2(2) of Reg. 3385/94.

n. 50. See now Art. 2(3) of Reg. 3385/94.

n. 51. The official languages are now those of the Union: *i.e.*, Danish, Dutch, English, Finnish, French, German, Greek, Italian, Portuguese, Spanish and Swedish: Reg. 1/58 as amended, most recently by Council Decision 5/1/EC, Euratom, ECSC: OJ 1995 L1/1, 218. Art. 2(5) of Reg. 3385/94 provides that one of the official languages of the EFTA States (*i.e.* Icelandic, Norwegian) may be used for a notification relating to the EEA competition rules, but that in that case all documentation must be translated into a Community official language which then becomes the language of the proceeding. This provision appears to contravene Art. 12 of Protocol 23 to the EEA Agreement, which states that in the implementation of Arts. 53–54 undertakings shall be entitled to address and be addressed by the Commission and the ESA in a Community or

EFTA language of their choosing. But see Point H of the Form A/B for recommendations on which languages to use.

n. 52. See now Art. 2(4) of Reg. 3385/94.

n. 53. See now the Introduction to the new Form A/B: Appendix 6, *post.*

11–049 **Need to observe formal requirements.** Notifications are now deemed to be effective if the Commission has not within one month of receipt informed the notifying parties that the notification is incomplete: Art. 4(2) and 4(5) of Reg. 3385/94. See also para. 11–054, *infra.*

11–050 **Need for full and accurate disclosure.** The Fourth Recital to Regulation 3385/94 refers to "full and honest" disclosure. The information required by Form A/B must be correct and complete: Art. 3(1) of Reg. 3385/94. Certain provisions have been adopted from the merger procedure: first, the Commission may dispense with the obligation to provide particular information required by the Form A/B where it considers such information is not necessary for the examination of the case (Art. 3(3) of Reg. 3385/94); secondly, a notification will be accepted as complete if the notifying parties have good reasons for not being able to provide missing information (Point E of the Form A/B); thirdly, any material changes in the facts contained in the notification which the notifying party knows or ought to have known must be communicated to the Commission without delay (Art. 4(3) of Reg. 3385/94).

n. 56. See now Art. 3(1) of Reg. 3385/94 and Points E and F of the Form A/B, Appendix 6, *post.*

11–051 **Form A/B.** The current Form A/B, annexed to Regulation 3385/94, took effect from 1 March 1995 and is set out in Appendix 6, *post.* The Form A/B has been recast and is now divided into an Introduction, which sets out general information under Points A to K, and an operational part, which specifies the information to be provided to the Commission (divided into Chapters I to IV). All notifications must provide the information requested in Chapter I (concerning the parties, their groups, procedural matters and the arrangements) and Chapter IV (concerning the reasons for negative clearance and/or exemption, supporting documentation and a declaration). Chapters II and III request information concerning the relevant market and are alternatives; the more detailed information requested in Chapter III must be provided in notifications of structural joint ventures for which the benefit of the accelerated procedure is claimed. The drafting in particular of Chapter III is modelled on the Form CO used in the merger procedure. For the accelerated procedure, see paras. 5–009 *supra* and 11–059A, *infra*

11–053 **Agreements within Restrictive Trade Practices Act 1976.** The requirement to transmit information to the Director General of Fair

Trading has been revoked: Registration of Restrictive Trading Agreements (EEC Documents)(Revocation) Regulations 1994 (S.I. 1994 No. 1095).

Date when notification takes effect. Article 4(2) of Regulation 3385/94 provides that where the Commission finds that the information contained in the notification is incomplete, it shall without delay inform the notifying party and fix a time limit for the completion of the information; in such cases the notification takes effect on the date the complete information is received by the Commission. If the Commission does not act to inform the notifying party within one month of receipt of a notification, the notification is deemed to have taken effect on the date of its receipt by the Commission (or, presumably, the date on the postmark if sent by registered post): *ibid.* Article 4(5). **11–054**

n. 64. Art. 4(1) of Reg. 3385/94.

Renewals and variations. Regulation 3385/94 now requires that any material changes in the facts contained in the notification which the notifying party knows or ought to know must be communicated to the Commission without delay: Article 4(3). **11–055**

Secrecy. Where an undertaking claims that a document is confidential as against the competent national authorities, the Commission, by analogy with the procedure for disclosure to other parties to proceedings (see Chap. 12, para. 12–046), must before transmission adopt a reasoned decision amenable to challenge before the Court: Case C–36/92P *SEP v. Commission* [1994] I ECR 1911. That case concerned the requirement under Article 10(1) of Regulation 17 that the Commission transmit "copies of the most important documents lodged with the Commission"; the same principles would presumably apply to the requirement that the Commission transmit copies of applications and notifications. **11–057**

n. 69. Now 15 competent authorities in the Member States.

n. 70. The Court of Justice held that the Commission was not competent to conclude the 1991 agreement: Case C–327/91 *France v. Commission* [1994] I ECR 3641 [1994] 5 CMLR 517. The Agreement was subsequently approved by the Council (on behalf of the EC) and the Commission (on behalf of the ECSC), with minimal amendments, with effect from 23 September 1991. An accompanying exchange of interpretative letters indicates that information covered by Art. 20 of Reg. 17 may not be communicated by the Commission to the US competition authorities without the express agreement of the source of the information. See Decision 95/145/EC, ECSC, OJ 1995 L95/45 [1995] 4 CMLR 707.

11–058 **Publicity.** In certain cases, in particular notifications of structural joint ventures treated under the accelerated procedure, the Commission publishes a preliminary notice informing third parties of the notification and inviting comments. Such notices are sometimes referred to as *Carlsberg* notices, after the first such notice: *Carlsberg-Tetley*, OJ 1992 C97/21 and see XXIInd Report on Competition Policy (1992), point 116. For recent examples, see *Bayer/Monsanto*, OJ 1995 C298/8 (notification of a joint venture) and *P&I Clubs*, OJ 1995 C181/16 (request for renewal of individual exemption). The form and content of such a preliminary notice is similar to a notice published in respect of merger notifications pursuant to Article 4(3) of Regulation 4064/89 (the Merger Regulation) but it is not required by the implementing legislation. It should, in particular, be distinguished from the more detailed notices published pursuant to Article 19(3) of Regulation 17. Section 5 of the Form A/B requires the notifying parties to provide a non-confidential summary which can be used as the basis for a preliminary notice.

6. POST-NOTIFICATION PROCEDURE

11–059 **Post notification procedure.** There is a further, infrequently used alternative of a "discomfort" letter: see para. 11–066A, *infra*.

11–059A **Accelerated procedure for structural joint ventures.** Since 1 January 1993 the notification of the creation of a co-operative JV of a structural nature can benefit from accelerated treatment: XXIInd Report on Competition Policy (1992), point 124, and Point D of the Form A/B; and for the notion of a structural co-operative JV, see para. 5–020, *supra*. The procedure is based on that applicable to notifications of mergers. Under the procedure the Commission will publish a preliminary notice (para. 11–058, *supra*) and will within two months of effective receipt of the notification send the parties either a comfort letter or a warning letter indicating that the Commission has "serious doubts" and intends to carry out an in-depth examination of the case. Where a formal decision is envisaged, the Commission will give the parties a timetable. Parties notifying a co-operative JV of a structural nature that wish to claim the benefit of accelerated treatment must provide the more detailed market information required by Chapter III of the Form A/B. See further at para. 5–009, *supra*.

(b) *Opposition procedure*

11–062 **Exemption pursuant to opposition procedure**

n. 87. The relevant block exemptions require that the notification expressly invoke the opposition procedure; the new Form A/B no longer specifically asks if the benefit of the opposition procedure is claimed, but continues to require the notifying parties to identify restrictions that exceed those automatically exempted by the relevant block exemption.

(c) *Comfort letter*

Informal procedures

n. 88. Point A of the Form A/B states that the Commission issues negative clearance decisions only when an important problem of interpretation has to be solved, and reiterates that normally the Commission issues exemption decisions only in cases of particular legal, economic or political importance. Note that the Form A/B no longer asks notifying parties if they would be satisfied with a comfort letter. **11–063**

Comfort letters. A comfort letter will normally state whether the notified agreement is considered to fall outside Article 85(1), or to fall within Article 85(1) but to merit an exemption. An Article 85(1) comfort letter may further indicate that the agreement falls within the Notice on Co-operation Agreements, the Notice on Agreements of Minor Importance, or the Notice on Subcontracting Agreements. An Article 85(3) comfort letter will indicate if the agreement is considered to fall within a block exemption regulation, or, if not, the restrictive provisions of the agreement will be identified. All comfort letters state that the case may be reconsidered if the factual or legal situation changes as regards any essential aspect of the agreements which affects the view which should be taken of it. In certain cases an Article 85(3) comfort letter is stated to be valid only until a specified date. The Report on the application of the competition rules in the EU (1995) includes a list of cases closed by comfort letter for the year under review: pp. 308–12. **11–064**

n. 90. *Inntrepreneur Estates Ltd v. Mason* is reported at (1994) 68 P & CR 53, [1993] 2 CMLR 293.

Formal comfort letters. However, the Commission does inform the Advisory Committee, and the comfort letter is not sent until after members of the Committee have had the opportunity to ask for a discussion of the case at a meeting of the Committee: see Gyselen, "Publication Policy of the Commission with regard to Comfort Letters" in Slot and McDonnell (eds.), *Procedure and Enforcement in EC and US Competition Law* (Sweet & Maxwell, 1993), Chapter 27. **11–065**

Effect of comfort letters. Add under (c): The Commission may reopen the procedure where a complaint discloses appreciable changes that have **11–066**

occurred following a comfort letter which (1) had expressly reserved the right to reopen the procedure if there was any appreciable change and (2) had been sent following a provisional analysis of market conditions based essentially on information provided by the notifying party. Reopening the procedure is, moreover, in conformity with the Commission's obligation carefully to examine matters brought to its attention by a complainant. The fact that the Commission mentions the issue of a comfort letter and comments on it in an annual Report on Competition Policy does not alter its legal nature. Case T–7/93 *Langnese-Iglo v. Commission* [1995] II ECR 1533 [1995] CMLR 602 [1995] All ER (EC) 902, at paras. 37 to 41; Case T–9/93 *Schöller v. Commission* [1995] II ECR 1611 [1995] 5 CMLR 659 at paras. 111 to 115. For the procedure on investigating a complaint, see para. 12–023 of the main work.

11–066A **"Discomfort" letters.** Another outcome, albeit rare, is a "discomfort" letter signed by a senior official of DGIV indicating that the notified agreement contains certain restrictions within Article 85(1) which do not justify an exemption but are of insufficient importance for the Commission to take action to terminate; the letter indicates that the file will be closed. A discomfort letter will typically be sent where the effects of an agreement are localised in a single Member State and the matter can be expected to be taken up by the relevant national competition authority.

CHAPTER 12

ENFORCEMENT AND PROCEDURE

Plan of this chapter **12–001**

n. 1. See now Kerse, *EC Antitrust Procedure* (Sweet & Maxwell, 3rd ed., 1994); also Ortiz Blanco, *EC Competition Procedure* (Clarendon Press, 1996).

1. THE COMMISSION'S POWERS OF INVESTIGATION

Generally. For the EFTA Surveillance Authority, the equivalent provisions to Regulation 17 are set out in Chapter II of Protocol 4 to the Agreement between the EFTA States on the Establishment of a Surveillance Authority and a Court of Justice ("the EFTA Surveillance Agreement"), OJ 1994 L344/1 [1994] 4 CMLR 180, *Encyclopedia of European Union Law* (*Constitutional Texts*), Vol. 5, paras. 82.0619 *et seq.* **12–002**

n. 2. The backlog has been considerably reduced: as at 31 December 1994, 1052 cases were pending, of which 604 were applications or notifications (236 made in 1994), 332 were complaints (140 made in 1994) and 116 were cases opened on the Commission's own initiative (16 commenced in 1994): XXIVth Report on Competition Policy (1994), Annex III, point A.2. As at 31 December 1995, the total had risen to 1178 pending cases, including those transferred by the EFTA Surveillance Authority, *infra*. Both the number of notifications (368) and the number of cases opened on the Commission's own initiative (46) in 1995 represented a substantial increase over the previous two years: XXVth Report on Competition Policy (1995), point 96.

The EFTA Surveillance Authority opened 115 competition cases in 1994, its first year of operation: 103 were the result of applications or notifications, eight followed complaints and four were started on the Authority's own initiative; about two thirds of the cases were transferred to the Commission at the end of 1994 following the accession of Austria, Finland and Sweden, leaving 38 pending cases: EFTA Surveillance Authority Annual Report '94, point 4.9.2. Five notifications and six complaints were received during 1995 and 43 cases were pending at the end of the year: EFTA Surveillance Authority Annual Report '95, point 3.4.

(a) *Power to obtain information*

12–003 **Power to request information from undertakings**

n. 10. See now Case T–46/92 *Scottish Football Association v. Commission* [1994] II ECR 1039, where the CFI dismissed arguments that a request for information was inadequately reasoned, excessive and premature. The Court held that it was not necessary for the undertaking to be manifestly obstructing the investigation before the Commission was justified in adopting a decision: given that individuals have an obligation to co-operate actively in the procedure, a passive reaction to an initial request may justify the adoption of a formal decision.

12–004 **Addressees of requests for information**

n. 14. See also *Ukwal*, OJ 1992 L121/45 [1993] 5 CMLR 632 (a "dawn raid" under Art. 18 of Reg. 4056/86 at the office in the United Kingdom of a liner conference some of whose members were based outside the United Kingdom).

12–005 **"Necessity" for information requested.** The Court of First Instance rejected an appeal alleging insufficient particularity of a request for information in Case T–34/93 *Société Générale v. Commission* [1995] II ECR 545 [1996] 4 CMLR 665.

n. 17. See now Case C–36/92P *SEP v. Commission* [1994] I ECR 1911 (§ 21): the connection must be such that the Commission could reasonably suppose that the document would help it to determine whether the alleged infringement had taken place (*per* Advocate General Jacobs at 1919).

n. 19. The fact that an undertaking complies with a request for information does not preclude it from challenging the legality of that request: *Scottish Football Association v. Commission, supra.*

12–008 **Power to require information from Member States**

n. 31. See now Case C–36/92P *SEP v. Commission* [1994] I ECR 1911 and para. 11–057, *supra*.

Co-operation with the EFTA Surveillance Authority. Under Articles 58 and 109 EEA, the Commission and the EFTA Surveillance Authority co-operate, exchange information and consult each other on general policy issues and individual cases: see also Protocol 23 (co-operation as regards competition rules) and Protocol 24 (co-operation as regards concentrations). They inform each other of complaints received that concern the application of the EEA Agreement. **12–008A**

Exchange of information with the US antitrust authorities. Under the EEC-USA Competition Laws Co-operation Agreement 1991 (see para. 1–070, *supra*), each party agreed to provide the other with "any significant information" that comes to its attention about anti-competitive activities that may warrant "enforcement activity" by the other party: Article III(3). For the implications of this provision as regards confidentiality, see para. 12–046, *infra*. **12–008B**

(b) *Power of investigation*

Penalties in respect of investigations **12–014**

n. 67. See also *AKZO Chemicals* Press Release, IP (93) 893 of 19 October 1993 [1993] 5 CMLR 431.

(c) *Ancillary matters*

Privilege against self-incrimination **12–016**

n. 76. In Case C–60/92 *Otto v. Postbank* [1993] I ECR 5683, the ECJ held that a national court considering a claim based on Arts. 85 and 86 is not bound to apply the Community law regarding privilege against self-incrimination.

Confidentiality. For recent case law and the position under EEC-USA Co-operation Agreement, see para. 12–046, *infra*. **12–017**

Independent action by Member States' authorities **12–018**

n. 87. See now also Case C–36/92P *SEP v. Commission* [1994] I ECR 1911.

2. COMPLAINTS

12–019 **Generally**

n. 88. As at 31 December 1994, 332 complaints (140 made in 1994) were outstanding: XXIVth Report on Competition Policy (1994), Annex III.A.

12–021 **Legitimate interest: generally**

n. 94. In Case T–37/92 *BEUC and NCC v. Commission* [1994] II ECR 285 [1995] 4 CMLR 167, the *locus* of consumers associations to make a complaint was not contested by the Commission.

12–022 **Legitimate interest: the practice.** In Case T–114/92 *BEMIM v. Commission* [1995] II ECR 147 [1996] 4 CMLR 305, the Court of First Instance held that an association of undertakings has a legitimate interest in lodging a complaint if, first, it is entitled (according to its governing instruments) to represent the interests of its members and, secondly, if the conduct complained of is liable adversely to affect the interests of its members.

n. 9. See now Case T–37/96 *Luftfartsfunktionaererne v. Commission*, not yet decided (professional staff association whose members are employed by one party to a JV).

12–023 **Procedure on investigating a complaint.** If the complainant alleges infringement of both Articles 85 and 86, the Commission's decision rejecting the complaint must deal expressly with both allegations: see *BEMIM*, *supra*; Case T–5/93 *Tremblay and Others v. Commission* [1995] II ECR 185 [1996] 4 CMLR 305; and Case T–74/92 *Ladbroke v. Commission* [1995] II ECR 115.

n. 13. See also Case C–39/93P *SFEI v. Commission* [1994] I ECR 2681. However, an Art. 6 letter is sufficient definition of the Commission's position to defeat an action under Art. 175 for failure to act: Case T–186/94 *Guérin Automobiles v. Commission* [1995] II ECR 1753 [1996] 4 CMLR 685, on appeal Case C–282/95P.

n. 14. See also the parallel judgments in *BEMIM* and *Tremblay and Others*, *supra*, where the CFI upheld the Commission's rejection of complaints on the grounds of lack of Community interest. In Case T–37/92 *BEUC and NCC v. Commission* [1994] II ECR 285 [1995] 4 CMLR 167, the CFI investigated the three reasons given by the Commission for rejecting the complaint. It found that the first reason was based on an inaccurate assessment of the factual background, the second reason was based on an error of law and the third reason, lack of Community interest, was wrong in law and insufficiently reasoned. The Commission decision was therefore annulled.

n. 14. See also Case T–575/93 *Koelman v. Commission* [1996] 4 CMLR 636.

n. 15. See also *BEMIM* and *Tremblay and others*, *supra.*

Decisions following a complaint. The Commission's duties when dealing with complaints have been further elucidated by a series of cases in which the Ladbroke betting services group complained about various aspects of the French horse race betting industry. Complaints were made under Articles 85 and 86 against the Pari Mutuel Urbain which was also alleged to have secured an illegal State Aid. The complaints were also directed at the French state, Ladbroke alleging breach of Article 90 of the Treaty. In Case T–32/93 *Ladbroke v. Commission* [1994] II ECR 1015, the Court of First Instance held that the Commission was not obliged, following a letter before action under Article 175, to address a decision to a Member State and it was therefore not open to Ladbroke to bring an action for failure to act on the ground that the Commission had failed to make use of its powers under Article 90(3) of the Treaty. The Commission nevertheless initiated a procedure to examine the complaint under Article 90 in order to assess the compatibility of French domestic legislation with Articles 85 and 86. In Case T–74/92 *Ladbroke v. Commission* [1995] II ECR 115, Ladbroke brought an action under Article 175 in relation to the Commission's failure to act on its complaint that an agreement between two undertakings infringed Articles 85 and 86. The Court of First Instance rejected the complaint of failure to act under Article 85 on the ground that the Commission had been pursuing an investigation and Ladbroke had not given the Commission enough time to complete this before bringing the action. But the Court found that the Commission had failed to define its position with regard to Article 86. The Court held that whilst the Commission was free to initiate and pursue its investigation solely on the basis of Article 85 if that appeared to be in the Community's interest, it was bound to examine the complaint under Article 86 and to inform the complainant of the reasons why it did not pursue it. Subsequently, the Commission purported definitively to reject the complaints as regards both Articles 85 and 86. This decision was overturned by the Court of First Instance on the grounds that the Commission could not properly reject these complaints before completing its investigation into the Article 90 position: Case T–548/93 *Ladbroke Racing v. Commission* [1995] II ECR 2565 [1996] 4 CMLR 549. At the same time, the Court delivered judgment in Case T–471/93 *Tiercé Ladbroke v. Commission* [1995] II ECR 2537, in which it dismissed an application to annul the decision of the Commission rejecting Ladbroke's allegations about the illegal State Aid under Articles 92 and 93. Both of the last two decisions are under appeal: Cases C–359 & 379/95P and Case C– 353/95P, respectively. **12–024**

If the Commission considers that the conditions for exempting an agreement under Article 85(3) are satisfied, it may reject a complaint on that basis without taking a formal decision granting exemption: Case T–575/93 *Koelman v. Commission* [1996] 4 CMLR 637.

n. 17. See also *Guérin Automobiles*, *supra*, and Case T–37/92 *BEUC and NCC v. Commission* [1994] II ECR 285 [1995] 4 CMLR 167. In Case C–39/93P *SFEI v. Commission* [1994] I ECR 2701, the ECJ overruled the decision of the CFI, holding that the lower court had misdirected itself in finding that the disputed letter that communicated the Commission's decision to close the file was not a reviewable act. Since the ECJ held that the Art. 173 action was admissible, it referred the case back to the CFI for consideration on the merits.

12–026 **Judicial review by complainant**

n. 25. See also Case T–114/92 *BEMIM v. Commission* [1995] II ECR 147 [1996] 4 CMLR 305; and *Koelman*, *supra*.

3. COMMISSION'S FORMAL PROCEDURE PRIOR TO AN ADVERSE DECISION

(a) *Generally*

12–028 **An "administrative" procedure**

n. 30. See further the Report of House of Lords Select Committee on the European Communities, Session 1993–94, "Enforcement of Community Competition Rules" (HL Paper 7); and Ehlermann, "The European Administration and the Public Administration of Member States with regard to Competition Law" [1995] 8 ECLR 454. For a critical evaluation, see Brent, "The Binding of Leviathan?—The Changing Role of the European Commission in Competition Cases" (1995) 44 ICLQ 255.

12–029 **The rights of defence.** For the "presumption of innocence" in Commission procedure see Case T–30/91 *Solvay v. Commission*, [1995] II ECR 1775 [1996] 5 CMLR 57 [1995] All ER (EC) 600, para. 73, and Case T–36/91 *ICI v. Commission* [1995] II ECR 1847, para. 83.

12–030 **The right to be heard.** For the EFTA Surveillance Authority, the equivalent provisions to Regulation 99 are set out in Chapter IV of Protocol 4 to the EFTA Surveillance Agreement, para. 12–002 *supra*.

(Note that the Articles in Protocol 4 are not numbered consecutively throughout but only within each Chapter, and therefore correspond to the Articles in the analogous EC Regulation.)

(b) *Initiation of procedure and the Statement of Objections*

Procedure on issue of Statement of Objections **12–033**

n. 54. For the Commission's standard practice on deadlines see XXIIIrd Report on Competition Policy (1993), point 207.

Obligation to supply relevant documents. In Case T–148/89 *Tréfilunion v. Commission* [1995] II ECR 1063, the applicant complained that documents annexed to the Statement of Objections were in their original language rather than translated into the language of the case. The Court of First Instance held that there had been no breach of the rights of the defence. Documents annexed which do not emanate from the Commission itself are not covered by Article 3 of Regulation 1/58 and, indeed, must be disclosed "as they are". Moreover, translations of relevant extracts appeared in the body of the Statement of Objections. **12–035**

n. 63. *Per contra* see now Case T–37/91 *ICI v. Commission*, *infra*, §§ 64–65 and see also § 12–036, *infra*.

Access to the file. The position with regard to the supply of documents and access to the file has been reconsidered by the Court of First Instance in the appeals by ICI and Solvay against the Commission's decisions condemning them for breaches of Articles 85 and 86. In Cases T–30/91 *Solvay v. Commission* and T–36/91 *ICI v. Commission* [1995] II ECR 1775 and 1847 [1996] 5 CMLR 57 [1995] All ER (EC) 600, Solvay and ICI respectively appealed against the Commission's decision under Article 85 (OJ 1991 L152/1 [1994] 4 CMLR 454). In parallel judgments, the Court annulled the decisions because of breaches of the rights of the defence. First, it found that various inculpatory documents were not disclosed by the Commission during the course of the administrative procedure. This would not, however, have resulted in the annulment of the decision but only in the inadmissibility of such evidence to support the allegations which could be proved by other means. More importantly, each applicant complained of the non-disclosure of exculpatory documents acquired from the files of the other alleged participant. The Court held that in order to find that the rights of the defence had been infringed it was sufficient for it to be established that the non-disclosure of the documents in question might have influenced the course of the procedure and the content of the decision to the applicant's detriment. The possibility of such an influence can be established if a provisional examination of some **12–036**

of the evidence shows that the documents not disclosed might have had a significance which ought not to have been disregarded. The Court held that some of the documents in the Commission's file which were not sent to the applicants were capable of substantiating their defence to the allegation of concerted practice by supporting alternative explanations for their parallel conduct. The Court rejected the Commission's argument that it had carefully considered the documents and decided that they were not exculpatory. It held that where difficult and complex economic appraisals are to be made, the Commission must give the advisers of the undertakings involved the opportunity to examine the documents and make their own appraisal of their probative value. It did not matter that the applicants had or could have provided each other with the documents on a voluntary basis: this does not lessen the duty of the Commission to ensure that the rights of the defence are respected.

On the question of access to the file more generally, the Court of First Instance referred to the "general principle of equality of arms" which presupposes that the knowledge which the undertaking has of the file used in the proceedings is the same as that of the Commission. The Court held that the Commission was not entitled to separate the evidence relating to the allegations under Article 85 from that relating to Article 86 because they arose from the same factual background. The Court rejected reliance on confidentiality of the documents on the facts. Any confidentiality could have been protected by deleting sensitive passages and did not justify the wholesale withholding of documents.

In the third case, T–37/91 *ICI v. Commission* [1995] II ECR 1901, ICI appealed against the Commission's Article 86 decision (OJ 1991 L152/40). The Court of First Instance here found that there had been no infringement of the rights of the defence. The Commission was under no obligation to provide the applicant with a list of the documents emanating from the applicant's own premises and the failure to disclose other inculpatory documents had not, on the facts, hindered the defence. However, the decision was annulled because of irregularities in its adoption by the college of Commissioners, as was another decision against Solvay under Article 85: see para. 12–043 *infra*.

The Commission has outlined the logistics of providing access to documents in its XXIIIrd Report on Competition Policy (1993), points 201–202. It will now send copies of all relevant documents (whether inculpatory or exculpatory) to the parties together with a list describing all available documents. The Commission will also respond to any "reasoned request" from an undertaking that believes that not all documents have been disclosed.

For access to the file by third parties see Case T–17/93 *Matra Hachette v. Commission* [1994] II ECR 595 at 608–10.

n. 72. The CFI's decision in *BPB Industries* was upheld by the ECJ: Case C–310/93P *BPB Industries and British Gypsum v. Commission* [1995] I ECR 865. The ECJ also noted (at § 26–27) that in an Art. 86 investigation, correspondence with third parties may be confidential on the grounds that an undertaking in a dominant position might adopt retaliatory measures against third party complainants, suppliers or customers who co-operated in the investigation: *i.e.* a request for confidentiality should be honoured to protect their identity in those circumstances although no business secrets as such are involved.

n. 74. See also the Commission's comments in *Cartonboard* 1994 OJ L243/1 [1994] 5 CMLR 547 § 123 (on appeal Cases T–295/94, etc.) and XXIIIrd Report on Competition Policy (1993), point 199. These must now be read subject to the *ICI* and *Solvay* judgments, *supra*.

(c) *The hearing and subsequently*

Hearings. As to the need for exhaustive minutes of the hearing see Case T–83/91 *Tetra Pak v. Commission* [1994] II ECR 755, § 37. There is no requirement that all statements made at the hearing must be translated into the language of the case in the minutes: Case T–77/92 *Parker Pen v. Commission* [1994] II ECR 549 [1995] 5 CMLR 435, § 74. **12–037**

Hearing Officer **12–038**

n. 95. The terms of reference of Hearing Officers were issued on 12 December 1994: see Appendix 7, *post*, and Commission is commentary in XXIIIrd Report on Competition Policy (1993), point 203.

n. 96. Now Arts. 2 and 7. The revised terms of reference include requirements for reasoned decision on issues of disclosure: Art. 5.

n. 97. Now Art. 8. Art. 10 provides that where appropriate, the Competition Commissioner may decide, at the Hearing Officer's request, to attach his report to the draft decision submitted to the Commission.

n. 98. Now Art. 9.

Adoption of the decision. The judgment of the Court of First Instance in *PVC* was set aside by the Court of Justice: Case C–137/92P *Commission v. BASF and others* [1994] I ECR 2555. The Court of Justice held that the Commission's decision was not "non-existent" but that it should be annulled because of the procedural irregularities surrounding its adoption. The Commission subsequently adopted a decision to the same effect as that which had been annulled: *PVC II* 1994 OJ L239/14. This later decision is itself now under appeal on various procedural grounds: Cases T–307/94 etc. *BASF and others v. Commission* [1995] 4 CMLR 15, not yet decided. **12–043**

The judgment of the Court of Justice in *PVC* has been applied by the Court of First Instance on several occasions. In Cases T–80/89, etc., *BASF and others v. Commission* [1995] II ECR 729, it annulled the Commission's decision in *LdPE* and in Case T–31/91 *Solvay v. Commission* and Case T–37/91 *ICI v. Commission* [1995] II ECR 1821 and 1901, it annulled the Commission's decisions against Solvay and ICI on the grounds that they had not been properly authenticated at the time of their adoption. In Case T–29/92 *SPO and Others v. Commission* [1995] II ECR 289, the Court found that apparently serious and convincing evidence of changes to the text adopted by the Commissioners was in fact the result of a technical defect in the electronic mail system which caused the loss of a page. There were no grounds for annulment for procedural irregularity. In Case T–106/89 REV *Norsk Hydro v. Commission* [1994] II ECR 419, the Court rejected an attempt by the applicant to revise the earlier judgment of the Court declaring that the applicant's appeal from the *PVC* decision had been lodged out of time and was therefore inadmissible.

n. 21. On the correction of errors in the text of the decision see Case T–38/92 *AWS Benelux v. Commission* [1994] II ECR 211 [1995] 4 CMLR 43.

n. 25. The CFI has reiterated that it will not initiate an investigation into the procedure of adoption unless the applicant adduces evidence rebutting the presumption of validity: see, *e.g.* Case T–34/92 *Fiatagri and New Holland Ford v. Commission* [1994] II ECR 905. The ECJ has held that challenges to the adoption of the decision by the Commission cannot be raised for the first time on appeal from a decision of the CFI: Case C–195/91P *Bayer v. Commission* [1994] I ECR 5619, § 14.

12–044 **Content of decision.** The decision must specify the evidence on which the case hangs. It is not necessary for it to enumerate exhaustively all the evidence but it may refer to it in general terms: Case T–43/92 *Dunlop Slazenger v. Commission* [1994] II ECR 441.

(d) *Confidentiality*

12–046 **Confidentiality**

(1) See Case C–36/92P *SEP v. Commission* [1994] II ECR 1911 which concerned the confidentiality of a contract between SEP and Statoil, a supplier of natural gas in competition with the Dutch state owned supplier, Gasunie. The Commission requested a copy of the contract and SEP refused on the ground that the Commission would thereafter supply it to the Dutch competent authority which would gain sight of commercially sensitive information. SEP argued successfully that Article 20 did not provide an adequate safeguard against the misuse of the information by the Dutch authorities. Referring to the *Direccion General de Defensa*

de la Competencia decision, the Court of Justice held that despite Article 20, the Dutch authority officials who had sight of the Statoil contract could not effectively be required to disregard its terms if it fell to them to determine the commercial policy of Gasunie. However, the Court went on to hold that Article 10 of Regulation 17 did not in fact require the Commission to pass the contract on to the Dutch authorities so that SEP's appeal against the decision ordering it to produce the contract was dismissed.

In Case T–353/94R *Postbank v. Commission* [1994] II ECR 1141, the Commission had supplied copies of the Statement of Objections issued against Postbank to two Dutch companies who, although not formally complainants, had an interest in the proceedings. The Dutch companies then sought permission from the Commission to adduce the SO as evidence in private proceedings they were pursuing against Postbank in the Dutch courts. The Commission purported to grant such permission, indeed stating that they were free to make use of the SO without any such authorisation. Postbank challenged the grant of permission and sought interim measures from the Court of First Instance. The President of the Court held that the application was admissible and granted the measures sought stating that the question of whether the Commission was obliged to ensure that third parties to whom it provided documents used them only in connection with the Commission proceedings was an "extremely delicate" one.

(2) In *Cartonboard*, OJ 1994 L243/1 [1994] 5 CMLR 547, para. 124, the Commission stated that professional secrecy did not relate only to trade secrets but extended to all information obtained from the undertaking pursuant to Regulation 17 "except that which is so trivial that it is not worthy of confidentiality".

(3) For the view of the Court of First Instance that confidentiality must give way to the rights of the defence, see Cases T–30/91 *Solvay v. Commission* and T–36/91 *ICI v. Commission* [1995] II ECR 1775 and 1847 [1996] 5 CMLR 57 [1995] All ER (EC) 600.

(4) On the question of confidentiality of documents during the appeal process *vis-à-vis* complainants and interveners see Case T–57/91 *NALOO v. Commission* [1993] 5 CMLR 124, 129 (Order of President of CFI); Case T–17/93 *Matra Hachette v. Commission* [1994] II ECR 595; and Case T–66/94 *Auditel v. Commission* [1995] II ECR 239.

(5) The confidentiality provision in Article VIII of the EEC-USA Competition Laws Co-operation Agreement, para. 12–008B *supra*, states that neither party is required to make disclosure to the other that is prohibited by its law. Nonetheless, on the challenge to the Agreement before the Court of Justice the Advocate General expressed the view that the obligation of the Commission under

Article III to exchange information with the U.S. antitrust authorities was contrary to Article 20 of Regulation 17 as regards secrecy: Case C–327/91 *France v. Commission* [1994] I ECR 3641 [1994] 5 CMLR 517, para. 42. The Court did not address this aspect but on the subsequent approval of the Agreement (with amendments) in 1995, the interpretative letter exchanged with the U.S. Government stated that the information referred to in Article III may not include information covered by Article 20 of Regulation 17 without the express agreement of the source concerned: 1995 OJ L95/45, 1995 OJ L131/38; [1995] 4 CMLR 707.

n. 37. See now Kerse, *EC Antitrust Procedure* (3rd ed.) pp. 305–10.

n. 43. See now Kerse, *op. cit.* p. 306.

4. INTERIM MEASURES OF THE COMMISSION

12–048 **Criteria for interim measures: *La Cinq.*** See also *Sea Containers v. Stena Sealink* OJ 1994 L15/8 [1995] 4 CMLR 84. For a claim based on alleged damage to the public interest see *Goldstein v. General Medical Council* [1994] 4 CMLR 492.

n. 60. See now Cases T–24 & 28/92R; *Langnese-Iglo and Schöoller v. Commission* [1992] II ECR 1839. Interim measures were granted by the Commission in *Irish Continental v. CCI Morlaix* [1995] 5 CMLR 177 to allow the applicant access to port facilities controlled by the respondent.

5. THE COMMISSION'S POWERS TO TERMINATE INFRINGEMENTS

12–054 **Orders to terminate.** In two decisions concerning the network of exclusive supply agreements operated by the leading suppliers of ice-cream in Germany, the Commission had withdrawn from the suppliers the benefit of exemption under Regulation 1984/83 and ordered them not to enter into similar agreements in the future: *Schöller Lebensmittel*, OJ 1993 L183/1 [1994] 4 CMLR 51 and *Langnese-Iglo*, OJ 1993 L183/19 [1994] 4 CMLR 83. On appeal, the Court of First Instance annulled those decisions insofar as they withdrew the benefit of the block exemption from the suppliers for the future. The Court held that there was no legal basis for such orders, and noted that their effect would be to distort competition as the suppliers' competitors would remain free to conclude equivalent agreements. Cases T–7/93 *Langnese-Iglo v. Commission* [1995] II ECR 1533 [1995] 5 CMLR 602 [1995] All ER (EC) 902 (on appeal Case C–279/95P); and T–9193 *Schöller v. Commission* [1995] II ECR 1611 [1995] 5 CMLR 659.

Power to order positive action **12–055**

n. 94. See now: Cases C–241 & 242/91P *RTE and ITP v. Commission* [1995] I ECR 743 [1995] 4 CMLR 718 [1995] All ER (EC) 416: the orders were upheld by the ECJ which dismissed the appeals.

Informal termination of infringement **12–061**

n. 9. See now Kerse, *EC Antitrust Procedure* (3rd ed.), pp. 233–34.

n. 10. In 1994, the Commission took 33 formal decisions and resolved 525 cases by "informal procedure"; the number of cases pending on December 31, 1994 had been reduced to 1052: XXIVth Report on Competition Policy (1994), Annex III(3). In 1995, the Commission took only 14 formal decisions and resolved 419 cases by "informal procedure"; the number of cases pending on 31 December 1995 was 1178: XXVth Report on Competition Policy (1995), points 97–98. See also Bourgeois, "Undertakings in EC Competition Law" in Slot and McDonnell (Eds) *Procedure and Enforcement in EC and US Competition Law* (Sweet & Maxwell 1993).

6. FINES FOR SUBSTANTIVE INFRINGEMENTS

(a) *Generally*

The nature and purpose of fines **12–063**

n. 18. See also Gyselen, "The Commission's Fining Policy in Competition Cases" in Slot and McDonnell, *op. cit.*

Fines imposed to date. The Table of Fines should be updated as follows: **12–064**

Hilti AG	Appeal dismissed by ECJ: Case C–53/92P [1994] I ECR 667 [1994] 4 CMLR 614.

Welded Steel Mesh

Some fines reduced on appeal:

Boël	fine reduced to 440,000 ECU: Case T–142/89 [1995] II ECR 867
Cockerill Sambre	fine reduced to 252,000 ECU: Case T–144/89 [1995] II ECR 947
Baustahlgewebe	fine reduced to 3,000,000 ECU: Case T–145/89 [1995] II ECR 987
Tréfilunion	fine reduced to 1,235,000 ECU: Case T–148/89 [1995] II ECR 1063
Sotralentz	fine reduced to 57,000 ECU: Case T–149/89 [1995] II ECR 1127

All other appeals from this decision dismissed.

Solvay, ICI	Decisions annulled for procedural irregularities: Cases T–30/91, etc. [1995] II ECR 1775, 1821, 1825, 1847, 1901 [1996] 5 CMLR 57 (T–30/91) and 91 (T–32/91).
Tetra Pak II	Appeal dismissed by CFI: Case T–83/91 [1994] II ECR 755, on appeal to ECJ.
Building and construction industry in the Netherlands	Appeals dismissed by CFI and ECJ: Case T–29/92 *SPO and others v. Commission* [1995] II ECR 289; Case C–137/95P [1996] I ECR 1611.
Newitt/Dunlop	Dunlop's fine reduced from 5,000,000 ECU to 3,000,000 ECU: Case T–43/92 [1994] II ECR 441; All Weather Sports' fine annulled on procedural grounds: Case T–38/92 [1994] II ECR 211.
Eurocheque Helsinki Agreement	Fine of Groupement des Cartes Bancaires reduced by CFI to 2,000,000 ECU: Cases T–39 & 40/92 *CB and Europay v. Commission* [1994] II ECR 49.
Viho/Parker Pen	Parker Pen's fine reduced to 400,000 ECU: Case T–77/92 [1994] II ECR 549 [1995] 5 CMLR 435; Herlitz's appeal dismissed: Case T–66/92 [1994] II ECR 531 [1995] 5 CMLR 458.
Distribution of railway tickets by travel agents	Decision declared void for error of law: Case T–14/93 *Union Internationale des Chemins de Fer* [1995] II ECR 1503 [1996] 5 CMLR 40, on appeal to ECJ.

Recent Cases are as follows:

Case	Reference	Offence	Fine imposed (ECU)
Danish Shipowners v. CEWAL	OJ 1993 L34/2 [1995] 5 CMLR 198	market sharing, abuse of collective dominance	Total fines 10,000,000
Cartonboard	OJ 1994 L243/1 [1994] 5 CMLR 547	price fixing and market sharing	Total fines of 132,150,000
Steel beams cartel	OJ 1994 L116/1 [1994] 5 CMLR 353	price fixing, market sharing and information exchange	Total fines of 104,364,350
Cement	OJ 1994 L343/1 [1995] 4 CMLR 327	price fixing and market sharing	Total fines 248,000,000
Tretorn and others	OJ 1994 L378/45	export bans	600,000 on manufacturer and 10,000 on distributors
Far Eastern Freight Conference	OJ 1994 L378/17	price fixing in liner conference	10,000 imposed on 13 companies
HOV SVZ/ MCN	OJ 1994 L104/34	abusive price discrimination	11,000,000
BASF Lacke + Farben/Accinauto	OJ 1995 L272/16 [1996] 4 CMLR 811	export bans	2,700,000 on manufacturer and 10,000 on distributor
SCK and FNK	OJ 1995 L312/79 [1996] 4 CMLR 565	price fixing by trade association and ban on hiring from non-affiliated suppliers	11,500,000 in respect of price fixing and 300,000 for other infringement
ADALAT	OJ 1996 L201/1 [1996] 5 CMLR 416	export bans	3,000,000

(b) *Intentional or negligent infringement*

Knowledge of Treaty not prerequisite to intention **12–068**

n. 37. See also Case T–77/92 *Parker Pen v. Commission* [1994] II ECR 549 [1995] 5 CMLR 435; similarly Case T–66/92 *Herlitz v. Commission* [1994] II ECR 531.

Involuntary infringement. See also *BASF Lacke+Farben/Accinauto*, OJ 1995 L272/16 [1996] 4 CMLR 811, where a moderate fine was imposed on a distributor which had operated its supplier's policy of hindering parallel **12–072**

imports, taking into account the fact that it was economically dependent on the supplier and that this dependence had been used by the supplier to enforce its economic interests (para. 105).

12–073 **Article 4(2) agreements**

n. 57. See also *SCK and FNK*, OJ 1995 L312/79 [1996] 4 CMLR 565, on appeal Case T–18/96.

(c) *Matters relevant to gravity and duration*

(ii) *Market share and turnover*

12–077 **Turnover.** On the identification of turnover for a trade association which sells on behalf of its members in return for commission see the treatment of Finnboard in *Cartonboard*, OJ 1994 L243/1; [1994] 5 CMLR 547, paras. 173 *et seq*, on appeal Case T–295/94. However, where it is the association alone that is subject to a fine, the ceiling on that fine is calculated by reference to the turnover of all its members, at least where the rules of the association permit it to hold its members liable: Cases T–39 & 40/92 *CB and Europay v. Commission* [1994] II ECR 49; Case T–29/92 *SPO v. Commission* [1995] II ECR 289, para. 385 (appeal dismissed, Case C–137/95P [1996] I ECR 1611). It is the aggregate turnover of the members, not of the association itself, which reflects the economic power of the association.

12–078 **Turnover in products and markets affected**

n. 79. See also Case T–77/92 *Parker Pen v. Commission* [1994] II ECR 549; [1995] 5 CMLR 435.

12–079 **Present scale of fines in relation to turnover**

n. 89. The CFI dismissed Tetra Pak's appeal, holding that even when imposing a very large fine the Commission is not bound to break down the fine between the various aspects of the infringement: Case T–83/91 *Tetra Pak v. Commission* [1995] II ECR 755. The case is on appeal to the ECJ, Case C–333/94P.

12–080 **Relevance of profitability.** The capital of the infringer is not relevant to the amount of the fine: Case T–145/89 *Baustahlgewebe v. Commission*, [1995] II ECR 987, para. 159.

(iii) *The effects of the infringement*

Effect on third parties **12–082**

n. 4. The appeal was dismissed: see Case T–83/91 *Tetra Pak v. Commission* [1995] II ECR 755, on further appeal Case C–333/94P.

Benefits accruing from the infringement **12–083**

n. 26. However, the CFI held that an important aspect of the agreement relied on by the Commission had not been established and reduced the fine on the association of French banks to two million ECU to reflect the gravity of the offence; the decision against Eurocheque itself was annulled on procedural grounds: Cases T–39 & 40/92 *CB and Europay v. Commission* [1994] II ECR 49.

Other relevant circumstances. See the various factors which led the Commission not to impose a fine for the breach of Article 85 in *HOV SVZ/MCN*, OJ 1994 L104/34, paras. 104 *et seq.* **12–084**

n. 32. In *Re Steel Beams Cartel* OJ 1994 L116/1 [1994] 5 CMLR 353 (§ 311), the Commission imposed no fine for conduct prior to June 1988 in view of possible misunderstandings about the application of Art. 65 ECSC during a period of manifest crisis and the operation of a quota system in the industry. In *Re Ford New Holland Ltd* OJ 1993 L20/1 [1995] 5 CMLR 89, the Commission did not impose a fine because its own tolerance of Ford's claim to benefit from a block exemption contributed to allowing Ford to believe that its conduct was legitimate.

n. 36. In *Danish Shipowners v. CEWAL*, OJ 1993 L34/1, [1995] 5 CMLR 198, the Commission referred to the fact that it is customary to moderate the fines in cases of the first application of legislation. But it held that no such moderation was justified in that case where the parties were fully informed of the effect of the new law. The decision is under appeal, Cases T–24/93, etc. *Compagnie Maritime Belge v. Commission.* In *Far Eastern Freight Conference*, OJ 1994 L378/17, the Commission took into account the fact that the decision was the first to apply Reg. 1017/68 to the members of a liner conference and imposed only 'symbolic' fines.

(iv) *The behaviour of the parties*

Mitigation following initiation of proceedings. The Commission has acknowledged that undertakings participating in secret cartels may wish to terminate their involvement and inform the Commission but are **12–086**

deterred by the risk of high fines. The Commission has therefore published a Notice that sets out guidelines on possible exemption from fine, or the circumstances in which an informant can expect a significant reduction in the fine if it co-operates fully with the Commission: App. 8, *post*. The Notice sets out three categories of co-operation. The first is where the undertaking alerts the Commission to the existence of a cartel and provides documentation and evidence. Provided that the undertaking has been the instigator of the cartel or compelled others to join, it can expect a 75 per cent reduction or more in the fine imposed. A reduction of 50–75 per cent can be expected where the undertaking co-operates fully in a case where the Commission has already launched an investigation but would not have sufficient evidence of the cartel without the informant. A reduction of 10–50 per cent can be granted where the undertaking provides information which materially contributes to establishing the cartel or where the undertaking does not contest the facts in the Statement of Objections; in this latter instance if the undertaking thereafter contests the facts in national proceedings, the Commission will ask the national authority to increase the fine it imposes. Where an undertaking wishes to take advantage of the Notice it should contact DGIV.

n. 59. See also the treatment of Stora in *Cartonboard*, 1994 OJ L243/1 [1994] 5 CMLR 547 ("very substantial reduction in the fine" for spontaneous admission and provision of detailed evidence that assisted the investigation: § 171).

(v) *Duration*

12–088 **Legal considerations affecting duration.** For a case where the time bar in Regulation 2988/74 operated to shorten the duration of the infringement, see Case T–43/92 *Dunlop Slazenger v. Commission* [1994] II ECR 441, para. 84. See also *SCK and FNK*, OJ 1995 L312/79 [1996] 4 CMLR 565, on appeal Case T–18/96, where a fine was imposed in respect of an agreement operated after the adoption of an Article 15(6) decision lifting immunity from fines.

n. 73. See also *Re Steel Beams Cartel*, OJ 1994 L116/1 [1994] 5 CMLR 353, § 313 (no fine on Spanish suppliers for conduct prior to the expiry of transitional measures).

n. 74. See also *Far Eastern Freight Conference*, OJ 1994 L378/17 where a mitigating factor was that the existence of the practices condemned was widely known and the decision took longer to adopt than might otherwise have been the case: § 158.

(d) *Ancillary matters of law and practice*

Allocation of fines between infringing parties **12–090**

n. 85. See also Case T–77/92 *Parker Pen v. Commission* [1994] II ECR 549, § 86.

Fines on parents and subsidiaries. See the Commission's discussion of this issue in *Cartonboard*, OJ 1994 L243/1; [1994] 5 CMLR 547, paras. 140, *et seq.* (on appeal Cases T–295/94, etc.) In *ADALAT*, OJ 1996 L201/1 T–41/96 [1996] 5 CMLR 416, the Commission imposed a substantial fine on the parent company of the Bayer group, although the infringements in question concerned the relationships between Bayer's French and Spanish subsidiaries and their respective wholesalers. The Commission held that because the parent company had prompted its wholly-owned subsidiaries to take such action, of which it was well aware, it was responsible for the infringement. The Decision is under appeal, Case T–41/96 *Bayer v. Commission.* **12–091**

n. 92. An appeal on other grounds against the CFI decision was dismissed by the ECJ: Case C–310/93P *BPB Industries and British Gypsum v. Commission* [1995] I ECR 865.

Liability of successor undertaking. In *Cartonboard*, *supra* (paras. 140 *et seq.*) the Commission first considered the basis on which the Statement of Objections is addressed to the particular subsidiary involved in the infringement, rather than to the parent or to the group, and then considered the effect of the sale of that subsidiary. Where, but for the sale, proceedings would normally have been addressed to the subsidiary in its own right, responsibility for its conduct prior to the transfer passes with it. It is not necessary that the acquirer has subsequently approved, adopted or continued the unlawful conduct. On the other hand, where a parent company or group which is itself properly considered a party to the infringement transfers a subsidiary to another undertaking, responsibility for the period up to the date of the divestment does not pass to the acquirer but remains with the first group. The Commission proceeded to apply these principles to the complex facts of the timber industry. See also *Re Cement Cartel*, OJ 1994 L343/1 [1995] 4 CMLR 327, paras. 45(12) and 59(2). **12–092**

In Case T–38/92 *AWS Benelux v. Commission* [1994] II ECR 211 [1995] 4 CMLR 43, the Court of First Instance held that for the Commission to impute liability to the purchaser of the infringing undertaking there must be no dispute as to the identity of the legal entity which is the successor to the party committing the infringement or as to the reality of the continuance by that entity of the commercial activity carried on by the infringer. That was not the case where the infringing undertaking continues to exist as a legal person (for tax reasons) although all its commercial activity is now carried on by a different legal entity.

12–093 **Several infringements**

n. 97. See also Case T–83/91 *Tetra Pak v. Commission* [1994] II ECR 755, § 236, where the CFI held that the Commission was not bound to break down the fine between the various aspects of the abuse of a dominant position.

12–094 **Double jeopardy**

n. 1. See also Case T–149/89 *Sotralentz v. Commission* [1995] II ECR 1127, where the CFI found that the Commission had taken account of the fine already imposed by the French authorities.

12–095 **Notified agreements**

n. 5. For a recent Art. 15(6) decision see *SCK and FNK*, OJ 1994 L117/30, which was followed by a decision imposing fines, *SCK and FNK*, OJ 1995 L312/79 [1996] 4 CMLR 565 (on appeal, Case T–18/96).

12–096 **Limitation of actions.** The equivalent provisions to Regulation 2988/74 in the EEA regime are in Chapter V of Protocol 4 to the EFTA Surveillance Agreement: see para. 12–002, *supra*.

12–097 **Payment of fine.** For discussion of the Commission's powers to charge interest see Case T–275/94 *CB v. Commission* [1995] II ECR 2169 [1995] All ER (EC) 717.

n. 16. See also Case T–18/96R *SCK and FNK* [1996] 5 CMLR 307 §31.

12–099 **Suspension of payment pending appeal.** For recent case law on when the obligation to provide a bank guarantee will be dispensed with see para. 12–129, *infra*.

n. 23. For an unsuccessful challenge to the rate of interest charged see Case T–142/89 *Boël v. Commission* [1995] II ECR 867. Interest is payable even if the appeal succeeds in part: *CB v. Commission*, *supra*.

7. CONTROL BY THE COURT OF FIRST INSTANCE

Generally **12–100**

n. 25. See now Schermers and Waelbroeck, *Judicial Protection in the European Communities* (5th ed., 1992); Hartley, *op. cit.* (3rd ed., 1994); Lasok, *op. cit.* (2nd ed. 1994).

(a) *Review under Articles 172 and 173*

The Court of First Instance of the European Communities. The Court of First Instance is now directly constituted by the amended Article 168a adopted by the Treaty on European Union, which also enables the Council to vest jurisdiction in the Court to hear all cases except for references under Article 177. However, at present the Court's jurisdiction comprises all actions brought by natural or legal persons, (*i.e.*, not by Community institutions or Member States). **12–101**

n. 26. Further amended by Decision 94/149, OJ 1994 L66/29 (bringing anti-dumping appeals within the jurisdiction of the CFI).

(i) *The scope of review*

Article 172: unlimited jurisdiction in fines cases. In Case T–275/94 *CB v. Commission* [1995] II ECR 2169 [1995] All ER (EC) 717, the Court of First Instance held that in setting a new fine on appeal the Court is not replacing the fine but merely altering the level of fine imposed by the Commission. This means that if the fine is reduced, interest still accrues from the date for payment fixed in the decision and not from the date of judgment on the appeal. **12–103**

Review under Article 173: generally **12–104**

n. 32. On the question of who is directly and individually concerned see Case T–2/93 *Air France v. Commission* [1994] II ECR 323 (a competitor challenging a merger clearance); Cases T–96/92 *CCE de la Société Générale des Grandes Sources v. Commission* [1995] II ECR 1213 and T–12/93 *CCE de Vittel v. Commission* [1995] II ECR 1247 (recognised representatives of employees of an undertakings concerned in a concentration); Case T–83/92 *Zunis Holding and Others v. Commission* [1993] II ECR 1169 [1994] 5 CMLR 154; appeal dismissed on other grounds, Case C–480/93P [1996] I ECR 1 [1996] 5 CMLR 219, but see The Opinion of Adv. Gen. Lenz §§36 *et seq.*) (shareholders in company involved in concentration).

12–105 **Nature of a decision reviewable under Article 173.** A decision which merely confirms a previous decision is not a reviewable act: Case C–480/93P *Zunis Holding, supra.* But it is submitted that the position should be otherwise if, unlike the circumstances which the Court of Justice emphasised in that case, the second decision was taken in the light of material facts of which the Commission was unaware when it took its original decision.

(ii) *The grounds of annulment*

12–108 **Grounds of annulment generally**

n. 53. See now Kerse, *EC Antitrust Procedure* (Sweet & Maxwell, 3rd ed., 1994), Chap. 9.

12–109 **Procedural irregularities.** A striking recent example of an essential procedural irregularity resulting in a decision being declared void is Case T–14/93 *Union Internationale des Chemins de Fer v. Commission* [1995] II ECR 1503 [1996] 5 CMLR 40, where the Court of First Instance held that the Commission's proceedings in *Distribution of Railway tickets by travel agents* should have been governed by Regulation 1017/68 and not Regulation 17. The decision is on appeal by the Commission: Case C–264/95P.

12–111 **Inadequacy of reasoning.** In Case T–38/92 *AWS Benelux v. Commission* [1994] II ECR 211 [1995] 4 CMLR 43, the Court of First Instance stated that the adequacy of the statement of reasons must be assessed in the context of the circumstances of the case. Where the decision relates to several addressees and raises a problem as to which is liable for the infringement, the decision must include an adequate statement of reasons with respect to each of the addressees. Where the applicant during the administrative procedure challenges its liability and the Commission fails at that stage to clarify its position, the decision must contain an even more detailed account of the grounds for holding the applicant liable. As regards the analogous Article 16 of the EFTA Surveillance Agreement, the EFTA Court held that the provision of reasons over the telephone for a decision cannot satisfy the requirement for a proper statement of reasons: Case E–2/94 *Scottish Salmon Growers Association v. EFTA Surveillance Authority* [1994–5] Rep. EFTA Ct. 59 [1995] 1 CMLR 851.

(iii) *Procedural aspects*

12–116 **The Court's procedure**

n. 5. The Protocol on the Statute of the Court of Justice has been amended to enable the Rules of Procedure to take account of the nature of litigation in intellectual property matters: OJ 1995 L131/33. The Rules of the CFI have been amended: OJ 1994 L249/17, OJ 1995 L44/64 and OJ 1995 L172/3.

Time-limits for bringing actions **12–117**

n. 8. See now Case C–195/91P *Bayer v. Commission* [1994] I ECR 5619 [1996] 4 CMLR 32 (appeal dismissed by ECJ).

Measures of organisation and inquiry **12–119**

n. 21. For a recent unsuccessful request for production of documents on appeal see Case T–145/89 *Baustahlgewebe v. Commission* [1995] II ECR 987.

(b) *Action under Article 175 in respect of failure to act*

Generally. For Article 175 actions see also the recent cases discussed at para. 12–024, *supra*. **12–122**

Applications for exemption and Article 175 **12–125**

n. 47. See now Kerse, *op. cit.* p. 345.

(c) *Interim relief from the Court*

Interim relief to suspend fine. In Case T–308/94R *Cascades v. Commission* [1995] II ECR 265, the Court of First Instance granted a request to suspend for six months the applicant's obligation to provide a bank guarantee in lieu of paying the fine pending appeal. The Court stated that such a suspension will be granted only in exceptional circumstances. In order to assess a trader's ability to provide the guarantee, account should be taken of the group to which the undertaking belongs. The suspension was granted subject to the parent company giving an undertaking to the Court to provide a guarantee. In Case T–301/94R *Laakmann Karton v. Commission* [1994] II ECR 1279, the Court of First Instance rejected an application for dispensation from the obligation to provide a bank guarantee on the grounds that no proper evidence of the undertaking's inability to comply had been adduced. See also Case T–295/94R *Buchmann v. Commission* [1994] II ECR 1265; Case T–104/95R *Tsimenta Chalkidos v. Commission* [1995] II ECR 2235; and Case T–18/96R *SCK and FNK v. Commission* [1996] 5 CMLR 307. **12–129**

12–130 **Suspension of Commission order.** In Case T–88/94R *Société Commerciale des Potasses et de l'Azote v. Commission* [1994] II ECR 401, the Court of First Instance suspended the implementation of a decision under which the Commission, as a condition of clearing a merger, ordered one of the parties to the concentration to dispose of its shareholding in a separate company. An Article 173 action was brought by another shareholder in that separate company claiming that the condition was unnecessary. At the interim measures stage, the applicant established that the disposal of the shareholding was likely to cause the separate company to be dissolved resulting in serious and irreparable damage to the other shareholders. However, note that in Case T–322/94R *Union Carbide v. Commission* [1994] II ECR 1159, the Court rejected an application to suspend a merger clearance at the suit of a third party who had submitted objections to the merger during the consultation process. The Court held that it had no jurisdiction to grant orders addressed to the parties to the merger in this Article 173 action against the Commission decision. Finding that Union Carbide had failed to make out its case on the facts, the Court commented that the applicant's interest in suspending the clearance must be weighed against the public interest in the implementation of decisions under the Merger Regulation which was adopted primarily to ensure effectiveness of control and legal certainty to the undertakings to which it applies.

In Case T–41/96R *Bayer v. Commission* [1996] 5 CMLR 290, the Court notably suspended a decision requiring the applicant to cease conduct which the Commission had found had the effect of curtailing parallel exports of pharmaceutical products. It was held that Bayer had shown an arguable case of error of law in the Commission's assessment and that the likely effect of the Commission's order would be to cause an increase in lower priced parallel imports into United Kingdom: this threatened major, irrecoverable loss of profits for Bayer's United Kingdom subsidiary, to the extent that its pharmaceutical branch might cease to be viable.

The single judge hearing an application for interim relief has a broad discretion and the President of the Court of Justice has made clear that there is no specific scheme of analysis that has to be applied on such applications. In Case T–395/94R *Atlantic Container Line v. Commission* [1995] II ECR 595, the Court of First Instance suspended that part of the Commission's order that prohibited the shipping companies from jointly exercising rate-making authority in respect of the inland portons of through-intermodal transport on the ground that the resulting changes to the framework of operations would be difficult to reverse if the main appeal against the decision were successful. The Commission's appeal against the suspension was dismissed: Case C–149/95P(R) [1995] I ECR 2165 [1995] All ER (EC) 853 (making clear also that the requirement of serious and irreparable harm is satisfied if such harm is probable).

n. 61. See also Case T–543/93R *Gestevision Telecino v. Commission* [1993] II ECR 1409; Cases T–79 & 80/95R *SNCF and British Rail v. Commission*, [1995] II ECR 1433 [1996] 5 CMLR 26 and Case C–174/94R *France v. Commission* [1994] I ECR 5229.

8. APPEALS TO THE COURT OF JUSTICE

Appeal from judgments of the Court of First Instance. For the limited nature of appeals to the Court of Justice see, *e.g.* Case C–53/92P *Hilti v. Commission* [1994] I ECR 667; [1994] 4 CMLR 614. However, the Court of Justice has set aside some judgments of the Court of First Instance: see Case C–360/92P *Publishers' Association v. Commission* [1995] I ECR 23 [1995] 5 CMLR 33 [1996] ICR 121; Case C–39/93P *SFEI v. Commission* [1994] I ECR 2681. **12–132**

n. 66. Art. 46 of the Protocol was amended by Dec. 95/208, OJ 1995 L131/33.

9. THE EFTA COURT

The EFTA Court: jurisdiction and procedure. Article 108(2) of the EEA Agreement made provision for the establishment by the EFTA States of a Court with competence to hear "appeals concerning decisions in the field of competition" by the EFTA Surveillance Authority. Notwithstanding that provision, which is broader than anything in the EC Treaty, the powers and procedures of the EFTA Court are closely modelled on those of the Court of Justice: see generally the EFTA Surveillance Agreement, Articles 27–41, and the Statute of the Court in Protocol 5, as amended by the EFTA Transitional Arrangements Agreement and the EFTA Adjustment Agreement: *Encyclopedia of European Union Law* (*Constitutional Texts*), Vol. 4, paras. 62.1007 *et seq.* The Court officially commenced operation on 1 January 1994, sitting in Geneva but has now moved to Luxembourg. With the accession of Austria, Finland and Sweden, the effective scope of the EFTA Court's jurisdiction was substantially reduced and since 1 January 1995 it has comprised three judges. **12–134A**

Decisions. The EFTA Court seeks to follow the decisions of the Court of Justice and the Court of First Instance as regards analogous provisions to those in the EEA Agreement and the EFTA Surveillance Agreement: see Case E–2/94 *Scottish Salmon Growers Association v. EFTA Surveillance Authority* [1994–5] Rep. EFTA Ct. 59 [1995] 1 CMLR 851, paras. 11–13. As at 1 September 1996 the Court had not issued any decisions in the field of competition law, but see the *Scottish Salmon Growers* case as regards procedural requirements. **12–134B**

CHAPTER 13

THE ROLE OF THE STATE IN REGULATED INDUSTRIES

1. INTRODUCTION

13–001 **The Commission's policy**

n. 1. See also XXIIIrd Report on Competition Policy (1993), points 36 to 42; XXIVth Report (1994), points 13 and 215 to 217; and XXVth Report (1995), points 99 to 101.

2. STATE MONOPOLIES OF A COMMERCIAL CHARACTER

13–004 **State monopoly of a commercial character.** Where the activities of the body are concerned with dealing with applications to a minister and administering regulatory provisions it will not fall within Article 37: See Cases C–46/90 and C–93/91 *Lagauche* [1993] I ECR 5267.

In Case C–393/92 *Almelo* [1994] I ECR 1477, it was held that a regional electricity distributor which did not enjoy an exclusive concession in its territory but concluded exclusive purchasing agreements with local electricity distributors was not a state monopoly. The effect on imports arose by way of contract not by way of the delegation of its regional concession and thus it was not the State as such which exercised control over imports.

n. 3. See now Oliver, *Free Movement of Goods in the European Community* (Sweet & Maxwell, 3rd ed., 1996).

n. 4. Electricity constitutes goods for these purposes: Case C–393/92 *Almelo, supra.*

n. 9. Also Sweden, Finland and Austria: XXVth Report on Competition Policy (1995), points 126–127.

n. 12. See also XXIVth Report on Competition Policy (1994), point 228.

n. 20. See now *Almelo*, *supra*, where Advocate General Darmon considered (at § 69) that it was established that Art. 37 encompasses a situation where the monopoly covers only a region.

Extent of prohibition under Article 37(1). The Commission considers that it is not incompatible with Article 37(1) to maintain exclusive rights to the retail sale of alcohol where that is based upon legitimate national concerns about alcoholism, provided that this does not involve discrimination between national and imported products. By contrast, monopolies with regard to import, export or wholesale supply of alcohol are incompatible with Article 37(1). See the Commission's approach to the Swedish, Finish and Austrian alcohol monopolies as set out in XXVth Report on Competition Policy (1995), points 126–127. **13–005**

International agreements: Article 37(5) **13–008**

n. 33. See now Oliver, *op. cit.* 11.12, p. 351.

Remedies **13–009**

n. 35. The Commission has commenced Art. 169 proceedings against Austria regarding the national alcohol and manufactured tobacco monopolies: XXVth Report on Competition Policy (1995), points 127 and 129.

3. PUBLIC UNDERTAKINGS: ARTICLE 90

(a) *Generally*

The wider application of Article 90 **13–010**

n. 37. See also XXIVth Report (1994), point 13.

(b) *Article 90(1)*

Undertakings granted special or exclusive rights **13–014**

n. 51. In Directive 94/46, OJ 1994 L268/15 [1996] 4 CMLR 87, which amends the Telecoms terminal equipment and Telecoms services Directives, the Commission has now incorporated a more precise definition of special rights.

13–015 **Measures of the Member State**

n. 52. See now Cases C–46/90 and C–93/91 *Lagauche* [1993] I ECR 5267: a ministerial power of authorisation as such cannot constitute a measure; nor can the delegated power to administer such authorisations.

13–016 **The grant of special or exclusive rights can itself be a measure.** In Case C–323/93 *Centre d'Insémination de la Crespelle v. Coopérative de la Mayenne* [1994] I ECR 5077, the Court of Justice held that the mere grant of exclusive rights within the scope of Article 90(1) that create a dominant position is not as such incompatible with Article 86; a Member State contravenes those two provisions only if by exercising that exclusive right the undertaking in question cannot avoid abusing its dominant position. Hence in Case C–18/93 *Corsica Ferries* [1994] I ECR 1783, the grant to an undertaking of the exclusive right to offer compulsory piloting services at the port of Genoa, thereby creating a dominant position, was not in itself contrary to Article 90(1); but in approving the adoption by the undertaking of discriminatory tariffs within Article 86(c), the Italian authorities infringed the prohibition of those two articles. *Cf.* Case C–320/91 *Corbeau* [1993] I ECR 2533 [1995] 4 CMLR 621, where the Belgian law conferring a postal monopoly was held to infringe Article 90(1) subject to the application of Article 90(2): see further para. 13–025, *infra.*

13–017 **The extension of exclusive rights as a measure.** In the context of liberalisation of telecommunications services, the Commission has used its powers under Article 90(3) in attempting to ensure a "level playing-field" by taking action against Member States that discriminate in favour of the existing public operator in determining the conditions for new entrants. In *Re GSM radiotelephony services in Italy*, OJ 1995 L280/49 [1996] 4 CMLR 700, the Italian government required a substantial initial bid payment for the grant of a second concession to operate mobile telephony services using the pan-European digital system (GSM). The Commission held that this would subject the second operator to a significant cost burden not shared by the State owned operator (Telecom Italia) and so would give Telecom Italia a competitive advantage that would enable it to extend its existing dominant position on the fixed infrastructure and analogue mobile telephony markets into the market in GSM radiotelephony. The requirement was therefore held to be contrary to Article 90 in conjunction with Article 86. For action commenced against other Member States, see XXVth Report on Competition Policy (1995), points 110–111.

Application in conjunction with other Treaty provisions **13–018**

n. 68. See also *Corsica Ferries, supra*; *Port of Rødby*, OJ 1994 L55/52 [1994] 5 CMLR 457 (refusal by State-owned port owner to allow access to port facilities or to authorise construction of new facilities on adjacent land); *Brussels Airport.* OJ 1995 L216/8 [1996] 4 CMLR 232 (decree fixing airport landing fees charged by public airways authority which incorporated a system of discounts that had the effect of applying dissimilar conditions to airlines for landing and take-off services), on appeal Case C–291/95 *Belgium v. Commission; Port of Elsinore*, Press Release IP (96) 205 of 6 March 1996 [1996] 4 CMLR 728 (access to port facilities for competing ferry operator). See also XXIVth Report on Competition Policy (1994), point 227.

n. 72. Although Italy subsequently introduced a new law to reform its port system, local authorities continued to refuse to grant operating licences to competitors seeking to enter the market; for the consequent action by the Commission, see XXVth Report on Competition Policy (1995), point 123. See also *Corsica Ferries, supra*: higher tariffs charged for piloting services by the Corporation of Pilots of the Port of Genoa for vessels that did not have a cabotage licence (which was granted only to Italian vessels); *Brussels Airport, supra*: stepped discounts for landing fees at Brussels Zaventem Airport that favoured airlines with higher volumes of traffic thereby placing small airlines at a competitive disadvantage (and favouring in particular Sabena).

(c) *Article 90(2)*

In general. Article 90(2) may also serve to provide a derogation from the application of the rules on State aids in Articles 92–93 although its inter-relationship in practice with those provisions remains unclear: see Case C–387/92 *Banco Exterior de Espana* [1994] I ECR 877 [1994] 3 CMLR 473. **13–021**

Services of general economic interest. Eurocontrol, an international organisation that carries out certain air navigation control functions, co-ordinates national policies on air navigation on behalf of Contracting States and collects route charges, was held not to be an undertaking within Article 90. Its activities were considered "typically those of a public authority" and "not of an economic nature justifying the application of the Treaty rules of competition". Case C–364/92 *SAT Fluggesellschaft v. Eurocontrol* [1994] I ECR 43, 63–64. **13–023**

n. 94. See also Case C–393/92 *Almelo* [1994] I ECR 1477: regional electricity distribution.

Obstructing the performance of the tasks. In Case C–320/91 *Corbeau* [1993] I ECR 2523 [1994] 4 CMLR 621, the Court of Justice considered **13–025**

the law establishing a postal monopoly in Belgium in the context of the criminal prosecution of an individual who had established a special "home collection" service in Liège. The Court held that there was justification within Article 90(2) for restricting competition to an undertaking entrusted with the operation of a service of general economic interest that involved more and less profitable operations, where the entry by a competitor into only the more profitable sectors would undermine the economic balance of the service on which the undertaking depended. However, the exclusion of competition was not justified as regards a specific service, of a kind not offered by the protected undertaking, that met a distinct need. The assessment of whether those criteria were met was for the national court. Similarly, in *Almelo, supra*, the necessity for the grant of exclusive rights to a regional electricity distributor had to be assessed having regard to the distributor's obligation to ensure uninterrupted supply of electricity to all consumers in its territory and the economic conditions in which it operates, in particular the legislation concerning the environment to which it is subject. See also XXIVth Report on Competition Policy (1994), point 216.

n. 6. See also *EBU/Eurovision System*, OJ 1993 L179/28 [1995] 4 CMLR 56 (annulled on other grounds, Cases T–528/93, etc. *Métropole Télévision v. Commission* [1996] 5 CMLR 386).

13–027 **Article 90(2) in national courts.** It is now clear that Article 90(2) is directly applicable and that once a national court holds that an undertaking comes within the scope of that provision, it must determine whether the conditions of the derogation are satisfied, if necessary seeking assistance by way of preliminary ruling from the Court of Justice: see *Corbeau; Almelo; supra.*

(d) *Article 90(3)*

13–028 **Article 90(3).** The Commission considers that the implementation of this provision "will be increasingly necessary, as the single market exposes privileged enterprises more and more to competition": XXIVth Report on Competition Policy (1994), point 215 and see also at point 222. However, in many cases an approach from the Commission leads the Member State to amend its regulation and formal action is not required: *ibid.*, point 217.

13–029 **Enforcement.** A third party, even where it is a competitor of the undertaking favoured by a Member State, cannot compel enforcement action by the Commission under Article 90(3). In Case T–32/93 *Ladbroke v. Commission* [1994] II ECR 1015, the Court of First Instance held that

Ladbroke's competitive position did not make it a person directly and individually concerned in the Commission's failure to take action against France regarding the grant to a grouping of ten French racecourse operators of exclusive rights to off-course betting. Furthermore, the Commission had a wide margin of discretion under Article 90(3) and its decision not to take any or any particular form of action could not be challenged by a complainant.

The power to legislate under Article 90(3). The Commission maintains that its powers under Article 90(3) are not legislative or quasi-legislative because it can only specify the implications of existing Treaty rules and set up procedures to ensure compliance: XXIVth Report on Competition Policy (1994), point 215. Directives under this provision are issued where there have been many infringements of the fundamental rules of the Treaty, in order to avoid a multiplicity of infringement proceedings and so that the Commission can give operators "a minimum amount of legal certainty": XXVth Report on Competitive Policy (1995), point 100. **13–031**

Directive 80/723. The Directive was further amended in 1993 by Directive 93/84: Appendix 15, *post.* This introduced a requirement that each Member State shall supply to the Commission annually detailed financial information for all public undertakings with a turnover in excess of 250 million ECU that operate in the manufacturing sector (defined to mean that at least 50 per cent of their turnover is in manufacturing). The specified information includes details of relevant intra-group transactions: Article 5a(3). **13–032**

The Telecoms Directives. The Court of Justice has ruled that Article 6 of Directive 88/301 prohibits the application of a national regulatory regime which prevents undertakings from producing, importing, stocking, selling or distributing terminal equipment without holding a certificate of conformity or other equivalent document where the entity which grants such certificates and draws up the technical specifications is not independent from all undertakings offering goods or services in the telecommunications field: Cases C–46/90 and C–93/91 *Lagauche* [1993] I ECR 5267, Case C–69/91 *Decoster* [1993] I ECR 5335 and Case C–92/91 *Taillandier* [1993] I ECR 5383. However, Article 3 of the Directive does not preclude national rules that prohibit importation or possession with a view to sale of equipment that does not meet the specifications that such equipment has to satisfy for connection to the national network: Case C–314/93 *Rouffeteau and Badia* [1994] I ECR 3257. **13–033**

The deficiencies in Directives 88/301 and 90/388 that led to partial annulment by the Court of Justice (see at notes 32–33 and para. 13–014 of the main work) have been remedied by Directive 94/46, OJ 1994 L286/25 [1996] CMLR 87, which also brought satellite earth station equipment and satellite communications services within the scope of, respectively, the Telecoms equipment and Telecoms services Directives. Directive 90/388 has been further amended by three subsequent Directives and the Commission is therefore close to achieving its stated objective of full liberalisation of telecommunications services within the internal market: see XXVth Report on Competition Policy (1995), points 102–107. The amending Directives are the following:

(i) Directive 94/46, *supra*, on satellite communications;

(ii) Directive 95/51, OJ 1995 L256/49, on cable television. This requires Member States to abolish all restrictions on the supply of transmission capacity by the cable TV networks and to allow such networks to provide liberalised telecommunications services at the latest by September 1, 1996;

(iii) Directive 96/2, OJ 1996 L20/59, on mobile telephony. This brings mobile and personal communications systems within the scope of the Telecoms services Directive. It requires Member States to abolish all exclusive or reserved rights in the field of mobile communications and also to allow operators to offer their services via their own infrastructure or via alternative infrastructures;

(iv) Directive 96/19, OJ 1996 L74/13, on full competition in telecommunications markets. This completes the process of applying Directive 90/388 to the entire field of telecommunications services by extending its ambit to cover public voice telephony services. Special or exclusive rights to provide voice telephony services must be abolished by 1 January 1998, subject to a right to derogation of a further five years for Spain, Ireland, Greece and Portugal that have less developed networks, and of two years for Luxembourg on account of its very small network, to enable those States to make the necessary structural adjustments. Where the supply of voice telephony services or the provision of telecommunications networks is subject to licensing, that must be carried out on an objective, non-discriminatory and transparent basis, with a right to appeal against the refusal of a licence. Exclusive rights for the publication of directories or provision of directory enquiry services must also be lifted.

Spain and Portugal have challenged the competence of the Commission under Article 90(3) of the Treaty as regards part of Directive 95/51 on the grounds that it goes beyond specifying the obligations already in existence and seeks to impose a new obligation to liberalise the market: Cases C–ll & 12/96, not yet decided. If upheld, it seems that the same objections would lie against Directives 96/2 and 96/19.

4. MILITARY EQUIPMENT

13–035 **Application of Article 223.** The French government invoked Article 223 in directing the parties to a concentration concerning the manufacture of engines for missiles not to notify it to the Commission. After receiving information from the French authorities, the Commission was satisfied that the conditions of Article 223(1)(b) were fulfilled. See XXIIIrd Report on Competition Policy (1993), points 324 to 326. Similarly, the Commission allowed the United Kingdom government to invoke Article 223 to prevent notification under the Merger Regulation of the military aspects of bids by GEC and British Aerospace for VSEL; the limited, non-military aspects were notified; see *British Aerospace/VSEL* (Case IV/M.528, Decision of 24 November 1994), *GEC/VSEL* (Case IV/M.529, Decision of 7 December 1994) and XXIVth Report on Competition Policy (1994), point 336. The Commission's decision was predicated on the fact that there were no spill-over effects on the non-military activities of the bidders and that the proposed mergers would have no significant impact on suppliers, sub-contractors or the Ministries of Defence in other Member States. (The military aspects of the bids were subsequently referred to the Monopolies and Mergers Commission which considered both competition issues and public security issues while the Commission considered the non-military aspects of the proposed acquisitions.) See also *GEC/Thomson-CSF(II)* (Case IV/M.724, Decision of 20 May 1996) where the United Kingdom and French governments jointly invoked Article 223(1)(b) in respect of the military aspects of a merger of the parties' sonar business.

CHAPTER 14

AGRICULTURE

1. GENERALLY

14–001 **Generally.** Following the amendments made by the TEU, Article 3(*d*) and (*f*) are now Article 3(*e*) and 3(*g*) respectively. In Article 39, there has been added (as paragraph (*d*)) a further objective, *i.e.* "to assure the availability of supplies". Former paragraph (*d*) is now numbered (*e*).

2. REGULATION 26

14–003 **Annex II products**

n. 4. In Case C–250/92 *Gøttrup-Klim v. Dansk Landbrugs AmbA* [1994] I ECR 5641 [1996] 4 CMLR 191, the ECJ confirmed that for Reg. 26 to apply the products concerned must be listed in Annex II. As a derogation from other Treaty rules, Art. 42 had to be interpreted strictly: fertilizers and pesticides, which were merely ancillary to the production of Annex II products, consequently did not fall within Reg. 26.

14–004 **The first Article 2(1) exception: national market organisations**

n. 6. See also *Scottish Salmon Board*, OJ 1992 L246/37 [1993] 5 CMLR 602.

14–005 **The second Article 2(1) exception: necessary under Article 39.** The Commission has made it clear that it will not allow a national trade association to take discriminatory measures which deny market access to operators from other Member States: *British Cattle and Sheep Breeders' Associations*, XXIInd Report on Competition Policy (1992), point 167 and Annex III, page 416.

n. 13. In *Scottish Salmon Board, supra,* the Commission held that Reg. 26 did not permit fish trade associations, faced with falling prices due to undercutting by non-EC producers, to enter into a price-fixing agreement with those producers in order to stabilise prices. The agreement was not necessary because Community law already provided remedies in such a situation, including the possibility of anti-dumping proceedings and also Reg. 3796/81 (re. the common organisation of the market in fishery products) which provided in certain circumstances for the grant of compensation to producers of salmon to safeguard their income level and for the establishment of a minimum import price for fish.

n. 14. See also *Milk Marketing Board*, XXIInd Report on Competition Policy (1992), points 161–167, where the Commission concluded that there were no grounds for action under Art. 85 (or Art. 86) against a national voluntary co-operative accounting for more than 80 per cent of milk production. In particular, it was noted that the leaving terms for members were significantly less restrictive than those earlier accepted by the Commission in *Campina*.

Farmers' associations. The Court of Justice considered the inter-relationship of the first and second sentences of Article 2 of Regulation 26 in Cases C–319/93, etc., *Dijkstra and Others v. Friesland Coöperatie* [1995] I ECR 4471 [1996] 5 CMLR 178. The Court held that the inapplicability of Article 85(1) to agreements, decisions and practices falling within the scope of the second sentence of Article 2, having regard to its legislative history, is to be determined exclusively according to the conditions laid down in that sentence. **14–006**

The derogations in Article 2 are to be interpreted strictly. As regards the requirement in the second sentence of Article 2 that the objectives of the common agricultural policy are not jeopardised, the Court of Justice has observed that this condition may not be fulfilled if the rules of an association have the effect of tying its members for a long period, thereby depriving them of the opportunity of approaching competitors for better prices: Case C–399/93 *Oude Luttikhuis v. Coberco* [1995] 1 ECR 4515 [1996] 5 CMLR 178.

Commission's exclusive jurisdiction. The approach suggested at the conclusion of para. 14–007 of the main work has been confirmed by the Court of Justice in *Dijkstra, supra.* A national court, faced with a challenge to an agreement falling within the second sentence of Article 2(1), should approach the matter in the same way as any other agreement found to fall within Article 85(1) for which exemption had not yet been granted: *cf.* para. 10–016 of the main work. If it is clear, having regard to the case law of the Court of Justice and the practice of the Commission, that the agreement excludes competition or jeopardizes the objectives of Article 39, the national court may declare the agreement void if it is incapable of qualifying for individual exemption under Article 85(3). If **14–007**

on the other hand the national court considers that the agreement may fall within the exemption in the second sentence of Article 2(1), the court may stay the proceedings pending a determination by the Commission under Article 2(2). Although not at issue in *Dijkstra*, the same principles would presumably apply to a case falling within the first sentence of Article 2(1).

By way of derogation from Article 85(1), as regards producer groups in Belgium, Italy and parts of France for certain specified produce, a determination by the Commission under Article 2(2) that Article 85(1) is applicable to an agreement or decision does not have retroactive effect but applies only from the date of the decision: Article 17 of Regulation 1360/78, OJ 1978 L166/1.

3. STATE AIDS IN AGRICULTURE

14–008 **State aids.** The Commission considers that any aid which is liable to disturb Community market mechanisms (for example, aid per unit of input or output) is a breach both of State aid provisions and of the Regulations establishing the common market organisations. However, the Commission has not objected to State aid in agriculture which is of a structural and not an operational nature, (*e.g.* aid for improved marketing arrangements) on the grounds that the provisions of the relevant market organisations are not exhaustive with respect to producer groups. Nor has it objected to per hectare aid for the introduction or maintenance of farming practices which are compatible with environmental protection. See generally, XXIInd Report on Competition Policy (1992), points 503 to 505; XXIIIrd Report on Competition Policy (1993), points 547 to 548; XXVth Report on Competition Policy (1995), points 191 to 194. The Commission has published guidelines for the examination of State aids in the fisheries and aquaculture sector: OJ 1994 C260/3.

There are transitional provisions for State aids granted by Austria and Finland in Articles 138 to 141 of the Act annexed to the Treaty of Nordic and Austrian Accession. In addition, the Commission is directed to authorise Finland and Sweden to grant long-term aid to ensure that agricultural activities are maintained in northern areas where climatic conditions render agriculture particularly difficult: *ibid.* Art. 142.

CHAPTER 15

TRANSPORT

1. INTRODUCTION

Generally. Following the amendments made by the TEU, Article 3(*e*) of the Treaty is now Article 3(*f*). The references in the main work to Articles 84(1) and 84(2) are transposed. **15–002**

The Regulations applying the competition rules to the various transport sectors now apply to the EEA: EEA Agreement, Annex XIII, point 7 (regarding Regulation 1017/68) and point 50 (regarding Regulation 4056/86); and Chapter XI of Protocol 4 to the Agreement between the EFTA States on the Establishment of a Surveillance Authority and a Court of Justice (regarding Regulation 3975/87).

Transitional regime **15–003**

n. 8. See also Case C–185/91 *Reiff* [1993] I ECR 5801 [1995] 5 CMLR 145.

2. RAIL, ROAD AND INLAND WATERWAY TRANSPORT

Scope of Regulation 1017/68. In Case T–14/93 *Union Internationale des Chemins de Fer v. Commission* [1995] II ECR 1503 [1996] 5 CMLR 40, on appeal Case C–264/95P, the Court of First Instance held that the activities of travel agents involved in the sale of rail tickets were "operations of providers of services ancillary to transport" within the meaning Article 1 of Regulation 1017/68 and therefore came within the scope of the Regulation. The Court took the view that if the principal aspects of a case fall within Regulation 1017/68 the fact that other neighbouring transport markets may also be affected should not be taken into account. The Court **15–004**

annulled the Commission's decision taken under Article 85(1) and Regulation 17 requiring the parties to terminate the infringing agreements. In *Eurotunnel III*, OJ 1994 L354/66 [1995] 4 CMLR 801, the Commission held that the business of providing a railway infrastructure fell outside Regulation 1017/68 and Regulation 141 as it did not relate directly to the provision of transport services; it was therefore to be regulated under Regulation 17. See also *Fenex*, OJ 1996 L181/28 [1996] 5 CMLR 332 forwarding agents' activities regarding customs declarations and handling services fell outside Regulation 1017/68. In *Trans-Atlantic Agreement*, OJ 1994 L376/1, and *Far Eastern Freight Conference*, OJ 1994 L378/17, the Commission rejected arguments that the inland carriage of sea containers, as part off inter-modal transport, should fall within Regulation 4056/86 (which contains an exemption for liner conferences) and held that such inland price fixing by shipowners came under the terms of Regulation 1017/68. The decision in *Trans-Atlantic Agreement* is on appeal: see Case T–395/94R *Atlantic Container Line and others v. Commission* [1995] II ECR 595, where interim measures were granted suspending the operation of the Commission's decision in so far as it related to inland price-fixing (affirmed on appeal, Case C–149/95P(R) *Commission v. Atlantic Container Line and others* [1995] I ECR 2165 [1995] All ER (EC) 853). And see now Case C–339/95 *Compagnia di Navigazione Marittima v. Compagnie Maritime Belge*, not yet decided (Art. 177 reference from the English Commercial Court).

15–005 **Prohibition and invalidity.** The Commission imposed fines on the members of the liner conference in *Far Eastern Freight Conference, supra*.

n. 20. See also *Eurotunnel III, supra*.

15–006 **Exception for technical agreements**

n. 22. See the refusal of exemption under Art. 3 on these grounds to the joint ventures between rail companies in *Night Services*, OJ 1994 L259/2 [1995] 5 CMLR 76, on appeal Cases T–374/94, etc.; and *ACI*, OJ 1994 L224/28.

15–008 **General power of exemption.** The Commission has exempted a number of co-operation arrangements between public rail undertakings in relation to the Channel Tunnel on the basis of conditions designed to facilitate access by other operators. In *Eurotunnel III, supra*, the Commission granted an exemption for 30 years having regard to the exceptional circumstances in that case and subject to certain obligations and conditions, notably that other railway undertakings shall have available at least 25 per cent of the hourly capacity of the Channel Tunnel in each direction to run international passenger and freight trains. The decision is under appeal and an application for interim measures was refused: Cases T–79 & 80/95R *SNCF and British Railways v. Commission* [1995] II ECR 1433 [1996] 5 CMLR 26. In *Night Services, supra*, the Commission granted an exemption for eight years for a joint venture established to provide overnight passenger rail services between points in the United Kingdom and Continental Europe on condition that the participating railway undertakings supplied to other operators wishing to operate night passenger trains through the Channel Tunnel the same necessary rail services as they have agreed to supply to their joint venture. In *ACI, supra*, the Commission exempted for a period of five years agreements between a number of railway undertakings relating to a joint venture established to provide rail transport services between the United Kingdom and Continental Europe for goods loaded in road vehicles, containers or other units suitable for intermodal transport, subject to certain conditions enabling other operators to obtain rail services from the joint venture's parents on a non-discriminatory basis including the hiring of specialised wagons designed for use in the Channel Tunnel. The Commission has noted the importance of developing such high quality rail services which provide increased competition with traditional sea and air transport: XXIVth Report on Competition Policy (1994), point 190. See also *CIA*, OJ 1994 C130/3, XXIVth Report on Competition Policy (1994), point 191,where a co-operation agreement between 13 European rail companies for the international carriage of new motor vehicles was exempted under the objections procedure for three years on the basis that it served to promote the development of rail transport.

Abuse of a dominant position **15–010**

n. 31. In *HOV SVZ/MCN*, OJ 1994 L104/34, the Commission imposed a fine of 11 million ECU on Deutsche Bundesbahn for infringing Art. 86 by using its dominant position on the rail services market in Germany to impose discriminatory tariffs on the market for the combined transport of sea-borne containers.

Procedure **15–011**

n. 36. See *Eurotunnel III, supra*, renewing the exemption subject to conditions. For an agreement concerning a European network of express delivery services, mainly by road and secondarily by rail and by air, see *Ducros/DHL*. The Commission's initial notice stated that Reg. 1017/68 and Reg. 3975/87 concerning air services may jointly apply; but the agreement was subsequently cleared for three years under Reg. 1017/68 (the period for analogous deemed exemption under Reg. 3975/87 is six years): OJ 1994 C165/10 and XXIVth Report on Competition Policy (1994), point 192. See also *CIA*, *ibid.* point 191. And see now Case T–14/93 *UIC*, para. 15–004, *supra*, concerning the scope of Reg. 1017/68.

3. SEA TRANSPORT

(a) *Scope of application of the competition rules*

15–013 **Scope of Regulation 4056/86.** The Regulation now applies to maritime transport services from or to one or more EEA States: EEA Agreement, Annex XIII, point 50.

The Commission has held that the Regulation does not apply to the inland leg of multimodal transport of sea containers; it is unclear whether it applies to port handling services. See *Far Eastern Freight Conference*, OJ 1994 L378/17.

15–015 **Other agreements and practices.** A block exemption for consortia agreements has now been adopted: Regulation 870/95. See para. 15–028A, *infra.*

(b) *Procedure, enforcement and substantive appraisal*

15–017 **Individual exemptions**

n. 68. In *DSB/SFL/SJ*, which concerned the joint operation of a ferry service between a port in Sweden and a port in Denmark, the Commission allowed the 90 day objections period to expire after the parties agreed to delete a clause requiring them to co-operate on other ferry services between the two countries concerned: XXIInd Report on Competition Policy (1992), Annex III p. 418. For other examples of applications made under the Art. 12 procedure, see *Agreement regarding the ferry service between Dragør and Limhamn*, OJ 1995 C350/16; *HansaFerry*, OJ 1996 C–118/5; and *Stena Tor Line*, OJ 1996 C209/5.

15–018 **Enforcement**

n. 75. The *Cewal, Cowal and Ukwal* decision is under appeal: Cases T–24/93, etc., *Compagnie Maritime Belge v. Commission.*

15–019 **Substantive appraisal under Article 85.** In *Trans-Atlantic Agreement*, OJ 1994 L376/1, on appeal Case T–395/94 *Atlantic Container Line and Others v. Commission*, the Commission refused to grant an individual exemption to a liner conference that fell outside Article 3 of Regulation 4056/86. In *Irish Club Rules*, the Commission issued a comfort letter under Article 85(3) relating to an agreement between a number of shipping companies providing liner services between the Continent and Northern Ireland after certain amendments were made to their agreement: OJ 1993 C263/6, XXIIIrd Report on Competition Policy (1993), point 233.

Article 86. Following the Court of Justice decisions concerning the operation of the port of Genoa, Case C–179/90 *Merci Convenzionali Porto di Genova* [1991] I ECR 5891 and Case C–18/93 *Corsica Ferries* [1994] I ECR 1783, the Commission has taken a number of decisions (including the grant of interim measures) holding that refusal of access to port facilities for inter-state maritime operation constitutes an infringement of Article 86. See the cases listed at para. 9–016A, *supra*, and also the investigation regarding the *Port of Elsinore*, Press Release IP (96) 205 of 6 March 1996 [1996] 4 CMLR 728. **15–021**

n. 82. The *Cewal, Cowal and Ukwal* decision is under appeal: n. 75, *supra.*

(c) *Block exemption for liner conferences*

Scope of block exemption **15–023**

n. 88. See also *Far Eastern Freight Conference*, OJ 1994 L378/17, and § 15–004, *supra.* And see now Case C–339/95 *Compagnia di Navigazione Marittima v. Compagnie Maritime Belge*, not yet decided.

Agreements between liner conference members. In *Trans-Atlantic Agreement*, OJ 1994 L376/1, the Commission decided that a liner conference that establishes at least two rate levels or provides for the non-utilisation of capacity falls outside Article 3 of Regulation 4056/86; the decision is under appeal, Case T–395/94 *Atlantic Container Line and Others v. Commission*, and interim measures were granted regarding part of the decision: see para. 15–004, *supra.* The Commission has stated that the maximum period of notice required before a member can leave a liner conference without penalty should not as a rule exceed six months, and in some cases it might be shorter. See *East African Conference* where the Commission terminated proceedings after the notice period was reduced from 12 to 6 months: XXIIIrd Report on Competition Policy (1993), points 230 and 231. **15–024**

n. 89. The *Cewal, Cowal and Ukwal* decision is under appeal: n. 75 *supra.*

Conditions and obligations. See Case C–339/95 *Compagnia di Navigazione Marittima v. Compagnie Maritime Belge*, not yet decided (Article 177 reference from the English Commercial Court). **15–025**

(d) *Consortia*

15–027 **Generally.** In April 1995 the Commission issued a block exemption under Regulation 479/92 for consortia agreements: paras. 15–028A and 15–028B, *infra*.

15–028A **Regulation 870/95.** The Commission finally adopted a block exemption for consortia agreements, Regulation 870/95 which came into force on 22 April 1995: see Appendix 14, *post*. The Regulation lasts for a period of five years and has to be read in conjunction with the block exemption for liner conferences. The Regulation applies to consortia agreements between two or more vessel-operating carriers which provide regular international shipping services ("liner shipping") from or to one or more Community ports exclusively for the carriage of cargo, chiefly by container: Articles 1–2. The Regulation therefore does not apply to domestic maritime transport, tramp vessel services or passenger services. The exemption applies to consortia which have as their object the rationalisation of the members' operations through technical, operational or commercial arrangements. Pursuant to Article 3, only the following specified activities provided for in consortia agreements are exempt:

(1) the joint operation of liner shipping transport services which comprise solely certain specified activities;
(2) temporary capacity adjustments;
(3) the joint operation or use of port terminals and related services;
(4) the participation in one or more of the following pools: tonnage, revenue or net revenue;
(5) the joint exercise of voting rights concerning the consortium's activities in the relevant conference;
(6) a joint marketing structure;
(7) the issue of a joint bill of lading; and
(8) any other ancillary activity necessary for the implementation of these specified activities.

15–028B **Conditions for exemption.** The definition of "consortium" in Regulation 870/95 excludes an arrangement where one of the means of rationalisation is price-fixing. The Regulation further provides, in Article 4, that the exemption will not apply to arrangements concerning the non-utilisation of a certain percentage of the capacity of consortium members used within the framework of the consortium. Further, for the exemption to apply, one or more of the following conditions must be met: there must be effective price competition between the members of the conference within which the consortium operates; or there must exist within that conference a sufficient degree of effective competition in terms of the services provided; or the consortium members must be subject to effective competition, actual or potential, from shipping lines outside the consortium (Article 5). In addition, in respect of the ranges of ports served by the consortium, it must possess effectively a share of under 30 per cent of the direct trade when it operates within a conference and 35 per cent otherwise (Article 6). If a consortium exceeds these thresholds but does not exceed 50 per cent of the direct trade, the exemption will still apply provided that the agreements in question are notified and the Commission does not oppose exemption within six months (Article 7). The Regulation imposes other conditions, including provisions designed to ensure freedom of independent action to the members of the consortium and for the protection of users. Pursuant to Article 9, any consortium claiming the benefit of the Regulation must be able to demonstrate, at the Commission's request, compliance with the conditions and certain obligations imposed. See generally Clough, "The Devil and the Deep Blue Sea" (1995) 7 ECLR 417. For the first decisions authorising consortia agreements under Regulation 870/95, see Press Release IP(96) 400 of 8 May 1996 [1996] 5 CMLR 6.

4. AIR TRANSPORT

(a) *Scope of application of the competition rules*

Legislative background. The third package of liberalisation measures has been incorporated into the EEA Agreement making Norway, Iceland and Liechtenstein part of the single market in civil aviation: Decision 7/94 of the EEA Joint Committee, Annex II, OJ 1994 L160/87. **15–029**

The two block exemptions for capacity co-ordination and for computer reservation systems were replaced on their expiry with new block exemptions, respectively, Regulation 1617/93, OJ 1993 L155/18, and Regulation 3652/93, OJ 1993 L333/37. Both these exemptions last until 30 June 1998. See paras. 15–047 and 15–048, *infra*.

For the air transport sector generally, see Adkins, *Air Transport and EC Competition Law* (Sweet & Maxwell, 1994); Balfour, *European Community Air Law* (Butterworths, 1995).

n. 19. Reg. 2408/92 was amended to take account of the accession Austria, Finland and Sweden, by Dec. 95/1, OJ 1995 L1/1 at 119.

Further proposals. Agreement has been reached in principle by the Council to adopt the Commission's proposal for a Directive on access to the ground handling markets at Community airports, OJ 1995 C142/7. See XXVth Report on Competition Policy (1995), point 122. **15–030**

Scope of Regulation 3975/87. Because of the limitation of Regulation 3975/87 to transport between Community airports, the Commission has now invoked Article 89 of the Treaty in seeking to examine the **15–031**

transatlantic "alliances" between European and US airlines, notably British Airways and American Airlines: see para. 15–057, *infra*. Such examination is required to be conducted "in co-operation with the competent authorities in the Member States" and the Commission is dependent upon the Member States to enforce any resulting decisions. It remains to be seen how this will work out in practice.

(b) *Procedure and enforcement*

15–033 **Generally.** Regulation 4261/88 has been amended by Article 4 of Regulation 3666/93 with a view to implementing the competition provisions laid down in the EEA Agreement, OJ 1993 L336/1, and further amended by Council Decision 95/1 to take account of the accession of Austria, Finland and Sweden, OJ 1995 L1/1 at 19. The amendments are minor but include a new Form AER: see para. 15–034, *infra*.

15–034 **Individual exemptions**

n. 31. The Form AER annexed to the original Reg. 4621/88 has been replaced by Reg. 3666/93, App. 4, to take account of the application to the EEA: OJ 1993 L336/1.

(c) *Common types of agreement under Article 85*

15–043 **Agreements involving computer reservation systems.** *Global Logistics System*, OJ 1993 C76/5, involved joint venture agreements between Lufthansa, Air France, Cathay Pacific and Japan Airlines to establish and market computerised cargo information logistics systems. The Commission issued an Article 19(3) Notice indicating its intention to take a favourable view on condition that the parties gave undertakings to respect the principles contained in the block exemption for air transport CRS, in particular as regards non-discriminatory access and freedom to participate in other systems. See also *Re Galileo and Covia CRSs*, OJ 1993 C107/4 [1993] 4 CMLR 638.

n. 52. The code of conduct has been amended by Reg. 3089/93, OJ 1993 L278/1 and corrigendum OJ 1995 L17/18.

15–044 **IATA agreements.** IATA rules that prevent passengers from purchasing tickets outside the country of travel origin have been modified as a result of the Commission's intervention so that they no longer apply to travel within the Community and Norway; XXIIIrd Report on Competition Policy (1993), point 237. See also para. 15–048, *infra*.

(d) *The block exemption regulations*

Generally **15–045**

n. 61. Reg. 3976/87 was further amended by Ann. I to Council Dec. 95/1. OJ 1995 L1/1 at 17, inserting a transitional provision to take account of the accession of Austria, Finland and Sweden.

Agreements for ground handling services **15–046**

n. 71. The Commission has reported that the market for ground handling services has opened up at a number of airports as a result of its intervention, but that it is examining complaints under Art. 86 regarding anti-competitive practices at Frankfurt and Milan airports: XXVth Report on Competition Policy (1995), point 121.

Purchase, development and operation of CRS. Regulation 83/91 was extended to 31 December 1993 and replaced on its expiry by a new block exemption, Regulation 3652/93, OJ 1993 L333/37. The new Regulation has since been extended to apply to air carriers established in the territory covered by the EEA Agreement, OJ 1994 L160/129. Regulation 3652/93 introduced a number of important changes. An airline that is involved in the ownership or control of a CRS must not discriminate against a competing CRS, in particular by refusing to provide the same data with equal timelines as that which it provides to its own CRS (Article 4). A system vendor (defined as any entity responsible for the operation or marketing of the CRS) must separate its CRS distribution facilities in a clear and verifiable manner from any carrier's private inventory and management and marketing facilities (Article 6). See also *Sabre/Air France and Iberia*, XXIIIrd Report on Competition Policy (1993), point 239. **15–047**

n. 75. See now Art. 1, Reg. 3652/93.

n. 76. *ibid*., Art. 3.

n. 77. *ibid*., Art. 7.

n. 78. *ibid*., Art. 6.

n. 79. *ibid*., Art. 12.

n. 80. *ibid*., Art. 6.

n. 81. *ibid*., Art. 11.

n. 82. *ibid*., Art. 10.

n. 83. *ibid.*, Art. 13.

n. 84. *ibid.*, Art. 4.

n. 85. *ibid.*, Art. 9.

n. 86. *ibid.*, Art. 14.

n. 87. *ibid.*, Art. 15.

15–048 **Joint planning and co-ordination of capacity, tariff consultation and slot allocation: generally.** Regulation 84/91 expired on 30 June 1993 and was replaced by a new block exemption, Regulation 1617/93, OJ 1993 L155/18 (and notice at OJ 1993 C177/6), which was subsequently amended by Regulation 1523/96, OJ 1996 L190/11, so as to exclude consultations on cargo tariffs from the scope of the exemption. The new Regulation has also been extended to apply within the EEA, OJ 1994 L160/130. The exemptions granted under the new Regulation are similar to those adopted under Regulation 84/91 save that Regulation 1617/93 also covers the "joint operation of a scheduled air service on a new or on a low density route between Community airports" (Article 1). The conditions for exemption of joint operations are designed to ensure that it only benefits small carriers and applies to routes on which there was either no air service in the four preceding traffic seasons or limited capacity (Article 3).

The Commission did not accept that a global surcharge introduced by IATA on all freight movements could benefit from Regulation 1617/93 and the surcharge was accordingly withdrawn: XXIIIrd Report on Competition Policy (1993), point 238.

n. 89. See now Reg. 1617/93 Reg. 1617.93, Art. 1.

n. 91. *ibid.* Art. 1.

n. 92. *ibid.* Art. 3.

n. 93. *ibid.* Art. 6.

n. 94. *ibid.* Art. 7.

(e) *Abuse of a dominant position*

15–053 **Dominant position.** The Court of First Instance followed *Ahmed Saeed* on market definition in Case T–2/93 *Air France v. Commission* [1994] II ECR 323, a challenge to the Commission's decision under the Merger Regulation not to oppose the acquisition by British Airways of a substantial interest in TAT. Although the Court also noted with apparent approval that the Commission had taken into account the effect of the transaction on competition between airline networks, the Court expressly rejected Air France's contention that the relevant market was international air transport between Member States.

See also *Brussels Airport*, OJ 1995 L216/8 [1996] 4 CMLR 232, where the Commission found that services linked to access to infrastructures at Brussels National Airport was the relevant market, on which the airports authority held a legal monopoly.

(f) *Mergers, joint ventures and minority shareholdings*

15–057 **Links between major airlines in different Member States.** The Commission has recently taken decisions concerning a number of major airline alliances, in particular *Swissair/Sabena* (Case IV/M.616, Decision of 20 July 1995) under the Merger Regulation and *LH/SAS*, OJ 1996 L54/28 [1996] 4 CMLR 845, on appeal Case T–37/96 *Luftfartsfunktionaererne v. Commission*, under Article 85(3) concerning an agreement between Lufthansa and SAS to establish an integrated air transport system. The Commission appears to have adopted a consistent approach in these cases, requiring the parties to give undertakings to facilitate market access on the routes most affected by the alliances, *i.e.* the routes between the domestic airports of the carriers concerned. These undertakings have comprised essentially a frequency freeze, interline agreements for new entrants, access to frequent flyer programmes and slot concessions at congested airports to facilitate new entry on the most affected routes. In addition, the Commission has required the participating carriers to terminate their co-operative arrangements with certain other airlines and, in line with its approach in *Air France/Sabena*, where the affected routes are not covered by the third package of liberalising measures in air transport, the Commission has obtained commitments from the home States of the carriers involved to liberalise air traffic on those routes: see *Swissair/Sabena, supra*.

In July 1996, the Commission stated its intention to investigate for the first time alliances between European and US airlines that covered transatlantic routes: Reuters, 3 July 1996. This investigation was prompted by the announcement of a major strategic alliance between British Airways and American Airlines that would give the two airlines a combined share of some 70 per cent of the London–New York route. As the competition aspects of this arrangement were being examined by the U.S. antitrust authorities, the Commission considered that it should also have jurisdiction to assess the impact of the alliance in the EEA. However, the Commission is investigating also the following alliances, some of which have been in place for several years: Lufthansa/United Airlines; SAS/United Airlines; British Airways/US Air; Swissair/Sabena/Austrian Airlines/Delta Air Lines; KLM/Northwest. Because Regulation 3975/87 is restricted to transport between Community airports, the investigation as regards transport outside the Community has been commenced under the little-used residual power in Article 89 of the Treaty. Under that provision, the Commission does not have direct authority to enforce any decision that it may adopt, but is dependent upon the Member States to implement appropriate remedial measures.

15–058 Other links between airlines

n. 27. The CFI dismissed the application by Air France to annul the Commission's decision not to oppose the concentration: Case T–2/93 *Air France v. Commission* [1994] II ECR 323. See also *SAS/Icelandair*, OJ 1994 C201/9; [1994] 5 CMLR 480.

n. 28. The Commission noted that airlines that operate on the package holiday market may be significant potential competitors to scheduled airlines. A joint venture between two tour groups to create a new airline, in place of their existing separate airlines, was granted exemption for six years: *Premiair*, Report on the application of the competition rules in the EU (1995), page 134.

CHAPTER 16

ENERGY

1. INTRODUCTION

(a) *Community policy in the energy sector*

The ECSC, Euratom and EC Treaties. The amendments to the EC Treaty made by the TEU include the addition of "measures in the sphere [...] of energy", as one of the activities of the Community listed under Article 3: see Appendix 1, *post.* The new Title XII of the EC Treaty sets out provisions aimed at the promotion of trans-European networks in the field of transport, telecommunications and energy infrastructures: Articles 129b–129d. See further para. 16–006, *infra.* **16–001**

n. 1. In Case C–18/94 *Hopkins v. National Power* [1996] 4 CMLR 745, the ECJ held that discrimination practised by purchasers is covered exhaustively by the ECSC Treaty, leaving no scope for the application of Art. 86 of the EC Treaty to such practices. See also Case C–128/92 *Banks* [1994] I ECR 1209 [1994] 5 CMLR 30, *per* Advocate General Van Gerven at §§ 7–9.

Agreement on Community Energy Policy **16–002**

n. 4. Art. 8a has been renumbered Art. 7a under the amendments made by the TEU. The Commission has stated that the establishment of a single energy market in accordance with this provision continues to be a priority: XXIIIrd Report on Competition Policy (1993), point 133; see also XXIVth Report (1994), point 231.

The Energy Charter Treaty was signed on 17 December 1994 providing for closer co-operation between the EC and East European countries in areas including investment, supplies and market access; protocols on energy efficiency and nuclear safety will also be negotiated: Press Release

Memo/94/75 of 16 December 1994. The Commission has adopted a proposal for ratification: Press Release IP (95) 998 of 20 September 1995.

16–003 Special characteristics of energy markets

n. 5. See also the Green Paper, "For a European Union Energy Policy", COM (94) 659, 23 February 1995, § 171. The co-ordination of sales and purchases of electricity to and from Norway by the organisation of Swedish electricity producers, KSN, notified to the ESA, was terminated following the ESA's indication that it intended to take a negative decision: ESA Annual Report '94, point 4.9.2.

16–004 The importance of security of supply

n. 7. See also "For a European Union Energy Policy", n. 5 *supra*, Chap. 2.2.

n. 8. Estimated energy dependence could increase to 70 per cent by 2020: "For a European Union Energy Policy", n. 5 *supra*, § 17.

n. 9. The ECSC Consultative Committee has stated that energy diversification is one of the main goals of energy policy: *Europe*, 13 July 1995.

n. 10 See also "For a European Union Energy Policy", n. 5 *supra*, Annex C.

16–005 Energy and the internal market

n. 15. At the end of 1994, the Council (Energy) reached agreement in principle on four of the five key points in the proposal for a Directive on the electricity market: liberalisation of electricity generation, separation of accounts of vertically integrated enterprises, provisions on the operation and management of the networks and criteria governing the possible setting by Member States of requirements in the general economic interest on enterprises in the sector. The Council noted that a single buyer system (that would allow the opening up of markets beyond electricity generation) and TPA might co-exist subject to conditions to secure equivalent economic results between the two. However, this remains politically contentious and, to the evident frustration of the Commission, no substantial progress was made in 1995 and the Council was unable to agree on a common position with regard to the draft Directive. See XXIVth Report on Competition Policy (1994), point 230;

"For a European Union Energy Policy", n. 5 *supra*; XXVth Report on Competition Policy (1995), points 112–117.

(b) *Energy and the EC Treaty*

Relevant provisions of the EC Treaty **16–006**

Articles 129b–129d contain provisions with the stated intention of promoting inter-connection and inter-operability of, *inter alia*, national energy networks, as well as access to those networks. However, those provisions for the most part enable the adoption of Guidelines, the provision of financial support and the co-ordination of common national policies rather than directive action by the Community. See, *e.g.*, the adoption by the Council (under Art. 189b) of Common Position (EC) No. 12/95 on Guidelines for trans-European gas and electricity networks, including connection of isolated networks and development of interconnections: OJ 1995 C216/31.

n. 17. Case C–393/92 *Almelo* [1994] I ECR 1477, 1516; see §§ 16–011 to 16–012 *infra.*

n. 18. The Commission has decided to refer the matter to the ECJ: Cases C–94/156, etc., not yet decided. See XXIIIrd Report on Competition Policy (1993), point 363, and n. 30 *infra.*

n. 20. See also XXIIIrd Report on Competition Policy (1993), point 533 (the Commission found that rebates off natural gas tariffs to Dutch ammonia producers who were suffering heavy losses did not give them a competitive advantage over foreign producers).

n. 21. See also Directive 93/38/EEC co-ordinating the procurement procedures of entities operating in the water, energy, transport and telecommunications sectors, 1993 OJ L199/84; and now the proposal for the amendment of this Directive in the light of the Uruguay Round, OJ 1995 C138/49.

n. 23. The Commission approved a proposed Directive to introduce rational planning techniques in the electricity and gas distribution sectors and to reduce CO_2 emissions: OJ 1996 C1/6.

2. ELECTRICITY

Article 85 and the Commission's decisions. See now the decision of the Court of Justice in *Almelo*, para. 16–011 and 16–012 *infra.* **16–009**

n. 28. The agreements notified on the reorganisation of the electricity industry in the United Kingdom were transitional and came to an end on 31 March 1993. The new agreements that replaced them were notified and Art 19(3) Notices issued: OJ 1993 C281/5 [1994] 4 CMLR 585 (England and Wales); OJ 1994 C15/15 [1994] 5 CMLR 107 (National Power and regional coal producers); OJ 1994 C223/8 (Scotland). See also *Electricidade de Portugal/Pego project* XXIIIrd Report on Competition Policy (1993), point 222: § 16–019A *infra.*

(a) *IJsselcentrale*

16–010 **Power distribution: *IJsselcentrale.***

n. 29. See Case C–19/93P *Rendo and others v. Commission* [1995] I ECR 3319. The ECJ set aside the judgment of the CFI insofar as it had held that the Commission decision had had no legal effect in respect of the application of Art. 85 to the import restrictions applicable in the period before the 1989 Dutch Electricity Law came into effect, dismissed the remainder of the appeal and referred the case back to the CFI.

16–011 **Prevention of imports and exports condemned.** In Case C–393/92 *Almelo* [1994] I ECR 1477, the Court of Justice considered that the restriction in the Dutch electricity sector which prevented imports for public supply purposes infringed Article 85. The case arose from arbitration proceedings brought by local distributors against IJsselmij (formerly IJsselcentrale) about the model General Terms and Conditions for the supply of electricity and the equalisation supplement in particular. The national court referred the issue to the Court under Article 177 because it considered that without the import ban IJsselmij could probably not have imposed the equalisation charge. The exclusive purchasing obligation imposed on local distributors, through the regional distributors' general conditions for the supply of electricity, prohibited local distributors from obtaining supplies from other suppliers, including those in other Member States. The Court held that the use of such an exclusive purchasing obligation by a regional electricity distributor, which was a part of a group of undertakings occupying a collective dominant position in a substantial part of the EC, would breach Article 86. It was for the national court to determine whether the links between the regional electricity distributors were sufficient to constitute such collective dominance. The Court also held that Article 37 did not apply because IJsselmij had not been granted an exclusive concession giving it a monopoly in supply within the territory. The contracts were concluded between regional and local distributors, not with public authorities, and did not transfer to the local distributors the concession granted to the regional undertaking. The conditions for the application of Article 37, where national authorities are in a position to control or influence trade between Member States through a body established for that purpose or a delegated monopoly, were not present. See further at para. 16–012 *infra* and Hancher (1995) C.M.L. Rev. 305.

n. 30. In June 1994, France, Ireland, Italy, the Netherlands and Spain were referred by the Commission to the ECJ following the response by the national authorities to reasoned opinions sent out and the failure by these Member States to produce specific plans to abolish monopolies: Cases C–94/156, etc., not yet decided. XXIIIrd Report on Competition Policy (1993), point 363; XXIVth Report (1994), point 228. See also § 16–038, n. 66, *infra.*

Application of Article 90(2). In the *Almelo* case, para. 16–011 *supra*, the Court of Justice held that it was for the national court to determine whether performance of the regional electricity distributor's task of general economic interest required imposition of an exclusive purchasing obligation on local distributors that prevented imports. In making this determination, "it is necessary to take into consideration the economic conditions in which the undertaking operates, in particular the costs which it has to bear and the legislation, particularly concerning the environment, to which it is subject" (para. 49). **16–012**

(b) *United Kingdom privatisation*

Electricity pricing mechanisms **16–013**

n. 32. The Commission also held that British Coal's amended licensing arrangements did not violate Art. 66(7) of the ECSC Treaty: see *National Association of Licensed Opencast Operators v. British Coal Corporation* [1993] 4 CMLR 615. That part of the decision is subject to an action for annulment: Case T–57/91 *National Association of Licensed Opencast Operators v. Commission*, not yet decided. In addition, a group of independent Welsh mineowners have claimed damages against the electricity generators under Art. 86 or alternatively Arts. 4 and 63(1) of the ECSC Treaty. In its decision on an Art. 177 reference from the English High Court, the ECJ held that discrimination practised by purchasers against producers of coal are to be governed not by Art. 86 of the EC Treaty but exclusively by Arts. 4 and 63(1) of the ECSC Treaty. Those provisions do not create rights in individuals that are directly enforceable unless the Commission has made a recommendation that is unconditional and sufficiently precise. Case C–18/94 *Hopkins v. National Power* [1996] 4 CMLR 745. The case is now back before the English court to determine whether this Commission decision satisfies those criteria. See further §§ 17–004A to 17–005, *infra.*

16–016 **United Kingdom privatisations: favourable approach adopted.** Upon the expiry of the contracts for raw materials in 1993, new five year contracts were entered into between the generators and British Coal that were the subject of an Article 19(3) Notice: OJ 1993 C281/5 [1994] 4 CMLR 585. The same approach was adopted towards the notified agreements for supply of coal to National Power from 17 private coal producers: OJ 1994 C15/15 [1994] 5 CMLR 107; and between the Scottish generators and British Coal: OJ 1994 C223/8.

(c) *Other arrangements*

16–019A **Electricidade de Portugal/Pego project.** The Commission considered a set of agreements between Electricidade de Portugal (EDP), National Power, Electricité de France and Empresa Nacional de Electricidad for the purchase and operation of a coal-fuelled station at Pego in Portugal. The arrangements followed the introduction of gradual competition into the Portuguese energy sector, in both generation and supply, where EDP previously had a monopoly. The competitive system distinguished, according to a consumption threshold, between franchise customers (able to purchase electricity from only one source) and free market customers (able to buy from any source). Under the arrangements, the Generator owned by the consortium agreed to purchase the Pego power project from EDP and to supply the power generated to EDP. The Commission refused to accept a 28 year exclusive supply arrangement which would have prevented the Generator from delivering electricity to consumers other than EDP in Portugal or in other Member States. EDP therefore agreed that the capacity and output exclusivity would be limited to EDP for the first 15 years and that for the subsequent term there would be a first option enabling the Generator to supply outside the franchise system if there was surplus capacity not required by the grid. Following these changes, the Commission sent a comfort letter. XXIIIrd Report on Competition Policy (1993), point 222.

See also *REN/Turbogás*, OJ 1996 C118/7 [1996] 4 CMLR 881, concerning agreements for the supply of electricity from a gas-fired power station to be built at Tapada, Portugal, to a company in the EDP group. The Commission issued a notice under Article 19(3) indicating its intention to take a favourable view of a 15 year exclusive supply agreement after that had been amended to delete a clause giving the purchaser a first option to obtain power from the generator after the end of the 15 years. Similarly in *ISAB Energy*, OJ 1996 C138/3 [1996] 4 CMLR 889, concerning a power purchase agreement for the supply of electricity to the Italian national utility ENEL from an integrated and combined cycle power plant to be constructed in Sicily, the Commission issued an Article 19(3) notice indicating its intention to take a favourable view for a 15 year period when the case would be re-examined. The Commission had previously informed the parties that it could not view favourably the 20 year exclusivity provided for in the agreement.

Effect on trade between Member States. In the *Almelo* case, para. 16–011 *supra*, the Court of Justice followed *Brasserie de Haecht* and *Delimitis* (see paras. 2–072 to 2–076 of the main work) in holding that the cumulative effect of exclusivity agreements, similar to that which it was considering, needed to be taken into account in determining if there was an appreciable effect on trade between Member States. The contractual relationships under the model General Terms and Conditions drawn up by the electricity industry in the Netherlands were found to have the cumulative effect of compartmentalising the national market. They prohibited local Dutch distributors from obtaining supplies of electricity from distributors or producers in other Member States. See also the Article 19(3) Notices on the revised arrangements for the electricity industry in the United Kingdom, paras. 16–015 and 16–016 *supra.* The Commission noted that no input fuel for electricity generation originated in other Member States: the United Kingdom is the lowest cost coal producer in the Community, there is no gas pipeline for imports from other Member States and the five year contracts did not foreclose the markets. In *Electricidade de Portugal/Pego project*, *supra*, the Commission noted that the exclusive supply obligation had the effect of preventing delivery of electricity to consumers in other Member States. **16–020**

3. NUCLEAR ENERGY

(a) *Euratom Treaty*

Scope of the Euratom Treaty **16–021**

n. 47. For an annotated text of the Treaty incorporating the Maastricht amendments made by the TEU see *Encyclopedia of European Union Law (Constitutional Texts)*, Vol. 1, §§ 11–0001 *et seq.*

Joint Undertakings **16–023**

n. 50. See now *Encyclopedia of European Union Law (Constitutional Texts)*, Vol. 1, § 11–0337A.

(b) *Commission policy: EEC Treaty*

***Scottish Nuclear*: Article 85(3).** See also para. 16–032, *infra*. **16–031**

National policy considerations: United Kingdom. The Commission issued Notices under Article 19(3) indicating its intention to take a **16–032**

favourable approach to the agreements for the provision and management of fuel assemblies for the use in advanced gas cooled reactors (AGRs) because the only AGRs in existence are in the United Kingdom and it is unlikely that any more will be built: *Nuclear Electric/British Nuclear Fuels*, OJ 1996 C89/4 [1996] 4 CMLR 716; *Scottish Nuclear/British Nuclear Fuels*, OJ 1996 C89/6 [1996] 4 CMLR 718.

n. 56. The restriction on the United Kingdom Government's Fossil Fuel Levy, that was limited to eight years because of its nuclear component by the Commission when granting authorisation in 1990, has been lifted with respect to the financing of renewable-generated electricity which requires longer-term support: XXth Report on Competition Policy (1990), point 293; XXIIIrd Report on Competition Policy (1993), point 532.

16–034 **Research, safety and Eastern Europe**

n. 58. See also Art. 19(3) Notice for the European Nuclear Assistance Consortium (ENAC) formed by eight nuclear engineering companies to carry out studies on improvement in the safety of nuclear power stations for a three year period, OJ 1993 C175/12; Art. 19(3) Notice for the European Fuel Cycle Consortium (EFCC) formed by two companies operating in the nuclear fuel business to study, assess the safety and environmental consequences and recommend management of irradiated nuclear fuel and design and operation of industrial facilities, OJ 1993 C351/6 [1994] 4 CMLR 589.

4. GAS

16–036 **Generally**

n. 62. Imports of gas are currently nearly 40 per cent, projected to grow towards 70 per cent by 2010: "For a European Union Energy Policy", Green Paper COM (94) 659, 23 February 1995, § 99; and see generally, "European Community Gas Supply and Prospects", COM (95) 478.

n. 63. On the basis of commercial agreements, over 50 per cent, of gas consumed in the EC crossed one border and about 30 per cent crossed more than one border: *ibid.*

16–037 **Articles 85 and 86 and gas distribution.** The Commission has issued a comfort letter in respect of the network code established in the United Kingdom setting out rules for the safe and efficient use of the network under the regulatory regime established by the Gas Act 1995. It considered that the network code did not fall within Article 85 because it did not prevent, restrict or distort competition within the common market; Press Release IP(96) 462 of 31 May 1996.

n. 64. See also the notification of a joint venture for construction, operation and use of an underwater gas interconnector pipeline between the United Kingdom and Belgium. The parties are Amerada Hess, BP Exploration, British Gas, Conoco, Distrigaz, Elf Aquitaine, Elf Petroleum, National Power, RAO Gazprom and Ruhrgas: OJ 1995 C73/18.

Article 37 and import/export monopolies **16–038**

n. 66. France was referred by the Commission to the ECJ following the response of the French authorities to the reasoned opinion sent out in November 1992: Case C–94/159, not yet decided; see also § 16–011, n. 30 *supra*, for the position regarding similar monopolies in electricity. The proceedings initiated against Denmark were terminated following the Danish authorities' decision to repeal the monopoly in natural gas imports granted to Dansk Naturgas A/S: XXIIIrd Report on Competition Policy (1993), point 363; XXIVth Report (1994), point 228.

5. OIL

Strategy **16–041**

n. 72. See also "For a European Union Energy Policy", *supra*, §§ 45, 98.

Efficient distribution and economic progress **16–043**

n. 80. In *International Energy Agency*, OJ 1994 L68/35, the Commission recognised that the trend for increase in oil imports since 1985 was likely to continue and the exemption granted to the IEP was renewed for 10 years.

National policy and protection: import/export control **16–044**

n. 83 With the entry into force on 14 January 1993 of Spanish legislation on the oil industry whereby the Spanish oil monopoly held by Campsa ceased to exist, the infringement proceedings that the Commission had commenced against Spain were terminated: XXIIIrd Report on Competition Policy (1993), point 362. However, the Commission expressed concern that the statutory restrictions should not be replaced with contractual ones and examined the exclusive supply contracts between the Spanish refineries and operators of service stations under the former monopolised network. When those contracts were found to fall outside Reg. 1984/83 the refineries agreed to amend them to accord with the terms of the block exemption: *ibid.* point 226.

16–045 **Exploration**

n. 84 Under the Art. 189b procedure, the Council has adopted a common position on the proposed Directive: OJ 1994 C101/14.

16–046 **Article 85 and Environmental Protection.** In *Oliebranchens Faellesrad*, the Commission considered an agreement notified by the organisation of Danish oil companies for the creation of an Environmental Pool to distribute funds for cleaning polluted petrol station sites. The Commission considered that the penalty payable by a site owner on reopening a station within ten years of receipt of funds for a clean-up was in breach of Article 85(1). Furthermore, the selection criteria for cleaning stations should be based on environmental criteria and the costs should be fair and reasonable. The case was closed after the agreement had been amended to remove the penalty so that, apart from reimbursement of costs to the Environment Pool, the only obligation on a station owner who wanted to reopen within a ten year period would be to certify that insurance had been taken against the risk of future pollution. XXIVth Report on Competition Policy (1994), Annex II, A.2(j). See also *Disma*, XXIIIrd Report on Competition Policy (1993), points 223–4 (joint venture for storage of jet fuel at Milan Malpensa airport: comfort letter issued after the agreement was amended to ensure non-discriminatory access for third parties).

CHAPTER 17

COAL AND STEEL

The scope of the ECSC Treaty **17–001**

n. 1. For the text of the Treaty as amended by the TEU, see *Encyclopedia of European Union Law (Constitutional Texts)*, Vol. 1, §§ 10.0010 *et seq.*

1. PRODUCTION QUOTAS AND PRICING

Price discrimination. Article 63(1) provides that if the Commission finds that "discrimination is being systematically practised by purchasers, in particular under provisions governing contracts entered into by bodies dependent on a public authority", it shall make appropriate recommendations to the relevant Government. Unlike Articles 65 and 66, this provision applies to undertakings that are not themselves engaged in the production of coal or steel: *cf.* para. 17–005, *infra*. **17–004A**

Three associations of British independent mine operators brought complaints under both the ECSC and EC Treaties concerning the coal supply contracts between the British Coal Corporation (BCC) and the English electricity generators, National Power and PowerGen (both in their own right and as successors to the Central Electricity Generating Board), on the grounds that BCC had secured more favourable, and therefore discriminatory, purchase conditions for its supplies of coal than the generators' terms of purchase of coal produced by the independent mines. The Commission found that the complaint under Articles 63 ECSC and 86 EC against the generators and under Article 66(7) against BCC "were justified". However, because the terms of the contracts with the complainants had subsequently been amended with retroactive effect, the Commission rejected the complaint as "no longer valid": *National Association of Licensed Opencast Operators v. British Coal Corporation* [1993] 4 CMLR 615.

A group of Welsh mineowners thereupon commenced proceedings

against the generators for damages under Article 86 of the EC Treaty alternatively Article 63(1) of the ECSC Treaty. On a reference from the English High Court, the Court of Justice held that the question is governed exclusively by the ECSC Treaty and that Article 63(1) does not create rights that are directly enforceable. However, a recommendation by the Commission under Article 63(1) may be relied on by individuals before the national court if it is unconditional and sufficiently precise: Case C–18/94 *Hopkins v. National Power* [1996] 4 CMLR 745. In the light of that ruling, the defendants are applying to strike out the claim before the English court: see further para. 17–005, *infra*, as regards the analogous proceedings against BCC.

2. RESTRICTIVE AGREEMENTS

17–005 **Prohibited Agreements.** Article 65 applies only to agreements between at least two undertakings as defined by Article 80: "any undertaking engaged in production in the coal and steel industry within the territories [covered by the ECSC Treaty] and ... any undertaking or agency regularly engaged in distribution other than sale to domestic consumers or small craft industries". Accordingly, a supply agreement between a producer of coal and electricity generators does not come within Article 65: *National Association of Licensed Opencast Operators v. British Coal Corporation, supra.*

The Court of Justice has held that Articles 65 and 66(7) do not confer directly enforceable rights: Case C–128/92 *Banks* [1994] I ECR 1209; [1994] 5 CMLR 30. A national court has no jurisdiction to rule on the applicability of either provision and may not entertain an action for damages based upon them until the Commission has adopted a decision finding that Article 65 or 66(7) applies. Furthermore, the national court is bound by the Commission's decision although it may ask the Court of Justice to question its validity by way of a reference for a preliminary ruling under Article 41. It is not clear whether the national court has jurisdiction where the Commission has proceeded by comfort letter or rejection of a complaint.

The preliminary ruling in *Banks* was made on a reference by the English High Court in the proceedings brought to claim damages against BCC in the light of the Commission's decision on the supply contracts for electricity-generating coal, *supra*. Following the ruling of the Court of Justice, the High Court dismissed those proceedings, and refused a stay, on the grounds that until the Commission had made a determination establishing infringement of either Article 65 or 66(7), there was no cause of action and that the Commission's decision relied on was not sufficient for that purpose: *Banks v. British Coal Corporation*, judgment of 19 July 1994 (QBD). The judgment is under appeal.

n. 31. See also *European producers of beams* OJ 1994 L116/1 [1994] 5

CMLR 353, on appeal Cases T–134/94 etc., *NMH Stahlwerke GmbH and others v. Commission.*

Authorisation of agreements. The Commission has issued explanatory notes to assist in an application for authorisation under Articles 65 or 66: XXIst Report on Competition Policy (1991), Annex II, pages 281–87. **17–006**

n. 36. Where transitional arrangements are made preparatory to full integration, they will require authorisation under Art. 65(2): see *Empresa Nacional Siderurgica SA and the Aristrain Group*, OJ 1993 L48/54 (JV for joint selling and specialisation in production of steel beams).

Fines for infringement **17–008**

n. 39. In *European producers of beams, supra*, the Commission imposed fines ranging from 600 ECU to 32 million ECU. It distinguished *Cold-rolled stainless steelflat products* on the grounds that the manifest crisis had ended in 1988 and that there was no evidence that the agreements had been brought to the notice of the Commission.

3. CONCENTRATIONS

Authorisation of concentrations. For the Commission's explanatory notes, see para. 17–006, *supra*. **17–012**

4. ABUSE OF DOMINANT POSITION UNDER ARTICLE 66(7)

Abuse of a dominant position. See also *Banks*, para. 17–005, *supra*. **17–017**

n. 74. In its decision on the complaint brought by the British small mine operators, *National Association of Licensed Opencast Operators v. British Coal Corporation* [1993] 4 CMLR 615, the Commission found that the complaint that British Coal Corporation had abused a dominant position under Art. 66(7) in securing favourable purchase conditions for the supply of electricity generating coal to National Power and PowerGen "was justified". For the subsequent proceedings in the English court, see §§ 17–004A and 17–005, *supra*. The Commission rejected the complaint regarding the royalties levied by BCC on the opencast operators; that part of the decision is under appeal before the CFI, Case T–57/91, but those proceedings were stayed to await the decision of the ECJ in *Banks*.

5. STATE AIDS UNDER THE ECSC TREATY

17–019 **State aids on coal.** The current regime is governed by Decision 3632/93 (OJ 1993 L329/12) which replaced Decision 2064/86 and lays down certain general requirements for authorisation as well as specifying particular conditions for certain types of aid. The general requirements (laid down in Article 2) are (i) progress towards economic viability (ii) solving social and regional problems caused by reduction in activity and (iii) adjustment to environmental standards. The specific categories which may be approved are certain types of operating aid, aid for reduction in activity, aid for exceptional costs, aid for research and development and environmental aid (Articles 3 to 7). Annual prior notification is required. Decision 3632/93 expires on July 23, 2002, the expiration date of the ECSC Treaty. In 1995 the Commission authorised grants of aid to cover inherited liabilities and the cost of restructuring in France, Germany and the United Kingdom: XXVth Report on Competition Policy (1995), point 165.

17–020 **State aids on steel.** On 12 April 1994, the Commission took six decisions under Article 95 of the ECSC Treaty approving aid outside the terms of Decision 3855/91 to the Spanish, Italian, Portuguese and German state-controlled steel companies (OJ 1994 L112/45). These are now under appeal in Case T–244/94 *Wirtschaftsvereinigung Stahl and others v. Commission*, Case T–243/94 *British Steel v. Commission* and Case T-239/94 *EISA v. Commission*. Interim relief was refused in Case T–239/94R *EISA v. Commission* [1994] II ECR 703.

n. 84. In *ProfilARBED*, on appeal Case T–150/95 *The British Iron and Steel Producers' Association v. Commission*, the Commission held that environmental aid for new plant also fell within Art. 3: XXIVth Report or Competition Policy (1994), Annex II.E, p. 504.

n. 85. For the Commission's interpretation of Art. 4, see *Aid for restructuring the Italian steel industry*, XXIVth Report on Competition Policy (1994), Annex II.E, pp. 503–4.

CHAPTER 18

STATE AIDS

1. INTRODUCTION

Generally. The EEA Agreement, which entered into force on 1 January 1994, contains in Article 61 analogous provisions concerning State aids to those set out in Article 92 of the EC Treaty. The Commission is now required to take account of the effect of aid granted in EC Member States on undertakings in the EFTA States whereas the EFTA Surveillance Authority, which applies the EEA State aid rules to EFTA States that are members of the EEA (*i.e.* Iceland, Liechtenstein and Norway), similarly takes account of the effect of aid granted in those countries on undertakings in EC Member States: Article 62(1) of the EEA Agreement. Article 109 and Protocol 27 to the EEA Agreement contain provisions concerning co-operation between the EFTA Surveillance Authority and the Commission. *Encyclopedia of European Union Law (Constitutional Texts)*, Vol. 2. See also XXIVth Report on Competition Policy (1994), points 339 and 399; EFTA Surveillance Authority, Annual Report '94, point 4.7.2.2. There is also a Joint Declaration on aid granted through the EC Structural Funds or other financial instruments, annexed to the EEA Agreement: *Encyclopedia of European Union Law*, Vol. 2, para. 30.2430. **18–001**

In 1993 and 1994, a total of 985 aid proposals were notified to the Commission (excluding aid to agriculture, fisheries, transport and coal) and in 72 cases the Commission initiated the contentious procedure under Article 93(2) of the EC Treaty. The Commission adopted 9 final negative decisions and registered 153 cases of un-notified aid proposals: XXIIIrd Report on Competition Policy (1993), Annex III(e); XXIVth Report (1994), Annex IV.D. In 1995 the Commission registered 680 notifications and 113 cases of unnotified aid. In 57 cases it opened the procedure under Article 93(2) of the EC Treaty or Article 6(4) of Decision 3855/91/ECSC; it took 22 positive final decisions, nine negative final decisions and five conditional final decisions: see XXVth Report on Competition Policy (1995), points 148 to 156 and point 219. The EFTA Surveillance

Authority has decided on 54 notified aid cases in 1994 and 1995: ESA Annual Report '95, point 4.7.4.1.

The Competition Commissioner has stated that he expects about 2,000 Cases to be notified in 1996 (more than half of which will involve subsidies in eastern Germany). The Commission is working on a draft proposal for new and more systematic procedures for the handling of State aid cases, similar to those used to deal with mergers: *Financial Times*, 5 July 1996.

n. 1. Art. 92(3) was amended by the TEU: see § 18–016, *infra*. For commentary see also Hancher, Ottervanger and Slot, *EC State Aids*, (Chancery Law Publishing, 1993); and Harden (ed.), *State Aid: Community law and Policy* (Cologne: Bundesanzeiger, 1993).

2. THE CONCEPT OF AN AID

18–003 **Wide concept of aid**

n. 10. See also Case C–387/92 *Banco Exterior de España* [1994] I ECR 877 [1994] 3 CMLR 473 and Case C–39/94 *SFEI and Others v. La Poste and others* [1996] All ER (EC) 685.

18–004 **An advantage.** See also Cases C–72 & 73/91 *Sloman Neptun* [1993] I ECR 887 [1995] 2 CMLR 97; Advocate General Jacobs in Cases C–278/92, etc., *Spain v. Commission* [1994] I ECR 4103, 4113 and Case T–471/93 *Tiercé Ladbroke v. Commission* [1995] II ECR 2537, on appeal Case C–353/95P. In Case C–39/94 *SFEI v. La Poste, supra*, the Court of Justice held that the provision of logistical and commercial assistance by a public undertaking to its subsidiaries, which are governed by private law and carried on an activity open to free competition, was capable of constituting aid if the remuneration received in return was less than that which would have been demanded under normal conditions.

n. 19. See, *e.g.* the Commission's decision in *Dutch gas tariffs* in XXIIIrd Report on Competition Policy (1993), points 388 and 533.

18–007 **The application of the market economy investor principle to public undertakings.** In Cases C–278/92, etc., *Spain v. Commission, supra*, concerning a capital injection made by the Spanish Government to three loss-making public companies in the textile and footwear sectors, the Spanish Government justified the payments on the grounds that the cost of rescuing the companies was preferable to the high costs of liquidation which would entail the payment of redundancy and employment benefits and the restructuring of the industrial infrastructure. The Commission considered that the payments involved incompatible State aid according to the market economy investor principle because the capital contributions exceeded the State's debt liabilities in these limited companies. The Court of Justice ruled that a distinction must be drawn between the obligations which the State assumes as the owner of the share capital of a company and its obligation as a public authority. The private liability of the State was limited to the liquidation value of their assets. The expenditure arising in relation to, *e.g.* unemployment must not be taken into consideration for the purpose of applying the market economy investor principle. See also Case C–42/93 *Spain v. Commission* [1994] I ECR 4175 [1995] 2 CMLR 702; XXIVth Report on Competition Policy (1994), point 344; XXVth Report (1995), point 159. See also the Opinion of Advocate General Jacobs (at paras. 61–62) in Case C–39/94 *SFEI v. La Poste, supra.*

For a summary of the principles concerning State aid applied to the privatisation of State-owned companies, see XXIIIrd Report on Competition Policy (1993), points 402 *et seq.*

n. 26. In Case C–325/91 *France v. Commission* [1993] I ECR 3283, the ECJ annulled the Commission Communication as imposing a reporting obligation that went beyond Art. 5 of Directive 80/723. Following that judgment, the Commission re-issued the Communication with the offending points 45 to 53 omitted: OJ 1993 C307/03 (and repr. in XXIIIrd Report on Competition Policy (1993), pp. 438–449). See further § 18–008, *infra.*

18–008 **Directive 80/723.** The obligation to provide annual information laid down by the Commission in its Communication was held *ultra vires* by the Court of Justice in Case C–325/91 *France v. Commission* [1993] I ECR 3283. The Communication was re-issued by the Commission with points 45–53 omitted, and Directive 80/723 was amended by Directive 93/84 inserting a new Article 5a that requires Member States to supply financial information for public undertakings in the manufacturing sector: Appendix 15, *post.*

18–009 **By a Member State or through State resources.** A measure does not need to involve a transfer of State resources to constitute a State aid. In Case C–387/92 *Banco Exterior de España, supra*, the Court of Justice held that the grant of a tax exemption was a State aid within the meaning of Article 92 since it mitigated the charges normally included in the budgets of the taxpayers to whom it was granted. See also the Commission's decision on *Tax aid for investment (Basque country)*, OJ 1993 L134/25.

The proceeds of a levy are considered "State resources": XXIIIrd Report on Competition Policy (1993), point 391.

n. 35. See also Cases C–72 & 73/91 *Sloman Neptun, supra.*

18–010 **Favouring certain undertakings.** See also Case C–56/93 *Belgium v. Commission* [1996] I ECR 723, where the Court of Justice upheld a

Commission decision that a revised version of the gas tariff which had been condemned as a State aid in CdF Chimie AZF v. Commission was justified for commercial reasons and did not favour Dutch ammonia producers.

An aid that is restricted to entities operating exclusively in the State or region concerned may infringe the right of establishment in Article 52 and this discriminatory nature of the aid will prevent it being regarded as a general measure: see *Tax aid for investment (Basque country), supra*. See also XXIIIrd Report on Competition Policy (1993), point 390; XXIVth Report (1994), point 347. For aid to the postal sector see XXVth Report on Competition Policy (1995), point 198.

18–011 **Examples of State aids.** On export aids, see XXIIIrd Report on Competition Policy (1993), points 427–429; XXVth Report (1995), points 208–210. The Commission has opened a number of Article 93(2) procedures on aid to undertakings for investment on markets outside the EEA.

Further examples of State aid are:

(i) loan guarantees, *e.g. EFIM*, OJ 1993 C267/11, and see XXIVth Report on Competition Policy (1994), point 346 and Annex II, page 519 ("Prodi law");
(ii) sales of land at a preferential price by public authorities, *e.g. Fresenius*, OJ 1994 C21/04; *Kimberley-Clark*, OJ 1995 C283/2; and see XXIIIrd Report on Competition Policy (1993), point 393; XXIVth Report, point 345; XXVth Report, points 157–158.
(iii) environmental and infrastructure measures for the benefit of a particular undertaking, *e.g. Fritz Egger Spanplattenindustrie* OJ 1994 C–369/6; *Kimberley-Clark, supra*. See also Case C–225/91 *Matra v. Commission* [1993] I ECR 3203 at para. 29.

18–012 **The effect on competition.** See further Case C–42/93 *Spain v. Commission* [1994] I ECR 4175 [1995] 2 CMLR 702.

18–013 **Aid to small and medium-sized companies.** In *Matra v. Commission, supra*, at para. 36, the Court of Justice stated that the assessment of the compatibility of a State aid is concerned not so much with the amount of the aid but with its effect on inter-State trade.

In March 1996, the Commission issued a separate Notice setting out a *de minimis* rule on State aid: OJ 1996 C68/9. This raised from 50,000 ECU to 100,000 ECU the ceiling for aid to SMEs (excluding for export aid). Subsequently, the Commission published fully revised Guidelines on State aid for SMEs that replace the Guidelines of 1992: OJ 1996 C213/4. The definition of an SME has been amended by raising the various financial ceilings; it now means an enterprise that

(i) has fewer than 250 employees;
(ii) has either an annual turnover not exceeding 40 million ECU or a balance sheet total not exceeding 27 million ECU; and
(iii) satisfies "the criterion of independence" (which is similarly defined as before): Guidelines, point 3.2.

The effect on inter-State trade. In Cases T–447/93, etc., *AITEC and Others v. Commission* [1995] II ECR 1971, the Court of First Instance annulled a Commission decision approving aid granted to a Greek cement producer where the Commission had failed to examine the effect that the aid was likely to have on inter-state trade in the future. It was not sufficient to confine the examination to the time when the aid was granted. See also Advocate General Jacobs in Cases C–278/92; etc., *Spain v. Commission* [1994] I ECR 4103, 4114–4115. **18–014**

n. 76. A proposal for a Council Directive under Article 113 of the EC Treaty to harmonise the conditions of medium and long-term export credit insurance was put to the Council in July 1994: see XXIVth Report on Competition Policy (1994), point 390; see also XXIIIrd Report (1993), points 427–429.

3. AIDS THAT ARE COMPATIBLE WITH THE COMMON MARKET

Article 92(2). The Commission considers that the ban on discrimination in Article 92(2)(a) refers to the geographical origin of the supplier of the product concerned and not to measures distinguishing between that product and competing products: XXIVth Report on Competition Policy (1994), point 354. **18–015**

4. AIDS THAT MAY BE COMPATIBLE WITH THE COMMON MARKET

Generally. Article 92(3) was amended by the Treaty on European Union to add another category of aid which may be authorised by the Commission: **18–016**

(d) aid to promote culture and heritage conservation where such aid does not affect trading conditions and competition in the Community to an extent that is contrary to the common interest.

The previous Article 92(3)(d) is now Article 92(3)(*e*).

Although no corresponding amendment was made to the EEA Agreement, the EFTA Surveillance Authority adopts an equivalent approach to the assessment of aid schemes: see *Aid for audio-visual productions*, ESA Annual Report '95, point 4.7.4.2.

In Case T–49/93 *SIDE v. Commission* [1995] II ECR 2501, the Court of First Instance annulled a Commission decision approving aid for the export of French-language books, *inter alia* for cultural reasons under Article 92(3)(*c*), without the Commission having opened the procedure under Article 93(2). (The Commission's decision was taken prior to the entry into force of the new sub-paragraph (3)(*d*) to Article 92.)

18–017 **The exercise of the Commission's discretion.** The EFTA Surveillance Authority issued comprehensive State Aid Guidelines on the application and interpretation of the State aid provisions of the EEA Agreement: OJ 1994 L231/1. These Guidelines seek to codify the Commission's various guidelines and notices in a single document and also take account of decisions of the Court of Justice; the Guidelines have been amended periodically to reflect new developments. See ESA Annual Report '94, point 4.7.2.1; ESA Annual Report '95, *ibid*; and OJ 1996 L124/41.

18–019 **Aid for important projects or to remedy a serious disturbance: Article 92(3)(b).** See Cases T–447/93, etc., *AITEC and others v. Commission*, para. 18–014, *supra*.

18–021 **Development of certain economic areas.** For the development of the Commission's approach, see XXIVth Report on Competition Policy (1994), point 362.

18–022 **Development of certain economic activities.** In Case T–459/93 *Siemens v. Commission* [1995] II ECR 1675, the Court of First Instance found that the operation in question did not involve any technical or structural change or the promotion of Siemens' development otherwise than in an exclusively commercial manner. The Court also confirmed that operating aid (*i.e.*, for day to day management) as opposed to investment aid cannot in any circumstances be considered compatible with the common market pursuant to Article 92(3)(*c*) if its very nature is such as that it may affect trading conditions to an extent contrary to the general interest.

n. 9. See also Case C–42/93 *Spain v. Commission* [1994] I ECR 4175, concerning the conditions for exemption pursuant to Art. 92(3)(*c*).

18–023 **The tailpiece to Article 92(3)(*c*): not contrary to the common interest.** In Cases C–42/93 *Spain v. Commission, supra*, and C–278/92, etc., *Spain v. Commission* [1994] I ECR 4103, the Court of Justice restated the principle that aid to undertakings in difficulty must be bound to a restructuring programme in order for the aid to be compatible with the common market.

18–024 **The Commission's policy on sectoral and other non-regional aids.** The Commission takes a generally negative attitude to sectoral aid: XXIVth Report on Competition Policy (1994), point 363.

See the Community guidelines on State aid for rescuing and restructuring firms in difficulty, OJ 1994 C368/12 (repr. in XXIVth Report on Competition Policy, Annex II, pages 474–482). The guidelines codify existing practice on aid to ailing firms. They distinguish between rescue and restructuring aid. In order to be approved, rescue aid should in principle be a limited "holding" operation and must:

(1) consist of loan guarantees or loans at normal commercial rates of interest;
(2) be restricted to the amount needed to keep the undertaking in business and be paid only for the time needed (generally not exceeding 6 months) to devise a feasible recovery plan;
(3) be warranted on the grounds of serious social difficulties and have no undue adverse effects in other Member States.

Restructuring aid must:

(1) be linked to a detailed restructuring plan which will make it possible to restore the long-term viability of the undertaking;
(2) keep adverse effects on competitors to a minimum (*i.e.* in a situation of overcapacity, the restructuring must involve an irreversible reduction in capacity);
(3) be limited in amount and intensity to the strict minimum that is necessary;
(4) be conditional on the aided undertaking fully implementing the restructuring plan; and
(5) enable the Commission to monitor implementation of the restructuring plan.

For the application of these guidelines, see XXVth Report on Competition Policy (1995), points 211–214. The Commission has indicated that the restructuring aid should normally be a one-off operation (at point 213). The ESA adopted equivalent guidelines as Chapter 16 of its State Aid Guidelines: OJ 1994 L383/1.

In Case C–313/90 *CIRFS and others v. Commission* [1993] I ECR 1125, the Court of Justice held that the Commission's aid frameworks, where they have been recommended to the Member States and accepted by them under Article 93(1), were legally binding. The Commission's decision in that case was annulled: it was held that the Commission could not alter a measure of general scope by an individual decision.

For the Commission's approach to aid in the banking sector, see *Crédit Lyonnais*, OJ 1995 L308/92 and XXVth Report on Competition Policy (1995), point 197. The decision has been challenged on appeal: Cases T–31 & 32/96 *Credit Lyonnais v. Commission*, not yet decided.

For the Commission's approach to aid measures to promote employment, see the employment aid guidelines, OJ 1995 C–334/4. The guidelines confirm the generally positive approach to State aid for job creation, in particular aid granted to SMEs or firms located in regions eligible for regional aid, provided that the aid leads to a net increase in the number of jobs in the firm concerned. On the other hand, the guidelines confirm the Commission's unfavourable view of aid to maintain existing jobs on the grounds that this constitutes operating aid. Similarly, the Commission will look unfavourably at job creation measures available only to sectors that are sensitive, suffer from overcapacity or are in a crisis. See XXVth Report on Competition Policy (1995), points 202–204. See also the Commission Communication on State aid aimed at reducing labour costs: Press Release IP(96) 528 of 19 June 1996.

For the Commission's approach to the postal sector and the audiovisual sector, see the XXVth Report on Competition Policy (1995) at points 198 and 199–200 respectively.

n. 19. The Commission amended the research and development guidelines to take account, *inter alia*, of the WTO Subsidies Code: XXVth Report on Competition Policy (1995), point 201. The revised framework also provides guidance as to when public financing of R & D conducted by higher education or non-profit making public research bodies falls within the scope of Art. 92(1).

n. 20. New Community guidelines on State aid for environmental protection were issued with effect from 1 January 1994: OJ 1994 C72/3. See XXIIIrd Report on Competition Policy (1993), point 384 (and text repr. in XXIVth Report, Annex II, pp. 483–489) and XXVth Report at point 205 where the Commission explains the need to strike a balance between the "polluter pays" principle and environmental policy considerations.

n. 21. The code on aid to the synthetic fibres industry was repeatedly extended until 31 March 1996 and then replaced with a new code that is valid for 3 years: OJ 1996 C94/11. See also XXVth Report on Competition Policy (1995), point 172. For the equivalent ESA guidelines, see OJ 1996 L140/54.

n. 22. See XXIVth Report on Competition Policy (1994), point 367 for application of the motor vehicle framework to aid for production of components. In Case C–135/93 *Spain v. Commission* [1995] I ECR 1651, the ECJ ruled that the framework on state aid for the motor vehicle industry ceased to apply on 1 January 1995. As a result the Commission decided to extend the framework retroactively from 1 January 1995, see further XXVth Report at points 166–171.

18–025 **Categories of aid specified by the Council.** In Case C–400/92 *Germany v. Commission*, [1994] I ECR 4701 [1995] 2 CMLR 461, the Court of Justice held that since Directive 90/684, concerning aid to the shipbuilding sector, authorises aid which would otherwise be incompatible with the common market, an aid measure which did not comply with the provisions of the Directive is automatically incompatible with the common market without further investigation.

n. 27. Directive 90/684 was extended to, at the latest, 1 October 1996 pending the expected entry into force of Council Regulation 3094/95 implementing an OECD agreement with respect to normal competitive conditions in commercial shipbuilding and ship repair: see XXVth Report on Competition Policy (1995), point 163. The delay of the entry into force of Regulation 3094/95 was due to delays by other parties in ratifying the OECD Agreement.

18–026 **Council authorisation in exceptional circumstances.** In Case C–122/94 *Commission v. Council* [1996] I ECR 881, the Court of Justice upheld two Council decisions adopted under the third sub-paragraph of Article 93(2) granting special aid for the distillation of certain wines in Italy and France. The Court of Justice held that the Council, in deciding what constitutes exceptional circumstances, is called upon to carry out an assessment of a complex economic situation and that on the facts the Council had not committed a manifest error of assessment.

5. SUPERVISION UNDER ARTICLE 93

(a) *Review of existing aids, notification of new aids and their review*

18–027 **Review of the existing aid systems.** In Case C–44/93 *Namur-les Assurances du Crédit v. OND* [1994] I ECR 3829, the Court of Justice held that the question of whether aid is an existing, a new aid or an alteration of existing aid is to be determined by reference to the legislative or other provisions providing for it and not by its scale or amount. For an example of a pre-Accession aid being an existing aid, see Case C–387/92 *Banco Exterior de España* [1994] I ECR 877 [1994] 3 CMLR 473.

Existing aid may be implemented as long as the Commission has not found it to be incompatible with the common market: see Case C–47/91 *Italy v. Commission* [1994] I ECR 4635 at para. 25. In that case, the Court of Justice confirmed that once a general aid scheme had been approved, it was unnecessary for individual implementing measures to be notified and examined by the Commission unless the Commission has issued a particular reservation in the approval of the general aid scheme. The aid in question must first be assessed according to the decision and not directly in relation to the Treaty. If the Commission has doubts as to the conformity of an individual aid with the general aid scheme, it can require the Member State concerned to provide the necessary information. If the Member State fails to provide the relevant information, the Commission can take an interim decision suspending the aid. For an example of an individual aid under an approved general scheme of aid that required notification, see Cases T–447/93, etc., *AITEC and others v. Commission* [1995] II ECR 1971 at paras. 124 to 132.

The Court of First Instance has applied to State aid decisions the principles laid down by the Court of Justice in Case C–137/92P *Commission v. BASF and others* [1994] I ECR 2555 on the rules concerning the adoption procedure for Commission competition decisions: para. 12–043, *supra*. In Case T–435/93 *ASPEC and others v. Commission* [1995] II ECR 1281 and Case T–442/93 *AAC and others v. Commission* [1995] II ECR 1329, the Court of First Instance held that where the Commission's decision involves a thorough examination of complex factual and legal questions, it cannot be regarded as a measure of management or administration which can be taken under the habilitation procedure. Both those cases concerned the same decision to approve aid by the Italian Government for the establishment of an agri-foods complex and the Court concluded that an examination of whether a particular measure fell within a previously approved general aid scheme could not be regarded as a measure of management or administration. The Commission's decision was annulled since it violated the principle of collegiality: there were significant differences between the draft letter considered by the Commission and the letter signed by the Commissioner for Agriculture and Rural Questions.

n. 33. See now the new code on synthetic fibres, § 18–024, n. 21, *supra*.

18–028 **Pre-notification of new aids or of alteration to existing aid.** The Commission has adopted a system of standardised notification and annual reports. See XXIIIrd Report on Competition Policy (1993), point 385 and the Letter from the Commission to Member States, SG(94) D/2484 of 22 February 1994, *ibid.* Annex II, pp. 418–419.

18–029 **Notification of compatible aids**

n. 41. See now Art. 5a to Directive 80/723 as inserted by Directive 93/84, Appendix 15, *post*; and § 18–008, *supra*.

18–030 **Time limit for review of new aids and alteration to existing aids**

n. 45. See also Cases C–278/92, etc., *Spain v. Commission* [1994] I ECR 4103 §§ 14–15.

18–031 **Preliminary examination of compatibility.** In Case C–198/91 *Cook v. Commission* [1993] I ECR 2487 [1993] 3 CMLR 206 and Case C–225/91 *Matra v. Commission* [1993] I ECR 3203, the Court of Justice confirmed the circumstances in which the Commission is obliged to initiate proceedings under Article 93(2) in order to allow interested third parties to comment on aid proposals. The Court stated that the procedure is essential whenever the Commission has doubts as to whether an aid is compatible with the common market. In *Cook* the Court held that the figures and statistics available to the Commission were not sufficient to enable the Commission to make a proper assessment; a complex analysis after investigation under the Article 93(2) procedure was required. See also Case T–49/93 *SIDE v. Commission* [1995] II ECR 2501, where the Court of First Instance stated (at para. 58) that the Commission may restrict itself to a preliminary examination under Article 93(3) when it is convinced that the aid is compatible with the Treaty.

In Case T–95/94 *Sytraval and Brink's France v. Commission* [1995] II ECR 2651, the Court of First Instance held (at para. 78) that the initial process after receiving a complaint may in certain circumstances require an exchange of views with the complainant since, in order to justify to the requisite legal standard its assessment of the nature of the measure characterised by the complainant as State aid, the Commission needs to ascertain the views of the complainant with respect to the information gathered during the inquiry. The decision is on appeal, Case C–367/95P. See also *SIDE v. Commission, supra*, at para. 71.

(b) *The contentious procedure under Article 93(2)*

Imposition of conditions. In *TWD Textilwerke Deggendorf (No. 2)*, OJ 1991 L215/16, and *(No. 3)*, OJ 1992 L183/36, the Commission approved grants and loans by the German Government but required suspension of payment of those aids until recovery of the aid previously paid to the same company that had been held unlawful in *Textilwerke Deggendorf (No. 1)*, OJ 1986 L300/34. The Court of First Instance upheld that condition in Cases T–244 & 486/93 *TWD v. Commission* [1995] II ECR 2265 [1996] 1 CMLR 332, on appeal Case C–355/95P. **18–036A**

Failure to comply with an Article 93(2) decision. In Case C–188/92 *TWD Textilwerke Deggendorf* [1994] I ECR 833 [1995] 2 CMLR 145, the Court of Justice held, on an Article 177 reference, that a national court is bound by a decision under Article 93(2) where the recipient of the aid had failed to bring an action for annulment within the time limit laid down by Article 173 of the Treaty. See also *Lener Ignace SA v. Beauvois* [1994] 2 CMLR 419 (French Cour de Cass). (Lawyer could not be liable in negligence for failing to make timely application to French State for aid which had been declared incompatible with Article 92, although the French government failed to comply with the Commission decision and made payments to other applicants.) **18–037**

Unnotified aid not unlawful **18–038**

n. 79. See also Case T–49/93 *SIDE v. Commission, supra.*

Interim measures against unnotified or prematurely implemented aid. In Case C–47/91 *Italy v. Commission* [1994] I ECR 4635, the Court of Justice **18–039**

held that if the Commission has doubts as to whether an individual aid falls within a previously authorised general aid scheme and is therefore uncertain whether such aid should be classified as new or existing aid, it cannot order suspension but must first require the Member State to supply all information necessary to examine the compatibility of the aid with the previous authorisation. If the Member State fails to supply the requested information, the Commission can then seek suspension. See also Cases C–324 & 342/90 *Germany and Pleuger Worthington v. Commission* [1994] I ECR 1173 [1994] 3 CMLR 521, paras. 26 to 28; *SIDE v. Commission, supra*, at paras. 78 to 87.

(c) *Repayment of illegally granted aid*

18–041 **Generally.** See the Commission Communication to Member States, OJ 1995 C156/5, in which the Commission gave notice of its intention to take, in appropriate cases, a provisional decision ordering a Member State to recover any aid granted in breach of Article 93(3). The Commission considers that in some cases a decision requiring suspension of aid granted in breach of Article 93(3) will not go far enough.

n. 88. See *SIDE v. Commission, supra.* The CFI held that there is no obligation upon the Commission to order suspension and repayment of an unnotified aid. Where the Commission does not exercise its power to recover unnotified aid, the last sentence of Art. 93(3) is not deprived of its effectiveness due to the direct effect of the latter provision.

18–042 **The duty of a Member State to seek repayment.** In Case C–348/93 and Case C–350/93 *Commission v. Italy* [1995] I ECR 673 and 699, the Court of Justice held that repayment of an unlawful aid may take the form of repayment to a public body responsible for managing state funds, the principal objective of repayment being that the recipient forfeits the advantage which the aid had provided.

n. 90. See also Case C–349/93 *Commission v. Italy* [1995] I ECR 343.

n. 93. See also Cases C–278/92, etc., *Spain v. Commission, supra.*

n. 99. See also Case C–349/93 *Commission v. Italy, supra.*

n. 4. See also Cases C–278/92, etc., *Spain v. Commission* [1994] I ECR 4103 § 75; *Siemens v. Commission*, § 18–042A *infra.*

18–042A **Interest and tax.** In Case T–459/93 *Siemens v. Commission* [1995] II ECR 1675, the Court of First Instance stated that the Commission is not obliged when ordering recovery of the state aid to determine the incidence of tax on the amount of aid to be recovered since that calculation falls to be made under national law. The Court held that this does not preclude the national authorities from deducting certain sums where appropriate from the gross sum to be recovered (such as tax paid) pursuant to internal rules, provided that the application of such rules does not render recovery impossible in practice or discriminate in relation to similar cases governed by national law. The Court rejected the applicant's challenge to the payment of interest on the State aid, stating that the obligation to pay interest meets the requirement of eliminating a financial advantage which is ancillary to the amount of illegal aid initially granted and therefore justified under Article 93(2). It is for the Commission to determine the date from which the interest is to run. Since the payment of interest is intended to eliminate the advantage of an interest-free loan the date for payment of interest may not start to run before the date on which the recipient of the aid had actually received it.

In its Communication on interest rates to apply when recovering illegal aid or illegal and incompatible aid, Press Release IP (95) 87 of 1 February 1995, the Commission confirmed that the commercial rate of interest should be applied and stated that, in any decisions ordering the recovery of unlawfully granted aid, it will apply the reference rate used in the calculation of the net grant equivalent of regional aid measures as the basis for the commercial rate.

The position of the recipient of the aid. In *Siemens v. Commission, supra*, the Court of First Instance held that Community law does not prevent national law from having regard to the protection of legitimate expectation in connection with the recovery of State aid, provided that the conditions laid down are the same as those for the recovery of purely national financial benefits and that the interests of the Community are fully taken into account. **18–043**

n. 5. See also Cases T–244 & 486/93 *TWD Textilwerke Deggendorf v. Commission* [1995] II ECR 2265 [1996] 1 CMLR 332 (§ 69).

6. ARTICLE 94

Article 94. The text of Article 94 was amended by the Treaty on European Union, as follows: **18–044**

> "The Council, acting by a qualified majority on a proposal from the Commission and after consulting the European Parliament, may make any appropriate regulations for the application of Articles 92 and 93 and may in particular determine the conditions in which Article 93(3) shall apply and the categories of aid exempted from this procedure."

7. JUDICIAL REMEDIES

(a) *National courts*

18–044A **Commission's Notice on Co-operation between national courts and the Commission in the State aid field.** On 31 October 1995 the Commission adopted a Notice on Co-operation between national courts and the Commission in the State aid field: Appendix 16, *post*. The Notice is similar in nature to the Commission Notice on Co-operation between national courts and the Commission in applying Articles 85 and 86 of the EC Treaty: see para. 10–017 and Appendix 26 to the main work. The Notice sets out the respective powers and functions of the Commission and national courts and provides a procedure for national courts to ask the Commission for information of a procedural nature in a particular case and for assistance in the application of Articles 92(1) and 93(3) of the EC Treaty. The answers given by the Commission will not deal with the substance of the individual case or the compatibility of the measure with the common market. A summary of the answers given by the Commission pursuant to the Notice will be published in the annual Reports on Competition Policy.

In Case C–39/94 *SFEI and others v. La Poste and others* [1996] All ER (EC) 685, the Court of Justice, referring to the Commission's Notice, stated that the Commission is under an obligation to respond as quickly as possible to requests from national courts.

18–046 **New aids and alterations to existing aids.** See generally the Commission Notice on Co-operation between national courts and the Commission: Appendix 16, *post*. In Case C–39/94 *SFEI v. La Poste, supra*, the Court of Justice held that the initiation of a procedure by the Commission under either Article 93(3) or 93(2) does not relieve national courts of their duty to safeguard rights of individuals under Article 93(3). The Court stated that a finding that an aid had been granted in breach of the last sentence of Article 93(3) must in principle lead to its repayment in accordance with the procedural rules of domestic law, subject to exceptional circumstances.

18–046A **Damages.** In Cases C–46 & 48/93 *Brasserie du Pêcheur v. Germany* and *Factortame III* [1996] I ECR 1029 [1996] 1 CMLR 889 [1996] All ER (EC) 301 and Case C–5/94 *R. v. Ministry of Agriculture Fisheries and Food ex p. Hedley Lomas (Ireland) Ltd* [1996] 2 CMLR 391 [1996] All ER (EC) 493, the Court of Justice considered the nature and extent of State liability to make reparation to individuals for breach of the EC Treaty. Those cases involved breaches of Articles 30 and 52 of the EC Treaty, both of which have direct effect. Where a Member State acts in a field where it has a wide discretion, Community law confers a right to reparation where:

(a) the rule of law infringed must be intended to confer rights on individuals;
(b) the breach must be sufficiently serious; and
(c) there must be a direct causal link between the breach of the obligation resting on the State and the damage sustained by the injured parties.

See also Case C–392/93 *R. v. H.M. Treasury, ex p. British Telecommunications* [1996] All ER (EC) 411 where the Court of Justice applied the same test to the incorrect implementation of a Directive and the Opinion of Advocate General Tesauro of 28 November 1995 in Cases C–178/94 etc., *Dillenhofer v. Germany*, not yet decided. See further para. 10–039, *supra*.

In Case C–39/94 *SFEI v. La Poste*, *supra*, the Court of Justice stated (at paras. 72 to 75) that Community law did not itself create a cause of action against a recipient of an aid who had failed to verify that the aid received was duly notified to the Commission; but that did not prejudice the possible application of domestic law to the grant of aid in breach of Article 93(3) where under domestic law the acceptance by an economic operator of unlawful assistance occasioning damage to other economic operators creates a cause of action.

18–047 **Enforcement of Commission decisions.** In Case C–188/92 *TWD Textilwerke Deggendorf* [1994] I ECR 833 [1995] 2 CMLR 145, the Court of Justice held that a national court is bound by a decision under Article 93(2) when the recipient of the aid had failed to bring an action for annulment within the time laid down by the Article 173 of the Treaty.

n. 28. See also *The State (Belgium) v. Tubemeuse* [1994] 3 CMLR 93 (Belg. Cour de Cass.): state injection of capital in the form of shareholding in a company, which was held by the Commission to be a prohibited state aid, is tainted by illegality and can be reclaimed as a debt when the company went into liquidation.

(b) *The Court of Justice*

(i) *Reviewable acts*

18–048 **Generally.** On 1 August 1993, the Court of First Instance was vested with jurisdiction to hear appeals by private parties against Commission decisions in the field of State aid: Council Decision 93/350, OJ 1993 L144/21. Actions by Member States are still brought before the Court of Justice. Where the same measure is being challenged before the Court of First Instance and the Court of Justice, the Court of First Instance may decline jurisdiction or the Court of Justice may stay the proceedings before it.

In Case C–135/93 *Spain v. Commission* [1995] I ECR 1651, the Court of Justice held that a decision to extend the validity of the Community framework for State aid to the motor vehicle industry produced legal effects and was therefore reviewable under Article 173.

In Case T–477/93 *AITEC v. Commission (No. 2)*, judgment of 22 May 1996, the Court of First Instance held that a private party could not judicially review under either Article 173 or Article 175 a letter from the Commission which did not accede to a prior request by a complainant that the Commission should bring proceedings under the second subparagraph of Article 93(2) in respect of non-compliance by Greece with a State aid decision.

(ii) *The grounds of annulment*

18–050 **Procedural irregularities.** In Case T–435/93 *ASPEC and others v. Commission* [1995] II ECR 1281 and Case T–442/93 *AAC and others v. Commission* [1995] II ECR 1329, the Court of First Instance annulled a Commission decision authorising the grant of aid since it breached the principle of collegiality: see para. 18–027, *supra.*

n. 39. See also Case C–198/91 *Cook v. Commission* [1993] I ECR 2487; [1993] 3 CMLR 206 (decision annulled: when a complex market analysis is required, the contentious procedure under Art. 93(2) should be used); similarly Case T–49/93 *SIDE v. Commission* [1995] II ECR 2501. See Case C–225/91 *Matra v. Commission* [1993] I ECR 3203 on the inter-relationship between Articles 85–86 and Article 92 (see further § 18–061 *infra*).

n. 42. See also Case T–459/93 *Siemens v. Commission* [1995] II ECR 1675 §§ 38–41.

18–051 **Lack of reasoning.** In Cases C–324 & 342/90 *Germany and Pleuger Worthington v. Commission* [1994] I ECR 1173 [1994] 3 CMLR 94, the Court of Justice held that where the Commission could not identify a specific legal act granting the aid, in determining the *de facto* existence of an aid programme the Commission must indicate the legislative, administrative, financial and economic factors which indicate the existence of a separate programme of aid. Further, the Court rejected the Commission's submission that the failure of the German government adequately to fulfil its duty to provide information justified a decision based on the fragmentary information that the Commission had received. The Commission should have exercised its powers to request, by way of interim decision, all relevant information.

In Case T–95/94 *Sytraval and Brink's France v. Commission* [1995] II ECR 2651 on appeal Case C–367/95P, the Court of First Instance annulled a Commission decision which rejected a complaint (51 months after the initial complaint was lodged) on the ground that there was no State aid within the meaning of Article 92. In considering whether the statement of reasons is adequate it was necessary to look not only at its wording but also its context. The Court considered that the Commission could not rely on the alleged paucity of the complainant's evidence in order to justify the inadequacy of the reasons for its decision, particularly in the light of the relative difficulty that complainants face in gathering information. The Commission's obligation to state reasons may in certain circumstances require an exchange of views with the complainant in order to ascertain what view the complainant takes of the information gathered by the Commission in the course of its inquiry. See also para. 18–031, *supra.*

n. 46. See also Case C–364/90 *Italy v. Commission* [1993] I ECR 2097 §§ 44–45; *SIDE v. Commission, supra.*

Review of the exercise of the Commission's discretion. For the limits on the discretion of the Commission in deciding whether or not to open the contentious procedure under Article 93(2), see para. 18–031, *supra.* **18–052**

In Cases C–278/92, etc., *Spain v. Commission* [1994] I ECR 4103, the Court of Justice annulled the Commission's decision on the basis of inconsistent reasoning. The Commission had failed to follow the assessment criteria which it had established for itself in that decision. In Case C–313/90 *CIRFS and others v. Commission* [1993] I ECR 1125, the Commission's decision was annulled for error of law on the basis that a measure of general scope could not be amended by a subsequent individual decision. The principle of equal treatment and legitimate expectation could not justify the repetition of an earlier incorrect interpretation of the measure of general scope.

n. 53. See also Cases T–447/93, etc., *AITEC and others v Commission* [1995] II ECR 1971.

(iii) *Applicants before the Court of Justice*

Actions by the Commission **18–053**

n. 60. See also Case C–47/91 *Italy v. Commission* [1994] I ECR 4635, where the ECJ held that the Commission can seek suspension of an individual aid granted under an approved general aid scheme only if the Commission has concluded that the aid is a new aid which is subject to Art. 93(3) and falls outside the approved scheme.

Actions by private parties. Once the time limit for bringing an action under Article 173 has expired, legal certainty requires that the **18–055**

Commission's decision is treated as definitive. See Case C–188/92 *TWD Textilwerke Deggendorf*, para. 18–037, *supra.*

The Court of First Instance has stated that the judgment in *COFAZ* should not be interpreted to mean that undertakings unable to demonstrate the existence of the circumstances prevailing in that case can never be deemed to be individually concerned within the meaning of Article 173. An undertaking may be in a position to demonstrate that it is individually concerned by other means, by reference to its own distinguishing and specific circumstances. In Case T–435/93 *ASPEC and others v. Commission* and Case T–435/93 *AAC and others v. Commission*, para. 18–027 *supra*, it was held that a competitor was individually concerned by the termination of a procedure under Article 93(2) where the aid authorised by the Commission involved a very substantial increase in production which was likely to have a direct and substantial effect on the existing competitors. See also *AITEC and others v. Commission*, *supra*, where the actions brought by Greek and United Kingdom cement producers were held to be admissible.

A competitor was directly and individually concerned by a decision of the Commission not to open the contentious procedure under Article 93(2) and could being an action for annulment. See Case C–198/91 *Cook v. Commission* [1993} I ECR 2487 [1993] 3 CMLR 206; Case C–225/91 *Matra v. Commission* [1993] I ECR 3203. Similarly, the EFTA Court held that a competitor could challenge a decision that there is no jurisdiction to assess its complaint regarding a State aid: Case E–2/94 *Scottish Salmon Growers Association v. EFTA Surveillance Authority* [1994–95] Rep. EFTA Ct. 59, [1995] 1 CMLR 851. On the other hand, in Case T–398/94 *Scheepvaart v. Commission*, judgment of 5 June 1996, the Court of First Instance held that an action for annulment of a Commission decision approving a general aid scheme was not admissible even where that could have included a refusal by the Commission to open the procedure under Article 93(2). The Court of First Instance distinguished *Cook* and *Matra* as cases concerning individual, not general, aids.

In Case T–585/93 *Greenpeace and others v. Commission* [1995] II ECR 2205, the Court of First Instance held that a challenge by Greenpeace and 16 local inhabitants to the grant of financial assistance under the European Regional Development Fund ("ERDF") by the Commission to Spain for the construction of two power stations on the Canary Islands was inadmissible. Neither the individuals nor Greenpeace were affected by the contested decision in such a way as to differentiate them from all other persons and this conclusion was not altered by the fact that some of the individuals had submitted a complaint to the Commission. No specific procedures were provided for individuals to be associated with the adoption of decisions under the ERDF. Although the Court of First Instance accepted that special circumstances, such as the role played by an association in a procedure which led to the adoption of a decision, might render admissible an action brought by an association whose members were not directly and individually concerned, the correspondence at meetings between Greenpeace and the Commission in the present case was for information only and could not constitute special circumstances. The decision is under appeal: Case C–321/95P.

n. 73. See also Case C–313/90 *CIRFS and others v. Commission* [1993] I ECR 1125, §§ 29–30; *AITEC and others v. Commission, supra; Scottish Salmon Growers Association, supra.*

n. 76 *Cf.* Case T–443/93 *Casillo Grani v. Commission* [1995] II ECR 1375: a competitor which was subsequently declared bankrupt ceased to have an interest in bringing proceedings. In that case the contested aid had not been paid to the intended beneficiary. On the right of a trade association to intervene, see the order in Case T–330/94 *Salt Union v. Commission* [1995] II ECR 2881.

8. THE RELATIONSHIP BETWEEN ARTICLES 92 TO 94 AND OTHER PROVISIONS OF THE EC TREATY

18–061 **Article 85.** In Case C–225/91 *Matra v. Commission* [1993] I ECR 3203, the applicant claimed that, by authorising the grant of State aid to a joint venture before an exemption was granted to that joint venture, the Commission had prejudged the outcome of the procedure under Article 85(3). The Court of Justice dismissed the argument, stating that the Commission was entitled to give a decision on the compatibility of the proposed aid with Article 92 if it was satisfied that the recipient of the aid was not in breach of Articles 85 and 86 of the Treaty. The Commission must maintain consistency between Articles 92 and 93 on the one hand and Articles 85 and 86 on the other. In that case, the Commission had published a notice under Article 19(3) of Regulation 17 indicating its intention to exempt the joint venture prior to approving the State aid. See further Case T–17/93 *Matra Hachette v. Commission* [1994] II ECR 595 where the Court of First Instance rejected the application to annul the exemption under Article 85(3). If the Commission had, in the light of observations received in response to its Notice, refused an exemption the only consequence would be that the aid would have had to be repaid. See also Case T–49/93 *SIDE v Commission* [1995] II ECR 2501, para. 72.

18–062 **Article 90.** In Case C–387/92 *Banco Exterior de España* [1994] I ECR 877 [1994] 3 CMLR 473, the question arose in a reference for a preliminary ruling whether Article 90 in conjunction with Article 92 precluded the application of national legislation granting tax exemption to public enterprises. The Court of Justice stated that the power of the Commission under Article 93 to keep aid under constant review and supervision also covers aid granted to the undertakings referred to in Article 90(2). It followed that the distinction made in Article 93 between existing and new aid is equally applicable to aid to undertakings covered by Article 90(2). With respect to existing aid which the Commission has not found to be incompatible with the common market, it is therefore unnecessary to examine whether the aid is capable of falling outside the scope of the prohibition in Article 92 by virtue of Article 90(2). See further XXIVth Report on Competition Policy (1994), point 492, where the Commission deduces from that judgment that the procedure under Article 93 prevails over that in Article 90(3) and that a Member State may not invoke Article 90(2) to evade the notification requirements in Article 93(3).

APPENDIX 1

GENERAL PRINCIPLES (EC TREATY)

Article 1

By this Treaty, the High Contracting Parties establish among themselves a European Community.

Article 2

The Community shall have as its task, by establishing a common market and an economic and monetary union and by implementing the common policies or activities referred to in Articles 3 and 3a, to promote throughout the Community a harmonious and balanced development of economic activities, sustainable and non-inflationary growth respecting the environment, a high degree of convergence of economic performance, a high level of employment and of social protection, the raising of the standard of living and quality of life, and economic and social cohesion and solidarity among Member States.

Article 3

For the purposes set out in Article 2, the activities of the Community shall include, as provided in this Treaty and in accordance with the timetable set out therein:

(a) the elimination, as between Member States, of customs duties and of quantitative restrictions on the import and export of goods, and of all other measures having equivalent effect;
(b) a common commercial policy;
(c) an internal market characterised by the abolition, as between Member States, of obstacles to the free movement of goods, persons, services and capital;
(d) measures concerning the entry and movement of persons in the internal market as provided for in Article 100c;
(e) a common policy in the sphere of agriculture and fisheries;
(f) a common policy in the sphere of transport;
(g) a system of ensuring that competition in the internal market is not distorted;
(h) the approximation of the laws of Member States to the extent required for the proper functioning of the common market;
(i) a policy in the social sphere comprising a European Social Fund;
(j) the strengthening of economic and social cohesion;
(k) a policy in the sphere of the environment;

(l) the strengthening of the competitiveness of Community industry;
(m)the promotion of research and technological development;
(n) encouragement for the establishment and development of trans-European networks;
(o) a contribution to the attainment of a high level of health protection;
(p) a contribution to education and training of quality and to the flowering of the cultures of the Member States;
(q) a policy in the sphere of development co-operation;
(r) the association of the overseas countries and territories in order to increase trade and promote jointly economic and social development;
(s) a contribution to the strengthening of consumer protection;
(t) measures in the spheres of energy, civil protection and tourism.

Article 3b

The Community shall act within the limits of the powers conferred upon it by this Treaty and of the objectives assigned to it therein.

In areas which do not fall within its exclusive competence, the Community shall take action, in accordance with the principle of subsidiarity, only if and in so far as the objectives of the proposed action cannot be sufficiently achieved by the Member States and can therefore, by reason of the scale or effects of the proposed action, be better achieved by the Community.

Any action by the Community shall not go beyond what is necessary to achieve the objectives of this Treaty.

Article 4

1. The tasks entrusted to the Community shall be carried out by the following institutions:

a European Parliament,
a Council,
a Commission,
a Court of Justice,
a Court of Auditors.

Each institution shall act within the limits of the powers conferred upon it by this Treaty.

2. The Council and the Commission shall be assisted by an Economic and Social Committee and a Committee of the Regions acting in an advisory capacity.

Article 4a

A European System of Central Banks (hereinafter referred to as "ESCB") and a European Central Bank (hereinafter referred to as "ECB") shall be established in accordance with the procedures laid down in this Treaty; they shall act within the limits of the powers conferred upon them by this Treaty and by the Statute of the ESCB and of the ECB (hereinafter referred to as "Statute of the ESCB") annexed thereto.

Article 4b

A European Investment Bank is hereby established, which shall act within the limits of the powers conferred upon it by this Treaty and the Statute annexed thereto.

Article 5

Member States shall take all appropriate measures, whether general or particular, to ensure fulfilment of the obligations arising out of this Treaty or resulting from action taken by the institutions of the Community. They shall facilitate the achievement of the Community's tasks.

They shall abstain from any measure which could jeopardise the attainment of the objectives of this Treaty.

Article 6

Within the scope of application of this Treaty, and without prejudice to any special provisions contained therein, any discrimination on grounds of nationality shall be prohibited.

The Council, acting in accordance with the procedure referred to in Article 189c, may adopt rules designed to prohibit such discrimination.

Article 7a

The Community shall adopt measures with the aim of progressively establishing the internal market over a period expiring on 31 December 1992, in accordance with the provisions of this Article and of Articles 7b, 7c, 28, 57(2), 59, 70(1), 84, 99, 100a and 100b and without prejudice to the other provisions of this Treaty.

The internal market shall comprise an area without internal frontiers in which the free movement of goods, persons, services and capital is ensured in accordance with the provisions of this Treaty.

Article 7b

The Commission shall report to the Council before 31 December 1988 and again before 31 December 1990 on the progress made towards achieving the internal market within the time limit fixed in Article 7a.

The Council, acting by a qualified majority on a proposal from the Commission, shall determine the guidelines and conditions necessary to ensure balanced progress in all the sectors concerned.

Article 7c

When drawing up its proposals with a view to achieving the objectives set out in Article 7a, the Commission shall take into account the extent of the effort that certain economies showing differences in development will have to sustain during the period of establishment of the internal market and it may propose appropriate provisions.

If these provisions take the form of derogations, they must be of a temporary nature and must cause the least possible disturbance to the functioning of the common market.

APPENDIX 2

REGULATION 1475/95[1]

on the application of Article 85(3) of the Treaty to certain categories of motor vehicle distribution and servicing agreements

THE COMMISSION OF THE EUROPEAN COMMUNITIES

Having regard to the Treaty establishing the European Community.

Having regard to the Council Regulation No. 19/65/EEC of 2 March 1965 on the application of Article 85(3) of the Treaty to certain categories of agreement and concerted practices[2], as last amended by the Act of Accession of Austria, Finland and Sweden, and in particular Article 1 thereof,

Having published a draft of this Regulation[3],

Having consulted the Advisory Committee on Restrictive Practices and Dominant Positions,

Whereas:

(1) Under Regulation No. 19/65/EEC the Commission is empowered to declare by means of a Regulation that Article 85(3) of the Treaty applies to certain categories of agreements falling within Article 85(1) to which only two undertakings are party and by which one party agrees with the other to supply only to that other certain goods for resale within a defined area of the common market. The experience gained in dealing with many motor vehicle distribution and servicing agreements allows a category of agreement to be defined which can generally be regarded as satisfying the conditions laid down in Article 85(3). These are agreements for a definite or an indefinite period, by which the supplying party entrusts to the reselling party the task of promoting the distribution and servicing of certain products of the motor vehicle industry in a defined area and by which the supplier undertakes to supply contract goods for resale only to the dealer, or only to a limited number of undertakings within the distribution network besides the dealer, within the contract territory.

A list of definitions for the purpose of this Regulation is set out in Article 10.

(2) Notwithstanding that the obligations listed in Articles 1, 2 and 3 normally have as their object or effect the prevention, restriction or distortion of competition within the common market and are normally liable to affect trade between Member States, the prohibition in Article 85(1) of the Treaty may nevertheless be declared inapplicable to these agreements by virtue of Article 85(3), albeit only under certain restrictive conditions.

(3) The applicability of Article 85(1) of the Treaty to distribution and servicing agreements in the motor vehicle industry stems in particular from the fact that the restrictions on competition and obligations agreed within the framework of a manufacturer's distribution system, and listed in Articles 1 to 4 of this Regulation, are generally imposed in the same or similar form throughout the common market. The motor vehicle manufacturers cover the whole common market or substantial parts of it by means of a cluster of agreements involving similar restrictions on competition and affect in this way not only distribution and servicing within Member States but also trade between them.

(4) The exclusive and selective distribution clauses can be regarded as indispensable measures of rationalisation in the motor vehicle industry, because motor vehicles are consumer durables which at both regular and irregular intervals require expert maintenance and repair, not always in the same place. Motor vehicle manufacturers co-operate with the selected dealers and repairers in order to provide specialised servicing for the product. On grounds of capacity and efficiency alone, such a form of co-operation cannot be extended to an unlimited number of dealers and repairers. The linking of servicing an distribution must be regarded as more efficient than a separation between a distribution organisation for new vehicles on the one hand and a servicing organisation which would also distribute spare parts on the other, particularly as, before a new vehicle is delivered to the final consumer, the undertaking within the distribution system must give it a technical inspection according to the manufacturer's specification.

(5) However, obligatory recourse to the authorised network is not in all respects indispensable for efficient distribution. It should therefore be provided that the supply of contract goods to resellers may not be prohibited where they:

— belong to the same distribution system (Article 3(10)(a)), or
— purchase spare parts for their own use in effecting repairs or maintenance (Article 3(10)(b)).

Measures taken by a manufacturer or by undertakings within the distribution system with the object of protecting the selective distribution system are compatible with the exemption under this Regulation. This applies in particular to a dealer's obligation to sell vehicles to a final consumer using the services of an intermediary only where that consumer has authorised that intermediary to act as his agent (Article 3(11)).

(6) It should be possible to prevent wholesalers not belonging to the distribution system from reselling parts originating from motor vehicle manufacturers. It may be supposed that the system, beneficial to the consumer, whereby spare parts are readily available across the whole contract range, including those parts with a low turnover, could not be maintained without obligatory recourse to the authorised network.

(7) The ban on dealing in competing products may be exempted on condition that it does not inhibit the dealer from distributing vehicles of other makes in a manner which avoids all confusion between makes (Article 3(3)). The obligation to refrain from selling products of other manufacturers other than in separate sales premises, under separate management, linked to the general obligation to avoid confusion between different makes, guarantees exclusivity of distribution of each make in each place of sale. This last obligation has to be implemented in good faith by the dealer so that the promotion, sale and after-sales service cannot, in any manner, cause confusion in the eyes of the consumer or result in unfair practices on the part of the dealer with regard to suppliers of competing makes. In order to maintain the competitiveness of competing products, the separate management of different sales premises has to be carried out by distinct legal entities. Such an obligation provides an incentive for the dealer to develop sales and servicing of contract goods and thus promote competition in the supply of those products and competing products. These provisions do not prevent the dealer from offering and providing maintenance and repair services for competing makes of motor vehicle in the same workshop, subject to the option of obliging the dealer not to allow third parties to benefit unduly from investments made by the supplier (Article 3(4)).

(8) However, bans on dealing in competing products cannot be regarded in all circumstances as indispensable to efficient distribution. Dealers must be free to obtain from third parties supplies of parts which match the quality of those offered by the manufacturer, and to use and sell them. In this regard, it can be presumed that all parts coming from the same source of product are identical in characteristics and origin; it is for spare-part manufacturers offering parts to dealers to confirm, if need be, that such parts correspond to those supplies to the manufacturer of the vehicle. Moreover, dealers must retain their freedom to

choose parts which are usable in motor vehicles within the contract range and which match or exceed the quality standard. Such a limit on the ban on dealing in competing products takes account of both the importance of vehicle safety and the maintenance of effective competition (Article 3(5) and Article 4(1)(6) and (7)).

(9) The restrictions imposed on the dealer's activities outside the allotted area lead to more intensive distribution and servicing efforts in an easily supervised contract territory, to knowledge of the market based on closer contact with consumers, and to more demand-orientated supply (Article 3(8) and (9)). However, demand for contract goods must remain flexible and should not be limited on a regional basis. Dealers must not be confined to satisfying the demand for contract goods within their contract territories, but must also be able to meet demand from persons and undertakings in other areas of the common market. Advertising by dealers in a medium which is directed at customers outside the contract territory should not be prevented, because is does not run counter to the obligation to promote sales within the contact territory. The acceptable means of advertising do not include direct personal contact with the customer, whether by telephone or other form of telecommunication, doorstep canvassing or by individual letter.

(10) So as to give firms greater legal certainty, certain obligations imposed on the dealer that do not stand in the way of exemption should be specified regarding the observation of minimum distribution and servicing standards (Article 4(1)(1)), regularity of orders (Article 4(1)(2)), the achievement of quantitive sales or stock targets agreed by the parties or determined by an expert third party in the event of disagreement (Article 4(1)(3) to (5)) and the arrangements made for after-sales service (Article 4(1)(6) to (9). Such obligations are directly related to the obligations in Articles 1, 2 and 3, and influence their restrictive effect. They may therefore be exempted, for the same reasons as the latter, where they fall in individual cases under the prohibition contained in Article 85(1) of the Treaty (Article 4(2)).

(11) Pursuant to Regulation No. 19/65/EEC, the conditions which must be satisfied if the declaration of inapplicability is to take effect must be specified.

(12) Under Article 5(1)(1)(a) and (b) it is a condition of exemption that the undertaking should honour the guarantee and provide free servicing, vehicle recall work, and repair and maintenance services necessary for the safe and reliable functioning of the vehicle, irrespective of where in the common market the vehicle was purchased. These provisions are intended to prevent limitation of the consumer's freedom to buy anywhere in the common market.

(13) Article 5(1)(2)(a) is intended to allow the manufacturer to build up a co-ordinated distribution system, but without hindering the relationship of confidence between dealers and sub-dealers. Accordingly, if the supplier reserves the right to approve appointments of sub-dealers by the dealer, he must not be allowed to withhold such approval arbitrarily.

(14) Article 5(1)(2)(b) requires the supplier not to impose on a dealer within the distribution system any requirements, as defined in Article 4(1), which are discriminatory or inequitable.

(15) Article 5(1)(12)(c) is intended to counter the concentration of the dealer's demand on the supplier which might follow from cumulation of discounts. The purpose of this provision is to allow spare-parts suppliers which do not offer as wide a range of goods as the manufacturer to compete on equal terms.

(16) Article 5(1)(2)(d) makes the exemption subject ti the condition that the dealer must be able to purchase for customers in the common market volume-produced passenger cars with the technical features appropriate to their place of residence or to the place where the vehicle is to be registered, in so far as the corresponding model is also supplied by the manufacturer through undertakings within the distribution system in that place (Article 10(10)). This provision obviates the danger that the manufacturer and undertakings within the distribution network might make use of product differentiation as between parts of the common market to partition the market.

(17) Article 5(2) makes the exemption dependent on other minimum conditions which aim to prevent the dealer, owing to the obligations which are imposed on him, from becoming economically over-dependent on the supplier and from abandoning the competitive activity which is nominally open to him because to pursue it would be against the interests of the manufacturer or other undertakings within the distribution network.

(18) Under Article 5(2)(1), the dealer may, for objectively justified reasons, oppose the application of excessive obligations covered by Article 3(3).

(19) Article 5(2)(2) and (3) and Article 5(3) lay down minimum requirements for exemption concerning the duration and termination of the distribution and servicing agreement, because the combined effect of the investments the dealer makes in order to improve the distribution the servicing of contract goods and short-term agreement or one terminable at short notice is greatly to increase the dealer's dependence on the supplier. In order to avoid obstructing the development of flexible and efficient distribution structures, however, the suppliers should be entitled to terminate the agreement where there is a need to reorganise all or a substantial part of the network. To allow rapid settlement of any disputes, provision should be made for reference to an expert third party or arbitrator who will decide in the event of disagreement, without prejudice to the parties' right to bring the matter before a competent court in conformity with the relevant provisions of national law.

(20) Pursuant to Regulation No. 19/65/EEC, the restrictions or provisions which must not be contained in the agreements, if the declaration of inapplicability or Article 85(1) of the Treaty under this Regulation is to take effect, are to be specified (Article 6(1), (1) to (5)). Moreover, practices of the parties which lead to automatic loss of the benefit of exemption when committed systematically and repeatedly shall be defined (Article 6(1)(6) to (12)).

(21) Agreements under which one motor vehicle manufacturer entrusts the distribution of his products to another must be excluded from the block exemption, because of their far-reaching impact on competition (Article 6(1)(1)).

(22) In order to ensure that the parties remain within the limits of the Regulation, any agreements whose object goes beyond the products or services referred to in Article 1 or which stipulate restrictions of competition not exempted by this Regulation should also be excluded from the exemption (Article 6(1)(2) and (3)).

(23) The exemption similarly does not apply where the parties agree between themselves obligations concerning goods covered by this Regulation which would be acceptable in the combination of obligations which is exempted by Commission Regulation (EEC) No. 1983/83[4] or (EEC) No. 1984/83[5], as last amended by the Act of Accession of Austria, Finland and Sweden, regarding the application of Article 85(3) of the Treaty to categories of exclusive distribution agreements and exclusive purchasing agreements respectively, but which go beyond the scope of the obligations exempted by this Regulation (Article 6(1)(4)).

(24) In order to protect dealers' investments and prevent any circumvention by suppliers of the rules governing the termination of agreements, it should be confirmed that the exemption does not apply where the supplier reserves the right to amend unilaterally during the period covered by the contract terms of the exclusive territorial dealership granted to the dealer (Article 6(1)(5)).

(25) In order to maintain effective competition at the distribution stage, it is necessary to provide that the manufacturers or supplier will lose the benefit of exemption where he restricts the dealer's freedom to develop his own policy on resale prices (Article 6(1)(6)).

(26) The principle of a single market required that consumers shall be able to purchase motor vehicles wherever in the Community prices or terms are most favourable and even to resell them, provided that the resale is not effected for commercial purposes. The benefits of this Regulation cannot therefore be

accorded to manufacturers or suppliers who impede parallel imports or exports through measures taken in respect of consumers, authorised intermediaries or undertakings within the network (Article 6(1)(7) and (8)).

(27) So as to ensure, in the interests of consumers, effective competition on the maintenance and repair markets, the exemption must also be withheld from manufacturers or suppliers who impede independent spare-part producers' and distributors' access to the markets or restrict the freedom of resellers or repairers, whether or not they belong to the network, to purchase and use such spare parts where they match the quality of the original spare parts. The dealer's right to procure spare parts with matching quality from external undertakings of his choice and the corresponding right for those undertakings to furnish spare parts to resellers of their choice, as well as their freedom to affix their trade mark or logo, are provided for subject to compliance with the industrial property rights applicable to those spare parts (Article 6(1)(9) to (11)).

(28) In order to give final consumers genuine opportunities of choice as between repairers belonging to the network and independent repairers, it is appropriate to impose upon manufacturers the obligation to give repairers outside the network the technical information necessary for the repair and maintenance of their makes of car, whilst taking into account the legitimate interest of the manufacturers to decide itself the mode of exploitation of its intellectual property rights as well as its identified, substantial, secret know-how when granting licences to third parties. However, these rights must be exercised in a manner which avoids all discrimination or other abuse (Article 6(1)(12)).

(29) For reasons of clarity, the legal effects arising from inapplicability of the exemption in the various situations referred to in the Regulation should be defined (Article 6(2) and (3)).

(30) Distribution and servicing agreements can be exempted, subject to the conditions laid down in Articles 5 and 6, so long as the application of obligations covered by Articles 1 to 4 brings about an improvement in distribution and servicing to the benefit of the consumer and effective competition exists, not only between manufacturers' distribution systems but also to a certain extent within each system within the common market. As regards the categories of products set out in Article 1, the conditions necessary for effective competition, including competition in trade between Member States, may be taken to exist at present, so that European consumers may be considered in general to take an equitable share in the benefit from the operation of such competition.

(31) Since the provisions of Commission Regulation (EEC) No. 123/85 of 12 December 1984 on the application of Article 85(3) of the Treaty to certain categories of motor vehicle distribution and servicing agreements[6], as last amended by the Act of Accession of Austria, Finland and Sweden, are applicable until 30 June 1995, provision should be made for transitional arrangements in respect of agreements still running on that date which satisfy the exemption conditions laid down by that Regulation (Article 7). The Commission's powers to withdraw the benefit of exemption or to alter its scope in a particular case should be spelled out and several important categories of cases should be listed by way of example (Article 8). Where the Commission makes use of its power of withdrawal as provided for in Article 8(2), it should take into account any price differentials which do not principally result from the imposition of national fiscal measures or currency fluctuations between the Member States (Article 8).

(32) In accordance with Regulation No. 19/65/EEC, the exemption must be defined for a limited period. A period of seven years is appropriate for taking account of the specific characteristics of the motor vehicle sector and the foreseeable changes in competition in that sector. However, the Commission will regularly appraise the application of the Regulation by drawing up a report by 31 December 2000 (Articles 11 and 13).

(33) Agreements which fulfil the conditions set out in this Regulation need not be notified. However, in the case of doubt undertakings are free to notify their agreements to the Commission in accordance with Council Regulation No. 17[7] as last amended by the Act of Accession of Austria, Finland and Sweden.

(34) The sector-specific character of the exemption by category for motor vehicles broadly rules out any regulations containing general exemptions by category as regards distribution. Such exclusion should be confirmed in respect of Commission Regulation (EEC) No. 4087/88 of 30 November 1988 concerning the application of Article 85(3) of the Treaty to categories of franchise agreements[8], as last amended by the Act of Accession of Austria, Finland and Sweden, without prejudice to the right of undertakings to seek an individual exemption under Regulation No. 17. On the other hand, as regards Regulations (EEC) No. 1983/83 and (EEC) No. 1984/83, which make provision for a more narrowly drawn framework of exemptions for undertakings, it is possible to allow them to choose. As for Commission Regulations (EEC) No. 417/85[9] and (EEC) No. 418/85[10], as last amended by the Act of Accession of Austria, Finland and Sweden, which relate to the application of Article 85(3) of the Treaty of categories of specialisation agreements and to categories of research and development agreements, respectively, but whose emphasis is not on distribution, applicability is not called in question (Article 12).

(35) This Regulation is without prejudice to the application of Article 86 of the Treaty.

HAS ADOPTED THIS REGULATION

Article 1

Pursuant to Article 85(3) of the Treaty it is hereby declared that subject to the conditions laid down in this Regulation Article 85(1) shall not apply to agreements to which only two undertakings are party and in which one contracting party agrees to supply, within a defined territory of the common market.

— only to the other party, or
— only to the other party and to a specified number of other undertakings within the distribution system,

for the purpose of resale, certain new motor vehicles intended for use on public roads and having three or more road wheels, together with spare parts therefor.

Article 2

The exemption shall also apply where the obligation referred to in Article 1 is combined with an obligation on the supplier neither to sell contract goods to final consumers nor to provide them with servicing for contract goods in the contract territory.

Article 3

The exemption shall also apply where the obligation referred to in Article 1 is combined with an obligation on the dealer:

1. not, without the supplier's consent, to modify contract goods or corresponding goods, unless such modification has been ordered by a final consumer and concerns a particular motor vehicle within the range covered by the contract, purchased by that final consumer;
2. not to manufacture products which compete with contract goods;
3. not to sell new motor vehicles offered by persons other than the manufacturer *except* on separate sales premises, under separate management, in the form of a distinct legal entity and in a manner which avoids confusion between makes;

4. not to permit a third party to benefit unduly, through any after-sales service performed in a common workshop, from investments made by a supplier, notably in equipment or the training of personnel;

5. neither to sell spare parts which compete with contract goods without matching them in quality nor to use them for repair or maintenance of contract goods or corresponding goods;

6. without the supplier's consent, neither to conclude distribution or servicing agreements with undertakings operating in the contract territory for contract goods or corresponding goods not to alter or terminate such agreements;

7. to impose upon undertakings with which the dealer has concluded agreements in accordance with point 6 obligations comparable to those which the dealer has accepted in relation to the supplier and which are covered by Articles 1 to 4 and are in conformity with Articles 5 and 6;

8. outside the contract territory:

(a) not to maintain branches or depots for the distribution of contract goods or corresponding goods,
(b) not to solicit customers for contract goods or corresponding goods, by personalised advertising;

9. not to entrust third parties with the distribution or servicing of contract goods or corresponding goods outside the contract territory;

10. not to supply to a reseller:

(a) contract goods or corresponding goods unless the reseller is an undertaking within the distribution system, or
(b) spare parts within the contract range unless the reseller uses them for the repair or maintenance of a motor vehicle;

11. not to sell motor vehicles within the contract range or corresponding goods to final consumers using the services of an intermediary unless that intermediary has prior written authority from such consumers to purchase a specified motor vehicle or where it is taken away by him, to collect it.

Article 4

1. The exemption shall apply notwithstanding any obligation whereby the dealer undertakes to:

(1) comply, in distribution, sales and after-sales servicing with minimum standards, regarding in particular;

(a) the equipment of the business premises and the technical facilities for servicing;
(b) the specialised, technical training of staff;
(c) advertising;
(d) the collection, storage and delivery of contract goods or corresponding goods and sales and after-sales servicing;
(e) the repair and maintenance of contract goods and corresponding goods, particularly as regards the safe and reliable functioning of motor vehicles;

(2) order contract goods from the supplier only at certain times or within certain periods, provided that the interval between ordering dates does not exceed three months;

(3) endeavour to sell, within the contract territory and during a specified period, a minimum quantity of contract goods, determined by the parties by common agreement or, in the vent of disagreement between the parties as to the minimum number of contractual goods to be sold annually, by an expert third party, account is being taken in particular of sales previously achieved in the territory and of forecast sales for the territory and at national level;

(4) keep in stock such quantity of contract goods as may be determined in accordance with the procedure in (3);

(5) keep such demonstration vehicles within the contract range, or such number thereof, as may be determined in accordance with the procedure in (3);

(6) perform work under guarantee, free servicing and vehicle-recall work for contract goods and corresponding goods;

(7) use only spare parts within the contract range or corresponding spare parts for work under guarantee, free servicing and vehicle-recall work in respect of contract goods or corresponding goods;

(8) inform customers, in a general manner, of the extent to which spare parts from other sources might be used for the repair or maintenance of contract goods or corresponding goods;

(9) inform customers whenever spare parts from other sources have been used for the repair or maintenance of contract goods or corresponding goods.

2. The exemption shall also apply to the obligations referred to in (1) above where such obligations fall in individual cases under the prohibition contained in Article 85(1).

Article 5

1. In all cases, the exemption shall apply only if:

(1) the dealer undertakes:

(a) in respect of motor vehicles within the contract range or corresponding thereto which have been supplied in the common market by another undertaking within the distribution network;
- to honour guarantees and to perform free servicing and vehicle-recall work to an extent which corresponds to the dealer's obligation covered by Article 4(1)(6).
- to carry out repair and maintenance work in accordance with Article 4(1)(1)(e);

(b) to impose upon the undertakings operating within the contract territory with which the dealer has concluded distribution and servicing agreements as provided for in Article 3(6) an obligation to honour guarantees and to perform free servicing and vehicle-recall work at least to the extent to which the dealer himself is so obliged:

(2) the supplier:

(a) does not without objectively valid reasons withhold consent to conclude, alter or terminate sub-agreements referred to in Article 3(6);

(b) does not apply, in relation to the dealer's obligations referred to in Article 4(1), minimum requirements or criteria for estimates such that the dealer is subject to discrimination without objective reasons or is treated inequitably;

(c) distinguishes, in any scheme for aggregating quantities or values of goods obtained by the dealer from the supplier and from connected undertakings within a specified period for the purpose of calculating discounts, at least between supplies of
- motor vehicles within the contract range,
- spare parts within the contract range, for supplies of which the dealer is dependent on undertakings within the distribution network, and
- other goods;

(d) supplies to the dealer, for the purpose of performance of a contract of sale concluded between the dealer and a final customer in the common market, any passenger car which corresponds to a model within the contract range and which is marketed by the manufacturer or with the manufacturer's consent in the Member State in which the vehicle is to be registered.

2. Where the dealer has, in accordance with Article 4(1), assumed obligations for the improvement of distribution and servicing structures, the exemption shall apply provided that:

(1) the supplier releases the dealer from the obligations referred to in Article 3(3) where the dealer shows that there are objective reasons for doing so;
(2) the agreement is for a period of at least five years or, if for an indefinite period, the period of notice for regular termination of the agreement is at least two years for both parties; this period is reduced to at least one year where:
   — the supplier is obliged by law or by special agreement to pay appropriate compensation on termination of the agreement, or
   — the dealer is a new entrant to the distribution system and the period of the agreement, or the period of notice for regular termination of the agreement, is the first agreed by that dealer;
(3) each party undertakes to give the other at least six months' prior notice of intention not to renew an agreement concluded for a definite period.

3. The conditions for exemption laid down in (1) and (2) shall not affect:

— the right of the supplier to terminate the agreement subject to at least one year's notice in a case where it is necessary to reorganise the whole or a substantial part of the network,
— the right of one party to terminate the agreement for cause where the other party fails to perform one of its basic obligations.

In each case, the parties must, in the event of a disagreement, accept a system for the quick resolution of the dispute, such as recourse to an expert third party or an arbitrator, without prejudice to the parties' right to apply to a competent court in conformity with the provisions of national law.

Article 6

1. The exemption shall not apply where:

(1) both parties to the agreement or their connected undertakings are motor vehicle manufacturers; or
(2) the parties link their agreement to stipulations concerning products or services other than those referred to in this Regulation or apply their agreement to such products or services; or
(3) in respect of motor vehicles having three or more road wheel, spare parts or services therefor, the parties agree restrictions of competition that are not expressly exempted by this Regulation; or
(4) in respect of motor vehicles having three or more road wheels or spare parts therefor, the parties make agreements or engage in concerted practices which are exempted from the prohibition in Article 85(1) of the Treaty under Regulations (EEC) No. 1983/83 or (EEC) No. 1984/83 to an extent exceeding the scope of this Regulation; or
(5) the parties agree that the supplier reserves the right to conclude distribution and servicing agreements for contract goods with specified further undertakings operating within the contract territory, or to alter the contract territory; or
(6) the manufacturer, the supplier or another undertaking directly or indirectly restricts the dealer's freedom to determine prices and discounts in reselling contract goods or corresponding goods; or
(7) the manufacturer, the supplier or another undertaking within the network directly or indirectly restricts the freedom of final consumers, authorised intermediaries or dealers to obtain from an undertaking belonging to the network of their choice within the common market contract goods or corresponding goods or to obtain servicing for such goods, or the freedom of final consumers to resell the contract goods or corresponding goods, when the sale is not effected for commercial purposes; or

(8) the supplier, without any objective reason, grants dealers remunerations calculated on the basis of the place of destination of the motor vehicles resold or the place of residence of the purchaser; or
(9) the supplier directly or indirectly restricts the dealer's freedom under Article 3(5) to obtain from a third undertaking of his choice spare parts which compete with contract goods and which match their quality; or
(10) the manufacturer directly or indirectly restricts the freedom of suppliers of spare-parts to supply such products to resellers of their choice, including those which are undertakings within the distribution system, provided that such parts match the quality of contract goods; or
(11) the manufacturer directly or indirectly restricts the freedom of spare-part manufacturers to place effectively and in an easily visible manner their trade mark or logo on parts supplied for the initial assembly or for the repair or maintenance of contract goods or corresponding goods; or
(12) the manufacturer refuses to make accessible, where appropriate upon payment, to repairers who are not undertakings within the distribution system, the technical information required for the repair or maintenance of the contractual or corresponding goods or for the implementing of environmental protection measures, provided that the information is not covered by an intellectual property right or does not constitute identified, substantial, secret know-how; in such case, the necessary technical information shall not be withheld improperly.

2. Without prejudice to the consequences for the other provisions of the agreement, in the vases specified in paragraph 1(1) to (5), the inapplicability of the exemption shall apply to *all* the clauses restrictive of competition contained in the agreement concerned; in the cases specified in paragraph 1(6) to (12), it shall apply only to the clauses restrictive of competition agreed respectively on behalf of the manufacturer, the supplier or another undertaking within the network which is engaged in the practice complained of.

3. Without prejudice to the consequences for the other provisions of the agreement, in the cases specified in paragraph 1(6) to (12), the inapplicability of the exemption shall only apply to the clauses restrictive of competition in favour of the other manufacturer, the supplier or another undertaking within the network which appear in the distribution and servicing agreements concluded for a geographic area within the common market in which the objectionable practice distorts competition, and only for the duration of the practice complained of.

Article 7

The prohibition laid down in Article 85(1) of the Treaty shall not apply during the period from 1 October 1995 to 30 September 1996 to agreements already in force on 1 October 1995 which satisfy the conditions for exemption provided for in Commission Regulation (EEC) No. 123/85.

Article 8

The Commission may withdraw the benefit of the application of this Regulation, pursuant to Article 7 of Regulation No. 19/65/EEC, where it finds that in an individual case an agreement which falls within the scope of this Regulation nevertheless has effects which are incompatible with the provisions of Article 85(3) of the Treaty, and in particular:

(1) where, in the common market or a substantial part thereof, contract goods or corresponding goods are not subject to competition from products considered by consumers as similar by reason of their characteristics, price and intended use;

(2) where prices or conditions of supply for contract goods or for corresponding goods are continually being applied which differ substantially as between Member States, such substantial differences being chiefly due to obligations exempted by this Regulation;
(3) where the manufacturer or an undertaking within the distribution system in supplying the distributors with contract goods or corresponding goods apply, unjustifiably, discriminatory prices or sales conditions.

Article 9

This Regulation shall apply *mutatis mutandis* to concerted practices falling within the categories covered by this Regulation.

Article 10

For the purposes of this Regulation the following terms shall have the following meanings:

1. "distribution and servicing agreements" are framework agreements between two undertakings, for a definite or indefinite period, whereby the party supplying goods entrusts to the other the distribution and servicing of those goods;
2. "parties", are the undertakings which are party to an agreement within the meaning of Article 1: "the supplier" being the undertaking which supplies the contract goods, and "the dealer" the undertaking entrusted by the supplier with the distribution and servicing of contract goods;
3. the "contract territory" is the defined territory of the common market to which the obligation of exclusive supply in the meaning of Article 1 applies;
4. "contract goods" are new motor vehicles intended for use on public roads and having three or more road wheels, and spare parts therefor, which are the subject of an agreement within the meaning of Article 1;
5. the "contract range" refers to the totality of the contract goods;
6. "spare parts" are parts which are to be installed in or upon a motor vehicle so as to replace components of that vehicle. They are to be distinguished from other parts and accessories, according to trade usage;
7. the "manufacturer" is the undertaking:
   (a) which manufactures or procures the manufacture of the motor vehicles in the contract range, or
   (b) which is connected with an undertaking described at (a);
8. "connected undertakings" are:
   (a) undertakings one of which directly or indirectly;
   — holds more than half of the capital or business assets of the other, or
   — has the power to exercise more than half the voting rights in the other, or
   — has the power to appoint more than half the members of the supervisory board, board of directors or bodies legally representing the other, or
   — has the right to manage the affairs of the other;
   (b) undertakings in relation to which a third undertaking is able directly or indirectly to exercise such rights or powers as are mentioned in (a) above,
9. "undertakings within the distribution system" are, besides the parties to the agreement, the manufacturer and undertakings which are entrusted by the manufacturers or with the manufacturer's consent with the distribution of servicing of contract goods or corresponding goods;
10. a "passenger car which corresponds to a model within the contract range" is a passenger car:

— manufactured or assembled in volume by the manufacturer and
— identical as to body style, drive-line, chassis, and type of motor with a passenger car within the contract range;

11. "corresponding goods", "corresponding motor vehicles" and "corresponding parts" are those which are similar in kind to those in the contract range, are distributed by the manufacturer or with the manufacturer's consent, and are the subject of a distribution or servicing agreement with an undertaking within the distribution system;
12. "resale" includes all transactions by which a physical or legal person — "the reseller" — disposes of a motor vehicle which is still in a new condition and which he had previously acquired in his own name and on his own behalf, irrespective of the legal description applied under civil law or the format of the transaction which effects such resale. The terms resale shall include all leasing contracts which provide for a transfer of ownership or an option to purchase prior to the expiry of the contract;
13. "distribute" and "sell" include other forms of supply by the dealer such as leasing.

Article 11

1. The Commission will evaluate on a regular basis the application of this Regulation, particularly as regards the impact of the exempted system of distribution on price differentials of contract goods between the different Member States and on the quality of service to final users.
2. The Commission will collate the opinions of associations and experts representing the various interested parties, particularly consumer organisations.
3. The Commission will draw up a report on the evaluation of this Regulation on or before 31 December 2000, particularly taking into account the criteria provided for in paragraph 1.

Article 12

Regulation (EEC) No. 4087/88 is not applicable to agreements concerning the products or services referred to in this Regulation.

Article 13

This Regulation shall enter into force on 1 July 1995.
It shall apply from 1 October 1995 until 30 September 2002.
The provisions of Regulation (EEC) No. 123/85 shall continue to apply until 30 September 1995.

This Regulation shall be binding in its entirety and directly applicable in all Member States.
Done at Brussels, June 28, 1995.

[1] OJ 1995 L145/25.
[2] OJ 1965 L36/533.
[3] OJ 1994 C379/16.
[4] OJ 1983 L 173/1.
[5] OJ 1983 L 173/5.
[6] OJ 1985 L 15/16.
[7] OJ 1962 L 13/204.
[8] OJ 1988 L 359/46.
[9] OJ 1985 L 53//1.
[10] OJ 1985 L 53/5.

APPENDIX 3

DISTRIBUTION OF MOTOR VEHICLES
EUROPEAN COMMISSION EXPLANATORY BROCHURE

REGARDING REGULATION 1475/95

CONTENTS

Foreword

I. Clarification of the scope of exemption
  1. Scope of the Regulation
  2. "Black list" clauses and practices
  3. Withdrawal of the benefit of the exemption
  4. Duration of the Regulation

II. Strengthening the competitiveness of dealers
  1. Multi-dealerships
  2. Quantitative purchasing targets
  3. Duration and termination of the agreement
  4. Recourse to an expert third party or arbitrator
  5. Direct sales

III. Improved market access for spare part producers/distributors and for independent repairers
  1. Spare parts
  2. Technical information

IV. Increasing consumers choice in accordance with the principles of the single market
  1. Parallel imports
  2. Honouring of manufacturer's guarantee
  3. Advertising outside the contract territory
  4. Leasing

V. Interaction with other provisions of Community law

FOREWORD

In the Member States of the European Union, motor vehicle manufacturers distribute their products through selected dealer networks. The distribution agreements making up the networks contain provisions which restrict competition and which may affect trade between Member States. Therefore they fall within the scope of Article 85(1) of the EC Treaty.

The prohibition laid down in Article 85(1) of the EC Treaty may be declared inapplicable if the agreement as a whole brings about overall economic advantages which outweigh the disadvantages for competition. Exemptions may be granted on a case-by-case basis or by regulation for certain category of agreements. Commission Regulation (EEC) No. 123/85, which contained such a group exemption, expired on June 30, 1995 and has been replaced by Commission Regulation (EC) No. 1475/95 on the application of Article 85(3) of the Treaty to certain categories of motor vehicle distribution and servicing agreements.[1] The Commission adopted this Regulation on 28 June 1995.

The Regulation contains several adjustments to stimulate competition in the car sector, to improve the functioning of a single market in cars and to re-balance the diverse interests in question. These adjustments aim in particular to:

— give dealers, the great majority of whom are small or medium sized enterprises, greater commercial independence *vis-à-vis* manufacturers;
— give independent spare-part manufacturers and distributors easier access to the various markets, notably the outlets provided by the car manufacturers' networks;
— improve the position of consumers in accordance with the principles underlying the internal market;
— make the dividing line between acceptable and unacceptable agreements and behaviour clearer.

As these changes are important for the distribution and servicing of vehicles, this brochure is intended as a legally non binding guide to the Regulation which is aimed particularly at distributors and consumers. It is not a detailed commentary on each provision of the Regulation. Its objective is to give answers to questions which are likely to arise in practice while applying the new regulatory framework for manufacturers, dealers, spare part producers and independent repairers. Moreover, it is intended to provide consumers with information as to how the Regulation guarantees the freedom to buy a car anywhere in the Community in accordance with the principles of the single market.

I. Clarification of the Scope of Exemption:

1. Scope of the Regulation

[Article 1]

Pursuant to Article 85(3) of the Treaty it is hereby declared that subject to the conditions laid down in this Regulation Article 85(1) shall not apply to agreements to which only two undertakings are party and in which one contracting party agrees to supply, within a defined territory of the common market.

— only to the other party, or
— only to the other party and to a specified number of other undertakings within the distribution system.

for the purpose of resale, certain new motor vehicles intended for use on public roads and having three or more road wheels, together with spare parts therefor.

Question 1: Does the Regulation apply to the distribution and servicing of all kinds of motor vehicles? Does the Regulation apply to the separate distribution of vehicle spare parts?

The Regulation applies to the distribution of motor vehicles which (1) are new and (2) intended for use on public roads and (3) have three or more road wheels [Article 1].

Used motor vehicles are not subject to the Regulation. The dividing line between new and used motor vehicles has to be drawn in accordance with commercial usage in a manner which prevents any circumvention of the Regulation.

Agricultural vehicles such as tractors are not subject to the Regulation, as their main use is not on public roads.

The Regulation does not apply to the distribution and servicing of motorbikes.

The separate distribution of automotive replacement parts without any connection to the distribution of vehicles is not covered either.

2. "Black List" Clauses and Practices

[Article 6]

1. The exemption shall not apply where:

(1) both parties to the agreement or their connected undertakings are motor vehicle manufacturers; or

(2) the parties link their agreement to stipulations concerning products or services other than those referred to in this Regulation or apply their agreement to such products or services; or

(3) in respect of motor vehicles having three or more road wheels, spare parts or services therefor, the parties agree restrictions of competition that are not expressly exempted by this Regulation; or

(4) in respect of motor vehicles having three or more road wheels or spare parts therefor, the parties make agreements or engage in concerted practices which are exempted from the prohibition in Article 85(1) of the Treaty under Regulations (EEC) No. 1983/83 or (EEC) No. 1984/83 to an extent exceeding the scope of this Regulation; or

(5) the parties agree that the supplier reserves the right to conclude distribution and servicing agreements for contract goods with specified further undertakings operating within the contract territory, or to alter the contract territory; or

(6) the manufacturer, the supplier or another undertaking directly or indirectly restricts the dealer's freedom to determine prices and discounts in reselling contract goods or corresponding goods; or

(7) the manufacturer, the supplier or another undertaking within the network directly or indirectly restricts the freedom of final consumers, authorised intermediaries or dealers to obtain from an undertaking belonging to the network of their choice within the common market contract goods or corresponding goods or to obtain servicing for such goods, or the freedom of final consumers to resell the contract goods or corresponding goods, when the sale is not effected for commercial purposes; or

(8) the supplier, without any objective reason, grants dealers remunerations calculated on the basis of the place of destination of the motor vehicles resold or the place of residence of the purchaser; or

(9) the supplier directly or indirectly restricts the dealer's freedom under Article 3(5) to obtain from a third undertaking of this choice spare parts which compete with contract goods and which match their quality; or

(10) the manufacturer directly or indirectly restricts the freedom of suppliers of spare-parts to supply such products to resellers of their choice, including those which are undertakings within the distribution system, provided that such parts match the quality of contract goods; or

(11) the manufacturer directly or indirectly restricts the freedom of spare-part manufacturers to place effectively and in an easily visible manner their trade mark or logo on parts supplied for the initial assembly or for the repair or maintenance of contract goods or corresponding goods; or

(12) the manufacturer refuses to make accessible, where appropriate upon payment, to

repairers who are not undertakings within the distribution system, the technical information required for the repair or maintenance of the contractual or corresponding goods or for the implementing of environmental protection measures, provided that the information is not covered by an intellectual property right or does not constitute identified, substantial, secret know-how; in such case, the necessary technical information shall not be withheld improperly.

2. Without prejudice to the consequences for the other provisions of the agreement, in the cases specified in paragraph 1(1) to (5), the inapplicability of the exemption shall apply to all the clauses restrictive of competition contained in the agreement concerned; in the cases specified in paragraph 1(6) to (12), it shall apply only to the clauses restrictive of competition agreed respectively on behalf of the manufacturer, the supplier or another undertaking within the network which is engaged in the practice complained of.

3. Without prejudice to the consequences for the other provisions of the agreement, in the cases specified in paragraph 1(6) to (12), the inapplicability of the exemption shall only apply to the clauses restrictive of competition agreed in favour of the manufacturer, the supplier or another undertaking within the network which appear in the distribution and servicing agreements concluded for a geographic area within the common market in which the objectionable practice distorts competition, and only for the duration of the practice complained of.

Question 2: Are there any clauses and/or practices which, under this Regulation, may not be included in exclusive and selective distribution agreements?

(a) The Regulation includes in Article 6(1)(1) to (5) a list of *clauses* which should not be used in an agreement for the distribution of cars ("black clauses") and which render the Regulation inapplicable, namely leading to an automatic loss of the benefit of the group exemption, if incorporated into exclusive and selective distribution agreements.

The group exemption does not apply:

— if the two parties to an agreement are both motor vehicle manufacturers[2] [Article 6(1)(1)];
— if the obligations in the agreement are extended to products and services other than motor vehicles and spare parts [Article 6(1)(2)];
— if the agreement contains obligations in favour of the manufacturer or the dealer which are more far-reaching than permitted under the Regulation [Article 6(1)(3)];
— if the parties agree between themselves obligations which would be acceptable under Commission Regulation (EEC) No. 1983/83[3] concerning exclusive distribution agreements or under Commission Regulation (EEC) No. 1984/83[4] concerning exclusive purchasing agreements but which go further than is permitted by this Regulation [Article 6(1)(4)];
— If the manufacturer or supplier is given in the agreement the unilateral right to alter the contract territory during the period of the agreement, or to conclude distribution and service agreements with other companies in the contract territory [Article 6(1)(5)].

(b) Furthermore, the list contains "black practices" which also lead to the automatic loss of the exemption, if committed systematically or repeatedly [Article 6(1)(6) to (12), Recital 20].

"Repeatedly" means that the practice must have been committed several times. An isolated practice is sufficient only where it is part of a plan, in which case it is considered to be committed "systematically".

"Black practices" are:

— where the manufacturer, the supplier or another undertaking within the network fixes the resale price for vehicles, spare parts or other contract goods and corresponding goods [Article 6(1)(6)];

— where the manufacturer, the supplier or another undertaking within the network directly or indirectly impedes final consumers, their intermediaries or authorised dealers from buying a vehicle where they consider it to be most advantageous [Article 6(1)(7)];
— where the manufacturer or the supplier, without objective reasons, makes the remuneration of a dealer dependent on the destination of sale [Article 6(1)(8)];
— where the manufacturer or the supplier directly or indirectly interferes with its dealer(s) buying spare parts of equal quality from a spare part supplier of his choice [Article 6(1)(9)];
— where the manufacturer or the supplier directly or indirectly interferes with sales by a spare-part supplier although the spare part supplier offers spare-parts of equal quality to those bought by the manufacturer [Article 6(1)(10)];
— where the manufacturer directly or indirectly hinders spare-part manufacturers from affixing their trade mark or logo on spare parts bought by the manufacturer or supplied to the network [Article 6(1)(11)];
— where the manufacturer does not pass on technical information necessary for the maintenance of its vehicles to independent repairers without objectively justified reasons for this refusal [Article 6(1)(12)].

The content of the "Black List" clauses and practices are further explained below in the context of the rights of dealers (Chapter II), spare-part producers and resellers (Chapter III) and consumers (Chapter IV).

Question 3: What does the automatic loss of the benefit of the exemption mean for the distribution system?

The legal consequences differ depending on whether the inapplicability of the group exemption is due to the incorporation of "black clauses" in the exclusive and selective distribution agreement or whether this is due to a "black practice".

(a) "Black clauses" [Article 6(1)(1) to (5)]:

If the parties agree to include a prohibited clause in their distribution agreement, the group exemption is inapplicable not only with regard to the prohibited clause(s) but with regard to all other restrictions of competition which are included in the agreement concerned. Therefore, the restrictive provisions in the distribution agreement, which would normally be allowed by Article 1 to 4 of the Regulation, are no longer exempted. It makes no difference whether such restrictions are in favour of the manufacturer or of the dealer.

As the Regulation does not then apply to exempt these restrictive clauses, they are prohibited by EC Competition Law (Article 85(1) of the Treaty) and are null and void from the date of the agreement. In addition, the Commission is entitled to fine the parties to the agreement [Article 15(2)(a) of Council Regulation No 17/62].

The parties may notify an exclusive and selective distribution agreement containing "black clauses" to receive individual exemption. Such individual exemption will only be justifiable in an exceptional situation relating to the specific circumstances of an individual case. A notification provides immunity from fines unless and until the Commission informs the undertakings concerned that after preliminary examination it considers that Article 85(1) of the Treaty applies and that application of Article 85(3) is not justified [Article 15(6) of Council Regulation No. 17/62] and adopts a decision lifting immunity from fines.

The Regulation does not say whether the non-restrictive clauses in the exclusive and selective distribution agreement remain valid in such a situation. This is, in principle, a question of national law, and therefore for the competent national court to decide.

(b) "Black practices" [Article 6(1)(6) to (12)]:

These are mostly actions on the part of a manufacturer, importer or authorised dealer, and have consequences only for the company engaged in the practice [Article 6(2)].

In cases of "black practices", all clauses in an exclusive and selective distribution agreement which are restrictive of competition and which benefit the company responsible are no longer covered by the group exemption. The consequences of the misconduct are limited to the contract territory where the distortion of competition takes place. However, if competition is distorted in a larger area, the exemption is no longer applicable for all the distribution contracts concluded for this area. The benefit of the exemption is only lost for so long as the objectionable conduct lasts.

This means, in practice, that if the manufacturer or importer is responsible, the authorised dealers are released from any obligation which has been imposed on them in favour of the manufacturer/importer under the agreement.

Moreover, even where "black practices" are imposed, *e.g.* by the manufacturer, but accepted by the dealer because he complies with them, such behaviour is considered a concerted practice and prohibited (Article 85(1) of the Treaty). As in the case of the "black clauses" (see above), the Commission can fine the parties to the agreement [Article 15(2)(a) of Council Regulation No 17/62].

(c) National courts in Member States which find "black clauses" and "black practices" which infringe EC competition law (Article 85(1) of the Treaty) can—as well as finding that the agreement or parts of it are prohibited and void—grant injunctions and award damages.

3. Withdrawal of the Benefit of the Exemption

[Article 8]

The Commission may withdraw the benefit of the application of this Regulation, pursuant to Article 7 of Regulation No 19/65/EEC, where it finds that in an individual case an agreement which falls within the scope of is Regulation nevertheless has effects which are incompatible with the provisions of Article 85(3) of the Treaty, and in particular:

(1) where, in the common market of a substantial part thereof, contract goods or corresponding goods are not subject to competition from products considered by consumers as similar by reason of their characteristics, price and intended use;

(2) where prices or conditions of supply for contract goods or for corresponding goods are continually being applied which differ substantially as between Member States, such substantial differences being chiefly due to obligations exempted by this Regulation;

(3) where the manufacturer or an undertaking within the distribution system in supplying the distributors with contract goods or corresponding goods apply, unjustifiably, discriminatory prices or sales conditions.

Question 4: Are there any other circumstances in which an agreement may lose the benefit of the group exemption?

The Regulation lists in Article 8 examples of situations in which the Commission has the power to withdraw the benefit of the group exemption or to alter its scope in a particular case. In contrast to the effects of the Black List, in these cases the benefit of the exemption is not automatically lost but is subject to an official procedure by the Commission. The Commission may begin a procedure for withdrawal either upon complaint or on its own initiative.

Although the Commission may withdraw the benefit of the exemption for other reasons, the circumstances listed are those in which withdrawal is most likely. These are:

— where the contract goods are not subject to effective competition [Article 8(1)];
— where the distribution system leads over a considerable period to differentials in price and sales conditions between Member States [Article 8(2)];
— where the manufacturer or an undertaking within the distribution system applies, unjustifiably, discriminatory prices or sales conditions to its dealers [Article 8(3)].

The Commission has already published in connection with Regulation (EEC) No. 123/85 a Notice[5] which explains what are acceptable and unacceptable price differentials. This Commission Notice remains applicable under the new Regulation as well as the other Commission Notice concerning the clarification of the activities of motor vehicle intermediaries.[6]

4. Duration of the Regulation

[Article 7]

The prohibition laid down in Article 85(1) of the Treaty shall not apply during the period from 1 October 1995 to 30 September 1996 to agreements already in force on 1 October 1995 which satisfy the conditions for exemption provided for in Commission Regulation (EEC) No. 123/85.

[Article 13]

This Regulation shall enter into force on 1 July 1995.
It shall apply from 1 October 1995 until 30 September 2002.
The provisions of Regulation (EEC) No. 123/85 shall continue to apply until 30 September 1995.

Question 5: From what date does Regulation (EC) No. 1475/95 apply and when does it expire?

Regulation (EC) No. 1475/95 entered into force on 1 July 1995. It says that until 30 September 1995, the provisions of Regulation (EEC) No. 123/85 continue to apply [Article 13], in order to give the interested parties sufficient time to adapt their distribution systems to the changes brought about by the new Regulation.

A further transition period of one year is provided for exclusive and selective distribution agreements which are already in force on 1 October 1995 and which satisfy the conditions for exemption set by Regulation (EEC) No. 123/85 [Article 7]. Therefore, from 1 October 1996 onwards, all exclusive and selective distribution agreements which are to benefit from the group exemption have to comply with Regulation (EC) No. 1475/95.

Regulation (EC) No. 1475/95 will be in force for 7 years and expires on 30 September 2002.

II. Strengthening the Competitiveness of Dealers:

1. Multi-Dealerships

[Article 3]

The exemption shall also apply where the obligation referred to in Article 1 is combined with an obligation on the dealer:

...

3. not to sell now motor vehicles offered by persons other than the manufacturer except on separate sales premises, under separate management, in the form of a distinct legal entity and in a manner which avoids confusion between makes;

4. not to permit a third party to benefit unduly, through any after-sales service performed in a common workshop, from investments made by a supplier, notably in equipment or the training of personnel;

...

6. without the supplier's consent, neither to conclude distribution or servicing agreements with undertakings operating in the contract territory for contract goods or corresponding goods nor to alter or terminate such agreements; ...

[Article 4]

1. The exemption shall apply notwithstanding any obligation whereby the dealer undertakes to:

(1) comply, in distribution, sales and after-sales servicing with minimum standards, regarding in particular;

(a) the equipment of the business premises and the technical facilities for servicing;
(b) the specialised technical training of staff;
(c) advertising;
(d) the collection, storage and delivery of contract goods or corresponding goods and sales and after-sales servicing;
(e) the repair and maintenance of contract goods and corresponding goods, particularly as regards the safe and reliable functioning of motor vehicles;

(2) order contract from the supplier only at certain times or within certain periods, provided that the interval between ordering dates does not exceed three months;

(3) endeavour to sell, within the contract territory and during a specified period, a minimum quantity of contract goods, determined by the parties by common agreement or, in the event of disagreement between the parties as to the minimum number of contractual goods to be sold annually, by an expert third party, account being taken in particular of sales previously achieved in the territory and of forecast sales for the territory and at national level;

(4) keep in stock such quantity of contract goods as may be determined in accordance with the procedure in (3);

(5) keep such demonstration vehicles within the contract range, or such number thereof, as may be determined in accordance with the procedure in (3);

(6) perform work under guarantee, free servicing and vehicle-recall work for contract goods and corresponding goods;

(7) use only spare parts within the contract range or corresponding spare parts for work under guarantee, free servicing and vehicle-recall work in respect of contract goods or corresponding goods;

(8) inform customers, in a general manner, of the extent to which spare parts from other sources might be used for the repair of maintenance of contract goods or corresponding goods;

(9) inform customers whenever spare parts from other sources have been used for the repair or maintenance of contract goods or corresponding goods. ...

[Article 5]

1. In all cases, the exemption shall apply only if:

...

(2) the supplier:

(a) does not without objectively valid reasons withhold consent to conclude, alter or terminate sub-agreements referred to in Article 3(6);

...

2. Where the dealer has, in accordance with Article 4(1), assumed obligations for the improvement of distribution and servicing structures, the exemption shall apply provided that:

(1) the supplier releases the dealer from the obligations referred to in Article 3(3) where the dealer shows that there are objective reasons for doing so; ...

[Article 6]

1. The exemption shall not apply where:

...

(2) the parties link their agreement to stipulations concerning products or services other than those referred to in this Regulation or apply their agreement to such products or services; or

(3) in respect of motor vehicles having three or more road wheels, spare parts or services therefor, the parties agree restrictions of competition that are not expressly exempted by this Regulation; or ...

Question 6: Can a dealer sell more than one make of motor vehicle from the same sales premises?

If a manufacturer wishes to benefit from the group exemption, its dealers must be given the right to sell competing makes.

The Regulation, however, allows the manufacturer to oblige the dealer to have (1) separate sales premises (2) under separate management (3) in the form of a distinct legal entity and (4) in a manner which avoids confusion between makes [see Article 3(3), Recital 7].

"Separate sales premises" may be located in the same building.

"Separate management" means in principle keeping separate records, accounts and sales forces.

The third condition, "in the form of a distinct legal entity", makes it clear that for each dealership a company has to be set up. It is the national law of the Member State in question which defines the requirements for the legal structure of such a company.

"In a manner which avoids confusion between makes" means, for example, that promotional literature on one make of vehicle should be kept separate from literature on the other. The attire of sales personnel should also respect this condition since the fixing of several manufacturers trademarks might cause confusion for consumers.

Question 7: Can the manufacturer always impose on the dealer the four obligations designed to maintain the separation of makes?

No, if the manufacturer has obliged the dealer to comply with minimum standards for the improvement of distribution and servicing structures (*e.g.* the collection, storage and delivery of contract goods or corresponding goods and sales and after sales servicing [described in Article 4(1)]), he must release the dealer from obligations relating to the separating of makes (see Question 6), provided that the dealer shows that there are objective reasons for so doing [Article 5(2)(1)].

It will depend on the facts of the case whether the manufacturer must release the dealer from all four obligations or only from those which have a detrimental effect on the dealer's business in that particular case.

An objective reason will be considered to exist if the obligations designed to maintain the separation of makes turn out to be excessive in a particular case [Recital 18]. One example of an objective reason is where the obligation(s) prevent the dealer from operating on an economically viable basis.

Question 8: Can a manufacturer discourage the development of "multi-brand" dealerships?

The Regulation's main objective is to open markets in terms of geography, products and competitors. This is why the Regulation permits multimarketing dealerships in general and leaves it in the sole discretion of the dealer to decide whether he wants to sell a second make. The dealer's freedom to take an autonomous economic decision may not be restricted directly or indirectly by the manufacturer. Measures aimed at stipulating "one brand" dealerships by a manufacturer, *i.e.* by way of rebate systems which accord higher rebates to the dealer if he maintains an exclusive dealership, would be considered as a restriction of competition that is not expressly exempted by the Regulation [Article 6(1)(3)], leading to an automatic loss of the benefit of the exemption.

Question 9: Is a dealer entitled to repair different makes in one workshop?

Yes. The manufacturer may not ask his dealers to instal separate workshops [Article 3(4)].

On the other hand, he may ask his dealers not to permit a third party to benefit unduly from the investments made by him, for example where the manufacturer has borne the costs of purchasing technical equipment used in the dealer's workshop. The manufacturer may require that this equipment may not be used to repair vehicles of another make. However, the financing of the equipment by the manufacturer may not be imposed.

The requirement may be more difficult to fulfil with regard to training of personnel. In this respect "unduly" means that a dealer has to make sure that knowledge obtained from the manufacturer which is not simply useful for repair work but which imparts additional qualifications in form of specific know-how to the personnel may not be used for other makes. This may lead in practice to the result that a dealer may have to nominate the personnel working for a specific make.

Question 10: Can a dealer participate in the distribution of competing makes through investment in other undertakings?

Dealers are free, even within the contract territory, to own or invest in companies which belong to the networks of competing manufacturers.

Question 11: Can a dealer appoint subagents?

Yes, but subject to the manufacturer's prior consent. The manufacturer can only refuse its consent if it gives objectively valid reasons which should be applied without discrimination, and in an equitable and reasonable manner [Article 3(6) and 5(1)(2)(a)].

Question 12: Can a manufacturer oblige its dealers to cooperate with specific finance institutions or insurance companies?

The Regulation does not allow such a clause in the agreement. Bank or insurance services are not among the products and services dealt with in the Regulation. Under Article 6(1)(2), the exemption does not apply in such a case.

2. Quantitative Purchasing Targets

[Article 4]

1. The exemption shall apply notwithstanding any obligation whereby the dealer undertakes to:
...
(3) endeavour to sell, within the contract territory and during a specified period, a minimum quantity of contract goods, determined by the parties by common agreement or, in the event of disagreement between the parties as to the minimum number of contractual goods to be sold annually, by an expert third party, account being taken in particular of sales previously achieved in the territory and of forecast sales for the territory and at national level;
(4) keep in stock such quantity of contract goods as may be determined in accordance with the procedure in (3);
(5) keep such demonstration vehicles within the contract range, or such number thereof, as may be determined in accordance with the procedure in (3); ...

[Article 3]

The exemption shall also apply where the obligation referred to in Article 1 is combined with an obligation on the dealer:
...
10. not to supply to a reseller:
(a) contract goods or corresponding goods unless the reseller is an undertaking within the distribution system, or...

[Article 6]

1. The exemption shall not apply where:
...
(3) in respect of motor vehicles having three or more road wheels, spare parts or services therefor, the parties agree restrictions of competition that are not expressly exempted by this Regulation; or ...

Question 13: Can the dealer have sales targets and stock requirements imposed by the manufacturer?

Sales targets and stock requirements can only be set by agreement between the manufacturer and dealer. Neither party to the agreement is given the final say. In the event of disagreement between the parties on the annual agreement of these quantities, the matter must be referred to an expert third party [Article 4(1) points 3, 4, and 5; Questions 17 to 19] or to a national court.

The Regulation starts with the assumption that the parties normally agree on an annual basis the minimum number of sales, stock and demonstration vehicles. Minimum requirements agreed for a shorter period may only be of an indicative nature. If they are made binding, this may result in an automatic loss of the benefit of the group exemption [Article 6(1)(3)]. This means that the dealer is free from the obligation to endeavour to sell the agreed minimum quantity of contract goods within that shorter period.

Question 14: Is there a general right for a dealer within the distribution network to obtain new motor vehicles in other parts of the Common Market?

An authorised dealer may not be prevented from selling to or purchasing from another authorised dealer within the Community. The Regulation only permits the manufacturer to impose on its dealers the obligation not to sell to a reseller who does not belong to its distribution system [Article 3(10)(a)]. The dealer may not be obliged to purchase only from the manufacturer. If the distribution agreement contains an obligation of the dealer to purchase only from the manufacturer, such obligation would be a "black clause" and the exemption would not apply [Article 6(1)(3)].

3. Duration and Termination of the Agreement

[Article 5]

...

2. Where the dealer has, in accordance with Article 4(1), assumed obligations for the improvement of distribution and servicing structures, the exemption shall apply provided that:

...

(2) the agreement is for a period of at least five years or, if for an indefinite period, the period of notice for regular termination of the agreement is at least two years for both parties; this period is reduced to at least one year where:

— the supplier is obliged by law or by special agreement to pay appropriate compensation on termination of the agreement, or
— the dealer is a new entrant to the distribution system and the period of the agreement, or the period of notice for regular termination of the agreement, is the first agreed by that dealer;

(3) each party undertakes to give the other at least six months' prior notice of intention not to renew an agreement concluded for a definite period.

3. The conditions for exemption laid down in (1) and (2) shall not affect;

— the right of the supplier to terminate the agreement subject to at least one year's notice in a case where it is necessary to reorganise the whole or a substantial part of the network,
— the right of one party to terminate the agreement for cause where the other party fails to perform one of its basic obligations.

In each case, the parties must, in the event of disagreement, accept a system for the quick resolution of the dispute, such as recourse to an expert third party or an arbitrator, without prejudice to the parties' right to apply to a competent court in conformity with the provisions of national law.

[Article 6]

1. The exemption shall not apply where:

...

(5) the parties agree that the supplier reserves the right to conclude distribution and servicing agreements for contract goods with specified further undertakings operating within the contract territory, or to alter the contract territory; or ...

Question 15: What is the minimum duration of the agreement and the period of notice for termination?

The parties may conclude an agreement for a definite period, or for an indefinite period [Article 5(2)].

If the parties choose the former, then they have to agree on a minimum duration of five years. There must also be a clause that in case one party does not want to renew the agreement, this party has to inform the other of its intention at least six months before the agreement is due to expire [Article 5(2)(3)]. If the parties conclude the agreement for an indefinite period, then they are deemed to agree on a two year period of notice for termination. Agreements can be terminated on one year's notice if the manufacturer undertakes to pay damages [Article 5(2)(2) first indent] or if the agreement is concluded with a newcomer to the network [Article 5(2)(2) second indent].

Question 16: Are there any possibilities for early termination of the agreement?

The Regulation introduces the possibility of early termination in two cases:

(a) The manufacturer has the right to terminate the agreement early (on one year's notice) where it needs to restructure the whole or a substantial part of the network. Whether it is necessary to reorganise is established between the parties by agreement or at the dealer's request by an expert third party or an arbitrator. Recourse to an expert third party or an arbitrator does not affect the right of either party to apply to a national court under national law [Article 5(3)]. Where the supplier provides for himself in the contract unilateral rights of termination exceeding the limits set by the Regulation, he automatically loses the benefit of the group exemption [Article 6(1)(5); see above I.2.].

This possibility for early termination has been introduced to provide the manufacturer with an instrument for flexible adaptation to changes in distribution structures [Recital 19]. A need for reorganising may arise due to the behaviour of competitors or due to other economic developments, irrespective of whether these are motivated by internal decisions of a manufacturer or external influences, *e.g.* the closure of a company employing a large workforce in a specific area. In view of the wide variety of situations which may arise, it would be unrealistic to list all the possible reasons.

Whether or not a "substantial part" of the network is affected, must be decided in the light of the specific organisation of a manufacturer's network in each case. "Substantial" implies both an economic and a geographical aspect, which may be limited to the network, or a part of it, in a given Member State. The manufacturer has to reach an agreement—either with or without the intermediation of an expert third party or arbitrator—with the dealer, whose distribution agreement will be terminated, but not with other dealers (who are only indirectly affected by an early termination).

(b) Both parties to the agreement have the right to terminate the agreement at any time without notice, where the other party fails to perform one of its basic obligations. Again, the parties must establish whether the reason for early termination is sufficient, by common accord or, in case of disagreement, by recourse to an expert third party or an arbitrator and/or by application to a competent court in conformity with the provisions of national law [Article 5(3)]. One reason for early termination might be where a party infringes contractual obligations allowed under Articles 1 to 4 of the Regulation.

4. Recourse to Expert Third Party or Arbitrator

[Article 4]

1. The exemption shall apply notwithstanding any obligation whereby the dealer undertakes to:

. . .

(3) endeavour to sell, within the contract territory and during a specified period, a minimum quantity of contract goods, determined by the parties by common agreement or, in the event of disagreement between the parties as to the minimum number of contractual goods to be sold annually, by an expert third party, account being taken in particular of sales previously achieved in the territory and of forecast sales for the territory and at national level;

(4) keep in stock such quantity of contract goods as may be determined in accordance with the procedure in (3);

(5) keep such demonstration vehicles within the contract range, or such number thereof, as may be determined in accordance with the procedure in (3); . . .

[Article 5]

3. The conditions for exemption laid down in (1) and (2) shall not affect;

— the right of the supplier to terminate the agreement subject to at least one year's notice in a case where it is necessary to reorganise the whole or a substantial part of the network,
— the right of one party to terminate the agreement for cause where the other party fails to perform one of its basic obligations.

In each case, the parties, in the event of disagreement, accept a system for the quick resolution of the dispute, such as recourse to an expert third party or an arbitrator, without prejudice to the parties' right to apply to a competent court in conformity with the provisions of national law.

Question 17: In what circumstances does the Regulation call upon the manufacturer and dealer, in the event of disagreement between them, to refer to an expert third party or an arbitrator?

The Regulation says that the manufacturer and dealer should refer to an expert third party when they disagree with regard to the annual setting of (1) sales targets [Article 4(1)(3)]; (2) stock requirements [Article 4(1)(4)] and (3) the keeping of demonstration vehicles [Article 4(1)(5)].

Recourse to an expert third party or an arbitrator is provided for in the case of early termination of the agreement. The Regulation leaves the parties free to decide whether they wish to refer to an expert third party or to an arbitrator [Article 5(3)].

However, the parties are not restricted to the use of an expert third party or an arbitrator only in these cases. They can adopt such procedures in other cases of dispute if they both agree so to do.

Question 18: How will the right to apply to a competent court interact with recourse to an expert third party or arbitrator?

The Regulation says that to resolve disputes, to establish a quick and efficient system of settlement, the parties must first go to an expert or an arbitrator. However, this obligation is without prejudice to the parties' right to apply to a competent national court to the extent this is allowed under national law.

Question 19: Who can act as an expert third party or an arbitrator and how should an expert third party or arbitrator be nominated?

Any person, accepted by both parties as being qualified to act in such a capacity, may be appointed as expert third party or arbitrator.

The parties are free to decide, should the situation arise, whom they wish to nominate and whether they prefer to appoint one, two, three or more people to be the expert(s) or arbitrator(s). However, no party is allowed to decide unilaterally who will be the expert or arbitrator. In the event of disagreement the parties shall adopt the nomination procedures which are normally used in such cases, *e.g.* nomination by the president of the court of first instance, by the president of the chambers for commerce and industry. It seems advisable that the contract between the manufacturer and dealer should specify what kind of nomination procedure they wish to use should the situation arise.

5. Direct Sales

[Article 2]

The exemption shall also apply where the obligation referred to in Article 1 is combined with an obligation on the supplier neither to sell contract goods to final consumers nor to provide them with servicing for contract goods in the contract territory.

Question 20: May the manufacturer reserve the right to make direct sales to final consumers?

Article 2 of the Regulation exempts an obligation on the manufacturer neither to sell contract goods to final consumers nor to provide them with servicing for contract goods in the contract territory. It follows from this provision that in the absence of such a contractual obligation, the manufacturer is free to supply final consumers in the contract territory. On the other hand, it is clear that customer restrictions may not be imposed on the dealer and that they lead to the automatic loss of the benefit of the group exemption. Therefore, the manufacturer may not prevent the dealer from supplying those final consumers whom the manufacturer himself wishes to supply.

Moreover, the manufacturer should take care not to affect by such behaviour the economic viability of the dealer's business because, in such a case, the basis of the agreement itself may be destroyed. It is for a national court to solve any dispute.

III. Improved Market Access for Spare Part Producers/Distributors and for Independent Repairers:

1. Spare Parts

[Article 3]

The exemption shall also apply where the obligation referred to in Article 1 is combined with an obligation on the dealer:

...

5. neither to sell spare parts which compete with contract goods without matching them in quality nor to use them for repair or maintenance of contract goods or corresponding goods;

...

10. not to supply to a reseller:

(a) contract goods or corresponding goods unless the reseller is an undertaking within the distribution system, or
(b) spare parts within the contract range unless the reseller uses them for the repair or maintenance of a motor vehicle; ...

[Article 4]

1. The exemption shall apply notwithstanding any obligation whereby the dealer undertakes to

...

(7) use only spare parts within the contract range or corresponding spare parts for work under guarantee, free servicing and vehicle-recall work in respect of contract goods or corresponding goods;
(8) inform customers, in a general manner, of the extent to which spare parts from other sources might be used for the repair or maintenance of contract goods or corresponding goods;
(9) inform customers whenever spare parts from other sources have been used for the repair or maintenance of contract goods or corresponding goods. ...

[Article 5]

1. In all cases, the exemption shall apply only if:

(c) distinguishes, in any scheme for aggregating quantities or values of goods obtained by the dealer from the supplier and from connected undertakings within a specified period for the purpose of calculating discounts, at least between supplies of
- motor vehicles within the contract range,
- spare parts within the contract range, for supplies of which the dealer is dependent on undertakings within the distribution network, and
- other goods; ...

[Article 6]

1. The exemption shall not apply where:

...

(2) the parties link their agreement to stipulations concerning products or services other than those referred to in this Regulation or apply their agreement to such products or services; or

...

(9) the supplier directly or indirectly restricts the dealer's freedom under Article 3(5) to obtain from a third undertaking of his choice spare parts which compete with contract goods and which match their quality; or

(10) the manufacturer directly or indirectly restricts the freedom of suppliers of spare-parts to supply such products to resellers of their choice, including those which are undertakings within the distribution system, provided that such parts match the quality of contract goods; or

(11) the manufacturer directly or indirectly restricts the freedom of spare-part manufacturers to place effectively and in an easily visible manner their trade mark or logo on parts supplied for the initial assembly or for the repair or maintenance of contract goods or corresponding goods; or ...

[Article 10]

For the purposes of this Regulation the following terms shall have the following meanings:

...

4. "contract goods" are new motor vehicles intended for use on public roads and having three or more road wheels, and spare parts therefor, which are the subject of an agreement within the meaning of Article 1;

5. the "contract range" refers to the totality of the contract goods;

6. "spare parts" are parts which are to be installed in or upon a motor vehicle so as to replace components of that vehicle. They are to be distinguished from other parts and accessories, according to trade usage;

...

11. "corresponding goods", "corresponding motor vehicles" and "corresponding parts" are those which are similar in kind to those in the contract range, are distributed by the manufacturer or with the manufacturer's consent, and are the subject of a distribution or servicing agreement with an undertaking within the distribution system; ...

Question 21: Do all vehicle parts and accessories fall under the term "spare parts" as used in the Regulation?

No, only parts which are to be installed in or upon a motor vehicle so as to replace components of that vehicle are spare parts within the meaning of the Regulation. The distinction follows trade usage [Article 10(6)]. For example: oil and other liquids are not considered as "spare parts" under the Regulation. Consequently, dealers are free to get those products wherever they wish and the manufacturer cannot justify restrictions imposed on its dealers with regard to the sourcing of such parts and accessories through reference to the Regulation. Nor is it possible for the parties to include parts and accessories, which fall outside the definition of "spare part", within the scope of the Regulation by agreement. If they do so, they will automatically lose the benefit of the group exemption [Article 6(1)(2)].

Question 22: What control can be exercised by a manufacturer over the sourcing of spare parts for use in the normal repair and maintenance of contract vehicles?

So as to ensure effective competition on the maintenance and repair markets, the Regulation starts from the assumption that dealers must be free to out-source spare parts, as this is in the interest of consumers. Nevertheless, the Regulation enables the manufacturer to verify the quality of spare parts, as this is important with regard to safety and consumer satisfaction.

This is why the manufacturer may impose on its dealers the obligation neither to sell spare parts which compete with contract goods without matching them in quality nor to use parts of lower quality for repair or maintenance of contract goods or corresponding goods [Article 3(5)]. This means that dealers are free to out-source spare parts (1) if the parts do not compete with those promoted by the manufacturer or (2) if the parts compete with contract goods but they match the quality of those products.

However, the manufacturer can require its dealers to inform customers about the use of spare parts from other sources in repair and maintenance work, first in a general manner before repair work has been undertaken [Article 4(1)(8)] and second, after the completion of the repair work where out-sourced spare parts have been used, as to their specific use [Article 4(1)(9)].

Question 23: What is meant by "matching" the quality of the spare parts sourced by the manufacturer? How will the matching quality of spare parts furnished by independent suppliers be controlled?

Recital (8) of the Regulation says that it can be presumed that all parts coming from the same source of production, regardless of whether supplied to the car manufacturer or to a dealer belonging to the network, are identical in characteristics and origin. If the dealer wishes to be certain that the parts offered to him correspond to those supplied to the manufacturer of the vehicle, he should ask the spare parts supplier for confirmation.

Where such parts have not been supplied to the car manufacturer, the question of equivalence in quality must be solved according to the general rules of national law.

Question 24: Do the same rules apply to the use of spare parts in guarantee work?

No, the manufacturer may oblige its dealers to use only its spare parts (*i.e.* those within the contract range or corresponding spare parts) for work under guarantee, free servicing and vehicle recall-work [Article 4(1)(7)].

Spare parts within the contract range or corresponding spare parts are either sourced and distributed by the manufacturer to its dealers [Article 10(4) and (5)] or sold by another undertaking to the authorised dealers with the manufacturer's consent. In the latter case, such spare parts must additionally be the subject of a distribution or servicing agreement between an authorised dealer and the manufacturer or between the manufacturer and a spare-part supplier [Article 10(11)].

Question 25: Why must a manufacturer, in aggregating quantities or values of goods for the purpose of calculating discounts to be granted to a dealer, differentiate between discounts given for motor vehicles within the contract range and for spare parts and for other goods?

The purpose is to avoid dealers having to rely solely on the manufacturer's supply because of special discounts given by him, thus closing the distribution system to independent spare-part suppliers [Article 5(1)(2)(c)].

Therefore, the Regulation imposes the obligation on the manufacturer to differentiate between discounts given to the dealer (1) for the ordering of motor vehicles, (2) for the ordering of spare parts for supplies of which the dealer is dependent on undertakings within the distribution network, *e.g.* bodywork spare-parts and (3) other spare-parts which are used for the normal maintenance of a vehicle and which are equally available outside the distribution network. If these three "baskets" are not kept separate for the accounting of discounts, it could lead to the result that a dealer receives such a high discount from the manufacturer because of the high amount of goods purchased, that no other spare-part manufacturer or supplier could make a competitive price.

Question 26: What are the legal consequences if a manufacturer tries to hinder dealers from purchasing spare parts from competing producers which are of matching quality?

The manufacturer loses the benefit of the exemption, if, directly or indirectly, he restricts the freedom of authorised distributors to purchase from third parties spare parts which match the quality of the contract products [Article 6(1)(9)].

Question 27: What rights are protected by the Regulation on independent suppliers of spare parts and on resellers?

The Regulation opens the market for independent suppliers of spare parts (described above) and resellers. The supply of contract goods [Article 10(4)] to resellers may not be prohibited where they belong to the same distribution system [Article 3(10)(a)], or where the purchase of spare parts is for their own use in effecting repairs or maintenance [Article 3(10)(b)].

These rights of suppliers of spare parts and resellers are safeguarded by the Black List. The manufacturer will automatically lose the benefit of the group exemption, if he directly or indirectly restricts:

— the freedom of spare-part suppliers to supply such products of matching quality to resellers of their choice, including those which are undertakings within the distribution system [Article 6(1)(10)];
— the spare-part manufacturers are hindered from affixing effectively and in an easily visible manner their trade mark or logo on the spare parts bought by the manufacturer or supplied to the network [Article 6(1)(11)].

2. Technical Information

[Article 6]

1. The exemption shall not apply where:

...

(12) the manufacturer refuses to make accessible, where appropriate upon payment, to repairers who are not undertakings within the distribution system, the technical information required for the repair or maintenance of the contractual or corresponding goods or for the implementing of environmental protection measures, provided that the information is not covered by an intellectual property right or does not constitute identified, substantial, secret know-how; in such case, the necessary technical information shall not be withheld improperly ...

Question 28: To what degree is the manufacturer obliged under the Regulation to provide access for independent repairers to technical information required for the repair or maintenance of vehicles produced by the manufacturer?

Independent garage owners are often unable to provide repair services because the manufacturer makes the relevant technical knowledge available only to firms which are network members. The consumer is thus deprived of a considerable part of his freedom of choice for the maintenance and repair of his car.

The Regulation takes account of this problem by imposing the obligation on manufacturers to make accessible to non-network firms the technical information necessary for the repair and maintenance of their makes of motor vehicles, provided this information is not covered by the manufacturer's intellectual property rights or does not constitute identified, substantial and secret know-how. Even in such cases, the necessary technical information may not be withheld in a discriminatory or abusive manner [Article 6(1)(12), Recital 28].

However, the manufacturer may ask from the independent repairer payment for the supply of technical information. In such a case, the amount requested should be reasonable and neither discriminatory nor prohibitive.

The term "intellectual property right" includes rights such as patents, copyrights, registered designs and industrial and commercial property.

The wording "identified, substantial, secret know-how" is interpreted according to the definition given in Article 1(7)(1) to (4) of Regulation (EEC) No. 556/89[7] as amended by Commission Regulation (EEC) No 151/93.[8]

IV. Increasing Consumers' Choice in Accordance with the Principles of the Single Market:

1. Parallel Imports

[Article 3]

The exemption shall also apply where the obligation referred to in Article 1 is combined with an obligation on the dealer:

. . .

10. not to supply to a reseller:

(a) contract goods or corresponding goods unless the reseller is an undertaking within the distribution system, or
(b) spare parts within the contract range unless the reseller uses them for the repair or maintenance of a motor vehicle,

11. not to sell motor vehicles within the contract range or corresponding goods to final consumers using the services of an intermediary unless that intermediary has prior written authority from such consumers to purchase a specified motor vehicle or where it is taken away by him, to collect it.

[Article 5]

1. In all cases, the exemption shall apply only if:
(1) the dealer undertakes:

(a) in respect of motor vehicles within the contract range or corresponding thereto which have been supplied in the common market by another undertaking within the distribution network:

— to honour guarantees and to perform free servicing and vehicle-recall work to an extent which corresponds to the dealer's obligation covered by Article 4(1)(6).
— to carry out repair and maintenance work in accordance with Article 4(1)(1)(e);

(b) to impose upon the undertakings operating within the contract territory with which the dealer has concluded distribution and servicing agreements as provided for in Article 3(6) an obligation to honour guarantees and to perform free servicing and vehicle recall work at least to the extent to which the dealer himself is so obliged: ...

[Article 6]

1. The exemption shall not apply where:

(6) the manufacturer, the supplier or another undertaking directly or indirectly restricts the dealer's freedom to determine prices and discounts in reselling contract goods or corresponding goods; or
(7) the manufacturer, the supplier or another undertaking within the network directly or indirectly restricts the freedom of final consumers, authorised intermediaries or dealers to obtain from an undertaking belonging to the network of their choice within the common market contract goods or corresponding goods or to obtain servicing for such goods, or the freedom of final consumers to resell the contract goods or corresponding goods, when the sale is not effected for commercial purposes; or
(8) the supplier, without any objective reason, grants dealers remunerations calculated on the basis of the place of destination of the motor vehicles resold or the place of residence of the purchaser; or ...

[Article 10]

For the purposes of this Regulation the following terms shall have the following meaning.
...

12. "resale" includes all transactions by which a physical or legal person—"the reseller"—disposes of a motor vehicle which is still in a new condition and which he had previously acquired in his own name and on his own behalf, irrespective of the legal description applied under civil law or the format of the transaction which with effects such resale. The terms resale shall include all leasing contracts which provide for a transfer of ownerships or an option to purchase prior to the expiry of the contract; ...

Question 29: Is a consumer, who is a resident of a E.U. Member State, free to buy a vehicle wherever he considers it to be most advantageous within the Common Market?

The consumer's freedom to buy anywhere in the Common Market is one of the fundamental achievements of the European Community and the Regulation reinforces this right. The consumer's right is not accompanied by an obligation imposed on dealers to sell since it is normally in a dealer's interest to maximise sales. A dealer within the Common Market may not reject a consumer's offer to buy or ask for a higher price simply because the consumer is a resident of another E.U. Member State.

The Regulation reinforces the right of a consumer resident in one Member State to buy a motor vehicle in another Member State:

— The consumer can be requested to complete only the same documentation and in the usual manner as is normally and lawfully required of a consumer resident in the Member State where the vehicle is bought. Usually such documentation relates to the name and address of the consumer.

— Under the Regulation the producer and all dealers should honour the guarantee and provide free servicing, vehicle recall work, and repair and maintenance services necessary for the safe and reliable functioning of the vehicle, irrespective of where and from whom in the Common Market the vehicle was purchased [Article 5(1)(1)(a) and (b) and Recital 26].
— The manufacturer, the supplier or another undertaking within the network who directly or indirectly restricts the freedom of final consumers, authorised intermediaries or authorised dealers to obtain a new motor vehicle from whichever authorised dealer they choose within the Common Market automatically loses the benefit of the exemption [Article 6(1)(7)].

Question 30: What formalities apply if a consumer appoints an intermediary to purchase a motor vehicle in another Member State on the consumer's behalf?

The intermediary must have prior authorisation in writing from the consumer to purchase and/or to collect a specified vehicle [Article 3(11)]. The Commission has already published under Regulation (EEC) No. 123/85 a Commission Notice[9], which remains applicable.

The written authorisation must enable the dealer to identify the final consumer by name and address. The dealer may require such authorisation to include the name and address of the intermediary. Moreover, the authorisation has to specify the vehicle together with the essential details chosen by the consumer, such as make and model together with the signature of the consumer and the date of signing.

If an intermediary cannot show such authorisation the manufacturer may oblige his dealer(s) not to sell to him [Article 3(10)].

Question 31: Does the use of an intermediary alter the rights accorded to the consumer under the Regulation with regard to purchase or after-sales service?

The right of an authorised intermediary to purchase a motor vehicle on behalf of the final consumer in a Member State other than where the final consumer is resident is given the same protection as the consumer's right to conclude personally such a transaction [see Article 6(1)(7)].

Question 32: Can a manufacturer stipulate the resale price charged by or discounts given by a dealer to a consumer?

Although it is true that a manufacturer may recommend prices, he may neither directly nor indirectly impose on the dealer fixed prices. Neither minimum and maximum resale prices may be fixed by the manufacturer. It is up to the dealer to decide his own policy on resale prices and discounts. If the manufacturer restricts the dealer's freedom with regard to resale prices and discounts, such behaviour will lead to the automatic loss of the exemption for the manufacturer [Article 6(1)(6)].

Question 33: Is the consumer restricted in disposing of the car?

The consumer is free to sell the motor vehicle at any time provided he is not a disguised independent reseller [Article 6(1)(7), Article 10(12)]. The manufacturer, importer or another undertaking within the distribution network may not impose an obligation on the final consumer to sell the vehicle only after a certain period of time and/or after a certain mileage reading.

Question 34: In what way(s) does the Regulation prevent a manufacturer from interfering with parallel imports/exports?

The scope of the rights of consumers, intermediaries and dealers to conduct parallel imports/exports has been discussed above. The manufacturer is, therefore, unable to interfere with these rights without losing the benefit of the exemption.

Additionally, a manufacturer cannot base the payment to a dealer (including rebate systems) on the destination of the vehicle being sold, without having objective reasons [Article 6(1)(8), Recital 26]. "Objective reasons" should be applied without discrimination, and in an equitable and reasonable manner. The manufacturer is, for example, not allowed to give greater remuneration to the dealer for sales to customers resident within the contract territory without objective reason. This prohibition therefore avoids indirect pressure being imposed on the dealer to sell only within the contract territory. An objective reason would be if the legal situation changes in a given Member State, *e.g.* tax which has lead to a change in the calculation basis of list prices.

2. Honouring of Manufacturer's Guarantee

[Article 4]

1. The exemption shall apply notwithstanding any obligation whereby the dealer undertakes to:

(a) comply, in distribution, sales and after-sales servicing with minimum standards, regarding in particular; ...

(e) the repair and maintenance of contract goods and corresponding goods, particularly as regards the safe and reliable functioning of motor vehicles; ...

[Article 5]

1. In all cases, the exemption shall apply only if:

(1) the dealer undertakes:

(a) in respect of motor vehicles within the contract range or corresponding thereto which have been supplied in the common market by another undertaking within the distribution network:

— to honour guarantees and to perform free servicing and vehicle-recall work to an extent which corresponds to the dealer's obligation covered by Article 4(1)(6),

— to carry out repair and maintenance work in accordance with Article 4(1)(1)(e);

...

[Article 6]

1. The exemption shall not apply where:

...

(7) the manufacturer, the supplier or another undertaking within the network directly or indirectly restricts the freedom of final consumers, authorised intermediaries or dealers to obtain from an undertaking belonging to the network of their choice within the common market contract goods or corresponding goods or to obtain servicing for such goods, or the freedom of final consumers to resell the contract goods or corresponding goods, when the sale is not effected for commercial purposes; or ...

Question 35: Having purchased the motor vehicle in another Member State, where can the consumer have normal servicing or guarantee work carried out?

The consumer is entitled to seek to have such a vehicle serviced by any undertaking belonging to the network which distributed the vehicle. Hence it is unnecessary for the consumer to return to the dealer in the Member State of purchase [Article 5(1)(1)(a) and Article 4(1)(1)(e)]. The consumer can also turn for servicing to an independent repairer even though there is a risk that in this case the manufacturer can refuse to honour guarantee services thereafter.

Under the Regulation, authorised dealers are expressly obliged to honour the manufacturer's guarantee, to perform free servicing and vehicle recall work on vehicles within their contract or a corresponding range which were supplied in the Common Market by another undertaking within the same distribution network, but only to the extent to which the dealers are obliged under the terms of their distributorship to service vehicles which they themselves have supplied [Article 5 (1)(1)(a), Recital 12]. This provision ensures that a final consumer can have the benefit of the manufacturer's guarantee, free servicing and vehicle recall work available from every dealer of the manufacturer's network throughout the Community.

The guarantee period begins at the time when a car leaves the manufacturer's network, *i.e.* the delivery of a car by an authorised dealer. It makes no difference whether the consumer himself or an authorised intermediary collects the vehicle from the authorised dealer. A final consumer who purchases a car from an independent reseller, should be aware that a part of the guarantee period given by the manufacturer could already have expired as the reseller could have bought the car from an authorised dealer of the manufacturer's network some months previously.

Where a manufacturer, importer, dealer or another company within the network impedes the principle of Community-wide guarantee services, it will lose the benefit of the exemption [Article 6(1)(7)].

3. Advertising Outside the Contract Territory

[Article 3]

The exemption shall also apply where the obligation referred to in Article 1 is combined with an obligation on the dealer:

...

8. outside the contract territory:

(b) not to solicit customers for contract goods or corresponding goods, by personalised advertising; ...

Question 36: To what extent is a dealer free to advertise outside the contract territory?

As the Regulation aims at reinforcing flexible demand for contract goods, customers must be in a position to choose the offer which suits them best. The

Regulation, therefore, provides that the dealer must be free to seek customers outside his territory by means *e.g.* of media, posters, general brochures or advertisements in newspapers [Article 3(8)(b)]. The manufacturer can only oblige his dealer not to seek customers by personalised advertising, *i.e.* telephone or other form of telecommunication, doorstep canvassing or by direct mail.

[Article 3]

The exemption shall also apply where the obligation referred to in Article 1 is combined with an obligation on the dealer:

. . .

10 not to supply to a reseller:

(a) contract goods or corresponding goods unless the reseller is an undertaking within the distribution system, or
(b) spare parts within the contract range unless the reseller uses them for the repair or maintenance of a motor vehicle; . . .

[Article 10]

For the purposes of this Regulation the following terms shall have the following meanings:

. . .

12. "resale" includes all transactions by which a physical or legal person—"the reseller"—disposes of a motor vehicle which is still in a new condition and which he had previously acquired in his own name and on his own behalf, irrespective of the legal description applied under civil law or the format of the transaction which effects such resale. The terms resale shall include all leasing contracts which provide for a transfer of ownership or an option to purchase prior to the expiry of the contract;
13. "distribute" and "sell" include other forms of supply by the dealer such as leasing.

Question 37: What is the position if a consumer wishes to lease a vehicle from a dealer?

The Regulation makes it clear that a dealer can lease cars as well as selling them [Article 10(13)]. This ensures that any dealer who offers leasing contracts to customers may still benefit from exemption under the Regulation and will still be required to comply with obligations imposed under the Regulation for the protection of consumers, for example as to the servicing of vehicles.

Question 38: Is a dealer entitled to sell to leasing companies?

Yes, the supply to leasing companies is a legitimate part of the activities of dealers as leasing companies are normally considered to be final consumers. However, the supplier may prevent the dealer from supplying contract goods to leasing companies which in fact act as resellers and which do not belong to the distribution network [Article 3(10)]). Article 10(12) makes it clear that leasing contracts which involve a transfer of ownership or a purchase option prior to the expiry of the contract are in reality sales contracts, and that the leasing company in such cases is treated as a reseller.

V. Interaction with Other Provisions of Community Law

[Article 12]

Regulation (EEC) No. 4087/88 is not applicable to agreements concerning the products or services referred to in this Regulation.

[Article 6]

1. The exemption shall not apply where:

...

(4) in respect of motor vehicles having three or more road wheels or spare parts therefor, the parties make agreements or engage in concerted practices which are exempted from the prohibition in Article 85(1) of the Treaty under Regulations (EEC) No. 1984/83 or (EEC) No. 198/83 to an extent exceeding the scope of this Regulation, or ...

Question 39: What effect does the Regulation have on the other group exemption Regulations which relate to the distribution of goods or services?

The Regulation excludes the application of Commission Regulation (EEC) No. 4087/88 concerning franchising agreements[10] on agreements concerning the distribution and servicing of new motor vehicles and the spare parts therefor [Article 12]. The reason is that Regulation 1475/95 has been specifically written for car distribution and is intended to safeguard and balance all the interests involved. Producers can seek an individual exemption if they wish to organise their distribution network as a franchise system.

The other group exemption regulations concerning the distribution of goods, Commission Regulation (EEC) No. 1983/83[11] and (EEC) No 1984/83,[12] remain applicable to cars. This means that producers are free to choose to organise their distribution system according to Regulation 1475/95 or according to these two other group exemptions. It is, however, not possible to combine provisions of those Regulations with provisions of Regulation 1475/85 if the other Regulations allow the introduction of obligations which favour the manufacturer or the dealer and which are more far-reaching than those permitted under Regulation 1475/95 [Article 6(1)(4)].

The group exemption regulations concerning specialisation[13] and research and development agreements[14] are applicable without any restriction since their emphasis does not lay on the distribution of goods.

Question 40: Can Article 86 of the Treaty apply to an exclusive and selective distribution agreement which falls within the scope of Regulation 1475/95?

Yes, the application of Regulation 1475/95—as with any other group exemption regulation—does not preclude the application of Article 86 of the Treaty. The scope of application of Article 86 of the Treaty is different from that of Article 85 since Article 86 requires that the undertaking in question has a dominant position in the relevant market. Article 85 of the Treaty—under which a group exemption is granted—prohibits agreements and concerted practices which restrict competition within the Common Market.

[1] OJ 1996 L145/25.
[2] A reference to manufacturer includes, where appropriate, a reference to supplier.
[3] OJ 1983 L173/1.
[4] OJ 1983 L173/5.
[5] OJ 1985 C17/4
[6] OJ 1991 C329/20.
[7] OJ 1989 L61/1.
[8] OJ 1993 L21/8.
[9] OJ 1991 C329/20. [App. 15 to the main work].
[10] OJ 1988 L359/46.
[11] OJ 1983 L173/1.
[12] OJ 1983 L173/5.
[13] Commission Regulation (EEC) No. 417/85, OJ 1985 L53/1.
[14] Commission Regulation (EEC) No. 418/85, OJ 1985 L53/5.

APPENDIX 4

REGULATION 240/96[1]

on the application of Article 85(3) of the Treaty to certain categories of technology transfer agreements

THE COMMISSION OF THE EUROPEAN COMMUNITIES

Having regard to the Treaty establishing the European Community.

Having regard to Council Regulation No. 19/65/EEC 2 March 1965 on the application of Article 85(3) of the Treaty to certain categories of agreements and concerted practices[2] as last amended by the Act of Accession Austria, Finland and Sweden, and in particular Article 1 thereof,

Having published a draft of this Regulation,[3]

After consulting the Advisory Committee on Restrictive Practices and Dominant Positions,

Whereas:

(1) Regulation No. 19/65/EEC empowers the Commission to apply Article 85(3) of the Treaty by regulation to certain categories of agreements and concerted practices falling within the scope of Article 85(1) which include restrictions imposed in relation to the acquisition or use of industrial property rights—in particular of patents, utility models, designs or trademarks—or to the rights arising out of contracts for assignment of, or the right to use, a method of manufacture of knowledge relating to use or to the application of industrial processes.

(2) The Commission has made use of this power by adopting Regulation (EEC) No. 2349/84 of 23 July 1984 on the application of Article 85(3) of the Treaty to certain categories of patent licensing agreements,[4] as last amended by Regulation (EC) No. 2131/95,[5] and Regulation (EEC) No. 556/89 of 30 November 1988 on the application of Article 85(3) of the Treaty to certain categories of know-how licensing agreements,[6] as last amended by the Act of Accession of Austria, Finland and Sweden.

(3) These two block exemptions ought to be combined into a single regulation covering technology transfer agreements, and the rules governing patent licensing agreements and agreements for the licensing of know-how ought to be harmonized and simplified as far as possible, in order to encourage the dissemination of technical knowledge in the Community and to promote the manufacture of technically more sophisticated products. In those circumstances Regulation (EEC) No. 556/89 should be repealed.

(4) This Regulation should apply to the licensing of Member States' own patents, Community patents[7] and European patents[8] ("pure" patent licensing agreements). It should also apply to agreements for the licensing-of non-patented technical information such as descriptions of manufacturing processes, recipes, formulae, designs or drawings, commonly termed "know-how" ("pure" know-how licensing agreements), and

to combined patent and know-how licensing agreements ("mixed" agreements), which are playing an increasingly important role in the transfer of technology. For the purposes of this Regulation, a number of terms are defined in Article 10.

(5) Patent or know-how licensing agreements are agreements whereby one undertaking which holds a patent or know-how ("the licensor") permits another undertaking ("the licensee") to exploit the patent thereby licensed, or communicates the know-how to it, in particular for purposes of manufacture, use or putting on the market. In the light of experience acquired so far, it is possible to define a category of licensing agreements covering all or part of the common market which are capable of falling within the scope of Article 85(1) but which can normally be regarded as satisfying the conditions laid down in Article 85(3), where patents are necessary for the achievement of the objects of the licensed technology by a mixed agreement or where know-how—whether it is ancillary to patents or independent of them—is secret, substantial and identified in any appropriate form. These criteria are intended only to ensure that the licensing of the know-how or the grant of the patent licence justifies a block exemption of obligations restricting competition. This is without prejudice to the right of the parties to include in the contract provisions regarding other obligations, such as the obligation to pay royalties, even if the block exemption no longer applies.

(6) It is appropriate to extend the scope of this Regulation to pure or mixed agreements containing the licensing of intellectual property rights other than patents (in particular, trademarks, design rights and copyright, especially software protection), when such additional licensing contributes to the achievement of the objects of the licensed technology and contains only ancillary provisions.

(7) Where such pure or mixed licensing agreements contain not only obligations relating to territories within the common market but also obligations relating to non-member countries, the presence of the latter does not prevent this Regulation from applying to the obligations relating to territories within the common market. Where licensing agreements for non-member countries or for territories which extend beyond the frontiers of the Community have effects within the common market which may fall within the scope of Article 85(1), such agreements should be covered by this Regulation to the same extent as would agreements for territories within the common market.

(8) The objective being to facilitate the dissemination of technology and the improvement of manufacturing processes, this Regulation should apply only where the licensee himself manufactures the licensed products or has them manufactured for his account, or where the licensed products is a service, provides the service himself or has the service provided for his account, irrespective of whether or not the licensee is also entitled to use confidential information provided by the licensor for the promotion and sale of the licensed product. The scope of this Regulation should therefore exclude agreements solely for the purpose of sale. Also to be excluded from the scope of this Regulation are agreements relating to marketing know-how communicated in the context of franchising arrangements and certain licensing agreements entered into in connection with arrangements such as joint ventures or patent pools and other arrangements in which a licence is granted in exchange for other licences not related to improvements to or new applications of the licensed technology. Such agreements pose different problems which cannot at present be dealt with in a single regulation (Article 5).

(9) Given the similarity between sale and exclusive licensing, and the danger that the requirements of this Regulation might be evaded by presenting as assignments what are in fact exclusive licenses restrictive of competition, this Regulation should apply to agreements concerning the assignment

and acquisition of patents or know-how where the risk associated with exploitation remains with the assignor. It should also apply to licensing agreements in which the licensor is not the holder of the patent or know-how but is authorised by the holder to grant the licence (as in the case of sub-licences) and to licensing agreements in which the parties' rights or obligations are assumed by connected undertakings (Article 6).

(10) Exclusive licensing agreements, *i.e.* agreements in which the licensor undertakes not to exploit the licensed technology in the licensed territory himself or to grant further licences there, may not be in themselves incompatible with Article 85(1) where they are concerned with the introduction and protection of a new technology in the licensed territory, by reason of the scale of the research which has been undertaken, of the increase in the level of competition, in particular inter-brand competition, and of the competitiveness of the undertakings concerned resulting from the dissemination of innovation within the Community. In so far as agreements of this kind fall, in other circumstances, within the scope of Article 85(1), it is appropriate to include them in Article 1 in order that they may also benefit from the exemption.

(11) The exemption of export bans on the licensor and on the licensees does not prejudice any developments in the case law of the Court of Justice in relation to such agreements, notably with respect to Articles 30 to 36 and Article 85(1). This is also the case, in particular, regarding the prohibition on the licensee from selling the licensed product in territories granted to other licensees (passive competition).

(12) The obligations listed in Article 1 generally contribute to improving the production of goods and to promoting technical progress. They make the holders of patents or know-how more willing to grant licences and licensees more inclined to undertake the investment required to manufacture, use and put on the market a new product or to use a new process. Such obligations may be permitted under this Regulation in respect of territories where the licensed product is protected by patents as long as these remain in force.

(13) Since the point at which the know-how ceases to be secret can be difficult to determine, it is appropriate, in respect of territories where the licensed technology comprises know-how only, to limit such obligations to a fixed number of years. Moreover, in order to provide sufficient periods of protection, it is appropriate to take as the starting point for such periods the date on which the product is first put on the market in the Community by a licensee.

(14) Exemption under Article 85(3) of longer periods of territorial protection for know-how agreements, in particular in order to protect expensive and risky investment or where the parties were not competitors at the date of the grant of the licence, can be granted only by individual decision. On the other hand, parties are free to extend the term of their agreements in order to exploit any subsequent improvement and to provide for the payment of additional royalties. However, in such cases, further periods of territorial protection may be allowed only starting from the date of licensing of the secret improvements in the Community, and by individual decision. Where the research for improvements results in innovations which are distinct from the licensed technology the parties may conclude a new agreement benefiting from an exemption under this Regulation.

(15) Provision should also be made for exemption of an obligation on the licensee not to put the product on the market in the territories of other licensees, the permitted period for such an obligation (this obligation would ban not just active competition but passive competition too) should, however be limited to a few years from the date on which the licensed product is first put on the market in the Community by a licensee, irrespective of whether the licensed technology comprises know-how, patents or both in the territories concerned.

(16) The exemption of territorial protection should apply for the whole duration of the periods thus permitted, as long as the patents remain in force or the know-how remains secret and substantial. The parties to a mixed patent and know-how licensing agreement must be able to take advantage in a particular territory of the period of protection conferred by a patent or by the know-how, whichever is the longer.

(17) The obligations listed in Article 1 also generally fulfil the other conditions for the application of Article 85(3). Consumers will, as a rule, be allowed a fair share of the benefit resulting from the improvement in the supply of goods on the market. To safeguard this effect, however, it is right to exclude from the application of Article 1 cases where the parties agree to refuse to meet demand from users or resellers within their respective territories who would resell for export, or to take other steps to impede parallel imports. The obligations referred to above thus only impose restrictions which are indispensable to the attainment of their objectives.

(18) It is desirable to list in this Regulation a number of obligations that are commonly found in licensing agreements but are normally not restrictive of competition, and to provide that in the event that because of the particular economic or legal circumstances they should fall within Article 85(1), they too will be covered by the exemption. This list, in Article 2, is not exhaustive.

(19) This Regulation must also specify what restrictions or provisions may not be included in licensing agreements if these are to benefit from the block exemption. The restrictions listed in Article 3 may fall under the prohibition of Article 85(1), but in their case there can be no general presumption that, although they relate to the transfer of technology, they will lead to the positive effects required by Article 85(3), as would be necessary for the granting of a block exemption. Such restrictions can be declared exempt only by an individual decision, taking account of the market position of the undertakings concerned and the degree of concentration on the relevant market.

(20) The obligations on the licensee to cease using the licensed technology after the termination of the agreement (Article 2(1)(3)) and to make improvements available to the licensor (Article 2(1)(4)) do not generally restrict competition. The post-term use ban may be regarded as a normal feature of licensing, as otherwise the licensor would be forced to transfer his know-how or patents in perpetuity. Undertakings by the licensee to grant back to the licensor a licence for improvements to the licensed know-how and/or patents are generally not restrictive of competition if the licensee is entitled by the contract to share in future experience and inventions made by the licensor. On the other hand, a restrictive effect on competition arises where the agreement obliges the licensee to assign to the licensor rights to improvements of the originally licensed technology that he himself has brought about (Article 3(6)).

(21) The list of clauses which do not prevent exemption also includes an obligation on the licensee to keep paying royalties until the end of the agreement independently of whether or not the licensed know-how has entered into the public domain through the action of third parties or of the licensee himself (Article 2(1)(7)). Moreover, the parties must be free, in order to facilitate payment, to spread the royalty payments for the use of the licensed technology over a period extending beyond the duration of the licensed patents, in particular by setting lower royalty rates. As a rule, parties do not need to be protected against the foreseeable financial consequences of an agreement freely entered into, and they should therefore be free to choose the appropriate means of financing the technology transfer and sharing between them the risks of such use. However, the setting of rates of royalty so as to achieve one of the restrictions listed in Article 3 renders the agreement ineligible for the block exemption.

(22) An obligation on the licensee to restrict his exploitation of the licensed technology to one or more technical fields of application ("fields of use") or to one or more product markets is not caught by Article 85(1) either, since the licensor is entitled to transfer the technology only for a limited purpose (Article 2(1)(8)).

(23) Clauses whereby the parties allocate customers within the same technological field of use or the same product market, either by an actual prohibition on supplying certain classes of customer or through an obligation with an equivalent effect, would also render the agreement ineligible for the block exemption where the parties are competitors for the contract products (Article 3(4)). Such restrictions between undertakings which are not competitors remain subject to the opposition procedure. Article 3 does not apply to cases where the patent or know-how licence is granted in order to provide a single customer with a second source of supply. In such a case, a prohibition on the second licensee from supplying persons other than the customer concerned is an essential condition for the grant of a second licence, since the purpose of the transaction is not to create an independent supplier in the market. The same applies to limitations on the quantities the licensee may supply to the customer concerned (Article 2(1)(13)).

(24) Besides the clauses already mentioned, the list of restrictions which render the block exemption inapplicable also includes restrictions regarding the selling prices of the licensed product or the quantities to be manufactured or sold, since they seriously limit the extent to which the licensee can exploit the licensed technology and since quantity restrictions particularly may have the same effect as export bans (Article 3(1) and (5)). This does not apply where a licence is granted for use of the technology in specific production facilities and where both a specific technology is communicated for the setting-up, operation and maintenance of these facilities and the licensee is allowed to increase the capacity of the facilities or to set up further facilities for its own use on normal commercial terms. On the other hand, the licensee may lawfully be prevented from using the transferred technology to set up facilities for third parties, since the purpose of the agreement is not to permit the licensee to give other producers access to the licensor's technology while it remains secret or protected by patent (Article 2(1)(12)).

(25) Agreements which are not automatically covered by the exemption because they contain provisions that are not expressly exempted by this Regulation and not expressly excluded from exemption, including those listed in Article 4(2), may, in certain circumstances, nonetheless be presumed to be eligible for application of the block exemption. It will be possible for the Commission rapidly to establish whether this is the case on the basis of the information undertakings are obliged to provide under Commission Regulation (E.C.) No. 3385/94.[8] The Commission may waive the requirement to supply specific information required in form A/B but which it does not deem necessary. The Commission will generally be content with communication of the text of the agreement and with an estimate, based on directly available data, of the market structure and the licensee's marker share. Such agreements should therefore be deemed to be covered by the exemption provided for in this Regulation where they are notified to the Commission and the Commission does not oppose the application of the exemption within a specified period of time.

(26) Where agreements exempted under this Regulation nevertheless have effects incompatible with Article 85(3), the Commission may withdraw the block exemption, in particular where the licensed products are not faced with real competition in the licensed territory (Article 7). This could also be the case where the licensee has a strong position on the market. In assessing the competition the Commission will pay special attention to cases where the licensee has more than 40 per cent of the whole market for

the licensed products and of all the products or services which customers consider interchangeable or substitutable on account of their characteristics, prices and intended use.

(27) Agreements which come within the terms of Articles 1 and 2 and which have neither the object nor the effect of restricting competition in any other way need no longer be notified. Nevertheless, undertakings will still have the right to apply in individual cases for negative clearance or for exemption under Article 85(3) in accordance with Council Regulation No. 17,[9] as last amended by the Act of Accession of Austria, Finland and Sweden. They can in particular notify agreements obliging the licensor not to grant other licences in the territory, where the licensee's market share exceeds or is likely to exceed 40 per cent,

HAS ADOPTED THIS REGULATION:

Article 1

1. Pursuant to Article 85(3) of the Treaty and subject to the conditions set out below, it is hereby declared that Article 85(1) of the Treaty shall not apply to pure patent licensing or know-how licensing agreements and mixed patent and know-how licensing agreements, including those agreements containing ancillary provisions relating to intellectual property rights other than patents to which only two undertakings are party and which include one or more of the following obligations:

(1) an obligation on the licensor not to license other undertakings to exploit the licensed technology in the licensed territory;
(2) an obligation on the licensor not to exploit the licensed technology in the licensed territory himself;
(3) an obligation on the licensee not to exploit the licensed technology in the territory of the licensor within the common market;
(4) an obligation on the licensee not to manufacture or use the licensed product, or use the licensed process in territories within the common market which are licensed to other licensees;
(5) an obligation on the licensee not to pursue an active policy of putting the licensed product on the market in the territories within the common market which are licensed to other licensees, and in particular not to engage in advertising specifically aimed at those territories or to establish any branch or maintain a distribution depot there;
(6) an obligation on the licensee not to put the licensed product on the market in the territories licensed to other licensees within the common market in response to unsolicited orders;
(7) an obligation on the licensee to use only the licensor's trademark or get up to distinguish the licensed product during the term of the agreement, provided that the licensee is not prevented from identifying himself as the manufacturer of the licensed products;
(8) an obligation on the licensee to limit his production of the licensed product to the quantities he requires in manufacturing his own products and to sell the licensed product only as an integral part of or a replacement part for his own products or otherwise in connection with the sale of his own products, provided that such quantities are freely determined by the licensee.

2. Where the agreement is a pure patent licensing agreement, the exemption of the obligations referred to in paragraph 1 is granted only to the extent that and for as long as the licensed product is protected by parallel patents, in the territories respectively of the licensee (points (1), (2), (7) and (8)), the licensor (point (3)) and other licensees (points (4) and (5)). The exemption of the obligation referred to in point (6) of paragraph 1 is granted for a period not exceeding five years from the date when the licensed product is first put on the market within the common

market by one of the licensees, to the extent that and for as long as, in these territories, this product is protected by parallel patents.

3. Where the agreement is a pure know-how licensing agreement, the period for which the exemption of the obligations referred to in points (1) to (5) of paragraph 1 is granted may not exceed ten years from the date when the licensed product is first put on the market within the common market by one of the licensees.

The exemption of the obligation referred to in point (6) of paragraph 1 is granted for a period not exceeding five years from the date when the licensed product is first put on the market within the common market by one of the licensees.

The obligations referred to in points (7) and (8) of paragraph 1 are exempted during the lifetime of the agreement for as long as the know-how remains secret and substantial.

However, the exemption in paragraph 1 shall apply only where the parties have identified in any appropriate form the initial know-how and any subsequent improvements to it which become available to one party and are communicated to the other party pursuant to the terms of the agreement and to the purpose thereof, and only for as long as the know-how remains secret and substantial.

Where the agreement is a mixed patent and now-how licensing agreement, the exemption of the obligations referred to in points (1) to (5) of paragraph 1 shall apply in Member States in which the licensed technology is protected by necessary patents for as long as the licensed product is protected in those Member States by such patents if the duration of such protection exceeds the periods specified in paragraph 3.

The duration of the exemption provided in point (6) of paragraph 1 may not exceed the five-year period provided for in paragraphs 2 and 3.

However, such agreements qualify for the exemption referred to in paragraph 1 only for as long as the patents remain in force or to the extent that the know-how is quantified and for as long as it remains secret and substantiated, whichever period is the longer.

5. The exemption provided for in paragraph 1 shall also apply where in a particular agreement the parties undertake obligations of the types referred to in that paragraph but with a more limited scope than is permitted by that paragraph.

Article 2

1. Article 1 shall apply notwithstanding the presence in particular of any of the following clauses, which are generally not restrictive of competition:

(1) an obligation on the licensee not to divulge the know-how communicated by the licensor; the licensee may be held to this obligation after the agreement has expired;
(2) an obligation on the licensee not to grant sublicences or assign the licence;
(3) an obligation on the licensee not to exploit the licensed know-how or patents after termination of the agreement in so far and as long as the know-how is still secret or the patents are still in force;
(4) an obligation on the licensee to grant to the licensor a licence in respect of his own improvements to or his new applications of the licensed technology, provided:
- that, in the case of severable improvements, such a licence is not exclusive, so that the licensee is free to use his own improvements or to license them to third parties, in so far as that does not involve disclosure of the know-how communicated by the licensor that is still secret,
- and that the licensor undertakes to grant an exclusive or non-exclusive licence of his own improvements to the licensee;

(5) an obligation on the licensee to observe minimum quality specifications, including technical specifications, for the licensed product or to procure

goods or services from the licensor or from an undertaking designated by the licensor, in so far as these quality specifications, products or services are necessary for:

(a) a technically proper exploitation of the licensed technology; or
(b) ensuring that the product of the licensee conforms to the minimum quality specifications that are applicable to the licensor and other licensees;

and to allow the licensor to carry out related checks;

(6) obligations:
(a) to inform the licensor of misappropriation of the know-how or of infringements of the licensed patents; or
(b) to take or to assist the licensor in taking legal action against such misappropriation or infringements;

(7) an obligation on the licensee to continue paying the royalties:
(a) until the end of the agreement in the amounts, for the periods and according to the methods freely determined by the parties, in the event of the know-how becoming publicly known other than by action of the licensor, without prejudice to the payment of any additional damages in the event of the know-how becoming publicly known by the action of the licensee in breach of the agreement;
(b) over a period going beyond the duration of the licensed patents, in order to facilitate payment;

(8) an obligation on the licensee to restrict his exploitation of the licensed technology to one or more technical fields of application covered by the licensed technology or to one or more product markets;

(9) an obligation on the licensee to pay a minimum royalty or to produce a minimum quantity of the licensed product or to carry out a minimum number of operations exploiting the licensed technology;

(10) an obligation on the licensor to grant the licensee any more favourable terms that the licensor may grant to another undertaking after the agreement is entered into;

(11) an obligation on the licensee to mark the licensed product with an indication of the licensors name or of the licensed patent;

(12) an obligation on the licensee not to use the licensor's technology to construct facilities for third parties; this is without prejudice to the right of the licensee to increase the capacity of his facilities or to set up additional facilities for his own use on normal commercial terms, including the payment of additional royalties;

(13) an obligation on the licensee to supply only a limited quantity of the licensed product to a particular customer, where the licence was granted so that the customer might have a second source of supply inside the licensed territory; this provision shall also apply where the customer is the licensee, and the licence which was granted in order to provide a second source of supply provides that the customer is himself to manufacture the licensed products or to have them manufactured by a subcontractor;

(14) a reservation by the licensor of the right to exercise the rights conferred by a patent to oppose the exploitation of the technology by the licensee outside the licensed territory;

(15) a reservation by the licensor of the right to terminate the agreement if the licensee contests the secret or substantial nature of the licensed know-how or challenges the validity of licensed patents within the common market belonging to the licensor or undertakings connected with him;

(16) a reservation by the licensor of the right to terminate the licence agreement of a patent if the licensee raises the claim that such a patent is not necessary;

(17) an obligation on the licensee to use his best endeavours to manufacture and market the licensed product;

(18) a reservation by the licensor of the right to terminate the exclusivity

granted to the licensee and to stop licensing improvements to him when the licensee enters into competition within the common market with the licensor, with undertakings connected with the licensor or with other undertakings in respect of research and development, production, use or distribution of competing products, and to require the licensee to prove that the licensed know-how is not being used for the production of products and the provision of services other than those licensed.

2. In the event that, because of particular circumstances, the clauses referred to in paragraph 1 fall within the scope of Article 85(1), they shall also be exempted even if they are not accompanied by any of the obligations exempted by Article 1.

3. The exemption in paragraph 2 shall also apply where an agreement contains clauses of the types referred to in paragraph 1 but with a more limited scope than is permitted by that paragraph.

Article 3

Article 1 and Article 2(2) shall not apply where:

(1) one party is restricted in the determination of prices, components of prices or discounts for the licensed products;

(2) one party is restricted from competing within the common market with the other party, with undertakings connected with the other party or with other undertakings in respect of research and development, production, use or distribution of competing products without prejudice to the provisions of Article 2(1)(17) and (18);

(3) one or both of the parties are required without any objectively justified reason:

  (a) to refuse to meet orders from users or resellers in their respective territories who would market products in other territories within the common market:

  (b) to make it difficult for users or resellers to obtain the products from other resellers within the common market, and in particular to exercise intellectual property rights or take measures so as to prevent users or resellers from obtaining outside, or from putting on the market in the licensed territory products which have been lawfully put on the market within the common market by the licensor or with his consent;

or do so as a result of a concerted practice between them;

(4) the parties were already competing manufacturers before the grant of the licence and one of them is restricted, within the same technical field of use or within the same product market, as to the customers he may serve, in particular by being prohibited from supplying certain classes of user, employing certain forms of distribution or, with the aim of sharing customers, using certain types of packaging for the products, save as provided in Article 1(1)(7) and Article 2(1)(13);

(5) the quantity of the licensed products one party may manufacture or sell or the number of operations exploiting the licensed technology he may carry out or subject to limitations, save as provided in Article (1)(8) and Article 2(1)(13);

(6) the licensee is obliged to assign in whole or in part to the licensor rights to improvements to or new applications of the licensed technology;

(7) the licensor is required, albeit in separate agreements or through automatic prolongation of the initial duration of the agreement by the inclusion of any new improvements, for a period exceeding that referred to in Article 1(2) and (3) not to license other undertakings to exploit the licensed technology in the licensed territory, or a party is required for a period exceeding that referred to in Article 1(2) and (3) or Article 1(4) not to exploit the licensed technology in the territory of the other party or of other licensees.

Article 4

1. The exemption provided for in Articles 1 and 2 shall also apply to agreements containing obligations restrictive of competition which are not covered by those Articles and do not fall within the scope of Article 3, on condition that the agreements in question are notified to the Commission in accordance with the provisions of Articles 1, 2 and 3 of Regulation (EC) No. 3385/94 and that the Commission does not oppose such exemption within a period of four months.

2. Paragraph 1 shall apply, in particular, where:

(a) the licensee is obliged at the time the agreement is entered into to accept quality specifications or further licences or to procure goods or services which are not necessary for a technically satisfactory exploitation of the licensed technology or for ensuring that the production of the licensee conforms to the quality standards that are respected by the licensor and other licensees;

(b) the licensee is prohibited from contesting the secrecy or the substantiality of the licensed know-how or from challenging the validity of patents licensed within the common market belonging to the licensor or undertakings connected with him.

3. The period of four months referred to in paragraph 1 shall run from the date on which the notification takes effect in accordance with Article 4 of Regulation (EC) No. 3385/94.

4. The benefit of paragraphs 1 and 2 may be claimed for agreements notified before the entry into force of this Regulation by submitting a communication to the Commission referring expressly to this Article and to the notification. Paragraph 3 shall apply *mutatis mutandis*.

5. The Commission may oppose the exemption within a period of four months. It shall oppose exemption if it receives a request to do so from a Member State within two months of the transmission to the Member State of the notification referred to in paragraph 1 or of the communication referred to in paragraph 4. This request must be justified on the basis of considerations relating to the competition rules of the Treaty.

6. The Commission may withdraw the opposition to the exemption at any time. However, where the opposition was raised at the request of a Member State and this request is maintained, it may be withdrawn only after consultation of the Advisory Committee on Restrictive Practices and Dominant Positions.

7. If the opposition is withdrawn because the undertakings concerned have shown that the conditions of Article 85(3) are satisfied, the exemption shall apply from the date of notification.

8. If the opposition is withdrawn because the undertakings concerned have amended the agreement so that the conditions of Article 85(3) are satisfied, the exemption shall apply from the date on which the amendments take effect.

9. If the Commission opposes exemption and the opposition is not withdrawn, the effects of the notification shall be governed by the provisions of Regulation No. 17.

Article 5

1. This Regulation shall not apply to:

(1) agreements between members of a patent or know-how pool which relate to the pooled technologies;

(2) licensing agreements between competing undertakings which hold interests in a joint venture, or between one of them and the joint venture, if the licensing agreements relate to the activities of the joint venture;

(3) agreements under which one party grants the other a patent and/or

know-how licence and in exchange the other party, albeit in separate agreements or through connected undertakings, grants the first party a patent, trademark or know-how licence or exclusive sales rights, where the parties are competitors in relation to the products covered by those agreements;

(4) licensing agreements containing provisions relating to intellectual property rights other than patents which are not ancillary;

(5) agreements entered into solely for the purpose of sale.

2. This Regulation shall nevertheless apply:

(1) to agreements to which paragraph 1(2) applies, under which a parent undertaking grants the joint venture a patent or know-how licence, provided that the licensed products and the other goods and services of the participating undertakings which are considered by users to be interchangeable or substitutable in view of their characteristics, price and intended use represent:

— in case of a licence limited to production, not more than 20 per cent, and

— in case of a licence covering production and distribution, not more than 10 per cent;

of the market for the licensed products and all interchangeable or substitutable goods and services;

(2) to agreements to which paragraph 1(1) applies and to reciprocal licences within the meaning of paragraph 1(3), provided the parties are not subject to any territorial restriction within the common market with regard to the manufacture, use or putting on the market of the licensed products or to the use of the licensed or pooled technologies.

3. This Regulation shall continue to apply where, for two consecutive financial years, the market shares in paragraph 2(1) are not exceeded by more than one-tenth; where that limit is exceeded, this Regulation shall continue to apply for a period of six months from the end of the year in which the limit was exceeded.

Article 6

This Regulation shall also apply to:

(1) agreements where the licensor is not the holder of the know-how or the patentee, but is authorised by the holder or the patentee to grant a licence;

(2) assignments of know-how, patents or both where the risk associated with exploitation remains with the assignor, in particular where the sum payable in consideration of the assignment is dependent on the turnover obtained by the assignee in respect of products made using the know-how or the patents, the quantity of such products manufactured or the number of operations carried out employing the know-how or the patents:

(3) licensing agreements in which the rights or obligations of the licensor or the licensee are assumed by undertakings connected with them.

Article 7

The Commission may withdraw the benefit of this Regulation, pursuant to Article 7 of Regulation No. 19/65/EEC, where it finds in a particular case that an agreement exempted by this Regulation nevertheless has certain effects which are incompatible with the conditions laid down in Article 85(3) of the Treaty, and in particular where:

(1) the effect of the agreement is to prevent the licensed products from being exposed to effective competition in the licensed territory from identical

goods or services or from goods or services considered by users as interchangeable or substitutable in view of their characteristics, price and intended use, which may in particular occur where the licensee's market share exceeds 40 per cent;

(2) without prejudice to Article 1(1)(6), the licensee refuses, without any objectively justified reason, to meet unsolicited orders from users or resellers in the territory of other licensees;

(3) the parties:
 (a) without any objectively justified reason, refuse to meet orders from users or resellers in their respective territories who would market the products in other territories within the common market; or
 (b) make it difficult for users or resellers to obtain the products from other resellers within the common market, and in particular where they exercise intellectual property rights or take measures so as to prevent resellers or users from obtaining outside, or from putting on the market in the licensed territory products which have been lawfully put on the market within the common market by the licensor or with his consent;

(4) the parties were competing manufacturers at the date of the grant of the licence and obligations on the licensee to produce a minimum quantity or to use his best endeavours as referred to in Article 2(1), (9) and (17) respectively have the effect of preventing the licensee from using competing technologies.

Article 8

1. For purposes of this Regulation:

(a) patent applications;
(b) utility models;
(c) applications for registration of utility models;
(d) topographies of semiconductor products;
(e) *certificats d'utilité* and *certificats d'addition* under French law;
(f) application for *certificats d'utilité* and *certificats d'addition* under French law;
(g) supplementary protection certificates for medicinal products or other products for which such supplementary protection certificates may be obtained;
(h) plant breeder's certificates,

shall be deemed to be patents.

2. This Regulation shall also apply to agreements relating to the exploitation of an invention if an application within the meaning of paragraph 1 is made in respect of the invention for a licensed territory after the date when the agreements were entered into but within the time limits set by the national law or the international convention to be applied.

3. This Regulation shall furthermore apply to pure patent or know-how licensing agreements or to mixed agreements whose initial duration is automatically prolonged by the inclusion of any new improvements, whether patented or not, communicated by the licensor, provided that the licensee has the right to refuse such improvements or each party has the right to terminate the agreement at the expiry of the initial term of an agreement and at least every three years thereafter.

Article 9

1. Information acquired pursuant to Article 4 shall be used only for the purposes of this Regulation.

2. The Commission and the authorities of the Member States, their officials and other servants shall not disclose information acquired by them pursuant to this Regulation of the kind covered by the obligation of professional secrecy.

3. The provisions of paragraphs 1 and 2 shall not prevent publication of general information or surveys which do not contain information relating to particular undertakings or associations of undertakings.

Article 10

For purposes of this Regulation:

(1) "know-how" means a body of technical information that is secret, substantial and identified in any appropriate form;

(2) "secret" means that the know-how package as a body or in the precise configuration and assembly of its components is not generally known or easily accessible, so that part of its value consists in the lead which the licensee gains when it is communicated to him; it is not limited to the narrow sense that each individual component of the know-how should be totally unknown or unobtainable outside the licensor's business;

(3) "substantial" means that the know-how includes information which must be useful, *i.e.* can reasonably be expected at the date of conclusion of the agreement to be capable of improving the competitive position of the licensee, for example by helping him to enter a new market or giving him an advantage in competition with other manufacturers or providers of services who do not have access to the licensed secret know-how or other comparable secret know-how;

(4) "identified" means that the know-how is described or recorded in such a manner as to make it possible to verify that it satisfies the criteria of secrecy and substantiality and to ensure that the licensee is not unduly restricted in his exploitation of his own technology, to be identified the know-how can either be set out in the licence agreement or in a separate document or recorded in any other appropriate form at the latest when the know-how is transferred or shortly thereafter, provided that the separate document or other record can be made available if the need arises;

(5) "necessary patents" are patents where a licence under the patent is necessary for the putting into effect of the licensed technology in so far as, in the absence of such a licence, the realisation of the licensed technology would not be possible or would be possible only to a lesser extent or in more difficult or costly conditions. Such patents must therefore be of technical, legal or economic interest to the licensee;

(6) "licensing agreement' means pure patent licensing agreements and pure know-how licensing agreements as well as mixed patent and know-how licensing agreements;

(7) "licensed technology" means the initial manufacturing know-how or the necessary product and process patents, or both, existing at the time the first licensing agreement is concluded, and improvements subsequently made to the know-how or patents, irrespective of whether and to what extent they are exploited by the parties or by other licensees;

(8) "the licensed products" are goods or services the production or provision of which requires the use of the licensed technology;

(9) "the licensee's market share" means the proportion which the licensed products and other goods or services provided by the licensee, which are considered by users to be interchangeable or substitutable for the licensed products in view of their characteristics, price and intended use, represent the entire market for the licensed products and all other interchangeable or substitutable goods and services in the common market or a substantial part of it;

(10) "exploitation" refers to any use of the licensed technology in particular in

the production, active or passive sales in a territory even if not coupled with manufacture in that territory, or leasing of the licensed products;

(11) "the licensed territory" is the territory covering all or at least part of the common market where the licensee is entitled to exploit the licensed technology;

(12) "territory of the licensor" means territories in which the licensor has not granted any licences for patents and/or know-how covered by the licensing agreement;

(13) "parallel patents" means patents which, in spite of the divergences which remain in the absence of any unification of national rules concerning industrial property, protect the same invention in various Member States;

(14) "connected undertakings" means:

(a) undertakings in which a party to the agreement, directly or indirectly:
- owns more than half the capital or business assets, or
- has the power ro exercise more than half the voting rights, or
- has the power to appoint more than half the members of the supervisory board, board of directors. or bodies legally representing the undertaking, or

has the right to manage the affairs of the undertaking;

(b) undertakings which, directly or indirectly, have in or over a party to the agreement the rights or powers listed in (a);

(c) undertakings in which an undertaking referred to in (b), directly or indirectly, has the rights or powers listed in (a);

(d) undertakings in which the parties to the agreement or undertakings connected with them jointly have the rights or powers listed in (a): such jointly controlled undertakings are considered to be connected with each of the parties to the agreement;

(15) "ancillary provisions" are provisions relating to the exploitation of intellectual property rights other than patents, which contain no obligations restrictive of competition other than those also attached to the licensed know-how or patents and exempted under this Regulation;

(16) "obligation" means both contractual obligation and a concerted practice;

(17) "competing manufacturers" or manufacturers of "competing products" means manufacturers who sell products which, in view of their characteristics, price and intended use, are considered by users to be interchangeable or substitutable for the licensed products.

Article 11

1. Regulation (EEC) No. 556/89 is hereby repealed with effect from 1 April 1996.
2. Regulation (EEC) No. 2349/84 shall continue to apply until 31 March 1996.
3. The prohibition in Article 85(1) of the Treaty shall not apply to agreements in force on 31 March 1996 which fulfil the exemption requirements laid down by regulation (EEC) No. 2349/84 or (EEC) No. 556/89.

Article 12

1. The Commission shall undertake regular assessments of the application of this Regulation, and in particular of the opposition procedure provided for in Article 4.
2. The Commission shall draw up a report on the operation of this Regulation before the end of the fourth year following its entry into force and shall, on that basis assess whether any adaptation of the Regulation is desirable.

Article 13

This Regulation shall enter into force on 1 April 1996.
It shall apply until 31 March 2006.
Article 11(2) of this Regulation shall, however, enter into force on 1 January 1996.

This Regulation shall be binding in its entirety and directly applicable in all Member States.
Done at Brussels, 31 January 1996.

[1] OJ 1996 L31/2.
[2] OJ 1965 C36/533
[3] OJ 1994 C178/3.
[4] OJ 1974 L219/15
[5] OJ 1995 L214/6.
[6] OJ 1989 L61/1.
[7] Convention for the European patent for the common market (Community Patent Convention) of 15 December 1975, OJ 1976 L17/1.
[8] Convention on the grant of European patents (European Patent Convention) of 5 October 1973.

APPENDIX 5

ARTICLE 25 OF REGULATION 17/62 (as amended)

Article 25

1. As regards agreements, decisions and concerted practices to which Article 85 of the Treaty applies by virtue of accession, the date of accession shall be substituted for the date of entry into force of this regulation in every place where reference is made in this Regulation to this latter date.

2. Agreements, decisions and concerted practices existing at the date of accession to which Article 85 of the Treaty applies by virtue of accession shall be notified pursuant to Article 5(1) or Article 7(1) and (2) within six months from the date of accession.

3. Fines under Article 15(2)(a) shall not be imposed in respect of any act prior to notification of the agreements, decisions and practices to which paragraph 2 applies and which have been notified within the period therein specified.

4. New Member States shall take the measures referred to in Article 14(6) within six months from the date of accession after consulting the Commission.

5. The provisions of paragraphs (1) to (4) above shall apply in the same way in the case of accession of the Hellenic Republic, the Kingdom of Spain and of the Portuguese Republic.

6. The provisions of paragraphs 1 to 4 shall apply in the same way in the case of the accession of Austria. Finland and Sweden. However, they do not apply to agreements, decisions and concerted practices which at the date of the accession already fall under Article 53 of the EEA Agreement.

Note: In the publication of the amendments in the *Official Journal* (English edition), the word "still" appears in the first line of paragraphs (5) and (6). That appears to be a mistranscription that does not correspond to the foreign language versions; in the text above the word 'shall' has accordingly been substituted.

APPENDIX 6

REGULATION 3385/94[1]

on the form, content and other details of applications and notifications provided for in Council Regulation No. 17

THE COMMISSION OF THE EUROPEAN COMMUNITIES,

Having regard to the Treaty establishing the European Community,
Having regard to the Agreement on the European Economic Area,
Having regard to Council Regulation No. 17 of 6 February 1962, First Regulation implementing Articles 85 and 86 of the Treaty,[2] as last amended by the Act of Accession of Spain and Portugal, and in particular Article 24 thereof,
Whereas Commission Regulation No. 27 of 3 May 1962, First Regulation implementing Council Regulation No. 17,[3] as last amended by Regulation (EC) No. 3666/93,[4] no longer meets the requirements of efficient administrative procedure; whereas it should therefore be replaced by a new regulation;
Whereas, on the one hand, applications for negative clearance under Article 2 and notifications under Articles 4, 5 and 25 of Regulation No. 17 have important legal consequences, which are favourable to the parties to an agreement, a decision or a practice, while, on the other hand, incorrect or misleading information in such applications or notifications may lead to the imposition of fines and may also entail civil law disadvantages for the parties; whereas it is therefore necessary in the interests of legal certainty to define precisely the persons entitled to submit applications and notifications, the subject matter and content of the information which such applications and notifications must contain, and the time when they become effective;
Whereas each of the parties should have the right to submit the application or the notification to the Commission; whereas, furthermore, a party exrcising the right should inform the other parties in order to enable them to protect their interests; whereas applications and notifications relating to agreements, decisions or practices of associations of undertakings should be submitted only by such association;
Whereas it is for the applicants and the notifying parties to make full and honest disclosure to the Commission of the facts and circumstances which are relevant for coming to a decision on the agreements, decisions or practices concerned;
Whereas, in order to simplify and expedite their examination, it is desirable to prescribe that a form be used for applications for negative clearance relating to Article 85(1) and for notifications relating to Article 85(3); whereas the use of this form should also be possible in the case of applications for negative clearance relating to Article 86;
Whereas the Commission, in appropriate cases, will give the parties, if they so request, an opportunity before the application or the notification to discuss the intended agreement, decision or practice informally and in strict confidence; whereas, in addition, it will, after the application or notification, maintain close contact with the parties to the extent necesary to discuss with them any practical

or legal problems which it discovers on a first examination of the case and if possible to remove such problems by mutual agreement;

Whereas the provisions of this Regulation must also cover cases in which applications for negative clearance relating to Article 53(1) or Article 54 of the EEA Agreement, or notifications, relating to Article 53(3) of the EEA Agreement are submitted to the Commission,

HAS ADOPTED THIS REGULATION:

Article 1

Persons entitled to submit applications and notifications

1. The following may submit an application under Article 2 of Regulation No. 17 relating to Article 85(1) of the Treaty or a notification under Articles 4, 5 and 25 of Regulation No. 17:
   (a) any undertaking and any association of undertakings being a party to agreements or to concerted practices; and
   (b) any association of undertakings adopting decisions or engaging in practices;

   which may fall within the scope of Article 85(1).

Where the application or notification is submitted by some, but not all, of the parties, referred to in point (a) of the first subparagraph, they shall give notice to the other parties.

2. Any undertaking which may hold, alone or with other undertakings, a dominant position within the common market or in a substantial part of it, may submit an application under Article 2 of Regulation No. 17 relating to Article 86 of the Treaty.
3. Where the applicxation or notification is signed by representatives of persons, undertakings or associations of undertakings, such representatives shall produce written proof that they are authorized to act.
4. Where a joint application or notification is made, a joint representative should be appointed who is authorized to transmit and receive documents on behalf of all the applicants or notifying parties.

Article 2

Submission of applications and notifications

1. Applications under Article 2 of Regulation No. 17 relating to Article 85(1) of the Treaty and notifications under Articles 4, 5 and 25 of Regulation No. 17 shall be submitted in the manner prescribed by form A/B as shown in the Annex to this Regulation. Form A/B may also be used for applications under Article 2 of Regulation No. 17 relating to Article 86 of the Treaty. Joint applications and joint notifications shall be submitted on a single form.
2. Seventeen copies of each application and notification and three copies of the Annexes thereto shall be submitted to the Commission at the address indicated in Form A/B.
3. The documents annexed to the application or notification shall be either originals or copies of the originals; in the latter case the applicant or notifying party shall confirm that they are true copies of the originals and complete.

4. Applications and notifications shall be in one of the official languages of the Community. This language shall also be the language of the proceeding for the applicant or notifying party. Documents shall be submitted in their original language. Where the original language is not one of the official languages, a translation into the language of the proceeding shall be attached.
5. Where applications for negative clearance relating to Article 53(1) or Article 54 of the EEA Agreement or notifications relating to Article 53(3) of the EEA Agreement are submitted, they may also be in one of the official languages of the EFTA States or the working language of the EFTA Surveillance Authority. If the language chosen for the application or notification is not an official language of the Community, the applicant or notifying party shall supplement all documentation with a translation into an official language of the Community. The language which is chosen for the translation shall be the language of the proceeding for the applicant or notifying party.

Article 3

Content of applications and notifications

1. Applications and notifications shall contain the information, including documents, required by Form A/B. The information must be correct and complete.
2. Applications under Article 2 of Regulation No. 17 relating to Article 86 of the Treaty shall contain a full statement of the facts, specifying, in particular, the practice concerned and the position of the undertaking or undertakings within the common market or a substantial part thereof in regard to the products or services to which the practice relates.
3. The Community may dispense with the obligation to provide any particular information, including documents, required by Form A/B where the Commission considers that such information is not necessary for the examination of the case.
4. The Commission shall, without delay, acknowledge in writing to the applicant or notifying party receipt of the application or notification, and of any reply to a letter sent by the Commission pursuant to Article 4(2).

Article 4

Effective date of submission of applications and notifications

1. Without prejudice to paragraphs 2 to 5, applications and notifications shall become effective on the date on which they are received by the Commission. Where, however, the application or notification is sent by registered post, it shall become effective on the date shown on the postmark of the place of posting.
2. Where the Commission finds that the information, including documents, contained in the application or notification is incomplete in a material respect, it shall, without delay, inform the applicant or notifying party in writing of this fact and shall fix an appropriate time limit for the completion of the information. In such cases, the application or notification shall become effective on the date on which the complete information is received by the Commission.
3. Material changes in the facts contained in the application or notification

which the applicant or notifying party knows or ought to know must be communicated to the Commission voluntarily and without delay.

4. Incorrect or misleading information shall be considered to be incomplete information.
5. Where, at the expiry of a period of one month following the date on which the application or notification has been received, the Commission has not provided the applicant or notifying party with the information referred to in paragraph 2, the application or notification shall be deemed to have become effective on the date of its receipt by the Commission.

Article 5

Repeal

Regulation No. 27 is repealed.

Article 6

Entry into force

This Regulation shall enter into force on 1 March 1995.

This Regulation shall be binding in its entirety and directly applicable in all Member States.

Done at Brussels, 21 December 1994.

APPENDIX 6

FORM A/B

INTRODUCTION

Form A/B, as its Annex, is an integral part of the Commission Regulation (EC) No. 3385/94 of 21 December 1994 on the form, content and other details of applications and notifications provided for in Council Regulation No. 17 (hereinafter referred to as "the Regulation"). It allows undertakings and associations of undertakings to apply to the Commission for negative clearance agreements or practices which may fall within the prohibitions of Article 85(1) and Article 86 of the EC Treaty, or within Articles 53(1) and 54 of the EEA Agreement or to notify such agreement and apply to have it exempted from the prohibition set out in Article 85(1) by virtue of the provisions of Article 85(3) of the EC Treaty or from the prohibition of Article 53(1) by virtue of the provisions of Article 53(3) of the EEA Agreement.

To facilitate the use of the Form A/B the following pages set out:

- in which situations it is necessary to make an application or a notification (Point A),
- to which authority (the Commission or the EFTA Surveillance Authority) the application or notification should be made (Point B),
- for which purposes the application or notification can be used (Point C),
- what information must be given in the application or notification (Points D, E and F),
- who can make an application or notification (Point G),
- how to make an application or notification (Point H),
- how the business secrets of the undertakings can be protected (Point I),
- how certain technical terms used in the operational part of the Form A/B should be interpreted (Point J), and
- the subsequent procedure after the application or notification has been made (Point K).

A. In which situations is it necessary to make an application or a notification?

I. *Purpose of the competition rules of the EC Treaty and the EEA Agreement*

1. Purpose of the EC Competition Rules

The purpose of the competition rules is to prevent the distortion of competition in the common market by restrictive practices or the abuse of dominant positions. They apply to any enterprise trading directly or indirectly in the common market, wherever established.

Article 85(1) of the EC Treaty (the text of Articles 85 and 86 is reproduced in Annex I to this form) prohibits restrictive agreements, decisions or concerted practices (arrangements) which may affect trade between Member States, and Article 85(2) declares agreements and decisions containing such restrictions void (although the Court of Justice has held that if restrictive terms of agreements are severable, only those terms are void); Article 85(3), however, provides for exemption of arrangements with beneficial effects, if its conditions are met. Article 86 prohibits the abuse of a dominant position which may affect trade between Member States. The original procedures for implementing these Articles, which provide for "negative clearance" and exemption pursuant to Article 85(3), were laid down in Regulation No. 17.

2. Purpose of the EEA competition rules

The competition rules of the Agreement on the European Economic Area (concluded between the Community, the Member States and the EFTA States[5]) are based on the same principles as those contained in the Community competition rules and have the same purpose, i.e. to prevent the distortion of competition in the EEA territory by cartels or the abuse of dominant position. They apply to any enterprise trading directly or indirectly in the EEA territory, wherever established.

Article 53(1) of the EEA Agreement (the text of Articles 53, 54 and 56 of the EEA Agreement is reproduced in Annex I) prohibits restrictive agreements, decisions or concerted practices (arrangements) which may affect trade between the Community and one or more EFTA States (or between EFTA States), and Article 53(2) declares agreements or decisions containing such restrictions void; Article 53(3), however, provides for exemption of arrangements with beneficial effects, if its conditions are met. Article 54 prohibits the abuse of a dominant position which may affect trade between the Community and one or more EFTA States (or between EFTA States). The procedures for implementing these Articles, which provide for "negative clearance" and exemption pursuant to Article 53(3), are laid down in Regulation No. 17, supplemented for EEA purposes, by Protocols 21, 22 and 23 to the EEA Agreement.[6]

II. *The scope of the competition rules of the EC Treaty and the EEA Agreement*

The applicability of Articles 85 and 86 of the EC Treaty and Articles 53 and 54 of the EEA Agreement depends on the circumstances of each individual case. It presupposes that the arrangement or behaviour satisfies all the conditions set out in the relevant provisions. This question must consequently be examined before any application for negative clearance or any notification is made.

1. Negative clearance

The negative clearance procedure allows undertakings to ascertain whether the Commission considers that their arrangement or their behaviour is or is not prohibited by Article 85(1), or Article 86 of the EC Treaty or by Article 53(1) or Article 54 of the EEA Agreement. This procedure is governed by Article 2 of Regulation No. 17. The negative clearance takes the form of a decision by which the Commission certifies that, on the basis of the facts in its possession, there are no grounds pursuant to Article 85(1) or Article 86 of the EC Treaty or under Article 53(1) or Article 54 of the EEA Agreement for action on its part in respect of the arrangement or behaviour.

There is, however, no point in making an application when the arrangements or the behaviour are manifestly not prohibited by the abovementioned provisions. Nor is the Commission obliged to give negative clearance. Article 2 of Regulation No. 17 states that "... the Commission may certify ...". The Commission issues negative clearance decisions only where an important problem of interpretation has to be solved. In the other cases it reacts to the application by sending a comfort letter.

The Commission has published several notices relating the interpretation of Article 85(1) of the EC Treaty. They define certain categories of agreements which, by their nature or because of their minor importance, are not caught by the prohibition.[7]

2. Exemption

The procedure for exemption pursuant to Article 85(3) of the EC Treaty and Article 53(3) of the EEA Agreement allows companies to enter into arrangements which, in fact, offer economic advantages but which, without exemption, would be prohibited by Article 85(1) of the EC Treaty or by Article 53(1) of the EEA Agreement. This procedure is governed by Articles 4, 6 and 8 and, for the new Member States, also by Articles 5, 7 and 25 of Regulation No. 17. The exemption takes the form of a decision by the Commission declaring Article 85(1) of the EC Treaty or Article 53(1) of the EEA Agreement to be inapplicable to the arrangements described in the decision. Article 8 requires the Commissioner to specify the period of validity of any such decision, allows the Commission to attach conditions and obligations and provides for decisions to be amended or revoked or specified acts by the parties to be prohibited in certain circumstances, notably if the decisions were based on incorrect information or if there is any material change in the facts.

The Commission has adopted a number of regulations granting exemptions to categories of agreements.[8] Some of these regulations provide that some agreements may benefit from exemption only if they are notified to the Commission pursuant to Article 4 or 5 of Regulation No. 17 with a view to obtaining exemption, and the benefit of the opposition procedure is claimed in the notification.

A decision granting exemption may have retroactive effect, but, with certain exceptions, cannot be made effective earlier than the date of notification (Article 6 of Regulation No. 17). Should the Commission find that notified arrangements are indeed prohibited and cannot be exempted and, therefore, take a decision condemning them, the participants are nevertheless protected, between the date of the notification and the date of the decision, against fines for any infringement described in the notification (Article 3 and Article 15(5) and (6) of Regulation No. 17).

Normally the Commission issues exemption decisions only in cases of particular legal, economic or political importance. In the other cases it terminates the procedure by sending a comfort letter.

B. To which authority should application or notification be made?

The applications and notifications must be made to the authority which has competence for the matter. The Commission is responsible for the application of the competition rules of the EC Treaty. However there is shared competence in relation to the application of the competition rules of the EEA Agreement.

The competence of the Commission and of the EFTA Surveillance Authority to apply the EEA competition rules follows from Article 56 of the EEA Agreement. Applications and notifications relating to agreements, decisions or concerted practices liable to affect trade between Member States should be addressed to the Commission unless their effects on trade between Member States or on competition within the Community are not appreciable within the meaning of the Commission notice of 1986 on agreements of minor importance.[9] Furthermore, all restrictive agreements, decisions or concerted practices affecting trade between one Member State and one or more EFTA States fall within the competence of the Commission, provided that the undertakings concerned achieve more than 67 per cent of their combined EEA-wide turnover within the Community.[10] However, if the effects of such agreements, decisions or concerted practices on trade between Member States or on competition within the Community are not appreciable, the notification should, where necessary, be addressed to the EFTA Surveillance Authority. All other agreements, decisions and concerted practices falling under Article 53 of the EEA Agreement should be notified to the EFTA Surveillance Authority (the address of which is given in Annex III).

Applications for negative clearance regarding Article 54 of the EEA Agreement should be lodged with the Commission if the Dominant position exists only in the Community, or with the EFTA Surveillance Authority, if the dominant position exists only in the whole of the territory of the EFTA States, or a substantial part of it. Only where the dominant position exists within both territories should the rules outlined above with respect to Article 53 be applied.

The Commission will apply, as a basis for appraisal, the competition rules of the

EC Treaty. Where the case falls under the EEA Agreement and is attributed to the Commission pursuant to Article 56 of that Agreement, it will simultaneously apply the EEA rules.

C. The Purpose of this Form

Form A/B lists the questions that must be answered and the information and documents that must be provided when applying for the following:

— a negative clearance with regard to Article 85(1) of the EC Treaty and/or Article 53(1) of the EEA Agreement, pursuant to Article 2 of Regulation No. 17, with respect to agreements between undertakings, decisions by associations of undertakings and concerted practices,
— an exemption pursuant to Article 85(3) of the EC Treaty and/or Article 53(3) of the EEA Agreement with respect to agreements between undertakings, decisions by associations of undertakings and concerted practices,
— the benefit of the opposition procedure contained in certain Commission regulations granting exemption by category.

This form allows undertakings applying for negative clearance to notify, at the same time, in order to obtain an exemption in the event that the Commission reaches the conclusion that no negative clearance can be granted.

Applications for negative clearance and notifications relating to Article 85 of the EC Treaty shall be submitted in the manner prescribed by form A/B (see Article 2(1), first sentence of the Regulation).

This form can also be used by undertakings that wish to apply for a negative clearance from Article 86 of the EC Treaty or Article 53 of the EEA Agreement, pursuant to Article 2 of Regulation No. 17. Applicants requesting negative clearance from Article 86 are not reqired to use form A/B. They are nonetheless strongly recommended to give all the information requested below to ensure that their application gives a full statement of the facts (see Article 2(1), second sentence of the Regulation).

The applications or notifications made on the form A/B issued by the EFTA side are equally valid. However, if the agreements, decisions or practices concerned fall solely within Articles 85 or 86 of the EC Treaty, i.e. have no EEA relevance whatsoever, it is advisable to use the present form established by the Commission.

D. Which chapters of the form should be completed?

The operational part of this form is sub-divided into four chapters. Undertakings wishing to make an application for a negative clearance or a notification must complete Chapters I, II and IV. An exception to this rule is provided for in the case where the application or notification concerns an agreement concerning the creation of a cooperative joint venture of a structural character if the parties wish to benefit from an accelerated procedure. In this situation Chapters I, III and IV should be completed.

In 1992, the Commission announced that it had adopted new internal administrative rules that provided that certain applications and notifications—those of cooperative joint ventures which are structural in nature—would be dealt with within fixed deadlines. In such cases the services of the Commission will, within two months of receipt of the complete notification of the agreement, inform the parties in writing of the results of the initial analysis of the case and, as appropriate, the nature and probable length of the administrative procedure they intend to engage.

The contents of this letter may vary according to the characteristics of the case under investigation:

- in cases not posing any problems, the Commission will send a comfort letter confirming the compatibility of the agreement with Article 85(1) or (3),
- if a comfort letter cannot be sent because of the need to settle the case by formal decision, the Commission will inform the undertakings concerned of its intention to adopt a decision either granting or rejecting exemption,
- if the Commission has serious doubts as to the compatibility of the agreement with the competition rules, it will send a letter to the parties giving notice of an in-depth examination which may, depending on the case, result in a decision neither prohibiting, exempting subject to conditions and obligations, or simply exempting the agreement in question.

This new accelerated procedure, applicable since 1 January 1993, is based entirely on the principle of self-discipline. The deadline of two months from the complete notification—intended for the initial examination of the case—does not constitute a statutory term and is therefore in no way legally binding. However, the Commission will do its best to abide by it. The Commission reserves the right, moreover, to extend this accelerated procedure to other forms of cooperation between undertakings.

A cooperative joint venture of a structural nature is one that involves an important change in the structure and organization of the business assets of the parties to the agreement. This may occur because the joint venture takes over or extends existing activities of the parent companies or because it undertakes new activities on their behalf. Such operations are characterized by the commitment of significant financial, material and/or non-tangible assets such as intellectual property rights and know how. Structural joint ventures are therefore normally intended to operate on a medium- or long-term basis.

This concept includes certain "partial function" joint ventures which take over one or several specific functions within the parents' business activity without access to the market, in particular research and development and/or production. It also covers those "full function" joint ventures which give rise to coordination of the competitive behaviour of independent undertakings, in particular between the parties to the joint ventures or between them and the joint venture.

In order to respect the internal deadline, it is important that the Commission has available on notification all the relevant information reasonably available to the notifying parties that is necessary for it to assess the impact of the operation in question on competition. Form A/B therefore contains a special section (Chapter III) that must be completed only by persons notifying cooperative joint ventures of a structural character that wish to benefit from the accelerated procedure.

Persons notifying joint ventures of a structural character that wish to claim the benefit of the aforementioned accelerated procedure should therefore complete Chapters I, III and IV of this form. Chapter III contains a series of detailed questions necessary for the Commission to assess the relevant market(s) and the position of the parties to the joint venture on that (those) market(s).

Where the parties do not wish to claim the benefit of an accelerated procedure for their joint ventures of a structural character they should complete Chapters I, II and IV of this form. Chapter II contains a far more limited range of questions on the relevant market(s) and the position of the parties to the operation in question on that (those) market(s), but sufficient to enable the Commission to commence its examination and investigation.

E. The need for complete information

The receipt of a valid notification by the Commission has two main consequences. First, it affords immunity from fines from the date that the valid notification is received by the Commission with respect to applications made in order to obtain exemption (see Article 15(5) of Regulation No. 17). Second, until a valid notification is received, the Commission cannot grant an exemption pursuant to Article 85(3) of the EC Treaty and/or Article 53(3) of the EEA Agreement, and any exemption that is granted can be effective only from the date of receipt of a valid notification.[11] Thus, whilst there is no legal obligation to notify as such, unless and until an arrangement that falls within the scope of Article 85(1) and/or Article 53(1) has not been notified and is, therefore, not capable of being exempted, it may be declared void by a national court pursuant to Article 85(2) and/or Article 53(2).[12]

Where an undertaking is claiming the benefit of a group exemption by recourse to an opposition procedure, the period within which the Commission must oppose the exemption by category only applies from the date that a valid notification is received. This is also true of the two months' period imposed on the Commission services for an initial analysis of applications for negative clearance and notifications relating to cooperative joint ventures of a structural character which benefit from the accelerated procedure.

A valid application or notification for this purpose means one that is not incomplete (see Article 3(1) of the Regulation). This is subject to two qualifications. First, if the information or documents required by this form are not reasonably available to you in part or in whole, the Commission will accept that a notification is complete and thus valid notwithstanding the failure to provide such information, providing that you give reasons for the unavailability of the information, and provide your best estimates for missing data together with the sources for the estimates. Indications as to where any of the requested information or documents that are unavailable to you could be obtained by the Commission must also be provided. Second, the Commission only requires the submission of information relevant and necessary to its inquiry into the notified operation. In some cases not all the information required by this form will be necessary for this purpose. The Commission may therefore dispense with the obligation to provide certain information required by this form (see Article 3(3) of the Reglation. This provision enables, where appropriate, each application or notification to be tailored to each case so that only the information strictly necessary for the Commission's examination is provided. This avoids unnecessary administrative burdens being imposed on undertakings, in particular on small and medium-sized ones. Where the information or documents required by this form are not provided for this reason, the application or notification should indicate the reasons why the information is considered to be unnecessary to the Commission's investigation.

Where the Commission finds that the information contained in the application or notification is incomplete in a material respect, it will, within one month from receipt, inform the applicant or the notifying party in writing of this fact and the nature of the missing information. In such cases, the application or notification shall become effective on the date on which the complete information is received by the Commission. If the Commission has not informed the applicant or the notifying party within the one month period that the application or notification is incomplete in a material respect, the application or notification will be deemed to be complete and valid (see Article 4 of the Regulation).

It is also important that undertakings inform the Commission of important changes in the factual situation including those of which they become aware after the application or notification has been submitted. The Commission must, therefore, be informed immediately of any changes to an agreement, decision or practice which is the subject of an application or notification (see Article 4(3) of the Regulation). Failure to inform the Commission of such relevant changes could result in any negative clearance decision being without effect or in the withdrawal of any exemption decision[13] adopted by the Commission on the basis of the notification.

F. The need for accurate information

In addition to the requirement that the application or notification be complete, it is important that you ensure that the information provided is accurate (see Article 3(1) of the Regulation). Article 15(1)(a) of Regulation No. 17 states that the Commission may, by decision, impose on undertakings or associations of undertakings fines of up to ECU 5000 where, intentionally or negligently, they supply incorrect or misleading information in an application for negative clearance or notification. Such information is, moreover, considered to be incomplete (see Article 4(4) of the Regulation), so that the parties cannot benefit from the advantages of the opposition procedure or accelerated procedure (see above, Point E).

G. Who can lodge an application or a notification?

Any of the undertakings party to an agreement, decision or practice of the kind described in Articles 85 or 86 of the EC Treaty and Articles 53 or 54 of the EEA Agreement may submit an application for negative clearance, in relation to Article 85 and Article 53, or a notification requesting an exemption. An association of undertakings may submit an application or a notification in relation to decisions taken or practices pursued into in the operation of the association.

In relation to agreements and concerted practices between undertakings it is common practice for all the parties involved to submit a joint application or notification. Although the Commission strongly recommends this approach, because it is helpful to have the views of all the parties directly concerned at the same time, it is not obligatory. Any of the parties to an agreement may submit an application or notification in their individual capacities, but in such circumstances the notifying party should inform all the other parties to the agreement, decision or practice of that fact (see Article 1(3) of the Regulation). They may also provide them with a copy of the completed form, where relevant once confidential information and business secrets have been deleted (see below, operational part, question 1.2).

Where a joint application or notification is submitted, it has also become common practice to appoint a joint representative to act on behalf of all the undertakings involved, both in making the application or notification, and in dealing with any subsequent contacts with the Commission (see Article 1(4) of the Regulation). Again, whilst this is helpful, it is not obligatory, and all the undertakings jointly submitting an application or a notification may sign it in their individual capacities.

H. How to submit application or notification

Applications and notifications may be submitted in any of the official languages of the European Community or of an EFTA State (see Article 2(4) and (5) of the Regulation). In order to ensure rapid proceedings, it is, however, recommended to use, in case of an application or notification to the EFTA Surveillance Authority one of the official languages of an EFTA State or the working language of the EFTA Surveillance Authority, which is English, or, in case of an application or notification to the Commission, one of the official languages of the Community or the working language of the EFTA Surveillance Authority. This language will thereafter be the language of the proceeding for the applicant or notifying party.

Form A/B is not a form to be filled in. Undertakings should simply provide the information requested by this form, using its sections and paragraph numbers, signing a declaration as stated in Section 19 below, and annexing the required supporting documentation.

Supporting documents shall be submitted in their original language; where this is not an official language of the Community they must be translated into the language of the proceeding. The supporting documents may be originals or copies of the originals (see Article 2(4) of the Regulation).

All information requested in this form shall, unless otherwise stated, relate to the calendar year preceding that of the application or notification. Where information is not reasonably available on this basis (for example if accounting periods are used that are not based on the calendar year, or the previous year's figures are not yet available) the most recently available information should be provided and reasons given why figures on the basis of the calendar year preceding that of the application or notification cannot be provided.

Financial data may be provided in the currency in which the official audited accounts of the undertaking(s) concerned are prepared or in Ecus. In the latter case the exchange rate used for the conversion must be stated.

Seventeen copies of each application or notification, but only three copies of all supporting documents must be provided (see Article 2(2) of the Regulation).

The application or notification is to be sent to:

Commission of the European Communities,
Directorate-General for Competition (DG IV),
The Registrar,
200, Rue de la Loi,
B-1049 Brussels.

or be delivered by hand during Commission working days and official working hours at the following address:

Commission of the European Communities,
Directorate-General for Competition (DG IV),
The Registrar,
158, Avenue de Cortenberg,
B-1040 Brussels.

I. Confidentiality

Article 214 of the EC Treaty, Article 20 of Regulation No. 17, Article 9 of Protocol 23 to the EEA Agreement, Article 122 of the EEA Agreement and Articles 20 and 21 of Chapter II of Protocol 4 to the Agreement between the EFTA States on the establishment of a Surveillance Authority and of a Court of Justice require the Commission, the Member States, the EEA Surveillance Authority and EFTA States not to disclose information of the kind covered by the obligation of professional secrecy. On the other hand, Regulation No. 17 requires the Commission to publish a summary of the application or notification, should it intend to take a favourable decision. In this publication, the Commission "... shall have regard to the legitimate interest of undertakings in the protection of their business secrets" (Article 19(3) of Regulation No. 17; see also Article 21(2) in relation to the publication of decisions). In this connection, if an undertaking believes that its interests would be harmed if any of the information it is asked to supply were to be published or otherwise divulged to other undertakings, it should put all such information in a separate annex with each page clearly marked "Business Secrets". It should also give reasons why any information identified as confidential or secret should not be divulged or published. (See below, Section 5 of the operational part that requests a non-confidential summary of the notification.)

J. Subsequent Procedure

The application or notification is registered in the Registry of the Directorate-General for Competition (DG IV). The date of receipt by the Commission (or the date of posting if sent by registered post) is the effective date of the submission (see Article 4(1) of the Regulation). However, special rules apply to incomplete applications and notifications (see above under Point E).

The Commission will acknowledge receipt of all applications and notifications in writing, indicating the case number attributed to the file. This number must be used in all future correspondence regarding the notification. The receipt of acknowledgement does not prejudge the question whether the application or notification is valid.

Further information may be sought from the parties or from third parties (Articles 11 to 14 of Regulation No. 17) and suggestions might be made as to amendments to the arrangements that might make them acceptable. Equally, a short preliminary notice may be published in the C series of the *Official Journal of the European Communities*, stating the names of the interested undertakings, the groups to which they belong, the economic sectors involved and the nature of the arrangements, and inviting third party comments (see below, operational part, Section 5).

Where a notification is made together for the purpose of the application of the opposition procedure, the Commission may oppose the grant of the benefit of the group exemption with respect to the notified agreement. If the Commission opposes the claim, and unless it subsequently withdraws its opposition, that notification will then be treated as an application for an individual exemption.

If, after examination, the Commission intends to grant the application for negative clearance or exemption, it is obliged (by Article 19(3) of Regulation No. 17) to publish a summary and invite comments from third parties. Subsequently, a preliminary draft decision has to be submitted to and discussed with the Advisory Committee on Restrictive Practices and Dominant Positions composed of officials of the competent authorities of the Member States in the matter of restrictive practices and monopolies (Article 10 of Regulation No. 17) and attended, where the case falls within the EEA Agreement, by representatives of the EFTA Surveillance Authority and the EFTA States which will already have received a copy of the application or notification. Only then, and providing nothing has happened to change the Commission's intention, can it adopt the envisaged decision.

Files are often closed without any formal decision being taken, for example, because it is found that the arrangements are already covered by a block exemption, or because they do not call for any action by the Commission, at least in circumstances at that time. In such cases comfort letters are sent. Although not a Commission decision, a comfort letter indicates how the Commission's departments view the case on the facts currently in their possession which means that the Commission could where necessary—for example, if it were to be asserted that a contract was void under Article 85(2) of the EC Treaty and/or Article 53(2) of the EEA Agreement—take an appropriate decision to clarify the legal situation.

K. Definitions used in the operational part of this form

Agreement: The word "agreement" is used to refer to all categories of arrangements, i.e. agreements between undertakings, decisions by associations of undertakings and concerted practices.

Year: All references to the word "year" in this form shall be read as meaning calendar year, unless otherwise stated.

Group: A group relationship exists for the purpose of this form where one undertaking:

- owns more than half the capital or business assets of another undertaking, or
- has the power to exercise more than half the voting rights in another undertaking, or
- has the power to appoint more than half the members of the supervisory board, board of directors or bodies legally representing the undertaking, or

— has the right to manage the affairs of another undertaking.

An undertaking which is jointly controlled by several other undertakings (joint venture) forms part of the group of each of these undertakings.

Relevant product market: Questions 6.1 and 11.1 of this form require the undertaking or individual submitting the notification to define the relevant product and/or service market(s) that are likely to be affected by the agreement in question. That definition(s) is then used as the basis for a number of other questions contained in this form. The definition(s) thus submitted by the notifying parties are referred to in this form as the relevant product market(s). These words can refer to a market made up either of products or of services.

Relevant geographic market: Questions 6.2 and 11.2 of this form require the undertaking or individual submitting the notification to define the relevant geographic market(s) that are likely to be affected by the agreement in question. That definition(s) is then used as the basis for a number of other questions contained in this form. The definition(s) thus submitted by the notifying parties are referred to in this form as the relevant geographic market(s).

Relevant product and geographic market: By virtue of the combination of their replies to questions 6 and 11 the parties provide their definition of the relevant market(s) affected by the notified agreement(s). That (those) definition(s) is (are) then used as the basis for a number of other questions contained in this form. The definition(s) thus submitted by the notifying parties is referred to in this form as the relevant geographic and product market(s).

Notification: This form can be used to make an application for negative clearance and/or a notification requesting an exemption. The word "notification" is used to refer to either an application or a notification.

Parties and notifying party: The word "party" is used to refer to all the undertakings which are party to the agreement being notified. As a notification may be submitted by only one of the undertakings which are party to an agreement, "notifying party" is used to refer only to the undertakings actually submitting the notification.

OPERATIONAL PART

PLEASE MAKE SURE THAT THE FIRST PAGE OF YOUR APPLICATION OR NOTIFICATION CONTAINS THE WORDS "APPLICATION FOR NEGATIVE CLEARANCE/NOTIFICATION IN ACCORDANCE WITH FORM A/B"

CHAPTER I

Sections concerning the parties, their groups and the agreement (to be completed for all notifications)

Section 1

Identity of the undertakings or persons submitting the notification

1.1. Please list the undertakings on behalf of which the notification is being submitted and indicate their legal denomination or commercial name, shortened or commonly used as appropriate (if it differs from the legal denomination).

1.2. If the notification is being submitted on behalf of only one or some of the undertakings party to the agreement being notified, please confirm that the remaining undertakings have been informed of that fact and indicate whether they have received a copy of the notification, with relevant confidential information and business secrets deleted.[14] (In such circumstances a copy of the edited copy of the notification which has been provided to such other undertakings should be annexed to this notification.)

1.3. If a joint notification is being submitted, has a joint representative[15] been appointed[16]?
If yes, please give the details requested in 1.3.1 to 1.3.3 below.
If no, please give details of any representatives who have been authorized to act for each or either of the parties to the agreement indicating who they represent.

1.3.1. Name of representative.
1.3.2. Address of representative.
1.3.3. Telephone and fax number of representative.

1.4. In cases where one or more representatives have been appointed, an authority to act on behalf of the undertaking(s) submitting the notification must accompany the notification.

Section 2

Information on the parties to the agreement and the groups to which they belong

2.1. State the name and address of the parties to the agreement being notified, and the country of their incorporation.

2.2. State the nature of the business of each of the parties to the agreement being notified.

2.3. For each of the parties to the agreement, give the name of a person that can be contacted, together with his or her name, address, telephone number, fax number and position held in the undertaking.

2.4. Identify the corporate groups to which the parties to the agreement being notified belong. State the sectors in which these groups are active, and the world-wide turnover of each group.[17]

Section 3

Procedural matters

3.1. Please state whether you have made any formal submission to any other competition authorities in relation to the agreement in question. If yes, state which authorities, the individual or department in question, and the nature of the contact. In addition to this, mention any earlier proceedings or informal contacts, of which you are aware, with the Commission and/or the EFTA Surveillance Authority and any earlier proceedings with any national authorities or courts in the Community or in EFTA concerning these or any related agreements.

3.2. Please summarize any reasons for any claim that the case involves an issue of exceptional urgency.

3.3. The Commission has stated that where notifications do not have particular political, economic or legal significance for the Community they will normally be dealt with by means of comfort letter.[18] Would you be satisfied with a comfort letter? If you consider that it would be inappropriate to deal with the notified agreement in this manner, please explain the reasons for this view.

3.4. State whether you intend to produce further supporting facts or arguments not yet available and, if so, on which points.[19]

Section 4

Full details of the arrangements

4.1. Please summarize the nature, content and objectives pursued by the agreement being notified.

4.2. Detail any provisions contained in the agreements which may restrict the parties in their freedom to take independent commercial decisions, for example regarding:
- buying or selling prices, discounts or other trading conditions,
- the quantities of goods to be manufactured or distributed or services to be offered,
- technical development or investment,
- the choice of markets or sources of supply,
- purchases from or sales to third parties,
- whether to apply similar terms for the supply of equivalent goods or services,
- whether to offer different services separately or together.

If you are claiming the benefit of the opposition procedure, identify in this list the restrictions that exceed those automatically exempted by the relevant regulation.

4.3. State between which Member States of the Community and/or EFTA States[20] trade may be affected by the arrangements. Please give reasons for your reply to this question, giving data on trade flows where relevant. Furthermore please state whether trade between the Community or the EEA territory and any third countries is affected, again giving reasons for your reply.

Section 5

Non-confidential Summary

Shortly following receipt of a notification, the Commission may publish a short notice inviting third party comments on the agreement in question.[21] As the objective pursued by the Commission in publishing an informal preliminary notice is to receive third party comments as soon as possible after the notification has been received, such a notice is usually published without first providing it to the notifying parties for their comments. This section requests the information to be used in an informal preliminary notice in the event that the Commission decides to issue one. It is important, therefore, that your replies to these questions do not contain any business secrets or other confidential information.

1. State the names of the parties to the agreement notified and the groups of undertakings to which they belong.
2. Give a short summary of the nature and objectives of the agreement. As a guideline this summary should not exceed 100 words.
3. Identify the product sectors affected by the agreement in question.

Chapter II

Section concerning the relevant market (to be completed for all notifications except those relating to structural joint ventures for which accelerated treatment is claimed)

Section 6

The relevant market

A relevant product market comprises all those products and/or services which are regarded as interchangeable or substitutable by the consumer, by reason of the products' characteristics, their prices and their intended use.

The following factors are normally considered to be relevant to the determination of the relevant product market and should be taken into account in this analysis[22]:

— the degree of physical similarity between the products/services in question,
— any differences in the end use to which the goods are put,
— differences in price between two products,
— the cost of switching between two potentially competing products,
— established or entrenched consumer preferences for one type or category of product over another,
— industry-wide product classifications (e.g. classifications maintained by trade associations).

The relevant geographic market comprises the area in which the undertakings concerned are involved in the supply of products or services, in which the conditions of competition are sufficiently homogeneous and which can be distinguished from neighbouring areas because, in particular, conditions of competition are appreciably different in those areas.

Factors relevant to the assessment of the relevant geographic market include[23] the nature and characteristics of the products or services concerned, the existence of entry barriers or consumer preferences, appreciable differences of the undertakings' market share or substantial price differences between neighbouring areas, and transport costs.

6.1 In the light of the above please explain the definition of the relevant product market or markets that in your opinion should form the basis of the Commission's analysis of the notification.
In your answer, please give reasons for assumptions or findings, and explain how the factors outlined above have been taken into account. In particular, please state the specific products or services directly or indirectly affected by the agreement being notified and identify the categories of goods viewed as substitutable in your market definition.
In the questions figuring below, this (or these) definition(s) will be referred to as "the relevant product market(s)".

6.2. Please explain the definition of the relevant geographic market or markets that in your opinion should form the basis of the Commission's analysis of the notification. In your answer, please give reasons for assumptions or findings, and explain how the factors outlined above have been taken into account. In particular, please identify the countries in which the parties are active in the relevant product market(s), and in the event that you consider the relevant geographic market to be wider than

the individual Member States of the community or EFTA on which the parties to the agreement are active, give reasons for this.
In the questions below, this (or these) definition(s) will be referred to as "the relevant geographic market(s)".

Section 7

Group members operating on the same markets as the parties

7.1. For each of the parties to the agreement being notified, provide a list of all undertakings belonging to the same group which are:
7.1.1. active in the relevant product market(s);
7.1.2. active in markets neighbouring the *relevant market(s)* (i.e. active in products and/or services that represent imperfect and partial substitutes for those included in your definition of the relevant product market(s)).

Such undertakings must be identified even if they sell the product or service in question in other geographic areas than those in which the parties to the notified agreement operate. Please list the name, place of incorporation, exact product manufactured and the geographic scope of operation of each group member.

Section 8

The position of the parties on the affected relevant product markets

Information requested in this section must be provided for the groups of the parties as a whole. It is not sufficient to provide such information only in relation to the individual undertakings directly concerned by the agreement.

8.1. In relation to each relevant product market(s) identified in your reply to question 6.1 please provide the following information:
8.1.1. the market shares of the parties on the *relevant geographic market* during the previous three years;
8.1.2. where different, the market shares of the parties in (a) the EEA territory as a whole, (b) the Community, (c) the territory of the EFTA States and (d) each EC Member State and EFTA State during the previous three years.[24] For this section, where market shares are less than 20 per cent, please state simply which of the following bands are relevant 0 to 5 per cent, 5 to 10 per cent, 10 to 15 per cent, 15 to 20 per cent.

For the purpose of answering these questions, market share may be calculated either on the basis of value or volume. Justification for the figures provided must be given. Thus, for each answer, total market value/volume must be stated, together with the sales/turnover of each of the parties in question. The source or sources of the information should also be given (e.g. official statistics, estimates, etc.), and where possible, copies should be provided of documents from which information has been taken.

Section 9

The position of competitors and customers on the relevant product market(s)

Information requested in this section must be provided for the group of the parties as a whole and not in relation to the individual companies directly concerned by the agreement notified.

For the (all) relevant product and geographic market(s) in which the parties have a combined market share exceeding 15 per cent, the following questions must be answered.

9.1. Please identify the five main competitors of the parties. Please identify the company and give your best estimate as to their market share in the relevant geographic market(s). Please also provide address, telephone number and fax number, and, where possible, the name of a contact person at each company identified.

9.2. Please identify the five main customers of each of the parties. State company name, address, telephone and fax numbers, together with the name of a contact person.

Section 10

Market entry and potential competition in product and geographic terms

For the (all) relevant product and geographic market(s) in which the parties have a combined market share exceeding 15 per cent, the following questions must be answered.

10.1 Describe the various factors influencing entry in product terms into the *relevant product market(s)* that exist in the present case (i.e. what barriers exist to prevent undertakings that do not presently manufacture goods within the relevant product market(s) entering this market(s)). In so doing take account of the following where appropriate:
- to what extent is entry to the markets influenced by the requirement of government authorization or standard setting in any form? Are there any legal or regulatory controls on entry to these markets?
- to what extent is entry to the markets influenced by the availability of raw materials?
- to what extent is entry to the markets influenced by the length of contracts between an undertaking and its suppliers and/or customers?
- describe the importance of research and development and in particular the importance of licensing patents, know-how and other rights in these markets.

10.2 Describe the various factors influencing entry in geographic terms into the relevant geographic market(s) that exist in the present case (i.e. what barriers exist to prevent undertakings already producing and/or marketing products within the relevant product market(s) but in areas outside the relevant geographic market(s) extending the scope of their sales into the relevant geographic market(s)?). Please give reasons for your answers, explaining where relevant, the importance of the following factors:
- trade barriers imposed by law, such as tariffs, quotas etc.,
- local specification or technical requirements,
- procurement policies,
- the existence of adequate and available local distribution and retailing facilities,
- transport costs,
- entrenched consumer preferences for local brands or products,
- language.

10.3 Have any new undertakings entered the relevant product market(s) in geographic areas where the parties sell during the last three years? Please provide this information with respect to both new entrants in product terms and new entrants in geographic terms. If such entry has occurred, please identify the undertaking(s) concerned (name, address, telephone and fax numbers, and, where possible, contact person), and provide your best estimate of their market share in the relevant product and geographic market(s).

CHAPTER III

Section concerning the relevant market only for structureal joint ventures for which accelerated treatment is claimed

Section 11

The relevant market

A relevant product market comprises all those products and/or services which are regarded as interchangeable or substitutable by the consumer, by reason of the products' characteristics, their prices and their intended use.

The following factors are normally considered to be relevant[25] to the determination of the relevant product market and should be taken into account in this analysis:

- the degree of physical similarity between the products/services in question,
- any differences in the end use to which the goods are put,
- differences in price between two products,
- the cost of switching between two potentially competing products,
- established or entrenched consumer preferences for one type or category of product over another,
- different or similar industry-wide product classifications (e.g. classifications maintained by trade associations).

The relevant geographic market comprises the area in which the undertakings concerned are involved in the supply of products or services, in which the conditions of competition are sufficiently homogeneous and which can be distinguished from neighbouring areas because, in particular, conditions of competition are appreciably different in those areas.

Factors relevant to the assessment of the relevant geographic market include[26] the nature and characteristics of the products or services concerned, the existence of entry barriers or consumer preferences, appreciable differences of the undertakings' market share or substantial price differences between neighbouring areas, and transport costs.

Part 11.1

The notifying parties' analysis of the relevant market

11.1.1. In the light of the above, please explain the definition of the relevant product market or markets that in the opinion of the parties should form the basis of the Commission's analysis of the notification.
In your answer, please give reasons for assumptions or findings, and explain how the factors outlined above have been taken into account.
In the questions figuring below, this (or these) definition(s) will be referred to as "the relevant product market(s)".

11.1.2. Please explain the definition of the relevant geographic market or markets that in the opinion of the parties should form the basis of the Commission's analysis of the notification.

In your answer, please give reasons for assumptions or findings, and explain how the factors outlined above have been taken into account.

Part 11.2

Questions on the relevant product and geographic market(s)

Answers to the following questions will enable the Commission to verify whether the product and geographic market definitions put forward by you in Section 11.1 are compatible with definitions figuring above.

Product market definition

11.2.1. List the specific products or services directly or indirectly affected by the agreement being notified.

11.2.2. List the categories of products and/or services that are, in the opinion of the notifying parties, close economic substitutes for those identified in the reply to question 11.2.1. Where more than one product or service has been identified in the reply to question 11.2.1, a list for each product must be provided for this question.
The products identified in this list should be ordered in their degree of substitutability, first listing the most perfect substitute for the products of the parties, finishing with the least perfect substitute.[27]
Please explain how the factors relevant to the definition of the relevant product market have been taken into account in drawing up this list and in placing the products/services in their correct order.

Geographic market definition

11.2.3. List all the countries in which the parties are active in the relevant product market(s). Where they are active in all countries within any given groups of countries or trading area (e.g. the whole Community or EFTA, the EEA countries, world-wide) it is sufficient to indicate the area in question.

11.2.4. Explain the manner in which the parties produce and sell the goods and/or services in each of these various countries or areas. For example, do they manufacture locally, do they sell through local distribution facilities, or do they distribute through exclusive, or non-exclusive, importers and distributors?

11.2.5. Are there significant trade flows in the goods/services that make up the relevant product market(s) (i) between the EC Member States (please specify which and estimate the percentage of total sales made up by imports in each Member State in which the parties are active), (ii) between all or part of the EC Member States and all or part of the EFTA States (again, please specify and estimate the percentage of total sales made up by imports), (iii) between the EFTA States (please specify which and estimate the percentage of total sales made up by imports in each such State in which the parties are active), and (iv) between all or part of the EEA territory and other countries? (again, please specify and estimate the percentage of total sales made up by imports.)

11.2.6. Which producer undertakings based outside the Community or the EEA territory sell within the EEA territory in countries in which the parties are active in the affected products? How do these undertakings market their products? Does this differ between different EC Member States and/or EFTA States?

Section 12

Group members operating on the same markets as the parties to the notified agreement

12.1. For each of the parties to the agreement being notified, provide a list of all undertakings belonging to the same group which are:

12.1.1. active in the relevant product market(s);

12.1.2. active in markets neighbouring the relevant product market(s) (i.e. active in products/services that represent imperfect and partial substitutes[28] for those included in your definition of the relevant product market(s);

12.1.3. active in markets upstream and/or downstream from those included in the relevant product market(s).

Such undertakings must be identified even if they sell the product or service in question in other geographic areas than those in which the parties to the notified agreement operate. Please list the name, place of incorporation, exact product manufactured and the geographic scope of operation of each group member.

Section 13

The position of the parties on the relevant product market(s)

Information requested in this section must be provided for the group of the parties as a whole and not in relation to the individual companies directly concerned by the agreement notified.

13.1 In relation to each relevant product market(s), as defined in your reply to question 11.1.2, please provide the following information:

13.1.1. the market shares of the parties on the relevant geographic market during the previous three years;

13.1.2. where different, the market shares of the parties in (a) the EEA territory as a whole, (b) the Community, (c) the territory of the EFTA States and (d) each EC Member State and EFTA State during the previous three years.[29] For this section, where market shares are less than 20 per cent, please state simply which of the following bands are relevant: 0 to 5 per cent, 5 to 10 per cent, 10 to 15 per cent, 15 to 20 per cent in terms of value or volume.

For the purpose of answering these questions, market share may be calculated either on the basis of value or volume. Justification for the figures provided must be given. Thus, for each answer, total market value/volume must be stated, together with the sales/turnover of each the parties in question. The source of sources of the information should also be given, and where possible, copies should be provided of documents from which information has been taken.

13.2. If the market shares in question 13.1 were to be calculated on a basis other than that used by the parties, would the resultant market shares differ by more than 5 per cent in any market (i.e. if the parties have calculated market shares on the basis of volume, what would be the relevant figure if it was calculated on the basis of value?) If the figure were to differ by more than 5 per cent please provide the information requested in question 13.1 on the basis of both value and volume.

13.3. Give your best estimate of the current rate of capacity utilization of the parties and in the industry in general in the relevant product and geographic market(s).

Section 14

The position of competitors on the relevant product market(s)

Information requested in this section must be provided for the group of the parties as a whole and not in relation to the individual companies directly concerned by the agreement notified.

For the (all) relevant product market(s) in which the parties have a combined market share exceeding 10 per cent in the EEA as a whole, the Community, the EFTA territory or in any EC Member State or EFTA Member State, the following questions must be answered.

14.1. Please identify the competitors of the parties on the relevant product market(s) that have a market share exceeding 10 per cent in any EC Member State, EFTA State, in the territory of the EFTA States, in the EEA, or world-wide. Please identify the company and give your best estimate as to their market share in these geographic areas. Please also provide the address, telephone and fax numbers, and, where possible, the names of a contact person at each company identified.

14.2. Please describe the nature of demand on the relevant product market(s). For example, are there few or many purchasers, are there different categories of purchasers, are government agencies or departments important purchasers?

14.3. Please identify the five largest customers of each of the parties for each *relevant product market(s).* State company name, address, telephone and fax numbers, together with the name of a contact person.

Section 15

Market entry and potential competition

For the (all) relevant product market(s) in which the parties have a combined market share exceeding 10 per cent in the EEA as a whole, the Community, the EFTA territory or in any EC Member State or EFTA State, the following questions must be answered.

15.1. Describe the various factors influencing entry into the relevant product market(s) that exist in the present case. In so doing take account of the following where appropriate:
- to what extent is entry to the markets influenced by the requirement of government authorization or standard setting in any form? Are there any legal or regulatory controls on entry to these markets?
- to what extent is entry to the markets influenced by the availability of raw materials?
- to what extent is entry to the markets influenced by the length of contracts between an undertaking and its suppliers and/or customers?
- what is the importance of research and development and in particular the importance of licensing patents, know-how and other rights in these markets.

15.2. Have any new undertakings entered the relevant product market(s) in geographic areas where the parties sell during the last three years? If so, please identify the undertaking(s) concerned (name, address, telephone and fax numbers, and, where possible, contact person), and provide your best estimate of their market share in each EC Member State and EFTA State that they are active and in the Community, the territory of the EFTA States and the EEA territory as a whole.

15.3. Give your best estimate of the minimum viable scale for the entry into the relevant product market(s) in terms of appropriate market share necessary to operate profitably.

15.4. Are there significant barriers to entry preventing companies active on the relevant product market(s):

15.4.1. in one EC Member State or EFTA State selling in other areas of the EEA territory;

15.4.2. outside the EEA territory selling into all or parts of the EEA territory.

Please give reasons for your answers, explaining, where relevant, the importance of the following factors:

— trade barriers imposed by law, such as tariffs, quotas etc.,
— local specification or technical requirements,
— procurement policies,
— the existence of adequate and available local distribution and retailing facilities,
— transport costs,
— entrenched consumer preferences for local brands or products,
— language.

Chapter IV

Final sections
To be completed for all notifications

Section 16

Reasons for the application for negative clearance

If you are applying for negative clearance state:

16.1. why, i.e. state which provision or effects of the agreement or behaviour might, in your view, raise questions of compatibility with the Community's and/or the EEA rules of competition. The object of this subheading is to give the Commission the clearest possible idea of the doubts you have about your agreement or behaviour that you wish to have resolved by a negative clearance.

Then, under the following three references, give a statement of the relevant facts and reasons as to why you consider Article 85(1) or 86 of the EC Treaty and/or Article 53(1) or 54 of the EEA Agreement to be inapplicable, i.e.:

16.2. why the agreements or behaviour do not have the object or effect of preventing, restricting or distorting competition within the common market or within the territory of the EFTA State to any appreciable extent, or why your undertaking does not have or its behaviour does not abuse a dominant position; and/or

16.3. why the agreements or behaviour do not have the object or effect of preventing, restricting or distorting competition within the EEA territory to any appreciable extent, or why your undertaking does not have or its behaviour does not abuse a dominant position; and/or

16.4. why the agreements or behaviour are not such as may affect trade between Member States or between the Community and one or more EFTA States, or between EFTA States to any appreciable extent.

Section 17

Reasons for the application for exemption

If you are notifying the agreement, even if only as a precaution, in order to obtain an exemption under Article 85(3) of the E.C. Treaty and/or Article 53(3) of the EEA Agreement, explain how:

17.1. the agreement contributes to improving production or distribution, and/or promoting technical or economic progress. In particular, please explain the reasons why these benefits are expected to result from the collaboration; for example, do the parties to the agreement possess complementary technologies or distribution systems that will produce important synergies? (if, so, please state which). Also please state whether any documents or studies were drawn up by the notifying parties when assessing the feasibility of the operation and the benefits likely to result therefrom, and whether any such documents or studies provided estimates of the savings or efficiencies likely to result. Please provide copies of any such documents or studies;

17.2. a proper share of the benefits arising from such improvement or progress accrues to consumers;

17.3. all restrictive provisions of the agreement are indispensable to the attainment of the aims set out under 17.1 (if you are claiming the benefit of the opposition procedure, it is particularly important that you should identify and justify restrictions that exceed those automatically exempted by the relevant Regulations). In this respect please explain how the benefits resulting from the agreement identified in your reply to question 17.1 could not be achieved, or could not be achieved so quickly or efficiently or only at higher cost or with less certainty of success (i) without the conclusion of the agreement as a whole and (ii) without those particular clauses and provisions of the agreement identified in your reply to question 4.2;

17.4 the agreement does not eliminate competition in respect of a substantial part of the goods or services concerned.

Section 18

Supporting documentation

The completed notification must be drawn up and submitted in one original. It shall contain the last versions of all agreements which are the subject of the notification and be accompanied by the following:

(a) sixteen copies of the notification itself;

(b) three copies of the annual reports and accounts of all the parties to the notified agreement, decision or practice for the last three years;

(c) three copies of the most recent in-house or external long-term market studies or planning documents for the purpose of assessing or analysing the affected markets) with respect to competitive conditions, competitors (actual and potential), and market conditions. Each document should indicate the name and position of the author;

(d) three copies of reports and analyses which have been prepared by or for any officer(s) or director(s) for the purposes of evaluating or analysing the notified agreement.

Section 19

Declaration

The notification must conclude with the following declaration which is to be signed by or on behalf of all the applicants or notifying parties.[30]

"The undersigned declare that the information given in this notification is correct to the best of their knowledge and belief, that complete copies of all documents requested by form A/B have been supplied to the extent that they are in the possession of the group of undertakings to which the applicant(s) or notifying party(ies) belong(s) and are accessible to the latter, that all estimates are identified as such and are their best estimates of the underlying facts and that all the opinions expressed are sincere.

They are aware of the provisions of Article 15(1)(a) of Regulation No. 17.

Place and date:

Signatures:"

Please add the name(s) of the person(s) signing the application or notification and their function(s).

Annex I

TEXT OF ARTICLES 85 AND 86 OF THE EC TREATY, ARTICLES 53, 54 AND 56 OF THE EEA AGREEMENT, AND OF ARTICLES 2, 3 AND 4 OF PROTOCOL 22 TO THAT AGREEMENT

Article 85 of the Treaty

1. The following shall be prohibited as incompatible with the common market: all agreements between undertakings, decisions by associations or undertakings and concerted practices which may affect trade between Member States and which have as their object or effect the prevention, restriction or distortion of competition within the common market, and in particular those which:

(a) directly or indirectly fix purchase or selling prices or any other trading conditions;
(b) limit or control production, markets, technical development, or investment;
(c) share markets or sources of supply;
(d) apply dissimilar conditions to equivalent transactions with other trading parties, thereby placing them at a competitive disadvantage;
(e) make the conclusion of contracts subject to acceptance by the other parties of supplementary obligations which, by their nature or according to commercial usage, have no connection with the subject of such contracts.

2. Any agreements or decisions prohibited pursuant to this Article shall be automatically void.

3. The provisions of paragraph 1 may, however, be declared in applicable in the case of:

— any agreement or category of agreements between undertakings,
— any decision or category of decisions by associations or undertakings,
— any concerted practice or category of concerted practices,

which contributes to improving the production or distribution of goods or to promoting technical or economic progress, while allowing consumers a fair share of the resulting benefit, and which does not:

(a) impose on the undertakings concerned restrictions which are not indispensable to the attainment of these objectives;
(b) afford such undertakings the possibility of eliminating competition in respect of a substantial part of the products in question.

Article 86 of the EC Treaty

Any abuse by one or more undertakings of a dominant position within the common market or in a substantial part of it shall be prohibited as incompatible with the common market in so far as it may affect trade between Member States.

Such abuse may, in particular, consist in:

(a) directly or indirectly imposing unfair purchase or selling prices or other unfair trading conditions;
(b) limiting production, markets or technical development to the prejudice of consumers;
(c) applying dissimilar conditions to equivalent transactions with other trading parties, thereby placing them at a competitive disadvantage;
(d) making the conclusion of contracts subject to acceptance by the other parties of supplementary obligations which, by their nature or according to commercial usage, have no connection with the subject of such contracts.

Article 53 of the EEA Agreement

1. The following shall be prohibited as incompatible with the functioning of this Agreement: all agreements between undertakings, decisions by associations of undertakings and concerted practices which may affect trade between Contracting Parties and which have as their object or effect the prevention, restriction or distortion of competition within the territory covered by this Agreement, and in particular those which:

(a) directly or indirectly fix purchase or selling prices or any other trading conditions;
(b) limit or control production, markets, technical development, or investment;
(c) share markets or sources of supply;
(d) apply dissimilar conditions to equivalent transactions with other trading parties, thereby placing them at a competitive disadvantage;
(e) make the conclusion of contracts subject to acceptance by the other parties of supplementary obligations which, by their nature or according to commercial usage, have no connection with the subject of such contracts.

2. Any agreement or decisions prohibited pursuant to this Article shall be automatically void.

3. The provisions of paragraph 1 may, however, be declared inapplicable in the case of:

— any agreement or category of agreements between undertakings,
— any decision or category of decisions by associations of undertakings,
— any concerted practice or category of concerted practices,

which contributes to improving the production or distribution of goods or to promoting technical or economic progress, while allowing consumers a fair share of the resulting benefit, and which does not:

(a) impose on the undertakings concerned restrictions which are not indispensable to the attainment of these objectives;
(b) afford such undertakings the possibility of eliminating competition in respect of a substantial part of the products in question.

APPENDIX 6

Article 54 of the EEA Agreement

Any abuse by one or more undertakings of a dominant position within the territory covered by this agreement or in a substantial part of it shall be prohibited as incompatible with the functioning of this Agreement in so far as it may affect trade between Contracting Parties.

Such abuse may, in particular, consist in:

(a) directly or indirectly imposing unfair purchase or selling prices or other unfair trading conditions;
(b) limiting production, markets or technical development to the prejudice of consumers;
(c) applying dissimilar conditions to equivalent transactions with other trading parties, thereby placing them at a competitive disadvantage;
(d) making the conclusion of contracts subject to acceptance by the other parties of supplementary obligations which, by their nature or according to commercial usage, have no connection with the subject of such contracts.

Article 56 of the EEA Agreement

1. Individual cases falling under Article 53 shall be decided upon by the surveillance authorities in accordance with the following provisions:

(a) individual cases where only trade between EFTA States is affected shall be decided upon by the EFTA Surveillance Authority;
(b) without prejudice to subparagraph (c), the EFTA Surveillance Authority decides, as provided for in the provisions set out in Article 58, Protocol 21 and the rules adopted for its implementation, Protocol 23 and Annex XIV, on cases where the turnover of the undertakings concerned in the territory of the EFTA States equals 33 per cent or more of their turnover in the territory covered by this Agreement;
(c) the EC Commission decides on the other cases as well as on cases under (b) where trade between EC Member States is affected, taking into account the provisions set out in Article 58, Protocol 21, Protocol 23 and Annex XIV.

2. Individual cases falling under Article 54 shall be decided upon by the surveillance authority in the territory of which a dominant position is found to exist. The rules set out in paragraph 1(b) and (c) shall apply only if dominance exists within the territories of both surveillance authorities.

3. Individual cases falling under paragraph 1(c), whose effects on trade between EC Member States or on competition within the Community are not appreciable, shall be decided upon by the EFTA Surveillance Authority.

4. The terms "undertaking" and "turnover" are, for the purpose of this Article, defined in Protocol 22.

Articles 2, 3, and 4 of Protocol 22 to the EEA Agreement

Article 2

"Turnover" within the meaning of Article 56 of the Agreement shall comprise the amounts derived by the undertaking concerned, in the territory covered by this Agreement, in the preceding financial year from the sale of products and the provision of services falling within the undertaking's ordinary scope of activities after deduction of sales rebates and of value-added tax and other taxes directly related to turnover.

Article 3

In place of turnover the following shall be used:

(a) for credit institutions and other financial institutions, their total assets multiplied by the ratio between loans and advances to credit institutions and customers in transactions with residents in the territory covered by this Agreement and the total sum of those loans and advances;

(b) for insurance undertakings, the value of gross premiums received from residents in the territory covered by this Agreement, which shall comprise all amounts received and receivable in respect of insurance contracts issued by or on behalf of the insurance undertakings, including also outgoing reinsurance premiums, and after deduction of taxes and parafiscal contributions or levies charged by reference to the amounts of individual premiums or the total value of premiums.

Article 4

1. In derogation of the definition of the turnover relevant for the application of Article 56 of the Agreement, as contained in Article 2 of this Protocol, the relevant turnover shall be constituted:

(a) as regards agreements, decisions of associations of undertakings and concerted practices related to distribution and supply arrangements between non-competing undertakings, of the amounts derived from the sale of goods or the provision of services which are the subject matter of the agreements, decisions or concerted practices, and from the other goods or services which are considered by users to be equivalent in view of their characteristics, price and intended use;

(b) as regards agreements, decisions of associations of undertakings and concerted practices related to arrangements on transfer of technology between non-competing undertakingss, of the amounts derived from the sale of goods or the provision of services which result from the technology which is the subject matter of the agreements, decisions or concerted practices, and of the amounts derived from the sale of those goods or the provision of those services which that technology is designed to improve or replace.

2. However, where at the time of the coming to existence of arrangements as described in paragraph 1(a) and (b) turnover as regards the sale of products or the provision of services is not in evidence, the general provision as contained in Article 2 shall apply.

ANNEX II

LIST OF RELEVANT ACTS

(as of 1 March 1995)

(If you think it possible that your arrangements do not need to be notified by virtue of any of these regulations or notices it may be worth your while to obtain a copy.)

IMPLEMENTING REGULATIONS[31]

Council Regulation No. of 6 February 1992: First Regulation implementing Articles 85 and 86 of the Treaty (OJ No. 13, 21.2.1962, p. 204/62, English Special

Edition 1959–1962, November 1972, p. 87) as amended (OJ No. 58, 10.7.1962, p. 1655/62; OJ No. 162, 7.11.1963, p. 2696/63; OJ No. L285, 29.12.1971, p. 49; OJ No. L73, 27.3.1972, p. 92; OJ No. L291, 19.11.1979, p. 94 and OJ No. L302, 15.11.1985, p. 165).

Commission Regulation (EC) No. 3385/94 of 21 December 1994 on the form, content and other details of applications and notifications provided for in Council Regulation No. 17.

Regulations Granting Block Exemption in Respect of a Wide Range of Agreements

Commission Regulation (EC) No. 1983/83 of 22 June 1983 on the application of Article 85(3) of the Treaty to categories of exclusive distribution agreements (OJ No. L173, 30.6.1983, p. 1, as corrected in OJ No. L281, 13.10.1983, p. 24), as well as this Regulation as adapted for EEA purposes (see point 2 of Annex XIV to the EEA Agreement).

Commission Regulation (EEC) No. 1984/83 of 22 June 1983 on the application of Article 85(3) of the Treaty to categories of exclusive purchasing agreements (OJ No. L173, 30.6.1983, p. 5, as corrrected in OJ No. L281, 13.10.1983, p. 24), as well as this Regulation as adapted for EEA purposes (see point 3 of Annex XIV to the EEA Agreement).

See also the Commission notices concerning Regulations (EEC) No. 1983/93 and (EEC) No. 1984/83 (OJ No. C101, 13.4.1984, p. 2 and OJ No. C121, 13.5.1992, p. 2).

Commission Regulation (EEC) No. 2349/84 of 23 July 1984 on the application of Article 85(3) of the Treaty to certain categories of patent licensing agreements (OJ No. L219, 16.8.1984, p. 15, as corrected in OJ No. L113, 26.4.1985, p. 34), as amended (OJ No. L12,18.1.1995, p. 13), as well as this Regulation as adapted for EEA purposes (see point 5 of Annex XIV to the EEA Agreement). Article 4 of this Regulation provides for an opposition procedure.

Commission Regulation (EEC) No. 123/85 of 12 December 1984 on the application of Article 85(3) of the Treaty to certain categories of motor vehicle distributing and servicing agreements (OJ No. L15, 18.1.1985, p. 16); as well as this Regulation as adapted for EEA purposes (see point 4 of Annex XIV to the EEA Agreement). See also the Commission notices concerning this Regulation (OJ No. C17, 18.1.1985, p. 4 and OJ No. C329, 18.12.1991, p. 20).

Commission Regulation (EEC) No. 417/85 of 19 December 1984 on the application of Article 85(3) of the Treaty to categories of specialization agreements (OJ No. L53, 22.2.1985, p. 1), as amended (OJ No. L21, 29.1.1993, p. 8), as well as this Regulation as adapted for EEA purposes (see point 6 of Annex XIV to the EEA Agreement). Article 4 of this Regulation provides for an opposition procedure.

Commission Regulation (EEC) No. 418/85 of 19 December 1984 on the application of Article 85(3) of the Treaty to categories of research and development cooperation agreements (OJ No. L53, 22.2.1985, p. 5), as amended (OJ No. L21, 29.1.1993, p. 8), as well as this Regulation as adapted for EEA purposes (see point 7 of Annex XIV to the EEA Agreement). Article 7 of this Regulation provides for an opposition procedure.

Commission Regulation (EEC) No. 4087/88 of 30 November 1988 on the application of Article 85(3) of the Treaty to categories of franchise agreements (OJ No. L359, 28.12.1988, p. 46), as well as this Regulation as adapted for EEA purposes (see point 8 of Annex XIV to the EEA Agreement). Article 6 of this Regulation provides for an opposition procedure.

Commission Regulation (EEC) No. 556/89 of 30 November 1988 on the application of Article 85(3) of the Treaty to certain categories of know-how licensing agreements (OJ No. L61, 4.3.1989, p. 1), as amended (OJ No. L21, 29.1.1993, p. 8), as well as this Regulation as adapted for EEA purposes (see point

9 of Annex XIV to the EEA Agreement). Article 4 of this Regulation provides for an opposition procedure.

Commission Regulation (EEC) No. 3932/92 of 21 December 1992 on the application of Article 85(3) of the Treaty to certain categories of agreements, decisions and concerted practices in the insurance sector (OJ No. L398, 31.12.1992, p. 7). This Regulation will be adapted for EEA purposes.

Notices of a General Nature[32]

Commission notice on exclusive dealing contracts with commercial agents (OJ No. 139, 24.12.1962, p. 2921/62). This states that the Commission does not consider most such agreements to fall under the prohibition of Article 85(1).

Commission notice concerning agreements, decisions and concerted practices in the field of cooperation between enterprises (OJ No. C75, 29.7.1968, p. 3, as corrected in OJ No. C84, 28.8.1968, p. 14). This defines the sorts of cooperation on market studies, accounting, R & D, joint use of production, storage of transport, ad hoc consortia, selling or after-sales service, advertising or quality labelling that the Commission considers not to fall under the prohibition of Article 85(1).

Commission notice concerning its assessment of certain subcontracting agreements in relation to Article 85(1) of the Treaty (OJ No. C1, 3.1.1979, p. 2).

Commission notice on agreements, decisions and concerted practices of minor importance which do not fall under Article 85(1) of the Treaty (OJ No. C231, 12.9.1986, p. 2) as amended by Commission notice (OJ No. C368, 23.12.1994, p. 20)—in the main, those where the parties have less than 5 per cent of the market between them, and a combined annual turnover of less than ECU 300 million.

Commission guidelines on the application of EEC competition rules in the telecommunications sector (OJ No. C233, 6.9.1991, p. 2). These guidelines aim at clarifying the application of Community competition rules to the market participants in the telecommunications sector.

Commission notice on cooperation between national courts and the Commission in applying Articles 85 and 86 (OJ No. C39, 13.2.1993, p. 6). This notice sets out the principles on the basis of which such cooperation takes place.

Commission notice concerning the assessment of cooperative joint ventures pursuant to Article 85 of the EC Treaty (OJ No. C43, 16.2.1993, p. 2). This notice sets out the principles on the assessment of joint ventures.

A collection of these texts (as at 31 December 1989) was published by the Office for Official Publications of the European Communities (references Vol. 1: ISBN 92-826-1307-0, catalogue No. CV-42-90-001-EN-C). An updated collection is in preparation.

Pursuant to the Agreement, these texts will also cover the European Economic Area.

Annex III

LIST OF MEMBER STATES AND EFTA STATES, ADDRESS OF THE COMMISSION AND OF THE EFTA SURVEILLANCE AUTHORITY, LIST OF COMMISSION INFORMATION OFFICES WITHIN THE COMMUNITY AND IN EFTA STATES AND ADDRESSES OF COMPETENT AUTHORITIES IN EFTA STATES

The Member States as at the date of this Annex are: Austria, Belgium, Denmark, Finland, France, Germany, Greece, Ireland, Italy, Luxembourg, the Netherlands, Portugal, Spain, Sweden and the United Kingdom.

The EFTA States which will be Contracting Parties of the EEA Agreement, as at the date of this Annex, are: Iceland, Liechtenstein and Norway.

APPENDIX 6

The address of the Commission's Directorate-General for Competition is:

Commission of the European Communities
Directorate-General for Competition
200 rue de la Loi
B-1049 Brussels
Tel. (322) 299 11 11

The address of the EFTA Surveillance Authority's Competition Directorate is:

EFTA Surveillance Authority
Competition Directorate
1–3 rue Marie-Thérèse
B-1040 Brussels
Tel. (322) 286 17 11

The addresses of the Commission's Information Offices in the Community are:

BELGIUM
73 rue Archimède
B-1040 Bruxelles
Tel. (322) 299 11 11

DENMARK
Højbrohus
Østergade 61
Postboks 144
DK-1004 København K
Tel. (4533) 14 41 40

FEDERAL REPUBLIC OF GERMANY
Zitelmannstraße 22
D-53113 Bonn
Tel. (49228) 53 00 90

Kurfürstendamm 102
D-10711 Berlin 31
Tel. (4930) 896 09 30
Erhardtstraße 27
D-80331 München
Tel. (4989) 202 10 11

GREECE
2 Vassilissis Sofias
Case Postale 11002
GR-Athina 10674
Tel. (301) 724 39 82/83/84

SPAIN
Calle de Serrano 41
5a Planta
E-28001 Madrid
Tel. (341) 435 17 00

Av. Diagonal, 407 bis
18 Planta
E-08008 Barcelona
Tel. (343) 415 81 77

FRANCE
288, boulevard Saint-Germain
F-75007 Paris
Tel. (331) 40 63 38 00

CMCI
2, rue Henri Barbusse
F-13241 Marseille, Cedex 01
Tel. (3391) 91 46 00

IRELAND
39 Molesworth Street
IRL-Dublin 2
Tel. (3531) 71 22 44

ITALY
Via Poli 29
I-00187
Roma
Tel. (396) 699 11 60

Corso Magenta 61
I-20123 Milano
Tel. (392) 480 15 05

LUXEMBURG
Bâtiment Jean-Monnet
rue Alcide de Gasperi
L-2920 Luxembourg
Tel. (352) 430 11

NETHERLANDS
Postbus 30465 NL-2500 GL Den Haag
Tel. (3170) 346 93 26

AUSTRIA
Hoyosgasse 5
A-1040 Wien
Tel. (431) 505 33 79

PORTUGAL
Centro Europeu Jean Monnet
Largo Jean Monnet, 1-10°
P-1200 Lisboa
Tel. (3511) 54 11 44

FINLAND
31 Pohjoisesplanadi
00100 Helsinki
Tel. (3580) 65 64 20

SWEDEN
PO Box 16396
Hamngatan 6
11147 Stockholm
Tel. (468) 611 11 72

UNITED KINGDOM
8 Storey's Gate
UK-London SW1P 3AT
Tel. (4471) 973 19 92

Windsor House
9/15 Bedford Street
UK-Belfast BT2 7EG
Tel. (44232) 24 07 08

4 Cathedral Road
UK-Cardiff CF1 9SG
Tel. (44222) 37 16 31

9 Alva Street
UK-Edinburgh EH2 4PH
Tel. (4431) 225 20 58

The addresses of the Commission's Information Offices in the EFTA States are:

NORWAY
Postboks 1643 Vika 0119 Oslo 1
Haakon's VII Gate No. 6
0161 Oslo 1
Tel. (472) 83 35 83

Forms for notification and applications, as well as more detailed information on the EEA competition rules, can also be obtained from the following offices:

AUSTRIA
Federal Ministry for Economic Affairs
Tel. (431) 71 100

FINLAND
Office of Free Competition
Tel. (3580) 73 141

ICELAND
Directorate of Competition and Fair Trade
Tel. (3541) 27 422

LIECHTENSTEIN
Office of National Economy
Division of Economy and Statistics
Tel. (4175) 61 11

NORWAY
Price Directorate
Tel. (4722) 40 09 00

SWEDEN
Competition Authority
Tel. (468) 700 16 00

[1] OJ 1994 L377/1.
[2] OJ No. 13, 21.2.1962, p. 204/62.
[3] OJ No. 35, 10.5.1962, p. 1118/62.
[4] OJ No. L336, 31.12.1993, p. 1.
[5] See list of Member States and EFTA States in Annex III.
[6] Reproduced in Annex I.
[7] See Annex II.
[8] See Annex II.
[9] OJ No. C231,12.9.1986, p. 2.
[10] For a definition of "turnover" in this context, see Articles 2, 3 and 4 of Protocol 22 to the EEA Agreement reproduced in Annex I.
[11] Subject to the qualification provided for in Article 4(2) of Regulation No. 17.
[12] For further details of the consequences of non-notification see the Commission notice on co-operation between national Courts and the Commission (OJ No. C39, 13.2.1993, p. 6).
[13] See point (a) of Article 8(3) of Regulation No. 17.
[14] The Commission is aware that in exceptional cases it may not be practicable to inform non-notifying parties to the notified agreement of the fact that it has been notified, or to provide them a copy of the notification. This may be the case, for example, where a standard agreement is being notified that is concluded with a large number of undertakings. Where this is the case you should state the reasons why it has not been practicable to follow the standard procedure set out in this question.

[15] *Note:* For the purposes of this question a representative means an individual or undertaking formally apointed to make the notification or application on behalf of the party or parties submitting the notification. This should be distinguished from the situation where the notification is signed by an officer of the company or companies in question. In the latter situation no representative is appointed.

[16] *Note:* It is not mandatory to appoint representatives for the purpose of completing and/or submitting this notification. This question only requires the identification of representatives where the notifying parties have chosen to appoint them.

[17] For the calculation of turnover in the banking and insurance sectors see Article 3 of Protocol 22 to the EEA Agreement.

[18] See paragraph 14 of the notice on cooperation between national courts and the Commission in applying Articles 85 and 86 of the EC Treaty (OJ No. C39, 13.2.1993, p. 6).

[19] *Note:* In so far as the notifying parties provide the information required by this form that was reasonably available to them at the time of notification, the fact that the parties intend to provide further supporting facts of documentation in due course does not prevent the notification being valid at the time of notification and, in the case of structural joint ventures where the accelerated procedure is being claimed, the two month deadline commencing.

[20] See list in Annex II.

[21] An example of such a notice figures in Annex I to this Form. Such a notice should be distinguished from a formal notice published pursuant to Article 19(3) of Regulation No. 17. An Article 19(3) notice is relatively detailed, and gives an indication of the Commission's current approach in the case in question. Section 5 only seeks information that will be used in a short preliminary notice, and not a notice published pursuant to Article 19(3).

[22] This list is not, however, exhaustive, and notifying parties may refer to other factors.

[23] This list is not, however, exhaustive, and notifying parties may refer to other factors.

[24] *i.e.* Where the relevant geographic market has been defined as world wide, these figures must be given regarding the EEA, the Community, the territory of the EFTA States, and each EC Member State. Where the relevant geographic market has been defined as the Community, these figures must be given for the EEA, the territory of the EFTA States, and each EC Member State. Where the market has been defined as national, these figures must be given for the EEA, the Community and the territory of the EFTA States.

[25] This list is not, however, exhaustive, and notifying parties may refer to other factors.

[26] This list is not, however, exhaustive, and notifying parties may refer to other factors.

[27] Close economic substitute; most perfect substitute; least perfect substitute these definitions are only relevant to those filling out Chapter III of the form, i.e. those notifying structural joint ventures requesting the accelerated procedure).

For any given product (for the purposes of this definition "product" is used to refer to products or services) a chain of substitutes exists. This chain is made up of all conceivable substitutes for the product in question, *i.e.* all those products that will, to a greater or lesser extent, fulfil the needs of the consumer in question. The substitutes will range from very close (or perfect) ones (products to which consumers would turn immediately in the event of, for example, even a very small price increase for the product in question) to very distant (or imperfect) substitutes (products to which customers would only turn to in the event of a very large price rise for the product in question). When defining the relevant market, and calculating market shares, the Commission only takes into account close economic substitutes of the products in question. Close economic substitutes are ones to which customers would turn to in response to a small but significant price increase for the product in question (say 5 per cent). This enables the Commission to assess the market power of the notifying companies in the context of a relevant market made up of all those products that consumers of the products in question could readily and easily turn to.

However, this does not mean that the Commission fails to take into account the constraints on the competitive behaviour of the parties in question resulting from the existence of imperfect substitutes (those to which a consumer could not turn to in response to a small but significant price increase (say 5 per cent) for the products in question). These effects are taken into account once the market has been defined, and the market shares determined.

It is therefore important for the Commission to have information regarding both close economic substitutes for the products in question, as well as less perfect substitutes.

For example, assume two companies active in the luxury watch sector conclude a research and development agreement. They both manufacture watches costing ECU 1800 to 2000. Close economic substitutes are likely to be watches of other manufacturers in the same or similar price category, and these will be taken into account when defining the relevant product market. Cheaper watches, and in particular disposable plastic watches, will be imperfect substitutes, because it is unlikely that a potential purchaser of a ECU 2000 watch will turn to one costing ECU 20 if the expensive one increased its price by 5 per cent.

[28] The following are considered to be partial substitutes: products and services which may replace each other solely in certain geographic areas, solely during part of the year or solely for certain uses.

[29] i.e. Where the relevant geographic market has been defined as world wide, these figures must be given regarding the EEA, the Community, the territory of the EFTA States, and each E.C. Member State and EFTA State. Where the relevant geographic market has been defined as the Community, these figures must be given for the EEA, the territory of the EFTA States, and each E.C. Member State and EFTA State. Where the market has been defined as national, these figures must be given for the EEA, the Community and the territory of the EFTA States.

[30] Applications and notifications which have not been signed are invalid.

[31] As regards procedural rules applied by the EFTA Surveillance Authority, see Article 3 of Protocol 21 to the EEA Agreement and the relevant provisions in Protocol 4 to the Agreement between the EFTA States on the establishment of a Surveillance Authority and a Court of Justice.

[32] See also the corresponding notices published by the EFTA Surveillance Authority.

APPENDIX 7

COMMISSION DECISION[1]

on the terms of reference of hearing officers in competition procedures before the Commission

THE COMMISSION OF THE EUROPEAN COMMUNITIES,

Having regard to the Treaty establishing the European Coal and Steel Community,

Having regard to the Treaty establishing the European Community,

Whereas the treaties establishing the Communities and the rules implementing those treaties in relation to competition matters provide for the right of the parties concerned and of third parties to be heard before a final decision affecting their interests is taken;

Whereas the Commission must ensure that that right is guaranteed in its competition proceedings;

Whereas it is appropriate to entrust the organisation and conduct of the administrative procedures designed to protect the right to be heard to an independent person experienced in competition matters, in the interest of contributing to the objectivity, transparency and efficiency of Commission's competition proceedings;

Whereas the Commission created the post of Hearing Officer for these purposes in 1982 and laid down his terms of reference;

Whereas it is necessary to adapt and consolidate those terms of reference in the light of subsequent developments in Community law,

HAS DECIDED AS FOLLOWS:

Article 1

1. The hearings provided for in the provisions implementing Articles 65 and 66 of the ECSC Treaty, Articles 85 and 86 of the EC Treaty and Council Regulation (EEC) No. 4064/89[2] shall be organised and conducted by the Hearing Officer in accordance with Articles 2 to 10 of this Decision.

2. The implementing provisions referred to in paragraph 1 are:

(a) Article 36(1) of the ECSC Treaty;
(b) Regulation No. 99/63/EEC of the Commission of 25 July 1963 on the hearings provided for in Article 19(1) and (2) of Council Regulation No. 17;[3]
(c) Regulation (EEC) No. 1630/69 of the Commission of 8 August 1969 on the hearings provided for in Article 26(1) and (2) of Council Regulation (EEC) No. 1017/68 of 19 July 1968;[4]
(d) Commission Regulation (EEC) No. 4260/88 of 16 December 1988 on the communications, complaints and applications and the hearings provided for

in Council Regulation (EEC) No. 4056/86 laying down detailed rules for the application of Articles 58 and 86 of the treaty to maritime transport;[5]

(e) Commission Regulation (EEC) No. 4261/88 of 16 December 1988 on the complaints, applications and hearings provided for in Council Regulation (EEC) No. 3975/87 laying down the procedure for the application of the rules on competition to undertakings in the air transport sector;[6]

(f) Commission Regulation (EEC) No. 2367/90 of 25 July 1990, on the notifications, time limits and hearings provided for in Council Regulation (EEC) No. 4064/89 on the control of concentrations between undertakings.[7]

3. Administratively the Hearing Officer shall belong to the Directorate-General for Competition. To ensure the independence of the Hearing Officer in the performance of his duties, he has the right of direct access, as defined in Article 9, to the Member of the Commission with special responsibility for competition.

4. Where the Hearing Officer is unable to act, the Director-General, where appropriate after consultation of the Hearing Officer, shall designate another official, who is least in the grade A3 and is not involved in the case in question, to carry out the duties described herein.

Article 2

1. The Hearing Officer shall ensure that the hearing is properly conducted and thus contribute to the objectivity of the hearing itself and of any decision taken subsequently. The Hearing Officer shall seek to ensure in particular that in the preparation of draft Commission decisions in competition cases due account is taken of all the relevant facts, whether favourable or unfavourable to the parties concerned.

2. In performing his duties the Hearing Officer shall see to it that the rights of the defence are respected, while taking account of the need for effective application of the competition rules in accordance with the regulations in force and the principles laid down by the Court of First Instance and the Court of Justice.

Article 3

1. Decisions as to whether third parties, be they natural or legal persons, are to be heard shall be taken after consulting the Director responsible for investigating the case which is the subject of the procedure.

2. Applications to be heard on the part of third parties shall be submitted in writing, together with a written statement explaining the applicant's interest in the outcome of the procedure.

3. Where it is found that an applicant has not shown a sufficient interest to be heard, he shall be informed in writing of the reasons for such finding. A time limit shall be fixed within which he may submit any further written comments.

Article 4

1. Decisions whether persons are to be heard orally shall be taken after consulting the Director responsible for investigating the case which is the subject of the procedure.

2. Applications to be heard orally shall be made in the applicant's written comments on letters which the Commission has addressed to him and shall contain a reasoned statement of the applicant's interest in an oral hearing.

3. The letters referred to in paragraph 2 are those:

— communicating a statement of objections,
— inviting the written comments of a natural or legal person having shown sufficient interest to be heard as a third party,
— informing a complainant that in the Commission's view there are insufficient grounds for finding an infringement and inviting him to submit any further written comments,
— informing a natural or legal person that in the Commission's view that person has not shown sufficient interest to be heard as a third party.

4. Where it is found that the applicant has not shown a sufficient interest to be heard orally, he shall be informed in writing of the reasons for such finding. A time limit shall be fixed within which he may submit any further written comments.

Article 5

1. Where a person, an undertaking or an association of persons or undertakings who or which has received one or more of the letters listed in Article 4(3) has reason to believe that the Commission has in its possession documents which have not been disclosed to it and that those documents are necessary for the proper exercise of the right to be heard, he or it may draw attention to the matter by a reasoned request.

2. The reasoned decision on any such request shall be communicated to the person, undertaking or association that made the request and to any other person, undertaking or association concerned by the procedure.

3. Where it is intended to disclose information which may constitute a business secret of an undertaking, it shall be informed in writing of this intention and the reasons for it. A time limit shall be fixed within which the undertaking concerned may submit any written comments.

4. Where the undertaking concerned objects to the disclosure of the information but it is found that the information is not protected and may therefore be disclosed, that finding shall be stated in a reasoned decision which shall be notified to the undertaking concerned. The decision shall specify the date after which the information will be disclosed. This date shall not be less than one week from the date of notification.

5. Where an undertaking or association of undertakings considers that the time limit imposed for its reply to a letter referred to in Article 4(3) is too short, it may, within the original time limit, draw attention to the matter by a reasoned request. The applicant shall be informed in writing whether the request has been granted.

Article 6

1. Where appropriate in view of the need to ensure that the hearing is properly prepared and particularly that questions of fact are clarified as far as possible, the Hearing Officer may, after consulting the Director responsible for investigating the case, supply in advance to the firms concerned a list of the questions on which he or she wishes them to explain their point of view.

2. For this purpose, after consulting the Director responsible for investigating the case which is the subject of the hearing, the Hearing Officer may hold a meeting with the parties concerned and, where appropriate, the Commission staff, in order to prepare for the hearing itself.

3. For the same purpose the Hearing Officer may ask for prior written notification of the essential contents of the intended statement of persons whom the undertakings concerned have proposed for hearing.

Article 7

1. After consulting the Director responsible for investigating the case, the Hearing Officer shall determine the date, the duration and the place of the

hearing, and, where a postponement is requested, the Hearing Officer shall decide whether or not to allow it.

2. The Hearing Officer shall be fully responsible for the conduct of the hearing.

3. In this regard, the Hearing Officer shall decide whether fresh documents should be admitted during the hearing, what persons should be heard on behalf of a party and whether the persons concerned should be heard separately or in the presence of other persons attending the hearing.

4. The Hearing Officer shall ensure that the essential content of the statement made by each person heard shall be recorded in minutes which, where appropriate, shall be read and approved by that person.

Article 8

The Hearing Officer shall report to the Director-General for Competition on the hearing and the conclusions he draws from it. The Hearing Officer may make observations on the further progress of the proceedings. Such observations may relate among other things to the need for further information, the withdrawal of certain objections, or the formulation of further objections.

Article 9

In performing the duties defined in Article 2, the Hearing Officer may, if he deems it appropriate, refer his observations direct to the Member of the Commission with special responsibility for competition.

Article 10

Where appropriate, the Member of the Commission with special responsibility for competition may decide, at the Hearing Officer's request, to attach the Hearing Officer's final report to the draft decision submitted to the Commission, in order to ensure that when it reaches a decision on an individual case it is fully apprised of all relevant information.

Article 11

This Decision revokes and replaces the Commission Decisions of 8 September 1982 and 23 November 1990 on the implementation of hearings in connection with procedures for the application of Articles 65 and 66 of the ECSC Treaty and Articles 85 and 86 of the EC Treaty.

Article 12

This Decision shall enter into force on the day following its publication in the *Official Journal of the European Communities*.

Done at Brussels, 12 December 1994.

[1] OJ 1994 L330/67.
[2] OJ L395, 30.12.1989, p. 1 (corrected version OJ l 257, 21.9.1990, p. 13).
[3] OJ 1963 127/2268/63.
[4] OJ 1969 L209/11.
[5] OJ 1988 L376/1.
[6] OJ 1988 L376/10.
[7] OJ 1990 L219/5.

APPENDIX 8

COMMISSION NOTICE[1]
on the non-imposition or reduction of fines in cartel cases

A. INTRODUCTION

1. Secret cartels between enterprises aimed at fixing prices, production or sales quotas, sharing markets or banning imports or exports are among the most serious restrictions of competition encountered by the Commission.

Such practices ultimately result in increased prices and reduced choice for the consumer. Furthermore, they not only prejudice the interests of Community consumers, but they also harm European industry. By artifically limiting the competition that would normally prevail between them, Community enterprises avoid exactly those pressures that lead them to innovate, both in terms of product development and with regard to the introduction of more efficient production processes. Such practices also lead to more expensive raw materials and components for the Community enterprises that buy from such producers. In the long term, they lead to a loss of competitiveness and, in an increasingly global market-place, reduced employment opportunities.

For all those reasons, the Commission considers that combating cartels is an important aspect of its endeavours to achieve the objectives set out in its 1993 White Paper on Growth, Competitiveness and Employment. This explains why it has increased its efforts to detect cartels in recent years.

2. The Commission is aware that certain enterprises participating in such agreements might wish to terminate their involvement and inform the Commission of the existence of the cartel, but are deterred from doing so by the risk of incurring large fines.

3. In order to take account of this fact, the Commission has decided to adopt the present notice, which sets out the conditions under which enterprises co-operating with the Commission during its investigation into a cartel may be exempted from fines, or may be granted reductions in the fine which would otherwise have been imposed upon them. The Commission will examine whether it is necessary to modify this notice as soon as it has acquired sufficient experience in applying it.

4. The Commission considers that it is in the Community interest in granting favourable treatment to enterprises which co-operate with it in the circumstances set out below. The interests of consumers and citizens in ensuring that such practices are detected and prohibited outweigh the interest in fining those enterprises which co-operate with the Commission, thereby enabling or helping it to detect and prohibit a cartel.

5. Co-operation by an enterprise is only one of several factors which the Commission takes into account when fixing the amount of a fine. This notice does not prejudice the Commission's right to reduce a fine for other reasons.

B. NON-IMPOSITION OF A FINE OR A VERY SUBSTANTIAL REDUCTION IN ITS AMOUNT

An enterprise which:

(a) informs the Commission about a secret cartel before the Commission has undertaken an investigation, ordered by decision, of the enterprises involved, provided that it does not already have sufficient information to establish the existence of the alleged cartel;
(b) is the first to adduce decisive evidence of the cartel's existence;
(c) puts an end to its involvement in the illegal activity no later than the time at which it discloses the cartel;
(d) provides the Commission with all the relevant information and all the documents and evidence available to it regarding the cartel and maintains continuous and complete co-operation throughout the investigation;
(e) has not compelled another enterprise to take part in the cartel and has not acted as an instigator or played a determining role in the illegal activity,

will benefit from a reduction of at least 75% of the fine or even from total exemption from the fine that would have been imposed if they had not co-operated.

C. SUBSTANTIAL REDUCTION IN A FINE

Enterprises which both satisfy the conditions set out in Section B, points (b) to (e) and disclose the secret cartel after the Commission has undertaken an investigation ordered by decision on the premises of the parties to the cartel which has failed to provide sufficient grounds for initiating the procedure leading to a decision, will benefit from a reduction of 50% to 75% of the fine.

D. SIGNIFICANT REDUCTION IN A FINE

1. Where an enterprise co-operates without having met all the conditions set out in Sections B or C, it will benefit from a reduction of 10% to 50% of the fine that would have been imposed it it had not co-operated.
2. Such cases may include the following:

— before a statement of objections is sent, an enterprise provides the Commission with information, documents or other evidence which materially contribute to establishing the existence of the infringement;
— after receiving a statement of objections, an enterprise informs the Commission that it does not substantially contest the facts on which the Commission bases its allegations.

E. PROCEDURE

1. Where an enterprise wishes to take advantage of the favourable treatment set out in this notice, it should contact the Commission's Directorate-General for Competition. Only persons empowered to represent the enterprise for that purpose may take such a step. This notice does not therefore cover requests from individual employees of enterprises.
2. Only on its adoption of a decision will the Commission determine whether or not the conditions set out in Sections B, C and D are met, and thus whether or not to grant any reduction in the fine, or even waive its imposition altogether. It would not be appropriate to grant such a reduction or waiver before the end of the administrative procedure, as those conditions apply throughout such period.
3. Nonetheless, provided that all the conditions are met, non-imposition or reductions will be granted. The Commission is aware that this notice will create legitimate expectations on which enterprises may rely when disclosing the existence of a cartel to the Commission. Failure to meet any of the conditions set out in Section B or C at any stage of the administrative procedure will, however, result in the loss of the favourable treatment set out therein. In such circumstances

an enterprise may, however, still enjoy a reduction in the fine, as set out in Section D above.

4. The fact that leniency in respect of fines is granted cannot, however, protect an enterprise from the civil law consequences of its participation in an illegal agreement. In this respect, if the information provided by the enterprise leads the Commission to take a decision pursuant to Article 85(1) of the EC Treaty, the enterprise benefiting from the leniency in respect of the fine will also be named in that decision as having infringed the Treaty and will have the part it played described in full therein. The fact that the enterprise co-operated with the Commission will also be indicated in the decision, so as to explain the reason for the non-imposition or reduction of the fine.

Should an enterprise which has benefited from a reduction in a fine for not substantially contesting the facts then contest them for the first time in proceedings for annulment before the Court of First Instance, the Commission will normally ask that court to increase the fine imposed on that enterprise.

[1] OJ 1996 C207/4.

APPENDIX 9

REGULATION 3384/94[1]

on the notifications, time limits and hearings provided for in Council Regulation (EEC) No. 4064/89 on the control of concentrations between undertakings

THE COMMISSION OF THE EUROPEAN COMMUNITIES,

Having regard to the Treaty establishing the European Community and the Agreements on the European Economic Area,

Having regard to the Agreement on the European Economic Area,

Having regard to Council Regulation (EEC) No. 4064/89 of 21 December 1989 on the control of concentrations between undertakings,[2] and in particular Article 23 thereof,

Having regard to Council Regulation No. 17 of 6 February 1962, First Regulation implementing Articles 85 and 86 of the Treaty,[3] as last amended by the Act of Accession of Spain and Portugal, and in particular Article 24 thereof,

Having regard to Council Regulation (EEC) No. 1017/68 of 19 July 1968 applying rules of competition to transport by rail, road and inland waterway,[4] as last amended by the Act of Accession of Greece and in particular Article 29 thereof,

Having regard to Council Regulation (EEC) No. 4056/86 of 22 December 1986 laying down detailed rules for the application of Articles 85 and 86 of the Treaty to maritime transport,[5] and in particular Article 26 thereof,

Having regard to Council Regulation (EEC) No. 3975/87 of 14 December 1987 laying down detailed rules for the application of the competition rules to undertakings in air transport,[6] as last amended by Regulation (EEC) No. 2410/92,[7] in particular Article 19 thereof,

Having consulted the Advisory Committee on Concentrations,

(1) Whereas experience in the application of Commission Regulation (EEC) No. 2367/90,[8] as amended by Regulation (EC) No. 3666/93,[9] which implements Regulation (EEC) No. 4064/89, has shown the need to improve certain procedural aspects thereof, whereas it should therefore be replaced by a new regulation;

(2) Whereas Regulation (EEC) No. 4064/89 is based on the principle of compulsory notification of concentrations before they are put into effect; whereas, on the one hand, a notification has important legal consequences which are favourable to the parties to the concentration plan, while, on the other hand, failure to comply with the obligation to notify renders the parties liable to a fine and may also entail civil law disadvantages for them; whereas it is therefore necessary in the interests of legal certainty to define precisely the subject matter and content of the information to be provided in the notification;

(3) Whereas it is for the notifying parties to make full and honest disclosure to the Commission of the facts and circumstances which are relevant for taking a decision on the notified concentration;

(4) Whereas in order to simplify and expedite examination of the notification it is desirable to prescribe that a form be used;
(5) Whereas since notification sets in motion legal time limits for initiating proceedings and for decisions, the conditions governing such time limits and the time when they become effective must also be determined;
(6) Whereas rules must be laid down in the interests of legal certainty for calculating the time limits provided for in Regulation (EEC) No. 4064/89, and whereas in particular, the beginning and end of the period and the circumstances suspending the running of the period must be determined, with due regard to the requirements resulting from the exceptionally short legal time limits referred to above, whereas in the absence of specific provisions the determination of rules applicable to periods, dates and time limits should be based on the principles of Council Regulation (EEC, Euratom) No. 1182/71;[10]
(7) Whereas the provisions relating to the Commissions procedure must be framed in such a way as to safeguard fully the right to be heard and the rights of defence; whereas for these purposes the Commission should distinguish between the parties who notify the concentration, other parties involved in the concentration plan, third parties and parties regarding whom the Commission intends to take a decision imposing a fine or periodic penalty payments;
(8) Whereas the Commission will give the notifying parties and other parties involved, if they so request, an opportunity before notification to discuss the intended concentration informally and in strict confidence; whereas in addition it will, after notification, maintain close contact with those parties to the extent necessary to discuss with them any practical or legal problems which it discovers on a first examination of the case and if possible to remove such problems by mutual agreement;
(9) Whereas in accordance with the principle of the rights of defence, the notifying parties must be given the opportunity to submit their comments on all the objections which the Commission proposes to take into account in its decisions; whereas other parties involved should also be informed of the Commission's objections and granted the opportunity to express their views;
(10) Whereas third parties having sufficient interest must also be given the opportunity of expressing their views where they make a written application;
(11) Whereas the various persons entitled to submit comments should do so in writing, both in their own interest and in the interest of good administration, without prejudice to their right to request a formal oral hearing where appropriate to supplement the written procedure; whereas in urgent cases, however, the Commission must be able to proceed immediately to formal oral hearings of the notifying parties, other parties involved or third parties;
(12) Whereas it is necessary to define the rights of persons who are to be heard, to what extent they should be granted access to the Commissions's file and on what conditions they may be represented or assisted;
(13) Whereas the Commission must respect the legitimate interest of undertakings in the protection of their business secrets;
(14) Whereas, in order to enable the Commission to carry out a proper assessment of modifications to the original concentration plan, and to ensure due consultation with other parties involved, third parties and the authorities of the Member States as provided for in Regulation (EEC) No. 4064/89, in particular Article 18(1) and (4) thereof, a time limit for submitting modifications to the concentration plan as provided for in Article 10(2) of Regulation (EEC) No. 4064/89 must be laid down;
(15) Whereas it is also necessary to define the rules for fixing and calculating the time limits for reply fixed by the Commission;
(16) Whereas the Advisory Committee on Concentrations must deliver its

opinion on the basis of a preliminary draft decision; whereas it must therefore be consulted on a case after the inquiry in to that case has been completed; whereas such consultation does not, however, prevent the Commission from reopening an inquiry if need be,

HAS ADOPTED THIS REGULATION

SECTION I

NOTIFICATIONS

Article 1

Persons entitled to submit notifications

1. Notifications shall be submitted by the persons or undertakings referred to in Article 4(2) of Regulation (EEC) No. 4064/89.
2. Where notifications are signed by representatives of persons or of undertakings, such representatives shall produce written proof that they are authorised to act.
3. Joint notifications should be submitted by a joint representative who is authorised to transmit and to receive documents on behalf of all notifying parties.

Article 2

Submission of notifications

1. Notifications shall be submitted in the manner prescribed by Form CO as shown in Annex I. Joint notifications shall be submitted on a single form.
2. Twenty-four copies of each notification and 19 copies of the supporting documents shall be submitted to the Commission at the address indicated in Form CO.
3. The supporting documents shall be either originals or copies of the originals; in the latter case the notifying parties shall confirm that they are true and complete.
4. Notifications shall be in one of the official languages of the Community. This language shall also be the language of the proceeding for the notifying parties. Supporting documents shall be submitted in their original language. Where the original language is not one of the official languages, a translation into the language of the proceeding shall be attached.
5. Where notifications are made pursuant to Article 57 of the EEA Agreement, they may also be in one of the official languages of the EFTA States or the working language of the EFTA Surveillance Authority. If the language chosen for the notifications is not an official language of the Community, the notifying parties shall simultaneously supplement all documentation with a translation into an official language of the Community. The language which is chosen for the translation shall determine the language used by the Commission as the language of the proceedings for the notifying parties.

Article 3

Information and documents to be provided

1. Notifications shall contain the information, including documents, requested by Form CO. The information must be correct and complete.
2. The Commission may dispense with the obligation to provide any particular information, including documents, requested by Form CO where the Commission considers that such information is not necessary for the examination of the case.
3. The Commission shall without delay acknowledge in writing to the notifying parties or their representatives receipt of the notification and of any reply to a letter sent by the Commission pursuant to Article 4(2) and 4(4).

Article 4

Effective date of notification

1. Subject to paragraphs 2, 3 and 4, notifications shall become effective on the date on which they are received by the Commission.
2. Where the information, including documents, contained in the notification is incomplete in a material respect, the Commission shall without delay inform the notifying parties or their representatives in writing and shall set an appropriate time limit for the completion of the information. In such cases, the notification shall become effective on the date on which the complete information is received by the Commission.
3. Material changes in the facts contained in the notification which the notifying parties know or ought to have known must be communicated to the Commission voluntarily and without delay. In such cases, when these material changes could have a significant effect on the appraisal of the concentration, the notification may be considered by the Commission as becoming effective on the date on which the information on the material changes is received by the Commission; the Commission shall inform the notifying parties or their representatives of this in writing and without delay.
4. Incorrect or misleading information shall be considered to be incomplete information.
5. When the Commission publishes the fact of the notification pursuant to Article 4(3) of Regulation (EEC) No. 4064/89, it shall specify the date upon which the notification has been received. Where, further to the application of paragraphs 2, 3 and 4, the effective date of notification is later than the date specified in this publication, the Commission shall issue a further publication in which it will state the later date.

Article 5

Conversion of notifications

1. Where the Commission finds that the operation notified does not constitute a concentration within the meaning of Article 3 of Regulation (EEC) No. 4064/89 it shall inform the notifying parties or their representatives in writing. In such a case, the Commission shall, if requested by the notifying parties, as appropriate and subject to paragraph 2, treat the notification as an application within the meaning of Article 2 or a notification within the meaning of Article 4 of Regulation No. 17,

as an application within the meaning of Article 12 or a notification within the meaning of Article 14 of Regulation (EEC) No. 1017/68, as an application within the meaning of Article 12 of Regulation (EEC) No. 4056/86 or as an application within the meaning of Article 3(2) or of Article 5 of Regulation (EEC) No. 3975/87.

2. In cases referred to in paragraph 1, second sentence, the Commission may require that the information given in the notification be supplemented within an appropriate time limit fixed by it in so far as this is necessary for assessing the operation on the basis of the above-mentioned Regulations. The application or notification shall be deemed to fulfil the requirements of such Regulations from the date of the original notification where the additional information is received by the Commission within the time limit fixed.

SECTION II

TIME LIMITS FOR INITIATING PROCEEDINGS AND FOR DECISIONS

Article 6

Beginning of the time period

1. The periods referred to in Article 10(1) of Regulation (EEC) No. 4064/89 shall start at the beginning of the working day (as defined under Article 22) following the effective date of the notification, within the meaning of Article 4 of this Regulation.

2. The period referred to in Article 10(3) of Regulation (EEC) No. 4064/89 shall start at the beginning of the working day (as defined under Article 22) following the day on which proceedings were initiated.

Article 7

End of the time period

1. The time period referred to in Article 10(1) first subparagraph of Regulation (EEC) No. 4064/89 shall end with the expiry of the day which in the month following that in which the time period began falls on the same date as the day from which the period runs. Where such a day does not occur in that month, the period shall end with the expiry of the last day of that month.

2. The time period referred to in Article 10(1) second subparagraph of Regulation (EEC) No. 4064/89 shall end with the expiry of the day which in the sixth week following that in which the period began is the same day of the week as the day from which the period runs.

3. The time period referred to in Article 10(3) of Regulation (EEC) No. 4064/89 shall end with the expiry of the day which in the fourth month following that in which the period began falls on the same date as the day from which the period runs. Where such a day does not occur in that month, the period shall end with the expiry of the last day of that month.

4. Where the last day of the period is not a working day within the meaning of Article 22, the period shall end with the expiry of the following working day.

Article 8

Recovery of holidays

Once the end of the time period has been determined in accordance with Article 7, if public holidays or other holidays of the Commission as defined in Article 22 fall within the periods referred to in Article 10(1) and in Article 10(3) of Regulation (EEC) No. 4064/89, a corresponding number of working days shall be added to those periods.

Article 9

Suspension of the time limit

1. The period referred to in Article 10(3) of Regulation (EEC) No. 4064/89 shall be suspended where the Commission, pursuant to Articles 11(5) and 13(3) of the same Regulation, has to take a decision because:

(a) information which the Commission has requested pursuant to Article 11(1) of Regulation (EEC) No. 4064/89 from one of the notifying parties or another involved party (as defined in Article 11 of this Regulation) is not provided or not provided in full within the time limit fixed by the Commission;
(b) one of the notifying parties or another involved party (as defined in Article 11 of this Regulation) has refused to submit to an investigation deemed necessary by the Commission on the basis of Article 13(1) of Regulation (EEC) No. 4064/89 or to co-operate in the carrying out of such an investigation in accordance with the above-mentioned provision;
(c) the notifying parties have failed to inform the Commission of material changes in the facts contained in the notification.

2. The period referred to in Article 10(3) of Regulation (EEC) No. 4064/89 shall be suspended:

(a) in the cases referred to in subparagraph 1(a), for the period between the end of the time limit fixed in the request for information and the receipt of the complete and correct information required by decision;
(b) in the cases referred to in subparagraph 1(b), for the period between the unsuccessful attempt to carry out the investigation and the completion of the investigation ordered by decision;
(c) in the cases referred to in subparagraph 1(c), for the period between the occurrence of the change in the facts referred to therein and the receipt of the complete and correct information requested by decision or the completion of the investigation ordered by decision.

3. The suspension of the time limit shall begin on the day following that on which the event causing the suspension occurred. It shall end with the expiry of the day on which the reason for suspension is removed. Where such a day is not a working day within the meaning of Article 22, the suspension of the time limit shall end with the expiry of the following working day.

Article 10

Compliance with the time limit

The time limits referred to in Article 10(1) and (3) of Regulation (EEC) No. 4064/89 shall be met where the Commission has taken the relevant decision before the end of the period. Notification of the decision to the notifying parties must follow without delay.

SECTION III

HEARING OF THE PARTIES AND OF THIRD PARTIES

Article 11

Parties to be heard

For the purposes of the rights to be heard pursuant to Article 18 of Regulation (EEC) No. 4064/89, the following parties are distinguished:

(a) notifying parties, that is, persons or undertakings submitting a notification pursuant to Article 4(2) of Regulation (EEC) No. 4064/89;
(b) other involved parties, that is, parties to the concentration plan other than the notifying parties, such as the seller and the undertaking which is the target of the concentration;
(c) third parties, that is, natural or legal persons showing a sufficient interest, including customers, suppliers and competitors, and especially members of the administration or management organs of the undertakings concerned or recognised workers' representatives of those undertakings;
(d) parties regarding whom the Commission intends to take a decision pursuant to Article 14 or Article 15 of Regulation (EEC) No. 4064/89.

Article 12

Decisions on the suspension of concentrations

1. Where the Commission intends to take a decision pursuant to Article 7(2) of Regulation (EEC) No. 4064/89 or a decision pursuant to Article 7(4) of that Regulation which adversely affects the parties, it shall, pursuant to Article 18(1) of that Regulation, inform the notifying parties and other involved parties in writing of its objections and shall fix a time limit within which they may make known their views.

2. Where the Commission pursuant to Article 18(2) of Regulation (EEC) No. 4064/89 has taken a decision referred to in paragraph 1 provisionally without having given the notifying parties and other involved parties the opportunity to make known their views, it shall without delay and in any event before the expiry of the suspension send them the text of the provisional decision and shall fix a time limit within which they may make known their views.

Once the notifying parties and other involved parties have made known their views, the Commission shall take a final decision annulling, amending or confirming the provisional decision. Where they have not made known their views within the time limit fixed, the Commission's provisional decision shall become final with the expiry of that period.

3. The notifying parties and other involved parties shall make known their views in writing or orally within the time limit fixed. They may confirm their oral statements in writing.

Article 13

Decisions on the substance of the case

1. Where the Commission intends to take a decision pursuant to Article 8(2), second subparagraph, Article 8(3), (4) or (5) of Regulation (EEC) No. 4064/89 it shall, before consulting the Advisory Committee on Concentrations, hear the parties pursuant to Article 18(1) and (3) of that Regulation.

2. (a) The Commission shall address its objections in writing to the notifying parties.
The Commission shall, when giving notice of objections, set a time limit within which the notifying parties may inform the Commission of their views in writing.
(b) The Commission shall inform other involved parties in writing of these objections. The Commission shall also set a time limit within which these other involved parties may inform the Commission of their views in writing.

3. (a) After having addressed its objections to the notifying parties, the Commission shall, upon request, give them access to the file for the purpose of enabling them to exercise their rights of defence.
(b) The Commission shall, upon request, also give the other involved parties who have been informed of the objections access to the file in so far as this is necessary for the purposes of preparing their observations.

4. The parties to whom the Commission's objections have been addressed or who have been informed of these objections shall, within the time limit fixed, make known in writing their views on the objections. In their written comments, they may set out all matters relevant to the case and may attach any relevant documents in proof of the facts set out. They may also propose that the Commission hear persons who may corroborate those facts.

5. Where the Commission intends to take a decision pursuant to Article 14 or Article 15 of Regulation (EEC) No. 4064/89 it shall, before consulting the Advisory Committee on Concentrations, hear (pursuant to Article 18(1) and (3) of that Regulation) the parties regarding whom the Commission intends to take such a decision.

The procedure provided pursuant to subparagraphs 2(a), 3(a), and paragraph 4 is applicable, *mutatis mutandis*

Article 14

Oral Hearings

1. The Commission shall afford the notifying parties who have so requested in the written comments the opportunity to put forward their arguments orally in a formal hearing if such parties show a sufficient interest. It may also in other cases afford such parties the opportunity of expressing their views orally.

2. The Commission shall afford other involved parties who have so requested in their written comments the opportunity to express their views orally in a formal hearing if they show a sufficient interest. It may also in other cases afford such parties the opportunity of expressing their views orally.

3. The Commission shall afford parties in relation to whom it proposes to impose a fine or periodic penalty payment who have so requested in their written comments the opportunity to put forward their arguments orally in a formal hearing. It may also in other cases afford such parties the opportunity of expressing their views orally.

4. The Commission shall summon the persons to be heard to attend on such date as it shall appoint.

5. The Commission shall immediately transmit a copy of the summons to the competent authorities of the Member States, who may appoint an official to take part in the hearing.

Article 15

Conduct of formal oral hearings

1. Hearings shall be conducted by persons appointed by the Commission for that purpose.

2. Persons summoned to attend shall either appear in person or be represented by legal representatives or by representatives authorised by their constitution. Undertakings and associations of undertakings may be represented by a duly authorised agent appointed from among their permanent staff.

3. Persons heard by the Commission may be assisted by lawyers or university teachers who are entitled to plead before the Court of Justice of the European Communities in accordance with Article 17 of the Protocol on the Statute of the Court of Justice, or by other qualified persons.

4. Hearings shall not be public. Persons shall be heard separately or in the presence of other persons summoned to attend. In the latter case, regard shall be had to the legitimate interest of the undertakings in the protection of their business secrets.

5. The statements made by each person heard shall be recorded.

Article 16

Hearing of third parties

1. If third parties apply in writing to be heard pursuant to Article 18(4) of Regulation (EEC) No. 4064/89, the Commission shall inform them in writing of the nature and subject matter of the procedure and shall fix a time limit within which they may make known their views.

2. The third parties referred to in paragraph 1 shall make known their views in writing within the time limit fixed. The Commission may, where appropriate, afford the parties who have so requested in their written comments, the opportunity to participate in a formal hearing. It may also in other cases afford such parties the opportunity of expressing their views orally.

3. The Commission may likewise afford to any other third parties the opportunity of expressing their views.

Article 17

Confidential information

Information, including documents, shall not be communicated or made accessible in so far as it contains business secrets of any person or undertaking, including the notifying parties, other involved parties or of third parties, or other confidential information the disclosure of which is not considered necessary by the Commission for the purpose of the procedure, or where internal documents of the authorities are concerned.

SECTION IV

MODIFICATIONS OF THE CONCENTRATION PLAN

Article 18

Time limit for modifications to the concentration plan

1. The modifications to the original concentration plan made by the undertakings concerned as provided for pursuant to Article 10(2) of Regulation (EEC) No. 4064/89 which are intended by the parties to form the basis for a decision pursuant to Article 8(2) shall be submitted to the Commission within not more than three months of the date on which proceedings were initiated. The Commission may in exceptional circumstances extend this period.
2. The time period referred to in paragraph 1 shall be determined according to the same rules as those contained in Articles 6 to 9 of this Regulation.

SECTION V

MISCELLANEOUS PROVISIONS

Article 19

Transmission of documents

1. Transmission of documents and summonses from the Commission to the addressees may be effected in any of the following ways:

(a) delivery by hand against receipt;
(b) registered letter with acknowledgment of receipt;
(c) telefax with a request for acknowledgment of receipt;
(d) telex;
(e) electronic mail with a request for acknowledgment of receipt.

2. Subject to Article 21(1), paragraph 1 also applies to the transmission of documents from the notifying parties, from other involved parties or from third parties to the Commission.
3. Where a document is sent by telex, by telefax or by electronic mail, it shall be presumed that it has been received by the addressee on the day on which it was sent.

Article 20

Setting of time limits

1. In fixing the time limits provided for pursuant to Article 4(2), 5(2), 12(1) and (2), 13(2) and 16(1), the Commission shall have regard to the time required for

preparation of statements and to the urgency of the case. It shall also take account of working days as defined under Article 22 as well as public holidays in the country of receipt of the Commission's communication.

2. These time limits shall be set in terms of a precise calendar date.

Article 21

Receipt of documents by the Commission

1. Subject to the provisions of Article 4(1) of this Regulation, notifications must be delivered to the Commission at the address indicated in Form CO or have been dispatched by registered letter to the address indicated in Form CO before the expiry of the period referred to in Article 4(1) of Regulation (EEC) No. 4064/89.

Additional information requested to complete notifications pursuant to Article 4(2) and (4) or to supplement notifications pursuant to Article 5(2) of this Regulation must reach the Commission at the aforesaid address or have been dispatched by registered letter before the expiry of the time limit fixed in each case.

Written comments on Commission communications pursuant to Articles 12(1) and (2), 13(2) and 16(1) must be delivered to the Commission or must have reached the Commission at the aforesaid address before the expiry of the time limit fixed in each case.

2. Time limits referred to in subparagraphs two and three of paragraph 1 shall be determined in accordance with Article 20.

3. Should the last day of a time limit fall on a day which is not a working day (as defined under Article 22), or which is a public holiday in the country of dispatch, the time limit expires on the following working day.

Article 22

Definition of working days

The expression "working days" in this Regulation means all days other than Saturdays, Sundays, public holidays and other holidays as determined by the Commission and published in the *Official Journal of the European Communities* before the beginning of each year.

Article 23

Repeal

Regulation (EEC) No. 2367/90 is repealed.

Article 24

Entry into force

This Regulation shall enter into force on 1 March 1995.

This Regulation shall be binding in its entirety and directly applicable in all Member States.

Done at Brussels, 21 December 1994

ANNEX

FORM CO-RELATING TO THE NOTIFICATION OF A CONCENTRATION PURSUANT TO REGULATION (EEC) No. 4064/89

INTRODUCTION

A. The purpose of this Form

This Form specifies the information that must be provided by an undertaking or undertakings when notifying the Commission of a concentration with a Community dimension. A "concentration" is defined in Article 3 and "Community dimension" by Article 1 of Regulation (EEC) No. 4064/89.

Your attention is drawn to Regulation (EEC) No. 4064/89 and to Regulation (EC) No. 3384/94 (hereinafter referred to as the "Implementing Regulation") and to the corresponding provisions of the Agreement of the European Economic Area.[11]

Experience has shown that prenotification meetings are extremely valuable to both the notifying party(ies) and the Commission in determining the precise amount of information required in a notification and, in the large majority of cases, will result in a significant reduction of the information required. Accordingly, notifying parties are encouraged to consult the Commission regarding the possibility of dispensing with the obligation to provide certain information (see Section B(b) discussing the possibility of waivers).

B. The need for a correct and complete notification

All information required by this Form must be correct and complete (Article 4 of the Implementing Regulation). In particular you should note that:

(a) if the information required by this Form is not reasonably available to you in part or in whole (for example, because of the unavailability of information on a target company during a contested bid), the Commission will accept that the notification is complete and thus valid notwithstanding the failure to provide such information, providing that you give reasons for the unavailability of said information, and provide your best estimates for missing data together with the sources for the estimates. Where possible, indications as to where any of the requested information that is unavailable to you could be obtained by the Commission should also be provided; unless all material information required by this Form is supplied in full or good reasons are given explaining why this has not been possible the notification will be incomplete and will only become effective on the date on which all such information required is received;

(b) the Commission only requires the submission of information relevant and necessary to its inquiry into the notified operation. If you consider that any particular information requested by this Form, in the full- or short-form version, may not be necessary for the Commission's examination of the case, you may explain this in your notification and ask the Commission to dispense with the obligation to provide that information, pursuant to Article 3(2) of the implementing Regulation;

(c) incorrect or misleading information in the notification will be considered to be incomplete information. In such cases, the Commission will inform the notifying parties or their representatives of this in writing and without delay. The notification will only become effective on the date on which the complete and accurate information is received by the Commission (Article 4(2) and (4) of the Implementing Regulation). Article 14(1)(b) of Regulation (EEC) No. 4064/89 provides that incorrect or misleading information where supplied intentionally or negligently can make the notifying party or parties liable to fines of up to ECU 50,000. In addition, pursuant to point (a) of Article 8(5) of Regulation (EEC) No. 4064/89 the Commission may also revoke its decision on the compatibility of a notified concentration where it is based on incorrect information for which one of the undertakings is responsible.

C. Notification in short-form

(a) In cases where a joint venture has no, or *de minimis*, actual or foreseen activities within the EEA territory, the Commission intends to allow notification of the operation by means of short-form. Such cases occur where joint control is acquired by two or more undertakings, and where:
  (i) the turnover[12] of the joint venture and/or the turnover of the contributed activities,[13] is less than ECU 100 million in the EEA territory; and
  (ii) the total value of assets[14] transferred to the joint venture is less than ECU 100 million in the EEA territory.[15]

(b) If you consider that the operation to be notified meets these qualifications, you may explain this in your notification and ask the Commission to dispense with the obligation to provide the full-form notification, pursuant to Article 3(2) of the Implementing Regulation, and to allow you to notify by means of short-form.

(c) Short-form notification allows the notifying parties to limit the information provided in the notification to the following sections and questions:
  — Section 1,
  — Section 2, except questions 2.1(a, b and d), 2.3.4, and 2.3.5,
  — Section 3, only question 3.1 and 3.2(a),
  — Section 5, only questions 5.1 and 5.3,
  — Section 6,
  — Section 10, and
  — Section 9, only questions 9.5 and 9.6 (optional for the convenience of the parties).

(d) In addition, with respect to the affected markets of the joint venture as defined below in Section 6, indicate the following for the EEA territory, for the Community as a whole, for each Member State and EFTA State, and where different, in the opinion of the notifying parties, for the relevant geographic market:
  — the sales in value and volume, as well as the market shares, for the year preceding the operation, and
  — the five largest customers and the five largest competitors in the affected markets in which the joint venture will be active. Provide the name, address, telephone number, fax number and appropriate contact person of each such customer and competitor.

(e) The Commission may require full, or where appropriate partial, notification under the Form CO where:
  — the notified operation does nor meet the short-form thresholds, or
  — this appears to be necessary for an adequate investigation with respect to possible competition problems on affected markers.

In such cases, the notification may be considered incomplete in a material respect pursuant to Article 4(2) of the Implementing Regulation. The Commission will inform the notifying parties or their representatives of this in writing and without delay and will fix a deadline for the submission of a full or, where appropriate partial, notification. The notification will only become effective on the date on which all information required is received.

D. Who must notify

In the case of a merger within the meaning of Article 3(1)(a) or the acquisition of joint control in an undertaking within the meaning of Article 3(1)(b), the notification shall be completed jointly by the parties to the merger or by those acquiring joint control as the case may be.

In case of the acquisition of a controlling interest in an undertaking by another, the acquirer must complete the notification.

In the case of a public bid to acquire an undertaking, the bidder must complete the notification.

Each party completing the notification is responsible for the accuracy of the information which it provides.

E. How to notify

The notification must be completed in one of the official languages of the European Community. This language shall thereafter be the language of the proceedings for all notifying parties. Where notifications are made in accordance with Article 12 of Protocol 24 to the EEA Agreement in an official language of an EFTA State which is not an official language of the Community, the notification shall simultaneously be supplemented with a translation into an official language of the Community.

The information requested by this Form is to be set out using the sections and paragraph numbers of the Form, signing a declaration as provided in Section 10, and annexing supporting documentation.

Supporting documents shall be submitted in their original language; where this is not an official language of the Community they shall be translated into the language of the proceeding (Article 2(4) of the Implementing Regulation).

Requested documents may be originals or copies of the originals. In the latter case the notifying party shall confirm that they are true and complete.

Twenty-four copies of each notification and 19 copies of all supporting documentation must be provided.

The notification should be delivered by registered mail or by hand (or courier service) during normal Commission working hours at the following address:

Commission of the European Communities,
Directorate- General for Competition (DG IV),
Merger Task Force,
150 avenue de Cortenberg/Kortenberglaan 150,
B–1049 Brussels.

F. Confidentiality

Article 214 of the Treaty and Article 17(2) of Regulation (EEC) No. 4064/89 as well as the corresponding provisions of the EEA Agreement[16] require the Commission, the Member States, the EFTA Surveillance Authority and the EFTA States, their officials and other servants not to disclose information they have acquired through the application of the Regulation of the kind covered by the obligation of professional secrecy. The same principle must also apply to protect confidentiality between notifying parties.

If you believe that your interests would be harmed if any of the information you are asked to supply were to be published or otherwise divulged to other parties, submit this information separately with each page clearly marked "Business Secrets". You should also give reasons why this information should not be divulged or published.

In the case of mergers or joint acquisitions, or in other cases where the notification is completed by more than one of the parties, business secrets may be submitted under separate cover, and referred to in the notification as an annex.

All such annexes must be included in the submission in order for a notification to be considered complete.

G. Definitions and instructions for purposes of this Form

Notifying party or parties: in cases where a notification is submitted by only one of the undertakings party to an operation, "notifying parties" is used to refer only to the undertaking actually submitting the notification.

Party(ies) to the concentration or, parties: these terms relate to both the acquiring and acquired parties, or to the merging parties, including all undertakings in which a controlling interest is being acquired or which is the subject of a public bid.

Except where otherwise specified, the terms "notifying party(ies)" and "party(ies) to the concentration" include all the undertakings which belong to the same groups as those "parties".

Affected markets: Section 6 of this Form requires the notifying parties to define the relevant product and/or service markers, and further to identify which of those relevant markers are likely to be affected by the notified operation. This definition of affected market is used as the basis for requiring information for a number of other questions contained in this Form. The definitions thus submitted by the notifying parties are referred to in this Form as the affected market(s). This term can refer to a relevant market made up either of products or of services.

Year: all references to the word "year" in this Form shall be read as meaning calendar year, unless otherwise stated. All information requested in this Form shall, unless otherwise specified, relate to the year preceding that of the notification.

The financial data requested in Section 2.4 must be provided in ecus at the average conversion rates prevailing for the years or other periods in question.

All references contained in this Form are to the relevant Articles and paragraphs of Council Regulation (EEC) No. 4064/89, unless otherwise stated.

SECTION 1

Background information

1.1. *Information on notifying party (or parties)*

Give details of:

1.1.1. name and address of undertaking;

1.1.2. nature of the undertaking's business;

1.1.3. name, address, telephone number, fax number and/or telex of, and position held by, the appropriate contact person.

1.2. *Information on other parties*[17] *to the concentration*

For each party to the concentration (except the notifying party or parties) give details of:

1.2.1. name and address of undertaking;

1.2.2. nature of undertaking's business;

1.2.3. name, address, telephone number, fax number and/or telex of, and position held by the appropriate contact person.

1.3. *Address for service*

Give an address (in Brussels if available) to which all communications may be made and documents delivered.

1.4. *Appointment of representatives*

Where notifications are signed by representatives of undertakings, such representatives shall produce written proof that they are authorised to act.

If a joint/notification is being submitted, has a joint representative been appointed?

If yes, please give the details requested in Sections 1.4.1 to 1.4.4.

If no, please give details of information of any representatives who have been authorised to act for each of the parties to the concentration, indicating whom they represent:

1.4.1. name of representative;
1.4.2. address of representative,
1.4.3. name of person to be contacted (and address, if different from 1.4.2);
1.4.4. telephone number, fax number and/or telex.

SECTION 2

Details of the concentration

2.1. *Briefly describe the nature of the concentration being notified.* In doing so state:

(a) whether the proposed concentration is a full legal merger, an acquisition of sole or joint control, a concentrative joint venture or a contract or other means of conferring direct or indirect control within the meaning of Article 3(3);
(b) whether the whole or parts of parties are subject to the concentration;
(c) a brief explanation of the economic and financial structure of the concentration;
(d) whether any public offer for the securities of one party by another party has the support of the former supervisory boards of management or other bodies legally representing that party;
(e) the proposed or expected date of any major events designed to bring about the completion of the concentration;
(f) the proposed structure of ownership and control after the completion of the concentration;
(g) any financial or other support received from whatever source (including public authorities) by any of the parties and the nature and amount of this support.

2.2. *List the economic sectors involved in the concentration.*

2.3. *For each of the undertakings concerned by the concentration*[18] *provide the following data*[19] *for the last financial year:*

2.3.1. world-wide turnover;
2.3.2. Community-wide turnover;
2.3.3. EFTA-wide turnover,
2.3.4. turnover in each Member State;
2.4.5. turnover in each EFTA State;
2.3.6. the Member State, if any, in which more than two-thirds of Community-wide turnover is achieved;[20]
2.3.7. the EFTA State, if any, in which more than two-thirds of EFTA-wide turnover is achieved.[20]

2.4. *Provide the following information with respect to the last financial year:*

2.4.1. does the combined turnover of the undertakings concerned in the territory of the EFTA States equal 25 per cent or more of their total turnover in the EEA territory?

2.4.2. does each of at least two undertakings concerned have a turnover exceeding ECU 250 million in the territory of the EFTA States?

SECTION 3

Ownership and control[21]

For each of the parties to the concentration provide a list of all undertakings belonging to the same group.

This list must include:

3.1. all undertakings or persons controlling these parties, directly or indirectly;

3.2. all undertakings active on any affected market[22] that are controlled, directly or indirectly:
(a) by these parties;
(b) by any other undertaking identified in 3.1.

For each entry listed above, the nature and means of control shall be specified.

The information sought in this section may be illustrated by the use of organisation charts or diagrams to show the structure of ownership and the control of the undertakings.

SECTION 4

Personal and financial links and previous acquisitions

With respect to the parties to the concentration each undertaking or person identified in response to Section 3 provide:

4.1. a list of all other undertakings which are active on affected markers (affected markers are defined in Section 6) in which the undertakings, or persons, of the group hold individually or collectively 10 per cent or more of the voting rights, issued share capital or other securities;
in each case identify the holder and stare the percentage held;

4.2. a list for each undertaking of the members of their boards of management who are also members of the boards of management or of the supervisory boards of any other undertaking which is active on affected markets; and (where applicable) for each undertaking a list of the members of their supervisory boards who are also members of the boards of management or any other undertaking which is active on affected markets;
in each case identify the name of the other undertaking and the positions held;

4.3. details of acquisitions made during the last three years by the groups identified above (Section 3) of undertakings active in affected markets as defined in Section 6.

Information provided here may be illustrated by the use of organisation charts or diagrams to give a better understanding.

SECTION 5

Supporting documentation

Notifying parties shall provide the following:

5.1. copies of the final or most recent versions of all documents bringing about the concentration, whether by agreement between the parties to the concentration, acquisition of a controlling interest or a public bid;

5.2. in a public bid, a copy of the offer document; if unavailable on notification, should be submitted as soon as possible and not later than when it is posted to shareholders);

5.3. copies of the most recent annual reports and accounts of all the parties to the concentration;

5.4. where at least one affected marker is identified:
copies of analyses, reports, studies and surveys submitted to or prepared for any member(s) of the board of directors, the supervisory board, or the shareholders' meeting, for the purpose of assessing or analysing the concentration with respect to competitive conditions, competitors (actual and potential), and market conditions.

SECTION 6

Market definitions

The relevant product and geographic markets determine the scope within which the market power of the new entity resulting from the concentration must be assessed.

The notifying party or parties shall provide the data requested having regard to the following definitions:

I. *Relevant product markets*

A relevant product market comprises all those products and/or services which are regarded as interchangeable or substitutable by the consumer, by reason of the products' characteristics, their prices and their intended use. A relevant product market may in some cases be composed of a number of individual products and/or services which present largely identical physical or technical characteristics and are interchangeable.

Factors relevant to the assessment of the relevant product market include the analysis of why the products or services in these markets are included and why others are excluded by using the above definition, and having regard to, *e.g.* substitutability, conditions of competition, prices, cross-price elasticity of demand or other factors relevant for the definition of the product markets.

II. *Relevant geographic markets*

The relevant geographic market comprises the area in which the undertakings concerned are involved in the supply of relevant products or services, in which the conditions of competition are sufficiently homogeneous and which can be distinguished from neighbouring geographic areas because, in particular, conditions of competition are appreciably different in those areas.

Factors relevant to the assessment of the relevant geographic market include the nature and characteristics of the products or services concerned, the existence of entry barriers, consumer preferences, appreciable differences of the undertakings' market shares between neighbouring geographic areas or substantial price differences.

III. *Affected markets*

For purposes of information required in this Form, affected markets consist of relevant product markets where in the EEA territory, in the Community, in the territory of the EFTA States, in any Member State or in any EFTA State:

(a) two or more of the parties to the concentration are engaged in business activities in the same product market and where the concentration will lead to a combined market share of 15%; or more. These are horizontal relationships;
(b) one or more of the parties to the concentration are engaged in business activities in a product market, which is upstream or downstream of a product market in which any other party to the concentration is engaged, and any of their individual or combined market share is 25%; or more, regardless of whether there is or is not any existing supplier/customer relationship between the parties to the concentration. These are vertical relationships.

On the basis of the above definitions and market share thresholds, provide the following information:

6.1. Identify each affected market within the meaning of Section III, within the EEA territory, the Community, the territory of the EFTA States, in any Member State or in any EFTA State

6.2. Briefly describe the relevant product and geographic markets concerned by the notified operation, including those which are closely related to the relevant product market(s) concerned (in upstream, downstream and horizontal neighbouring markets), where two or more of the parties to the concentration are active and which are not affected markets within the meaning of Section III.

SECTION 7

Information on affected markets

For each affected relevant product market, for each of the last three financial years:

(a) for the EEA territory;
(b) for the Community as a whole;
(c) for the territory of the EFTA States as a whole;
(d) individually for each Member State and EFTA State where the parties to the concentration do business;
(e) and, where in the opinion of the notifying parties, the relevant geographic market is different;

provide the following:

7.1. an estimate of the total size of the market in terms of sales value (in ecus) and volume (units).[23] Indicate the basis and sources for the calculations and provide documents where available to confirm these calculations;

7.2. the sales in value and volume, as well as an estimate of the market shares, of each of the parties to the concentration;

7.3. an estimate of the market share in value (and where appropriate volume) of all competitors (including importers) having at least 10%; of the geographic market under consideration. Provide documents where available to confirm the calculation of these market shares and provide the name, address, telephone number, fax number and appropriate contact person, of these competitors;

7.4. an estimate of the total value and volume and source of imports from outside the EEA territory and identify:
(a) the proportion of such imports that are derived from the groups to which the parties to the concentration belong;
(b) an estimate of the extent to which any quotas, tariffs or non-tariff barriers to trade, affect these imports, and
(c) an estimate of the extent to which transportation and other costs affect these imports;

7.5. the extent to which trade among States within the EEA territory is affected by:
(a) transportation and other costs; and
(b) other non-tariff barriers to trade;

7.6. the manner in which the parties to the concentration produce and sell the products and/or services; for example, whether they manufacture locally, or sell through local distribution facilities;

7.7. a comparison of price levels in each Member State and EFTA State by each party to the concentration and a similar comparison of price levels between the Community, the EFTA States and other areas where these products are produced (*e.g.* Eastern Europe, the United States of America, Japan, or other relevant areas);

7.8. the nature and extent of vertical integration of each of the parties to the concentration compared with their largest competitors.

SECTION 8

General conditions in affected markets

8.1. Identify the five largest suppliers to the notifying parties and their individual shares of purchases from each of these suppliers (or raw materials or goods used for purposes to producing the relevant products). Provide the name, address, telephone number, fax number and appropriate contact person, of these suppliers.

Structure of supply in affected markets

8.2. Explain the distribution channels and service networks that exist on the affected markets. In so doing, take account of the following where appropriate:

(a) the distribution systems prevailing on the market and their importance. To what extent is distribution performed by third parties and/or undertakings belonging to the same group as the parties identified in Section 3?
(b) the service networks (for example, maintenance and repair) prevailing and their importance in these markets. To what extent are such services performed by third parties and/or undertakings belonging to the same group as the parties identified in Section 3?

8.3. Where appropriate, provide an estimate of the total Community-wide and EFTA-wide capacity for the last three years. Over this period what proportion of this capacity is accounted for by each of the parties to the concentration, and what have been their respective rates of capacity utilisation.

Structure of demand in affected markets

8.4. Identify the five largest customers of the notifying parties in each affected market and their individual share of total sales for such products accounted for by each of those customers. Provide the name, address, telephone number, fax number and appropriate contact person, of each of these customers.

8.5. Explain the structure of demand in terms of:
(a) the phases of the markets in terms of, for example, take-off, expansion, maturity and decline, and a forecast of the growth rate of demand;
(b) the importance of customer preferences, in terms of brand loyalty, products differentiation and the provision of a full range of products;
(c) the degree of concentration or dispersion of customers;
(d) segmentation of customers into different groups and describe the 'typical customer' of each group;
(e) the importance of exclusive distribution contracts and other types of long-term contracts;
(f) the extent to which public authorities, government agencies, state enterprises or similar bodies are important participants as a source of demand.

Market Entry

8.6. Over the last five years, has there been any significant entry into any affected markets? If the answer is 'yes', where possible provide their name, address, telephone number, fax number and appropriate contact person, and an estimate of their current market shares.

8.7. In the opinion of the notifying parties are there undertakings (including those at present operating only in extra-Community or extra-EEA markets) that are likely to enter the market? If the answer is 'yes', please explain why and identify such entrants by name, address, telephone number, fax number and appropriate contact person, and an estimate of the time within which such entry is likely to occur.

8.8. Describe the various factors influencing entry into affected markets that exist in the present case, examining entry from both a geographical and product viewpoint. In so doing, take account of the following where appropriate:

(a) the total costs of entry (R&D, establishing distribution systems, promotion, advertising, servicing, etc.) on a scale equivalent to a significant viable competitor, indicating the market share of such a competitor:
(b) any legal or regulatory barriers to entry, such as government authorisation or standard setting in any form;
(c) any restrictions created by the existence of patents, know-how and other intellectual property rights in these markets and any restrictions created by licensing such rights;
(d) the extent to which each of the parties to the concentration are licensees or licensors of patents, know-how and other rights in the relevant markets;
(e) the importance of economies of scale for the production of products in the affected markets;
(f) access to sources of supply, such as availability of raw materials.

Research and Development

8.9. Give an account of the importance of research and development in the ability of a firm operating on the relevant market(s) to compete in the long-term. Explain the nature of the research and development in affected markets carried out by the undertakings to the concentration.
In so doing, take account of the following, where appropriate:

(a) the research and development intensities[24] for these markets and the relevant research and development intensities for the parties to the concentration;
(b) the course of technological development for these markets over an appropriate time period (including developments in products and/or services, production processes, distribution systems, etc.);
(c) the major innovations that have been made in these markets and the undertakings responsible for these innovations;
(d) the cycle of innovation in these markets and where the parties are in this cycle of innovation.

Cooperative Agreements

8.10. To what extent do cooperative agreements (horizontal or vertical) exist in the affected markets?

8.11. Give details of the most important cooperative agreements engaged in by the parties to the concentration in the affected markets, such as research and development, licensing, joint production, specialisation, distribution, long-term supply and exchange of information agreements.

Trade Associations

8.12. With respect to the trade associations in the affected markets:

(a) identify those in which the parties to the concentration are members;

(b) identify the most important trade associations to which the customers and suppliers of the parties to the concentration belong.

Provide the name, address, telephone number, fax number and appropriate contact person of all trade associations listed above.

SECTION 9

General Matters

Market data on conglomerate aspects

Where any of the parties to the concentration hold individually a market share of 25%; or more for any product market in which there is no horizontal or vertical relationship as described above, provide the following information:

9.1. a description of each product market and explain why the products and/or services in these markets are included (and why others are excluded) by reasons of their characteristics, prices and their intended use;

9.2. an estimate of the value of the market and the market shares of each of the groups to which the parties belong for each product market identified in 9.1. for the last financial year:
(a) for the EEA territory as a whole;
(b) for the Community as a whole;
(c) for the territory of the EFTA States as a whole;
(d) individually for each Member State and EFTA State where the groups to which the parties belong do business;
(e) and where different for the relevant geographic market.

Overview of the markets

9.3. Describe the world-wide context of the proposed concentration, indicating the position of each of the parties to the concentration outside of the EEA territory in terms of size and competitive strength.

9.4. Describe how the proposed concentration is likely to affect the interests of intermediate and ultimate consumers and the development of technical and economic progress.

Ancillary restraints

9.5. Operations which have as their object or effect the co-ordination of the competitive behaviour of undertakings which remain independent fall, in principle, within Articles 85 and 86 of the Treaty of Rome. However, if the parties to the concentration, and/or other involved parties (including the seller and minority shareholders), enter into ancillary restrictions directly related and necessary to the implementation of the concentration, these restrictions may be assessed in conjunction with the concentration itself (see in particular the 25th recital to Regulation (EEC) No. 4064/89 and Commission notice on restrictions ancillary to concentrations.[25]

(a) Identify each ancillary restriction in the agreements provided with the notification for which you request an assessment in conjunction with the concentration; and
(b) explain why these are directly related and necessary to the implementation of the concentration.

Transfer of notification

9.6. In the event that the Commission finds that the operation notified does not constitute a concentration within the meaning of Article 3 of Regulation (EEC) No. 4064/89 do you request that it be treated as an application for negative clearance from, or a notification to obtain an exemption from Article 85 of the Treaty of Rome?

SECTION 10

Declaration

Article 1(2) of the Implementing Regulation states that where notifications are signed by representatives of undertakings, such representatives shall produce written proof that they are authorised to act. Such written authorisation must accompany the notification.

The notification must conclude with the following declaration which is to be signed by or on behalf of all the notifying parties.

The undersigned declare that, to the best of their knowledge and belief, the information given in this notification is true, correct, and complete, that complete copies of documents required by Form CO, have been supplied, and that all estimates are identified as such and are their best estimates of the underlying facts and that all the opinions expressed are sincere.

They are aware of the provisions of Article 14(1)(b) of Regulation (EEC) No. 4064/89.

Place and date:

Signatures:

GUIDANCE NOTE I[26]

Calculation of turnover for credit and other financial institutions

(Article 5(3)(a))

For the calculation of turnover for credit institutes and other financial institutions, we give the following example (proposed merger between bank A and bank B).

APPENDIX 9

I. *Consolidated balance sheets*

(ECU million)

Assets	Bank A		Bank B	
Loans and advances to credit institutions	20,000		1,000	
— to credit institutions within the Community		(10,000)		(500)
— to credit institutions within one (and the same Member State X		(5,000)		(500)
Loans and advances to customers	60,000		4,000	
— to Community residents		(30,000)		(2,000)
— to residents of one (and the same) Member State X		(15,000)		(500)
Other assets:	20,000		1,000	
Total assets:	100,000		6,000	

II. *Calculation of turnover*

In place of turnover, the following figures shall be used:

	Bank A	Bank B
1. Aggregate world-wide turnover is replaced by one-tenth of total assets the total sum of which is more than ECU 5,000 million.	10,000	600

2. Community-wide turnover is replaced by, for each bank, one-tenth of total assets multiplied by the ratio between loans and advances to credit institutions and customers within the Community; to the total sum of loans and advances to credit institutions and customers.

	Bank A	Bank B
This is calculated as follows:		
one-tenth of total assets:	10,000	600
which is multiplied for each bank by the ratio between loans and advances to credit instituions and customers within the Community	10,000	500
	30,000	2,000
	40,000	2,500
and the total sum of loans and advances to credit institutions and customers	20,000	1,000
	60,000	4,000
	80,000	5,000

For:
— Bank A: 10,000 multiplied by (40,000:80,000) = 5,000
— Bank B: 600 multiplied by (2,500:5,000) = 300
which exceeds ECU 250 million for each of the banks.

3. Total turnover within one (and the same) Member State X

	Bank A	Bank B
is replaced by one-tenth of total assetts:	10,000	600

which is multiplied for each bank by the ratio between loans and advances to credit institutions and customers within one and the same Member State X; to the total sum of loans and advances to credit institutions and customers.

	Bank A	Bank B
This is calculated as follows:		
loans and advances to credit institutions	5,000	500
and customers	15,000	500
within one (and the same) Member State X	20,000	1,000
and the total sum of loans and advances to credit institutions and customers	80,000	5,000

For
— Bank A: 10,000 multiplied by (20,000:80,000) = 2,500
— Bank B: 600 multiplied by (1,000:5,000) = 120

Result:
50 per cent of bank A's and 40 per cent of bank B's Community-wide turnover are achieved in one (and the same) Member State X.

III. *Conclusion*

Since

(a) the aggregate world-wide turnover of bank A plus bank B is more than ECU 5,000 million;
(b) the Community-wide turnover of each of the banks is more than ECU 250 million; and
(c) each of the banks achieve less than two-thirds of its Community-wide turnover in one (and the same) Member State,

the proposed merger would fall under the scope of the Regulation.

GUIDANCE NOTE II

Calculation of turnover for insurance undertakings

(Article 5(3)(a))

For the calculation of turnover for insurance undertakings, we give the following example (proposed concentration between insurance A and B):

I. *Consolidated profit and loss account*

(ECU million)

Income	Insurance A		Insurance B	
Gross premiums written	5,000		300	
— gross premiums received from Community residents		(4,500)		(300)
— gross premiums received from residents of one (and the same) Member State X		(3,600)	(270)	
Other income	500		50	
Total income	5,500		350	

II. *Calculation of turnover*

1. Aggregate world-wide turnover is replaced by the value of gross premiums written world-wide, the sum of which is ECU 5,300 million.

2. Community-wide turnover is replaced, for each insurance undertakings, by the value of gross premiums written with Community residents. For each of the insurance undertakings, this amount is more than ECU 250 million.

3. Turnover within one (and the same) Member State X is replaced, for insurance undertakings, by the value of gross premiums written with residents of one (and the same) Member State X. For insurance A, it achieves 80 per cent of its gross premiums written with Community residents within Member State X, whereas for insurance B, it achieves 90 per cent of its gross premiums written with Community residents in that Member State X.

III. *Conclusion*

Since

(a) the aggregate world-wide turnover of insurances A and B, as replaced by the value of gross premiums written world-wide, is more than ECU 5,000 million;
(b) for each of the insurance undertakings, the value of gross premiums written with Community residents is more than ECU 250 million; but
(c) each of the insurance undertakings achieves more than two-thirds of its gross premiums written with Community residents in one (and the same) Member State X,

the proposed concentration would not fall under the scope of the Regulation.

GUIDANCE NOTE III

Calculation of turnover for joint undertakings

A. Creation of a joint undertaking (Article 3(2))

In a case where two (or more) undertakings create a joint undertaking that constitutes a concentration, turnover is calculated for the undertakings concerned.

B. Existence of a joint undertaking (Article 5(5))

For the calculation of turnover in case of the existence of a joint undertaking C between two undertakings A and B concerned in a concentration, we give the following example:

I. *Profit and loss accounts*

(ECU million)

Turnover	Undertaking A	Undertaking B
Sales revenues world-wide	10,000	2,000
— Community	(8,000)	(1,500)
— Member State Y	(4,000)	(900)

(ECU million)

Turnover	Joint undertaking C
Sales revenues world-wide	100
— with undertaking A	(20)
— with undertaking B	(10)
Turnover with third undertakings	70
— Community-wide	(60)
— in Member State Y	(50)

II. *Consideration of the joint undertaking*

(a) The undertaking C is jointly controlled (in the meaning of Article 3(3) and (4)) by the undertakings A and B concerned by the concentration, irrespective of any third undertaking participating in that undertaking C.
(b) The undertaking C is not consolidated A and B in their profit and loss accounts.
(c) The turnover of C resulting from operations which A and B shall not be taken into account.
(d) The turnover of C resulting from operations with any third undertaking shall be apportioned equally amongst the undertakings A and B, irrespective of their individual shareholdings in C.

III. *Calculation of turnover*

(a) Undertaking A's aggregate world-wide turnover shall be calculated as follows: ECU 10,000 million and 50 per cent of C's world-wide turnover with third undertakings (*i.e.* ECU 35 million), the sum of which is ECU 10,035 million.
Undertaking B's aggregate world-wide turnover shall be calculated as follows: ECU 2,000 million and 50 per cent of C's world-wide turnover with third undertakings (*i.e.* ECU 35 million), the sum of which is ECU 2,035 million.
(b) The aggregate world-wide turnover of the undertakings concerned is ECU 12,070 million.
(c) Undertaking A achieves ECU 4,025 million within Member State Y (50 per cent of C's turnover in this Member State taken into account), and a Community-wide turnover of ECU 8,030 million (including 50 per cent of C's Community-wide turnover).
Undertaking B achieves ECU 925 million within Member State Y (50 per cent of C's turnover in this Member State taken into account), and a Community-wide turnover of ECU 1,530 million (including 50 per cent of C's Community-wide turnover).

IV. *Conclusion*

Since

(a) the aggregate world-wide turnover of undertakings A and B is more than ECU 5,000 million;
(b) each of the undertakings concerned by the concentration achieves more than ECU 250 million within the Community;
(c) each of the undertakings concerned (undertaking A 50.1 per cent and undertaking B 60.5 per cent) achieves less than two-third of its Community-wide turnover in one (and the same) Member State Y;

the proposed concentration would fall under the scope of the Regulation.

GUIDANCE NOTE IV

Application of the two-thirds rule

(Article 1)

For the application of the two-thirds rule for undertakings, we give the following examples (proposed concentration between undertakings A and B):

I. *Consolidation profit and loss accounts*

Example 2(b)

Example 1

(ECU million)

Turnover	Undertaking A	Undertaking B
Sales revenues world-wide	10,000	500
— within the Community	(8,000)	(400)
— in Member State X	(6,000)	(200)

Example 2(a)

(ECU million)

Turnover	Undertaking A	Undertaking B
Sales revenues world-wide	4,800	500
— within the Community	(2,400)	(400)
— in Member State X	(2,100)	(300)

Sample figures as in example 2(a) but undertaking B achieves ECU 300 million in Member State Y.

II. *Application of the two-thirds rule*

Example 1

1. Community-wide turnover is, for undertaking A, ECU 8,000 million and for undertaking B ECU 400 million.
2. Turnover in one (and the same) Member State X is, for undertaking A (ECU 6,000 million), 75 per cent of its Community-wide turnover and is, for undertaking B (ECU 200 million), 50 per cent of its Community-wide-turnover.
3. Conclusion: In this case, although undertaking A achieves more than two-thirds of its Community-wide turnover in Member State X, the proposed concentration would fall under the scope of the Regulation due to the fact that undertaking B achieves less than two-thirds of its Community-wide turnover in Member State X.

Example 2(a)

1. Community-wide turnover of undertaking A is ECU 2,400 million and of undertaking B, ECU 400 million.
2. Turnover in one (and the same) Member State X is, for undertaking A, ECU 2,100 million (*i.e.* 87.5 per cent of its Community-wide turnover); and, for

undertaking B, ECU 300 million (*i.e.* 75 per cent of its Community-wide turnover).

3. Conclusion: In this case, each of the undertakings concerned achieves more than two-thirds of its Community-wide turnover in one (and the same) Member State X, the proposed concentration would not fall under the scope of the Regulation.

Example 2(b)

Conclusion: In this case, the two-thirds rule would not apply due to the fact that undertakings A and B achieve more than two-thirds of their Community-wide turnover in different Member States X and Y. Therefore, the proposed concentration would fall under the scope of the Regulation.

[1] OJ 1994 L377/1.
[2] OJ 1989 L395/1.
[3] OJ 1962 13/204/62.
[4] OJ 1968 L175/1.
[5] OJ 1986 L378/4.
[6] OJ 1987 L374/1.
[7] OJ 1992 L240/18.
[8] OJ 1990 L219/5.
[9] OJ 1993 L336/7.
[10] OJ 1981 L124/1.
[11] Hereinafter referred to as the "EEA Agreement", in particular Article 57 of the EEA Agreement (point 1 of Annex XIV to the EEA Agreement and Protocol 4 to the Agreement between the EFTA States on the establishment of a Surveillance Authority and a Court of Justice), as well as Protocols 21 and 24 to the EEA Agreement and Article 1, and the Agreed Minutes of the Protocol adjusting the EEA Agreement. In particular, any reference to EFTA States shall be understood to mean those EFTA States which are Contracting Parties to the EEA Agreement.
[12] The turnover of the joint venture should be determined according to the most recent audited accounts of the parent companies, or the joint venture itself, depending upon the availability of separate accounts for the resources combined in the joint venture.
[13] The expression "and/or" refers to the variety of situations covered by the short-form; for example:
— in the case of the joint acquisition of a target company, the turnover to be taken into account is the turnover of this target (the joint venture)
— in the case of the creation of a joint venture to which the parent companies contribute their activities, the turnover to be taken into account is that of the contributed activities,
— in the case of entry of a new controlling party into an existing joint venture, the turnover of the joint venture and the turnover of the activities contributed by the new parent company (if any) must be taken into account.
[14] The total value of assets of the joint venture should be determined according to the last regularly prepared and approved balance sheet of each parent company. The term "assets" includes (1) all tangible and intangible assets that will be transferred to the joint venture (examples of tangible assets include production plants, wholesale or retail outlets, and inventory of goods) and (2) any amount of credit or any obligations of the joint venture which any parent company of the JV has agreed to extend or guarantee.
[15] Where the assets transferred generate turnover, then neither the value of the assets nor that of the turnover may exceed ECU 100 million.
[16] See, in particular, Article 122 of the EEA Agreement, Article 9 of Protocol 24 to the EEA Agreement and Article 17(2) of Chapter XIII of Protocol 4 to the Agreement between the EFTA States on the establishment of a Surveillance Authority and a Court of Justice (ESA Agreement).
[17] This includes the target company in the case of a contested bid, in which case the details should be completed as far as is possible.
[18] See Commission notice on the notion of undertakings concerned.
[19] See, generally, the Commission notice on "Calculation of turnover". Turnover of the acquiring party or parties to the concentration shall include the aggregated turnover of all undertakings within the sense of Article 5(4). Turnover of the acquired party or parties shall include the turnover relating to the parts subject to the transaction in the sense of Article

5(2). Special provisions are contained in Articles 5(3), (4) and 5(5) for credit, insurance, other financial institutions and joint undertakings.

[20] See guidance note IV for the calculation of turnover in one Member State with respect to Community-wide turnover.

[21] See Articles 3(3) to 3(5) and 5(4).

[22] See Section 6 for the definition of affected markets.

[23] The value and volume of a market should reflect output less exports plus imports for the geographic areas under consideration.

[24] Research and development intensity is defined as research and development expenditure as a proportion of turnover.

[25] OJ C203, 14.8.1990, p. 5.

[26] In the following guidance notes, the terms 'institution' or 'undertaking' are used subject to the exact delimitation in each case.

APPENDIX 10

COMMISSION NOTICE ON THE DISTINCTION BETWEEN CONCENTRATIVE AND CO-OPERATIVE JOINT VENTURES[1]

Under Council Regulation (EEC) No. 4064/89 of 21 December 1989 on the control of concentrations between undertakings

I. INTRODUCTION

1. The purpose of this notice is to provide guidance as to how the Commission interprets Article 3 of Regulation (EEC) No. 4064/89[2] (hereinafter referred to as "the Merger Regulation") in relation to joint ventures.

2. This notice replaces the notice on the same subject adopted by the Commission on 25 July 1990.[3] Changes made in the current notice reflect the experience gained by the Commission in applying the Merger Regulation since its entry into force on 21 September 1990. The principles set out in this notice will be followed and further developed by the Commission's practice in individual cases.

3. Under the Community competition rules joint ventures are undertakings which are jointly controlled by two or more other undertakings.[4] In practice joint ventures encompass a broad range of operations, from merger-like operations to co-operation for particular functions such as R&D, production or distribution.

4. Joint ventures fall within the scope of the Merger Regulation if they meet the requirements of a concentration set out in Article 3 thereof.

5. According to recital 23 of the Merger Regulation "it is appropriate to define the concept of concentration in such a manner as to cover only operations bringing about a lasting change in the structure of the undertakings concerned . . . it is therefore necessary to exclude from the scope of this Merger Regulation those operations which have as their object or effect the co-ordination of competitive behaviour of undertakings which remain independent . . ."

6. The structural changes brought about by concentrations frequently reflect a dynamic process of restructuring in the markets concerned. They are permitted under the Merger Regulation unless they result in serious damage to the structure of competition by creating or strengthening a dominant position.

In this respect concentrations are to be contrasted with arrangements between independent undertakings whereby they co-ordinate their competitive behaviour. The latter do not, in principle, involve a lasting change in structure of undertakings. It is therefore appropriate to submit such arrangements to the prohibition laid down in Article 85(1) of the EEC Treaty where they affect trade between Member States and have as their object or effect the prevention, restriction or distortion of competition within the common market, and they can be exempted from this prohibition only where they fulfil the requirements of Article 85(3). For this reason, co-operative arrangements are dealt with under Regulation (EEC) No. 17,[5] (EEC) No. 1017/68,[6] (EEC) No. 4056/86,[7] or (EEC) No. 3975/87[8] implementing Articles 85 and 86.[9]

7. The Merger Regulation deals with the distinction between concentrative and co-operative operations in Article 3(2)[10] as follows:

"An operation, including the creation of a joint venture, which has as its object or effect the co-ordination of the competitive behaviour of undertakings which remain independent shall not constitute a concentration within the meaning of paragraph 1(b).

The creation of a joint venture performing on a lasting basis all the functions of an autonomous economic entity, which does not give rise to co-ordination of the competitive behaviour of the parties amongst themselves or between them and the joint venture, shall constitute a concentration within the meaning of paragraph 1(b)."

8. Although Article 3(2), second subparagraph, refers to co-ordination between parent companies and the joint venture, this has to be interpreted in the light of recital 23 and Article 3(2), first subparagraph, the purpose of which is to exclude from the scope of the Merger Regulation operations which lead to the co-ordination of behaviour between "undertakings which remain independent". For the purposes of the distinction between co-operative and concentrative joint ventures therefore, the co-ordination between the parent companies and the joint venture referred to in the second subparagraph is relevant only in so far as it is an instrument for producing or reinforcing the co-ordination between the parent companies.

II. JOINT VENTURES UNDER ARTICLE 3 OF THE MERGER REGULATION

9. In order to be a concentration within the meaning of Article 3 of the Merger Regulation an operation must fulfil the following requirements:

1. Joint control

10. A joint venture may fall within the scope of the Merger Regulation where there is an acquisition of joint control by two or more undertakings, that is, its parent companies (Article 3(1)(b)). The concept of control is set out in Article 3(3). This provides that control is based on the possibility of exercising decisive influence on an undertaking, which is determined by both legal and factual considerations.

11. The principles for determining joint control are set out in detail in the Commission's notice on the notion of concentration.[11]

2. Structural change of the undertakings

12. Article 3(2), second subparagraphs stipulates that the joint venture must perform, on a lasting basis, all the functions of an autonomous economic entity.

13. Essentially this means that the joint venture must operate on a market, performing the functions normally carried out by other undertakings operating on the same market. In order to do so the joint venture must have sufficient financial and other resources including finance, staff, and assets (tangible and intangible) in order to operate a business activity on a lasting basis. In respect of intellectual property rights it is sufficient that these rights are licensed to the joint venture for its duration.[12] Joint ventures which satisfy this requirement are commonly described as "full-function" joint ventures.

14. A joint venture is not full-function venture if it only takes over one specific function within the parent companies' business activities without access to the market. This is the case, for example, for joint ventures limited to R&D or production. Such joint ventures are auxiliary to their parent companies' business activities. This is also the case where a joint venture is essentially limited to the distribution or sales of its parent companies' products and, therefore, acts

principally as a sales agency. However, the fact that a joint venture makes use of the distribution network or outlet of one or more of its parent companies, normally will not disqualify it as "full-function" as long as the parent companies are acting only as agents of the joint venture.[13]

15. The strong presence of the parent companies in upstream or downstream markets is a factor to be taken into consideration in assessing the full-function character of a joint venture where this presence leads to substantial sales or purchases between the parent companies and the joint venture. The fact that the joint venture relies almost entirely on sales to its parent companies or purchases from them only for an initial start-up period does not normally affect the full-function character of the joint venture. Such a start-up period may be necessary in order to establish the joint venture on a market. It will normally not exceed a time period of three years, depending on the specific conditions of the market in question.[14]

Where sales from the joint venture to the parent companies are intended to be made on a lasting basis the essential question is whether regardless of these sales the joint venture is geared to play an active role on the market. In this respect the relative proportion of these sales compared with the total production of the joint venture is an important factor. Another factor is that sales to the parent companies are made on the basis of normal commercial conditions.[15]

In relation to purchases made by the joint venture from its parent companies, the full-function character of the joint venture is questionable in particular where little value is added to the products or services concerned at the level of the joint venture itself. In such a situation, the joint venture may be closer to a joint sales agency. However, in contrast to this situation where a joint venture is active in a trade market and performs the normal functions of a trading company in such a market, it normally will not be an auxiliary sales agency but a full-function joint venture. A trade market is characterised by the existence of companies which specialise in the selling and distribution of products without being vertically integrated in addition to those which may be integrated, and where different sources of supply are available for the products in question. In addition, many trade markets may require operators to invest in specific facilities such as outlets, stockholding, warehouses, depots, transport fleets and sales personnel. In order to constitute a full-function joint venture in a trading market, it must have the necessary facilities and be likely to obtain a substantial proportion of its supplies not only from its parent companies but also from other competing sources.[16]

16. Furthermore, the joint venture must be intended to operate on a lasting basis. The fact that the parent companies commit to the joint venture the resources described above normally demonstrates that this is the case. In addition, agreements setting up a joint venture often provide for certain contingencies, for example, the failure of the joint venture or fundamental disagreement as between the parent companies.[17] This may be achieved by the incorporation of provisions for the eventual dissolution of the joint venture itself or the possibility for one or more parent companies to withdraw from the joint venture. This kind of provision does not prevent the joint venture from being considered as operating on a lasting basis. The same is normally true where the agreement specifies a period for the duration of the joint venture where this period is sufficiently long in order to bring about a lasting change in the structure of the undertaking concerned,[18] or where the agreement provides for the possible continuation of the joint venture beyond this period. By contrast, the joint venture will not be considered to operate on a lasting basis where it is established for a short finite duration. This would be the case, for example, where a joint venture is established in order to construct a specific project such as a power plant, but it will not be involved in the operation of the plant once its construction has been completed.

3. Co-operative aspects

17. The creation of a full-function joint venture normally constitutes a concentration within the meaning of Article 3 of the Merger Regulation unless its

object or effect is co-ordination of the competitive behaviour of independent undertakings which is likely to result in a restriction of competition within the meaning of Article 85(1). In order to assess whether a joint venture is co-operative in nature it is necessary to determine whether there is co-ordination between the parent companies in relation to prices, markets, output or innovation. The co-ordination between the parent companies and the joint venture referred to in the second subparagraph of Article 3(2) is relevant only in so far as it is an instrument for producing or reinforcing the co-ordination between the parent companies. Where there is a restriction of competition of this kind the Commission will have to examine the applicability of Article 85 to the whole operation by means of Regulation No. 17. Where the factors leading to this restriction of competition can be separated from the creation of the joint venture itself, the former will be assessed under Regulation No. 17, the latter under the rules on merger control.[19]

3.1. Product market

18. The following typical situations illustrate where co-ordination of the competitive behaviour of the parent companies resulting in an appreciable restriction of competition may or may not occur:

— there is no possibility of co-ordination of the competitive behaviour of independent undertakings where the parent companies transfer their entire business activities to the joint venture or their total activities in a given industrial sector,
— co-ordination can normally be excluded where the parent companies are not active in the market of the joint venture or transfer to the joint venture all their activities in this market or where only one parent company remains active in the joint venture's market. The same is true where the parent companies retain only minor activities in the market of the joint venture,
— by contrast to the above, there is normally a high probability of co-ordination where two or more parent companies retain to a significant extent activities in the same product market as the joint venture itself in so far as these activities are in the same geographic market,[20]
— there is also a probability of co-ordination where the, parent companies or the joint venture specialise in specific segments of an overall product market, unless these segments are of minor importance in view of the main activities of the parent companies or the joint venture respectively or there are objective reasons for the parent companies to retain their activities outside the joint venture, *e.g.* technology related to other activities of the parent companies. In the latter case each of the parent companies retains a genuine interest in their specific segments. The existence of the joint venture therefore does not normally of itself justify the assumption that they would co-ordinate their behaviour with regard to these activities,
— where a network of co-operative links already exists between the parent companies in the joint venture's market the main object or effect of the joint venture may be to add a further link and thereby strengthen already existing co-ordination of competitive behaviour,[21]
— where the parent companies are active in a market which is downstream from the joint venture's market co-ordination of their competitive behaviour may occur where the joint venture is their main supplier and relatively little further value is added at the level of the parent companies; equally, where the parent companies are active in a market which is upstream from the joint venture's market co-ordination of their competitive behaviour may occur where their main customer is the joint venture either in general or in a particular geographic market,
— where two or more parent companies have a significant activity in a neighbouring market and this neighbouring market is of significant

economic importance compared with that of the joint venture, the collaboration within the joint venture may lead to the co-ordination of the parent companies' competitive behaviour on this neighbouring market.[22] In this context a neighbouring market is a separate but closely related market to the market of the joint venture, both markets having common characteristics including technology, customers or competitors.

3.2. Geographic market

19. The parent companies and the joint venture may be active in the same product market but in different geographic markets. In this context two situations may be particularly relevant: the parent companies and the joint venture are each in different geographic markets, or the parent companies are in the same geographic market which is nevertheless different from that of the joint venture. In these situations co-ordination may or may not occur as follows:

— where the parent companies and the joint venture are all in different geographic markets, the Commission will examine closely the likelihood of co-ordination between the parent companies. In doing so the Commission will consider interaction between markets, and foreseeable developments in the emergence of wider geographic markets particularly in the light of the market integration process in the Community.[23] The same applies where one parent company and the joint venture are in the same geographic market while the other parent companies are all in different geographic markets,

— where the parent companies are in the same geographic market, which is different from that of the joint venture, there is scope for co-ordination of the competitive behaviour of the parent companies where the joint venture's activities have a substantial economic importance when compared with the parent companies' activities on their home market ant where there is interaction between the parent companies' and joint venture's markets or such interaction is likely to evolve in the near future. By contrast, where the joint venture's activities account for only a small proportion of the overall activities of the parent companies in the products concerned, the conclusion that collaboration in the joint venture would lead to co-ordination on the parent companies' market would be justified only in exceptional cases,

— in any event, where the co-ordination of competitive behaviour of the parent companies takes place on geographic markets outside the Community or the EEA and has no appreciable effect on competition within the Community/EEA the joint venture is considered to be concentrative despite this co-ordination;

20. In relation to the abovementioned paragraphs, the fact that a joint venture leads to co-ordination of the competitive behaviour of the parent companies does not prevent the assumption of a concentration where these co-operative elements are only of minor economic importance relative to the operation as a whole (*de minimis*).

However a high accumulation of minor elements of co-ordination may lead to a situation where the operation as a whole has to be considered as co-operative.

III. FINAL

21. The Commission's interpretation of Article 3 with respect to joint ventures is without prejudice to the interpretation which may be given by the Court of Justice or the Court of First Instance of the European Communities.

[1] OJ 1994 C385/1.
[2] OJ 1989 C395/1, corrected version OJ 1990 L257/13.
[3] OJ 1990 C203/10.
[4] The concept of joint control is set out in the notice on the notion of a concentration.
[5] OJ 1962 13/204.
[6] OJ 1968 L175/1.
[7] OJ 1986 L378/4.
[8] OJ 1987 L374/1.
[9] See Commission Notice concerning the assessment of co-operative joint ventures pursuant to Article 85 of the EEC Treaty, OJ 1993 C43/2.
[10] Whilst Article 3(2) first subparagraph, is not confined to joint ventures, its application to operations other than joint ventures is not dealt with in the context of the present notice.
[11] Paragraphs 18 to 39.
[12] Case IV/M.236, Ericsson/Ascom of 8 July 1992 (paragraph 11).
[13] Case IV/M.102, TNT/Canada Post etc. of 2 December 1991; Case IV/M.149, Lucas/Eaton of 9 December 1991.
[14] Case IV/M.394, Mannesmann/RWE/Deutsche Bank of 22 December 1983 (paragraph 9).
[15] Case IV/M.266, Rhône-Poulenc Chimie/SITA of 26 November 1992 (paragraph 15), to be contrasted with Case IV/M.168, Flachglas/VEGLA of 13 April 1992.
[16] Case IV/M.179, Spar/Dansk Supermarked of 3 February 1992 (food retail); Case IV/M.326, Toyota Motor Corp./Walter Frey Holding/Toyota France 1 July 1993 (car distribution).
[17] Case IV/M.408, RWE/Mannesmann of 28 February 1994 (paragraph 6).
[18] Case IV/M.259, British Airways/TAT of 27 October 1992 (paragraph 10).
[19] Case IV/M.179, Spar/Dansk Supermarked of 3 February 1992 (paragraph 8).
Case IV/M.263, Ahold/Jeronimo Martins of 29 September 1992 (paragraph 8).
[20] Case IV/M.088, Elf Enterprise of 24 July 1991 (paragraph 6); Case IV/M.117 Koipe—Tabacalera/Elosua of 28 July 1992 (paragraphs 10 to 14). In principle, the same would apply where, following the creation of the joint venture, the parent companies, while no longer active in the joint venture's market, nevertheless remain potential competitors in this market. However, this can normally be excluded since it is unlikely that the parents would re-enter the market on their own, in particular, where they have transferred their respective activities to the joint venture, or where they commit significant investment to the joint venture.
[21] Case IV/M.176, Sunrise of 13 January 1992 (paragraph 34).
[22] Case IV/M.293, Philips/Thomson/SAGEM of 18 January 1993 (paragraph 19).
[23] See Case IV/M.207, Eureko of 27 April 1992 (paragraph 16(b)) which can be contrasted with Case IV/M.319, BHF/CCF/Charterhouse of 30 August 1993 (paragraph 6).

APPENDIX 11

COMMISSION NOTICE ON THE NOTION OF A CONCENTRATION[1]

Under Council Regulation (EEC) No. 4064/89 of 21 December 1989 on the control of concentrations between undertakings

I. INTRODUCTION

1. The purpose of this notice is to provide guidance as to how the Commission interprets the notion of a concentration under Article 3 of Regulation (EEC) No. 4064/89[2] (hereinafter referred to as the "Merger Regulation"). It forms part of the initiatives which the Commission envisaged in its report[3] to the Council of Ministers of 28 July 1993 in order to improve the transparency and legal security of all decisions taken in application of the Regulation. This formal guidance on the interpretation of Article 3 should enable firms to establish more quickly whether and to what extent their operations may be covered by Community merger control in advance of any contact with the Commission's services.

This notice deals with paragraphs (1), (3), (4) and (5) of Article 3. The interpretation of Article 3 in relation to joint ventures, dealt with in particular under Article 3(2), is set out in the Commission's notice on the distinction between concentrative and co-operative joint ventures.[4]

2. The guidance set out in this notice reflects the experience of the Commission in applying the Merger Regulation since it entered into force on 21 December 1990. The principles contained here will be applied and further developed by the Commission in individual cases.

3. According to recital 23 of the Merger Regulation the concept of a concentration is defined as covering only operations which bring about a lasting change in the structure of the undertakings concerned. Article 3(1) provides that such a structural change is brought about either by a merger between two previously independent undertakings or by the acquisition of control over the whole or part of another undertaking.

4. The determination of the existence of a concentration under the Merger Regulation is based upon qualitative rather than quantitative criteria, focusing on the notion of control. These criteria include considerations of both law and fact. It follows, therefore, that a concentration may occur on a legal or a *de facto* basis.

5. Article 3(1) of the Regulation defines two categories of concentration:

- those arising from a merger between previously independent undertakings (point (a));
- those arising from an acquisition of control (point (b)).

These are treated respectively in sections II and III below.

II. MERGERS BETWEEN PREVIOUSLY INDEPENDENT UNDERTAKINGS

6. A merger within the meaning of point (a) of Article 3(1) of the Merger Regulation occurs when two or more independent undertakings amalgamate into a new undertaking and cease to exist as different legal entities. A merger may also occur when an undertaking is absorbed by another, the latter retaining its legal identity while the former ceases to exist as a legal entity.

7. A merger within the meaning of point (a) of Article 3(1) may also occur where, in the absence of a legal merger, the combining of the activities of previously independent undertakings results in the creation of a single economic unit.[5] This may arise in particular where two or more undertakings, while retaining their individual legal personalities, establish contractually a common economic management.[6] If this leads to a *de facto* amalgamation of the undertakings concerned into a genuine common economic unit, the operation is considered to be a merger. A prerequisite for the determination of a common economic unit is the existence of a permanent, single economic management. Other relevant factors may include internal profit and loss compensation as between the various undertakings within the group, and their joint liability externally. The *de facto* amalgamation may be reinforced by cross-shareholdings between the undertakings forming the economic unit.

III. ACQUISITION OF CONTROL

8. Point (b) of Article 3(1) provides that a concentration occurs in the case of an acquisition of control. Such control may be acquired by one undertaking acting alone or by two or more undertakings acting jointly.

Control may also be acquired by a person in circumstances where that person already controls (whether solely or jointly) at least one other undertaking or, alternatively, by a combination of persons (which control another undertaking) and/or undertakings. The term "person" in this context extends to public bodies[7] and private entities, as well as individuals.

As defined, a concentration within the meaning of the Merger Regulation is limited to changes in control. Internal restructuring within a group of companies, therefore, cannot constitute a concentration.

An exceptional situation exists where both the acquiring and acquired undertakings are public companies owned by the same State (or by the same public body). In this case, whether the operation is to be considered as an internal restructuring or not depends in turn on the question whether both undertakings were formerly part of the same economic unit within the meaning of recital 12 of the Merger Regulation. Where the undertakings were formerly part of different economic units having an independent power of decision the operation will be deemed to constitute a concentration and not an internal restructuring.[8] Such independent power of decision does not normally exist, however, where the undertakings are within the same holding company.

9. Whether an operation gives rise to an acquisition of control depends on a number of legal and/or factual elements. The acquisition of property rights and shareholders' agreements are important but are not the only elements involved: purely economic relationships may also be determinant. Therefore, in exceptional circumstances a situation of economic dependence may lead to control on a factual basis where, for example, very important long term-supply agreements or credits provided by suppliers or customers, coupled with structural links, confer decisive influence.[9]

There may also be acquisition of control even if it is not the declared intention of the parties.[10] Moreover the Merger Regulation clearly defines control as "having the possibility of exercising decisive influence" rather than the actual exercise of such influence.

10. Control is nevertheless normally acquired by persons or undertakings which are the holders of the rights or are entitled to rights conferring control (point (a) of Article 3(4)). There may be exceptional situations where the formal holder of a controlling interest differs from the person or undertaking having in fact the real power to exercise the rights resulting from this interest. This may be the case, for example, where an undertaking uses another person or undertaking for the acquisition of a controlling interest and exercises the rights through this person or undertaking, even though the latter is formally the holder of the rights. In such a situation control is acquired by the undertaking which in reality is behind the operation and in fact enjoys the power to control the target undertaking (point (b) of Article 3(4)). The evidence needed to establish this type of indirect control may include factors such as the source of financing or family links.

11. The object of control can be one or more undertakings which constitute legal entities, or the assets of such entities, or only some of these assets.[11] In the last mentioned situation, which could apply to brands or licenses, the assets in question must constitute a business to which a market turnover can be clearly attributed.

12. The acquisition of control may be of sole or joint control. In both cases control is defined as the possibility to exercise decisive influence on an undertaking on the basis of rights, contracts or any other means (Article 3(3)).

1. Sole control

13. Sole control is normally acquired on a legal basis where an undertaking acquires a majority of the voting rights of a company. It is not in itself significant that the acquired shareholding is 50 per cent of the share capital plus one share[12] or that it is 100 per cent of the share capital.[13] In the absence of other elements an acquisition which does not include a majority of the voting rights does not normally confer control even if it involves the acquisition of a majority of the share capital.

14. Sole control may also be acquired in the case of a "qualified minority". This can be established on a legal and/or *de facto* basis.

On a legal basis it can occur where specific rights are attached to the minority shareholding. These may be preferential shares leading to a majority of the voting rights or other rights enabling the minority shareholder to determine the strategic commercial behaviour of the target company, such as the power to appoint more than half of the members of the supervisory board or the administrative board.

A minority shareholder may also be deemed to have sole control on a *de facto* basis. This is the case, for example, where the shareholder is highly likely to achieve a majority in the shareholders' meeting, given that the remaining shares are widely dispersed.[14] In such a situation it is unlikely that all the smaller shareholders will be present or represented at the shareholders' meeting. The determination of whether or not sole control exists in a particular case is based on the evidence resulting from the presence of shareholders in previous years. Where, on the basis of the number of shareholders attending the shareholders' meeting, a minority shareholder has a stable majority of the votes in this meeting, then the large minority shareholder is taken to have sole control.[15]

Sole control can also be exercised by a minority shareholder who has the right to manage the activities of the company and to determine its business policy.

15. An option to purchase or convert shares cannot in itself confer sole control unless the option will be exercised in the near future according to legally binding agreements.[16] However the likely exercise of such an option can be taken into account as an additional element which, together with other elements, may lead to the conclusion that there is sole control.

16. A change from joint to sole control of an undertaking is deemed to be a concentration within the meaning of the Merger Regulation because decisive influence exercised solely is substantially different to decisive influence exercised jointly.[17] For the same reason, an operation involving the acquisition of joint control of one part of an undertaking and sole control of another part, are in principle regarded as two separate concentrations under the Merger Regulation.[18]

17. The concept of control under the Merger Regulation may be different from that applied in specific areas of legislation concerning, for example, prudential rules, taxation, air transport or media. In addition, national legislation within a Member State may provide specific rules on the structure of bodies representing the organisation of decision-making within an undertaking, in particular, in relation to the rights of representatives of employees. While such legislation may confer a certain power of control upon persons other than the shareholders, the concept of control under the Merger Regulation is related only to the means of influence normally enjoyed by the owners of an undertaking. Finally, the prerogatives exercised by a State acting as a public authority rather than as a shareholder, in so far as then are limited to the protection of the public interest, do not constitute control within the meaning of the Merger Regulation to the extent that they have neither the aim nor the effect of enabling the State to exercise a decisive influence over the activity of the undertaking.[19]

2. Joint control

18. As in the case of sole control, the acquisition of joint control (which includes changes from sole control to joint control) can also be established on a legal or *de facto* basis. There is joint control if the shareholders (the parent companies) must reach agreement on major decisions concerning the controlled undertaking (the joint venture).

19. Joint control exists where two or more undertakings or persons have the possibility to exercise decisive influence over another undertaking. Decisive influence in this sense normally means the power to block actions which determine the strategic commercial behaviour of an undertaking. Unlike sole control, which confers the power upon a specific shareholder to determine the strategic decisions in an undertaking, joint control is characterised by the possibility of a deadlock situation resulting from the power of two or more parent companies to reject proposed strategic decisions. It follows, therefore, that these shareholders must reach a common understanding in determining the commercial policy of the joint venture.

2.1. Equality in voting rights or appointment to decision-making bodies

20. The clearest form of joint control exists where there are only two parent companies which share equally the voting rights to the joint venture. In this case it is not necessary for a formal agreement to exist between them. However, where there is a formal agreement, it must not contradict the principle of equality between the parent companies, by laying down, for example, that each is entitled to the same number of representatives in the management bodies and that none of the members has a casting vote.[20] Equality may also be achieved where both parent companies have the right to appoint an equal number of members to the decision-making bodies of the joint venture.

2.2 Veto rights

21. Joint control may exist even where there is no equality between the two parent companies in votes or in representation in decision-making bodies or where there are more than two parent companies. This is the case where minority shareholders have additional rights which allow them to veto decisions which are essential for the strategic commercial behaviour of the joint venture.[21] These veto rights may be set out in the statute of the joint venture or conferred by agreement between its parent companies. The veto rights themselves may operate by means of a specific quorum required for decisions taken in the shareholders' meeting or in the board of directors to the extent that the parent companies are represented

on this board. It is also possible that strategic decisions are subject to approval by a body, *e.g.*: supervisory board, where the minority shareholders are represented and form part of the quorum needed for such decisions.

22. These veto rights must be related to strategic decisions on the business policy of the joint venture. They must go beyond the veto rights normally accorded to minority shareholders in order to protect their financial interests as investors in the joint venture. This normal protection of the rights of minority shareholders is related to decisions on the essence of the joint venture, such as, changes in the statute, increase or decrease of the capital or liquidation. A veto right, for example, which prevents the sale or winding up of the joint venture, does not confer joint control on the minority shareholder concerned.[22]

23. In contrast, veto rights which confer joint control typically include decisions and issues such as the budget, the business plan, major investments or the appointment of senior management. The acquisition of joint control, however, does not require that the acquiror has the power to exercise decisive influence on the day-to-day running of an undertaking. The crucial element is that the veto rights are sufficient to enable the parent companies to exercise such influence in relation to the strategic business behaviour of the joint venture. Moreover, it is not necessary to establish that an acquiror of joint control of the joint venture will actually make use of its decisive influence. The possibility to use this influence and, hence, the mere existence of the veto rights, is sufficient.

24. In order to acquire joint control, it is not necessary for a minority shareholder to have all the veto rights mentioned above. It may be sufficient that only some, or even one such right, exists. Whether or not this is the case depends upon the precise content of the veto right itself and also the importance of this right in the context of the specific business of the joint venture.

Appointment of management and determination of budget

25. Normally the most important veto rights are those concerning decisions on the appointment of the management and the budget. The power to co-determine the structure of the management confers upon the holder the power to exercise decisive influence on the commercial policy of an undertaking. The same is true with respect to decisions on the budget since the budget determines the precise framework of the activities of the joint venture and, in particular, the investments it may make.

Business plan

26. The business plan normally provides details of the aims of a company together with the measures to be taken in order to achieve those aims. A veto right over this type of business plan may be sufficient to confer joint control even in the absence of any other veto right. In contrast, where the business plan contains merely general declarations concerning the business aims of the joint venture, the existence of a veto right will be only one element in the general assessment of joint control but will not, on its own, be sufficient to confer joint control.

Investments

27. In the case of a veto right on investments the importance of this right depends on, first, the level of investments which are subject to the approval of the parent companies and secondly, the extent to which investments constitute an essential feature of the market in which the joint venture is active. In relation to the first, where the level of investments necessitating parental approval is extremely high, this veto right may be closer to the normal protection of the interests of a minority shareholder than to a right conferring a power of co-determination over the commercial policy of the joint venture. With regard to the second, the investment policy of an undertaking normally is an important element in assessing whether or not there is joint control. However, there may be

some markets where investment does not play a significant role in the market behaviour of an undertaking.

Market-specific rights

28. Apart from the typical veto rights mentioned above, there exist a number of other veto rights related to specific decisions which are important in the context of the particular market on the joint venture. One example is the decision on the technology to be used by the joint venture where technology is a key feature of the joint venture's activities. Another example relates to markets characterised by product differentiation and a significant degree of innovation. In such markets a veto right over decisions relating to new product lines to be developed by the joint venture may also be an important element in establishing the existence of joint control.

Overall context

29. In assessing the relative importance of veto rights, where there are a number of them, these rights should not be evaluated in isolation. On the contrary, the determination of the existence or not of joint control is based upon an assessment of these rights as a whole. However, a veto right which does not relate either to commercial policy and strategy or to the budget of business plan cannot be regarded as giving joint control to its owner.[23]

2.3. Common exercise of voting rights

30. Even in the absence of specific veto rights, two or more undertakings acquiring minority shareholdings in another undertaking may obtain joint control. This may be the case where the minority shareholdings together provide the means for controlling the target undertaking. This means that the minority shareholders, together, will have a majority of the voting rights; and they will act together in exercising these voting rights. This can result from a legally binding agreement to this effect, or it may be established on a *de facto* basis.

31. The legal means to ensure the common exercise of voting rights can be in the form of a holding company to which the minority shareholders transfer their rights, or an agreement by which they engage themselves to act in the same way (pooling agreement).

32. Very exceptionally, collective action can occur on a *de facto* basis where strong common interests exist between the minority shareholders to the effect that they would not act against each other in exercising their rights in relation to the Joint venture.

33. In the case of acquisitions of minority shareholdings the prior existence of links between the minority shareholders or the acquisition of the shareholdings by means of concerted action will be factors indicating such a common interest.

34. In the case where a new joint venture is established, as opposed to the acquisition of minority shareholdings in an already existing company, there is higher probability that the parent companies are carrying out a deliberate common policy. This is true, in particular, where each parent company provides a contribution to the joint venture which is vital for its operation (*e.g.* specific technologies, local know-how or supply agreements). In these circumstances the parent companies may be able to operate the joint venture in full co-operation only with each other's agreement on the most important strategic decisions even if there is no express provision for any veto rights. The greater the number of parent companies involved in such a joint venture, however, the likelihood of this situation occurring becomes increasingly remote.

35. In the absence of strong common interests such as those outlined above, the possibility of changing coalitions between minority shareholders will normally

exclude the assumption of joint control. Where there is no stable majority in the decision-making procedure and the majority can on each occasion be any of the various combinations possible amongst the minority shareholders, it cannot be assumed that the minority shareholders will jointly control the undertaking. In this context, it is not sufficient that there are agreements between two or more parties having an equal shareholding in the capital of an undertaking which establish identical rights and powers between the parties. For example, in the case of an undertaking where three shareholders each own a third of the share capital and each elect a third of the members of the Board of Directors, the shareholders do not have joint control since decisions are required to be taken on the basis of a simple majority. The same considerations also apply in more complex statutes, for example, where the capital of an undertaking is equally divided between three shareholders and whose Board of Management is composed of 12 members of which two are each elected by shareholders A, B and C, two by A B and C jointly, and the remaining four by the other eight members. In this case also there is no joint control, and hence no control at all within the meaning of the Merger Regulation.

2.4. Other considerations related to joint control

36. Joint control is not incompatible with the fact that one of the parent companies enjoys specific knowledge of and experience in the business of the joint venture. In such a case, the other parent company can play a modest or even non-existent role in the daily management of the joint venture where its presence is motivated by considerations of a financial, long-term-strategy, brand image or general policy nature. Nevertheless, it must always retain the real possibility of contesting the decisions taken by the other parent company, without which there would be sole control.

37. For joint control to exist, there should not be a casting vote for one parent company only. However, there can be joint control when this casting vote can be exercised only after a series of stages of arbitration and attempts at reconciliation or in a very limited field.[24]

2.5. Joint control for a limited period

38. Where an operation leads to joint control for a starting-up period[25] but, according to legally binding agreements, this joint control will be converted to sole control by one of the shareholders, the whole operation will normally be considered as an acquisition of sole control.

3. Control by a single shareholder on the basis of veto rights

39. An exceptional situation exists where, in the course of an acquisition, only one shareholder is able to veto strategic decisions in an undertaking but this shareholder does not have the power, on his own, to impose such decisions. This situation occurs either where one shareholder holds 50 per cent in an undertaking whilst the remaining 50 per cent is held by two or more minority shareholders, or where there is a quorum required for strategic decisions which in fact confers a veto right upon only one minority shareholder.[26] In these circumstances, a single shareholder, possesses the same level of influence as that normally enjoyed by several jointly—controlling shareholders, *i.e.* the power to block the adoption of strategic decisions. However, this shareholder does not enjoy the powers which are normally conferred on an undertaking with sole control, *i.e.* the power to impose strategic decisions. Since this shareholder can produce the same deadlock situation as in the normal cases of joint control he acquires decisive influence and therefore control within the meaning of the Merger Regulation.[27]

4. Changes in the structure of control

40. A concentration may also occur where an operation leads to a change in the structure of control. This includes the change from joint control to sole control as well as an increase in the number of shareholders exercising joint control. The principles for determining the existence of a concentration in these circumstances are set out in detail in the notice on the notion of undertakings concerned.[28]

IV. EXCEPTIONS

41. Article 3(5) sets out three exceptional situations where the acquisition of a controlling interest does not constitute a concentration under the Merger Regulation.

42. First, the acquisition of securities by companies, the normal activities of which include transactions and dealings for their own account or for the account of others, is not deemed to constitute a concentration if such an acquisition is made in the framework of businesses and where the securities are held only on a temporary basis (point (a) of Article 3(5)). In order to fall within this exception, the following requirements must be fulfilled:

- the acquiring undertaking must be a credit or other financial institution or insurance company the normal activities of which are described above,
- the securities must be acquired with a view to their resale,
- the acquiring undertaking must not exercise the voting rights with a view to determining the strategic commercial behaviour of the target or must exercise these rights at least only with a view to preparing the total or partial disposal of the undertaking, its assets or securities,
- the acquiring undertaking must dispose of its controlling interest within one year of the date of the acquisition, that is, it must reduce its shareholding within this one-year period at least to a level which no longer confers control. This period, however, may be extended by the Commission where the acquiring undertaking can show that the disposal was not reasonably possible within the one-year period.

43. Secondly, there is no change of control, and so no concentration within the meaning of the Merger Regulation, where control is acquired by an office-holder according to the law of a Member State relating to liquidation, winding-up, insolvency, cessation of payments, compositions or analogous proceedings (point (b) of Article 3(5));

44. Thirdly, a concentration does not arise where a financial holding company within the meaning of the Fourth Council Directive 78/660/EEC[29] acquires control, provided that this company exercise its voting rights only to maintain the full value of its investment and does not otherwise determine directly or indirectly the strategic commercial conduct of the controlled undertaking.

45. In the context of the exceptions under Article 3(5), the question may arise whether a rescue operation constitutes a concentration under the Merger Regulation. A rescue operation typically involves the conversion of existing debt into a new company, through which a syndicate of banks may acquire joint control of the company concerned. Where such an operation meets the criteria for joint control, as outlined above, it will normally be considered to be a concentration.[30] Although the primary intention of the banks is to restructure the financing of the undertaking concerned for its subsequent resale, the exception set out in point (a) of Article 3(5) is normally not applicable to such an operation. This is so because the restructuring programme normally requires the controlling banks to determine the strategic commercial behaviour of the rescued undertaking. Furthermore, it is not normally realistic to transfer a rescued company into a commercially viable entity and to resell it within the permitted one-year period. Moreover, the length of time needed to achieve this aim may be so uncertain that it would be difficult to grant an extension of the disposal period.

V. FINAL

46. The Commission's interpretation of Article 3 as set out in this notice is without prejudice to the interpretation which may be given by the Court of Justice or the Court of First Instance of the European Communities.

[1] OJ 1994 C385/5.

[2] OJ 1989 L395/1, corrected version OJ 1990 L257/13.

[3] Doc. COM(93) 385 final, as amended by COM(93) 385 final/2.

[4] Commission notice regarding the distinction between concentrative and co-operative joint ventures under Council Regulation (EEC) No. 4064/89 of 21 December 1989 on the control of concentrations between undertakings.

[5] In determining the previous independence of undertakings the issue of control may be relevant. Control is considered generally in paragraphs 12, *et seq.*, below. For this specific issue minority shareholders are deemed to have control if they have previously obtained a majority of votes on major decisions at shareholders meetings. The reference period in this context is normally three years.

[6] This could apply for example in the case of "Gleichordnungskonzern" in German law, certain "Groupements d'Intérêts Economiques" in French law, and certain partnerships.

[7] Including the State itself, *e.g.* Case IV/M.157—Air France/Sabena, of 5 October 1992 in relation to the Belgian State, or other public bodies such as the Treuhand in Case IV/M.308—Kali und Salz/MDK/Treuhand, of 14 December 1993.

[8] Case IV/M.097—Péchiney/Usinor, of 24 June 1991; IV/M.216—CEA Industrie/France Télécom/SGS—Thomson, 22 February 1993.

[9] For example in the Usinor/Bamesa decision adopted by the Commission under the ECSC Treaty. See also Case IV/M.258 CCIE/GTE, of 25 September 1992.

[10] Case IV/M.157—Air France/Sabena, of 5 October 1992.

[11] Case IV/M.286 Zürich/MMI, of 2 April 1993.

[12] Case IV/M.296—Crédit Lyonnais/BFG Bank, of 11 January 1993.

[13] Case IV/M.299 Sara Lee/BP Food Division, of 8 February 1993.

[14] Case IV/M.025 Arjomari/Wiggins Teape, of 10 February 1990.

[15] Case IV/M.343—Société Générale de Belgique/Générale de Banque, of 3 August 1993

[16] Case T–2/93 *Air France v Commission* (judgment of 19 May 1994, not yet published).

[17] This issue is dealt with in paragraphs 30 to 32 of the notice on the notion of undertakings concerned.

[18] Case IV/M.409 ABB/Renault Automation, of 9 March 1994.

[19] Case IV/M.493—Tractebel/Distrigaz II, of 1 September 1994.

[20] Case IV/M.292 Matra/CAP Gemini Sogeti, of 17 March 1993.

[21] Case T–2/93, *Air France v Commission* (*ibid.*). Case IV/M.0010 Conagra/Idea, of 3 May 1991.

[22] Case IV/M.062—Eridania/ISI, of 30 July 1991.

[23] Case IV/M.295—SITA-RPC/SCORI, of 19 March 1993.

[24] Case IV/M.425—British Telecom/Banco Santander, of 28 March 1994.

[25] This starting-up period must not exceed three years. Case IV/M.425—British Telecom/ Banco Santander, *ibid*.

[26] Case IV/M.258—CCIE/GTE, of 25 September 1992, where the veto rights of only one shareholder were exercisable through a member of the board appointed by this shareholder.

[27] Since this shareholding is the only undertaking acquiring a controlling influence only this shareholder is obliged to submit a notification under the Merger Regulation.

[28] Paragraphs 30 and 48.

[29] OJ 1978 L222/11, as last amended by Directive 84/569/EEC, OJ 1984 L314/28. Article 5(3) of this Directive, defines financial holding companies as "those companies the sole objective of which is to acquire holdings in other undertakings, and to manage such holdings and turn them to profit, without involving themselves directly or indirectly in the management of those undertakings, the aforegoing without prejudice to their rights as shareholders".

[30] Case IV/M.116—Kelt/American Express, of 28 August 1991.

APPENDIX 12

COMMISSION NOTICE ON THE NOTION OF UNDERTAKINGS CONCERNED[1]

Under Council Regulation (EEC) No. 4064/89 of 21 December 1989 on the control of concentrations between undertakings

I. INTRODUCTION

1. This Commission notice aims at clarifying the Commission's interpretation of the notion of undertakings concerned in Articles 1 and 5 of Regulation (EEC) No. 4064/89,[2] as well as at helping to identify the undertakings concerned in the most typical situation which have arisen in cases dealt with by the Commission to date. The principles set out in this notice will be followed and further developed by the Commission's practice in individual cases.

2. According to Article 1 of the Merger Regulation, this Regulation only applies to operations that satisfy a double condition. First, several undertakings must merge, or one or more undertakings must acquire control of the whole or part of other undertakings through the proposed operation, which must qualify as concentrations within the meaning of Article 3 of the Regulation. Secondly, those undertakings must meet the three turnover thresholds set out in Article 1.

3. From the point of view of determining jurisdiction, the undertakings concerned are, broadly speaking, the actors in the transaction in so far as they are the merging, or acquiring and acquired parties; in addition, their total aggregate economic size in terms of turnover will be decisive to determine whether the thresholds are fulfilled. The concept of undertakings concerned is used only for the purposes of determining jurisdiction, as the Commission's assessment of the competitive impact of the operation on the market place will then focus not only on the activities of those undertakings concerned party to the concentration, but also on the activities of the groups to which these undertakings belong.

4. The Commission's interpretation of Articles 1 and 5 with respect to the notion of undertakings concerned is without prejudice to the interpretation which may be given by the Court of Justice or by the Court of First Instance of the European Communities.

II. THE NOTION OF UNDERTAKING CONCERNED

5. Undertakings concerned are the direct participants in a merger or acquisition of control. In this respect, Article 3(1) of the Merger Regulation provides that:

"A concentration shall be deemed to arise where:
(a) two or more previously independent undertakings merge, or

(b) —one or more persons already controlling at least one undertaking, or
—one or more undertakings

acquire, whether by purchase of securities or assets, by contract or by any other means, direct or indirect control of the whole or parts of one or more undertakings."

6. In the case of a merger, the undertakings concerned will be the undertakings that are merging.

7. In the remaining cases, it is the concept of "acquiring control" that will determine which are the undertakings concerned. On the acquiring side, there can be one or several companies acquiring sole or joint control. On the acquired side, there can be one or more companies as a whole or parts thereof, when only one of their subsidiaries or some of their assets are the subject of the transaction. As a general rule, each of these companies will be an undertaking concerned within the meaning of the Merger Regulation. However, the particular features of specific transactions require a certain refinement of this principle, as will be seen below when analysing different possible scenarios.

8. In those concentrations other than mergers or the setting up of new joint ventures, *i.e.* in cases of sole or joint acquisition of pre-existing companies or part of them, there is an important party to the agreement that gives rise to the operation who is to be ignored when identifying the undertakings concerned: the seller. Although it is clear that the operation cannot proceed without its consent, its role ends when the transaction is completed since, by definition, from the moment the seller has relinquished all control over the company, its links with it disappear. Where the seller retains joint control with the acquiring company (or companies) it will be considered as one of the undertakings concerned.

9. Once the undertakings concerned have been identified in a given transaction, their turnover for the purposes of determining jurisdiction should be calculated according to the rules set out in Article 5 of the Merger Regulation.[3] One of the main provisions of Article 5 is that where the undertaking concerned belongs to a group, the turnover of the whole group should be included in the calculation. All references to the turnover of the undertakings concerned in Article 1 should be therefore understood as the turnover of their entire respective groups.

10. The same can be said with respect to the substantive appraisal of the impact of a concentration in the market place. When Article 2 of the Merger Regulation provides that the Commission shall take into account "the market position of the undertakings concerned and their economic and financial power", this includes the groups to which they belong.

11. It is important not to confuse the concept of undertakings concerned under Articles 1 and 5, with those other terms used in the Merger Regulation and in the Implementing Regulation[4] in referring to the various undertakings which may be involved in a procedure. These other notions are notifying parties, other involved parties, third parties and parties who may be subject to fines or periodic penalty payments. They are defined in Section III of the Implementing Regulation, along with their respective rights and duties.

III. IDENTIFYING THE UNDERTAKINGS CONCERNED IN DIFFERENT TYPES OF OPERATIONS

1. Mergers

12. In a merger, several previously independent companies come together to create a new company or, while remaining separate legal entities, to create a single economic unit. As mentioned earlier, the undertakings concerned are each of the merging entities.

2. Acquisition of sole control

2.1. Acquisition of sole control of the whole company

13. Acquisition of sole control of the whole company is the most straightforward case of acquisition of control; the undertakings concerned will be the acquiring company and the acquired or target company.

2.2. Acquisition of sole control of part of a company

14. The first subparagraph of Article 5(2) of the Merger Regulation stipulates that when the operation concerns the acquisition of parts of one or more undertakings, only those parts which are the subject of the transaction shall be taken into account with regard to the seller. The concept of "parts" is to be understood as one or more separate legal entities (such as subsidiaries), internal subdivisions within the seller (such as a division or unit), or specific assets which in themselves could constitute a business (*e.g.* in certain cases brands or licences) to which a market turnover can clearly be attributed. In this case, the undertakings concerned will be the acquirer and the acquired part(s) of the target company.
15. The second subparagraph of Article 5(2) includes a special provision on staggered operations or follow-up deals whereby if several acquisitions of parts by the same purchaser from the same seller occur within a two-year period, these transactions shall be treated as one and the same operation arising on the date of the last transaction. In this case, the undertakings concerned are the acquirer and the different acquired part(s) of the target company taken as a whole.

2.3. Acquisition of sole control of previously reduced or enlarged companies

16. The undertakings concerned are the acquiring company and the target company(ies), in their configuration at the date of the operation.
17. The Commission bases itself on the configuration of the undertakings concerned at the date of the event triggering the obligation to notify under Article 4(1) of the Merger Regulation, namely the conclusion of the agreement, the announcement of the public bid, or the acquisition of a controlling interest. If the target company has divested an entity or closed a business prior to the date of the event triggering notification or where such a divestment or closure is a pre-condition for the operation,[5] then sales of the divested entity or closed business would not be included when calculating turnover. Conversely if the target company has acquired an entity prior to the date of the event triggering notification, the sales of the latter would be added.[6]

2.4. Acquisition of sole control through a subsidiary of a group

18. Where the target company is acquired by a group through one of its subsidiaries, the undertakings concerned for the purpose of calculating turnover are the target company and the acquiring subsidiary. However, regarding the actual notification, this can be made by the subsidiary concerned or by its parent company.
19. All the companies within a group (parent companies, subsidiaries, etc. constitute a single economic entity, and therefore there can only be one undertaking concerned within the one group—*i.e.* the subsidiary and the parent company cannot each be considered as separate undertakings concerned, either

for the purposes of ensuring that the threshold requirements are fulfilled (for example, if the target company docs not meet the ECU 250 million Community-turnover threshold), or that they are not (for example if a group was split in two companies each with a Community turnover below ECU 250 million).

20. However, even though there can only be one undertaking concerned within a group, Article 5(4) of the Merger Regulation provides that it is the turnover of the whole group to which the undertaking concerned belongs that will be included in the threshold calculations.[7]

3. Acquisition of joint control

3.1. Acquisition of joint control of a newly-created company

21. In the case of acquisition of joint control of a newly-created company, the undertakings concerned are each of the companies acquiring control of the newly set-up joint venture (which, as it does not yet exist, cannot yet be considered as an undertaking concerned and furthermore has no turnover of its own yet).

3.2. Acquisition of joint control of a pre-existing company

22. In the case of acquisition of joint control of a pre-existing company or business,[8] the undertakings concerned are each of the companies acquiring joint control on the one hand, and the pre-existing acquired company on the other.

23. Where the pre-existing company was under the sole control of one company and one or several new shareholders acquire joint control but the initial parent company remains, the undertakings concerned are each of the jointly-controlling companies (including this initial shareholder) and the target company. This situation is a passage from sole to joint control. In so far as sole control and joint control have a different nature, the Commission has consistently considered that passing from one type of control to another normally constitutes a concentration.

3.3. Acquisition of joint control in order to split assets immediately

24. In the case where several undertakings come together solely for the purpose of acquiring another company and agree to divide up the acquired assets according to a pre-existing plan immediately upon completion of the transaction, there is no effective concentration of economic power between the acquirers and the target company as the assets acquired are only jointly held and controlled for a "legal instant". This type of acquisition in order to split assets up immediately will in fact be considered as several operations, whereby each of the acquiring companies acquires its relevant part of the target company. For each of these operations, the undertakings concerned will therefore be the acquiring company, and that part of the target which it is acquiring just as if there was an acquisition of sole control of part of a company).

25. This scenario is referred to in the recital 24 of the Merger Regulation, which stipulates that the Merger Regulation applies to agreements whose sole object is to divide up the assets acquired immediately after the acquisition.

4. Acquisition of control by a joint venture

26. In transactions where a joint venture acquires control of another company, the question arises whether or not, from the point of view of the acquiring party, the joint venture should be taken as a single undertaking concerned (the turnover of which would include the turnover of its parent companies), or whether each of its parent companies should individually be considered as undertakings concerned. In other words, the issue is whether or not to "lift the corporate veil" of the

intermediate undertaking (the vehicle). In principle, the undertaking concerned is the direct participant in the acquisition of control. However, there may be circumstances where companies set up "shell" companies, which have no or insignificant turnover of their own, or use an existing joint venture which is operating on a different market from that of the target company in order to carry out acquisitions on behalf of the parent companies. Where the acquired or target company has a Community turnover of less than ECU 250 million the question of determining the undertakings concerned may be decisive for jurisdictional purposes.[9] In this type of situation the Commission will look at the economic reality of the operation to determine which are the undertakings concerned.

27. Where the acquisition is carried out by a full-function joint venture, *i.e.* a joint venture which has sufficient financial and other resources to operate a business activity on a lasting basis,[10] which is already operating on a market, the Commission will normally consider the joint venture itself and the target company to be the undertakings concerned (and not the joint venture's parent companies).

28. Conversely, where the joint venture can be regarded as a vehicle for an acquisition by the parent companies, the Commission will consider each of the parent companies themselves to be the undertakings concerned, rather than the joint venture, together with the target company. This is the case in particular where the joint venture is set up especially for the purpose of acquiring the target company, where the joint venture has not yet started to operate, where an existing joint venture has no legal personality or full-function character as referred to above; or where the joint venture is an association of undertakings. The same applies where there are elements which demonstrate that the parent companies are in fact the real players behind the operation. These elements may include a significant involvement by the parent companies themselves in the initiative, organization and financing of the operation. Moreover, where the acquisition leads to a substantial diversification in the nature of the joint venture's activities this may also indicate that the parent companies are the real players in the operation. This will normally be the case when the joint venture acquires a target company operating on a different product market. In those cases the parent companies should be regarded as undertakings concerned.

29. In the TNT case,[11] joint control over a joint venture (JVC) was to be acquired by a joint venture (GD NET BV) between five postal administrations and another acquiring company (TNT Ltd) (see below). In this case, the Commission considered that the joint venture GD NET BV was simply a vehicle set up to enable the parent companies (the five postal administrations) to participate in the resulting JVC joint venture in order to facilitate decision-making amongst themselves and to ensure that the parent companies spoke and acted as one; this configuration would ensure that the parent companies could exercise a decisive influence with the other acquiring company, TNT, over the resulting joint venture JVC and would avoid the situation where that other acquirer could exercise sole control because of the postal administrations' inability to reach a unified position on any decision.

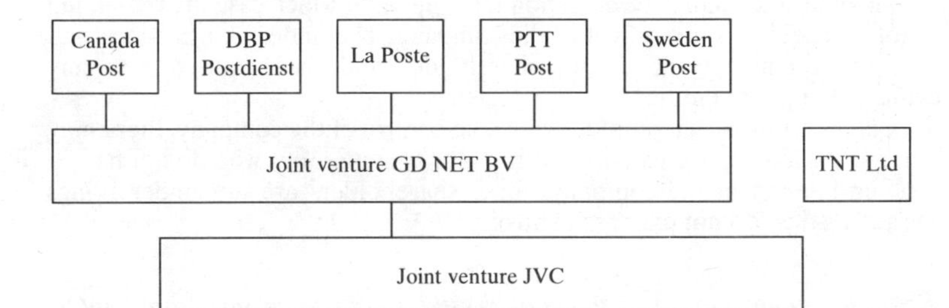

5. Passage from joint control to sole control

30. In the case of passage from joint control to sole Control, one shareholder acquires the stake previously held by the other shareholder(s). In the case of two

shareholders, each of them has joint control over the entire joint venture, and not sole control over 50 per cent of the joint venture; hence the sale of all of his shares by one shareholder to the other does not lead the sole remaining shareholder to pass from sole control over 50 per cent to sole control over 100 per cent of the joint venture, but rather to pass from joint control to sole control of the entire company (which, subsequently to the operation, ceases to be a "joint" venture).

31. In this situation, the undertakings concerned are the remaining (acquiring) shareholder and the joint venture. As is the case for any other seller, the "exiting" shareholder is not an undertaking concerned.

32. The ICI/Tioxide case[12] was precisely such a passage from joint (50/50) control to sole control. The Commission considered that '... decisive influence exercised solely is substantially different to decisive influence exercised jointly, since the latter has to take into account the potentially different interests of the other party or parties concerned ... By changing the quality of decisive influence exercised by ICI on Tioxide, the transaction will bring about a durable change of the structure of the concerned parties ...'. In this case, the undertakings concerned were held to be ICI (as acquirer) and Tioxide as a whole (as acquired), but not the seller Cookson.

6. Change in the shareholding in cases of joint control of an existing joint venture

33. The decisive element in assessing in the shareholding of a company is whether the operation leads to a change in the quality of control. The Commission assesses each operation on a case-by-case basis, but in certain hypotheses, there will be a presumption that the given operation leads, or respectively does not lead, to such a change in the quality of control, and thus constitutes a notifiable concentration.

34. A distinction must be made according to the circumstances of the change in the shareholding; first, one or more existing shareholder(s) can exit; secondly, one or more new additional shareholder(s) can enter, and thirdly, one or more existing shareholder(s) can be replaced by one or more new shareholder(s).

6.1. Reduction in the number of shareholders leading to passage from joint to sole control

35. It is not the reduction of shareholders *per se* which is important, but rather the fact that if some shareholders sell their stakes in a given joint venture, these stakes are then acquired by other (new or existing) shareholders, and thus that the acquisition of these stakes or additional contractual rights may lead to the acquisition of control or may strengthen an already existing position of control (*e.g.* additional voting rights or veto rights, additional board members, etc.).

36. Where the number of shareholders is reduced, there may be passage from joint control to sole control (see Section III.5. also), in which case the remaining shareholder acquires sole control of the company. The undertakings concerned will be the remaining (acquiring) shareholder and the acquired company (previously the joint venture).

37. In addition to the shareholder with sole control of the company, there may be other shareholders, for example with minority stakes, but who do not have a controlling interest in the company; these shareholders are not undertakings concerned as they do not exercise control.

6.2 Reduction in the number of shareholders not leading to passage from joint to sole control

38. Where the operation involves a reduction in the number of shareholders having joint control, without leading to the passage from joint to sole control and

without any new entry or substitution of shareholders acquiring control (see Section III.6.3.), the proposed transaction will normally be presumed not to lead to a change in the quality of control, and therefore not be a notifiable concentration. This would be the case where, for example, five shareholders initially have equal stakes of 20 per cent each, and where after the operation, one share-holder would exit, and the remaining four shareholders would each have equal stakes of 25 per cent.

39. However, this situation would be different where there is a significant change in the quality of control such as where the reduction of shareholders gives the remaining shareholders additional veto rights or additional board members which create a new acquisition of control by at least one of the shareholders, either through the application of the existing or a new shareholders' agreement. In this case, the undertakings concerned will be each of the remaining shareholders which exercise joint control and the joint venture. In Avesta II,[13] the fact that the number of major shareholders decreased from four to three led to one of the remaining shareholders acquiring negative veto rights (which it had not previously enjoyed) because of the provisions of the shareholders' agreement which remained in force.[14] This acquisition of full veto rights was considered by the Commission to represent a change in the quality of control.

6.3. Any other changes in the composition of the shareholding

40. Finally, in the case where following changes in the shareholding, one or more shareholders acquire control, the operation will constitute a notifiable operation as there is a presumption that the operation will normally lead to a change in the quality of control.

41. Irrespective of whether the number of shareholders decreases, increases or remains the same subsequent to the operation, this acquisition of control can take any of the following forms:

- entry of new shareholder(s) (either leading to the passage from sole to joint control, or situation of joint control both before and after the operation);
- acquisition of a controlling interest by minority shareholder(s) (either leading to the passage from sole to joint control, or situation of joint control both before and after the operation);
- substitution of shareholder(s) (situation of joint control both before and after the operation).

42. The question is whether the undertakings concerned are the joint venture and the new shareholder(s) who would together acquire control of a pre-existing company, or whether all of the shareholders (existing and new) are to be considered as undertakings concerned acquiring control of a new joint venture. This question is particularly relevant when there is no express agreement between one (or several) of the existing shareholders and the new shareholder(s), who might only have had an agreement with the "exiting" shareholder(s), *i.e.* the seller(s).

43. A change in the shareholding through the entry or ,substitution of shareholders is considered as leading to a change in the quality of control. This is because the entry of a new parent company, or the substitution of one parent company for another, is not comparable to the simple acquisition of part of a business as it implies a change in the nature and quality of control of the whole joint venture, even when, both before and after the operation, joint control is exercised by a given number of shareholders.

44. The Commission therefore considers that the undertakings concerned in cases where there are changes in the shareholding are the shareholders (both existing and new) who exercise joint control and the joint venture itself. As mentioned earlier, non-controlling shareholders are not undertakings concerned.

45. An example of such a change in the shareholding is the Synthomer/Yule

Catto case,[15] in which one of two parent companies with Joint control over the pre-existing joint venture was rcplaccd by a new parent company. Both parent companies with joint control the existing one and the new one) and the joint venture were considered as undertakings concerned.

7. "Demergers" and the break-up of companies

46. When two undertakings merge or set up a joint venture, then subsequently de-merge or break up their joint venture, and the assets[16] are split between the "demerging" parties differently from under the original configuration, there will normally be more than one acquisition of control (see the Annex).

47. For example, undertakings A and B merge and then subsequently demerge with a new asset configuration. There will be the acquisition by undertaking A of various assets (which may have been previously owned by itself, as well as assets previously owned by undertaking B and assets jointly acquired by the entity resulting from the merger), with similar acquisitions for undertaking B. Similarly, a break-up of a joint venture can be considered as the passage from joint control over the joint venture's entire assets to sole control over the divided assets. (See Solvay-Laporte/Interox.)[17]

48. A break-up of a company in this way is "asymmetrical". For such a demerger, the undertakings concerned (for each break-up operation) will be, on the one hand, the original parties to the merger and on the other, the assets that each original party is acquiring. For the break-up of a joint venture, the undertakings concerned (for each break-up operation) will be, on the one hand, the original parties to the joint venture, each as acquirer, and on the other, that part of the joint venture that each original party is acquiring.

8. Swaps of Assets[18]

49. In those transactions where two (or more) companies exchange assets, regardless of whether these constitute legal entities or not, each acquisition of control constitutes an independent concentration. Although it is true that both transfers of assets in a swap are usually considered by the parties to be interdependent, that they are often agreed in a single document, and that they may even take place simultaneously, the purpose of the Merger Regulation is to assess the impact of the operation resulting from the acquisition of control by each of the companies. The legal or even economic link between those operations is not sufficient for them to qualify as a single concentration.

50. Hence the undertakings concerned will for each property transfer be the acquiring companies, and the acquired companies or assets.

9. Acquisitions of control by individual persons

51. Article 3(1) of the Merger Regulation specifically provides that a concentration shall be deemed to arise, *inter alia*, where "one or more persons already controlling at least one undertaking" acquire control of the whole or parts of one or more undertakings. This text indicates that acquisitions of control by individuals will only bring about a lasting change in the structure of the companies concerned if those individuals carry out economic activities of their own. The Commission considers that the undertakings concerned are the target company and the individual acquirer (with the turnover of the undertaking(s) controlled by that individual being included in the calculation of turnover).

52. This was the view taken in the Commission decision in the Asko/Jacobs/Adia case,[19] where Asko, a German holding company with substantial retailing assets, and Mr Jacobs, a private Swiss investor, acquired joint control of Adia, a Swiss company active mainly in personnel services. Mr Jacobs was considered to be an undertaking concerned because of the economic interests he held in the industrial chocolate, sugar confectionary and coffee sectors.

10. Management buy-outs

53. An acquisition of control of a company by its own managers is also an acquisition by individuals, and what has been said above is therefore also applicable here. However, the management of the company may pool its interests through a "vehicle company", so that it acts with a single voice and also to facilitate decision making. Such a vehicle company may be, but is not necessarily, an undertaking concerned. The general rule on acquisitions of control by a joint venture applies here (see Section III.4.).

54. With or without a vehicle company, the management may also look for investors in order to finance the operation. Very often, the rights granted to these investors according to their shareholding may be such that control within the meaning of Article 3 of the Merger Regulation will be conferred on them and not on the management itself, which may simply enjoy minority rights. In the CWB/Goldman Sachs/Tarkett decision,[20] the two companies managing the investment funds taking part in the transaction were in fact those acquiring joint control, and not the managers.

11. Acquisition of control by a State-owned company

55. In those situations where a State-owned company merges with or acquires control of another company controlled by the same State,[21] the question arises as to whether these transactions really constitute concentrations within the meaning of Article 3 of the Regulation or rather internal restructuring operations of the "public sector group of companies".[22] In this respect, recital 12 of the Merger Regulation sets forth the principle of non-discrimination between the public and the private sectors and declares that "in the public sector, calculation of the turnover of an undertaking concerned in a concentration needs, therefore, to take account of undertakings making up an economic unit with an independent power of decision, irrespective of the way in which their capital is held or of the rules of administrative supervision applicable to them".

56. A merger or acquisition of control arising between two companies owned by the same State may constitute a concentration and, if it does, both of them will qualify as undertakings concerned, since the mere fact that two companies are both owned by the same State does not necessarily mean that they belong to the same "group". Indeed, the decisive issue will be whether or not these companies are both part of the same industrial holding and are subject to a certain co-ordinated strategy. This was the approach taken in the SGS/Thomson decision.[23]

[ANNEX]

"DE-MERGERS" AND BREAK UP OF COMPANIES[24]

Merger scenario

Before merger

Company A		Company B

After merger

Merged company
Combined assets

After breaking up the merger

Company A:	Company B:
Divided Assets of merged company: – some (initial) assets of A – some (initial) assets of B – some (subsequent) assets of the merged company	Divided Assets of merged company: – some (initial) assets of A – some (initial) assets of B – some (subsequent) assets of the merged company

Joint venture scenario

Before JV

Company A	Assets of A for the JV		Assets of B for the JV	Company B

After JV

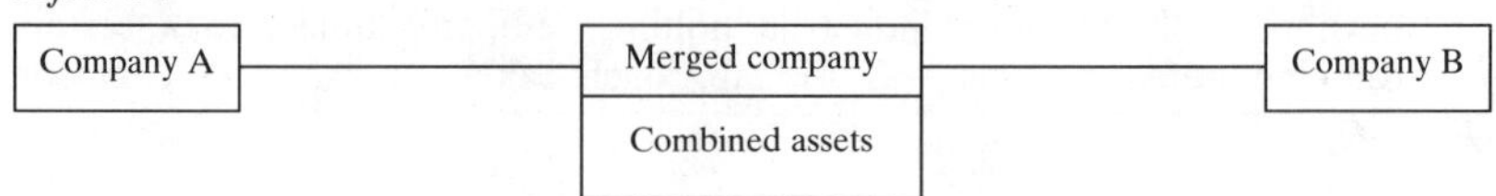

After breaking up the JV

Company A	Divided Assets of joint venture: – some (initial assets of A – some (initial) assets of B – some (subsequent) assets of the JV		Company B	Divided Assets of joint venture: – some (initial assets of A – some (initial) assets of B – some (subsequent) assets of the JV

[1] OJ 1994 C385/12.

[2] Council Regulation (EEC) No. 4064/89 of 21 December 1989 on the control of concentrations between undertakings (hereafter referred to as "the Merger Regulation"), OJ 1989 L395/1, corrected version OJ 1990 L257/13.

[3] The rules for calculating turnover in accordance with Article 5 are detailed in the Commission Notice on Calculation of Turnover.

[4] Commission Regulation (EC) No. 3384/94 of 21 December 1994 on the notifications, time limits and hearings provided for in Council Regulation (EEC) No. 4064/89 (thereafter referred to as the "Implementing Regulation") (OJ 1994 L377).

[5] See Judgment of the Court of First Instance of 24 March 1994 in Case T–3/93—*Air France v. Commission* not yet published).

[6] The calculation of turnover in the case of acquisitions or divestments subsequently to the date of the last audited accounts is dealt with in the Commission Notice on Calculation of Turnover, paragraph 27.

[7] The calculation of turnover in the case of company groups is dealt with in the Commission Notice on Calculation of Turnover, paragraphs 36 to 42.

[8] *i.e.* two or more companies (companies A, B, etc.) acquire a pre-existing company (company X). For changes in the shareholding in cases of joint control of an existing joint venture see Section III.6.

[9] The target company hypothetically has an aggregate Community turnover of less than ECU 250 million, and the acquiring parties are two (or more) undertakings, each with a Community turnover exceeding ECU 250 million. If the target is acquired by a "shell" company set up between the acquiring undertakings, there would be only one company (the "shell" company) with a Community turnover exceeding ECU 250 million, and thus one of the cumulative threshold conditions for Community jurisdiction would fail to be fulfilled (namely, the existence at least two undertakings with a Community turnover exceeding ECU 250 million). Conversely, if instead of acting through a "shell" company, the acquiring undertakings acquire the target company themselves, then the turnover threshold would be met and the Merger Regulation would apply to this transaction.

[10] The rules determining the full-function nature of a joint venture are contained in the Commission Notice regarding the distinction between concentrative and co-operative joint ventures, paragraphs 13 to 15.

[11] Case IV/M.102—TNT/Canada Post, DBP Postdienst, La Poste, PTT Post and Sweden Post, of 2 December 1991.

[12] Case IV/M.023—ICI/Tioxide, of 28 November 1990.

[13] Case IV/M.452—Avesta II, of 9 June 1994.

[14] In this case, a shareholder party to the shareholders' agreement sold its stake of approximately 7 per cent. As the exiting shareholder had shared veto rights with another shareholder who remained, and as the shareholders' agreement remained unchanged, the remaining shareholder now acquired full veto rights.

[15] Case IV/M.376—Synthomer/Yule Catto, of 22 October 1993.

[16] By "assets", reference is made to specific assets which in themselves could constitute a business (*e.g.* a subsidiary, a division of a company, in some cases brands or licences, etc.) to which a market turnover can clearly be attributed.

[17] Case No. IV/M.197—Solvey-Laporte/Interox, of 30 April 1992.

[18] See footnote 15.

[19] Case IV/M.082—Asko/Jacobs/Adia, of 16 May 1991.

[20] Case IV/M.395—CWB/Goldman Sachs/Tarkett, of 21 February 1994.

[21] By "State", reference is made to any legal public entity, *i.e.* Member States but also regional or local public entities such as provinces, departments, Länder, etc.

[22] See also Commission Notice on the notion of a concentration, paragraph 8.

[23] Case IV/M.216—CEA Industrie/France Telecom/Finmeccanica/SGS-Thomson, of 22 February 1993.

[24] By "assets", reference is made to specific assets which in themselves could constitute a business (*e.g.* a subsidiary, a division of a company, in certain cases brands or licences) to which a market turnover can clearly be attributed.

Appendix 13

COMMISSION NOTICE ON CALCULATION OF TURNOVER[1]

Under Council Regulation (EEC) No. 4064/89 of 21 December 1989 on the control of concentrations between undertakings[2]

The purpose of this notice is to expand upon the text of Articles 1 and 5 of Council Regulation (EEC) No. 4064/89 (hereinafter referred to as "the Merger Regulation") and in so doing to elucidate certain procedural and practical questions which have caused doubt or difficulty.

2. This notice is based on the experience gained by the Commission in applying the Merger Regulation to date. The principles it sets out will be followed and further developed by the Commission's practice in individual cases.

3. The Merger Regulation has a two-fold test for Commission jurisdiction. One test is that the transaction must be a concentration within the meaning of Article 3.[3] The second comprises the three turnover thresholds contained in Article I and which are designed to identify those transactions which have an impact upon the Community and can be deemed to be of "Community interest". In particular, the world-wide turnover threshold is intended to measure the overall dimension of the undertakings concerned, the Community turnover threshold seeks to determine whether they carry on a minimum level of activities in the Community and the two-thirds rule aims to exclude purely domestic transactions from Community jurisdiction. Turnover is used as a proxy for the economic resources and activity being combined in a concentration, and it is allocated geographically to reflect the geographic distribution of these resources and activity.

4. The thresholds as such are designed to establish jurisdiction and not to assess the market position of the parties to the concentration nor the impact of the operation. In so doing they include turnover derived from, and thus the resources devoted to, all areas of activity of the parties, and not just those directly involved in the concentration. Article 1 of the Merger Regulation sets out the thresholds to be used to determine a concentration of "Community dimension" while Article 5 explains how turnover should be calculated.

5. The fact that the thresholds of Article 1 of the Merger Regulation are purely quantitative, since they are only based on turnover calculation instead of market share or other criteria, shows that their aim is to provide a simple and objective mechanism that can be easily handled by the companies involved in a merger in order to determine if their transaction is of Community dimension and therefore notifiable.

6. The decisive issue for Article 1 of the Merger Regulation is to measure the economic strength of the undertakings concerned as reflected in their respective turnover figures, regardless of the sector where such turnover was achieved and of whether those sectors will be at all affected by the transaction in question. The Merger Regulation has thereby given priority to the determination of the overall economic and financial resources that are being combined through the merger in order to decide whether the latter is of Community interest.

7. In this context, it is clear that turnover should reflect as accurately as possible

the economic strength of the undertakings involved in a transaction. This is the purpose of the set of rules contained in Article 5 of the Merger Regulation which are designed to ensure that the resulting figures are a true representation of economic reality.

8. The Commission's interpretation of Articles 1 and 5 with respect to calculation of turnover is without prejudice to the interpretation which may be given by the Court of Justice or the Court of First Instance of the European Communities.

I. "ACCOUNTING" CALCULATION OF TURNOVER

1. Turnover as a reflection of activity

1.1 The concept of turnover

9. The concept of turnover as used in Article 5 of the Merger Regulation refers explicitly to "the amounts derived from the sale of products and the provision of services". Sale, as a reflection of the undertaking's activity, is thus the essential criterion for calculating turnover, whether for products or the provision of services. "Amounts derived from sale" generally appear in company accounts under the heading "sales".

10. In the case of products, turnover can be determined without difficulty, namely by identifying each commercial act involving a transfer of ownership.

11. In the case of services, the factors to be taken into account in calculating turnover are much more complex since the commercial act involves a transfer of "value".

12. Generally speaking, the method of calculating turnover in the case of services does not differ from that used in the case of products: the Commission takes into consideration the total amount of sales. Where the service provided is sold directly by the provider to the customer, the turnover of the undertaking concerned consists of the total amount of sales for the provision of services in the last financial year.

13. Because of the complexity of the service sector, this general principle may have to be adapted to the specific conditions of the service provided. Thus, in certain sectors of activity (such as tourism and advertising), the service may be sold through the intermediary of other suppliers. Because of the diversity of such sectors, many different situations may arise. For example, the turnover of a service undertaking which acts as an intermediary may consist solely of the amount of commissions which it receives.

14. Similarly, in a number of areas such as credit, financial services and insurance, technical problems in calculating turnover arise which will be dealt with in section III.

1.2. Ordinary activities

15. Article 5(1) states that the amounts to be included in the calculation of turnover must correspond to the "ordinary activities" of the undertakings concerned.

16. With regard to aid granted to undertakings by public bodies, any aid relating to one of the ordinary activities of an undertaking concerned is liable to be included in the calculation of turnover if the undertaking is itself the recipient of the aid and if the aid is directly linked to the sale of products and the provision of services by the undertaking and is therefore reflected in the price.[4] For example, aid towards the consumption of a product allows the manufacturer to sell at a higher price than that actually paid by consumers.

17. With regard to services, the Commission looks at the undertaking's ordinary activities involved in establishing the resources required for providing the service. In its Decision in the Accor/Wagons-Lits case,[5] the Commission decided to take into account the item "other operating proceeds" included in Wagons-Lits' profit and loss account. The Commission considered that the components of this item which included certain income from its car-hire activities were derived from the sale of products and the provision of services by Wagons-Lits and were part of its ordinary activities.

2. "Net" turnover

18. The turnover to be taken into account is "net" turnover, after deduction of a number of components specified in the Regulation. The Commission's aim is to adjust turnover in such a way as to enable it to decide on the real economic weight of the undertaking.

1.2.1. The deduction of rebates and taxes

19. Article 5(1) provides for the "deduction of sales rebates and of value added tax and other taxes directly related to turnover". The deductions thus relate to business components (sales rebates) and tax components (value added tax and other taxes directly related to turnover).

20. "Sales rebates" should be taken to mean all rebates or discounts which are granted by the undertakings during their business negotiations with their customers and which have a direct influence on the amounts of sales.

21. As regards the deduction of taxes, the Merger Regulation refers to VAT and "other taxes directly related to turnover". As far as VAT is concerned, its deduction does not in general pose any problem. The concept of "taxes directly related to turnover" is a clear reference to indirect taxation since it is directly linked to turnover, such as, for example, taxes on alcoholic beverages.

2.2 The deduction of "internal" turnover

22. The first subparagraph of Article 5(1) states that "the aggregate turnover of an undertaking concerned shall not include the sale of products or the provision of services between any of the undertakings referred to in paragraph 4", *i.e.* those which have links with the undertaking concerned (essentially parent companies or subsidiaries).

23. The aim is to exclude the proceeds of business dealings within a group so as to take account of the real economic weight of each entity. Thus, the "amounts" taken into account by the Merger Regulation reflect only the transactions which take place between the group of undertakings on the one hand and third parties on the other.

3. Adjustment of turnover calculation rules for the different types of operations

3.1. The general rule

24. According to Article 5(1) of the Merger Regulation "aggregate turnover within the meaning of Article 1(2) shall comprise the amounts derived by the undertakings concerned in the preceding financial year from the sale of products and the provision of services . . .". The basic principle is thus that for each undertaking concerned the turnover to be taken into account is the turnover of the closest financial year to the date of the transaction.

25. This provision shows that since there are usually no audited accounts of the year ending the day before the transaction, the closest representation of a whole year of activity of the company in question is the one given by the turnover figures of the most recent financial year.

26. The Commission seeks to base itself upon the most accurate and reliable figures available. As a general rule therefore, the Commission will refer to audited or other definitive accounts. However, in cases where major differences between the Community's accounting standards and those of a non-member country are observed, the Commission may consider it necessary to restate these accounts in accordance with Community standards in respect of turnover. The Commission is, in any case, reluctant to rely on provisional, management or any other form of provisional accounts in any but exceptional circumstances (see the next paragraph). Where a concentration takes place within the first months of the year and audited accounts are not yet available for the most recent financial year, the figures to be taken into account are those relating to the previous year. Where there is a major divergence between the two sets of accounts, and in particular, when the final draft figures for the most recent years are available, the Commission may decide to take those draft figures into account.

27. Notwithstanding paragraph 26, an adjustment Must always be made to account for acquisitions or divestments subsequent to the date of the audited accounts. This is necessary if the true resources being concentrated are to be identified. Thus if a company disposes of a subsidiary or closes a factory at any time before the signature of the final agreement or the announcement of the public bid or the acquisition of a controlling interest bringing about a concentration, or where such a divestment or closure is a pre-condition for the operation[6] the turnover generated by that subsidiary or factory must be subtracted from the turnover of the notifying party as shown in its last audited accounts. Conversely, the turnover generated by assets of which control has been acquired subsequent to the preparation of the most recent audited accounts must be added to a company's turnover for notification purposes.

28. Other factors that may affect turnover on a temporary basis such as a decrease of the orders of the product or a slow-down of the production process within the period prior to the transaction will be ignored for the purposes of calculating turnover. No. adjustment to the definitive accounts will be made to incorporate them.

29. Regarding the geographical allocation of turnover, since audited accounts often do not provide a geographical breakdown of the sort required by the Merger Regulation, the Commission will rely on the best figures available provided by the companies in accordance with the rule laid down in Article 5(1) of the Merger Regulation (see Section II.1).

3.2. Acquisitions of parts of companies

30. Article 5(2) of the Merger Regulation provides that "where the concentration consists in the acquisition of parts, whether or not constituted as legal entities, of one or more undertakings only the turnover relating to the parts which are the subject of the transaction shall be taken into account with regard to the seller or sellers".

31. This provision states that when the acquiror does not purchase an entire group, but only one or part of it businesses, whether or not constituted as a subsidiary, only the turnover of the part effectively acquired should be included in the turnover calculation. In fact, although in legal terms the seller as a whole (with all its subsidiaries) is an essential party to the transaction, since the sale-purchase agreement cannot be concluded without him, he plays no role once the agreement has been implemented. The possible impact of the transaction ir the marketplace will exclusively depend on the combination of the economic and financial

resources that are the subject of a property transfer with those of the acquiror and not on the part of the seller who remain independent.

3.3. Staggered operations

32. Sometimes certain successive transactions are only individual steps within a wider strategy between the same parties. Considering each transaction alone, even if only for determining jurisdiction, would imply ignoring economic reality. At the same time, whereas some of these staggered operations may be designed in this fashion because they will better. meet the needs of the parties, it is not excluded than others could be structured like this in order to circumvent the application of the Merger Regulation.

33. The Merger Regulation has foreseen these scenarios in Article 5(2), second subparagraph, which provides that "two or more transactions within the meaning of the first subparagraph which take place within a two-year period between the same persons or undertakings shall be treated as one and the same concentration arising on the date of the last transaction".

34. In practical terms, this provision means that if company A buys a subsidiary of company B that represents 50 per cent of the overall activity of B and one year later it acquires the other subsidiary (the remaining 50 per cent of B), both transactions will be taken as one. Assuming that each of the subsidiaries only attained a turnover in the Community of ECU 200 million, the first transaction would not be notifiable. However, since the second takes place within the two-year period, both have to be notified as a single transaction when the second occurs.

35. The importance of the provision is that previous transactions (within two years) become notifiable with the most recent transactions once the thresholds are cumulatively met.

3.4. Turnover of groups

36. When an undertaking concerned in a concentration within the meaning of Article 1 of the Merger Regulation,[7] belongs to a group, the turnover of the group as a whole is to be taken into account in order to determine whether the thresholds are met. The aim is again to capture the total volume of the economic resources that are being combined through the operation.

37. The Merger Regulation does not define the concept of group in abstract terms but focuses on whether the companies have the right to manage the undertaking's affairs as the yardstick to determine which of the companies that have some direct or indirect links with an undertaking concerned should be regarded as part of its group.

38. Article 5(4) of the Merger Regulation provides the following:

> "Without prejudice to paragraph 2 (acquisitions of parts) the aggregate turnover of an undertaking concerned within the meaning of Article 1(2) shall be calculated by adding together the respective turnovers of the following:
> (a) The undertaking concerned;
> (b) those undertakings in which the undertaking concerned directly or indirectly:
> — owns more than half the capital or business assets, or
> — has the power to exercise more than half the voting rights, or
> — has the power to appoint more than half the members of the supervisory board, the administrative board or bodies legally representing the undertakings, or
> — has the right to manage the undertakings' affairs;
> (c) those undertakings which have in the undertaking concerned the rights or powers listed in (b);

(d) those undertakings in which an undertaking as referred to in (c) has the rights or powers listed in (b);

(e) those undertakings in which two or more undertakings as referred to in (a) to (d) jointly have the rights or powers listed in (b)."

This means that the turnover of the company directly 3 involved in the transaction (subparagraph (a)) should include its subsidiaries (b), its parent companies (c), the other subsidiaries of its parent companies (d) and any other undertaking jointly controlled by two or more of the companies belonging to the group (e). A graphic example is as follows:

The undertaking concerned and its group:

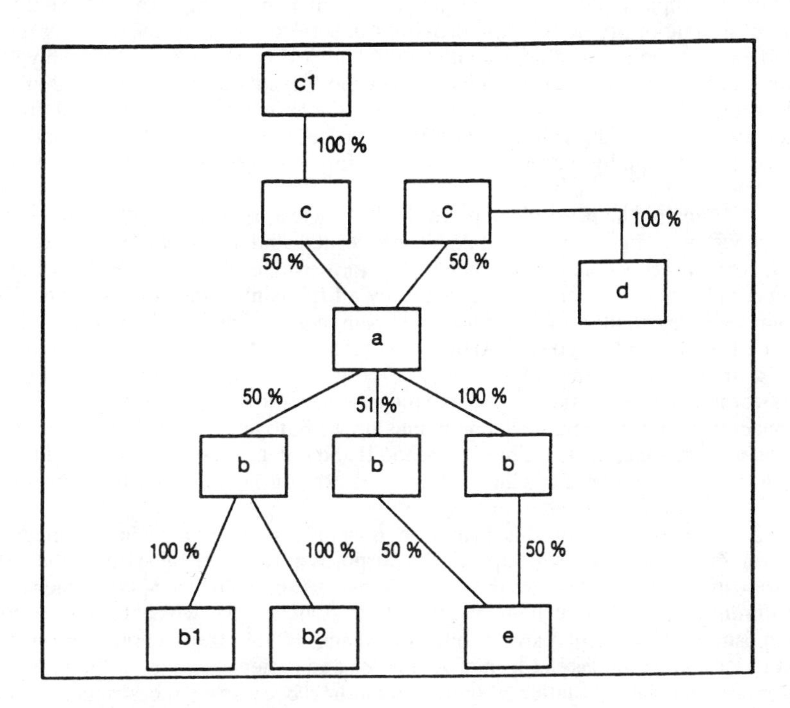

a: The undertaking concerned.
b: Its subsidiaries and their own subsidiaries (b1 and b2).
c: Its parent companies and their own parent companies (c1).
d: Other subsidiaries of the parent companies of the undertaking concerned.
e: Companies jointly controlled by two (or more) companies of the group.

Note: These letters correspond to the relevant subparagraphs of Article 5(4).

Several remarks can be made from this chart:

(1) As long as the test of control of subparagraph (b) is fulfilled, the whole turnover of the subsidiary in question will be taken into account regardless of the actual shareholding of the controlling company. In the example, the whole turnover of the three subsidiaries (called b) of the undertaking concerned (a) will be included.

(2) When any of the companies identified as belonging to the group also control others, these should also be incorporated to in the calculation. In the example, one of the subsidiaries of a (called b) has in turn its own subsidiaries b1 and b2.

(3) When two or more companies jointly control the undertaking concerned (a) in the sense that the agreement of each and all of them is needed in order to

manage the undertakings affairs, the turnover of all of them should be included.[8] In the example, the two parent companies (c) of the undertaking concerned (a) would be taken into account as well as their own parent companies (c1 in the example). Although the Merger Regulation does not explicitly mention this rule for those cases where the undertaking concerned is in fact a joint venture, it is inferred from the text of subparagraph (c), which uses the plural when referring to the parent companies. This interpretation has been consistently applied by the Commission.

(4) Any intra-group sale should be subtracted from the turnover of the group (see paragraph 22).

39. The Merger Regulation also deals with the specific scenario that arises when two or more undertakings concerned in a transaction exercise joint control of another company. Pursuant to point (a) of Article 5(5), the turnover resulting from the sale of products or the provision of services between the joint venture and each of the undertakings concerned or any other company concerned with any one of them should be excluded. The purpose of such a rule is to avoid double counting. With regard to the turnover of the joint venture generated from activities with third parties, point (b) of Article 5(5) provides that it shall be apportioned equally amongst the undertakings concerned, to reflect the joint control.[9]

40. Following the principle of point (b) of Article 5(5) by analogy, in the case of joint ventures between undertakings concerned and third parties, the Commission's practice has so far been to allocate to each of the undertakings concerned the turnover shared equally by all the controlling companies in the joint venture. In all these cases however, joint control has to be demonstrated.

41. It should be noted that Article 5(4) refers only to the groups that already exist at the time of the transaction, *i.e.* the group of each of the undertakings concerned in an operation, and not to the new structures created as a result of the concentration. For example, if companies A and B, together with their respective subsidiaries, are going to merge, it is A and B and not the new entity that qualify as undertakings concerned, which implies that the turnover of each of the two groups should be calculated independently.

42. Since the aim of this provision is simply to identify. The companies belonging to the existing groups for the purposes of turnover calculation, the test of having the right to manage the undertaking's affairs in Article 5(4) is somewhat different to the test of control set out in Article 3(3), which refers to the acquisition of control carried out by means of the transaction subject to examination. Whereas the former is simpler and easier to prove on the basis of factual evidence, the latter is more demanding because in the absence of an acquisition of control no concentration arises.

3.5. Turnover of State-owned companies

43. While Article 5(4) sets out the method to determine the economic grouping to which an undertaking concerned belongs for the purpose of calculating turnover, the Article's provisions should be read in conjunction with recital 12 of the Regulation in respect of State-owned enterprises. This recital states that in order to avoid discrimination between the public and private sector, account should be taken "of undertakings making up an economic unit with an independent power of decision irrespective of the way in which their capital is held or of the rules of administrative supervision applicable to them". Thus the mere fact that two companies are both State-owned should not automatically lead to the conclusion that they are part of a group for Article 5 purposes. Rather it should be considered whether there are grounds to consider that both companies constitute an independent economic unit.

44. Thus where a State-owned company is not part of an overall industrial holding company and is not subject to any co-ordination with other State-

controlled holdings, it should be treated as an independent group for the purposes of Article 5, and the turnover of other companies owned by that State should not be taken into account. Where, however, a Member State's interests are grouped together in holding companies, are managed together, or where for other reasons it is clear that State-owned companies form part of an "economic unit with an independent power of decision", then the turnover of those businesses should be considered part of the undertaking concerned's group for the purposes of Article 5.

II. GEOGRAPHICAL ALLOCATION OF TURNOVER

1. General rule

45. The second and third thresholds set by Article 1 select cases which have sufficient Community turnover to be of Community interest and which are primarily crossborder in nature. They both require turnover to be allocated geographically to achieve this. The second subparagraph of Article 5(1) provides that the location of turnover is determined by the location of the customer at the time of the transaction.

> "Turnover, in the Community or in a Member State, shall comprise products sold and services provided to undertakings or consumers, in the Community or in that Member State as the case may be."

46. The reference to "products sold" and "services provided" is not intended to discriminate between goods and services by focusing on where the sale takes place in the case of goods but the place where a service is provided (which might be different from where the service was sold) in the case of services. In both cases turnover should be attributed to the place where the customer is located because that is, in most circumstances, where a deal was made, where the turnover for the supplier in question was generated and where competition with alternative suppliers took place.[10] The second subparagraph of Article 5(1) does not focus on where a good or service is enjoyed or the benefit of the good or service derived. In the case of a mobile good, a motor car may well be driven across Europe by its purchaser but it was purchased at only one place—Paris, Berlin or Madrid say. This is also true in the case of those services where it is possible to separate the purchase of a service from its delivery. Thus in the case of package holidays, competition for the sale of holidays through travel agents takes place locally, as with retail shopping, even though the service may be provided in a number of distant locations. This turnover is, however, earned locally and not at the site of an eventual holiday.

47. This applies even where a multinational corporation has a Community buying strategy and sources all its requirements for a good or service from one location. The fact that the components are subsequently used in 10 different plants in a variety of Member States does not alter the fact that the transaction with a company outside the group occurred in only one country. The subsequent distribution to other sites is purely an internal question for the company concerned.

48. Certain sectors do, however, pose very particular problems with regard to the geographical allocation of turnover (see Section III).

2. Conversion of turnover into ecus

49. When converting turnover figures into ecus great care should be taken with the exchange rate used. The annual turnover of a company should be converted at the average rate for the 12 months concerned. This average can be obtained from the Commission. The audited annual turnover figures should not be broken down into component quarterly, monthly, or weekly sales figures and converted individually at the corresponding average quarterly, monthly or weekly rates and then the ecus figures summed to give a total for the year.

50. When a company has sales in a range of currencies, the procedure is no different. The total turnover given in the consolidated audited accounts and in that company's reporting currency is converted into ecus at the average rate for the 12 months. Local currency sales should not be converted directly into ecus since these figures are not from the consolidated audited accounts of the company.

III. CREDIT AND OTHER FINANCIAL INSTITUTIONS AND INSURANCE UNDERTAKINGS

1. Definitions

51. The specific nature of banking and insurance activities is formally recognised by the Merger Regulation which includes specific provisions dealing with the calculation of turnover for these sectors.[11] Although the Merger Regulation does not provide a definition of the terms, "credit institutions and other financial institutions" within the meaning of point (a) of Article 5(3), the Commission in its practice has consistently adopted the definitions provided in the first and second banking directives:

— "*Credit institution* means an undertaking whose business is to receive deposits or other repayable funds from the public and to grant credits for its own account".[12]
— "*Financial institution* shall mean an undertaking other than a credit institution, the principal activity of which is to acquire holdings or to carry one or more of the activities listed in points 2 to 12 in the Annex".[13]

52. From the definition of "financial institution" given above it is clear that on the one hand holding companies shall be considered as financial institutions and, on the other hand, that undertakings which perform on a regular basis as a principal activity one or more activities expressly mentioned in points 2 to 12 of the abovementioned Annex shall also be considered as financial institutions within the meaning of point (a) of Article 5(3) of the Merger Regulation. These activities include:

— lending (*inter alia*, consumer credit, mortgage credit factoring, . . .),
— financial leasing,
— money transmission services,
— issuing and managing instruments of payment (credit cards, travellers' cheques and bankers' drafts),
— guarantees and commitments,
— trading on own account or on account of customers in money market instruments, foreign exchange, financial futures and options, exchange and interest rate instruments, and transferable securities,
— participation in share issues and the provision of services related to such issues,
— advice to undertakings on capital structure, industrial strategy and related questions and advice and services relating to mergers and the purchase of undertakings,
— money broking,
— portfolio management and advice,
— safekeeping and administration of securities.

2. Calculation of turnover

53. The methods of calculation of turnover for credit and other financial institutions and for insurance undertakings are described in Article 5(3) of the Merger Regulation and examples are provided in guidance notes one and two respectively, annexed to Form CO. These provisions remain in force. The purpose

of this section is to provide an answer to supplementary questions related to turnover calculation for the abovementioned types of undertaking which were raised during the first years of the application of the Merger Regulation.

2.1. Credit and financial institutions (other than financial holding companies)

2.1.1. General

54. There are normally no particular difficulties in applying the rule of one-tenth of total assets for the definition of the world-wide turnover to credit institutions and other kinds of financial institutions. However, difficulties may arise with regard to the calculation of Community-wide turnover and the determination of the turnover within Member States for the purpose of application of the two-thirds rule.

55. Difficulties also arise with some financial institutions which do not provide loans and advances "*stricto sensu*" or when the credit granted, if any exists, is not a relevant indicator of the economic activity and weight of he undertakings concerned. This is the case, for example, with asset management companies, merchant banks, credit card companies, tradings in foreign exchange, money market instruments, financial futures and options, as the companies in question are mainly firms providing financial services rather than granting credit to business or individuals. In such cases, the determination of Community-wide turnover using the criteria established by the Merger Regulation cannot be applied meaningfully.

56. Therefore, with regard to the calculation of Community-wide turnover and turnover within a Member State, the concept of "loans and advances" should be interpreted broadly in order to include any kind of activity which could be assimilated to some form of credit activity. For example, the fact that a financial institution has a portfolio of bonds and other interest-bearing securities has been assimilated for the purpose of the application of the Merger Regulation to a means of granting credit and therefore the securities held have been considered as loans and advances.[14]

2.1.2. Turnover of leasing companies

57. There is a fundamental distinction to be made, for the purpose of application of point (a) of Article 5(3) of the Merger Regulation, between financial leases and operating leases. Basically, financial leases are made for longer periods than operating leases and ownership is generally transferred to the lessee at the end of the lease term by means of a bargain purchase option included in the lease contract. Under an operating lease, on the contrary, ownership is not transferred to the lessee at the end of the lease term and the cost of maintenance, repair and insurance of the leased equipment are included in the lease payments. A financial lease therefore functions as a loan by the lessor to enable the lessee to purchase a given asset. A financial leasing company is thus a financial institution within the meaning of point (a) of Article 5(3) and its turnover has to be calculated by applying the specific rules related to the calculation of turnover for credit and other financial institutions. Given that operational leasing activities do not have this lending function, they are not considered as carried out by financial institutions, at least as primary activities, and therefore the general turnover calculation rules of Article 5(1) should apply.[15]

2.1.3. Turnover of fund management companies

58. In the case of a fund management company, the relevant assets to be taken into account in the calculation of turnover by the one-tenth of assets rule are only those belonging to the fund management company itself and not the assets being managed on behalf of clients. The assets being managed do not belong to the fund

management company; they are held on a fiduciary basis and therefore either they are booked in "off balance sheet" accounts (not included in the total assets figure of the fund management company) or they have to be booked in financial statements completely independent of the accounts of the fund management company. However, commission generated by asset management should be counted, as such, as turnover of a fund management company. Hence the turnover of a fund management company, which manages both its own assets and assets belonging to clients, will be calculated as follows:

Own assets × $\frac{1}{10}$	= x
Commission or fees generated by management of clients' assets	= y
Total turnover	= x + y

2.2. Insurance undertakings

2.2.1. Gross premiums written

59. The application of the concept of gross premiums written as a measure of turnover for insurance undertakings has raised supplementary questions notwithstanding the definition provided in point (b) of Article 5(3) of the Merger Regulation. The following clarifications are appropriate:

— "gross" premiums written is the sum of received premiums (which may include received reinsurance premiums if the undertaking concerned has activities in the field of reinsurance). Outgoing or outward reinsurance premiums, *i.e.* all amounts paid and payable by the undertaking concerned to get reinsurance cover, are already included in the gross premiums written within the meaning of the Merger Regulation,

— wherever the word "premiums" is used (gross premiums, net (earned) premiums, outgoing reinsurance premiums etc.) these premiums are related not only to new insurance contracts made during the accounting year being considered but also to all premiums related to contracts made in previous years which remain in force during the period taken into consideration.

2.2.2. Investments of insurance undertakings

60. In order to constitute appropriate reserves allowing for the reimbursement of claims, insurance undertakings, which are also considered as institutional investors, usually hold a huge portfolio of investments in shares, interest-bearing securities, land and property and other assets which provide an annual revenue which is not considered as turnover for insurance undertakings.

61. However, with regard to the application of the Merger Regulation, a major distinction should be made between pure financial investments, in which the insurance undertaking is not involved in the management of the undertakings where the investments have been made, and those investments leading to the acquisition of a controlling interest in a given undertaking thus allowing the insurance undertaking to exert a decisive influence on the business conduct of the subsidiary or affiliated company concerned. In such cases Article 5(4) of the Merger Regulation would apply, and the turnover of the subsidiary or affiliated company should be added to the turnover of the insurance undertaking for the determination of the thresholds laid down in the Merger Regulation.[16]

2.3. Financial holding companies

62. A financial holding company is a financial institution and therefore the calculation of its turnover should follow the criteria established in point (a) of

Article 5(3) for the calculation of turnover for credit and other financial institutions. However, as the main purpose of a financial holding is to acquire and manage participation in other undertakings, Article 5(4) also applies, (as for insurance undertakings), with regard to those participations allowing the financial holding company to exercise a decisive influence on the business conduct of the undertakings in question. In such cases, the turnover figures of those undertakings obtained directly from the audited financial statements, or requiring special calculations (for example, turnover of banking and insurance undertakings) are simply added together in order to obtain the relevant turnover which will be used to determine whether the case falls under the Merger Regulation.

63. In these cases different accounting rules, in particular those related to the preparation of consolidated accounts, which are to some extent harmonised but not identical within the Community, may need to be taken into consideration. This applies to any type of undertaking concerned by the Merger Regulation but it is particularly important in the case of financial holding companies[17] where the number and the diversity of enterprises controlled and the degree of control the holding holds on its subsidiaries, affiliated and participated companies requires careful examination.

64. This method of calculation, of which an example is given in the following paragraphs, may in practice prove onerous. Therefore a strict and detailed application of this method will be necessary only in cases where it seems that the turnover of a financial holding company is likely to be close to the Merger Regulation thresholds; in other cases it may well be obvious that the turnover is far from the thresholds of the Merger Regulation, and therefore the published accounts are adequate for the establishment of jurisdiction.

Example of the calculation of turnover of financial holding companies

(a) Initially, it is necessary to consider the non-consolidated balance sheet of the financial holding company instead of the group consolidated accounts. Although this type of undertaking may have assets such as cash, plant property and equipment, the major part of the assets of a financial holding company are normally constituted by investments in shares, bonds and other interest bearing securities.

At the end of the most recent financial year the non-consolidated balance sheet of a financial holding company may be presented as follows, according to published financial statements:

(ECU million)

Assets		Liabilities	
Marketable Securities	2,000[1]	Debt	1,500
Participations	2,000[2]	Equity	2,500
Total Assets	4,000	Total Liabilities	4,000

[1] Marketable Securities are constituted by bonds and other interest bearing securities and shares held as pure financial investment in undertakings on which the holding company does not exercise any kind of influence.

[2] Participations represent investment in shares on a long-term basis in companies on which the holding company exerts some kind of influence.

(b) As the assets as presented do not provide the necessary information for the calculation of turnover under the Merger Regulation, a different break-down of assets is required:

	(ECU million)
(i) Bonds and other interest bearing securities	1,500
(ii) Shares in undertakings not controlled by the financial holding[18]	1,500
	3,000
(iii) Shareholding in undertakings controlled:	
of which insurance undertakings	500
industrial undertakings	500
	1,000
Total Assets	4,000

(c) To calculate the aggregate world-wide turnover of the financial holding company account should be taken separately of the turnover of the different activities of the group (industrial, financial and insurance) and then the amounts should be added in order to get the final amount. Turnover for insurance and industrial activities are already given (ECU 300 million and 2,000 million respectively). Assets which are not related to shareholding in undertakings controlled amount to ECU 3,000 million (see (i) and (ii) above). Therefore total world-wide turnover is as follows:

		ECU million
– Turnover related to financial activities $\frac{1}{10} \times 3{,}000$	=	300
– Turnover related to insurance activities gross premiums written	=	300
– Turnover of industrial activities		2,000
Total worldwide turnover Group ABC		2,600

Community-wide turnover and turnover in Member States calculations should follow the same principle. For Community-wide and Member States turnover calculations related to financial activities, bonds and other interest-bearing securities should be considered as loans and advances.

3. Geographical allocation of turnover of banking and insurance undertakings

65. The geographical turnover of banking and insurance undertakings is in principle allocated according to the place of residence of the beneficiaries of loans and advances for credit and other financial institutions, and of customers who pay insurance premiums in the case of insurance undertakings as stated in Article 5(3) of the Merger Regulation.

66. A particular problem which arises with financial institutions is how to allocate loans, and in particular the frequently large volumes of overnight interbank loans when the client is not a subsidiary as such, but a branch or division of a company or bank incorporated in a different country. Since the branch or division to which the loan is made is most likely to be the place where the loan will be used, it is only rational to allocate geographically that loan to the branch or division rather than the place of incorporation of the debtor company or bank, even if this is what the banks themselves take into account for risk assessment purposes.[19]

67. The current practice of the Commission is to consider, for banking and insurance undertakings, that branches, divisions and other undertakings operating on a lasting basis but not having a legal personality should be considered as residents in the countries in which they have been established.

4. Ecu exchange rate applicable to credit and financial institutions

68. The question of the appropriateness of average annual exchange rates for financial institutions arises, since for such institutions turnover calculations are based on data derived from the balance sheet, which represents a financial situation at a particular date, rather than the profit and loss account which

represents financial flows through time. However, in order to avoid using a separate method for this particular sectors the balance sheet asset values should be converted at the average rate for the 12 months preceding the balance sheet date, in conformity with the general rule.

[1] OJ 1994 C385/21.

[2] OJ 1989 L395/1, corrected version OJ 1990 L257.

[3] The concept of concentration is defined in the Notice on "the notion of concentration".

[4] See Case IV/M.156—Cereol/Continentale Italiana of 27 November 1991. In this case, the Commission excluded Community aid from the calculation of turnover because the aid was not intended to support the sale of products manufactured by one of the undertakings involved in the merger, but the producers of the raw materials (grain) used by the undertaking, which specialised in the crushing of grain.

[5] Case IV/M.126—Accor/Wagons-Lits, of 28 April 1992.

[6] See Judgment of 24 March 1994 of the Court of First Instance in Case T–3/93—*Air France v. Commission* (not yet published).

[7] See Commission Notice on the notion of undertakings concerned.

[8] See Commission Notice on the notion of undertakings concerned for acquisitions of control by a joint venture (paragraphs 26 to 29).

[9] For example, company A and company B set up a joint venture C. These two parent companies exercise at the same time joint control of company D, although A has 60 per cent and B 40 per cent of the capital. When calculating the turnover of A and B at the time they set up the new joint venture C, the turnover of D with third parties is attributed in equal parts to A and B.

[10] Where the place where the customer was located when purchasing the goods or service and the place where the billing was subsequently made are different, turnover should be allocated to the former.

[11] See Article 5(3) of the Merger Regulation.

[12] First Council Directive (77/780/EEC) of 12 December 1977 on the co-ordination of laws, regulations and administrative provisions relating to the taking up and pursuit of the business of credit institutions, Article 1 (OJ 1977 L322/30).

[13] Second Council Directive (89/646/EEC) of 15 December 1989 on the co-ordination of laws, regulations and administrative provisions relating to the taking up and pursuit of the business of credit institutions, Article 1(6) (OJ 1989 L386/1).

[14] See Case IV/M.166—Torras/Sarrió, of 24 February 1992.

[15] See Case IV/M.234—GECC/Avis Lease, 15 July 1992.

[16] See Case IV/M.018—AG/AMEV, of 21 November 1990.

[17] See for example Case IV/M.166—Torras Sarrió, of 24 February 1992, Case IV/M.213—Hong Kong and Shanghai Bank/Midland, of 21 May 1992, IV/M.192—Banesto/Totta, of 14 April 1992.

[18] "Controlled" in the sense of Article 5(4)(b) of the Merger Regulation.

[19] See Case IV/M.213—Hong Kong and Shanghai Bank/Midland, of 21 May 1992.

[20] OJ 1987 L256/1.

[21] OJ 1993 L241.

[22] OJ 1994 C342.

APPENDIX 14

COMMISSION REGULATION 870/95[1]

On the application of Article 85(3) of the Treaty to certain categories of agreements, decisions and concerted practices between liner shipping companies (consortia) pursuant to Council Regulation (EEC) No. 479/92

THE COMMISSION OF THE EUROPEAN COMMUNITIES,

Having regard to the Treaty establishing the European Community,

Having regard to Council Regulation (EEC) No. 479/92 of 25 February 1992 on the application of Article 85(3) of the Treaty to certain categories of agreements, decisions and concerted practices between liner shipping companies (consortia),[2] as amended by the Act of Accession of Austria, Finland and Sweden, and in particular Article 1 thereof,

Having published a draft of this Regulation,[3]

Having consulted the Advisory Committee on Restrictive Practices and Dominant Positions in Maritime Transport,

(1) Whereas certain categories of agreements, decisions and concerted practices between shipping companies relating to the joint operation of liner transport services (consortia), through the co-operation they bring about between the shipping companies that are parties thereto, are liable to restrict competition within the common market and to affect trade between Member States and may therefore be caught by the prohibition contained in Article 85(1) of the Treaty;

(2) Whereas the analysis carried out by the Commission of consortium agreements indicates that a large number of agreements may nevertheless normally be regarded as fulfilling the requirements of Article 85(3); whereas this category of consortia should be defined;

(3) Whereas the Commission has taken due account of the special features of maritime transport; whereas those features will also constitute a material factor in any Commission assessment of consortia not covered by this block exemption:

(4) Whereas consortia, as defined in this Regulation, generally help to improve the productivity and quality of available liner shipping services by reason of the rationalization they bring to the activities of member companies and through the economies of scale they allow in the operation of vessels and utilization of port facilities; whereas they also help to promote technical and economic progress by facilitating and encouraging greater utilization of containers and more efficient use of vessel capacity;

(5) Whereas users of the shipping services provided by consortia generally obtain a fair share of the benefits resulting from the improvements in productivity and service quality which they bring about; whereas these benefits may also take the form of an improvement in the frequency of sailings and port calls, or an improvement in scheduling as well as better quality and personalised services through the use of more modern vessels and other equipment including port facilities; whereas users can benefit

effectively from consortia only if there is sufficient competition in the trades in which the consortia operate;

(6) Whereas these agreements should therefore benefit from a block exemption, provided they do not give the companies concerned the possibility of eliminating competition in a substantial part of the trade in question; whereas in order to take account of the constant fluctuations in the maritime transport market and the frequent changes made by the parties to the terms of consortium agreements or to the activities covered by the agreements, an object of this Regulation is to clarify the conditions to be met by consortia in order to benefit from the block exemption it grants;

(7) Whereas, for the purpose of establishing and running a joint service, an essential feature inherent in consortia is the ability to make capacity adjustments; whereas the non-utilization of a certain percentage of vessel capacity within a consortium is not an essential feature of consortia;

(8) Whereas the block exemption granted by this Regulation covers both consortia operating within a liner conference and consortia operating outside such conferences, except that it does not cover the joint fixing of freight rates;

(9) Whereas rate fixing activities come under Council Regulation (EEC) No. 4056/86,[4] as amended by the Act of Accession of Austria, Finland and Sweden; whereas consortium members that wish to fix rates jointly and do not satisfy the criteria of Regulation (EEC) No. 4056/86 must apply for individual exemption;

(10) Whereas the first of the conditions attaching to the block exemption should be that a fair share of the benefits resulting from the improved efficiency, as well as the other benefits offered by consortia, are passed on to transport users;

(11) Whereas this requirement of Article 85(3) should be regarded as being met when a consortium is in one or more of the three situations described below:

— there is effective price competition between the members of the conference within which the consortium operates as a result of independent rate action,

— there exists within the conference within which the consortium operates a sufficient degree of effective competition in terms of services provided between consortium members and other conference members that are not members of the consortium, as a result of the fact that the conference agreement expressly allows consortia to offer their own service arrangements, *e.g.* the provision by the consortium alone of a "just-in-time delivery" service or an advanced "electronic data interchange" (EDI) service allowing users to be kept informed at all times of the whereabouts of their goods, or a significant increase in the frequency of sailings and calls in the service offered by a consortium compared with that offered by the conference,

— consortium members are subject to effective, actual or potential competition from non-consortium lines, whether or not a conference operates in the trade in question;

(12) Whereas, in order to satisfy this same requirement of Article 85(3), provision should be made for a further condition aimed at promoting individual competition as to quality of service between consortium members as well as between consortium members and other shipping companies operating in the trade;

(13) Whereas it should be a condition that consortia and their members do not, in respect of a given route, apply rates and conditions of carriage which are differentiated solely by reference to the country of origin or destination of the goods carried and thus cause within the Community deflections of trade that are harmful to certain ports, shippers, carriers or providers of services ancillary to transport, unless such rates or conditions can be economically justified;

(14) Whereas the aim of the conditions should also be to prevent consortia from imposing restrictions of competition which are not indispensable to the attainment of the objectives justifying the grant of the exemption; whereas, to this end, consortium agreements should contain a provision enabling each shipping line party to the agreement to withdraw from the consortium provided it gives reasonable notice; whereas, however, provision should be made in the case of highly integrated and/or high-investment consortia. for a longer notice period in order to take account of the higher investments undertaken to set them up and the more extensive reorganization entailed in the event of a member leaving; whereas it should also be stipulated that, where a consortium operates with a joint marketing structure, each member must have the right to engage in independent marketing activities provided it gives reasonable notice;

(15) Whereas exemption must be limited to consortia which do not have the possibility of eliminating competition in a substantial part of the services in question;

(16) Whereas for the purposes of block exemption and for reasons of legal certainty, reference will be made to the consortium's share of direct trade between the ranges of ports it serves, calculated on the overall basis of all of those ports;

(17) Whereas in order to determine for the purposes of individual exemption whether effective competition exists, account should be taken both of direct trade between the ranges of ports covered by a consortium as well as of any competition from other liner services sailing from ports which may be substituted for those served by the consortium and also, where appropriate, of other modes of transport;

(18) Whereas the block exemption granted by this Regulation is hence applicable only on condition that this share of the trade held by a consortium does not exceed a given size;

(19) Whereas the share of the trade held by a consortium within a conference should be smaller in view of the fact that the agreements in question are superimposed on an existing restrictive agreement in the trade;

(20) Whereas, however, it is appropriate to offer consortia which exceed the limits laid down in this Regulation by a given percentage but which continue to be subject to effective competition in the trades in which they operate a simplified procedure so that they may benefit from the legal certainty afforded by block exemptions; whereas such a procedure must also enable the Commission to carry out effective monitoring and simplify the administrative control of agreements;

(21) Whereas, however, consortia which exceed the latter limit may benefit from exemption by individual decision provided they satisfy the tests of Article 85(3), taking account of the special features of maritime transport;

(22) Whereas this Regulation applies only to agreements concluded between the members of a consortium; whereas, therefore, the block exemption does not cover restrictive agreements concluded between, on the one hand, consortia or one or more of their members, and, on the other hand, other shipping companies; whereas it also does not apply to restrictive agreements between different consortia operating in the same trade or between the members of such consortia;

(23) Whereas certain obligations must also be attached to the exemption; whereas in this respect transport users must at all times be in a position to acquaint themselves with the conditions for the provision of the maritime transport services jointly operated by the members of the consortium; whereas provision should be made for real and effective consultations between the consortia and transport users on the activities covered by the agreements; whereas this Regulation also specifies what is meant by real and effective consultations and what main procedural stages are to be followed for such consultations; whereas provision is made for such

mandatory consultation, limited to the activities of consortia as such, in view of the present degree of openness of the market in question; whereas maintenance of this requirement in the event of amendment of this Regulation will have to be reviewed in the light of market trends;

(24) Whereas such consultations are likely to secure a more efficient operation of maritime transport services which takes account of users' requirements; whereas, consequently, certain restrictive practises which could ensue from such consultations should be exempted;

(25) Whereas, for the purposes of this Regulation, the concept of *force majeure* is that laid down by the Court of Justice of the European Communities in its established case law;

(26) Whereas provisions should be made that awards given at arbitration and recommendations made by conciliators and accepted by the parties be modified forthwith to the Commission in order to enable it to verify that consortia are not thereby exempted from the conditions and obligations provided for in the Regulation and thus do not infringe the provisions of Articles 85 and 86;

(27) Whereas this Regulation should provide, in accordance with Article 3 of Regulation (EEC) No. 479/92, that it applies with retroactive effect to agreements, decisions and concerted practices which were in existence at the date of its entry into force, provided they meet the conditions and obligations established in this Regulation;

(28) Whereas it is necessary to provide that, for the duration of the specified period, the prohibition laid down in Article 85(1) of the Treaty does not apply to consortium agreements existing at the date of its entry into force and not satisfying the conditions of Article 85(3) as specified in this Regulation, if they have been modified in the six months following the entry into force of this Regulation in order to meet its conditions and if the amendments are modified to the Commission;

(29) Whereas provision should be made for fair and positive treatment of consortia which exist at the time of entry into force of this Regulation and which, whilst exceeding the limits on the share of trade laid down by this Regulation as a condition for exemption, satisfy the other conditions of this Regulation;

(30) Whereas it is necessary to specify, in accordance with Article 6 of Regulation (EEC) No. 479/92; the cases in which the Commission may withdraw from companies the benefit of the block exemption;

(31) Whereas no applications under Article 12 of Regulation (EEC) No. 4056/86 need be made in respect of agreements automatically exempted by this Regulation; whereas, however, when real doubts exist, companies may request the Commission to declare whether their agreements comply with this Regulation;

(32) Whereas this Regulation is without prejudice to the application of Article 86 of the Treaty,

HAS ADOPTED THIS REGULATION:

CHAPTER I

DEFINITIONS AND SCOPE

Article 1

Definitions

For the purposes of this Regulation:

— "*consortium*" means an agreement between two or more vessel-operating carriers which provide international liner shipping services exclusively for the carriage of cargo, chiefly by container, relating to a particular trade and the object of which is to bring about co-operation in the joint operation of a maritime transport service, which improves the service which would be offered individually by each of its members in the absence of the consortium, in order to rationalize their operations by means of technical, operational and/or commercial arrangements, with the exception of price fixing,

— "*liner shipping*" means the transport of goods on a regular basis on a particular route or routes between ports and in accordance with timetables and sailing dated advertised in advance and available, even on an occasional basis, to any transport user against payment,

— "*service arrangement*" means a contractual arrangement concluded between one or more transport users and an individual member of a consortium or a consortium itself under which a user, in return for an undertaking to have the latter transport a certain quantity of goods over a given period of time, receives an individual undertaking from the consortium member or the consortium to provide an individualised service of a given quality and which is specially tailored to its needs,

— "*transport user*" means any undertaking (*e.g.* shipper, consignee, forwarder, etc.) which has entered into, or demonstrated an intention to enter into, a contractual agreement with a consortium (or one of its members) for the shipment of goods, or any association of shippers,

— "*independent rate action*" means the right of a maritime conference member to offer, on a case-by-case basis and in respect of goods, freight rates which differ from those laid down in the conference tariff, provided notice is given to the other conference members.

Article 2

Scope

This regulations shall apply to consortia only in so far as they provide international liner transport services from or to one or more Community ports.

CHAPTER II

EXEMPTIONS

Article 3

Exempted agreements

1. Pursuant to Article 85(3) of the E.C. Treaty and subject to the conditions and obligations laid down in this Regulation, it is hereby declared that Article 85(1) of the Treaty shall not apply to the activities listed in paragraph 2 of this Article when contained in consortia agreements as defined in Articles 1 and 2 of this Regulation.

2. The declaration of non-applicability shall apply only to the following activities:

(a) joint operation of liner shipping transport services which comprise solely the following activities:

(i) co-ordination and/or joint fixing of sailing timetables and the determination of ports of call;

(ii) the exchange, sale or cross-chartering of space or slots on vessels;
(iii) the pooling of vessels and/or port installations;
(iv) the use of one or more joint operations offices;
(v) the provision of containers, chassis and other equipment and/or rental, leasing or purchase contracts for such equipment;
(vi) the use of a computerized data exchange system and/or joint documentation system;

(b) temporary capacity adjustments;
(c) the joint operation or use of port terminals and related services (*e.g.* lighterage or stevedoring services);
(d) the participation in one or more of the following pools; tonnage, revenue or net revenue;
(e) the joint exercise of voting rights held by the consortium in the conference within which its members operate, in so far as the vote being jointly exercised concerns the consortium's activities as such;
(f) a joint marketing structure and/or the issue of a joint bill of lading; ;
(g) any other activity ancillary to those referred to above in points (a) to (f) which is necessary for their implementation.

Article 4

Non-utilization of capacity

The exemption provided for in Article 3 shall not apply to a consortium when the consortium includes arrangements concerning the non-utilization of existing capacity whereby shipping line members of the consortium refrain from using a certain percentage of the capacity of vessels operated within the framework of the consortium.

CHAPTER III

CONDITIONS ATTACHING TO EXEMPTION

Article 5

Basic condition for the grant of exemption

The exemption provided for in Article 3 shall apply only if more of the conditions set out below are met:

— there is effective price competitions between the members of the conference within which the consortium operates due to the fact that the members are expressly authorized by the conference agreement, whether by virtue of a statutory obligation or otherwise, to apply independent rate action to any freight rate provided for in the conference tariff, or
— there exists within the conference within which the consortium operates a sufficient degree of effective competition between the conference members in terms of the services provided, due to the fact that the conference agreement expressly allows the consortium to offer its own service arrangements, irrespective of form, concerning the frequency and quality of trans port services provided as well as freedom at all times to adapt the services it offers in response to specific requests from transport users, or
— whether or not a conference operates in the trade in question, the consortium members are subject to effective competition, actual or potential, from shipping lines which are not members of that consortium.

Article 6

Conditions relating to share or trade

1. In order to benefit from the exemption provided for An Article 3, a consortium must possess, in respect of the ranges of ports it serves, a share of the direct trade of under 30 per cent, calculated by reference to the volume of goods carried (freight tonnes or 20-foot equivalent units) when it operates within a conference, and under 35 per cent when it operates outside a conference.

2. The exemption provided for in Article 3 shall continue to apply if the share of the trade referred to in paragraph 1 of this Article is exceeded during any period of two consecutive calendar years by not more than one 10th.

3. Where one of the limits specified in paragraphs 1 and 2 is exceeded, the exemption provided for in Article 3 shall continue to apply for a period of six months following the end of the calendar year during which it was exceeded. This period shall be extended to 12 months if the excess is due to the withdrawal from the trade of a carrier which is not a member of the consortium.

Article 7

Opposition procedure

1. The exemption provided for in Articles 3 and 10 shall also apply to consortia whose share of the trade exceeds the limit laid down in Article 6 but does not, however, exceed 50 per cent of the direct trade, on condition that the agreements in question are notified to the Commission in accordance with the provisions of Commission Regulation (EEC) No. 4260/88,[5] and that the Commission does not oppose such exemption within a period of six months.

2. The period of six months shall run from the date on which notification is received by the Commission. Where, however, the notification is made by registered post, the period shall run from the date shown on the postmark of the place of posting.

3. Paragraph 1 shall apply only if:

(a) express reference is made to this Article in the notification or in a communication accompanying it;
(b) the information furnished with the notification is complete and in accordance with the facts.

4. The benefit of paragraph 1 may also be claimed for agreements notified before the entry into force of this Regulation by submitting a communication to the Commission referring expressly to this Article and to the notification. Paragraphs 2 and 3(b) shall apply *mutatis mutandis*.

5. The Commission may oppose the exemption. It shall oppose the exemption if it receives a request to do so from a Member State within three months of the forwarding to the Member State of the notification referred to in paragraph 1 or of the communication referred to in paragraph 4. This request must be justified on the basis of considerations relating to the competition rules of the Treaty.

6. The Commission may withdraw its opposition to the exemption at any time. However, where the opposition was raised at the request of a Member State and this request is maintained, it may be withdrawn only after consultation of the Advisory Committee on Restrictive Practices and Dominant Positions in Maritime Transport.

7. If the opposition is withdrawn because the undertakings concerned have shown that the conditions of Article 85(3) are fulfilled, the exemption shall apply from the date of notification.

8. If the opposition is withdrawn because the undertakings concerned have amended the agreement so that the conditions of Article 85(3) are fulfilled, the exemption shall apply from the date on which the amendments take effect.

9. If the Commission opposes exemption and its opposition is not withdrawn, the effects of the notification shall be governed by the provisions of Section 11 of Regulation (EEC) No. 4056/86.

Article 8

Other conditions

Eligibility for the exemptions provided for in Articles 3 and 10 shall be subject to the following conditions:

1. The consortium must allow each of its members to offer, on the basis of an individual contract, its own service arrangements.

2. The consortium agreement must give member companies the right to withdraw from the consortium without financial or other penalty such as, in particular, an obligation to cease all transport activity in the trade, whether or not coupled with the condition that such activity may be resumed only after a certain period has elapsed. This right shall be subject to a maximum notice period of six months which may be given after an initial period of 18 months starting from the entry into force of the agreement.

However, in the case of a highly integrated consortium which has a net revenue pool and/or high level of investment due to the purchase or charter by its members of vessels specifically for the purpose of setting up the consortium, the maximum notice period shall be six months, which may be given after an initial period of 30 months starting from the entry into force of the agreement.

3. Where a consortium operates with a joint marketing structure, each member of the consortium must be free to engage in independent marketing without penalty subject to a maximum period of notice of six months.

4. Neither the consortium nor consortia members shall, within the common market, cause detriment to certain ports, users or carriers by applying to the carriage of the same goods and in the area covered by the agreement, rates and conditions of carriage which differ according to the country of origin or destination or port of loading or discharge, unless such rates or conditions can be economically justified.

CHAPTER IV

OBLIGATIONS

Article 9

Obligations attaching to exemption

The following obligations shall be attached to the exemption provided for in Article 3:

1. There shall be real and effective consultations between users or their representative organizations, on the one hand, and the consortium, on the other hand, for the purpose of seeking solutions on all important matters, other than purely operational matters of minor importance, concerning the conditions and quality of scheduled maritime transport services offered by the consortium or its members.

These consultations shall take place whenever requested by any of the abovementioned parties.

The consultations must take place, except in cases of *force majeure*, prior to the implementation of the measure forming the subject of the consultation. If, for reasons of *force majeure*, the members of the consortium are obliged to put a decision into effect before consultations have taken place, any consultations requested shall take place within 10 working days of the date of the request. Save in the case of such *force majeure*, to which reference shall be made in the notice announcing the measure, no public announcement of the measure shall be made before the consultations.

The consultations shall take place in accordance with following procedural stages:

(a) prior to the consultation, details of the subject-matter of the consultation shall be notified in writing by the consortium to the other party;
(b) an exchange of views shall take place between the parties either in writing or at meetings or both in the course of which the representatives of the consortium members and of the shippers taking part will have authority to reach a common point of view and the parties shall use their best efforts to achieve that end;
(c) where no common point of view can be reached despite the efforts of both parties, the disagreement shall be acknowledged and publicly announced. It may be brought to the Commission's attention by either party;
(d) a reasonable period for the completion of consultations may be fixed, if possible, by common agreement between the two parties. That period shall be not less than one month, save in exceptional cases or by agreement between the parties.

2. The conditions concerning the maritime transport services provided by the consortium and its members, including those relating to the quality of such services and all relevant modifications, shall be made available on request to transport users at reasonable cost and shall be available for examination without cost at the offices of the consortium members, or the consortium itself, and their agents.

3. Arbitration awards and recommendations of conciliators that have been accepted by the parties and settle disputes concerning practices of consortia covered by this Regulation shall be notified forthwith to the Commission by the consortium.

4. Any consortium claiming the benefit of this Regulation must be able, on being given a period of notice which the Commission shall determine on a case-by-case basis and which shall be not less than one month, to demonstrate at the Commission's request that the conditions and obligations imposed by Articles 5 to 8 and points 1 and 2 of this Article are met and must submit to it the consortium agreement in question within this period.

Article 10

Exemption for agreements between transport users and consortia concerning the use of scheduled maritime transport services

Agreements, decisions and concerted practices between transport users or their representative organizations, on the one hand, and a consortium exempted under Article 3, on the other hand, concerning the conditions and quality of liner shipping services provided by the consortium and all general questions connected with such services, in so far as they arise out of the consultations provided for in point 1 of Article 9, are hereby exempted from the prohibition laid down in Article 85(1) of that Treaty.

CHAPTER V

MISCELLANEOUS PROVISIONS

Article 11

Professional secrecy

1. Information acquired as a result of the application of Article 7 and point 4 of Article 9 shall be used only for the purposes of this Regulation.

2. The Commission and the authorities of the Member States, their officials and other servants shall not disclose information acquired by them as a result of the application of this Regulation which is of the kind covered by the obligation of professional secrecy.

3. The provisions of paragraphs 1 and 2 shall not prevent publication of general information or studies which do not contain information relating to particular undertakings or associations of undertakings.

Article 12

Withdrawal of block exemption

The Commission may withdraw the benefit of this Regulation, in accordance with Article 6 of Regulation (EEC) No. 479/92, where it finds in a particular case that an agreement, decision or concerted practice exempted under this Regulation nevertheless has certain effects which are incompatible with the conditions laid down by Article 85(3) or are prohibited by Article 86 of the Treaty, in particular where:

1. In a given trade, competition from outside the conference within which the consortium operates or from outside a particular consortium is not effective;
2. a consortium fails repeatedly to comply with the obligations provided for in Article 9;
3. the behaviour of a consortium produces effects that are incompatible with Article 86 of the Treaty;
4. such effects result from an arbitration award.

Article 13

Final provisions

This Regulation shall enter into force on the day following its publication in the *Official Journal of the European Communities*. It shall be valid for a period of five years starting from the date of its entry into force.

It shall apply with retroactive effect to agreements, decisions and concerted practice which were in existence at the date of its entry into force, from the time when the conditions for exemption were met.

In the case of agreements, decisions and concerted practices which were in existence on the date of entry into force of this Regulation and which did not on that date meet the conditions and obligations set out herein, the prohibition laid down in Article 85(1) of the Treaty shall not apply to the period before they were amended in order to satisfy those conditions, provided such amendment is made within six months of such entry into force and is communicated to the Commission within the same period.

However, during a period of six months following the entry into force of this Regulation the opposition procedure provided for in Article 7 may be applied to consortia which, whilst exceeding the limit on the share of trade, nevertheless satisfy the other conditions set out in this Regulation.

This Regulation shall be binding in its entirety and directly applicable in all Member States.

Done at Brussels, 20 April 1995.

[1] OJ 1995 L89/7.
[2] OJ 1955 L55/3.
[3] OJ 1994 C63/8.
[4] OJ 1986 L378/4.
[4] OJ 1988 L376/1.

APPENDIX 15

DIRECTIVE 93/84/EEC[1]

Amending Directive 80/723/EEC on the transparency of financial relations between Member States and public undertakings

THE COMMISSION OF THE EUROPEAN COMMUNITIES,

Having regard to the Treaty establishing the European Economic Community, and in particular Article 90(3) thereof,

Whereas Commission Directive 80/723/EEC,[2] as amended by Directive 85/413/EEC,[3] introduced a system whereby Member States were placed under an obligation to ensure that financial relations between public authorities and public undertakings are transparent; whereas that Directive required certain financial information to be retained by Member States and supplied to the Commission when requested;

Whereas Directive 80/723/EEC contains provisions, particularly in Articles 3 and 5, which may facilitate the Commission's task in meeting the obligations it has assumed;

Whereas public undertakings play an important role in the economies of Member States; whereas the need for transparency of financial relations between the Member States and their public undertakings has proved greater than before, on account of developments in the competitive situation in the common market, especially as the Community is moving towards close economic integration and social cohesion;

Whereas the Member States have adopted a Single European Act which in turn has led to the creation of the Single Market with effect from January 1, 1993; whereas this will lead to greater competitive pressures and to a need for the Commission to be vigilant in ensuring that the benefits of the Single Market are achieved; whereas the Single Market makes it increasingly necessary to ensure that an equality of opportunity exists between both public and private undertakings;

Whereas it has been established that a significant part of the financial flows between a State and its public undertakings pass though a variety of forms of financial transfers and do not simply take the form of capital or quasi-capital injections;

Whereas it is predominantly in the manufacturing sector that the Commission has established that a considerable amount of aid has been granted to undertakings but not notified pursuant to Article 93(3) of the Treaty; whereas the first,[4] second,[5] and third[6] State aid surveys confirm that large amounts of State aid continue to be granted illegally;

Whereas a reporting system based on *ex post facto* checks of the financial flows between public authorities and public undertakings will enable the Commission to fulfil its obligations; whereas that system of control must cover specific financial information; whereas such information is not always publicly available and, as it is found in the public arena, is insufficiently detailed to allow a proper evaluation of the financial flows between the State and public undertakings;

Whereas all of the information requested can be regarded as being proportional to the objective pursued, taking account of the fact that such information is already subject to the disclosure obligations under the Fourth Council Directive 78/660/EEC[7] concerning the annual accounts of companies, as last amended by Directive 90/605/EEC;[8]

Whereas, in order to limit the administrative burden on Member States, the reporting system should make use of both publicly available data and information available majority shareholders; whereas the presentation of consolidated reports is to be permitted; whereas incompatible aid to major undertakings operating in the manufacturing sector will have the greatest distortive effect on competition in the common market; whereas, therefore, such a reporting system may at present be limited to undertakings with a yearly turnover of more that ECU 250 million;

Whereas, although the Commission, when notifying the Directive in 1980, took the view that movements of funds within a public undertakings or group of public undertakings were not subject to the requirements of Directive 80/723/EEC, the inclusion of such information is called for by the new requirements of economic life, which is often influenced by State intervention via public undertakings; whereas, as has been underlined in the case-law of the Court of Justice since 1980,[9] infringements of the provisions of Article 93(3) by Member States have increased appreciably, thereby making the Commission's monitoring tasks in the field of competition more and more difficult; whereas the Commission's powers of vigilance must therefore be increased,

HAS ADOPTED THIS DIRECTIVE;

Article 1

Directive 80/723/EEC is amended as follows:

1. in Article 2 the following indent is added:
   "public undertakings operating in the manufacturing sector" means:
   all undertakings whose principal area of activity, defined as being at least 50 per cent of total annual turnover, is in manufacturing. These undertakings are those whose operations fall to be included in Section D—Manufacturing (being subsection DA up to and including subsection DN) of the NACE (Rev. 1) classification.[10]
2. Article 5a is inserted as follows:
   "*Article 5a*
   1. Member States whose public undertakings operate in the manufacturing sector shall supply the financial information as set out in paragraph 2 to the Commission on an annual basis within the timetable contained in paragraph 4.
   2. The financial information required for each public undertaking operating in the manufacturing sector and in accordance with paragraph 3 shall be as follows:
   (i) The annual report and annual accounts, in accordance with the definition of Council Directive 78/660/EEC.[11] The annual accounts and annual report include the balance sheet and profit/loss account, explanatory notes, together with accounting policies, statements by directors, segmental and activity reports. Moreover, notices of shareholders' meetings and any other pertinent information shall be provided.

   The following details, in so far as not disclosed in the annual report and annual accounts of each public undertaking, shall also be provided:
   (ii) the provision of any share capital or quasi-capital funds similar in nature to equity, specifying the terms of its or their provision (whether ordinary, preference, deferred or convertible shares and interest rates; the dividend or conversion rights attaching thereto);

(iii) non-refundable grants, or grants which are only refundable in certain circumstances;
(iv) the award to the enterprise of any loans, including overdrafts and advances on capital injections, with a specification of interest rates and the terms of the loan and its security, if any, given to the lender by the enterprise receiving the loan;
(v) guarantees given to the enterprise by public authorities in respect of loan finance (specifying terms and any charges paid by enterprises for these guarantees);
(vi) dividends paid out and profits retained;
(vii) any other forms of State intervention, in particular, the forgiving of sums due to the State by a public undertaking, including, *inter alia*, the repayment of loans, grants, payment of corporate or social taxes or any similar charges.

3. The information required by paragraph 2 shall be provided for all public undertakings whose turnover for the most recent financial year was more than ECU 250 million.
The information required above shall be supplied separately for each public undertaking including those located in the Member States, and shall include, where appropriate, details of all intra- and inter-group transactions between different public undertakings, as well as transactions conducted direct between public under taking and the State. The share capital referred to in paragraph 2(ii) shall include share capital contributed by the State direct and any share capital received contributed by a public holding company or other public undertaking (including financial institutions), whether inside or outside the same group, to a given public undertaking. The relationship between the provider of the finance and the recipient shall always be specified. Similarly, the reports required in paragraph 2 shall be provided for each individual public undertakings separately, as well as for the (sub)-holding company which consolidates several public undertakings in so far as the consolidated sales of the (sub)-holding company lead to its being classified as "manufacturing".
Certain public enterprises split their activities into several legally distinct undertakings. For such enterprises the Commission is willing to accept one consolidated report. The consolidation should reflect the economic reality of a group of enterprises operating in the same or closely related sectors. Consolidated reports from diverse, and purely financial, holdings shall not be sufficient.

4. The information required under paragraph 2 shall be supplied to the Commission on an annual basis. The information in respect of the financial year 1992 shall be forwarded to the Commission within two months of publication of this Directive.
For 1993 and subsequent years, the information shall be provided within 15 working days of the date of publication of the annual report of the public undertaking concerned. In any case, and specifically for undertakings which do not publish an annual report the required information shall be submitted not later than nine months following the end of the undertaking's financial year.
In order to assess the number of companies covered by this reporting system, Member States shall supply to the Commission a list of the companies covered by this Article and their turnover, within two months of publication of this Directive. The list is to be updated by 31 March of each year.

5. This Article is applicable to companies owned or controlled by the Treuhandanstalt only from the expiry date of the special reporting system set up for Treuhandanstalt investments.

6. Member States will furnish the Commission with any additional information that it deems necessary in order to complete a thorough appraisal of the data submitted."

Article 2

Member States shall adopt the provision necessary to comply with this Directive by 1 November 1993. They shall inform the Commission thereof immediately.

When Member States adopt these provisions, these shall contain a reference to this Directive or shall be accompanied by such reference at the time of their official publication. The procedure for such reference shall be adopted by Member States.

Article 3

This Directive is addressed to the Member States.

Done at Brussels, 30 September 1993.

[1] OJ 1993 L254/16.
[2] OJ 1980 L195/35.
[3] OJ 1985 L229/20.
[4] ISBN 92–825–9535.
[5] ISBN 9–826–0386.
[6] ISBN 92–826–4637.
[7] OJ 1978 L222/11.
[8] OJ 1990 L317/60.
[9] See, for example, the Judgments in Case 290/83 *Commission v. France* [1985] ECR 439 (agriculture credit fund), Joined Cases 67, 68 and 70/85 *Van der Kooy v. Commission* [1988] ECR, p. 219, Case 303/88 *Italy v. Commission* [1991] ECR-I, p. 1433 (ENI-Lanerossi) and Case C–305/89 *Italy v. Commission* [1991] I ECR 1603 (IRI, Finmeccanica and Alfa Romeo).
[10] OJ 1993 L83.
[11] OJ 1978 L222/11.

APPENDIX 16

COMMISSION NOTICE ON CO-OPERATION BETWEEN NATIONAL COURTS AND THE COMMISSION IN THE STATE AID FIELD[1]

The purpose of this Notice is to offer guidance on co-operation between national courts and the Commission in the State aid field. The Notice does not in any way limit the rights conferred on Member States, individuals or undertakings by Community law. It is without prejudice to any interpretation of Community law which may be given by the Court of Justice and the Court of First Instance of the European Communities. Finally, it does not seek to interfere in any way with the fulfilment by national courts of their duties.

I. INTRODUCTION

1. The elimination of internal frontiers between Member States enables undertakings in the Community to expand their activities throughout the internal market and consumers to benefit from increased competition. These advantages must not be jeopardized by distortions of competition caused by aid granted unjustifiably to undertakings. The completion of the internal market thus reaffirms the importance of enforcement of the Community's competition policy.

2. The Court of Justice has delivered a number of important judgments on the interpretation and application of Articles 92 and 93 of the E.C. Treaty. The Court of First Instance now has jurisdiction over actions by private parties against the Commission's State aid decisions and will thus also contribute to the development of case law in this field. The Commission is responsible for the day-to-day application of the competition rules under the supervision of the Court of First Instance and the Court of Justice. Public authorities and courts in the Member States, together with the Community's courts and the Commission each assume their own tasks and responsibilities for the enforcement of the E.C. Treaty's State aid rules, in accordance with the principles laid down by the case law of the Court of Justice.

3. The proper application of competition policy in the internal market may require effective co-operation between the Commission and national courts. This Notice explains how the Commission intends to assist national courts by instituting closer co-operation in the application of Articles 92 and 93 in individual cases. Concern is frequently expressed that the Commission's final decisions in State aid cases are reached some time after the distortions of competition have damaged the interests of third parties. While the Commission is not always in a position to act promptly to safeguard the interests of third parties in State aid matters, national courts may be better placed to ensure that breaches of the last sentence of Article 93(3) are dealt with and remedied.

II. POWERS[2]

4. The Commission is the administrative authority responsible for the implementation and development of competition policy in the Community's public interest. National courts are responsible for the protection of rights and the

enforcement of duties, usually at the behest of private parties. The Commission must examine all aid measures which fall under Article 92(1) in order to assess their compatibility with the common market. National courts must make sure that Member States comply with their procedural obligations.

5. The last sentence of Article 93(3) [*sic.*] has direct effect in the legal order of the Member States:

"The Commission shall be informed, in sufficient time to enable to submit its comments, of any plans to grant or alter aid. If it considers that any such plan is not compatible with the common market having regard to Article 92, it shall without delay initiate the procedure provided for in paragraph 2. The Member State concerned shall not put its proposed measures into effect until this procedure has resulted in a final decision."

6. The prohibition on implementation referred to in the last sentence of Article 93(3) extends to all aid which has been implemented without being notified[3] and, in the event of notification, operates during the preliminary period and, if the Commission sets in motion the contentious procedure, until the final decision.[4]

7. Of course a court will have to consider whether the "proposed measures" constitute State aid within the meaning of Article 92(1)[5] before reaching a decision under the last sentence of Article 93(3). The Commission's decisions and the Court's case law devote considerable attention to this important question. Accordingly, the notion of State aid must be interpreted widely to encompass not only subsidies, but also tax concessions and investments from public funds made in circumstances in which a private investor would have withheld support.[6] The aid must come from the "State", which includes all levels, manifestations and emanations of public authority.[7] The aid must favour certain undertakings or the production of certain goods: this serves to distinguish State aid to which Article 92(1) applies from general measures to which it does not.[8] For example, measures which have neither as their object nor as their effect the favouring of certain undertakings or the production of certain goods, or which apply to persons in accordance with objective criteria without regard to the location, sector or undertaking in which the beneficiary may be employed, are not considered to be State aid.

8. Only the Commission can decide that State aid is "compatible with the common market", *i.e.* authorised.

9. In applying Article 92(1), national courts may of course refer preliminary questions to the Court of Justice pursuant to Article 177 of the E.C. Treaty and indeed must do so in certain circumstances. They may also request assistance from the Commission by asking it for "legal or economic information" by analogy with the Court's Delimitis[9] judgment in respect of Article 85 of the E.C. Treaty.

10. The national court's role is to safeguard rights which individuals enjoy as a result of the direct effect of the prohibition laid down in the last sentence of Article 93(3). The court should use all appropriate devices and remedies and apply all relevant provisions of national law to implement the direct effect of this obligation placed by the Treaty on Member States.[10] A national court must, in a case within its jurisdiction, apply Community law in its entirety and protect rights which that law confers on individuals; it must therefore set aside any provision of national law which may conflict with it, whether prior or subsequent to the Community rule.[11] The judge may, as appropriate and in accordance with applicable rules of national law and the developing case law of the Court of Justice,[12] grant interim relief, for example by ordering the freezing or return of monies illegally paid, and award damages to parties whose interests are harmed.

11. The Court of Justice has held that the full effectiveness of Community rules would be impaired and the protection of the rights which they grant would be weakened if individuals were unable to obtain redress when their rights are infringed by a breach of Community law for which a Member State can be held responsible,[13] the principle whereby a State must be liable for loss and damage caused to individuals as a result of breaches of Community law for which the State can be held responsible is inherent in the system of the Treaty,[14] a national court which considers, in a case concerning Community law, that the sole obstacle

precluding it from granting interim relief is a rule of national law, must set aside that rule.[15]

12. These principles apply in the event of a breach of the Community's competition rules. Individuals and undertakings must have access to all procedural rules and remedies provided for by national law on the same conditions as would apply if a comparable breach of national law were involved. This equality of treatment concerns not only the definitive finding of a breach of directly effective Community law, but extends also to all legal means capable of contributing to effective legal protection.

III. THE COMMISSION'S LIMITED POWERS

13. The application of Community competition law by the national courts has considerable advantages for individuals and undertakings. The Commission cannot award damages for loss suffered as a result of an infringement of Article 93(3). Such claims may be brought only before the national courts. National courts can usually adopt interim measures and order the termination of infringements quickly. Before national courts, it is possible to combine a claim under Community law with a claim under national law. This is not possible in a procedure before the Commission. In addition, courts may award costs to the successful applicant. This is never possible in the administrative procedure before the Commission.

IV. APPLICATION OF ARTICLE 93(3)

14. Member States are required to notify to the Commission all plans to grant aid or to alter aid plans already approved. This also applies to aid that may qualify for automatic approval under Article 92(2), because the Commission has to check that the requisite conditions are met. The only exception to the notification obligation is for aid classed as *de minimis* because it does not affect trade between Member States significantly and thus does not fall within Article 92(1).[16]

15. The Commission receives notification of general schemes or programmes of aid, as well as of plans to grant aid to individual firms. Once a scheme has been authorized by the Commission, individual awards of aid under the scheme do not normally have to be notified. However, under some of the aid codes or frameworks for particular industries or particular types of aid, individual notification is required of all awards of aid or of awards exceeding a certain amount. Individual notification may also be required in some cases by the terms of the Commission's authorization of a given scheme. Member States must notify aid which they wish to grant outside the framework of an authorized scheme. Notification is required in respect of planned measures, including plans to make financial transfers from public funds to public or private sector enterprises, which may involve aid within the meaning of Article 92(1).

16. The first question which national courts have to consider in an action under the last sentence of Article 93(3) is whether the measure constitutes new or existing State aid within the meaning aid of Article 92(1). The second question to be answered is whether the measure has been notified either individually or under a scheme and if so, whether the Commission has had sufficient time to come to a decision.[17]

17. With respect to aid schemes, a period of two months is considered by the Court of Justice to be "sufficient time", after which the Member State concerned may, after giving the Commission prior notice, implement the notified measure.[18] This period is reduced by the Commission voluntarily to 30 working days for individual cases and 20 working days under the "accelerated" procedure. The periods run from the time the Commission is satisfied that the information provided by the Member State is sufficient to enable it to reach a decision.[19]

18. If the Commission has decided to initiate the procedure provided for in Article 93(2), the period during which the implementation of an aid measure is prohibited runs until the Commission has reached a positive decision. For

non-notified aid measures, no deadline exists for the Commission's decision-making process, although the Commission will act as speedily as possible. Aid may not be awarded before the Commission's final decision.

19. If the Commission has not ruled on an aid measure, national courts can always be guided, in interpreting Community law, by the case-law of the Court of First Instance and the Court of Justice, as well as by decisions issued by the Commission. The Commission has published a number of general notices which may be of assistance in this regard.[20]

20. National courts should thus be able to decide whether or not the measure at issue is illegal under Article 93(3). Where national courts have doubts, they may and in some cases must request a preliminary ruling from the Court of Justice in accordance with Article 177

21. Where national courts give judgment finding that Article 93(3) has not been complied with, they must rule that the measure at issue infringes Community law and take the appropriate measures to safeguard the rights enjoyed by individuals and undertakings.

V. EFFECTS OF COMMISSION DECISIONS

22. The Court of Justice has held[21] that a national court is bound by a Commission decision addressed to a Member State under Article 93(2) where the beneficiary of the aid in question seeks to question the validity of the decision of which it had been informed in writing by the Member State concerned and where it had failed to bring an action for annulment of the decision within the time limits prescribed by Article 173 of the EC Treaty.

VI. CO-OPERATION BETWEEN NATIONAL COURTS AND THE COMMISSION

23. The Commission realises that the principles set out above for the application of Articles 92 and 93 by national courts are complex and may sometimes be insufficiently developed to enable them to carry out their judicial duties properly. National courts may therefore ask the Commission for assistance.

24. Article 5 of the EC Treaty establishes the principle of loyal and constant co-operation between the Community institutions and the Member States with a view to attaining the objectives of the Treaty, including implementation of Article 3(g), which provides for the establishment of a system ensuring that competition in the internal market is not distorted. This principle involves obligations and duties of mutual assistance, both for the Member States and for the Community institutions. Under Article 5, the Commission has a duty of co-operation with the judicial authorities of the Member States which are responsible for ensuring that Community law is applied and respected in the national legal order.

25. The Commission considers that such co-operation is essential in order to guarantee the strict, effective and consistent application of Community competition law. In addition, participation by the national courts in the application of competition law in the field of State aid is necessary to give effect to Article 93(3). The Treaty obliges the Commission to follow the procedure laid down in Article 93(2) before it can order reimbursement of aid which is incompatible with the common market.[22] The Court has ruled that Article 93(3) has direct effect and that the illegality of an aid measure, and the consequences that flow therefrom, can never be validated retroactively by a positive decision of the Commission on an aid measure. Application of the rules on notification in the field of State aid therefore constitutes an essential link in the chain of possible legal action by individuals and undertakings.

26. In the light of these considerations, the Commission intends to work towards closer co-operation with national courts in the following manner.

27. The Commission is committed to a policy of openness and transparency. The Commission conducts its policy so as to give the parties concerned useful information on the application of competition rules. To this end, it will continue to

publish as much information as possible about State aid cases and policy. The case-law of the Court of Justice and Court of First Instance, general texts on State aid published by the Commission, decisions taken by the Commission, the Commission's annual reports on competition policy and the monthly Bulletin of the European Union may assist national courts in examining individual cases.

28. If these general pointers are insufficient, national courts may, within the limits of their national procedural law, ask the Commission, for information of a procedural nature to enable them to discover whether a certain case is pending before the Commission, whether a case has been the subject of a notification or whether the Commission has officially initiated a procedure or taken any other decision.

29. National courts may also consult the Commission where the application of Article 92(1) or Article 93(3) causes particular difficulties. As far as Article 92(1) is concerned, these difficulties may relate in particular to the characterisation of the measure as State aid, the possible distortion of competition to which it may give rise and the effect on trade between Member States. Courts may therefore consult the Commission on its customary practice in relation to these issues. They may obtain information from the Commission regarding factual data, statistics, market studies and economic analyses. Where possible, the Commission will communicate these data or will indicate the source from which they can be obtained.

30. In its answer, the Commission will not go into the substance of the individual case or the compatibility of the measure with the common market. The answer given by the Commission will not be binding on the requesting court. The Commission will make it clear that its view is not definitive and that the court's right to request a preliminary ruling from the Court of Justice pursuant to Article 177 is unaffected.

31. It is in the interests of the proper administration of justice that the Commission should answer requests for legal and factual information in the shortest possible time. Nevertheless, the Commission cannot accede to such requests unless several conditions are met. The requisite data must actually be at its disposal and the Commission may communicate only non-confidential information.

32. Article 214 of the EC Treaty requires the Commission not to disclose information of a confidential nature. In addition, the duty of loyal co-operation under Article 5 applies to the relationship between courts and the Commission, and does not concern the parties to the dispute pending before those courts. The Commission is obliged to respect legal neutrality and objectivity. Consequently, it will not accede to requests for information unless they come from a national court, either directly, or indirectly through parties which have been ordered by the court concerned to request certain information.

VII. FINAL REMARKS

33. This Notice applies *mutatis mutandis* to relevant State aid rules, in so far as they have direct effect in the legal order of Member States, of:

- the Treaty establishing the European Coal and Steel Community and provisions adopted thereunder, and
- the Agreement on the European Economic Area.

34. This Notice is issued for guidance and does not in any way limit the rights conferred on Member States, individuals or undertakings by Community law.

35. This Notice is without prejudice to any interpretation of Community law which may be given by the Court of Justice and Court of First Instance of the European Communities.

36. A summary of the answers given by the Commission pursuant to this Notice will be published annually in the Report on Competition Policy.

Done at Brussels, 31 October 1995.

[1] DOC C(95) 2436 final.

[2] The Court of Justice has described the roles of the Commission and the national courts in the following way:

"9. As far as the role of the Commission is concerned, the Court pointed out in its Judgment in Case 78/96, *Steinlike and Weinlig v. Germany* [1977] ECR 595, at paragraph 9, that the intention of the Treaty, in providing through Article 93 for aid to be kept under constant review and supervised by the Commission, is that the finding that aid may be incompatible with the common market is to be arrived at, subject to review by the court by means of an appropriate procedure which it is the Commission's responsibility to set in motion.
10. As far as the role of national courts is concerned, the Court held in the same judgment that proceedings may be commenced before national courts requiring those courts to interpret and apply the concept of aid contained in Article 92 in order to determine whether State aid introduced without observance of the preliminary examination procedure provided for in Article 93(3) ought to have been subject to this procedure.
11. The involvement of national courts is the result of the direct effect which the last sentence of Article 93(3) of the Treaty has been held to have. In this respect, the Court stated in its judgment in Case 120/73, *Lorenz v. Germany* [1973] ECR 1471 that the immediate enforceability of the prohibition on implementation referred to in that article extends to all aid which has been implemented without being notified and, in the event of notification, operates during the preliminary period, and if the Commission sets in motion the contentious procedure, until the final decision.
14. ... The principal and exclusive role conferred on the Commission by Articles 92 and 93 of the Treaty, which is to hold aid to bc incompatible with the common market where this is appropriate, is fundamentally different from the role of national courts in safeguarding rights which individuals enjoy as a result of the direct effect of the prohibition laid down in the last sentence of Article 93(3) of the Treaty. Whilst the Commission must examine the compatibility of the proposed aid with the common market, even where the Member State has acted in breach of the prohibition on giving effect to aid, national courts do no more than preserve, until the final decision of the Commission, the rights of individuals faced with a possible breach by State authorities of the prohibition laid down by the last sentence of Article 93(3)."

Case C–354/90, *Fédération nationale du commerce extérieur des produits alimentaires and Syndicat national des négociants et transformateurs de saumon v. France* [1991] ECR I–5505 paras. 9, 10, 11 and 14, at pp. 5527 and 5528.

[3] With the exception of "existing" aid. Such aid may be implemented until the Commission has decided that is it incompatible with the common market: see Case C–387/92, *Banco de Crédito Industrial*, now *Banco Exterior de Espana v. Ayuntamiento de Valencia* [1994] ECR I–877 and Case C–44/93, *Namur—Les Assurances du Crédit v. Office National du Ducroire and Belgium* [1994] ECR I–3829.

[4] Case C–354/90, cited at footnote 1, § 11 at p. 5527.

[5] See the Court of Justice's judgment in Case 78/76, *Steinlike and Weinlig v. Germany* [1977] ECR 595, § 14: "... a national court may have cause to interpret and apply the concept of aid contained in Article 92 in order to determine whether State aid introduced without observance of the preliminary examination procedure provided for in Article 93(3) ought to have been subject to this procedure."

[6] For a recent formulation, see Adv. Gen. Jacobs' Opinion in Joined Cases C–278/92, C–279/92 and C–280/92, *Spain v. Commission*, § 28: "... State aid is granted whenever a Member State makes available to an undertaking funds which in the normal course of events would not be provided by a private investor applying normal commercial criteria and disregarding other considerations of a social, political or philanthropic nature."

[7] The Court of Justice held in Case 290/83, *Commission v. France* [1985] ECR 439, that "... The prohibition contained in Article 92 covers all aid granted by a Member State or through State resources and there is no necessity to draw any distinction according to whether the aid is granted directly by the State or by public or private bodies established or appointed by it to administer the aid" (§ 4 at p. 449).

[8] A clear statement of this distinction is to be found in Adv. Gen. Darmon's Opinion in Joined Cases C–72 and C–73/91, *Sloman Neptun* [1993] ECR I–887.

[9] Case C–234/89, *Delimitis v. Henninger Bräu* [1991] ECR I–935; Commission notice on co-operation between national courts and the Commission in applying Articles 85 and 86 of the EC Treaty, OJ 1993 C39/6. See Adv. Gen. Lenz's Opinion in Case C–44/93, cited at footnote 2 (para. 106). See also Case C–2/88, Imm. Zwartveld [1990] ECR I–3365 and I–4405: "the Community institutions are under a duty of sincere co-operation with the judicial authorities of the Member States, which are responsible for ensuring that

Community law is applied and respected in the national legal system" (§ 1 at p. I–3366 and para. 10 at pp. 4410 and 4411, respectively).

[10] As the Court of Justice held in Case C–354/90, cited at footnote 1, § 12 at p. 5528: "... the validity of measures giving effect to aid is affected if national authorities act in breach of the last sentence of Article 93(3) of the Treaty. National courts must offer to individuals in a position to rely on such breach the certain prospect that all the necessary inferences will be drawn, in accordance with their national law, as regards the validity of measures giving effect to the aid, the recovery of financial support granted in disregard of that provision and possible interim measures."

[11] Case 106/77, *Amministrazione delle Finanze dello Stato v. Simmenthal* [1978] ECR 629, (§ 1 at p. 644). See also Case C–213/89, *The Queen v. Secretary of State for Transport, ex parte Factortame Ltd et al.* [1990] ECR I–2433, at p. 2475.

[12] Joined Cases C–6/90 and C–9/90, *Andrea Francovich et al. v. Italy* [1991] ECR I–5357. Other important cases are pending before the Court concerning the responsibilities of national courts in the application of Community law: Case C–48/93, *The Queen v. Secretary of State for Transport, ex parte Factortame Ltd and others*, OJ 1993 C94/13; Case C–46/93, *Brasserie du Pêcheur SA v. Germany*, OJ 1993 C92/4; Case C–312/93, *SCS Peterbroeck, Van Campenhout & Cie v. Belgian State*, OJ 1993 C189/9; Cases C–430 and C–431/93, *J. Van Schindel and J.N.C. Van Veen v. Stichting Pensioenfonds voor Fysiotherapeuten*, OJ 1993 C338/10.

[13] *Francovich*, cited at footnote 11, para. 33 at p. 5414.

[14] *Francovich*, cited at footnote 11, para. 35 at p. 5414.

[15] *The Queen v. Secretary of State for Transport, ex parte Factortame Ltd et al.*, cited at footnote 10.

[16] See point 3.2 of the Community guidelines on State aid for SMEs, OJ 1992 C213/2, and the letter to the Member States ref. IV/D/06878 of 23 March 1993, Competition Law in the European Communities, Volume II.

[17] Case 120/73, *Lorenz v. Germany* [1973] ECR 1471.

[18] Case 120/73, *Lorenz v. Germany*, cited at footnote 16, para. 4 at p. 1481; see also Case 84/42, *Germany v. Commission* [1984] ECR 1451, para. 11 at p. 1488.

[19] The Commission has issued a Guide to its procedures in State aid cases: see Competition Law in the European Communities, Volume II.

[20] The Commission publishes and updates from time to time a compendium of State aid rules (Competition Law in the European Communities, Volume II).

[21] Case C–188/92, *TWD Textilwerke Deggendorf GmbH v. Germany* [1994] ECR I–833; see also Case 77/72, *Capolongo v. Maya* [1973] ECR 611.

[22] The Commission has informed the Member States that "... in appropriate cases it may—after giving the Member State concerned the opportunity to comment and to consider alternatively the granting of rescue aid, as defined by the Community guidelines—adopt a provisional decision ordering the Member State to recover any monies which have been disbursed in infringement of the procedural requirements. The aid would have to be recovered in accordance with the requirements of domestic law; the sum repayable would carry interest running from the time the aid was paid out." (Commission Communication to the Member States supplementing the Commission's letter No. SG(91) D/4577 of 4 March 1991 concerning the procedures for the notification of aid plans and procedures applicable when aid is provided in breach of the rules of Article 93(3) of the EEC Treaty), not yet published.

INDEX

Abuse of dominant position. *See* Dominant position
Accession Treaties,
  agreements, 2–029
  historical background, 1–004
  notification of agreements, 11–008, 11–033, 11–034, 11–044
  text, 1–004
Acquisitions. *See* Mergers
Adoption of Treaty provisions, 1–069
Agency,
  independent trader, agent as, 7–005
  true agreements, 7–004
  vertical agreements, 7–004, 7–005
Agreements,
  Accession, 2–029
  air transport sector, 3–012
  assignments, 2–024
  commission, rates appointed by, 2–021
  concerted practice, duration of, 2–048
  conditions of sale, 2–019
  duration of concerted practice, 2–048
  duress, 2–020
  exclusive licences, 2–024
  gentlemen's agreement, 2–016
  Government measures, 2–021
  horizontal. *See* Horizontal agreements
  incorporation of terms, 2–017
  industry appointed commissions, 2–021
  informal, 2–016
  information. *See* Information agreements
  judicial settlements, 2–026
  national measures, 2–021
  price. *See* Price
  spent, 2–025
  standard conditions of sale, 2–019
  subsidiary undertakings, with, 2–053, 2–054
  tariff fixing, 2–021
  termination, terms of, 2–022, 2–025
  terms, incorporation of, 2–017
  unilateral action, 2–022
Agriculture,
  Annex II products, 14–003
  Commission's exclusive jurisdiction, 14–007
  farmers' associations, 14–006
  generally, 14–001
  national market organisations, 14–004
  necessary discrimination, 14–005
  state aids, 14–008
Air transport sector,
  abuse of dominant position, 15–053
  agreements, 3–012
  block exemption, 3–012
    capacity, 15–048
    computerised reservation system, 15–047
    ground handling services, 15–046
Air transport sector—*cont.*
  block exemption—*cont.*
    slot allocation, 15–048
    tariff consultation, 15–048
  block exemptions, 15–045
  capacity, 15–048
  collective exclusive dealing, 4–082
  common agreements, 15–043
  computerised reservation systems, 3–012, 15–047
  dominant position, 9–016A
  enforcement, 15–033
  ground handling services, 15–046
  IATA agreements, 15–044
  individual exemption, 15–034
  joint ventures, 15–057
  legislative background, 15–029
  links between airlines, 15–057, 15–058
  mergers, 15–057
  minority shareholdings, 15–057
  procedure, 15–033
  reform proposals, 15–030
    scope of regulation, 15–031
  relevant market, 9–016A
  scope of application of rules, 15–029
  slot allocation, 15–048
  sources of law, 1–038
  tariff consultation, 15–048
Altering structure of competition, 2–131
Appeal,
  fines, 12–099
Appreciable effect,
  co-operative joint ventures, 5–062
  Commission's notice, 2–142, 2–144
  de limitis, application of, 2–144
  EFTA Treaties, 2–165
  general, 2–139
  Israel, Treaty with, 2–167
  parallel networks, 2–143
  third countries, treaties with, 2–168
Article 86, 9–005, 9–006. *See also* Dominant position
Asset swaps,
  concentrations, 6–019
Assignments,
  agreements, 2–024
Auctions, 4–079
Audiovisual media,
  purchasing, joint, 4–095
Banking sector,
  state aids, 18–024
Beer supply agreements,
  brewery ties, 7–126
  competing brewers, 7–144
  Delimitis case, 7–127, 7–128
  drinks, specified, 7–135
  minor brewery networks, 7–129
  permitted tie, requirements for, 7–131
  revocation, 7–146
  transitional provisions, 7–145

Block exemption,
air transport agreements, 3–012
Commission regulations, 3–005
consortium agreements, 3–016
EEA Agreements, 3–016A
liner consortia, 3–015A, App 13
maritime transport services, 3–004
motor vehicles, selective distribution for, 3–009, App 2, App 3
patient licences, 3–008
power to grant, 3–004
proposed, 3–016
technology transfer. *See* Technology transfer block exemption
Bundling. *See* Typing clauses
Burden of proof, 10–047
evidence, 10–047
national law, effect on,
different approaches, 10–051
generally, 10–050
United Kingdom, application of law in,
Community principles, 10–059
exempt agreements, 10–060
generally, 10–055
INNO principle, 10–064
restrictive trade practices, 10–056, 10–057
Business sale. *See* Mergers
Cartels. *See* Common horizontal agreements
Cartonboard,
price-fixing, 4–014B
production limitation, 4–038
Cement,
price, 4–014C
production limitation, 4–038
Channel tunnel, 4–054
Co-operative joint ventures,
accelerated consideration, 5–009, 11–059A
agreement to form,
ancillary restriction, 5–025
approach, 5–025
autonomy, loss of parent's, 5–038
dominant position, parent in, 5–040A
foreclosure effects, 5–039
Merger regulation test, 5–025
network effect, 5–042
parallel interlocking, 5–042
prohibition test, 5–025
restriction of competition, 5–035
spillover effect, 5–041
third parties, effect of foreclosure on, 5–039
ancillary restrictions, 5–054, 5–060
appreciable effect, 5–062
assessment, 2–093
character, 5–022
Commission initiative, 5–009
compatibility, determining, 5–023
concentrations distinguished, 1–056, 2–095, App 9
definition, 5–012
determining compatibility, 5–023
distribution and sale, 5–051
Co-operative joint ventures—*cont.*
diversity, 5–013
EFTA Surveillance Authority notice, 2–059
exemption,
advanced technology products, 5–049
conditions, 5–053, 5–077
distribution and sale, 5–051
duration, 5–053
improvements in competitive structure, 5–048
indispensability, 5–052
individual, 5–045
R&D joint ventures, 5–106
substantial elimination of competition, 5–046
fast track treatment, 5–009
Ford/Volkswagen case, 5–074, 5–077
full function, 5–020
function, 5–021
functional diversity, 5–013
increase in use, 2–095
Interface Notice, 1–056, 2–095, 5–012
joint ventures, 5–012
leading cases, 5–074, 5–077
limited function, 5–020
meaning, 5–012
merger regulation,
impact, 5–008
review, 5–009A
non-complete restrictions, 5–055, 5–056
parallel interlocking, 5–042
permitted co-operation, 2–116
production,
cases, 5–019
comfort letter, cases concluded by, 5–019
examples, 5–019
R&D,
agreements, 5–088
agreements covered, 5–122
downstream extension of co-operation, 5–094
establishment, 5–087
individual exemption, 5–106
plus production, 5–087
pure, 5–087
sales, production through to, 5–087
rule of reason, application of, 5–007
specialisation agreements, 5–135, 5–155
strategic alliances,
Commission's approach, 5–131B
meaning, 5–131A
spillover issue, 5–131B
structural, 5–020
technology transfer block exemption, 8–164E
See also Mergers
Co-operative joint ventures exclusive purchasing obligation, 7–192
Coal and steel,
abuse of dominant position, 17–017
authorisation of agreements, 17–006
concentrations, 17–012
ECSC Treaty, 17–001

Coal and steel—*cont.*
fines for infringement, 17–008
infringement, 17–008
price discrimination, 17–004A
production quotas, 17–004A
prohibited agreements, 17–005
restrictive agreements, 17–005
state aids,
coal, 17–019
steel, 17–020
Comfort letters, 3–019
notification, 11–004, 11–064, 11–066
Commission,
abuse of dominant position, approach to, 9–043
agriculture jurisdiction, 14–007
appreciable effect, notice on, 2–142, 2–144
co-operative joint venture initiative, 5–009
collective exclusive dealing, attitude to, 4–086
Directorates-General, 1–013, 1–014. *See also* Directorate-General for Competition
electricity decisions, 16–009
enforcement. *See* Enforcement
exemptions. *See* Individual exemptions
individual exemptions. *See* Individual exemptions
investigations by. *See* Investigations
Legal Services, 1–013
membership, 1–012
mergers, implementing regulations on, 6–003
nuclear energy policy, 16–032, 16–034
Secreteriat-General, 1–013
services of, 1–013
state's role, 13–001
strategic alliances, approach to, 7–050
Title I agreement revocation, 7–124
Complaints,
decision following, 12–024
duties when dealing with, 12–024
generally, 12–019
investigation procedure, 12–023
judicial review by complainant, 12–026
legitimate interest,
generally, 12–021
practice, 12–022
procedure on investigation, 12–023
Computer programs,
copyright, 8–063
Concentrations,
asset swaps, 6–019
co-operation procedure, 6–138
co-operative joint ventures distinguished, 1–056, 2–095, App 9
coal and steel, 17–012
control,
changes in nature of, 6–011
joint, 6–010
nature of, 6–010, 6–011
notice, App 11
regulation, App 6, App 8
Concentrations—*cont.*
control—*cont.*
shareholder reduction, 6–011
sole, 6–010, 6–013
Court's role, 6–140
decisive influence in acquisition of control, 6–008, 6–009
deemed absence,
financial holding companies, acquisitions by, 6–024
generally, 6–021
liquidations, 6–023
EFTA Surveillance Authority role, 6–138
Form CO, 6–096
interim measures, 6–140A
interpretation Notice, App 10
liquidations, 6–023
loans, 6–009
meaning, 6–006
merger concept, 6–007
Notice, 1–056, 6–006, App 10
notification,
derogation, 6–110
documentation, 6–097
Form CO, 6–096
full and accurate disclosure, 6–099
language, 6–098
Merger Task Force role, 6–100
obligation, 6–103
one week to notify, 6–103
regulation, App 6
supporting documentation, 6–097
suspension period, 6–108
time limits, App 6, App 8
options, 6–009
rationalisation agreements, 6–019
relevant market,
geographic market, 6–065, 6–066
product market, 6–064
technology licensing, 6–064A
shareholding,
changes in, 6–011
minority, 6–012
reductions, 6–011
sole control through, 6–013
two or more,
asset swaps, 6–019
break-up, 6–017
generally, 6–016
rationalisation agreements, 6–019
Undertakings Concerned Notice, 6–016
undertaking, 6–006
Concerted practice,
duration, 2–048
Confidentiality,
formal procedure, 12–046
independent action by Member States' authorities, 12–018
investigations, 12–017
notification, 11–057
Consortium agreements,
block exemption, 3–016
Constitutional challenges, 1–006

Consumption of product,
  place of, 2–106
  relevant market, 2–106
Copyright,
  Community's approach, 8–047
  computer programs, 8–063
  licences, 8–173, 8–173A, 8–176
  literary works, 8–055
  sound recordings, 8–052
  television broadcasts, 8–060
  See also Intellectual property rights
Council. *See* European Council
Court of Auditors, 1–008, 1–023
Court of First Instance,
  appeals from, 12–132
  Court of Justice, appeals to, 12–132
  enforcement by. *See* Enforcement
  judges, 19–019
  procedural rules, 1–017
  structure, 1–018
Court of Justice,
  appeals to, 12–132
  judges, 1–019
  procedural rules, 1–017
Damages, 10–039
Dawn raids, 12–004
De limitis,
  appreciable effect, 2–144
  beer supply agreements, 7–127, 7–128
  restriction of competition, 2–079
De minimis,
  mergers, 6–042
Direct effect, 10–002
Directorate-General for Competition,
  composition, 1–015
  structure, 1–015
Discrimination,
  agriculture, 15–05
  price,
    coal and steel, 17–004A
    generally, 9–055
    United brands, in, 9–056
  tying clauses, 9–077
Distortion of competition,
  Maastricht amendments, 2–108
  national laws, by, 2–122
Distribution agreements,
  Community approach, 7–014
  customer service, 7–046
  exclusive distribution, 7–011
  exclusive supply to distributor, 7–027
  exemption, individual, 7–069
  export ban prohibition, 7–019
  export restriction, 7–020
  guarantee service, 7–046
  individual,
    Commission's notice, 7–050
    customer service, 7–046
    exclusive supply to distributor, 7–027
    generally, 7–048
    guarantee service, 7–046
    net book agreement, 7–036
    resale price maintenance, 7–036
    revocation, 7–067
  net book agreement, 7–036
Distribution agreements—*cont.*
  parallel imports, measures obstructing,
      7–019–7–021
  pricing to restrict exports, 7–020
  product differentiation, 7–021
  territorial protection for distributor,
      7–013
Distributors,
  exchange of information between, 4–031
  territorial protection, 7–013
  vertical agreements. *See* Distribution
      agreements
Dominant position
  abuse,
    air transport, 15–053
    coal and steel, 17–017
    Commission approach, 9–043
    exclusionary, 9–046
    exploitative, 9–046
    general considerations, 9–042
    intellectual property rights,
      licences refused, 9–065
      remedies, 9–066
    kinds, 9–047
    links, 9–045
    objective concept, 9–044
    principles governing, 9–043
    transport, 15–010
  airports, 9–016A
  collective, decisions on, 9–039
  definition, 9–007
  demand substitutability, 9–009
  dominance defined, 9–020
  elements of, 9–007
  exclusionary abuse, 9–046
  exploitative abuse, 9–046
  fidelity rebates, 9–057
  geographic market, 9–040
  intellectual property rights, 9–032
  interchangeability, 9–010
  licences refused, 9–065
  luxury goods, 9–015
  narrow market justification, 9–014,
      9–015
  need to take account of competitive
      conditions, 9–017
  ports, 9–016A
  predatory pricing, 9–054
  price discrimination, 9–055, 9–056
  private undertakings, 9–029
  product market, relevant, 9–008
  public undertakings, 9–029
  refusal to supply,
    essential facilities, 9–063A
    generally, 9–059
    narrow markets, 9–062
  relevant product market, 9–008
  substantial part of common market,
      9–041
  tying clauses,
    ancillary services, 9–074
    exclusive purchasing obligations
        distinguished, 9–073
    Hilti case, 9–071
    Tetra Pak II, 9–073

Double jeopardy, 12–094
Duress,
  agreements, 2–020
Eastern Aluminium case, 4–058
EC Treaty,
  activities, expansion, 1–023
  adoption of provisions, 1–069
  aims, 1–024
  alteration of structure, 1–022, 1–023
  economic and monetary union, 1–022, 1–023
  interpretation, 1–050
  mergers, 6–001
  part one, 1–022, App 1
  repealed provisions, 1–038
  social policy provisions, 1–038
  subsidiarity, 1–026A
  tasks, statement of, 1–022
ECJ. *See* Court of Justice
Economic and monetary union, 1–023, 1–024
ECSC Treaty,
  historical background, 1–001
  merger, 6–001
  scope, 16–001, 17–001
  text, 1–001
EEA Agreement,
  3–003A
  block exemption, 3–016A
  commencement, 1–007
  horizontal agreements, application to, 4–001A
  individual exemption. *See* Individual exemption
  membership, 1–007
  mergers, 6–004A. *See also* Mergers
  notification. *See* Notification
  signatories, 1–007
  state aids, 18–001
EEA Treaty. *See* European Economic Area Agreement
EEC Treaty,
  energy and, 16–001, 16–006
  historical background, 1–002
EFTA Court,
  decisions, 12–134B
  jurisdiction, 12–134A, 1084
  procedure, 12–134A
EFTA Surveillance Authority,
  individual exemptions, 3–057
  investigations, co-operation in, 12–008A
  practice, 3–057
Electricity. *See* Energy
Energy,
  Agreement on Community Energy policy, 16–002
  characteristics of markets, 16–003
  Charter Treaty, 16–002
  Community policy, 16–002
  dependence, 16–004
  ECSC Treaty, 16–001
  EEC treaties, 16–001, 16–006
  electricity,
    Article 90(2), application of, 16–012
    Commission decisions, 16–009
Energy—*cont.*
  electricity—*cont.*
    distribution, 16–010
    Electricidade de Portugal, 16–019A
    export prevention, 16–011
    IJsselcentrale case, 16–010
    import prevention, 16–011
    privatisation in United Kingdom, 16–013, 16–016
    trade between Member States, 16–020
  Euratom Treaty, 16–001
  gas,
    distribution, 16–037
    export monopolies, 16–038
    generally, 16–036
    import monopolies, 16–038
  internal market, 16–005
  nuclear energy,
    Commission policy, 16–032, 16–034
    Eastern Europe, 16–034
    Euratom Treaty, 16–021, 16–023
    national policy considerations, 16–032
    research, 16–034
    safety, 16–034
  oil,
    distribution, efficient, 16–043
    economic progress, 16–043
    environmental protection, 16–046
    exploration, 16–045
    national policy, 16–044
    strategy, 16–041
  policy, 16–002
  security of supply, 16–004
  special characteristics of markets, 16–003
Enforcement,
  adverse decision, Commission's formal procedure prior to,
    access to file, 12–036
    administrative nature, 12–028
    adoption of decision, 12–043
    confidentiality, 12–046
    content of decision, 12–044
    defence, 12–029
    documentation, 12–035
    errors in text of decision, 12–043
    heard, right to be, 12–030
    hearing, 12–037
    hearing officer, 12–038
    initiation of procedure, 12–033–12–036
    minutes, 12–037
    Statement of Objections, 12–033
  Article 4(2) agreements, 12–073
  case law, recent, 10–039
  complaints. *See* Complaints
  consistency,
    assistance from Commission, 10–019
    avoidance of inconsistent decisions, 10–016
    Commission's Notice, 10–017
    earlier Commission decisions, 10–022
    generally, 10–015
    informal view of Commission, 10–023

Enforcement—*cont.*
  Court of First Instance control,
    annulment grounds, 12–108, 12–109, 12–111
    appeals, 12–132
    Article 173, under, 12–104
    constitution of Court, 12–101
    failure to act, 12–122, 12–125
    fines, 12–103, 12–129
    grounds of annulment, 12–108, 12–109, 12–111
    inadequacy of reasoning, 12–111
    interim relief, 12–129, 12–130
    jurisdiction, 12–103
    organisational measures, 12–119
    procedural irregularities, 12–109
    procedure, 12–116
    scope of review, 12–103
    suspension of Commission order, 12–130
    suspension of fine, 12–129
    time limits, 12–117
  damages, 10–039
  direct effect, 10–002
  European Communities Act, 10–003
  fines. *See* Fines
  Francovich case, 10–041
  intentional infringement, 12–068
  interim measures, criteria for, 12–048
  investigations by Commission. *See* Investigations
  involuntary infringement, 12–072
  jurisdiction,
    Article 177 references, 10–010
    national courts, 10–006
    non-Member State, contract subject to, 10–011
  nexus, contractual, 10–033
  nullity, consequences of, 10–030
  pleading, 10–043
  positive action ordered, 12–055
  sea transport, 15–018
  severance, 10–029
  sincere co-operation, duty of, 10–015
  supremacy of Community law, 10–002
  termination of infringements,
    informal, 12–061
    orders, 12–054
    positive action ordered, 12–055
  voidness of contractual provisions, 10–028
Euratom Treaty,
  historical background, 1–003
  nuclear energy, 16–021, 16–023
  scope, 16–001
  text, 1–003
European Community,
  naming, 1–002
European Community Treaty. *See* EC Treaty
European Council,
  constitution, 1–006, 1–010
  functions, 1–010
  recognition, 1–006
European Court of Justice. *See* Court of Justice
European Economic Area Agreement. *See* EEA Agreement
European Parliament,
  co-decision procedure, 1–009
  importance, 1–009
  membership, 1–009
  powers, 1–009
  role, 1–006
European Union,
  establishment, 1–006
  meaning, 1–006
  structure, 1–006
Exclusive purchasing agreements for resale,
  anti-competitive effect, 7–111
  Article 86, 7–116
  beer supply agreements. *See* Beer supply agreements
  block exemption, 7–117A
  generally, 7–109
  import hindrance, 7–113
  individual exemption, 7–116
  joint ventures, 7–192
  minimum quantities, 7–112
  service station agreements. *See* Service station agreements
  Title I agreements,
    duration, permitted, 7–123
    exclusive purchasing obligation, 7–118
    revocation by Commission, 7–124
Exemptions,
  Article 86, infringement of, 3–003
  block. *See* Block exemption
  EEA Agreement, 3–003A
  free movement of workers, 3–003
  individual. *See* Individual exemption
  institutions granting, 3–003A
  patent licences, 3–008
  technology transfer agreements, 3–008A. *See also* Technology transfer block exemption
Exports,
  agreement prohibiting, 2–099
Fair dealing,
  promotion of, 1–071
Farmers' associations, 14–006
Fidelity rebates, 9–057
Financial services,
  collective exclusive dealing, 4–081
Fines,
  allocation between infringing parties, 12–090
  appeal, 12–099
  Article 4(2) agreements, 12–073
  behaviour of parties, 12–086
  benefits accruing from infringement, 12–083
  circumstances relevant, 12–084
  coal and steel, 17–008
  Court of First Instance jurisdiction, 12–103, 12–129
  double jeopardy, 12–094
  duration of infringement, 12–088

Fines—*cont.*
gravity, 12–077–12–080
intentional infringement, 12–068
involuntary infringement, 12–072
limitation of actions, 12–096
mitigation following proceedings, 12–086
nature, 12–063
negligent infringement, 12–068
notified agreements, 12–095
parents and subsidiaries, 12–091
payment, 12–097
profitability, 12–080
purpose, 12–063
scale in relation to turnover, 12–079
several infringements, 12–093
successor undertaking's liability, 12–092
suspension of payment pending appeal, 12–099
Table of, 12–064
third parties, effect of infringement on, 12–082
turnover identification, 12–077, 12–078
Franchising,
block exemption application, 7–172
competing goods, 7–177
Court of Justice attitude, 7–165
generally, 7–163
non-competition, 7–177
optional purchasing system, 7–177
prices, 7–185
sources of supply, 7–177
Free movement of workers,
exemptions and, 3–003
Gas. *See* Energy
Gentlemen's agreement, 2–016
Hearing officers, terms of reference, App 7
Helsinki Agreement, 4–017
Historical background,
accession Treatys, 1–004
ECSC Treaty, 1–001
EEC Treaty, 1–002
Euratom Treaty, 1–003
member States, 1–005
treaty on European Union (TEU), 1–006
Horizontal agreements,
collective exclusive dealing,
airline industry, 4–082
Article 85(3), under, 4–075
auctions, 4–079
Commission attitude to membership rules, 4–086
financial services, 4–081
membership rules, 4–086
unreasonable refusal of membership, 4–084
Commission, approach, 4–0011
EEA Agreement, application of, 4–001A
Eurocheque case, 4–017
Helsinki Agreement, 4–017
information agreements. *See* Information agreements
Horizontal agreements—*cont.*
inter-state price cartels, 4–005
markets. *See* Markets
price recommendations, 4–004. *See also* Price
price-fixing. *See* Price
production limitation. *See* Production limitation
purchasing, joint. *See* Purchasing, joint
selling, joint, 4–096, 4–102
service industries, 4–016
technical standards, 4–047
two-tier approach, 4–001
Ice cream, 2–017
Individual exemption,
air transport sector, 15–034
banking sector exemptions, 3–037
co-operative joint ventures, 5–045
comfort letters, 3–019
Commission,
delay, problem of, 3–018
economic progress, 3–034
expedited procedure, 3–018
margin of appreciation, 3–021
opposition procedures, 3–020
policy, 3–024
powers, 3–017–3–019
refusal of exemption, 3–021
technical progress, 3–033
conditions, 3–052
consumer benefits,
fair share, 3–039
generally, 3–038
resulting benefit, 3–040
delay, problem of, 3–018
distribution agreements, 7–069
duration, 3–047, 3–050
economic progress, 3–034
EEA Agreement,
exempted before commencement, 3–053
notification of agreement to Commission, 3–054
other agreements, 3–055
post-commencement agreements, 3–056
EFTA Surveillance Authority, 3–057
exclusive purchasing agreements for resale, 7–116
expedited procedure, 3–018
fair share for consumers, 3–038
likely duration, 3–050
margin of appreciation, 3–021
no substantial elimination of competition, 3–045
obligations, 3–052
opposition procedures, 3–020
policy of Commission, 3–024
R&D joint ventures, 5–106
refusal by Commission, 3–021
restrictions indispensable,
meaning, 3–042
unnecessary restrictions, 3–043
retroactive effect, 3–047
sea transport, 15–017

Individual exemption—*cont.*
service station agreements, 7–162
technical progress, 3–033
Individual exemptions,
EFTA Surveillance Authority, 3–057
Informal agreements, 2–016
Information agreements,
distributors, exchange of information between, 4–031
market sharing, 4–036
operation, 4–029
output information, 4–034
price-fixing, 4–036
production limitation, 4–036
purpose, 4–029
sales information, 4–034
Information. *See* Information agreements; Investigations
Inland waterway transport. *See* Transport
INNO principle, 10–064
Institutional structure,
Commission. *See* Commission
council. *See* European Council
courts. *See* Court of First Instance; Court of Justice
generally, 1–008
Parliament. *See* European Parliament
Intellectual property rights,
abuse of,
licences refused, 9–065
remedies ordered, 9–066
copyright,
collective licences, 8–173A
Community's approach, 8–047
computer programs, 8–063
licences, 8–173, 8–173A, 8–176
literary works, 8–055
performing rights, 8–052
sound recordings, 8–052
television broadcasts, 8–060
dominant position, 9–032
exercise, existence distinguished, 8–003
exhaustion, 8–005
existence, exercise distinguished, 8–003
free movement of goods,
chronological checklist, 8–010
effect of rules, 8–010
generally, 8–002
generally, 8–001
goods, free movement of, 8–002
infringement actions,
generally, 8–064
trademark actions, 8–067
TV Guide cases, 8–071
Volvo case, 8–072, 8–073
know-how licences, 8–150, 8–151. *See also* Technology transfer block exemption
licensing, 2–113, 8–007. *See also* Licences
patents,
consent, 8–021
cross licences, 8–116
discriminatory restrictions, 8–025
disguised restrictions, 8–025
Intellectual property rights—*cont.*
patents—*cont.*
exhaustion of rights, 8–018
exploitation of technology, 8–114A
jointly held, 8–115
licences,
balancing conflicts, 8–080
block exemption, 8–093
exclusive provisions, 8–089
export restrictions, 8–089
limited, 8–078
royalties, 8–096, 8–109
sales by licensee, 8–090
territorial provisions, 8–025
unjustified restrictions, 8–025
plant breeders' rights licences, 8–177
technical information,
duration of regulation, 8–125
regulation, 8–118, 8–119
scope of regulation, 8–119
trade related aspects, 8–007A
trademarks,
consent for importing, 8–027
enforcement of rights, 8–040
exhaustion of rights, 8–029
importation, 8–027
licences, 8–165
packaging, 8–038
passing off, 8–042
repackaging, 8–036, 8–037
reputation gained in other Member States, 8–045
subject matter, 8–030
summary of rules, 8–028
unfair competition, 8–042
United Kingdom law, 8–027
Interface Notice, 1–056, 2–095, 5–012
Intermediaries,
importance of trading by, 1–075
Internal market, 9–002
energy, 16–005
International conventions,
additional, 1–068
Investigations,
backlog, 12–002
confidentiality, 12–017
generally, 12–002
information provision,
addressees, 12–004
dawn raids, 12–004
EFTA Surveillance Authority co-operation, 12–008A
Member State, from, 12–008
necessity of, 12–005
power to require, 12–008
requests from undertakings, 12–003
undertaking, from, 12–003
US antitrust authorities, 12–008B
penalties, 12–014
privilege against self-incrimination, 12–016
self-incrimination, privilege against, 12–016
Israel,
appreciable effect, treaty on, 2–167

Joint ventures. *See* Co-operative joint ventures
Judicial review,
  complainant, by, 12–026
Know how licensing, 3–008A, 3–014. *See also* Technology transfer block exemption
Legal Services,
  commission, 1–014
Licences,
  abuse of dominant position, 9–065
  copyright, 8–173, 8–173A, 8–176
  European standards, 8–179
  patent. *See* Intellectual property rights
  plant breeders' rights, 8–177
  policies, 8–178
  refusal, 9–065
  restrictions, 8–175
  software, 8–178
  trademarks, 8–165
Limitation of production. *See* Production limitation
Liner consortia, 3–015A, App 13
Liquidations,
  concentrations, 6–023
Lome Convention, 2–168
Maritime transport services,
  block exemption, 3–004
Markets,
  Channel tunnel, 4–054
  division between distributors, 4–067
  emergency allocation of supplies, 4–059
  export control, 4–071
  import control, 4–071
  limitation, 4–054
  selling rights, exclusive, 4–065
  sharing,
    bilateral, 4–064
    distributors, division between, 4–067
    domestic agreements, 4–070
    Eastern Aliminium case, 4–058
    emergency allocation of supplies, 4–059
    exclusive dealing, 4–057
    export control, 4–071
    import control, 4–071
    producers, between, 4–055
    selling rights, 4–065
Maastricht treaty,
  political pressures, 1–006
  See also Treaty on European Union
Member States,
  historical background, 1–005
  number of, 1–005, 2–127
  trade between. *See* trade between Member States
Mergers,
  aggregation of turnover, 6–048, 6–051
  air transport sector, 15–057
  Ancillary Restrictions Notice, 6–003
  Article 85, under, 6–161, 6–164, 6–165
  Article 86, under, 6–161, 6–164, 6–165
  autonomy,
    full-function undertakings, 6–033
    functional independence, 6–034
Mergers—*cont.*
  autonomy—*cont.*
    legal dependence, 6–035
    meaning, 6–033
  banking income, 6–005A
  co-ordination in market, absence of, 6–037
  Commission Implementing Regulations, 6–003
  compatibility assessment, 6–074A
  complete, 6–036
  Concentration Notice, 6–003
  concentrations. *See* Concentrations
  de minimis considerations, 6–042
  defence sector, 6–157
  definition of market, significance of, 6–041
  dissemination of merger decisions, 6–004
  EC Treaty, 6–001
  ECSC Treaty, 6–001
  EEA regime, 6–004A
  EA states, in,
    decisions, 6–146
    defence sector mergers, 6–157
    distinct market concept, 6–148
    grounds for referral, 6–153
    media, plurality of, 6–151
    Member State requesting investigation, 6–154
    national competition authorities, referral to, 6–144-6–148
    public security, 6–150
    timing of referral, 6–147
  exclusivity of jurisdiction, 6–142, 6–143
  failing firm defence, 6–074A
  formal investigations,
    amendment of transaction, 6–113
    communication of decisions, 6–118
    initial investigation, 6–112
    mixed decisions, 6–116
    serious doubts investigations. *See* serious doubt investigations *below*
    withdrawal of notification, 6–113A
  half of board, power to appoint, 6–053
  industrial policy issues, non-competition notices, 6–077
  Interface Notice, 6–003, 6–027
  interpretative notes, 6–004
  joint control,
    absence of agreement, 6–032
    agreement based, 6–031
    concept, 6–028
    factors indicating, 6–030
    identification, 6–030
    limited period, 6–032A
    temporary, 6–032A
  joint ventures, 6–005A
  jurisdictional criteria, 6–046
  minority shareholdings, 6–164, 6–165
  multiple notifications, 6–005A
  non-competition notices, 6–077
  notices, 1–056
  oligopoly control, 6–076

Mergers—*cont.*
one parent active, 6–039
part, sale of, 6–050
partial, 6–036
pre-existing joint ventures, interests in, 6–044
procedural improvements, 6–005A
regulation,
Green Paper on review, 5–009A, 6–005A
impact, 5–008
review, 5–009A, 6–005A
related markets, 6–038
relevant turnover, 6–049
reporting decisions, 6–004
review of regulation, 5–009A
risk of co-ordinations between parents, 6–040
serious doubts investigations,
access to file, 6–121
decisions following, 6–124
defence rights, 6–121
duration, 6–119
modifications to concentration plan, 6–123A
objections, 6–1120
oral hearing, 6–123
reply, 6–122
statement of objections, 6–120
state controlled undertakings, 6–054
task force,
constitution, 1–016
provision of information, 6–102
role, 6–100
thresholds, 6–005A
turnover,
aggregation of, 6–051
calculating, 6–056–6–058, App 12
credit institutions, 6–056
financial institutions, 6–056
insurance companies, 6–057
jointly controlled undertakings, 6–052
mixed activity groups, 6–058
Notice, 6–003
parent, sale of, 6–050
state controlled undertakings, 6–054
Undertakings Concerned Notice, 6–003
See also Concentrations
Military equipment, 13–035
Minor importance, agreements of,
mergers, 6–042
Minority shareholdings,
air transport sector, 15–057
concentrations, 6–012
mergers, 6–164, 6–165
Monopolies, state,
commercial character of, 13–004
International agreements, 13–008
prohibition, 13–005
remedies, 13–009
Motor vehicles,
block exemption, 3–009, 7–108A–7–108J, App 2, App 3
selective distribution block exemption, 3–009, App 2, App 3
Multimodal transport, 4–003
National courts,
burden of proof, 10–050, 10–051
enforcement, 10–006
state aids, 18–044A–18–047
National law,
burden of proof, 10–051, 10–070
distortion of competition by, 2–122
energy policy, 16–032
nuclear energy policy, 16–032
oil policy, 16–044
Negative clearance, 11–005
Net book agreement, 7–036
Notification,
Accession Agreements, 11–008, 11–033, 11–034, 11–044
allocation of responsibility, 11–001A
comfort letters, 11–004, 11–064
confidentiality, 11–057
consequences, 11–003
date for notification, 11–035
discomfort letters, 11–066A
EEA Agreement, under, 11–001A, 11–034A
exempted agreements, 11–006
exemption, to obtain, 11–002
fines, 12–095
formal procedure, 11–048
informal approaches, 11–047
loss of provisional validity, 11–041
negative clearance application, 11–005
new agreements,
accelerated procedure, 11–014
Article 4(2), within, 11–024, 11–025
civil validity, 11–022
demerits, 11–023
effect of notification, 11–017
joint ventures, 11–014
meaning, 11–010
merits, 11–023
retroactive exemption, 11–018
time-scale, 11–014
numbers, 11–002
one-stop shop principle, 11–001A
opposition procedure, 11–062
post-notification procedure,
accelerated procedure, 11–059A
comfort letters, 11–064–11–066
discomfort letters, 11–066A
effect of comfort letters, 11–066
formal comfort letters, 11–064
informal procedures, 11–063
joint ventures, 11–059A
opposition procedure, 11–062
uses, 11–059
pre-notification discussions, 11–047
preliminary notices, 11–058
procedure,
confidentiality, 11–057
date of effect, 11–054
Form A/B, 11–046, 11–051
formal, 11–048
full and accurate disclosure, 11–050
generally, 11–046
informal approaches, 11–047

Notification—*cont.*
procedure—*cont.*
preliminary notices, 11–058
publicity, 11–058
renewals, 11–055
requirements, 11–049
restrictive trade agreements, 11–053
rules, 11–001A
secrecy, 11–057
variations, 11–055
publicity, 11–058
renewals, 11–055
secrecy, 11–057
structural joint ventures, 11–059A
transitional rules,
accession agreements, 11–033, 11–034
date for notification, 11–035
EEA Agreements, 11–034A
loss of provisional validity, 11–041
Perfumes case, 11–041
retroactive exemptions, 11–038
timely notification, effect of, 11–036
variations, 11–055
Nuclear energy,
Commission policy, 16–032, 16–034
Eastern Europe, 16–034
Euratom Treaty, 16–021, 16–023
joint undertakings, 16–023
national policy considerations, 16–032
research, 16–034
safety, 16–034
Oil. *See* Energy
Oligopolies, 6–076
Ombudsman,
appointment, 1–009
Parallel networks of agreements, 2–143
Parliament,
European. *See* European Parliament
Passing off trademarks, 8–042
Patents,
licences, 3–008. *See also* Intellectual property rights; Technology transfer block exemption
Penalties. *See* Fines
Plant breeders' rights licences,
intellectual property rights, 8–177
Pleading, 10–043
Policy Newsletter, EC Competition, 1–061
Postal sector,
state aids, 18–024
Predatory pricing, 9–054
Price,
Article 85(3), under, 4–027
cartonboard, 4–014B
cement, 4–014C
collective fixing of trading conditions, 4–025
collective resale price maintenance, 4–023
discrimination,
coal and steel, 17–004A
generally, 9–055
United brands, in, 9–056
domestic agreements,
extending to exports/imports, 4–020
Price—*cont.*
domestic agreements—*cont.*
not extending to exports/imports, 4–021
whole Member State, covering, 4–022
Eurocheque case, 4–017
exports, domestic agreements extending to, 4–020
fixing,
cartonboard, 4–014B
cement, 4–014C
LdPE decision, 4–011
meaning, 4–003
multimodal transport, 4–003
polypropelene case, 4–010
prohibition, 4–002
PVC decision, 4–011
railway ticket distribution, 4–003
steel beams, 4–014A
Helsinki Agreement, 4–017
imports, domestic agreements extending to, 4–020
inter-state cartels, 4–005
predatory pricing, 9–054
recommendations, 4–004
resale price maintenance, collective, 4–023
service industries, agreements in, 4–016
steel beams, 4–014A
Privilege against self-incrimination,
investigations, 12–016
Production limitation,
cartonboard, 4–014B, 4–038
cement, 4–014C, 4–038
information agreements, 4–036
restructuring agreements, 4–040
steel beams, 4–038, 4–014A
Public undertakings,
application in conjunction with other Treaty provisions, 13–018
Article 90(2),
generally, 13–021
national courts, 13–027
obstructing performance of tasks, 13–025
services of general economic interest, 13–023
Article 90(3),
enforcement, 13–029
generally, 13–028
legislative power under, 13–031
Telecoms Directives, 13–033
exclusive rights granted, 13–014, 134–016, 13–017
extension of exclusive rights, 13–017
generally, 13–010
information provision, 13–032
measure of Member State, 13–015
services of general economic interest, 13–023
special rights granted, 13–014, 13–016
Telecoms Directives, 13–033
Purchasing,
exclusive. *See* Exclusive purchasing agreements for resale

Purchasing—*cont.*
joint,
audiovisual media, 4–095
raw materials, 4–090
Purpose of competition rules, 1–071
R&D joint ventures. *See* Co-operative joint ventures
Rail transport,
ticket sales, 15–004
Rationalisation agreements,
concentrations, 6–019
Relevant product market, 2–106
Research and development. *See* Co-operative joint ventures
Restriction of competition,
appreciable effect, 2–105
conceptual issues, 2–057
distortion of competition, 2–108
essential, 2–063
export prohibition agreement, 2–099
horizontal restrictions, 2–059
intellectual property licences, 2–113
main decisions,
Delimitis case, 2–079
generally, 2–064
market analysis, 2–063
objects restrictive *per se*, 2–098
principle, general, 2–064
Pronuptia case, 2–091
relevant product market, 2–106
rule of reason, 2–063
whole economic context, 2–104
workable competition, 2–082
Restructuring agreements, 4–040
Retroactive effect,
individual exemption, 3–047
notification of new agreements, 11–018
Road transport. *See* Transport
Rule of reason, 2–063
Sami people, 1–005
Sea transport,
Article 86, 15–021
block exemption, 15–015
consortia,
conditions for exemption, 15–028B
definition, 15–028B
exemption, 15–028B
generally, 15–027
regulation, 15–028A
consortia agreements, 15–015
enforcement, 15–018
individual exemptions, 15–017
liner conferences block exemption,
agreements between members, 15–024
conditions, 15–025
obligations, 15–025
scope, 15–023
scope of regulation, 15–013
substantive appraisal, 15–019
Secretariat-General, 1–014
Selective distribution systems. *See* Vertical agreements
Selling, joint, 4–096, 4–102
Service industries,
price agreements, 4–016
Service station agreements,
advertising, 7–157
duration of tie, 7–155
exemption, 7–162
fuels, 7–150
goods, 7–154
individual exemption, 7–162
lubricants, 7–153
minimum quantities, 7–158
solus agreements, 7–147
transitional provisions, 7–160
Shareholdings. *See* Concentrations; Minority shareholdings
Sharing markets. *See* Markets
Sound recordings,
copyright, 8–052
performing rights, 8–052
Sources of law,
air transport sector, 1–038
Directives, 1–052–1–070
generally, 1–039
interpretation of Treaty, 1–050
regulations, 1–052–1–070
Specialisation agreements, 5–135, 5–155
State aids,
agriculture, 14–008
alteration to existing aids, 18–030
Article 94, 18–044
banking sector, 18–024
categories of specified, 18–025
coal, 17–019
common interest, 18–023
compatibility,
aids that are compatible, 18–015
categories of specified aid, 18–025
common interest, 18–023
Council authorisation, 18–026
discretion of Commission, 18–017
economic activities, development of, 18–022
economic areas, development of, 18–021
important projects, 18–019
non-regional aids, 18–024
possibly compatible, 18–016 *et seq*
preliminary examination, 18–031
sectoral aids, 18–024
serious disturbance remedied, 18–019
competition, effect on, 18–012
concept of aid,
advantage, as, 18–004
market economy investor principle, 18–007
wide concept, 18–003
conditions, 18–036A
contentious procedure,
conditions, 18–0036A
imposition of conditions, 18–036A
non-compliance, 18–037
unnotified aid, 18–038
Council authorisation, 18–026
Court of Justice,
annulment grounds, 18–050, 18–051, 18–052
applicants, 18–053, 18–055

State aids—*cont.*
Court of Justice—*cont.*
Commission, action by, 18–053
private party action, 18–055
procedural irregularities, 18–050
reasoning, lack of, 18–05
review of exercise of discretion, 18–052
reviewable acts, 18–048
EC Treaty, relationship of provisions with, 18–061, 18–062
EEA Agreement, 18–001
effect on competition, 18–012
employment promotion, 18–024
environmental protection, 18–024
examples, 18–011
favouring certain undertakings, 18–010
generally, 18–001
illegally granted aid,
duty to seek repayment, 18–042
generally, 18–041
interest, 18–042A
recipient's position, 18–043
repayment, 18–042
tax, 18–042A
important projects, 18–019
information obligation, 18–008
inter-State trade, effect on, 18–014
judicial remedies,
alterations to existing aids, 18–046
Commission's Notice, 18–044A
Court of Justice. *See* Court of Justice *above*
damages, 18–046A
enforcement of Commission decisions, 18–047
national courts, 18–044A–18–047
new aids, 18–046
market economy investor principle, 18–007
medium sized companies, 18–013
Member State, through, 18–009
new aid,
notification, 18–028
pre-notification, 18–028
review, 18–030
time limit for review, 18–030
non-regional aids, 18–024
Notice, App 15
notification,
compatible aids, 18–029
new aids, 18–028
unnotified aids, 18–038, 18–039
postal sector, 18–024
pre-notification of new aids, 18–028
prematurely implemented, 18–039
procedural irregularities, 18–050
restructuring, 18–024
review of existing aids, 18–027
sectoral aids, 18–024
serious disturbance remedied, 18–019
small companies, 18–013
statistics, 18–001
steel, 17–020
synthetic fibres industry, 18–024
State aids—*cont.*
time limit for review, 18–030
unnotified aid, 18–038
State, role of,
Commission's policy, 13–001
military equipment, 13–035
monopolies,
commercial character of, 13–004
International agreements, 13–008
prohibition, 13–005
remedies, 13–009
public undertakings. *See* Public undertakings
Steel beams,
price-fixing, 4–014A
Steel. *See* Coal and steel
Strategic alliances,
Commission's approach, 5–131B
meaning, 5–131A
spillover issue, 5–131B
Strategic alliances, 2–095
Structural joint ventures,
accelerated notification procedure, 11–059A
meaning, 5–070
Sub-contracting, 7–198
Subsidiarity, 1–026A
Subsidiary undertakings,
agreements with, 2–053, 2–054
whole economic unit, comprising, 2–053
Supply,
vertical agreements. *See* Vertical agreements
Supremacy of Community law, 10–002
Swiss Protocol, 1–007
Synthetic fibres industry,
state aids, 18–024
Tariff fixing agreements, 2–021
Technical standards,
horizontal agreements, 4–047
Technology licensing,
market, 6–064A
Technology transfer block exemption,
ambit, 3–008A
ancillary provisions, 3–008A
application of, 3–008A
commencement, 3–008A, 8–164A
exclusions, 3–008A
joint ventures, 8–164E
notification form, 8–164V
opposition procedure, 3–008A, 8–146
patent licensing, 8–164B–8–164T
prevention of competition, 3–008A
purpose, 8–164A
scope, 3–008A, 8–164D
structure, 8–164C
text of, App 4
withdrawal of benefit, 3–008A, 8–164F
Television broadcasts,
copyright, 8–060
TEU. *See* Treaty on European Union
Three Pillars, 1–006
Trade between Member States,
altering structure of competition, 2–131
barriers to entry, 2–135

Trade between Member States—*cont.*
confined to one member state, agreements, 2–137
definition of trade, 2–128
degree of effect required, 2–132
effect,
degree required, 2–133
whole agreement, 2–133
flows, alteration of, 2–129
one Member State, agreements covering, 2–134
trade, 2–128
whole agreement, effect of, 2–133
Trademarks. *See* Intellectual property rights
Transparency,
Directive, App 14
importance given to, 1–061
Transport,
abuse of dominant position, 15–010
air. *See* Air transport sector
applicable regulations, 15–002
exemption, 15–008
generally, 15–002
invalidity, 15–005
procedure for exemption, 15–011
prohibition, 15–005
rail ticket sales, 15–004
sea. *See* Sea transport
technical agreement exception, 15–006
transitional regime, 15–003
Treaty on a European Economic Area. *See* European Economic Area Agreement
Treaty on European Union (TEU),
commencement, 1–006
EEC Treaty amended by, 1–002
effect, 1–006
historical background, 1–006
ratification, 1–006
structure, 1–006
Turnover,
identification, 12–077
mergers and. *See* Mergers
Tying clauses,
ancillary services, 9–074
contractual conditions, 9–075
discrimination, 9–077
exclusive purchasing obligations distinguished, 9–073
Hilti case, 9–071
Tetra Pak II, 9–073
Undertakings,
activities, 2–004
aim, 2–004
economic or commercial activity, 2–004

Undertakings—*cont.*
identification, 2–004
individuals as, 2–008
legal personality, 2–003
liberal professions, 2–008
member states, 2–010
subsidiary companies, 2–005. *See also* Subsidiary undertakings
Unfair competition,
not deserving protection, 2–121
United States,
antitrust law, 1–070
information exchange with, 12–008B
Vertical agreements,
agency,
independent trader, agent as, 7–005
true agency agreements, 7–004
distribution agreements. *See* Distribution agreements
franchising. *See* Franchising
overview, 7–003
purchasing agreements for resale. *See* Exclusive purchasing agreement for resale
selective distribution systems,
additional obligations, 7–089
admission to network, procedure for, 7–087
authorised dealers, 7–100, 7–102
basic principles, 7–075
block exemptions, 7–096
customer restrictions, 7–095
enforcement, 7–107A
leading cases, 7–075
luxury products, 7–085
motor vehicle block exemption, 7–108A–7–108J, App 2, App 3
non-applicability of Regulations, 7–106
objective technical requirements, 7–084
permitted restrictions, 7–100
prestige products, 7–085
qualitative criteria, 7–086
removal from prohibition, 7–098
restrictions on sale, 7–090
revocation of block exemption, 7–107
sales promotion obligations, 7–093
severance, 7–107A
suitable products, 7–084
territorial limitation of outlets, 7–094
territorial restrictions on sale, 7–090
transitional provisions, 7–018, 7–108A
sub-contracting, 7–198
Workable competition, 2–082